NAUVOO

THE
WORK
AND THE
GLORY

Praise to the Man

Building the Nauvoo Temple

VOLUME 6

THE
WORK
AND THE
GLORY

Praise to the Man

A HISTORICAL NOVEL

Gerald N. Lund

BOOKCRAFT
Salt Lake City, Utah

THE WORK AND THE GLORY

Volume 1: Pillar of Light
Volume 2: Like a Fire Is Burning
Volume 3: Truth Will Prevail
Volume 4: Thy Gold to Refine
Volume 5: A Season of Joy
Volume 6: Praise to the Man

Library of Congress Catalog Card Number: 95-81231
ISBN 0-88494-999-0

First Printing, 1995

Printed in the United States of America

For behold, this is my work and my glory—to bring to pass the immortality and eternal life of man.

—Moses 1:39

To Jewell G. Lund
(1910–1995)

He was a man who considered himself uneducated but who loved truth and sought for it all of his days. He was a man who never lost his love for learning. He was a man who never faltered in the quest to improve his understanding of the world, the people who inhabit it, and, most important, the God who rules us all.

It was from him that I first learned about the greatness of God's work and glory. It was at his feet that I first gained a testimony of the greatness of the Prophet Joseph Smith. And it was from him that I learned that truth is of such inestimable value that it is worth a lifetime of searching.

Preface

On a beautiful morning in the spring of 1820, Joseph Smith walked into a grove of trees near his home to seek an answer to the question that troubled him. Even as he knelt to pray, the powers of darkness gathered around him and tried to destroy him and stop the work of restoration that was about to unfold. Those powers were turned aside and Joseph was delivered by a blazing pillar of light.

That initial experience would prove to be a type and a shadow of much of the life of Joseph Smith. Opposition rose on every side. Neighbors mocked him, ministers railed at their congregations against him, newspaper editors vilified him, families disowned those who dared to believe in his teachings. He was cursed and condemned, spit upon and slapped, tarred and feathered, jailed and shot at. Ambushes were laid, conspiracies hatched, plots initiated. He was hounded by mobs, betrayed by friends, sentenced to be executed by firing squad.

Time and again, the powers of darkness tried to bring him and the work down. Time and again, higher powers intervened. "Thy days are known," the Lord once told him, "and thy years shall not be numbered less." And so it proved to be. He was protected, shielded, warned, and safeguarded. Sometimes this protective power was subtle and unseen, sometimes clearly miraculous.

During the time period covered in *Praise to the Man*, volume 6 in the series *The Work and the Glory*, the season of joy described in volume 5 came to an end. At first, the forces that would eventually bring down a firestorm on the heads of the Saints were hidden, silent, treacherous. But that would end soon enough, and before it was over even the governor of the state would become part of the movement to destroy the Prophet. And this time the mobs would not be turned aside. This time the cries for blood would not be stilled. This time the rifles and the pistols would not misfire or miss the mark. Joseph's work was done. The keys had been placed on the shoulders of others, and his Father said, "Come home." Under the muzzles of more than a hundred blazing rifles fired by men with blackened faces, the life of the man whom God had chosen to usher in the last dispensation came to an abrupt and violent end.

In the world and among the followers of darkness a great shout of triumph went up. How little did they understand that they had slain the man but not the work. Even the Saints, who waited in stunned, silent grief, did not fully comprehend that what Joseph had set in place and moved forward so boldly could not be ended with powder and ball. They had not yet remembered that as early as 1828, long before Joseph fully knew that his path would take him to Carthage Jail, the Lord said to him: "The works, and the designs, and the purposes of God cannot be frustrated, neither can they come to naught. . . . Remember, remember that it is not the work of God that is frustrated, but the work of men."

Volume 6 may prove to be a troublesome book for some readers. In the late months of 1841 and on into 1842, Joseph Smith began to teach a select circle of leaders the doctrine of plural marriage. Even today, some one hundred fifty years later, that issue continues to be controversial and disturbing in the minds of some people. Plural marriage proved to be so highly divisive in the Church during the Prophet's time that even some in the highest councils found it impossible to accept. One member of the Twelve was excommunicated, and a former member of the First Presidency ended up in a conspiracy to kill Joseph and Hyrum. That was how volatile this issue became. Plural marriage was a major factor in creating the emotions that led to the Martyrdom.

Writing of this time in history proved to be an interesting challenge for this author. Because of its highly explosive emotional ramifications, plural marriage generated a hurricane of reaction in the nineteenth century. Much of that reaction has been preserved to our time. There are journal entries, letters, affidavits, recollections, reminiscences, and formal historical accounts. Sorting through those sources—trying to decide what was truth, what was rumor and innuendo, what was hearsay and embellishment, and what was downright slander and fabrication—proved to be an almost overwhelming task. One cannot even get the most careful of historians to agree on exactly how many women were sealed to Joseph Smith and which of those he actually lived with as husband and wife. But I can assure the reader that those sources were carefully read again and again as this book was written.

There are surely some readers who will think I spent far too much time on this subject and will be uncomfortable with what is given and how it is treated. There will surely be others who believe I have deliberately sidestepped far too much and that a fuller treatment was called for. The fundamental issue—for those back then and for us today—comes down to one basic question: Did God reveal this law to Joseph and require him and others to live it, or was it purely the product of Joseph's own mind? In *Praise to the Man* I have tried to let Joseph and those who believed in him speak for themselves. I have also tried to accurately depict the reactions of those who heard about the restoration of the practice of plural marriage—both those who accepted it and those who bitterly and totally rejected it. Ultimately each reader must answer that fundamental question for himself or herself. Was this of God, or was it of man?

Though I am solely responsible for the work in this volume, there are many who have had tremendous influence in bringing it about. Editors, researchers, artists, secretaries, readers, and publishing staff have all been thanked in previous volumes. With this latest installment, their contribution continues to be as significant as ever, if not more so. And my not naming them again here in no way lessens my debt to them all.

My wife, Lynn, proved to be a sure voice pointing out various snares, pitfalls, and land mines as I tried to negotiate this particularly hazardous terrain. She has a wonderful sense of what works and what does not work and has the courage to express it. That good sense and the honesty to say what she feels are more valuable than even she knows.

Kim Moe and his wife, Jane, continue to be a steadying influence and to offer unflagging support. We have come through this together now for almost seven years and find our friendship and partnership all the more treasured.

I have, more than ever, a deep sense of gratitude and admiration for the numerous historians who have so tirelessly put together the sources upon which I rely so heavily. Though they may not agree with what I have done with their research, without it the historical accuracy of this series would not be possible.

Finally, I should like to pay tribute to my father. Jewell G. Lund, a bright and promising student in high school, came to Salt Lake City from a small town in central Utah and enrolled at the University of Utah. That was in September 1929. In October the stock market crashed and the Great Depression began. Thus his formal higher education ended less than a month after it began. He often referred to himself as an uneducated man and always mourned for that lost opportunity.

Education and learning, however, are not always the same thing. Though he spent his life as a smelter worker and had no further formal education of any kind, he was a learner for all of his life. He read widely, consistently, and constantly. He loved to know and understand things. He worked with his hands and explored with his mind. Most important, he made it a lifelong quest to search for truth and then, when he found it, to incorporate it into his life.

His influence on me both as a person and as a writer is incalculable. In all my growing-up years, our family circle was characterized by a constant focus on the importance of truth and how to find it. You didn't have to agree with Dad, but you'd sure as certain better be prepared to defend your position. He constantly challenged us to see beyond platitudes, cliches, generalities, or fuzzy-headed thinking. "Chapter and verse?" was a demand he often threw at us when we pronounced that this or that was true. By his own personal example, he taught me to dig through the overburden of information so as to reach the ore of truth that lay beneath it. From him and my mother I learned my love of God, my reverence for the scriptures, my admiration for the Prophet Joseph and his teachings, and the importance of truth and true principles.

He influenced me in another important way that would later prove to be of great worth in writing *The Work and the Glory*. He kept a garden larger than most modern building lots. Partly that was to supplement our family's food supply; mostly it was to teach his children to work. He planted rows and rows of raspberries not only for the fruit they would produce but also for the character they would help build. (For those who have not experienced it personally, I can testify that picking raspberries is a character-building experience, though I certainly did not see it that way at the time.) He taught us not only how to work but that work can be ennobling, edifying, and exalting.

Without that legacy he gave to us, this series would never have come into existence. It has been seven years since I began the first work on this series. It has taken literally thousands of hours sitting in front of a computer, hunched over books, lying awake at night mulling over what this or that character should be doing. Without my father's gentle—and sometimes not so gentle—demands to weed the garden, pick raspberries, clean out the chicken coop, haul load after load of "gold dust" from the corral, I would have never had the stamina to continue onward in telling the story as it demanded to be told.

He died without a great accumulation of worldly wealth, but the inheritance he gave to each of us is a treasure of far greater worth. I tried at times before his death to express in words my gratitude for what he has done for me. He would always brush it aside. So I now take this opportunity to more fully and permanently thank him. With each passing year his legacy to me grows in value and worth. Dad, this is small thanks indeed.

GERALD N. LUND

Bountiful, Utah
September 1995

Characters of Note in This Book

The Steed Family

Benjamin, father and grandfather; fifty-six as the book begins.

Mary Ann Morgan, wife of Benjamin, and mother and grandmother; almost fifty-five as the story opens.

Joshua, the oldest son (thirty-four), and his wife, **Caroline Mendenhall** (thirty-four).

    William ("Will"), from Caroline's first marriage; seventeen.

    Olivia ("Livvy"), from Caroline's first marriage; almost fourteen.

    Savannah; four.

    Charles Benjamin; seventeen months.

Jessica Roundy Steed Griffith, Joshua's first wife, widow of John Griffith; thirty-seven.

    Rachel, from marriage to Joshua; nine and a half.

    Luke and Mark, sons from John Griffith's first marriage; almost nine and seven, respectively.

    John Benjamin, from marriage to John; three.

Nathan, the second son (thirty-two), and his wife, **Lydia McBride** (not quite thirty-two).

    Joshua Benjamin ("Young Joshua"); ten.

    Emily; just barely nine.

    Elizabeth Mary ("Lizzie"); three.

    Josiah Nathan; six months.

Melissa, the older daughter (thirty), and her husband, **Carlton ("Carl") Rogers** (thirty-one).

    Carlton Hezekiah; nine.

    David Benjamin; not quite seven.

    Caleb John; almost five.

    Sarah; two and a half.

Rebecca, the younger daughter (twenty-three), and her husband, **Derek Ingalls** (almost twenty-four).
Christopher Joseph; two.
Matthew, the youngest son (just turning twenty-one), and his new bride, **Jennifer Jo McIntire** (nineteen and a half).

Note: Deceased children are not included in the above listing.

The Smiths

* Lucy Mack, the mother.
* Hyrum, Joseph's elder brother; almost six years older than Joseph.
* Mary Fielding, Hyrum's wife.
* Joseph, age thirty-five as the story opens.
* Emma Hale, Joseph's wife; a year and a half older than Joseph.
* Joseph and Emma's children: Julia Murdock, Joseph III, Frederick Granger Williams, Alexander Hale, and Don Carlos.
* Don Carlos, Joseph's youngest brother; ten years younger than Joseph.

Note: There are sisters and other brothers to Joseph, but they do not play major roles in the novel.

Others

* John C. Bennett, converted to the Church in 1840, elected mayor of Nauvoo in 1841.
Jean Claude Dubuque, lumberman in Wisconsin.
* Thomas Ford, governor of the state of Illinois.
* Robert Foster, member of the Church in Nauvoo.

*Designates actual people from Church history.

Solomon Garrett, supervisor of "common schools" in Ramus, Illinois.

Peter Ingalls, Derek's younger brother; seventeen.

* Heber C. Kimball, friend of Brigham Young's and a member of the Quorum of the Twelve Apostles.

Kathryn Marie McIntire, Jennifer Jo's sister; four years younger than Jennifer.

Abigail Pottsworth, a convert to the Church during Heber C. Kimball's first mission to England in 1837.

Jenny Pottsworth, English convert; not quite sixteen as the story begins.

* Willard Richards, member of the Quorum of the Twelve Apostles.

* Orrin Porter Rockwell, close friend and bodyguard of Joseph Smith.

* George A. Smith, member of the Quorum of the Twelve Apostles.

* John Taylor, member of the Quorum of the Twelve Apostles.

* Wilford Woodruff, member of the Quorum of the Twelve Apostles.

* Brigham Young, President of the Quorum of the Twelve Apostles.

Though too numerous to list here, there are many other actual people from the pages of history who are mentioned by name in the novel. Stephen Markham, Israel Barlow, Sidney Rigdon, William and Wilson Law, and many others mentioned in the book were real people who lived and participated in the events described in this work.

*Designates actual people from Church history.

The Benjamin Steed Family[†]

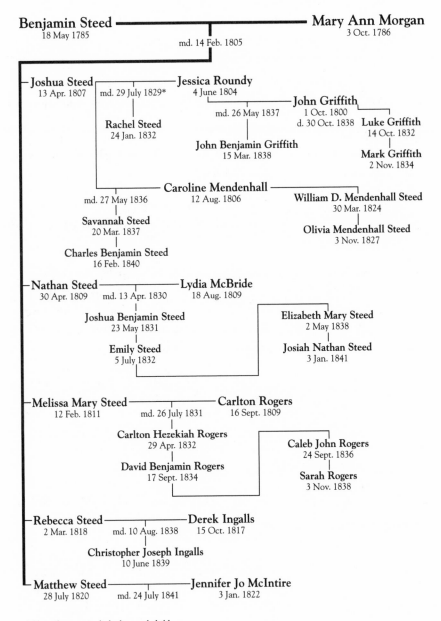

Benjamin Steed ——————————————— **Mary Ann Morgan**
18 May 1785   3 Oct. 1786
                        md. 14 Feb. 1805

— **Joshua Steed** ———————— **Jessica Roundy**
13 Apr. 1807   md. 29 July 1829*   4 June 1804
                                                                    —— **John Griffith**
                                        md. 26 May 1837   1 Oct. 1800
                                                                    d. 30 Oct. 1838   **Luke Griffith**
                        Rachel Steed   14 Oct. 1832
                        24 Jan. 1832
                                        John Benjamin Griffith   **Mark Griffith**
                                        15 Mar. 1838   2 Nov. 1834

                        ———————— **Caroline Mendenhall** ————————
        md. 27 May 1836   12 Aug. 1806   **William D. Mendenhall Steed**
                                                                                        30 Mar. 1824
                        Savannah Steed
                        20 Mar. 1837   **Olivia Mendenhall Steed**
                                                                                    3 Nov. 1827
                Charles Benjamin Steed
                16 Feb. 1840

— **Nathan Steed** ———————— **Lydia McBride**
30 Apr. 1809   md. 13 Apr. 1830   18 Aug. 1809
                        Joshua Benjamin Steed   **Elizabeth Mary Steed**
                        23 May 1831   2 May 1838

                        Emily Steed   **Josiah Nathan Steed**
                        5 July 1832   3 Jan. 1841

— **Melissa Mary Steed** ———————— **Carlton Rogers**
12 Feb. 1811   md. 26 July 1831   16 Sept. 1809
                        Carlton Hezekiah Rogers   **Caleb John Rogers**
                        29 Apr. 1832   24 Sept. 1836

                        David Benjamin Rogers   **Sarah Rogers**
                        17 Sept. 1834   3 Nov. 1838

— **Rebecca Steed** ———————— **Derek Ingalls**
2 Mar. 1818   md. 10 Aug. 1838   15 Oct. 1817
                Christopher Joseph Ingalls
                10 June 1839

— **Matthew Steed** ———————— **Jennifer Jo McIntire**
28 July 1820   md. 24 July 1841   3 Jan. 1822

†Chart does not include deceased children
*Divorced Jan. 1833

Key to Abbreviations Used in Chapter Notes

Throughout the chapter notes, abbreviated references are given. The following key gives the full bibliographic data for those references.

American Moses   Leonard J. Arrington, *Brigham Young: American Moses* (New York: Alfred A. Knopf, 1985.)

CHFT   *Church History in the Fulness of Times* (Salt Lake City: The Church of Jesus Christ of Latter-day Saints, 1989.)

HC   Joseph Smith, *History of The Church of Jesus Christ of Latter-day Saints*, ed. B. H. Roberts, 7 vols. (Salt Lake City: The Church of Jesus Christ of Latter-day Saints, 1932–51.)

In Old Nauvoo   George W. Givens, *In Old Nauvoo: Everyday Life in the City of Joseph* (Salt Lake City: Deseret Book Co., 1990.)

JD   *Journal of Discourses*, 26 vols. (London: Latter-day Saints' Book Depot, 1854–86.)

LHCK   Orson F. Whitney, *Life of Heber C. Kimball*, Collector's Edition (Salt Lake City: Bookcraft, 1992.)

Restoration   Ivan J. Barrett, *Joseph Smith and the Restoration: A History of the Church to 1846* (Provo, Utah: Brigham Young University Press, 1973.)

Women of Covenant   Jill Mulvay Derr, Janath Russell Cannon, and Maureen Ursenbach Beecher, *Women of Covenant: The Story of Relief Society* (Salt Lake City: Deseret Book Co., 1992.)

Women of Nauvoo   Richard Neitzel Holzapfel and Jeni Broberg Holzapfel, *Women of Nauvoo* (Salt Lake City: Bookcraft, 1992.)

Praise *to the* Man

Praise to the man who communed with Jehovah!
Jesus anointed that Prophet and Seer.
Blessed to open the last dispensation,
Kings shall extol him, and nations revere.

Praise to his mem'ry, he died as a martyr;
Honored and blest be his ever great name!
Long shall his blood, which was shed by assassins,
Plead unto heav'n while the earth lauds his fame.

Hail to the Prophet, ascended to heaven!
Traitors and tyrants now fight him in vain.
Mingling with Gods, he can plan for his brethren;
Death cannot conquer the hero again.

—William W. Phelps

W e've got a live one!"

The man darted away, running hard for the nearest outcropping of rock. Behind him, a length of black fuse ran along the ground, then up the sheer rock face. A tiny, sputtering tongue of fire puffed little clouds of white smoke into the air as it ate its way relentlessly along the cord. Nathan, positioned behind his own rock, watched until the flame reached the point just a foot or so from where the fuse disappeared into a neatly drilled hole in the limestone cliff. He dropped to a crouch, clasping his hands over his ears, his head down near the ground. Benjamin didn't need that signal to follow suit. He was already hunched over and covering his head.

For one brief moment, there was an eerie silence over the stone quarry, then *whummph!* The earth beneath Nathan's face shook, and just in front of his nose small pebbles momentarily danced on the hard surface. The noise of the explosion was followed almost simultaneously by an earsplitting *crack!*

Nathan straightened slowly, then stood up. Benjamin pushed up to stand beside him, brushing off the knees of his trousers. All around the quarry the men were standing, each one looking at where the charges had been planted only minutes before. A cloud of smoke and dust was roiling upward in the sultry morning air. As it cleared, Nathan nodded in satisfaction. It always amazed him how black powder in such small amounts could so completely work its will on virgin stone. Twenty feet of the sheer face of the rock wall had cracked cleanly in nearly straight lines which led from hole to hole. These holes had been drilled by another team the previous day with point drills and eight-pound sledgehammers called double jacks or jack sledges.

"That should last us most of the day," Benjamin grunted as the quarry foreman and the black-powder man walked across the floor of the quarry to take a closer look.

"Yeah," Nathan mumbled, "maybe longer." He reached in his pocket for his bandanna and wiped the back of his neck. The cloth came away dark and wet. It was barely nine o'clock in the morning, but already the sky above had a brassiness to it, holding sure promise of another scorching July day. Already the air in the quarry was stifling. He shrugged, and stuffed the bandanna back in his pants. This was his and his father's "tithing day"—an offering of one day in ten to work on the temple—and you took whatever task the building committee assigned. You also accepted whatever old Mother Nature happened to offer for weather that day too, and complaining about it hadn't ever changed it much.

Off to the side, Benjamin watched his son, guessing at the thoughts going through his mind. He smiled inwardly. They were getting to be so much alike, he thought, that he knew what Nathan was thinking. Back in Vermont, when his two sons were growing into manhood, everyone had talked about how much Joshua was like his father and Nathan like his mother. Much of that came from their physical appearance. Nathan wasn't much more than five feet ten inches tall and was slight of build. Benjamin and Joshua were both about six feet and much stockier through the body. Nathan's eyes were a pale brown, almost like a dusty road, and his hair was only slightly darker. His features were quite nondescript. He wasn't really plain, but neither did he have Joshua's rugged handsomeness that caused women to turn and glance in admiration. Nathan's beard, when he grew it, was even lighter in color than his hair and grew slowly enough that he could go several days before one noticed he hadn't shaved. Joshua and Benjamin both had dark hair and heavy whisker growth, though Benjamin's hair and whiskers were now liberally touched with gray. So with regard to physical appearance, their friends and neighbors had been right. Joshua was the son most like his father.

But with regard to temperament, that was something else again. For years Benjamin had told himself that the ongoing battles and the seemingly never-ending clashes between him and Joshua were the result of Joshua's hotheadedness and a streak of independence that wouldn't be tamed. But as Mary Ann was wont to frequently remind him, Benjamin Steed had carried a pretty wide stubborn streak of his own back then, and a temper that sometimes seemed bound by nothing stronger than a single strand of a spider's web.

He grinned openly now. Fortunately, she always used the past tense when she described him that way. And he knew she was right. How strange—and yet how fitting—that life, and the gospel, and living with a wonderful woman for nigh onto thirty-seven years had brought Benjamin Steed to a point where he was far more like his second son than his first. Since his return to the family circle some years before, Joshua had grown quite close to his father. But Benjamin and Nathan had become almost as one. *Like now,* he thought. Here they both were, dreading the heat of the day, and yet knowing there was not one thing to be done about it and so you simply pushed it aside and refused to brood about it.

He decided to test his theory. He stepped over to his son. "Hot enough, isn't it?"

Nathan glanced up at the sky, then pulled his hat down a

little lower over his eyes. "Not much point in complaining about it, though. It just adds to the supply of hot air."

Benjamin chuckled softly, pleased to have his validation. He slapped his son on the shoulder. "Right. Brother Garnett says he wants you and me on the jib crane this morning. May as well get to it."

———— • ————

By eleven-thirty, they had the first block of stone down and squared sufficiently to send it up to the stonemasons at the temple site. Benjamin and Nathan were manning the winch on the jib crane. They watched as four men snaked two thick cables underneath the block, using the space between the logs. In a moment, they had the cables secure.

Nathan pushed on the jib, turning the crane partially around its circular base until the jib, or the boom, of the derrick was over the four men. As he did so, Benjamin spun the winch and let the ropes and the big hook start to lower. With practiced ease the men secured the hook to the cables.

"All right," Benjamin said, tightening his grip on the winch handle as Nathan joined him there. "Here we go."

Benjamin and Nathan were both grunting now as they leaned into the crank. The stone lifted off the floor of the quarry and began to rise slowly but steadily as father and son kept the winch turning.

"That's good!" One of the men by the block was in a crouch, eyeing the height of the waiting wagon to see when the stone was high enough to clear the long bed. Nathan reached out and slapped the ratchet lever with the heel of his hand, making sure it was engaged in the gears, and then he and Benjamin let the winch ease back just a hair until it caught and held. Now both of them leaned against the jib as the four men pulled on the stone. The boom responded slowly, the bull wheel at the base of the mast creaking ominously now with the weight, as they moved the block around a hundred-and-eighty-degree arc until it hung directly over the wagon.

The nearest man eyed the lineup of stone and wagon, then turned and held up both thumbs. Benjamin and Nathan sprang back into action. Feet planted firmly to prevent them from slipping, straining until the veins in their foreheads stood out like a mole's burrow across a meadow, they pushed the winch handle forward just enough to take the pressure off the catch. Carefully, they let the winch come back toward them now, and slowly, ever so slowly, the huge limestone block lowered onto the wagon bed, settling as gently as a baby being laid in a crib.

The teamster, who had been standing back watching the quarry team work, now swung up into his wagon seat. As he took out his whip, he turned to Albert Rockwood, the quarry foreman. "That reminds me. Brother Cutler says he's shorthanded up at the temple site for unloading. Can you spare a couple of men?"

Rockwood frowned, but immediately nodded. Alpheus Cutler was a member of the building committee. If he said he needed men, then he needed men.

"Brother Steed? Nathan? You wanna go up to the temple site and help them out?"

"Whatever you say," Benjamin said with a wave.

"Absolutely," Nathan chortled. It would be hot up on the bluffs too, but at least there would be the possibility of a breeze from time to time. He turned and hopped up on the wagon, holding out his hand to help his father do the same.

Carlton Rogers pulled back on the reins gently as they entered the shade of a large oak tree. "Whoa there!" he called.

The team of horses needed no urging and immediately stopped their forward progress. The animals were pulling nearly a half ton of brick in the big flatbed wagon, brick that was to be laid as the basement floor of the temple. They had come up the hill to the temple site in the afternoon's worst heat. The horses' shoulders and withers were dripping sweat, and even the straps of the harnessing were darkened clear through. Carl could see flecks of foam around their nostrils as they raised their heads and shook them, glad to be relieved, even if only for a few moments.

"Can we get down and play, Pa?"

Carl turned and looked at his three sons lined up on the wagon bench beside him. Caleb, who, at nearly five, was the youngest, had been the one to ask, but from the excitement in their eyes it was obvious that he spoke for his brothers as well. Then he looked across an open field where a group of boys were playing stickball and rolling metal hoops.

"All right, but you stay off the road."

"Yes, Pa." It came in a chorus.

"And keep an eye out. I don't want to have to come lookin' for you once I'm unloaded."

"Yes, Pa."

He let the sternness in his face soften. "Then why are you standing around here?"

With a whoop they were across the road and gone.

Taking off his hat and wiping his brow with the sleeve of his shirt, Carl looked around. There were plenty of men working at the site today, but he couldn't see either of the two foremen who usually came out to take the consignment of bricks. But there were three wagons from the quarry ahead of him waiting to unload, so there was no sense getting in a hurry. He put his hat back on and turned to the wagon.

Carl Rogers was not a member of The Church of Jesus Christ of Latter-day Saints. In that, he and his brother-in-law Joshua were alike, but there the similarity ended. After years of hostility, Joshua had come to an uneasy truce with the Church. He married Caroline Mendenhall, who wasn't a member either. But now Caroline wanted to be baptized. Joshua couldn't accept that, and so a note of tension had crept into their marriage. Melissa Steed had been a Mormon when Carl married her. Carl's family had been opposed to the Church and Carl had inherited a little of that attitude for a while. So there had been tension between him and Melissa over religion too, but that was completely gone now. He wasn't interested at all in the Church, but he respected Melissa's right to worship as she chose. Though he had not openly admitted this to her, he was actually pleased to be living among the Mormons now. They were a good people, and they made for a strong community for him and his family. Unlike Joshua, he had no residual feelings about Mormonism.

Carl turned to the box beneath the wagon seat and found a large rag and a currycomb. He moved forward and began to rub down his team. He worked slowly and methodically, first drying them off, then taking long strokes with the currycomb, watching the flesh of the horses ripple with pleasure as he worked them over. Carl was donating these bricks to the temple project. It was his third load now. The building committee sent the men down to the kilns to provide the labor, but Carl provided the materials and hauled the bricks up here at no cost. It pleased Melissa greatly that he would do so, and it hadn't hurt his relationship with her family either.

He finished, slapping the near horse's rump affectionately as he moved to put the comb away again. Sure, donating the bricks cost him out-of-pocket money, but his kilns were running two shifts a day now trying to keep up with the demand by the Mormons for new housing. He could afford to be a little generous. And besides, his relationship with Melissa was as happy as it had ever been in their ten years of marriage.

His head came up with a jerk. *Ten years?* They had been married on July twenty-sixth, 1831. Today was July twenty-sixth! He groaned and hit his head with his hand. Today was his tenth wedding anniversary and he had totally forgotten. Then almost instantly he felt relieved. He *had* remembered now, before it was too late. He would swing past the woodworking shop where Brigham Young and Matthew Steed worked in partnership and buy her that rocking chair. Melissa had admired it openly more than once and now he understood. That was her way of telling him what he should get her.

"Ho! Carl!"

Carl turned around. Another wagon from the quarry was approaching. He lifted a hand to shade his eyes, then immediately raised a hand to wave. "Afternoon, Israel."

Israel Barlow pulled his team in behind Carl's wagon, and jumped down. Carl walked to meet him and they shook hands.

"Another load today, huh?" Barlow commented, eyeing the stacks of bricks in Carl's wagon.

"Yes. And one more for you too." Carl turned and looked at the man's team. Israel Barlow had one of the finest working teams in Nauvoo—a beautifully matched pair of black mares— and often he was at the quarry whether it was his tithing day or not. Barlow had hauled more than one load of brick for Carl Rogers as a way of supplementing his farm income and they had become good friends.

"How are the two lovebirds doing?"

Carl turned. "Lovebirds?"

"Yes. Didn't I hear your brother-in-law got married on Saturday?"

"Oh." Carl's mind hadn't been thinking in terms of Matthew and Jennifer Jo, and the question had caught him off guard. He smiled. "Yes. Well, it's a little hard to tell. They're both off in a world of their own."

As Barlow nodded and chuckled, Carl squinted into the afternoon sun, looking at Israel's wagon. As in most wagons, there was a small metal tube fastened to the side of the wagon seat. It was designed to hold the teamster's whip, easily at hand when needed, but leaving his hands free when it wasn't. Israel's wagon had the holder but nothing in it.

"I see you haven't come to your senses and bought yourself a whip for your team yet."

Barlow gave him a look reserved for those who had been too long in the sun, and Carl grinned. This was a running gibe between the two of them. Israel also took a lot of joshing from the other teamsters around town for his refusal to carry a whip for his team.

"Treat an intelligent animal with love and respect and you won't be needing no whip to make him obey you," Barlow grunted. "Not that I'd be holding it against a man who can't control his animals if he bought one." He gave a meaningful look toward

Carl's wagon, where a long buggy whip stood in its holder.

Carl laughed easily. You didn't top Israel Barlow easily in a joshing contest. Carl wasn't a man to whip his teams either, but a sharp pop of the whip over their ears was sometimes necessary to get a reluctant team to listen to you. He turned and looked at the fine-looking mares harnessed to Barlow's wagon. "You're probably right," he mused. "If I had a couple of high-spirited animals like those, with a mind of their own, I suppose a whip wouldn't make a lot of difference one way or the other. They'll just go their own way, no matter what you want them to do."

Barlow frowned, and Carl knew he had hit the mark. These two horses were particularly high-spirited, but they were amazingly responsive to Barlow's every command. He rarely even raised his voice to them. And Israel Barlow took great pride in that. He started a retort, then saw the satisfaction on Carl's face, and bit it off. "Only a cretin needs a whip to control his animals," he grumbled.

Then, happy for a respite, Barlow looked beyond Carl at two approaching men. "Well, there's a couple of your in-laws. Looks like it's about your turn to unload."

Carl turned in surprise as Benjamin and Nathan came up. "I thought you were working down in the quarry today."

"We were," Nathan grinned, "but Pa looked so plumb tuckered out, they took pity on us and sent us up for some lighter duty."

Benjamin ignored that. "Hello, Carl. Hello, Israel." Then to Carl, "Did Joshua and Will get off?"

Carl shook his head. "They were catching that noon steamboat, but then Joshua decided he has some business in Warsaw. They'll leave tonight, then catch a boat on down to St. Louis from there tomorrow."

"Oh," Benjamin said, his mind already caught by something else. He was squinting up at Barlow's wagon. "I see you haven't got yourself a whip yet, Israel."

There was a low rumble, noncommittal, incomprehensible. Then before Benjamin could pursue it further, Barlow looked at

Carl. "Come on, Rogers," he groused, "get your wagon up in line so I can get out of here and on with my work."

———•———

Rebecca Steed Ingalls knocked lightly on the door to Nathan and Lydia's cabin, then opened it up slowly. This was standard procedure along Granger Street. Six Steed homes sat either side by side or facing each other across the street. Anyone in the family was family. One only knocked to give warning in case someone might not be dressed properly inside. Inside, Lydia's four children were all occupied. Young Joshua had little Josiah on the floor, letting him wrestle him. Emily and Elizabeth Mary were at the table, drawing with a piece of chalk on a slate.

"Oh, hello, Aunt Rebecca," Joshua said.

"Hello, Joshua. Is your mother at home?"

"No. She just left to go up to the store a few minutes ago. She said she'll probably stay until closing time."

"All right. Thank you. I'll go over there."

A few minutes later, Rebecca stood on the store porch, waiting until the couple inside the store came out. There was a brief exchange of pleasantries—Rebecca knew them only as having recently arrived from Tennessee—then they moved to their carriage. As they drove away, Rebecca peered through the store window just to be sure. It was Monday afternoon, which was usually a slow time at the store, and she hoped there would not be any other customers for a time. Lydia was at the rear shelves, straightening bolts of cloth. Caroline was at the counter, making entries in a ledger. Relieved, Rebecca went inside.

Lydia and Caroline both looked up, and both spoke at once. "Oh, hello, Rebecca."

"Good afternoon." She moved across the room, looking around to see if Nathan or Jenny was nearby.

"Where's Christopher?" Caroline asked.

"Derek had to get some tools fixed at the blacksmith's, so he took him along." She didn't add that taking Christopher had been her suggestion.

"That's good," Lydia said. "I'll bet it feels good to you not to be lugging him around for once. He's such a little chunk, that one."

Rebecca smiled and nodded. Christopher was two now, and built like a stone fence. He also went everywhere on a dead run, letting his body lean forward until he was ready to fall, then making his feet race to keep it from happening. But he still wanted his mother to hold him from time to time, which was enough to make anyone's arms ache after a few moments.

Rebecca looked over to the corner, where the potbellied stove sat cold and unused now. In the winter it would glow cherry red and always have two or three persons gathered round it, passing the time or playing this game or that. Almost every store in the western part of the United States had such a corner, often with a small table whose top was an inlaid board and a corncob cut into narrow slices to serve as checker pieces. It was an important gathering place, even in cities the size of Nauvoo. She turned to her two sisters-in-law. "Do you have a minute to sit down?"

"Of course," Caroline said, giving Lydia a quick look. They came around from the counter and moved to the wicker chairs by the stove. As they sat down, Rebecca looked around again. "Where's Jenny?" she asked innocently.

"Taking inventory on some stuff delivered today," Lydia said, openly curious now. Rebecca was not a good one at pulling off feigned casualness. "And Nathan is at the quarry today."

"So how are you feeling?" Caroline asked, watching Rebecca closely. "Are you still having problems?"

"Yes." Rebecca looked up and tried to smile but it was not very convincing. "I . . ." Her face flushed a little and she looked down at her hands again. "I've been thinking about going to a doctor."

Again a quick look passed between Lydia and Caroline.

"It's not that serious," Rebecca went on in a rush. "Really. It's just that, well, ever since Christopher was born, it's just . . ." She was coloring now, even though she was speaking to two women who not only were related to her by marriage but also were as close to her as her own sister. "I don't know. I just worry a little. Christopher's weaned now, and now that Derek is home again, he and I are thinking maybe it's time to have another baby. I . . . I would just like to know that everything is all right, I guess."

"Then you should see a doctor," Lydia said firmly.

"Absolutely," Caroline agreed.

Rebecca finally looked up, first at Caroline and then to Lydia. "I was thinking about Doctor Bennett, but . . ." She let it trail off, watching for their reaction.

"Mayor Bennett?" Lydia asked in surprise. "But that's a wonderful idea, Rebecca. They say he is very well trained."

"I agree," Caroline said enthusiastically. "He started a medical college in Ohio, you know. And I'm told he has especially studied in . . . in womanly concerns."

"Yes, I'd heard that," Rebecca murmured. "Actually, I have a time with him tomorrow morning."

"Good," Caroline said. "I'm glad. He'll probably tell you everything is fine, but you need to find out for sure."

But Lydia was still watching Rebecca's face. "You're not worried about all those awful rumors, are you?"

Rebecca's chin dropped and there was the briefest of nods. "I know I shouldn't be, Lydia, but what if they're true?"

Caroline was suddenly agitated. Joshua Steed was one of Nauvoo's most prosperous businessmen, and because of that he and Caroline had been invited on more than one occasion to have dinner with John C. Bennett. She was very impressed with the man. She found him to be witty, urbane, very learned, and a man of great charm. The rumors floating around the city about his past had been bad enough. Now there were the whisperings about questionable behavior.

"I think it is terrible that anyone would give those wild stories one moment's thought," she said. "He's the temporary Assistant President of the Church, remember. He's helping out while Sidney Rigdon is sick. Do you think Joseph would allow that if there was anything at all to those stories?"

That was something Rebecca hadn't considered, and it cheered her considerably. "No," she mused, "I suppose not."

"Of course not." Lydia leaned forward. "I agree with Caroline. You need to be sure there's nothing wrong, Rebecca. And everyone agrees, Doctor Bennett is the best."

Rebecca sat back in her chair, greatly relieved. This was why she had come to talk to them. "You're right," she said. "It wouldn't be fair to act on the basis of backyard gossip."

———•———

Alpheus Cutler set down his mason's hammer and looked out west over the river to where the sun hung low in the sky. He reached in the vest pocket of his leather apron and pulled out a watch. Flipping the lid of it open, he saw that it was nearly six o'clock.

He turned and looked around with satisfaction. They had made good progress today. Ten more blocks, maybe twelve, and the next course of the basement level would be done. Yes, Cutler thought, they were making good progress, and the Lord's commandments would be fulfilled.

In January, Joseph Smith had received a revelation concerning work for the dead and the importance of the temple. It had been published in the Church newspaper, the *Times and Seasons*, just last month. The Lord had been most specific. The building committee, chaired by Cutler, Elias Higbee, and Reynolds Cahoon, had committed one particular passage to memory and referred to it often so as to motivate them continually to make their best efforts. He half closed his eyes, letting the words sweep through his mind once again:

Build a house to my name, for the Most High to dwell therein; for there is not place found on earth, that he may come and restore again that which was lost unto you, or, which he hath taken away, even the fulness of the priesthood; for a baptismal font there is not upon the earth; that they, my saints, may be baptized for those who are dead.

It would be many months before the temple was completed, but Joseph had asked William Weeks, the temple architect, to draw up plans for the font, which would go in the basement. Brother Weeks had now presented that draft to the Prophet and the Twelve. Joseph was pleased, and Cutler and the others who led the building committee knew that there was a very good chance that within a few days the formal approval would be given and work on the font would begin. That meant the building committee had to have the basement ready or there would be no place for the font to go.

But he was no longer worried. Today was the twenty-sixth day of July. He guessed it would take a month or two to build the font, once it was approved. With the cellar walls within a few feet of ground level around the whole perimeter of the temple and a third of the basement floor now laid with brick, Cutler knew that they could be ready for the font in another three or four weeks, maybe five at the most.

Glancing at his watch again, Cutler saw that it was now six o'clock straight up. He turned and looked across the work site. He tipped his head back. "Brethren!" he shouted. "It's six o'clock. That's all for today. Thank you, one and all."

———◆———

As the men laid aside their tools and started for home, Nathan walked over to the well, filled the dipper from the bucket, removed his hat, and dumped the water squarely on top of his head. He got another dipperful and did it again. A little shudder of pleasure ran through him as the water cascaded down his neck and across his face. Sunset was only a couple of hours away now, but the afternoon heat was still fierce and draining.

Suddenly he felt a hand clapped on his shoulder. "Hot enough for you, Brother Nathan?"

"It sure is." Nathan turned, wiping the water from his eyes with the sleeve of his shirt. It was Joseph. He had his hat off as well. His normally fair hair was plastered to his forehead. He had been assigned to work with the stonemasons today, and his clothes, face, arms, and hands were covered with gray dust. Sweat had trickled down his face, leaving him with streaks through the layers of dirt.

Nathan turned and got a fresh dipper of water. He held it out with a mischievous look. "You ready for a drink?" Without waiting for an answer, Nathan drank it down.

Joseph's eyes narrowed. "Ah," he said softly, "now there's a real Christian for you. Thank you, Brother Nathan."

"Most assuredly," Nathan said, handing him the empty dipper.

Joseph's head came up a bit. "Well," he said, looking on past Nathan, "here comes your father."

Nathan swung around. To his surprise, Benjamin was still bent over, holding a plumb line against the side of the stone for one of the masons. Nathan turned back, about to make a comment about Joseph's eyesight, just in time to catch a blur out of the corner of his eye. He ducked, but Joseph had anticipated it. The full force of the bucket of water caught Nathan squarely in the face, knocking him back a step and leaving him gasping.

Joseph dropped the bucket back. "There you go," he said with satisfaction. "One good Christian turn deserves another, don't you think?"

Chapter Notes

The stone quarry, which became the primary source of building material for the Nauvoo Temple, was located near the river on the northwest end of the city, a few blocks north of the current LDS visitors' center. It yielded a fine whitish-gray to light tan limestone that was easily worked by stonemasons. After being blasted off, the blocks were usually shaped to a uniform size at the quarry and then were taken by wagon to the temple site, where they were given their final chiseling and polishing. Working in the quarry was the most grueling and dangerous work done in connection with the building of the temple, but also the most interesting. Often townspeople and visitors would come to watch the blasting and the other work there. At the height of the construction project about a hundred men were employed at the quarry, and in a period of three and a half years over a hundred casks of blasting powder were used. (See *Encyclopedia of Mormonism*, s.v. "Nauvoo Temple"; *In Old Nauvoo*, pp. 150–51.)

The scripture recalled by Alpheus Cutler is now D&C 124:27–29. It was received by Joseph on 19 January 1841.

"C ome, old friends," Joseph said as Benjamin finished drinking deeply from the dipper, "I'll walk with you back down the hill."

Other than Alpheus Cutler and Reynolds Cahoon, who were still over in the stonecutting yard, the two Steeds and the Prophet Joseph were the last men at the site.

They moved off slowly, feeling the weariness of a day's hard labor. They had gone only half a block before they reached the edge of the bluff that overlooked the city proper. Joseph stopped and his two companions followed suit. Nathan often did the same thing whenever he was at this spot. It provided one of the loveliest of views in all of Hancock County. The main part of Nauvoo lay below them in a grand panorama. The Mississippi River encircled the city on three sides like some vast, protective arm. Across it, the green plains of Iowa stretched to the horizon. Through the summer's haze they could make out the buildings that marked the site of Zarahemla on the other side of the river.

Near to Montrose, the Saints had named it after the great capital city of the Nephites, mentioned so often in the Book of Mormon.

Nathan let his eyes drop slightly. The land below them was marked off into squares by the neat pattern of streets. To the south, just coming into view, a riverboat was churning the water behind it white. To the southwest, the ferry, carrying a wagon and team and several standing passengers, was in midriver, coming back from the Iowa side. They could see the tiny figures of two men, pulling mightily on the rope to move the ferry against the current.

"Nauvoo the Beautiful," Joseph said softly.

They both looked at him, then Benjamin nodded. "You were inspired to call it that, Joseph." He chuckled. "Though at the time, I must admit, I had some questions about the appropriateness of the name."

Nathan laughed too. *Nauvoo* was a Hebrew word, according to Joseph. It meant a "beautiful location or place of rest." At that point back in the summer of 1839, Commerce hardly seemed up to the name. Now no one denied the prophetic nature of the title.

Nathan let his mind go back. He remembered the almost impassable swampland, the hordes of mosquitoes, the unseen chiggers in the grass that always managed to work their way above a man's boot line and dig in under the skin, driving any normal person insane with the itching. There was the "Nauvoo fly," as the Saints now called it, which was a particularly troublesome mothlike insect peculiar to this place and which plagued the city every summer. There were snakes and muskrats and gophers and mice and all sorts of creeping things that left the men frustrated trying to control them and the women squeamish about their presence.

Two years ago, there hadn't been much that was beautiful. Now, the changes were dramatic. The swamps, with few exceptions, were now neat checkerboards of corn and rye, sorghum and barley, tomatoes, beans, melons, squash, and half a dozen other crops. The land below them was crisscrossed with streets running straight as an arrow north and south, and east and west. Houses, barns, stores, shops, and sheds were going up everywhere. There were still the cabins and a few shanties down by the river, but there were also the spacious frame homes, handsome cottages with picket fences and richly colored flower gardens, two-story brick houses that would hold their own nicely in New York City or Philadelphia. There were three thriving brickyards, at least half a dozen stores in addition to the Steeds', two blacksmith shops, a gunsmith shop, two printing establishments, and several woodworking shops, including the recent one begun in partnership between Brigham Young and Matthew Steed.

Joseph stirred, as if ready to move on, but Benjamin, seeing it, spoke quickly. "May I ask you a question, Joseph?"

"Of course."

Benjamin looked out across the panorama before them. "Is this to be our permanent home?"

That brought the Prophet's head around. The blue eyes were level and calm. "Why do you ask that?"

"Because I remember something you once said back in Kirtland, about the destiny of the Church." He paused, trying to remember the exact words.

Joseph knew exactly what he meant. "I said that someday the Church would fill North and South America, and eventually it would fill the world." He stopped, sobering, realizing now why Benjamin had asked what he did. "And I prophesied that someday there will be tens of thousands of Latter-day Saints gathered in the Rocky Mountains."

Nathan didn't move. He had not thought of that meeting for a long time, but he could clearly remember the little shiver of—what? excitement, anticipation, dread?—that ran through all who were present that night. It was one of those times they had come to recognize, when the spirit of prophecy lay heavily on Joseph. His face would almost transform itself. His skin would seem to glow. His eyes would get a faraway look in them, as though they were gazing on the very breadth of eternity.

"So this isn't to be our final stop?" Benjamin asked softly.

Joseph looked at him for several long seconds; then he just smiled, and started off down the hill. Benjamin gave Nathan a quizzical look, then shrugged, and they moved off to fall into step beside the Prophet. They walked for nearly five minutes in silence before Joseph moved closer to Benjamin and laid a hand on his shoulder. "Benjamin, my friend."

"Yes, Joseph?"

"There's a favorite passage of mine in one of the revelations. It says simply, 'Let your hearts be comforted concerning Zion; for all flesh is in my hands. Therefore . . .'" He let it hang, inviting Benjamin to finish it for him.

Benjamin looked puzzled, but Nathan knew it well. "'Therefore,'" he said for his father, "'be still, and know that I am God.'"

"Exactly," Joseph said soberly. He was still looking at Benjamin. "I don't know how long we shall be allowed to stay here in this beautiful place. I do have a strong feeling that this is not our final destiny. But in the meantime?" He smiled, and now any discernible worry in his countenance had disappeared. "It's a beautiful place. Let's enjoy it to the fullest."

Jenny Pottsworth was busy in the back room of the store, taking inventory of two wagonloads of barrels and boxes brought in from Springfield earlier in the day. She enjoyed being out front behind the counter, visiting with the people and helping them find what they needed, but she found satisfaction in the more menial things as well. Perhaps that was a legacy from being brought up in the slums of Preston, England, the only daughter of a widow who grubbed out a living in the great cotton factories there. There was something innately pleasing to her in the process of tallying things and then organizing them neatly on the shelves and in the bins, having a place for each thing and each thing in its place. That kind of order made it easier to satisfy the needs of the customers, and Jenny took pride in the fact that in this store the needs of their customers were met with efficient and cheerful regularity.

She reached up and brushed a damp lock of hair back from her forehead. Jenny would turn sixteen in another month. That surprised most people, for she seemed much older than that. Perhaps her maturity was a product of her early life as well. English childhood labor laws allowed children to work in the cotton mills once they turned nine, and Jenny had begun two days after her birthday. Jenny was a woman now, both in body and in mind. She knew that men considered her attractive. Even those with absolutely no romantic interest in her seemed to enjoy being around her and talking with her. She accepted that fact simply and without pride, viewing it as one of the many gifts with which God had blessed her. Her long golden hair, the wide-set eyes, her clear features, and the smile that flashed so quickly and so naturally were no better in her mind than what others were given. But she was also honest enough to know that some men didn't agree with that assessment.

She was humming softly to herself as she counted the spools of twine packed neatly in a long, narrow box and then marked the number in her ledger book. Then she smiled. In a way, it was fortunate that she did like this part of the store work. She was the only one who felt this way. Lydia and Caroline didn't mind it, and would do it simply because they felt guilty if they always left it to Jenny. But Nathan made no bones about it: taking inventory drove him to distraction, and he was constantly and profusely thanking Jenny for taking care of things back here. He didn't particularly enjoy being behind the counter out front either, but that at least was bearable to him.

So what happened next on that late Monday afternoon came as a substantial surprise to Jenny. The door opened behind her, and when she turned to look, Nathan was standing there. That alone was unexpected. Nathan and Father Steed had gone to work in the quarry, and Lydia said they wouldn't see Nathan at the store all day. But here he was, obviously come straight from the work site.

"Hello, Jenny," he said, surveying the clutter with a faint air of distaste.

"Hello, Nathan," she answered. "I didn't expect to see you today."

"I was headed home." Moving over beside her, he looked around. "Looks like you're making good progress."

She lowered the book to her side and brushed the hair back out of her eyes with the back of one hand. "Yes. It's been kind of slow this afternoon, so I thought I'd get it done."

"Well, I'll take over now," he said.

Her head came up quickly and she couldn't help but stare at him.

There was a sheepish grin. "I can do it, Jenny."

"I know that," she started, embarrassed that she had looked so shocked.

He took the book and pen from her. "I'll take over now. You go home."

"Go home? But Nathan, what about helping Lydia close? I—"

"Go on now," he said, giving her a gentle shove toward the door. "I promise not to do too much damage in here."

Bewildered, and a little hurt, she surrendered the pen and stepped back. She moved to the door, watching him closely. This wasn't like Nathan at all. Did he think she might be pilfering something back here?

"Go on," he said again, this time with a smile that let her know that it was all right.

Lydia looked up as she came into the main part of the store and also smiled at her.

"Nathan—" Jenny looked over her shoulder. "Nathan said I should go home now."

"A wonderful idea," Lydia said, with just a little too much enthusiasm.

"But—"

"You've put in some long days this week, Jenny. We'll finish up here."

"Are you sure?" It was hard to keep the hurt from her voice.

"I'm sure." Lydia waved her toward the door, then went back to her work.

———————

Jenny stopped once more as she stepped off the porch, looking back at the store, still puzzled and feeling a tiny bit betrayed. But then, reveling in the fresh air, she shrugged it off and started away. She reached up and pulled the comb that held her hair in a bun atop her head. She shook her hair out, letting it fall down her back.

"Hello."

Jenny jumped visibly as Will Steed stepped out from beside the corner of the store.

"Oh! Will."

"How are you?"

"I'm fine. But—" She stopped. He had really quite startled her. "I thought you and your father went to St. Louis."

"In about an hour. Pa needs to take a wagonload of something or other to Warsaw. We'll catch a boat from there. So I thought I'd come and say good-bye."

"What a nice surprise. I—" Jenny stopped short, turning back to peer suspiciously at the store. "How long have you been waiting here?"

He colored slightly. "About fifteen minutes. But I didn't expect you for another half an hour or more."

"Did you talk to Nathan?"

"When?"

"Just now."

"I said hello as he went by."

Now she was smiling and nodding, greatly relieved. "But you didn't ask him to have me come out?"

He was surprised at that. "No, of course not. Why?"

"Never mind." There was a soft chuckle. Maybe she would end up doing that inventory after all.

———————

They walked west from the store, to the end of Knight Street, then cut across the open fields, skirting around those few patches of swampland that hadn't yet been drained. They passed several men working in the fields who called out cheerfully to Jenny. Will smiled, faintly jealous, and yet proud as well. Everyone knew Jenny.

When they finally reached the river, they walked along the edge of the water, moving slowly. "How long will you be gone?" Jenny finally asked, frowning slightly.

Will's shoulders lifted briefly. "Oh, a week or so. Pa thinks five or six days with his business associates in St. Louis should be plenty."

"Will you be taking your Book of Mormon?"

Now it was Will who frowned. "Jenny, I *am* trying, you know."

She was instantly contrite and laid her hand on his arm. "I'm sorry, Will. I know you are. It's just that I'm so anxious to have you get an answer."

"I read in the scriptures every night, and I pray a lot. But answers are what I'm not getting. Everybody keeps telling me I've just got to be patient."

She read clearly the silent rebuke. How like his father he was in so many ways. Even though they were not natural father and son, they were so similar. Will's hair was not as dark as Joshua's and had touches of auburn in it—a legacy from his mother—but they both had the same thick, dark eyebrows, the same brown eyes, the same muscular build, though Will was just slightly taller than his father. They were much alike in temperament too—deep thinkers but seldom letting the thoughts come out, quick sense of humor but often as not sober and reflective.

There was one thing that Will and Joshua Steed did not share in common, however, and that was affection for Jenny Pottsworth. From the moment the Pottsworths had arrived in Nauvoo, his father had sensed Will's feelings toward the English girl and made little pretense of hiding his disapproval of that. He had been very kind to her mother, providing the small cabin where they lived now, but he was only barely polite to Jenny. She had tried hard to change that, but—

"You're a long ways away," Will said, watching her with a faint smile. "Care to tell me about it?"

She waved one hand airily. "Oh, I was just thinking about your leaving. Come on," she said, "let's not talk about that anymore. Let's see who can skip a rock across the water the farthest."

———◆———

When Will finally woke up, the first thing he saw was that the sun was up fully, backlighting the drapes that covered the one window in their hotel room. Outside, he heard the rattle of a wagon, and someone was yelling at a child to come home. He lay there for a moment, staring at the drapes, letting his mind start to focus. Will and his father had left Nauvoo later than they had planned the previous evening, and by the time they covered the fifteen or so miles to Warsaw, the next river town south of Nauvoo, it had been well after midnight before they got to bed. He turned his head and saw that his father was not lying beside him any longer. With a low groan, he came up on one elbow. Last night his father's clothes had been laid across the one chair in the room; they were gone too, which meant Joshua wasn't just down the hall shaving.

Will rolled over and sat up, wanting to stay where he was but knowing he'd better not. He didn't have a watch of his own, and there was no clock in the room. Their boat was scheduled to leave at 11:30 this morning, and if the hour was very late there would be no getting breakfast, and he was ravenous. With a reluctant sigh, he hauled himself up and moved to the rod where his clothes hung. It was then he saw the note on the dressing table.

W—

Have to take care of that wagonload of freight. Back by ten. Then we'll have breakfast. If it weren't for that English girl, the night would have been longer for the both of us.

—Pa

Will shook his head as he pulled on his shirt. Even in a note Joshua couldn't pass up an opportunity to take another swipe at her. "Her name is Jenny," Will muttered at the small mirror above the dressing table. "She's not 'that English girl.'" Will had lingered a little too long with Jenny down by the river, and by the time he got to the freight office, he was fifteen minutes late. His father was fuming. Even though the team wasn't yet hitched to the wagon, even though Joshua lingered another ten minutes after Will's arrival checking details and leaving instructions with his foreman, Will still got all the credit for their late departure.

Ten minutes later, freshly shaved and washed, Will came down into the lobby of the hotel and looked at the clock on the wall. He frowned, his irritation deepening. It was only five minutes to nine. He knew his grumpiness was mostly a product of the short night and long wagon ride, but his father could have left his watch for him. Then Will could have slept almost another full hour. His stomach was like a hollow drum, and it would be three-quarters of an hour before his father returned. Frowning even more deeply, he thought of the note, now lying crumpled on the floor in one corner of the room upstairs, and turned to the desk. "Where can I get some breakfast?" he asked the desk clerk.

The man smiled broadly. "Callahan's. Just three doors up from the newspaper office."

"And where's that?" Will asked.

"Straight up the street," he answered, pointing to show the direction.

Will turned and went out without another word.

———•———

"Appreciate you waitin' for me," his father grunted as he sat down in the chair across the table from Will.

"Sorry," Will mumbled, glancing up, then looking back down at what little was left of his plate of ham, eggs, biscuits, and fried potatoes. "I was real hungry. You said you wouldn't be back till ten." It was barely nine-thirty now.

Joshua shook his head and turned to look for the girl waiting on the tables. It was his way of saying, "It's not worth a battle." Which was a relief to Will. With some breakfast and a little time walking around, he was feeling just a bit guilty for being so mulish.

As the girl came over, Joshua laid a folded-up newspaper on the table. The masthead was partially visible and Will saw that it was the *Warsaw Signal*. That brought the corners of his mouth down. This paper, though a local one, was well known in Nauvoo. In fact, it had been the topic of more than one conversation in the Steed family. The editor, a man by the name of Thomas Sharp, had moved to Warsaw just last September. Two months later he and a partner had bought Warsaw's newspaper, the *Western World*, Sharp thus becoming its editor. This past May, the paper's name had been changed to the *Warsaw Signal*. From the issues making their way north, it was clear that Thomas Sharp had two very strong biases. The paper was obviously pro-Whig and violently anti-Mormon.

Will pulled his eyes away from the paper as Joshua finished ordering and the girl walked away. Will put his fork down. "So, did you get things taken care of?"

"Yes. The wagon is down at the warehouse being unloaded right now. They're expecting that consignment of tools from Pittsburgh in the next day or two, so they should have everything ready for us by the time we return."

"Good. Anything else you have to do before we leave, then?"

His father grinned. "Nope. We've got time to walk around town a bit, see if there are any young fillies worth looking at."

Will's head came up sharply. He knew his father wasn't talking about horses. "Don't, Pa."

"Ah, come on, Will," Joshua said, keeping his voice light. "It isn't like you're promised to that English girl or—"

"Pa!" Will cut in, sharply enough that he saw the two men at the next table turn to look at him. He lowered his voice, then went on tightly. "Her name is Jenny, Pa. Not 'that English girl.'"

"All right, Jenny, then," Joshua said. He was still trying to smile, but his brows were lowering in warning. "You're not promised to her, are you?"

"You know I'm not," Will said wearily.

"Then it'll do you good to look around. I'm just joking about here in Warsaw. But one of my partners in St. Louis has got a daughter who is three times the young woman this Jenny is and—"

Will pushed his plate back and stood abruptly. "I'll be outside, Pa."

"Will!" Joshua said, looking up at his son. He was half-surprised, and more than half-annoyed. "You're more tender than a pig with sunburn. Just sit down."

Will shook his head, taking a half-dollar from his pocket and setting it beside his plate.

"Sit down, Will!" Joshua hissed, mindful that more than one person was watching them now.

"I'll be at the boat landing by eleven," Will said, and walked away.

Chapter Notes

The description given here of Nauvoo at this time (summer of 1841) is an accurate one. On his return from England, Heber C. Kimball said that he had left when Nauvoo had no more than thirty buildings and returned to twelve hundred, with hundreds more under construction. He also noted that at the Independence Day celebration of 1841 there were about eight thousand people in attendance, which gives some indication of the incredible growth that was taking place in the city. (See *LHCK*, pp. 313–15.)

Joseph's reference to the Rocky Mountains was given in April 1834 (see *Restoration*, p. 278).

Thomas C. Sharp and the *Warsaw Signal* were to play an important role in events in Illinois. In a move to promote goodwill, the Saints invited Thomas Sharp to Nauvoo for the laying of the cornerstones of the temple in April 1841. Listening to the Church leaders speak about the prospects for continuing growth of Nauvoo and the kingdom of God probably awakened concern in Sharp. Eventually he became convinced that Mormonism was far more than a religion. He saw it as a political movement ultimately designed to create a vast empire. Soon, in the pages of the *Warsaw Signal* he launched a bitter campaign against the Church, claiming it was Joseph Smith's intent, contrary to Constitutional principles, to unite church and state together in a powerful political organization. In the mind of the fiery young newspaperman, the liberal Nauvoo Charter and the creation of the Nauvoo Legion were proof of this. In June, Sharp helped to form a new anti-Mormon political party in Hancock County and began a relentless campaign against the Church and Joseph Smith. (See CHFT, p. 265.)

Chapter Three

My, my, Sister Ingalls, you are very tense."

Rebecca was sitting on a padded settee in the back room of John C. Bennett's house, the room that served as his medical office. The morning sun flooded through the east windows, filling the room with light. The mayor was standing by her side, holding her wrist and feeling for a pulse. He laughed lightly, giving her his most reassuring look. "Does coming to the doctor make you so nervous?"

Rebecca managed a fleeting smile. "I . . . I suppose so. We were in Missouri for most of the time when I was carrying my first child, and . . . well, there was only a midwife and . . ."

He finished with her wrist and let it drop back, but almost instantly he had her hand in both of his and was patting it solicitously. "Now, now, you absolutely must relax. I'm not going to hurt you and I promise I'll do my best not to embarrass you."

"I know," she murmured, her face flaming red. But even as she willed herself to relax a little she felt a tiny chill of revulsion.

He had held her hand for just a moment too long, and there had been the slightest brush of his fingers up her arm as he released his hold on her. Now she chided herself for rejecting Lydia's offer to come with her this morning. She had felt foolish, like a child afraid to go into a dark room alone, and so she had said no.

She watched him as he turned to a desk and started to make some notes on a sheet of paper. He was strikingly handsome, and in spite of her discomfort, Rebecca understood why most of the single women and not a few of the married ones in Nauvoo were half swooning over the man. He was not particularly tall—maybe five feet seven or eight—and weighed no more than a hundred and fifty pounds, maybe less. His face was thin but his features were finely shaped. Though he was only thirty-seven, just a year older than the Prophet, there was the first sprinkling of gray in his black hair; but this only added to his suaveness and overall good looks. His smile was quick and could flash like a ray of sun through a break in the clouds. He was witty, stimulating, charming—but his eyes! He had dark, restless eyes that were constantly moving. When she had stepped through the door ten minutes before, she had seen his eyes move slowly up and down her frame and had seen the open admiration in them. "Why, Sister Ingalls," he said as he introduced himself with a broad, welcoming smile, "I hadn't expected someone quite so young and lovely as you."

It was meant as a sincere compliment, she supposed, but it had immediately set her nerves on edge. Then he had taken her by the elbow to guide her down the hallway to his offices, as though she were a partial invalid or something. Now there was the caress along her arm.

She stopped, getting stern with herself. Caress? He had barely touched her. She was simply letting her apprehension drive her imagination.

"There," Bennett said, turning back around. He had the pen and the paper in his hand. "Let me ask you some questions." He moved a chair over and sat down facing her, very professional now. "Are you having any pain or cramps?"

"No."

"But you say that you have not felt like things have been normal since the birth of your last child?"

"No."

Rebecca inwardly steeled herself, fighting the temptation to either turn away and stare out the window as he gently kept asking the questions or get up and bolt. It seemed like an eternity, though she knew it was no more than two or three minutes. After each answer, he would write something on his paper, very brief, and with quick, bold strokes.

Finally, he lowered the pad. "Well," he said, "that should do it for today. I think you are right in having some cause for concern. A woman needs to listen to what her body is telling her. But on the other hand, I see no real cause for alarm at this stage."

"That's good. Thank you, Doctor Bennett."

Rebecca stood up quickly, once again aware of his eyes on her.

"Oh, please," he laughed, "call me Brother Bennett." There was the tiniest hint of a sly smile. "Or even John if you'd like."

He stood now too. "I'd like to see you next week," he said. "Would you like to come in the evening? That way we won't be disturbed." There was open invitation in his eyes now. "Perhaps we might even have dinner together."

Instantly, the crawly feeling along her flesh was back. It was as though he had taken off his doctor's persona and laid it aside. And what she saw in its place gave her the chills. "I . . . I'm not sure," she stammered. "I'll let you know." She plunged toward the door. "Thank you, Doctor Bennett," she called over her shoulder.

She saw him frown at her use of the formal title, but she didn't wait to see if he would correct her again. She was out the door and down the walk, not turning back.

⸻ • ⸻

When Lydia looked up and saw Rebecca standing in the

doorway, she brightened and started to call out a greeting. Then she saw her face. Instantly she turned. "Jenny!"

Rebecca nodded gratefully and backed out again.

"Jenny! Can you come up front and watch the store for a few minutes?"

———◆———

They crossed the field behind the store and found a shady spot behind a large barn. Now they sat side by side, speaking quietly to each other. They were quite different, these two Steed women. Lydia, the only child of a well-to-do storekeeper in Palmyra, New York, had come into the Steed family when she married Nathan. Even now, in her early thirties, and after having borne six children, Lydia was strikingly beautiful. She had dark, lustrous hair, dark brown eyes, clear skin, and beautiful facial features. Being an only child, she was of a determined mind and not afraid to speak it.

Rebecca was much like her mother, both in looks and temperament. She had Mary Ann's quiet gentleness and patience. Her hair was light brown and combed straight so that it fell below her shoulders. Her eyes were a pale blue and reflected her more serious nature. But when she smiled, a dimple in her left cheek would appear with startling swiftness. Some of her slenderness had been lost when she gave birth to Christopher, but she still carried herself with a grace that Lydia envied. Rebecca was a peacemaker and a stabilizing influence in the family. It was little wonder that everyone loved this sweet and gentle woman.

"I'm going to tell Nathan."

Rebecca swung around. "No, Lydia!"

"Why not?" Lydia asked. "Nathan won't say anything to anyone unless you tell him it's all right."

"I know. It's just that . . ." She looked down, the color spreading across her face again.

"It's just what?" Lydia urged, being gentle now.

"I'm not even sure about it, Lydia. So he said I was lovely—it made me uncomfortable, but maybe that's just his manner."

"But what about the other things he said? Evening appointments? Dinner?"

Rebecca could only nod.

Lydia reached out and took Rebecca's shoulders. "Rebecca, you're not an excitable person. If you felt that uncomfortable, then you have reason to be upset. This isn't just all in your head. Especially in light of all the rumors that have been going around about him." She shook her head, berating herself for not insisting on going with her. She gave Rebecca a long look. "Are you going to tell Derek?"

"No!" Rebecca blurted it out in panic.

Lydia didn't have to say anything. Her look said it all.

Rebecca shook her head slowly. "I know, I know. But if I tell Derek, you know what he'll do? It takes a lot to get Derek angry," she went on, "but he's very protective of me. He'll march right down there and slug Bennett or something."

Lydia didn't move. "Are you going back to him again?"

Rebecca's resolve was instantaneous. "No!" Then she straightened, giving a little shudder. "I don't care how good a doctor he is, I won't go back."

Lydia nodded. "I'll talk to Emma. She always has Frederick G. Williams attend her. She thinks he's a wonderful doctor." She leaned over, touching Rebecca's arm. "Becca?"

"Yes?"

"You think about letting me talk to Nathan. If you change your mind, just let me know. All right?"

It was nearly four o'clock when Rebecca Ingalls came to the front door of Lydia's cabin and stuck her head in. Lydia was at the table with Emily. A copy of the Book of Mormon was in front of them, and Emily was reading out loud in carefully measured cadence. Young Joshua had the baby on his lap, listening. Off in the corner, Elizabeth Mary and her cousin Savannah were playing dolls.

When Lydia saw her, she started to rise. "Joshua?"

He looked up. "Yes, Mama?"

"Do you think you could help Emily with her reading? I need to speak with your Aunt Rebecca."

"No, Lydia," Rebecca said. "Don't get up. I just wanted to tell you that I've changed my mind about Nathan."

Lydia's eyes flew open. "Good," she said immediately. "Good. He's at the store. I'll go find him right now."

"Thank you." And Rebecca backed out the door again.

———————

They were walking along Mulholland, moving slowly eastward in the late afternoon sunlight. They had come up on the eastern bluffs now, about a block from the temple site. Lydia's arm was in the crook of Nathan's elbow, her shoulder lightly touching his. It was hot, but she didn't mind. She always loved walking with Nathan.

"Tell me about John C. Bennett," she said suddenly.

Nathan's stride faltered and he peered at her closely.

"I know you don't like him. Why?"

"What's this all about?" he said.

"I just want to know."

He took her hand, teasing her now. "Come on. You snatch me away from the store as though our lives were in mortal danger. Now you ask me in a low voice what I know about our mayor. What's going on, Lydia?"

She laughed briefly, realizing just how strangely she had acted. But just as quickly, her face grew solemn again. "I'll tell you in a moment. First I want you to tell me why you have such strong feelings about him, all right?"

He searched her face, then finally nodded. "All right. Let's find a place where we can sit."

Nathan looked around. A short distance away, a small lane took off to the left, threading its way between two lines of rail fencing. He took her hand. "Come," he said. "This may take a few minutes."

"You must realize, Lydia, that some of what I'm about to tell you is not public knowledge. You must not tell anyone unless you hear Joseph or another leader say it first. There has just been too much gossip."

Lydia moved her head slowly up and down, stirred by the solemnity she saw in his eyes.

Nathan leaned back against the bottom rail of the fence. "It all started a few months after Brother Bennett joined the Church. One day Joseph got an anonymous letter. It said that Brother Bennett had a wife and two or three children back in a town called McConnelsville, Ohio. At that point, of course, there was no knowing if it was true or not. The spirit of the letter was bitter and vindictive. It said Bennett was an evil man and that he had abandoned his wife and children, leaving them to fend for themselves. It also said he had treated her shamefully and had been unfaithful to her."

"How did Joseph respond to that?"

"Obviously he was troubled, but he was also very cautious about overreacting. Joseph knows what it's like to be accused falsely. And, as you know, he also is very trusting by nature."

"Yes," she replied. "That's one reason why everyone loves him."

"Exactly. Well, Joseph said that it was not uncommon for good men, especially prominent men, to have evil spoken of them."

"Did he confront Brother Bennett with this?"

"Right at first? I don't know. He didn't say. But it troubled him enough that last February, he sent George Miller off to Ohio to investigate. In early March, Brother Miller wrote to Brother Joseph and reported what he found."

"And?"

"It wasn't a good report," Nathan admitted. "The people said that John Bennett was a vain man who believed he was the smartest man in the nation, and that if he cannot be placed at the head of the heap in whatever situation he finds himself, then he goes off in another direction. In short, they confirmed the accusations made in the earlier letter."

"But . . ." The dismay was written clearly in her eyes. "But why, then, hasn't Joseph released him as Assistant President?"

Nathan took a deep breath, then let it out in a long sigh. "You have to understand, Lydia. It's not my place to ask, and Joseph hasn't told me everything. My guess is that he confronted Bennett with what he had learned from Brother Miller. Knowing Bennett, I think he told Joseph that it was all in the past, before he had found the Church and given his life to Jesus." There was faint mockery in those final words.

He watched the doubt fill her eyes. Suddenly he felt a need to defend Joseph, even though he had asked himself some of these same questions. "You need to remember something, Lydia. John C. Bennett came to us with an impressive set of credentials. He founded a medical college in Ohio. That's a fact. At the time he first came to us, he was the quartermaster general for the Illinois militia. That's the most important military position in the state, an appointment that comes straight from the governor. That's a fact. And Nauvoo has a charter that is the envy of every city in the state of Illinois. And without John C. Bennett's work in Springfield, we wouldn't have that charter. That's a fact too. Everything about the man seemed legitimate. This was not some shifty character that came in by canoe on some moonless night. So when these terrible rumors started coming in, Joseph had every reason to question them."

Lydia was a little ashamed. "Yes, I can see that. I didn't mean to sound critical of Joseph."

Nathan watched her face, seeing the play of emotions there, pleased when the doubt gradually faded.

He almost hated to take this any further, but the matter was far too serious. "Then Hyrum left for a mission to the East a couple of months ago. I don't know if Joseph asked him to investigate further or whether Hyrum did it on his own, but when Hyrum got to Pittsburgh he wrote a letter to Joseph. That arrived just a couple of weeks ago."

"And what did it say?"

"Hyrum confirmed that all the accusations against Bennett were true." He paused, looking away from her now, lost in his own feelings about the whole situation. "You know how much Joseph trusts Hyrum's counsel. That letter shook him deeply. I think Joseph has now started a formal investigation into the charges."

"But if he has Hyrum's letter, what more is there to investigate?"

Nathan gave her a long look, then shook his head. "I'm not talking about investigating what happened in Ohio."

Her eyes widened perceptibly. "You mean . . . ?"

"I mean that Joseph wants to know if there is any truth to the rumors about what has been happening here."

"Suppose," Lydia said, choosing her words carefully now, "you had strong evidence that there is some truth to those rumors. What would you do?"

He turned in surprise. "I'd go straight to Joseph."

"Good."

He was searching her face. "Why do you ask that?"

She took a deep breath. "I think you'd better hear about an experience your sister had today."

———•———

At about the same time Lydia and Nathan were talking, Joshua and Will were still about sixty miles out of St. Louis. The boat was making good time, but when darkness came it would have to slow considerably. So it would be well past sunrise tomorrow before they reached their destination. As Will walked along the outside railing, he could hear the young boy at the bow calling out the depths of the water at periodic intervals as he dropped a lead-weighted rope into the water.

Will found his father near the back of the boat, leaning on the railing, staring down into the water beneath them. Behind him, the great paddle wheels turned steadily, churning the muddy water into a long white trail behind them. Will stopped for a moment, watching the man he had been fighting with earlier in the morning. Though they had called an unspoken truce, the strain between them was still there. Now it was time to put it away.

Somehow his father heard him approaching over the roar of the engine and the loud *swish-swish* of the paddle wheel. He turned; then seeing who it was, he nodded. "Evenin', Will."

"Evenin', Pa." He joined Joshua at the rail. "We'll be slowing down soon, won't we?" The awkwardness was still there.

"Good thing," Joshua grunted. "And not just because it'll be dark. I slipped into the engine room of this old barge a while ago. It's an older model boiler, the kind with no safety valve and no pressure gauges. And it's pretty rusty."

"And that's bad?" Will's specialty was sailing ships, not steamers.

"Only if we keep up these full-speed runs."

Will frowned. He might not be an expert, but he had traveled the river enough to know that explosions and fires aboard the riverboats were commonplace, and often with horrendous loss of life. Feeling a little uneasy, he decided to change the subject. He glanced sideways at his father. "Sorry about this morning, Pa."

Joshua shrugged it off. "It's done with," he said simply.

Will bobbed his head once, relieved to have it said. He looked down at the brown water rushing past them. He wanted to ask his father what it was about Jenny Pottsworth that he detested so much, but he knew that in that direction lay only more anger and frustration. So they both lapsed into silence, continuing to gaze at the water below them.

About five minutes later, from above them there was a shout. They both straightened and turned. One of the crew was on the top deck, pointing forward and yelling something indistinguishable over the noise of the paddles. "Uh-oh," Joshua muttered.

"What?"

He shook his head and walked quickly around to the other side of the boat. As he reached the other side, Joshua lifted an arm to point. "That's what I was afraid of."

Up ahead of them, perhaps three-quarters of a mile off still, just coming into view around a bend of the river, they could see another boat, a big one, probably half again as big as theirs, with two paddle wheels on each side amidships. Now above them, several members of the crew were shouting at each other. Some of the passengers who were out on deck came around to the starboard side to see what was going on.

"What is it, Pa?"

"We are about to engage in a race," he said grimly.

The race wasn't much of a surprise, but the timing was. It seemed like anytime two boats got within a mile of each other going the same direction a race was on. Will had been in several going up and down this river, but never when it was nearly dark and never this late in the summer when the river was lower. This could prove to be pure insanity. But even as he thought that, the roar of the engine deepened, and the sound of the paddles quickened noticeably.

"But we can't possibly beat him," Will said. "He's way bigger than us."

"And with the double wheels, he'll have two big boilers for sure. But since when did that ever stop a riverboat captain from trying?"

News of what was happening spread fast. People poured out from their cabins and from the big dining hall to line the rails. Above them, the smokestacks were belching a huge quantity of dark black smoke which trailed out behind them for quarter of a mile.

"The race is on!" someone shouted five minutes later. They had closed the distance to about half a mile now. There was no question about it. The other boat was streaming huge clouds of smoke and the paddle wheels were a blur now. The smaller boat had been spotted, and the captain of the larger boat wasn't about to let this upstart little boat pass one of the great river queens.

"Ten dollars says the big boat wins!" someone shouted.

"I'll give you fifty that ours overtakes it within the next quarter hour."

Will turned to his father in disbelief. "They're betting on the race? Does the captain know that?"

"Know it?" Joshua snorted. "He'll be covering some of the bets himself. The stupid fool. Now he's got to win." He grabbed Will's arm. "Will, go to our cabin. Get all my papers. Don't worry about the rest of our stuff. I'll meet you at the bow."

Will just stared at him. "We're getting off?"

"Of course not, but if this thing blows, you and I are going to be as far from that boiler as possible. I'll go see if I can find something we can use to float ashore if we need to."

"Pa!" Will cried, truly alarmed now, but Joshua was already gone.

Two minutes later, Will pushed his way through the mob at the front of the boat, holding his father's small case in front of him as a wedge, winning himself several angry looks. He looked around but could not see his father anywhere. Two more minutes and Joshua was suddenly standing beside him.

"It's all right. I've got a couple of small casks put aside. We can get to them if we need to."

"So what now?"

His father grinned. "Now we see who wins." Will's gaping mouth made his father laugh. "Look, we've prepared for the worst, which probably won't happen. There's nothing more we can do."

Will turned and was surprised to see that they had cut the distance between the two boats by almost half again. "Look, Pa, we're closing on him."

"Yep," Joshua said lazily. "I put a word in with the captain."

"You did?" Will exclaimed. "What did you say?"

"I told him that if his boiler blows up, I will personally drag him out of the water and beat him to a pulp." There was an ironic grin. "In the meantime, I told him he darn well better win, because I put a hundred dollars down for us with a man from Natchez."

"You what?"

But Joshua just laughed.

Another ten minutes and a roar went up from the crowd. The big boat was up to full steam now and making almost twice the speed it had when they first saw it, but the distance was now down to a few hundred yards. The larger boat had started to turn, moving toward the faster current, directly where their boat was traveling. With the smaller boat making better speed, they were on a possible collision course now, depending on who got there first. That had brought the shout. Will saw that whoever got there first would be the winner, for the other boat would have to go out and around him, into the slower current.

"He's going for the current!" someone yelled.

"We'll crash!" another man cried.

Will, still dumbfounded, looked at his father, but Joshua seemed undaunted. "Our captain's already in the swiftest current. We may not have the boiler power of that one, but we're smaller and lighter and more maneuverable. You want to put some money down on this, Will?"

Will just shook his head. And then, seeing the look in his father's eyes, he realized what Joshua was doing. He was trying to keep Will's mind off the possibility of an explosion. And then Will smiled. They had done all they could do to prepare for it. They would fare better than most. And if it didn't happen, then all there was to worry about was the race. He laughed aloud, relieved and excited and proud of his father and cocky about their chances all in the same moment. He turned forward again and began to shout, urging their boat on faster and faster.

The crowd was going wild now. The boats were down to fifty yards apart. Even women and children were outside, screaming and shouting, cheering their captain on. This was a grand American tradition. Competition was a way of life here on the river. It was a way of life in many parts of America, especially on the frontier. And on the frontier, often you bet on that competition with your life. It was frightening and exhilarating and expanding and totally American.

Their boat was coming up hard on the other one now, and they could clearly see the people who lined its rails three and four deep also. And they too were shouting and screaming and waving their fists with wild abandon. As a seaman, Will was getting increasingly nervous. The distance between them was closing fast. You didn't turn boats and ships the way you did a wagon or a carriage. You needed room. A lot of room. And that was fast disappearing.

To his surprise, he saw his father looking up toward the wheelhouse. "Don't you do it," Joshua said in a low, commanding voice. "Don't lose your nerve. Hold steady, now."

With a start, Will suddenly realized that if the two boats collided, the bigger boat would get the better of it by far. "We're going to hit, Pa!" he exclaimed. He could feel his heart thudding in his chest as he eyed the two intersecting paths.

People had stopped shouting now. They were holding their breath, staring in horror as the two boats closed ominously. Now the big river queen towered over them, looking for all reality like a giant box bearing down on a bug. Will looked across the water and saw the horrified looks on the faces of the people there.

"Everybody back!" someone screamed. "We're going to hit!"

"Turn! Turn! Turn!" someone else was shouting.

Suddenly the crowds around him bolted, running for the back of the ship. Will staggered and nearly fell, then braced himself against the mass. The din was deafening—people screaming and sobbing, the high pitched whine of the big engines, the roar of great paddle wheels propelling them forward at ramming speed. Joshua reached out and grabbed Will's arm, holding him in place. His eyes were darting back and forth between the two riverboats, measuring the distance with a practiced eye. He shouted in Will's ear. "If we do hit, it's going to be at the back and not the front. Stay here and hang on."

Will grabbed the rail, digging his fingertips in and planting his feet, staring back at the massive shape coming at them like a juggernaut. He tensed, wanting to close his eyes but not able to. And then, at what seemed like the last possible moment, the huge stubby nose of the double paddle wheeler veered away, coming not more than ten to twelve feet from the side of their boat. He was turning. Their boat rocked violently as the wake from the bigger boat shook them like a dog shaking a rag. The side paddle wheel, which stuck out a good eight to ten feet wider than the rest of the big boat, still nearly clipped them. Will tensed again, expecting to hear the ripping sound of churning paddles chewing into hardwood. But then in another moment, the paddle wheel was clear and their boat shot forward as the big one went off at an angle.

A great cheer went up all along their boat. Hats flew in the air. People fell on each other, pounding one another and laughing and pointing. On the far boat, the other passengers were silent. A few shook their fists at them, but the rest just stared in bitter disappointment. Angling off, the big boat was dropping rapidly to stern. The race was over. Will felt a great sigh of relief as the boat slowed and the sound of the engine dropped in pitch.

Will looked at his father, and finally could only shake his head.

Joshua smiled, though Will could see the relief in his eyes as well. Then he took Will by the shoulder. "Why don't you take our stuff back to the cabin. I'll go collect my winnings, and then I'll buy you the biggest steak on board this old tub."

"That's a deal," Will agreed.

"And Will?"

"Yes, Pa?"

"We don't have to tell your mother about this, all right?"

He grinned. "Yes, Pa."

———◆———

As they sat lazily letting the dinner settle in their stomachs, Joshua stirred beside him. "Will?" It was said with some tentativeness.

"Yes, Pa?"

"Walter Samuelson's a good man, Will."

Will nodded, a little surprised at the sudden mention of his father's St. Louis business partner.

"He's been real good to me. Real fair. Never had one question about his integrity."

"That's good, Pa." He still wasn't sure where this was going.

"I didn't ask him to set something up, Will."

"Set something up?"

There was a long pause. "Yes."

"Like what, Pa?"

"Like dinner at his home."

Will went cold. "Oh."

"With his daughter."

"I figured that much out," Will said with a sudden bite to his voice.

"I was joking with you earlier today, Will. But I wouldn't be surprised if he has arranged something. He thinks you're one of the finest young men he's ever met."

"No, Pa."

"Will, it's not my doing. And I'll not have you be offending Mrs. Samuelson or their daughter. She's a fine young woman."

Will considered that. He believed his father when he said it wasn't his doing. But he also knew that whatever it was Samuelson was setting up, it wouldn't be going against Joshua Steed's wishes either. Well, it wasn't the girl's fault, was it? Maybe she felt as stupid about it as he did. Finally, he nodded. "I'll not be offending them, Pa."

"Good."

Will stood up. "I'm tired, Pa. I think I'll be turning in."

"I'll be along shortly."

"All right." Will turned and headed for their cabin, already dreading their arrival on the morrow.

Chapter Notes

The details surrounding John C. Bennett's life as given here—including his position of prominence, the anonymous letter from Ohio, the investigation by George Miller, and Hyrum Smith's subsequent letter—are described in several sources (see, for example, *HC* 5:36–37, 42–43; *Times and Seasons* 3

[1 July 1842]: 839–40, 842; and Andrew F. Smith, "The Saintly Scoundrel: The Life and Times of John Cook Bennett," [unpublished ms., Brooklyn, N.Y., 1994], pp. 117–18). Bennett was elected mayor of Nauvoo on 1 February 1841 and elected as major general in the Nauvoo Legion three days later (see *HC* 4:287, 296). Sidney Rigdon continued to have serious health problems incident to his long imprisonment in Missouri, and so during the April 1841 conference, John C. Bennett was appointed Assistant President in the First Presidency while Rigdon was ill (see *HC* 4:341).

To his surprise, as Nathan came around the corner onto Water Street later that same night, approaching the large two-story cabin that was known as the Homestead, he saw two figures standing just outside the fence, having an animated discussion. It was full dark now, and only as Nathan drew up on them did he see it was Brigham Young and Heber Kimball. They looked up as he strode over to them, immediately cutting their conversation short. Both looked grim. "Hello, Brother Nathan," Brigham said.

Nathan was still fuming over what Lydia had told him. Every time he thought of those oily eyes raking Rebecca up and down, and the smooth hands brushing at her arm, he felt himself boiling inside. So he didn't pay much attention to the state the two brethren were in. "Is Brother Joseph at home?" he asked abruptly.

"No," Brigham said. "We were just looking for him."

Nathan threw up his hands. "Did Emma say where he is? I must talk with him."

"No. As you probably know, Don Carlos Smith is very ill. Emma's gone to help his wife care for him. Only Emma's nephew is home now with the baby."

Nathan grunted at that. He knew that Emma's nephew, a young man in his early twenties, was visiting with them from out of town somewhere. "It is a matter of utmost urgency," he went on. "No idea where Joseph might be?"

"No," Brigham answered. "We have an urgent matter of our own." There was a snort of open disgust. "It concerns our esteemed mayor. We were just discussing where we might find Joseph so we can deal with it."

Nathan had started to turn away, but now he snapped back around. "Brother Bennett?"

"Yes," Heber growled. "We've been working on a problem concerning him. Now it is time for a resolution."

"Well, there's a thing or two you should know about this man before you go calling him our esteemed mayor," Nathan snapped.

The two Apostles exchanged a quick glance; then Brigham took Nathan by the arm. "When I called him our esteemed mayor, I was being somewhat sarcastic, Nathan. But I suggest that you tell Heber and me what it is that is of concern to you. There are some questions with John C. Bennett that we wish to take up with Brother Joseph." He gave his companion another quick look, and it was filled with a sudden dread. "And I pray this is not what I think it is, Nathan."

Nathan hesitated only a moment. Here were two senior members of the Quorum of the Twelve. If he couldn't tell Joseph, then there weren't two men in Nauvoo with more authority to tell it to. So he told them, trying to control his bitterness from spilling over into the narrative.

When he finished, there was a long silence, and then Brigham's face noticeably relaxed. "Thank heavens, Nathan."

"Thank heavens?" he echoed incredulously. "My sister goes

to the Assistant President of the Church and is made to feel like a common harlot, and all you can say is thank heavens?"

Heber turned Nathan to face him. "What Brigham means is that we are thankful that it progressed no further than that. At first we feared the report might be much worse."

"Oh." Nathan realized he was letting his feelings get the better of him. "I'm sorry, Brigham. I didn't mean to snap at you."

Brigham brushed that off as inconsequential. "When did all this happen?"

"This morning."

Brigham shook his head, his jaw tight, the blue-gray eyes looking like the advancing crest of a thunderstorm. "Nathan, I want you to come with us and find Joseph. He needs to hear your report along with ours. This is a very serious thing now."

As Nathan looked back and forth between these two lifelong friends, his bewilderment was evident. Heber watched him for a moment, then looked at Brigham. "I think he has a right to know what is going on."

There was a quick, curt nod.

Heber turned back to Nathan. "Are you aware of the letter Joseph got from Brother Hyrum a short time ago?"

"Yes, Joseph told my father and me about it."

"Joseph has opened an inquiry," Heber went on. "Brigham and I have been helping him."

"He hinted as much to us in that same conversation. What have you found?"

Brigham didn't answer that directly. "In the past few days, Joseph called in a young woman whose name has been linked with Bennett's in various rumors and gossip. He was hoping that she would refute the accusations."

"But she didn't?" Nathan asked, already knowing the answer.

"No, she didn't," Heber said.

"But it is far worse than any of us had supposed," Brigham broke in. "This woman, thinking Bennett was an unmarried man and hoping for a proposal of marriage from him, was quite flattered that his attentions had settled on her. But he began to press his affections upon her, begging her to let him gratify the passion he felt for her. The woman demurred, of course. She was a virtuous and innocent sister. She protested that such acts were against the laws of God."

Now Brigham's eyes were hard and very cold. "Was Bennett discouraged by such a show of chastity? Not in the least. He told her that she didn't understand the law properly. He said that promiscuous relations between the sexes was lawful and that there was no harm in it as long as it was kept a secret."

"No!" Nathan exclaimed.

"Oh, yes!" Brigham muttered. "She was shocked and refused his advances in the strongest terms, saying that she couldn't accept his word on a matter that important. She told him that what he was asking was wrong and it would bring shame and disgrace upon her and the Church."

"Good for her." Nathan's anger was quickly turning into cold fury.

"No," Heber corrected him, "not good. Even her vehement protests did not stop this man. When the mayor found that his line of argument was ineffectual, he took another tack. He reminded her of his position as Assistant President to Joseph, then told her that men of high position in the Church, including Joseph himself, had taught him this doctrine."

"What?" Nathan exploded.

"That's right. He swore that Joseph had given him permission to teach and live it."

Nathan was gaping at him.

Heber's voice had a ring of cold steel to it now. "He told her that Joseph and other leaders, including Brigham and me, were not only teaching that doctrine but living it as well. Knowledge of this was only being kept secret because it would cause an uproar among the people, and especially create problems with Emma. He swore that he was acting with our direct permission in teaching the doctrine to her."

Filled with revulsion and horror, Nathan exploded. "Surely the woman was not fool enough to believe that?"

For several moments both men were silent. Then, with a heavy heart, Brigham answered. "She did believe him. And she did succumb to his advances."

Nathan felt as if he had been kicked in the stomach. No wonder Brigham had been thankful when he learned that Rebecca's interaction with this man had ended as quickly as it did.

"That was what we were to meet about," Brigham went on. "All of this has only just come out in the last few days, some of it as recently as this morning. He asked us to investigate some of the reports."

"You mean there is more than one woman involved in all this?"

Brigham nodded. "There are at least five others that we know of." His jaw tightened. "And not all are unmarried."

Nathan straightened, now filled with implacable resolve. "What do you want me to do?"

"I suggest we split up," Brigham said. "Nathan, you go up to the temple site. Heber, you go to the city council office. Also check the mayor's office. Emma's nephew said those are some of the places Joseph specifically mentioned where he might be going. I'll check out the site of his new store and at the printing office. If we find him, we come back here. Let's all try to be back here in an hour either way."

They nodded and moved away, each heading off in a different direction.

When Emma's nephew opened the door, Nathan removed his hat. "Good evening. Has Brother Joseph returned home yet?"

"Good evening. No, but I expect him soon. May I help you?" Then recognition crossed the man's face. "Brother Steed, I think it is?"

Nathan nodded. "Yes, we met at the store. I'm sorry, I've forgotten your name."

"Lorenzo Wasson. I'm Emma's nephew."

"Yes." Nathan looked around. There was no sign of Brigham or Heber. "Have Brother Young or Brother Kimball returned here in the last few minutes?"

"No. They were here over an hour ago, but I haven't seen them since." He opened the door wider. "Look, why don't you come in and wait for Uncle Joseph. I expect him back any minute now."

Hesitating, Nathan considered that. Then he decided that Heber and Brigham would also inquire at the house when they returned. "All right, thank you."

As Wasson stepped back, Nathan entered the house. The young man moved through the main parlor and into the sitting room behind it. The house still held some of the day's heat, and this was the coolest room in it. "Have a seat, Brother Steed. As you probably know, Joseph's brother Don Carlos is very sick."

"Yes," Nathan responded. Don Carlos was Joseph's youngest brother, and especially close to Joseph and Emma. They had even named their last baby after him. "How is he doing?"

"A little better, but still quite serious. Aunt Emma has gone to help Agnes. Julia has the other children at Mother Smith's, but I'm watching little Don Carlos. So if you'll excuse me, I'll go check and make sure he's still asleep."

Nathan nodded absently as Wasson left the room, his thoughts already moving ahead to what this night would bring. He thought of the innocent women duped by the lying tongue of John Bennett. He thought of husbands who had been betrayed and wondered if they knew. And if they did, what did that do to their marital situation? How would he feel if he were to ever find out that Lydia had been unfaithful to him?

He shook his head, feeling slightly nauseated. Gratefully, he heard footsteps coming down the stairs and pulled out of his thoughts. Wasson came back into the room. "Uncle Joseph is coming up the street right now. I saw him from the window."

Nathan stood. "Good. Is anyone with him?"

"Yes. I think it's the mayor."

Nathan visibly started at that. "Brother Bennett?"

"Yes. I'm pretty certain that's who it is."

That was a totally unexpected turn. "And it's only the two of them?"

"Yes."

Where was Brigham? Where was Heber? Still puzzled, he turned and started toward the front door. His mind was racing. How did you report on John C. Bennett's behavior when John C. Bennett was standing there? But he didn't get a chance to answer that question. As he and Wasson entered the larger parlor that fronted the house, the sound of irate voices came through the open windows. Nathan stopped. It was Joseph's voice. And there was no mistaking it. He was angry. Very angry!

Nathan turned to Wasson. He was staring in the direction of the doorway, obviously shocked. That was not surprising, Nathan thought. He was reeling a little himself. He had known Joseph Smith for fourteen years now. Never once in all that time had he heard his voice filled with such fury as he was hearing now. Then Nathan realized that the two figures outside were coming up the walk. With a quick jerk of his head, he moved back into the smaller room. "I think it's best if we're not in here," he said in a low voice.

Wasson jumped, moving to follow Nathan. Nathan shut the door between the two rooms carefully, seeing the front door open just as he did so.

"Joseph! Joseph!" John C. Bennett's voice was close to a sob. "Please! Listen to me."

"Listen to what, John? More of your lies? More of your silk tongue?"

The voices came through the paneling of the door with only the slightest of muffling. Embarrassed to be listening to obviously privileged communication, Nathan gestured toward the hallway. "Can we get outside from here?" he whispered to Wasson.

"No. Not without them seeing us."

"How about upstairs?"

"Yes, that would be better."

Behind them the voices were still hammering at each other.

"I'm sorry, Joseph!" Bennett wailed. "I swear to you. I am truly sorry."

Nathan led the way, moving quickly up the stairs and into the far bedroom. It helped but it wasn't enough. The two men below them were speaking loudly enough that their voices carried into every corner of the house. There was no avoiding it. Nathan sat down on the edge of the bed, not wanting to listen, but not able not to.

"Sorry?" Joseph cried. "John, that's what you said months ago when I first confronted you about having abandoned your wife and children back in Ohio. 'I'm sorry,' you said. 'I'm sorry I left them. I'm sorry I lied to you, Joseph. Please forgive me, Brother Joseph. Now that I've joined the Church, I've changed. I'm a different man.'" There was mocking irony in the biting words. "Isn't that what you said, John? Aren't those your very words?"

"Yes, but—"

"And I believed you. When others were saying evil things about you, I believed you, John. I believed you meant what you said. I believed your promises. I supported you for mayor." Now Joseph's voice sounded choked. "I asked you to be the Assistant President of the Church! And all that time . . . all that time you were going on with your abominations."

There was a muttered sound, but the words were not distinguishable.

"No, John," came the thunderous reply. "I can't accept that. I won't accept words. Not anymore. Not after all the lies. Not now that your blackest doings have been exposed to the light."

"I'll do anything, Joseph. Just tell me what you want me to do." He was sobbing openly now, his voice desperate. "Please!"

It was as though Joseph hadn't heard him. "It is shocking beyond belief to think that you have given way to your basest instincts. You have dragged the innocent into submitting to your depravity. You have deprived them of that which is most precious and dear. That alone would be sin enough. But to compound the evil, you did so in the name of the Lord. You did so in the name of the Church. You used my name and the name of other leaders. You used your own position of authority to lie and deceive and seduce."

"I know, Joseph. I know. I am an evil person. I've tried to stop. I've tried to do better. I can't. These women, they weren't totally innocent either. They encouraged me with their—"

"No!" The roar of Joseph's voice almost made the lamps beside the bed tremble. "How dare you? How dare you shift the blame to them?"

There was silence. The lion had evidently cowed the wolf. The silence stretched on; then again there was the murmur of Bennett's voice, too soft to make out the words.

Joseph's answer was now heavy with weariness. "I have no choice, John. You leave me no choice."

"You can't expose me, Joseph. I'll repent. I'll change. I swear to you! Give me one more chance." The desperation was driving his voice into a high, shrill whine. "If you expose me, Joseph, my reputation here will be ruined. I won't be able to practice medicine. How can I face people?"

Again Joseph's voice thundered out. Nathan could visualize him, risen to full height, his blue eyes like twin swords. "How can you face God, John Bennett?" he cried. "That is the question that should be foremost in your mind at this moment. You have offended God with the enormity of your sins. And I fear for your everlasting soul."

"I know!" came the wailing reply. "I fear I have lost my soul too, Joseph. So please, don't make me lose everything else. Please don't expose me."

Again there was silence, and Nathan, though he was shamed at having to overhear, nevertheless found himself straining to hear. And then came the words, filled with utter, irrevocable finality. "I cannot let this pass, John," Joseph said. "You have gone too far this time. You have broken too many promises. I have no choice."

There was a strangled cry, the scrape of a chair, followed by the sound of the door slamming. And then the house was silent.

———•———

Emma's nephew left Nathan sitting on the bed when little Don Carlos started to fuss in the adjoining bedroom. He didn't come back to where Nathan was. Only when a knock sounded below about ten minutes later and Nathan heard Brigham's voice did he finally stand and make his way slowly back down the stairs. Both Heber and Brigham had returned. They were standing next to Joseph by the front door, talking quietly. At the sound of Nathan opening the door into the parlor, they all turned in surprise.

"Nathan?" Joseph said.

Nathan moved quickly to him. "Joseph, I'm sorry. I was here with Lorenzo, waiting for you, when you and Doctor Bennett came. I was going to come out, then I realized what was happening. We went upstairs, trying to get as far away as possible. We didn't mean to listen."

Joseph slowly nodded. "You heard it all?"

"Most of it." Nathan dropped his head, but not before he saw the haunted look in Joseph's eyes, the lines of weariness around his mouth.

Joseph was silent for a moment, then slowly nodded his head. "That's good. I am glad to have a second witness. And Lorenzo?"

"He heard it too. He's upstairs with the baby now."

Joseph sighed, accepting that. Then he motioned to the chairs behind them. "Can you stay for a while, brethren? Brigham, you need to hear what I've just done."

"We saw Bennett going toward his house," Brigham answered. "He looked like a whipped mongrel."

Nathan cleared his throat, feeling very awkward now. "I'd best be leaving now. Again, Joseph, I apologize. It was not my intent—"

"No," he said, "I understand. It's all right. I'd like you to stay, Nathan. Brigham was just telling me that you have something to report."

"Yes," Nathan said, "but there is no need now."

"There is need," Joseph said, sinking into a chair and pointing to another. "I need to hear it all, and then to counsel with you. This may take some time. Will your wives be upset if you don't return by bedtime?"

"Lydia knew I was coming to see you," Nathan answered. "She won't expect me until she sees me walk in the door."

"We're fine too," Brigham agreed.

Joseph leaned forward, putting his face in his hands, and began to massage his temples very slowly with his fingertips. "Then, brethren," he finally said, "let's see if we can't sort this whole thing out."

———•———

It was almost ten o'clock when a shout outside Joseph's house pulled the four men out of their huddle. Joseph got to his feet, peering out the window.

"Brother Joseph! Brother Joseph! Come quick!" It was a man's voice and it was filled with urgency.

Joseph went to the door and stepped out onto the porch. The other three stood and followed. As they came outside, Nathan saw the man. He was jogging toward them, waving his hands, coming from the direction of the main part of town.

It was Hosea Stout, clerk for the Nauvoo high council. He came through the gate and into the yard, then pulled up as he saw Joseph and the others. "Brother Joseph!" he gasped. "You must come."

"Yes, Hosea. What is it?"

"It's John Bennett, Joseph."

Joseph straightened perceptibly. "John Bennett? What about him?"

"He's tried to kill himself, sir. You'd better come quick. He's real bad."

———•———

Lydia sat up in bed, the pillows behind her back, watching Nathan slowly undress. "Does he even know that Rebecca has talked to us?"

Nathan was unbuttoning his shirt absently. "No. I had no chance to tell Joseph before the confrontation with Bennett. I told him later, but no, Bennett doesn't know anything about it."

"That's good. I wouldn't want him to ever come back against Rebecca."

Lydia scooted down in the bed, letting the black hair cascade out across the pillow. Now there was genuine sadness on her face. She knew Nathan wasn't—couldn't—tell her everything. But what he had told her was enough. She felt a great abhorrence for the man behind all this, and yet at the same time, she saw him as a tragic, broken figure. "So you think he'll live?"

"Yes. George Robinson was working furiously to save him. Bennett was fighting like a wild man. It took two of us just to hold him down. But he's past the crisis now."

He paused for a moment in front of the small mirror, passing a hand through his hair, then rubbing his eyes. He moved over and blew out the lamp. In a moment, he was in bed beside her, pulling her over to curl up in his arms.

"Thank you, Nathan."

"For what?"

"For doing that for Rebecca."

"It wasn't just for Rebecca. That man had to be stopped." Then he gave a quick shake of his head. "Let's not talk about it anymore."

"All right." She went up on one elbow and kissed him on the forehead. "I love you, Nathan Steed."

"And I love you, Lydia McBride." As she lay down again, he pulled her to him, suddenly fiercely protective of her. "Don't you ever leave me, Miss McBride."

"Leave you?" she said in surprise. "What ever made you say such a thing as that?"

He kissed her now, not with passion but with sweet tenderness and longing. "Just don't you ever leave me, all right?"

Chapter Notes

Lorenzo Wasson, a nephew of Emma Smith who would become a member of the Church in March 1842, was present on the day Joseph and Bennett had the blowup. According to his report, Joseph gave Bennett "a tremendous flagellation for practicing iniquity under the base pretence of authority from the heads of the church." (*Times and Seasons* 3 [15 August 1842]: 892; see Andrew F. Smith, "The Saintly Scoundrel: The Life and Times of John Cook Bennett" [unpublished ms., Brooklyn, N.Y., 1994], p. 118.)

It is difficult to pinpoint the exact timing of the events leading up to Bennett's attempted suicide. Joseph also reported the confrontation and said that soon afterwards Bennett made his suicide attempt (see HC 5:36–37, 42–43). Whether these took place on the same day is not clear. An article in the 23 July 1842 issue of the *Wasp*, a local paper published in Nauvoo, pinpointed the date of the suicide attempt as 27 July 1841, which has been followed here. There seems to be little doubt that it was Joseph's threat to expose him publicly that drove Bennett to take poison.

$\mathbf{M}$atthew came running out of the bedroom, pulling up his suspenders over his shoulders as he came. "Coming!" he called.

Whoever was outside their door either didn't hear him or didn't care. The heavy pounding started again. *Bam! Bam! Bam!*

"I'm coming, I'm coming!"

He reached the door and opened it, blinking at the bright morning sunlight.

"Well, what do you know," Brigham Young boomed, "there really is life in there after all."

"Good morning, Brigham," Matthew said, trying not to look too surprised.

Jennifer Jo came out of the bedroom. She was dressed except for her feet, which were bare. Her hands were up, pulling her hair into a braid at the back of her head. "Who is it, Matth— Oh, Brother Brigham. Good morning." Instantly the smile filled her face, wrinkling her nose and pushing the freckles into one another so as to make them all the more noticeable.

"Good morning, Jennifer." Though the family had taken to calling Matthew's sweetheart Jennifer Jo to distinguish her from Jenny Pottsworth, Brigham never called her anything but Jennifer.

"Do come in," Jennifer Jo said. "I'm just going to start breakfast. Will you join us?"

To Matthew's surprise, Brigham immediately nodded. "Don't mind if I do. We were up with the children last night, so I told Mary Ann to sleep in." He slapped his stomach, which had just a touch of paunch to it now. "Wouldn't hurt me at all to miss a meal or two, but I wouldn't want to hurt your feelings by turning down the invitation."

Matthew smiled, still a little bewildered by this early appearance. Brigham was not an early riser but preferred working late into the night. They never started at the carpentry shop before half past eight, and often Brigham wouldn't come until nine or later. It was barely seven o'clock now. "Come in and sit down," Matthew said, pushing aside his perplexity.

Brigham did so, dropping his hat on the bench inside the door. Then he moved over to the table. If he had had a late night, Matthew thought, he certainly didn't look it. Brigham had celebrated his fortieth birthday in June on their way home from England, but he looked younger than that. He wore his reddish hair down to his collar but was clean shaven. His face was normally round and a touch boyish, but was filling out even more with age. He had blue-gray eyes that could dance with amusement or crackle with anger. Now they were filled with humor.

As he sat down, he grinned up at Jennifer Jo, who had moved to the stove. "Actually, if the truth be known, I'm here to check up on this young man. I thought it best to do that without any warning so he couldn't cover his tracks."

"Check up? On me?" Matthew frowned. "What have I done wrong?"

"Don't know that you have," Brigham said solemnly. "That's what I'm here for. Now, Matthew, I'm going to ask your bride some questions, and I don't want you butting in and trying to answer them for her. Understood?"

Jennifer Jo was laughing, but her curiosity was piqued as well. "Questions for me?"

"Yep. Question number one. How long have you been married now?"

There was no hesitation. "Seven days."

"A whole week? And you still love this tall, gangly goose here?"

Her face melted as she looked at Matthew. "More than I thought possible."

"Is he treating you right?"

She giggled with delight. "Perfectly!"

"Hey," Matthew grumbled. "What about asking me if she's treating me right?"

"Just hush now, boy, or we'll send you out to do the chores." Brigham turned back to her. "You think you want to try another week of this wedded bliss?"

Jennifer Jo was completely into the game now. "Could I just commit to three or four days and see how it's looking by then?"

As Matthew let out a howl, Brigham nodded, ignoring him. "Wise choice. It never hurts to be cautious. And how about his Irish? Is he learning to speak to you like a true son of the Emerald Isle?"

"Alas," she said mournfully, "this is one area where he has completely failed me. After spending all that time in London, all he can manage is a poor imitation of a Cockney accent. It is an offense to my ears, to be completely frank."

"Aye," Brigham averred solemnly. "No wonder you're cautious about committing too heavily to the boy."

"Look," Matthew growled, moving over to the stove to stand beside his wife, "if you two are just going to sit here and jaw, and that looks like that's about all you're good for, let a hungry man get some breakfast started and on the table."

"Hmm," Jennifer Jo said, cocking her head to one side. "With that kind of offer, I just may extend my contract to another full week after all." She went up on tiptoes and kissed Matthew lightly.

"Away with you, girl," he warned ominously, actually not doing too badly with his attempt at an Irish accent. "You've wounded me deeply now, and there'll be no winning me back with your insincere and flattering ways."

Matthew watched Brigham mop up maple syrup with the last half of his fourth pancake. "By the way, did you see Bennett's grave?" Matthew asked.

There was a startled look. "His grave? He didn't die. He's past the crisis now."

Matthew chuckled. "I know that, but this was evidently the work of some wag with a sense of humor. It was a pile of sand and a fake tombstone."

"Really?" Brigham asked. "No, I hadn't heard about it."

"Tell him about the epitaph," Jennifer Jo urged Matthew.

"Well, we weren't sure what it all meant at first," Matthew started. "Fortunately, Peter was with us. And you know Peter. He always has his nose in a book. He seems to know everything."

"Yes," Brigham agreed, "that's Peter, all right."

"It said something like, 'In memory of Major General John C. Bennett, who died at the siege of Philter, in the defense of the cause of Venus, July 27, 1841.'"

"Philter?" Brigham asked with a blank look.

"Yes. Peter says that a philter is a drug or a potion which is supposed to cause someone to fall in love with you."

"Oh." Brigham's eyes sparkled. "Sounds like someone knew him pretty well."

"And Venus is the goddess of love," Jennifer Jo added shyly, blushing even now as she remembered the boldness of the statement.

Brigham speared the last piece, stuffed it in his mouth, and chased it down with the final two swallows of milk. He leaned back. "So, there are others who are skeptical too, eh?"

That caught Jennifer Jo's attention. "Skeptical?" she asked. "What do you mean?"

Brigham set the mug down. "There are some, including Matthew's own brother, who have doubts about whether this was a serious attempt at suicide or not."

Jennifer Jo looked dubious. She knew that Nathan didn't like John C. Bennett, but she hadn't heard anything about this. "How could that be? The man nearly died."

Brigham answered with some tartness, making Matthew wonder if he might not share in Nathan's doubts a little. "Bennett is a doctor. He specializes in medicines and herbs. It's likely that he would know exactly how much poison to take to make it look real but without actually risking his life."

It wasn't enough for Jennifer Jo, who by nature trusted everyone. "But Nathan said he fought off any attempts to keep him alive."

Brigham just grunted and said nothing more. Matthew reached over and took her hand and smiled at her. Jennifer Jo McIntire had come to America from Ireland with her mother and her younger sister, and they had eventually made their home in the sparsely settled area of northern Missouri. Their farm was some miles from the nearest town, and so for the two growing girls there hadn't been much of what the Latter-day Saints called the "worldly influences." That was one of the reasons Matthew had fallen in love with her so quickly. There was an innocence about her that was very precious to him.

He watched her now, admiring and loving her all over again. The freckles, once bright in childhood, had faded somewhat, but still provided a light sprinkling across her nose and upper cheeks. The tip of her nose turned up just slightly, as if she had bumped against something before the clay had set. All of that, combined with sky blue eyes and a smile that made him soften up like butter on the fireplace hearth, made her seem almost childlike sometimes. Brigham's skepticism about Bennett's motives was clearly distressing to her.

Matthew decided to change the subject. "Nathan says Joseph is going to give Brother Bennett another chance and not bring him before the council."

"That's true," Brigham agreed. He looked at Matthew thoughtfully. "He's willing to see if this deep outward remorse is really proof of an inward change." At Matthew's frown, he went on quickly. "This is not to say that Joseph has turned a blind eye to the whole matter. He has instructed the Twelve to watch the situation very carefully. If we see any signs that there has not been true repentance, we are to let Joseph know immediately."

"That's good," Matthew said. "I feel better about that."

"Me too," Jennifer Jo chimed in.

They were silent for a moment. Then Matthew gave Brigham a crooked grin. "So if you don't mind my asking, is the reason you dropped by this morning to have breakfast or to encourage my wife's continuing ill-treatment of me?"

"Ill-treatment in a pig's eye," Brigham snorted. "This girl is just wise enough to know that she's got a real job on her hands here, getting you made into something valuable. The breakfast was an accident of timing, nothing more." He slapped his stomach. "And a darn good one, I might add."

He stood up, and the smile slowly faded. "No, actually I came by to tell you I'm not going to be in the shop today either, Matthew. Joseph wants us to spend the day with him."

Matthew shrugged. "That's fine." Since their return from England, that was occurring with increasing frequency.

Brigham stood, walked to the door, and retrieved his hat. "If it doesn't take all day, I'll come over." He opened the door and stepped outside.

The young couple followed him. "When it comes time to do those fireplace mantels though," Matthew said, "I'm going to need you. That's still a little beyond me."

Brigham nodded absently, his mind already moving off to other things.

"Brother Joseph is spending a lot of time with the Twelve now, isn't he?" Jennifer Jo asked. "That must be wonderful."

Brigham turned, the surprise and then the pleasure showing in his eyes. "Yes," he said softly, "he really is."

He wasn't the only one surprised. Matthew was looking at his wife with a bit of amazement. Brigham was gone a lot, but Matthew hadn't really thought about what it meant for the Apostle.

"It is more than wonderful, Jennifer," Brigham said. "It is incredible. Joseph is so different now. So . . . So . . ." He shook his head in frustration. "I don't know how to describe it. So much broader. So much deeper. So much more—"

"So much more the Prophet?" Jennifer Jo guessed.

"Yes, exactly! It's marvelous. Ever since we returned from England. He's been opening the scriptures to us, teaching us the doctrines. He says that the time has come for the Twelve to take a larger role in the work of the kingdom."

He was eyeing this young Irish girl with open respect now. Then he put his hat on and turned to Matthew. "This is a fine young woman you've found for yourself, Matthew Steed. You treat her right or I'll be putting you through the lathe and trimming your head down to size."

Matthew put his arm around Jennifer Jo and pulled her shoulder up against his own. "I know, Brigham. I know."

———•———

By the middle of 1841, it was becoming increasingly common for the Saints to have two houses. Virtually everyone except the newest arrivals had a "first house." Usually it was a log cabin or a small hut made of mud and sticks, or even a rough lean-to put up against the side of a barn or some other outbuilding. Here the family did everything—eat, sleep, cook, socialize. Often these "homes" had only one large room and no doors or windows. It was not uncommon even after two years of remarkable growth to see some of these first houses with quilts hung across the front door to provide some privacy and to keep out the Nauvoo flies, those ever-present mothlike insects that plagued the city in summertime. Often the chimneys were no more than holes cut in the ceiling or wall, with a funnel or piece of tin twisted round to fit the hole and vent off at least some of the smoke from the cooking fires.

But with hard work came prosperity, and after two years of diligence more and more families were building a second home, what was commonly called the "big house." It was usually located beside or just behind the first house. This second home was normally made of brick and was two stories—thus its name. It would generally have a separate kitchen and eating area, a parlor or sitting room for company, and several bedrooms for the family.

The block on Granger Street between Ripley and Mulholland was rapidly coming to be known as "Steed Row." This was where all the Steeds had built their homes. Along the west side of Granger, from north to south, there was Jessica's combination house and school, then Benjamin and Mary Ann's cabin, flanked on the south by Nathan and Lydia's place. On the east side of the street, Derek and Rebecca (and Derek's brother, Peter) lived across from Nathan; Joshua and Caroline lived directly east of Benjamin and Mary Ann; and Carl and Melissa lived across from Jessica. All of these were what were known as "first homes."

While the Steeds had fared better than most with their first homes—largely thanks to Joshua's generosity—they were still fairly modest dwellings, with the exception of Joshua and Caroline's home. But by summer 1841, the Steeds were prospering also, and started to add their own big houses. Not surprisingly, Carl and Melissa were first. Using brick from his own kiln, Carl had built them a fine two-story Federal-style home with a large, airy kitchen and five upstairs bedrooms. That proved to be perfect timing for Matthew and Jennifer Jo, who immediately moved into their first house.

Now two additional big houses were under construction. With the store doing a steadily growing business, Lydia and

Nathan were just digging the foundations for a new home behind their old one. And over Benjamin and Mary Ann's consistent protests, Joshua had hired a crew to begin work on a big house for his parents. It was now up to the first five or six courses of brick—furnished at no cost from Carl's kilns—and though it would be smaller than either Joshua's or Nathan's, it would be a wonderful improvement for the patriarch and matriarch of the Steed clan.

Peter Ingalls was thinking about all of that as he left his house and started toward the store. Steed Row was a wonderful place to live. The families were constantly associating with each other, and the children were more like brothers and sisters living in adjacent bedrooms than cousins living in adjacent homes. Peter had turned seventeen in May, and he realized that he would soon have to find somewhere to live other than with Rebecca and Derek. Little Christopher was two now, and soon, he suspected, there would be a second on the way. While they would never say anything to him about it, Peter knew full well what it would mean to them to have his bedroom. And so without their knowing it, he had already visited with Joshua about underwriting Peter's efforts to finance the purchase of a lot just around the corner from Nathan and Lydia. Peter was working now. He had recently been hired as a typesetter at the *Times and Seasons* office. It would be a while before he could actually start construction, but now that he was salaried, he felt that he could negotiate something in good faith with Joshua.

As he passed Jessica's house he turned his head. Kathryn McIntire, Jennifer Jo's sister, was on the front porch, sweeping it with a straw broom. "Good morning, Kathryn," he called out.

She turned, raising a hand to shade her eyes from the sun. When she saw who it was, she immediately straightened, one hand going up quickly to brush back an errant strand of hair. "Oh, good morning, Peter."

He slowed his step and then stopped by the fence. "How are you this morning?"

"I . . . we're just fine."

"Getting ready to start school again?"

She smiled at that. "Yes. We start a week from Monday. Jessica has gone down to Warsaw with a couple of other people to see if they can find any arithmetic books."

"And I heard that you will actually be helping her teach."

"Yes." She lowered her eyes, coloring slightly. "Will you be coming to school at all this year, Peter?"

He shook his head, feeling the disappointment in him. It had been he who had served as Jessica's teaching assistant the previous school year. He would miss that more than he was willing to admit. "No," he answered. "I'm working every day now."

Kathryn nodded and Peter saw the disappointment in her eyes. He thought nothing of it, other than its being the reaction of a friend. "Well," he said, lifting one hand, "I'd better be going or I'll be late for work."

Kathryn waved; then as he started north again, she called out to him. "You haven't forgotten where the printing office is, have you?" she teased. The *Times and Seasons* was printed in the basement of a warehouse down on Water Street, near the Prophet's home. That was the opposite direction from the way he was headed now.

"Oh," Peter responded, "I've got to stop by the store. I've written a poem for Jenny."

It was as though someone had blown out the candle in Kathryn's eyes. Her face fell and her mouth pulled down. "Oh," was all she said. Then she turned to her sweeping again, swinging around so her back was to him.

Barely aware of her reaction, and forgetting it almost as quickly as he noted it, Peter started off again, striding out with resoluteness. As he rounded the corner, Kathryn stopped her sweeping and turned to watch him disappear. "Yes, that's right, Peter," she muttered. "Hurry and go see your precious Jenny. Will is gone to St. Louis. Now's your chance."

Angry at him, angry at herself, Kathryn swung the broom at the last vestiges of the dust on the porch, then spun around and went back in the house, slamming the door behind her.

———•———

The Steed Family Dry Goods and General Store was a low structure, made of logs chinked heavily with mud and mortar. Though Caroline had funded the store with twenty thousand dollars she had received from the sale of her home in Savannah, Georgia, most of that went into the stocking of the store rather than the construction of it. It had proved to be a wise move, for their store had a much wider variety of goods than most of the other stores in the city. But there had been no money for a second story. Instead, there were storage rooms all along the back of the store, and thus the low squat profile of the building.

Peter jumped up lightly onto the porch that ran the full length of the storefront. There was a sign in the window that announced the store was still closed, but he tried the door anyway. Jenny was almost always here by eight o'clock, getting things in order for the nine o'clock opening time. The door was unlocked and he pushed it open quietly. For a moment, he couldn't make out much in the dimmer light; then he saw Jenny over in the corner near the tools, straightening out items on the shelf. He pushed the door open wider and stepped inside.

Jenny heard the noise and turned, then smiled warmly. "Oh, hello, Peter."

"Hello, Jenny."

"You're up and about bright and early."

"I have to be at the print shop by half past."

"Oh, yes. That's right. You're a working man now."

"Yes." He felt a quick warmth to know that she knew about his new position. "And you're up early yourself," he said, walking over to where she was.

"Actually I was a little late this morning. It's a good thing Lydia and Caroline don't know what a lazy girl I am."

"One might call you a lot of things," Peter said, "but lazy isn't one of them."

She laughed lightly, seeing that for what it was. Peter blushed, feeling like a tongue-tied dolt. He and Jenny had been childhood friends back in Preston. Back then they had been able to talk about anything. But he had come to America, and Jenny had turned from a spunky little girl into a lovely young woman.

She stopped what she was doing and turned to face him squarely. The morning light from the window lit her face, showing the wideness of her eyes, the firmness of her lips, and the golden sheen of her hair. There was an elfin look in her eyes. "And just what might some of those other things be?"

"What things?" he asked, having lost the thread of the conversation.

"Those other things that you might call me?"

But before he could answer there was a sound behind them. They both turned to see a tall young man coming out of one of the back rooms, staggering beneath the weight of a large wooden box. "Jenny, where do you want these shoes?"

"Behind the counter, over there," she answered, pointing.

As Peter watched, the fellow moved across the main room of the store to the spot indicated and set the box down. Peter noticed that he did so with relative ease, barely making a bump as the box was placed. Then he straightened, brushing off his hands. He was tall, half a hand taller than Peter at least, and strongly built. His hair was almost as fair as Jenny's, and deep blue eyes were set amid striking features. Peter guessed he was twenty or thereabouts. As he came toward them, he eyed Peter curiously.

"Andrew," Jenny said, "come meet a fellow Britisher."

He came across the room in long, easy steps, then stuck out his hand. "Andrew Stokes," he said. "It's a pleasure to meet you."

Herefordshire, Peter thought as he took his hand. The accent was definitely that of a person from Herefordshire. "How do you do?" he said. "I'm Peter Ingalls."

Like Jenny, and many other children of the poor in England, Peter had started working in the cotton mills at the age of nine. He had not progressed out of the cutting rooms, and so had never done any of the hard-labor jobs as Derek had done. Peter was not solidly built. He was slender, and his shoulders stooped slightly—also a product of the cutting room. Suddenly he was keenly conscious of that fact as he stood beside this broad-shouldered Stokes fellow. He was also aware that his hair was ragged and needed cutting, and that his apron had ink stains from the latest edition of the paper. Without thinking, he wiped his free hand against his trousers.

"Ah, yes, Jenny's childhood friend. She's told me about you."

Peter flushed a little at that. So that was how she described him to others.

"That means you must be a Lancashire lad too."

"Yes," Peter replied, noting the use of the word *lad* with faint irritation. "And from what part of Herefordshire are you?"

Andrew released Peter's hand and stepped back. "Very good. You have a quick ear. I'm from Castle Froome, about fourteen miles south and west of Worcester." He pronounced it "Wooster," as the British do.

"You lived near Brother Benbow?"

The young man was surprised. "That's right. So you know Herefordshire?"

"Not really. My brother was with Elder Woodruff on his mission there, and I've heard him talk about Castle Froome. That's all."

"Your brother?" Then he snapped his fingers. "Of course, Elder Ingalls. Yes, he was there when my family and I were baptized. We lived just a mile or so from the Benbows. We were some of the first to hear the gospel."

"Andrew has just recently arrived from England," Jenny said. "He came in the store just a few weeks or so ago and we've already become fast friends, haven't we, Andrew?"

"Most assuredly," he said, smiling at her and showing evenly spaced teeth.

"And of late, he's been coming in early to help me lift the heavy stuff. It's been very nice."

Peter, watching the light in Jenny's eyes, realized that she was positively glowing with excitement. And with a lurch, he realized that it had nothing to do with him. She was looking up into Andrew's face, watching his every expression.

Finally she turned back to Peter. "So what brings you to the store at this early hour?" she asked.

Suddenly flustered, Peter stammered for a moment. "Uh, I was . . ." He thought about the folded paper in his pocket and knew there was nothing in the world that could make him tell her about that now. "I was just on my way to work and thought I'd stop by and say hello. Caroline said you're almost always here by this hour."

She laughed lightly, her eyes teasing him. "Isn't this kind of the long way to work?"

"Not really," he managed. "It's a beautiful morning, and I . . . uh . . . I wanted to drop something off for Nathan at the city council office." Then before she could pin him down further, he stuck out his hand toward Andrew. "It's good to meet you. I suppose we'll be seeing you again."

"Yes, I'm sure. Give my best regards to your brother."

"I will." And with that, he turned and made himself stroll casually to the door. He stopped one more time. "We'll see you later," he called, and then he was outside.

"Fool!" he muttered under his breath as he stepped off the porch. "Stupid dolt!" As he walked swiftly away, he reached in his pocket and withdrew the paper that was there. He didn't open it. He didn't have to. He knew every word by heart. He had pored over them for hours. There was no hesitation, even though this was the only copy. He simply tore the sheet in half, in half again, and then again a third time. Then he tossed the pieces over his shoulder, not turning to watch them flutter to the ground.

Chapter Notes

The mock grave and the satirical headstone of John C. Bennett's "final resting place" were referred to in the *Wasp*, a Nauvoo newspaper (see *Wasp* 1 [23 July 1842]: 2; Andrew F. Smith, "The Saintly Scoundrel: The Life and Times of John Cook Bennett" [unpublished ms., Brooklyn, N.Y., 1994], pp. 118–19).

W alter Samuelson's office was on the fourth floor of one corner of the huge cotton warehouse that faced the Mississippi River. From his window, Will could look upriver and downriver and watch the heart of what made St. Louis one of the thriving new cities in the American West. There was hardly a time when he couldn't count five or six boats moving upstream or downstream. Dozens of the great steamers lined the docks and wharves on both sides of the river. Hundreds of stevedores—Negro slaves, Irish immigrants, Chinese coolies, Indians from the Caribbean—ran about as though someone had just kicked their anthill. This was American commerce, and while it might not have the elegance and grace of the great ocean ports, it certainly had the same bustle and pulsing energy. And Will grudgingly had to admit he found it exciting.

It was grudging because he was still disgruntled about how things were going for him personally. Two nights ago Will and his father had gone to the dinner at Samuelson's house. The dinner itself hadn't been too awful—awkward, but not awful. Alice Samuelson, though not as pretty as Jenny, had proven to be witty, charming, and understanding of Will's cautious reserve. Before the evening was over, the two of them had gone for a walk. When she began telling him of her own response to "this arrangement," as she referred to the dinner, she had Will laughing uproariously. He guessed that given half a chance, they would become fast friends. But she was no more interested in being matched by her parents than he was in having his father work out something for him.

But when they returned to the house, they realized they had made a strategic mistake. What had been merely the desire of two young people to escape a boring evening with the old folks had been seen by the parents as something quite different. It was working!

Joshua started in on him the moment they left the house, pressing him to know how he felt about Alice now, suggesting they could prolong their departure a little if he wanted, and how would he feel about another dinner on their last evening here? They hadn't gone halfway back to their hotel before Will was glowering and had his father muttering to himself. Why couldn't he understand? he thought. All Will wanted was to make his own way in these matters.

And then this morning, the worst had happened. Alice appeared at the office with her father. She needed a ride to her violin lesson, Samuelson explained innocently. Mrs. Samuelson's carriage driver had suddenly taken ill and couldn't take her later in the day. She would just have to stay at the office until noon, when her father would take her. Perhaps Will might join her for a sight-seeing trip around the city.

The girl was mortified, totally humiliated, but neither father seemed aware of that. However, Will flatly refused to leave the task he had been given, which was to run an inventory on the cotton in the warehouse. Instead he invited Alice to join him, best dress and all. That had won him Samuelson's dismay, his father's fury, and Alice's gratitude. Finally, a couple of hours ago,

Samuelson, still clearly in a huff, left with Alice in tow to take her to her lesson. That left Will and Joshua to share the office with nothing but an icy wall between them.

Will turned around as the door to the office opened. He nearly groaned aloud. Samuelson was back, and right behind him was Alice again. But Samuelson didn't even look at Will. He walked right over to Joshua. "Steed," he said in a commanding voice, "put that pen down and come with us. We've got something to show you."

Joshua was surprised by the enthusiasm on his partner's face. "What's that?"

Samuelson grabbed his arm and started to tug him out of his chair. "There isn't any way to describe it. You've got to see this for yourself."

Alice went straight to Will. "Will, you too. It's wonderful. You've got to come."

He looked at her suspiciously. Was she in on the conspiracy now too?

Seeing his expression, she slugged him on the arm as if he were her little brother, which was the best thing she could have done to and for him. "It's not what you think," she said. "Come on."

"All right," Samuelson said. "This is it."

Will looked around in surprise. They were on a vacant lot in the heart of downtown St. Louis. Correction, he thought. It was normally a vacant lot. Now there was a medium-sized white canvas tent pitched just about in the center of the lot. A crowd was gathered around the front of it in a semicircle. Even from the road they could hear the excited rumble of voices.

Will stood up in the carriage so as to see better. And then, right in front of the tent, he saw a tall man in a black suit and high stovepipe hat. He was holding something up—from here it looked metallic—and that was bringing a chorus of oohs and aahs from the crowd.

Alice gave him a little shove. "Come on, Will."

He jumped out of the carriage, then helped her down. Behind them, Samuelson and Joshua were also climbing out. They moved across the grassy lot, and Will saw that off to one side there was a collection of strange-looking equipment—four or five large wooden trunks, a padded bench, three padded stools, several tripods which held nothing except some curious-looking braces, and a white square of canvas, easily six feet by six feet square, mounted on a light wooden frame and braced so that it stood almost vertically.

"What is this?" he asked Alice.

She merely smiled and took his arm, pulling him forward. Evidently many in the crowd recognized Samuelson and viewed him as someone of considerable importance. When they saw his party approaching, they moved back to make an aisle for him. It led right to the man in the black stovepipe hat. When he looked up to see what had caused the crowd to shift, his face instantly became wreathed in smiles. "Ah, Mr. Samuelson." He took Alice's hand and curtsied slightly. "And Miss Samuelson."

"Mr. Pickerell," Samuelson said, "may I introduce my business partner and his son—Joshua and Will Steed. This is Mr. William Pickerell from New York City, but presently on tour of the West demonstrating a—" He caught himself and laughed. "Well, I'll let him tell you that."

The black hat was swept off and the man bowed deeply. "A pleasure, sir."

"Is it ready?" Alice burst out.

The man smiled, pleased at her excitement. "It is. Just a moment."

He turned and disappeared into the tent. The crowd went silent, obviously knowing what to expect. "What is going on?" Will whispered, pulling Alice around to face him.

"You've got to see it for yourself. But it's better than anything you've ever seen," she promised. "Even in China."

"Most definitely," her father agreed.

A moment later Pickerell reappeared. In his hand he carried

a square of cloth. As the tent flap closed again, Will caught a whiff of something foul-smelling, something burning, as if some animal had been caught in a fire. No, he thought, as he tried to identify it. It had a chemical quality to it. More as if a printing office or an apothecary shop had caught fire.

Pickerell walked over to Alice and began to unwrap whatever it was he carried. By now the onlookers had closed in again. They craned their necks to see over and around Samuelson's group as an almost reverential hush fell over them. As Pickerell dropped the cloth away, Will saw that what he carried *was* metallic. It was a copper plate, about eight inches square, and no thicker than a piece of heavy parchment. He held it up for all to see. Will peered at it, but it was just a plain piece of copper sheeting. But the crowd knew more than Will. There was no collective sigh of disappointment. If anything, the air of expectancy heightened even more.

Then, with a flourish worthy of a master magician, Pickerell flipped the copper sheet around. "Behold the daguerreotype," he said grandly, holding the metal up for Alice to see.

A great "Aah!" went up, but Will was barely conscious of it. He stared dumbly at what he saw before him, not understanding. The side of the sheet now visible was apparently silver-plated, and etched into the metal was a tiny painting of Alice Samuelson. He leaned forward. No, not a painting. It was far too precise for that. It was her! Every detail was perfect. There was the thin tracing of feathers that lined her bonnet, the wide, teasing eyes looking directly at him, the eyelet pattern on the lace around her collar—even a wisp of hair plucked by a passing breeze. It was all there in absolute, exquisite clarity.

"Oh, it's lovely!" she cried. She reached out and took it, carefully holding it by the edges.

Will turned to see his father staring openmouthed as well. "What in the world . . . ?" he finally breathed.

Pickerell was delighted with the effect he was creating. "It's called a daguerreotype, sir. Da-*gehr*-o-type," he pronounced slowly. "It's named after the Frenchman who invented it. It's a real picture. Pho-*tahg*-ra-phee, we call it." Pickerell turned and took another plate from a small table next to the tent and handed it to Joshua. This was a picture of a young girl, about Savannah's age. Again, the detail was stunning, and Will and Joshua leaned over to stare at it in wonder.

"We take a silver-plated sheet of copper, polish the silver side so that it's bright like a mirror, and treat that same silver surface with certain chemicals to sensitize the plate to light. Then we put it in this box here." Pickerell turned and pointed to where a box about as big as a good-sized hatbox was perched atop one of the tripods. Will saw that in one end it had a glass lens. "When we take the cover off the lens, light is let into the box and strikes the silver side of the plate. It takes about half a minute, sometimes more, but—"

"He had to clamp my head in position," Alice broke in, "so I wouldn't move."

"That's right. The person must remain perfectly still until the picture is taken. Once the plate has been exposed, we treat the exposed side with fumes made by heated mercury, and the image forms on the plate. Then finally we treat it with a salt solution. That fixes the image—makes it permanent—on the plate, and voila! you have a daguerreotype."

Joshua turned to his partner. "You were right, this is incredible. I wouldn't have believed it if you hadn't let me see it."

"I still can't believe it," Will admitted.

"Oh," Alice exclaimed, "Mama is going to be so surprised."

That brought Joshua around with a jerk. "Mr. Pickerell, did I understand correctly that you move from place to place with this . . . process of yours?"

"Indeed I do, sir. I have been in St. Louis now for over a week. Before that, I was in Cincinnati."

Joshua took him by the arm and turned him away from the crowd. "That's wonderful. I think I have a business proposition for you."

Kathryn McIntire looked up in surprise. She was at a table in the schoolroom in Jessica Griffith's home. She was counting out papers, ten for each student, that would have to last for the better part of the school year. Peter Ingalls was standing at the doorway, hat in hand, looking around.

Slowly, she laid the papers down. "Hello," she murmured.

"Hello, Kathryn."

She smoothed her dress down and fought the temptation to brush at her hair. "You're not at work?" It was the only thing she could think of to say.

He shook his head. "Don Carlos asked me to take some papers to Heber Kimball. I saw you through the window." He stopped, looking around wistfully.

Kathryn sat silently, watching him. She guessed what was going through his mind. Peter Ingalls loved to learn. He took to books like a young colt to a bucket of oats. He couldn't consume them fast enough. And for the first time in quite a while, he wouldn't be sitting in Jessica's class, wouldn't be helping her as her teaching assistant. Kathryn would be doing that this year.

He sensed her watching him and forced a quick smile. "So it starts again in about a week?" he said.

"Yes."

He nodded, feeling suddenly awkward. "I . . . I wrote a poem, Kathryn." His hand moved toward the pocket of his trousers, then dropped back again.

One eyebrow came up. "Oh?" And then she couldn't hold it back. "You seem to have been doing a lot of that lately."

It was said evenly enough, but he still flinched. He knew full well what she was referring to. "Yeah," he finally said lamely.

She knew she had hurt him, and somewhere inside her a tiny voice chided her for her pettiness. But it wasn't as though he had been particularly mindful of her feelings, was it? "Is this another something for Jenny?" she asked, as though she were only marginally interested anyway.

For several moments he looked at her, then he shook his head. "Not really." And then, looking quite dejected, he raised one hand. "Well, I'd better get back, I guess." He put his hat on and, without another word, turned and left.

Few people in Nauvoo knew that Rachel Griffith was Joshua Steed's natural daughter. Joshua and Jessica had married in Jackson County, Missouri, in 1829. Joshua Steed had been a different man back then—bitter, hard-drinking, smoldering with resentment—and the marriage had been rocky from the start. They divorced when Rachel was only a year old, and she had never known Joshua as her father. But by then Jessica had joined the Church and met the Steeds. Though technically she was no longer part of the family, they had taken her in as though she were one of their own.

Then, after years of separation, Joshua and his family were reunited. By that time Jessica had married John Griffith, and Joshua had married Caroline Mendenhall. John had two boys from a previous marriage, and so while there had been no legal adoption of Rachel, it was only natural that she took the Griffith name along with her stepbrothers so there was no distinction between them. Given these arrangements, Joshua's return created an awkward situation. So by mutual agreement Joshua and Jessica decided that the best way to deal with the whole matter was to put aside the past. It wasn't a denial that the past had happened; it was just a determination not to let it intrude into the family structure now. They made a pact that Joshua would become "Uncle Joshua" to Rachel and just another one of the brothers-in-law to Jessica. It had been a little strained at first, but gradually all of the Steed family settled into the new role definitions. Even after John Griffith was killed at Haun's Mill and Jessica was left a widow, that did not change. Now, three years later, family members rarely thought about what once had been.

Rachel Steed Griffith was nine now. She had more of her natural father's physical characteristics than her mother's. Her hair was a dark brown, almost black in subdued light, and had a natural curl to it. Worn long and down her back, it tended to fall into natural ringlets. But in temperament, she was more like her mother, quite serious and reflective by nature, often content to sit quietly while her noisier cousins jabbered around her. But that didn't mean she was a melancholy child in any way. A favorite of her Grandfather Steed, she had a subtle but quick sense of humor, often making quiet comments that would startle the listener for a moment before bringing an appreciative smile. She was bright and learned very quickly, proving to be one of Jessica's most promising pupils in school. She was also a willing worker and was fast becoming surrogate mother to her three brothers—Luke and Mark, her stepbrothers, and little John Benjamin, her half brother.

Rachel also had two foster sisters now. Widow McIntire and her two daughters had been drawn into the Steed family circle when they joined the Church at Far West just about the time when the Saints were being driven from Missouri. Thus they had become part of that tragic exodus. The mother never quite recovered, and when ague swept through the ranks of the Mormons in the summer of 1839, Nancy McIntire was one of the casualties. Jessica took Jennifer Jo and Kathryn McIntire as her own, and Rachel gained two "sisters" on a permanent basis. Kathryn and Rachel had become especially close, in spite of the six years' difference in their ages.

Rachel was in the schoolroom too. She was supposed to be sorting the reading books but, as usual, had opened one and in a moment was deeply engrossed. Kathryn had forgotten she was there, and so when Peter came to the door, Rachel became a silent witness to the little interchange that followed. Now she watched her sister closely as she stared at the door where Peter had been standing just a few moments before.

"Kathryn?" Rachel asked quietly.

Kathryn jumped and turned. "Oh, Rachel. You're so quiet."

"Why are you angry with Peter?"

Kathryn came slowly over to join her. The book Rachel had been reading was forgotten now. "I'm not angry with Peter," Kathryn said slowly. "Why do you say that?"

It was not Rachel's nature to be disingenuous. She was only nine, and maybe she didn't fully understand when adults were angry, but it certainly looked to her like Kathryn was angry. "You acted angry."

Kathryn sat down wearily. "I'm not angry, Rachel. It's just that . . ." Her eyes drew away, remembering. "Ooh! He's so transparent! He's blind, and insensitive, and, and—" She stopped, frustrated that she couldn't think of any other appropriate words.

Just then the door opened and Jessica came into the room, carrying several books in her arms. Right behind her was Jennifer Jo. Peter was immediately forgotten. Rachel leaped up and ran to Jennifer Jo and gave her a hug. "Hi, Jennifer Jo."

"Hello, Rachel." She bent down and kissed Rachel on top of the head, then turned. "Good morning, Kathryn."

"Hello." It came out as little more than a growl.

Jennifer Jo gave Kathryn a sharp look, then turned to Jessica, who just shrugged. Finally, she looked back down at Rachel. "I thought I'd come help you all get ready for school. What needs to be done?"

"You could help me sort the books," Rachel answered. Then, looking at her mother sheepishly, she admitted, "I started reading a story and I haven't gotten very far."

Jessica smiled, not at all surprised.

"Are you excited for school?" Jennifer Jo asked Rachel.

"Oh, yes."

"Do you think you will be able to stand Kathryn as a teacher?" Jennifer Jo said, watching her sister out of the corner of her eye. "Your mother tells me that she's going to let Kathryn teach the reading groups."

Rachel giggled. "Mama says that Kathryn will get all the bad students, and she'll take all the good ones."

"That's right," Kathryn murmured, moving back to where she had been counting papers. "Jessica knows my capabilities well."

"Kathryn!" Jessica exclaimed in dismay. "You know I was

only teasing about that. You will make a fine teacher. And I'm going to give all of the teaching of reading—good and bad students—over to you."

Jennifer Jo was watching her sister carefully. This was not Kathryn. Kathryn's disposition was more sober than her own, but still she was usually sunny and cheerful, a legacy they had both inherited from their mother. So Jennifer Jo knew what to do. Both of them had long ago perfected the ability to pull each other out of blue moods.

She turned and looked at Jessica. "Maybe she just needs some help, Jessica. What if you got her a teaching assistant?"

Jessica caught on immediately. "Oh, now there's an idea for you." She smiled broadly at Kathryn. "But it would have to be someone who already has experience."

Kathryn's head came up for a moment. She knew what her sister was doing and she clearly didn't appreciate it. Then she looked down at the papers again. Jennifer Jo was still looking at Jessica and didn't see it. "What about that one boy? Let's see, what was his name?"

Kathryn kept her eyes down. "Jenny . . ." It came as a quiet warning.

Jessica's smile slowly died and she pulled back, sensing this was not the time for teasing. But Jennifer Jo was determined to bring her sister out of whatever it was that was bothering her. "Oh, yes," she said, snapping her fingers. "Ingalls, I think. Peter Ingalls. Wasn't that his name? Maybe he could help her out."

Kathryn whirled away, slamming the remaining papers down on the table. With an angry toss of her head, she stomped from the room. Jennifer Jo stared at her in disbelief. "Well," she said after a moment of awkward silence, "I didn't expect that to happen."

"Something's wrong," Jessica agreed.

Rachel quickly told her mother and Jennifer Jo what had happened.

"Oh, dear," Jennifer Jo said, deeply contrite. "This was not the time to try and cheer her up, I guess." She started for the door. "I'd better go make my peace with her."

It was like what the French called *déjà vu*. Will Steed rolled over in the bed, turning his head away from the window where the drapes blocked the direct rays of the sun but did very little to keep the light out. It was the same hotel room in Warsaw where they had stayed on their way to St. Louis. One difference was they had got in much later last night—or earlier this morning, to be more exact—than they had on the trip down. Just after dusk, their boat had run aground on a sandbar. No damage was done, but even with all of the power of the boiler put into the paddle wheel, they couldn't back off. Finally, a little after nine, another boat came by and threw them a line. That worked, but the captain was all the more cautious as they continued upriver, and it was almost two o'clock in the morning before they reached Warsaw. It took them another ten minutes to roust the hotel clerk from a deep sleep, and so it was past three before father and son finally were in bed.

Will cracked one eye open. Sure enough, the bed beside him was empty. His father had gone again. Well, that was just too bad, he thought, turning over and burying his head beneath the pillow. They were taking that wagonload of goods back to Nauvoo. This time there was no boat to miss. His body felt as if he had been dragged behind the boat. His mouth was dry and foul-tasting. Behind the closed lids his eyes burned. If he overslept, he decided, his father could just darn well wait.

But five minutes later, he knew it was futile. He was awake and there was going to be no changing that. Grumpy as a bear kicked awake in mid-December, Will dressed, shaved in the bathroom down the hall, and then went downstairs. It was ten-fifteen, he saw, and he was famished again. He started up the street for Callahan's, but then, remembering what had happened before, he slowed his step. Hungry or not, he would wait for his father. He stopped altogether now, trying to decide what to do.

Without realizing it, he had stopped directly next to the window of the newspaper office. As he looked around, his eye was

caught by the editions of the *Warsaw Signal* that had been posted there. Absently, still wondering where to look for his father,
he noticed that the nearest issue was dated with today's date.
Down the window a little, four earlier editions were posted with
a notice that copies were still available for sale. The one dated
July 21 caught his eye and he backed up a little.

After ten minutes of moving back and forth reading snip-
pets from the paper, Will was positively seething. He knew
about Thomas Sharp's helping to form an anti-Mormon political party here in Warsaw. That had been the talk of Nauvoo a
few weeks before. So it was no surprise that the paper contained announcements and propaganda related to this party
and its objectives. That was not what made Will angry. Most
newspapers in America were strongly partisan in one way or
another.

First there were several sarcastic attacks on Joe Smith. In
one place, Sharp challenged Joseph Smith to bring forth the
gold plates so they could be retranslated by a local expert. Will
shook his head in disgust. Did Sharp think that was an original
idea? In another place, an article called the Prophet the
"Presiding Great Devil" and the "Superior Ugly Devil." It said
that "Nauvoo" in "reformed Egyptian," the language of the Book
of Mormon plates, meant "a dwelling place for Devils, or where
their evil deities delighted to dwell."

Will hooted in open derision. This was like a spoiled child
who, when he doesn't get his way, reverts to petty name-calling.

He almost walked away then, thoroughly put off by the bla-
tant bias. But then another article in the earliest posted edition
caught his eye. Sharp had printed something from an Eastern
newspaper, a piece that claimed to expose the real story of
what had happened to the Saints in Missouri. As Will read the
article—along with another of Sharp's own editorials on the
same page—one of Sharp's purposes became clear in Will's
mind. No doubt he intended, among other things, to convey the
message that people in Illinois, and particularly Quincy, had
been duped into extending food, housing, and sometimes even

financial help to the Mormon exiles. While offering such aid was a noble thing, Sharp was suggesting it was misled.

Whoever had written the article for the Eastern paper claimed that his information came from an official U.S. report on the Missouri wars and was based on testimony of eyewitnesses. The only problem was, the ones interviewed were those who were enemies of the Church—members of the mob, generals who had directed the militia, the old settlers who had, Will knew, personally profited from the expulsion of the Saints from their farms. There were also several interviews with people Will knew were former Mormons who had turned against their own. Some of it was obviously downright fabrication.

One of the claims was so blatantly false that Will read it three times in total disbelief. Part of the tragedy was caused by Joseph Smith himself, it read. In a desperate attempt to win sympathy for his cause, Joseph had sent his own secret henchmen out to burn Mormon houses so the Saints would be enraged and rise up against the Missourians.

Almost before he knew it, Will was through the door and into the more subdued light of the newspaper office. He stopped, blinking a little to let his eyes adjust. There was a long counter that ran almost the full length of the room. Behind it, in the far corner, he could see the printing press. A movement to his right caught his eye and he turned. A man was at a table. In front of him, attached to the table, were cases that held thousands of pieces of type in tiny square dividers. Mounted on the wall directly in front of the man's face were other cases; these held the capital letters. Peter had taken Will to show him a similar layout in the *Times and Seasons* offices and explained that this was where the terms "upper case" and "lower case" letters came from.

The man turned at the sound of the door opening and closing. He stood. Will saw that he was carrying the line of type he was working on in one hand. "Yes? May I help you?"

He was a big man, with biceps like a blacksmith's—probably from pulling the press lever thousands upon thousands of times.

His features were porcine, his eyes narrow slits in heavy cheeks.

"I want to speak to the editor," Will barked, only now realizing where his anger had carried him.

The man set the line of type down carefully. He scowled darkly at Will across the counter. "Mr. Sharp is not here at the moment."

"When will he return?"

"I'm not sure. Is there a problem?" It was not spoken with the slightest touch of cordiality.

"Yeah," Will spat out. "I'll tell you what the problem is." He jerked a thumb in the direction of the window behind him. "Your paper is nothing but a pack of lies."

The eyes narrowed even more. "You a Mormon?" he rumbled menacingly.

Will wasn't cowed at all. You didn't stay bosun on a sailing ship for long if you couldn't hold your own with whatever kind of man had been hired as crew. "No," he snapped right back, "I'm not a Mormon. Never have been. But I know enough about them to know that what you've got here is not news. It's nothing but the most damnable lies."

For a moment, there was nothing but the glittering dark eyes behind the rolls of flesh. Then the man jerked his head toward the door. "Mister, I suggest you just turn yourself around and get out of here. You don't like what Mr. Sharp prints, don't buy Mr. Sharp's papers."

"I didn't buy one of these rags," Will said evenly.

The man gave a short laugh of derision. And then, with open contempt, he turned his back on Will and returned to the typesetting table, sitting down heavily. "Then you got no cause for sniveling, do you?" he tossed over his shoulder.

For a moment, Will stood there, breathing deeply, his fists clenching and unclenching. Then he knew what to do. "Only one," he responded. "I don't like passing open garbage on my way to breakfast." He spun around and walked to the window where the papers were pasted.

"Hey!" the man yelled as he saw Will's hands go up. "Get away from there!"

Will ripped one edition off the window with a brisk, downward yank. There was a crash as the man shot up, sending his chair flying. "What the—"

Will tore off another, then turned calmly, crumpling the paper in one hand while he reached in his pocket with the other. He found a coin, not caring what it was, and flipped it at the counter. "Tell Sharp that one of his paying customers doesn't like his newspaper, all right?" He spun on his heel and moved toward the door.

With a roar, the man darted down the counter. Will had expected no less and backed out the door swiftly, not wanting to be caught inside the narrow confines of the office. He shut the door calmly in the man's face; then, as the man ripped it open again, he moved out into the center of the street, nearly knocking two women off the sidewalk as he did so.

The man stopped for just a moment, dazzled by the bright sunlight. Then, seeing Will waiting for him, he lumbered out into the street, swinging the hamlike fists even as he came. Will didn't have time to entertain any second thoughts about the wisdom of what he had just done. Nor did he try to sidestep the rush. Instead, at the last second, he dropped into a crouch, as the first mate on his ship had once taught him, and let the man trip on him and hurtle over the top of him. There was a solid thud, and clouds of dust billowed up around them.

Will really had no desire to fight the man. He had done what he needed to do, and now he just wanted to disengage and get out of there. But he had made one miscalculation. As the man went over the top of him, his knee caught Will squarely in the side. It felt like someone punching a hole through the side of a barrel. Will too went sprawling, rolling over and over, clutching his chest, gasping for air.

The man was up again, and Will managed to stagger to his feet. People were shouting and running towards them. Already there was a small circle gathering around them. On the voyage to China, Will's ship had stopped at Lisbon, on the Iberian Peninsula, to get supplies and to provide some much-needed shore leave for the crew. That Sunday, the captain had taken the ship's officers to a bullfight. That was the image that came to Will's mind right now. The typesetter's head was down and swinging slowly back and forth, as though targeting his prey. Then he lunged. This time Will did try to sidestep, driving his fist into the man's tremendous girth as he passed by. But the man was too quick for him. He hooked left with one of those huge fists. Fortunately, Will's shoulder was still up from throwing his punch and that took the main force of the blow. But the man's fist, still hooking, glanced off the shoulder and smashed directly into Will's face.

Will went down and he went down hard. Blood spurted from his nose, and suddenly there were brightly colored lights flashing behind his eyes. Somewhere he heard a voice shouting at him. "Get up, Will! Get up!" He was conscious of the danger. If the man dropped on him while he was down, it would be over. He tried to push himself up, realizing with some wonder that the voice was his own and that it was only in his mind. And then his elbows gave way. With a low moan, he fell back down, face first into the dust of the street, and everything went black.

※

"I think he may have cracked a rib, and his shoulder is definitely sprained." The doctor glanced at Will, but then went on talking to his father. "The nose is fine, but I suspect he'll end up with an eye that is a real conversation piece."

"How long should he wear the sling?" Joshua asked.

"About a week, I'd guess." He turned now to Will. "You'll know. When it stops hurting when you move it, then you can get rid of the sling."

"What about the binding around my chest?"

"The same. When you can take a really deep breath and not

Fight on Main Street, Warsaw, Illinois

have it hurt you too badly, then it's fine. You'll still be tender, but you're young. You'll heal soon enough."

Joshua stood. "Thank you, Doctor. What do we owe you?"

"Two dollars will cover everything."

"I'll get it," Will said, trying to reach around for the purse he kept in his back pocket. He gasped, wincing with the pain.

Joshua just shook his head, trying to hold his patience, and paid the man.

As they came back out on the street again, Joshua looked at his son. "You ready to talk about it now?"

Will shook his head. "No."

"You know that Thomas Sharp is one of our customers, don't you?"

Will's head came up with a jerk.

"That's right. I've hauled many a load of paper for the *Signal*."

"Then I'd like to stop doing that."

Joshua's nostrils flared and there was a quick intake of breath. But Will wasn't up to any more battles today. Holding his damaged arm with the other, he moved away, not waiting for his father to say anything further.

———

Chapter Notes

It was 1837 when a French scenic artist named Louis Jacques Mandé Daguerre, having worked in partnership with an inventor, perfected the process of fixing photographic images permanently on sheets of silver-plated copper. This was to become the forerunner of modern photography. Daguerre's first photos required several minutes' exposure time. By the end of 1840, a change in the chemicals used, coupled with a significantly improved lens, not only greatly reduced the time necessary for the photo but also gave a richer image. Even then, head clamps were often used to ensure immobility during the picture taking. Though expensive, daguerreotypes were widely used in Europe and the United States until the 1850s when ambrotype, tintype, and paper photographs replaced them. (See *World Book Encyclopedia*, 1994 ed., s.v. "Daguerreotype.")

Though it may seem odd to modern readers to have school starting in early August, the traditional school year that we are familiar with was not yet established back in the mid-1800s. Many of the schools of that day, particularly in areas that depended heavily on farm labor, had very short terms, generally during the winter months only. But as cities, such as Nauvoo, began to develop, longer terms were tried by some schools. We know of one Nauvoo school which had a term that went from May to December. (See *In Old Nauvoo*, pp. 242–43.)

Thomas Sharp and the *Warsaw Signal* were to play an important role in the history of the Saints during the Nauvoo period. The editorial stance and accusations depicted here accurately reflect his bitter opposition to the Saints.

Caroline looked up as the bell in the front entry began to tinkle. "I got it," Savannah shouted from in the dining room. In a moment, she came racing around the corner on a dead run and nearly skidded into the wall as she hit the throw rug at the end of the hall.

"Careful, Savannah." Caroline sighed wearily. "Oh, that girl."

Olivia, who had been at the piano practicing, swung around to listen for who it was. Will, lying on the sofa reading, laid his book down and did the same.

"Well, good morning, young lady."

"Hello, Brother Joseph," Savannah's voice came back.

At the sound of Joseph's voice, Caroline straightened and put aside her knitting. Will groaned as he pulled himself up, careful not to bump his one shoulder. Olivia stood and walked to the parlor entry.

"And how is the prettiest redhead in all of Nauvoo today?" they heard Joseph say.

"Grandpa says I'm the prettiest redhead in the whole county," came the quick reply.

As they heard Joseph's explosion of laughter, Caroline stood too. Shaking her head, she moved to stand beside Olivia just in time to greet Joseph as he came, still chuckling, to where the entry hall opened into the parlor. "Hello, Brother Joseph," Caroline said. "I see you've already been greeted by my humble daughter."

"I have," he laughed. He reached down and picked Savannah up, lifting her until her face was right next to his. "Actually," he said in a conspiratorial whisper, "I would be surprised if you're not the prettiest redhead in *three* counties." She giggled, knowing now that she was being teased but accepting the compliment anyway. Joseph let her down again and stuck out his hand. "Good morning, Caroline. Morning, Olivia."

"Hello, Brother Joseph."

Joseph looked past Caroline into the room, and then his jaw dropped a little. "Oh, my!" he exclaimed.

"Hello, Brother Joseph," Will said, looking embarrassed but coming forth to shake hands too.

Joseph peered more closely at the blackness that covered all of Will's right eye and most of his upper cheek. Then he looked at the swollen nose. "Nathan wasn't exaggerating, was he?" he said with a low whistle.

Caroline looked at her son. "No, and I think we haven't seen the worst of it yet."

Joseph reached out and barely touched the sling. "And how's the arm?"

"Getting stiffer," Will admitted. "But the doctor said that would happen."

"Well," Joseph went on with a rueful smile, "when Nathan told me that I had a defender of the faith in Warsaw, I thought I'd better come and offer my personal thanks."

Will colored deeply. He had only told the family the details of what had happened under pressure from his father, who was still half-irritated by the whole affair and yet clearly proud of Will's courage in the matter. Will didn't want the incident getting around as common knowledge. "Uh, it just kind of happened," he said.

"Uh-huh," Joseph grinned. "That's kind of how Nathan described it too."

Caroline reached out her arms and Savannah transferred over from Joseph. "Come, Olivia. This is a good time to get those things from the store."

"Oh, you don't need to go," Joseph said.

"That's all right," Caroline answered. "We really were just talking about getting some things we need. That will give you and Will a chance to talk." Then to Will she added, "If you'll listen for the baby, he should sleep for another half an hour at least."

"Yes, Mama."

As they left, Will came back into the room and showed Joseph to a chair. The Prophet sat down and crossed his legs. "Tell me what happened, Will. I'd like to get it straight from you."

Will did, trying to explain some of his feelings as well as just reporting what had transpired. When he finished, Joseph was silent for a time. Then Will saw that his eyes were glistening a little. "Thank you, Will," he finally said in a husky voice. "It is a wonderful thing to have a friend who'll stand up for you like that."

"Well, actually," Will said with a deadpan face, "had I taken a little longer to size the man up, I may have decided just to mail in my complaint."

That won him a quick grin and a nod. "Nathan says your father said the man was huge."

"Ever seen one of those great big old bull buffalo out on the prairie?"

Joseph nodded.

"Well, I think this guy uses one of those for a back brush when he takes a bath."

Joseph laughed merrily. "And you just up and ripped that paper right off the window, right there in front of him."

"Yeah," Will admitted, for the first time starting to see the humor in it, "I guess I did."

"You're lucky Joshua didn't bring you back in a bucket." Now Joseph sobered a little. "But thank you, Will. I really do appreciate it."

"What made me the maddest was all that stuff about you sending people to burn your own houses. They were trying to make it look like the Mormons were to blame for everything. I think of Jessica at Haun's Mill. John being killed. Then I remembered what happened to Rebecca and Lydia and Grandma there at Grandpa's cabin in Far West." He shrugged. "I just saw red, I guess, and went in to do something about it."

Joseph leaned back in his chair, half closing his eyes. "You know, Will, it seems strange to me, though I am getting used to it now."

"What's that, Brother Joseph?"

He opened his eyes again. "I know you're not sure if the Church is true yet, but Nathan tells me you've got a pretty good testimony of the Book of Mormon."

Will nodded. "It makes me feel good when I read it."

"That's good. What I was going to say was, that first night in 1823, when the angel Moroni came to my room, he said something very significant to me."

"What?"

"After telling me that God had a work for me to do, he said that my name would be had for good and evil among all nations, kindreds, and tongues."

"Really? What did he mean by that?"

"I suppose that good and evil should be spoken of me among all people."

"Well, Thomas Sharp's paper calls you the 'Superior Ugly Devil,'" Will said with a grimace. "I suppose that would count for evil, right?"

Joseph's smile was fleeting. "I suppose. But Thomas Sharp is not the only one. Many newspapers are publishing lies about me by the wholesale. If I were to try to enumerate them, I could write nothing else. It would take all of my time. Suffice it to say that every falsehood wicked men can invent, assisted by their father the devil, is trumpeted to the world as sound and true doctrine."

"That must get awfully discouraging," Will said, thinking of the terrible feeling he had experienced just by reading the slanderous things Sharp had said, and it wasn't even about him personally.

Joseph brightened. "Do you have a Bible nearby, Will?"

Will pointed to the piano where their family Bible sat. Joseph stood and retrieved it, opening it even as he sat back down. He thumbed a few pages, then ran his finger down the page. Will saw that he was in the Gospel of John. Now Joseph looked up at him. "I *would* get discouraged, except for these words. It is the Savior speaking to his disciples the night before his life was taken."

He looked down again, found his place, and began to read. "'If the world hate you, ye know that it hated me before it hated you. If ye were of the world, the world would love his own: but because ye are not of the world, but I have chosen you out of the world, therefore the world hateth you.'" Now his voice slowed a little. "'Remember the word that I said unto you, The servant is not greater than his lord. If they have persecuted me, they will also persecute you; if they have kept my saying, they will keep yours also.'"

Will was nodding. "Yes, I understand, Joseph."

The Prophet shut the Bible and returned it to its place. He did not sit down again. "Well, I won't keep you, Will. I just wanted to personally come and say thank you and tell you that I'm really glad the man knocked you out with that first blow."

Will laughed softly. "I was afraid he was going to sit on me."

Joseph pulled a face. "Then Joshua wouldn't even have needed a bucket for you." Then he leaned forward a little. "Nathan also tells me you're having a bit of a struggle getting an answer to your prayers."

Now Will looked glum, an expression made all the worse by the huge black eye. "It just doesn't seem to come."

"Do you remember Brigham's advice to you on the ship?"

Will looked up in surprise. "You know about that?"

"Yes, Brigham has a great affection for you, you know."

"I think a lot of him too," Will said, greatly pleased.

"Well, you just remember that advice. You don't hurry the Lord. All you need to do is make sure you're listening when he finally speaks."

"And if the answer *does* come," Will said, quite depressed now, "I don't know if Pa will allow me to get baptized."

Joseph nodded slowly. "I know. I know what your mother is going through too. But your pa is a good man, Will."

"I know that. It's just that he's as stubborn as four span of mules."

Joseph laughed right out loud at that.

"What?" Will asked.

"It takes more than four span of mules to light into a man who uses a bull buffalo for a back scrub." And then he sobered again. "Just don't hurry the Lord, Will. He knows your heart, and he knows your mother's heart. And . . ."

Will thought he was going to say, "And he knows your father's heart," but he didn't. He just smiled and finished with, "And he knows a good man when he sees one."

———•———

It was just past noon when Joshua came running into the house. He stuck his head in the parlor and saw Will there. If he saw the Book of Mormon in Will's hands, he gave no sign of it.

"Will, where's your mother?"

"Upstairs with Charles."

"And the girls?"

"Over at Lydia's."

Joshua's voice dropped and he grinned openly. "He made it, Will. He's here."

For a moment that lost Will; then his eyebrows shot up. "Pickerell?"

"Yes. He was on the ten o'clock boat. He's down in the field behind the stables setting up right now. You get your mother. I'll go tell the rest of the family."

"All of them?" Will asked in surprise.

"You bet! We promised Pickerell we'd make it worth his while. Who better than the whole Steed clan to make that promise good?"

"Yes!" Will agreed instantly. "That's a wonderful idea."

As his father spun around and started out again, Will called after him. "Pa?"

Joshua stopped, turning back impatiently. "What?"

"You brought Livvy and Savannah back new dresses again from St. Louis. And Mama too."

"Yes." Joshua always did that. Every trip without fail. "So?"

"You have another daughter too," Will said quietly.

Joshua visibly flinched.

"I know why you don't talk about it much, Pa, and that's all right. But did you see Rachel's eyes last time when she saw Livvy's new dress?"

Joshua stood there for a moment, his face a mask. Then he looked down. "Sometimes a man can make a fool of himself by sticking his hand into a sack when he doesn't know what's in it." There was just a touch of bitterness to his voice now.

"I understand," Will said, accepting the rebuke. "Just remember that she's your flesh and blood too." And then he hauled himself up and started toward the stairs. "I'll go tell Mama."

"Tell her that everyone's got to be in their best dress," Joshua said, his enthusiasm returning now. "She'll shoot us if she finds out what this is all about and the girls don't look their best. I'll send Livvy and Savannah back here to change clothes."

———— ✦ ————

Joshua shook his head, feeling a sense of uneasiness even as he swelled with pride. Olivia was up on the driver's seat of the buckboard with Savannah and Peter, who was driving the team.

Joshua was in the carriage with Caroline and baby Charles, which left him free to study this stepdaughter whom he had adopted as his own. It was eerie. With every passing day, Olivia was looking more and more like Caroline. People who didn't know Livvy at all would come in the store and instantly say, "You're Caroline Steed's daughter, aren't you?" And there was no denying it. Her auburn hair, straight and past her shoulder blades now, had that same lustrous quality of her mother's, glinting like burnished copper in the sunlight. She had the same large green eyes that could be so arresting, the same flawless complexion, the same slenderness of body—though she would pass her mother by an inch or two before she was through growing. It was this similarity to her mother that gave Joshua his sense of uneasiness. Though just now becoming a young woman, Olivia was already keenly aware of her effect on the young men of Nauvoo, and what was worse, he knew she absolutely gloried in it.

He smiled at her as she turned to him, eyes pleading. "How much longer, Papa?"

"Yes," Savannah cried, turning now too. "How much longer?"

"It's just a few more minutes. It's down by the stables."

"What is it?" Caroline said.

Joshua laughed, delighted that he had her as completely mystified as the children, and just about as excited.

Caroline could see that there was no point in pressing Joshua further, but Savannah was dauntless in her attempts to get more information from her father. She climbed down from the seat and crawled up into his lap. She took his face in both of her hands and pulled him down to look into her deep blue eyes. "Please, Papa. I can't wait another minute. I'll give you a kiss if you tell me."

"You are shameless, you little imp," Joshua laughed. "No. You just wait."

Savannah would never be the striking beauty that her half sister was going to be. But both Caroline and Joshua knew that with Savannah it wouldn't matter one iota. The words which invariably were used when people talked about her were things like *adorable, enchanting, delightful.* In the last few months her hair had become long enough that Caroline now curled it into long ringlets at the back of her head. They danced and swayed whenever she moved, almost as alive as those mischievous blue eyes. Her face was more expressive than those of the traveling minstrels who went from town to town putting on shows from the back of their wagons. As comfortable around adults as she was around children, she could cajole, plead, persuade, rebuke, censure, or praise with the expertise of a born politician. She could be impudent and coy in the same moment; exasperate in one instant and totally melt the heart in the next. She was the pride and joy of both her father and her grandfather, and expertly milked their adoration on a regular basis.

Joshua turned his head, the excitement in him building. The whole family was stretched out in a small caravan behind them. They were all there but two. Melissa's husband, Carl, was delivering a load of brick out of town somewhere, and Derek was working in the fields and they decided it was better not to send for him. Jenny Pottsworth had been left in charge of the store so that no one in the family had to be there. With a nod to himself, he turned back. He felt like rubbing his hands. This was going to be the best surprise ever.

By the time Pickerell had his tripods in place and the camera ready on its perch, the Steeds had been joined by a small crowd. No one knew what was going on down behind the Steed freight stables, but whatever it was, word was spreading fast.

Joshua had given Pickerell strict instructions. No one was to have a clue. He would take the first picture—of Savannah, Joshua had decided—and they would wait while Pickerell went in the tent and "fixed" the image, as he called it. That way, the first unveiling of the daguerreotype would have the maximum effect.

"All right, Mr. Steed," Pickerell called out. "I'm ready for our first candidate."

The crowd went quiet as Joshua turned around. "All right," he said with great solemnity, "who shall we have be the very first?"

Instantly the children were dancing up and down. They didn't know what Joshua was up to, but they knew it must be something wonderful. Savannah was fairly leaping in front of her father, waving both arms. "Me, Papa. Me!"

Suddenly, just as he was about to reach out and touch her, out of the corner of his eye Joshua saw Will standing next to Nathan and Lydia. He wasn't even looking in this direction, but it was enough. Slowly Joshua straightened; then he walked down the line, as if faced with a great decision. Savannah and Elizabeth Mary, Lydia's younger daughter, were right on his heels, begging him to look in their direction. But he kept moving. When he came to Jessica and her family, the boys shot up their hands. "Me, Uncle Joshua! Please!"

Rachel stood behind them, patient as usual, smiling at their excitement, not even assuming she would be considered.

Joshua hesitated for only a moment; then he reached over the boys and laid a hand on her shoulder. "I say that we let Rachel be first, how's that?"

There was a collective wail behind him, but Rachel's eyes widened and she stiffened in surprise. "Me, Uncle Joshua?"

"Yes, Rachel." He looked up at Jessica. "Is that all right?"

Jessica's eyes were shining, something very rare for her. "That would be wonderful," she whispered. "Thank you."

———◆———

They were gathered in the backyard at Caroline's house, all come to supper to talk about the miraculous gift Joshua had brought the family from St. Louis. It was fully dark now, and kerosene lamps hung from hooks on the porch. The supper of roast duck, boiled potatoes and gravy, and Mary Ann's hot cherry pie had long since settled in their stomachs. The dishes were long since done. The two babies—Caroline's and Lydia's—were in cribs and settled for the night. It felt good to have the family together on a pleasant and leisurely summer's night.

Benjamin was content to listen as the family turned their attention to Peter and pumped him for details about his work at the *Times and Seasons* office. For some time, though he hadn't said anything to anyone but Mary Ann, Benjamin had worried about Peter. Matthew and Brigham had tried to persuade him to help them in the woodworking business. This was done more to help Peter than because he was needed there. He had thanked them, but respectfully, and wisely, declined. He could help Jessica at the school, but what little she could pay him wouldn't be much of a living for a young man who was, at seventeen, at an age where some men were already on their own or were apprenticed out to a craftsman of one kind or another. Caroline and Lydia had both tried to persuade him to do the books at the store with them. But mathematics was not his favorite thing either.

Thus Benjamin's concerns had grown. Peter was a fine young man, and a hard worker, but his strongest assets were in his head, not in his hands. He loved books, had a gift for poetry, and was an excellent teacher. In mechanical things he was barely adequate and often frustrated, able to learn but with little natural aptitude. So when Don Carlos Smith, who was the editor of the Church's newspaper, became quite ill, John Taylor recommended Peter to come in and help out. He was interviewed and immediately hired.

"Well," Joshua spoke up, "I was going to offer Peter an opportunity to go up to Wisconsin with us this winter."

"You were?" Nathan asked in surprise. The others looked at him with interest too. They all knew that Joshua was hiring crew to head north to cut timber in the pineries of Wisconsin, as they were called. Nathan, Joshua, Will, and Carl had gone north the previous winter to investigate the possibilities. Nauvoo and the surrounding settlements were in desperate need of cheap lumber, and the pineries held an almost inexhaustible supply. It was a new business venture. There was money to be made in it. That was normally all it took to get Joshua going. But he had never once said anything about taking Peter up with him.

"I was," Joshua said with a nod. "And as a matter of fact, the offer is still good. I'll pay double what they're giving you at the press."

"No thanks," Peter said, hoping that Joshua wasn't hinting that he was worried about the loan on the building lot they had talked about.

"Well, I didn't think I could tempt you," Joshua said with a smile, relieving Peter's concerns that he might be upset with him.

"Speaking of the pineries," Carl broke in, "when are you going north, Joshua?"

"About mid-September. We need to get up there and get everything ready so we can start cutting trees once the first snow flies."

"Joseph's group will be leaving about that same time," Nathan said.

"And Nathan will be going up with them," Lydia said quietly.

That brought an exclamation of surprise from nearly everyone. "You didn't tell me that, Nathan," Joshua said, with just a touch of rebuke in his voice.

"Joseph just asked me yesterday. I guess they figure that since I was up there last winter with you I might be of help."

"So," Joshua said lightly, but not completely covering his hurt, "you won't go up and work for me for money, but you will go up and work for Joseph for nothing." He shook his head. "That's some church you belong to."

"It's like a mission call," Lydia said, wishing now she hadn't brought it up before Nathan had had a chance to tell Joshua. "We're going to miss him, but they need lumber so badly for the temple and for the Nauvoo House."

"Will you be gone all winter?" Mary Ann asked, speaking to both of her sons.

"Joseph has given me permission to come home for a couple of weeks at Christmas," Nathan said.

Joshua was also shaking his head. "I'll go up and get the crew started, and maybe once or twice more, but then I'm going to leave Will in charge."

If his comment about Peter had caught people by surprise, this really caused a stir. Will had told everyone that he would be taking charge of the freight yard while his father was gone. He stared at his father in dismay, then shot his mother a beseeching look.

Joshua, who was looking toward his father and Nathan, didn't see the response his comment had drawn from Will. And he misread the surprise on his father's face for something else. He scowled a little. "Well, what's wrong with that? Will will be eighteen come March. It wasn't much past that that I was making my own way in life and running things at the warehouse in Palmyra. There'll be some good men to help him, but he's going to be in charge."

"It's not that," Nathan started, but when Lydia gave him a warning look, he backed off and let it die.

Joshua went on, warming to the topic quickly. "I figure if we can get a crew of fifteen or twenty men, we can float a hundred thousand board feet downriver come spring."

"Pa."

Joshua turned toward Will, responding absently. "Yes, son."

"I don't want to spend the winter in Wisconsin."

Joshua looked startled for a moment, then laughed, waving him off. "Don't be ridiculous. Come spring, you can be one of the most prosperous young men in Nauvoo. Then maybe that Jenny Pottsworth will pay you the attention you deserve."

Will's face instantly flamed and Caroline's mouth dropped. "Joshua!"

"Well?" he said, bristling a little. "She just sees Will as some young kid barely old enough to shave. You've got to remember, this 'boy' was nearly running my freight yard by the time he was fifteen. He was an officer on an ocean ship directing crew members twice his age. Will's a man, and it irritates me that she won't treat him like one." Looking at Will, he had a sudden thought.

"You been down to show her your wounds? That'll end any question about you being a man or not."

Caroline looked away. Will was staring at his hands, his face bright red now. The silence was heavy and awkward to the point that even Joshua began to look a little taken aback.

Suddenly, Benjamin cleared his throat and stood abruptly. He walked over to the long table set up on the back porch of the house. There, laid out in neat order, were all the daguerreotypes taken by William Pickerell earlier that day. He picked up the one of Rachel. "This is still my favorite," he said, holding it up.

That did the trick. Caroline got up and came over to stand beside him. Nathan and Lydia and Matthew and Jennifer Jo did the same. The Wisconsin pineries and Jenny Pottsworth were not forgotten, but there was a reason now to talk about something else.

"Do you really think so?" Caroline asked, picking up another one. "I love this one of you and Mother Steed."

"G'wan," he said in disgust. "The man in that picture looks like an old grandpa. Look at the wrinkles around his eyes. And his hair is almost completely gray now."

Caroline laid the picture back down, laughing. She slipped an arm around Benjamin's waist. "Well, we love that old grandpa just the way he is. We hope he never changes."

While they all leaned forward, looking more closely at Benjamin and Mary Ann, Will quietly got up and slipped out the gate. Joshua watched him go but said nothing.

———◆———

Benjamin's fingers stopped unbuttoning his shirt as he looked down at the daguerreotype picture of himself and Mary Ann sitting together stiffly on the two stools. He turned it so as to catch the lamplight better. His brow furrowed slightly and the corners of his mouth pulled down. When one had to hold a pose with perfect stillness for almost a minute, it was only natural that there was a certain grimness to the face. But he looked as though the goddess of tragedy were sitting between his shoulder blades. The details of both their faces were sharp and distinct, plain enough for anyone to read, and that was why he winced a little. Benjamin Steed didn't much care for what he saw. For nearly six decades now—he would be fifty-seven next May—life had been writing its history upon his face. He could see the effects of years spent behind a plow or wielding a scythe beneath a hot sun. There were lines that represented the loss of children and grandchildren, the long years of alienation from Joshua, the worry of a father and grandfather over his offspring. How deeply had the siege of Far West etched his face? Which lines represented those weeks of imprisonment in the unheated hellhole of a Missouri jail?

He gazed at the picture, strangely saddened. It was not his appearance that was bothering him. He cared not a fig for that. In fact, he had to admit, age had left him looking just a bit more distinguished than when he was younger. No, it was that this Mr. Pickerell and his "dagger-oh-type" had presented Benjamin with the irrefutable proof of his own mortality. How many years were left to him now?

Twice he had escaped the final nod from the angel of death—once in a Richmond jail, and once two years ago when the ague brought him close enough that he had even made his last farewells to his family. Both times only a prophet of God was able to pull him back from the brink. Those brushes with death had taken their toll, along with the years. He could feel the weariness permeate his body when he worked in the quarry or even when he and Mary Ann walked up to the temple site. He could feel the ache in his shoulders and knees at night if he lay too long without changing position. The knuckles in his hands took a while in the morning to limber up enough to do what he commanded his fingers to do. Would the next bout with the ague or pneumonia or yellow fever be the one to take him?

The frown deepened a little. He was finding himself doing this too much lately, giving in to what Mary Ann teasingly called his "walk through the valley of the shadow of death." He reached out, the tip of his right forefinger brushing lightly across

Mary Ann's face in the picture. The years had been kinder to her. She had a grandmotherly look—there was no disputing that—but the wrinkles were no more than light touches around her eyes and the corners of her mouth. If anything, they only heightened the gentleness and the warmth that lay within her.

Now his brow smoothed and his lips softened as he picked up the picture. How he loved this woman! Every day now he thanked God for leading him to her those thirty-seven years ago. More so, for it was more the miracle, he thanked God for softening her heart and blinding her eyes enough that she saw something attractive in the big-boned, rough-cut New England farmer named Benjamin Steed.

"It's like a miracle, isn't it?"

He turned. Mary Ann was already in bed. She always chided him about how much he puttered around as he got ready for bed. She could be in bed and asleep while he was still taking his boots off. But now she was looking at the picture in his hands.

He nodded. "It is. If someone had tried to tell me such a thing was possible, I would have said he was daft."

"I know."

He set the picture down and finished unbuttoning his shirt. In another moment he blew out the lamp and was in bed beside her. He reached out and clasped her hand as he always did if she was still awake. "I'm not sure I'm ready for it."

"Ready for what?"

"This new age were coming into."

"What do you mean by that?"

"It's a new age, Mary Ann. A new age. Imagine, pictures from a box. Now some man named Morse is claiming he can send messages over a piece of wire. The papers are saying they have demonstrated street lamps in France that are lit by electricity—like taking a little piece of lightning from the sky and holding it there forever. What's next, do you suppose?"

"Something wonderful, I'm sure. Does that worry you?"

"What?"

"Living in a new age."

"I'm getting too old for new things."

She laughed, squeezing his hand. "You certainly are."

He looked hurt. "You could disagree with me, you know."

"Why? Your mind is already made up."

Now he chuckled too. "Since when did that ever stop you?"

"Well," she mused, "I remember a man who once strongly believed that if you plowed the earth with metal, it would pollute the soil forever. But as I remember, you were one of the first to try one of those John Deere steel plows. And, if my recollection is right, it was that same man who had the first McCormick reaper in northern Missouri. Such a man as that would surely never be afraid of change."

He grinned at her. She always did this to him. He'd try to take off on one line of conversation, which he had worked out carefully in his mind, and she'd turn it inside out and upside down and head him in a whole different direction. "So you're saying maybe this old dog can handle a new bone every now and then?"

There was a long pause. "Well, maybe not a new bone. Maybe just a biscuit or two. "

"Thanks. You're always so comforting."

"Are you walking in the shadow again?"

He started to protest, then finally nodded. "Yeah, I suppose."

She turned and put one arm across his chest. "You've got a lot of good years left in you, Benjamin Steed," she said, completely serious now.

"*Are* they going to be good years?"

She came up on one elbow. "Of course! This is a wonderful time for us. We have all of our family together with us. They are all happily married now, except for Jessica, of course. We have seventeen beautiful grandchildren. We may not be well-to-do, but we are prospering. We have a prophet of God in our midst. We have the gospel—"

Benjamin surrendered. "All right, all right," he grumbled. "I'll stop complaining." Then he thought of the picture again. "I guess it's looking at us in that picture . . ." He let it go, not wanting to carry it further.

She lay back. "It is a good life, Ben. A good life."

He held her hand tightly. "I know."

And in fact, with a start, he realized that was exactly what lay at the root of his uneasiness. Life was so good right now. He was happier than at any time in his fifty-six years. He didn't need, nor did he want, a new age. He just wanted to keep what he had now. He turned toward his wife and kissed her gently on the cheek. "It *is* a good life, Mary Ann, and you make it so."

She laughed softly at him. "I know," she said.

———◆———

The night was warm, so they had nothing but a sheet over them; but with her long cotton nightdress, even that was too much, and Caroline threw the sheet back.

Joshua turned his head. "It's really muggy tonight, isn't it?"

She nodded, then slid over closer to him. He turned on his side and opened his arms. In a moment, in spite of the heat, she was snuggled up against him, her head cradled in the crook of his arm. This was her favorite position, particularly when she wanted to talk to him.

"It feels good to have you back," she murmured. "I never sleep well when you're gone."

"Me neither."

She poked him gently. "I'll bet you never even miss me, you're so busy with business."

"I do miss you," he responded firmly, turning and kissing her on the forehead. "I always miss you."

She smiled. That was the right answer and she wanted more of it. "I don't believe you."

"It's true. I think about you every day."

"At least once, hmm?" she teased. "How nice."

He chuckled. "One day I thought about you three different times."

She slugged him in the stomach and he jerked back laughing. Then almost instantly he sobered. "Do you know, I've always loved traveling, being on the road, being out making this deal or that come to pass. I've always liked seeing new places and having a change of scene."

"Yes, I know."

"But this time, it was like I was a homesick kid. We hadn't even stepped off the boat in St. Louis and all I could think about was how soon we could start back home again."

That pleased her, more deeply than he could have imagined. "Really?"

"Yes, really. I'm coming to realize that there's nowhere I'd rather be than home with my wife and family."

She went up on one elbow and kissed him softly. "I think that's one of the nicest things you've ever said to me, Joshua Steed."

"Well, it's true. I'm dreading having to go to Wisconsin."

There was a moment of silence; then she lay slowly back again. "So is Will, Joshua. He doesn't want to go."

Joshua berated himself for being so stupid. He had changed her mood instantly. "I know," he said wearily.

"He doesn't want to be away from Jenny for the whole winter. He's worried enough about making this work with her."

He rolled onto his back, knowing it was too late now to return the conversation to the way it was a moment before. "Well, sometimes we all have to do things we don't like. We had dinner with the Samuelsons while we were there in St. Louis. Remember their daughter, Alice?"

"Yes." And then before he could wax too enthusiastic, she added, "Will told me all about the dinner and what happened. She's not for him, Joshua."

"Oh." But he wasn't ready to back down. "And Jenny Pottsworth is?"

"I'm not saying that. I have questions about that myself. But it's not for you or me to say. That's Will's decision, and he has to come to it himself."

"Well, taking him north for the winter will get him away from her."

"And what if he won't go?" she said, her voice barely a whisper.

"He'll go!"

"He's a man now, Joshua. What if he just says no?"

"He's my son, and he's a partner in the business. This winter our business is cutting timber. I don't want to go either, but I'm going. That's part of growing up."

She didn't answer, and they lay together in silence for almost a minute.

Finally, he softened a little. "I won't say anything to him about Jenny."

She wanted to cry at that. Will told her there had hardly been a day while they were gone that Joshua hadn't made some snide comment about Jenny or tried to push him and Alice together. But instead she just said, "You won't have to."

Stung, he jerked around to face her. "This isn't about Will at all, is it?"

Surprised, she turned too. "What do you mean by that?"

"This is just another way you have of digging at me for not letting you be baptized."

Instantly there were tears burning at the corners of her eyes. "My being baptized hadn't even crossed my mind, Joshua."

"Oh no? Isn't that what it always comes back to? You think I'm stubborn and unbending on this. Just like I am about Will marrying Jenny. Well, I'll say it again. If you want to be baptized, be baptized."

Now her voice was low and sorrowful. "And I'll say it again. I won't be baptized until you *want* it for me."

There was a soft explosion of air. "Then it'll never happen."

There was a long pause, and then, very quietly, "I know."

Totally frustrated and angry now, he sat up on the edge of the bed. "I'm going to go downstairs and read for a while."

He got up and found his robe in the darkness. As he reached the door, she started to speak, wanting to take the hurt away, wanting to recapture what they had been feeling only moments before. But she hesitated for a moment too long and he was gone.

Chapter Notes

Joseph's comments about his name being vilified by the nation's newspapers were made in his journal history under date of 15 July 1841, just three weeks prior to when the scene with him and Will takes place in the novel. Though he does not quote the scripture (John 15:18–20) in its entirety in the journal entry, he does make reference to it. (See *HC* 4:383.)

A convert who moved to Nauvoo from New York in 1844 established the first daguerreotype shop in the Mormon city (see *Women of Nauvoo*, p. 136). Whether any of the many traveling photographers who were immensely popular throughout the United States at this time came to Nauvoo before that is not known.

It was a soft and gentle August rain, more like a mist, and it was almost warm to his skin. Through the night, it had washed the roadside dust from the grass and the trees and left the myriad shades of green all the deeper and the more lustrous. It was at times like this that Nauvoo was at its most beautiful. By comparison, St. Louis seemed like a dismal collection of hovels and soot-belching factories.

Will tipped his head back and breathed deeply, letting the mist caress his battered face and cool the darkened flesh. There was no smell of salt in the air, but other than that, this morning reminded him of the sea. The air was almost crisp, it was so clean and fresh. Suddenly his longing for the deck of a ship and a hundred yards of canvas cracking and popping in the wind over his head was so sharp it made him wince.

He shook it off, bringing his attention back to the scene ahead of him. He was just rounding the corner of Granger and Knight Streets. The Steed Family Dry Goods and General Store lay just a block ahead of him now. Even from here though, he could see that there were no wagons or carriages or horses tied up in front of it. *Good.* It was barely nine o'clock, and he was hoping that it was still too early for customers to be there. And since Jenny more and more was opening the store on her own, he might even strike it lucky and have a few minutes alone with her.

After he had walked out on his family the previous night, Will had gone to see Jenny, but the cabin had been dark and no one answered the door. Jenny's mother was often out gathering up laundry in the evenings, and once the store closed, Jenny would help her. Will waited around for almost half an hour, but they did not return. He hadn't seen her since returning to Nauvoo and wasn't even sure if she knew he was back yet. Anxious now, he squared his shoulders and strode out eagerly.

But as he neared the store, he slowed, and then stopped altogether. There were two people on the porch, and the sound of their laughter carried clearly in the morning air. The woman had her back to him, but that made no difference. Will knew Jenny Pottsworth from every angle, from every viewpoint, and in every shade of light. But he wasn't sure about the man. He was facing Will, but he was under the porch and in shadow.

Jenny laughed then, her head tipping back and her shoulders squaring. It was a full laugh. Whatever the man said, it had delighted her. The sound of it was like music on the air—soft, lilting. Will loved that sound. And then, in one instant, his mood was dashed.

"Oh, Andrew," Jenny cried. "You are so funny."

It was music, all right, Will thought with sudden bitterness. Music that pierced him like a fiery dart because now he knew who the man was. It was Andrew Stokes. Andrew Stokes was twenty-one years old and a full three inches taller than Will. Andrew Stokes was from England. Derek knew the family well and spoke highly of both the family in general and Andrew in particular. Just last night, when Peter had said something about Andrew Stokes to Derek, Lydia and Caroline had jumped in to sing his praises. What a fine young man he was. So helpful.

Always willing to carry things for them if Nathan wasn't around.

Will stared at the two figures on the porch, absently reaching up and rubbing his damaged shoulder, wanting the ache to go away. It didn't matter now that he couldn't see the man's face clearly. Andrew Stokes had a deep cleft in his chin and a solid jaw line that made him look strong without seeming too arrogant. And when he came in the store, Jenny became a totally different person.

Sick at heart, Will stood there in the road, fighting with himself. It was clear that Stokes was just leaving. Then she would be alone again. Will wanted to talk to her—needed to talk with her. On the other hand, any euphoria at the thoughts of seeing her again tasted like ashes in his mouth now. With a dejected shake of his head he turned and walked away, head down, eyes dark and brooding.

———•———

"Mother, can I talk with you?"

Caroline looked up in surprise. She was at the table, peeling potatoes. "Will? What are you doing home so early?"

"Pa asked me to make sure those five wagons headed for St. Joseph got loaded and off." He shrugged. "We got finished, so I came home."

"Did your father get back?"

"No. He said he'd be home in time for supper." He looked around. "Where's Charles?"

"Down for his nap. Livvy took Savannah to the store. So I thought I'd start supper early." She patted the bench beside her. "Come, sit here."

He moved over and sat down next to her.

"So," she said brightly, "what would you like to talk about?" There was a teasing smile. "Jenny Pottsworth?"

Instantly he frowned and shook his head. "No."

"Oh? Then what?" she asked.

He shook his head, blowing out his breath in frustration. "Oh, I don't know."

She waited, keeping her face expressionless, but inside she wanted to burrow in beneath that taciturn expression and find out what was going on behind the somber eyes. He was so much like Joshua in that regard, a thousand thoughts boiling beneath the surface, very few of them ever given verbal form. She wanted to take him by the shoulders and shout at him, "Just say it, Will!" But she knew that it was better to let him take this where he wanted.

After almost a full minute, his brow furrowed. "What do you think Pa will say if I decide to be baptized?"

She straightened slowly, turning her body so she could face him more directly. "*Are* you going to be baptized?" she asked gently.

His shoulders lifted and fell. "I . . . I'm not sure. Maybe."

Caroline kept her initial reaction, which was to throw her arms around him and shout for joy, in check. "And this isn't just for Jenny?" she asked carefully.

He was silent for a moment, his face concentrating as he turned his thoughts inward, searching his own motives. "Maybe it would be," he finally admitted.

She sighed, fighting a mother's instinctive wish to try and teach him about himself. Caroline well understood Will's pain. Jenny was frustrating him because she was adamant about marrying a member of the Church. But although he was terribly smitten with this winsome young woman, Will wasn't ready for marriage yet. He didn't know that, but Caroline did. The question of his conversion was only part of it.

There was a sudden irritation pulling at his mouth. "Why can't she understand that it just takes longer for some than for others?"

Caroline smiled, wanting to remind him that he didn't want to talk about Jenny. But instead she just said, "Jenny is one of those who was blessed to know the gospel is true immediately, Will. There are many like that. Nathan. Your grandmother. Jennifer Jo. But it wasn't like that for Lydia. Or for Grandpa Steed. They struggled just like you. And look at them now."

"I've thought about that." He leaned forward. "And so what is Pa going to say if I do decide I want to be a Mormon? We're already fighting about Jenny. And if I don't go to Wisconsin for him, it's only going to be worse."

She chose her words very carefully. "It's not right that you be baptized just to win Jenny," she said. "Baptism is a covenant with the Lord, and not just a way to influence someone. And so . . ." She bit her lip. "And so it's not right that you *not* be baptized just to please someone either."

"But then . . ." He stopped. She knew exactly what he was thinking, and she knew he wouldn't say it, because he didn't want to hurt her. If what she said was true, why wasn't *she* going to be baptized?

"It's different when people are married to each other, Will," she said slowly, answering his unasked question. "Someday you'll understand that better."

"If I am baptized, I want to be baptized with you, Mama."

She had to look away. "There is nothing that would please me more, Will. You know that. But when you're ready, you don't wait for anyone or anything." She was suddenly filled with a terrible fierceness. "Do you hear me, Will? Don't you wait for anything."

It was a hot and dirty morning. Heat waves shimmered off the stone floor and walls. The light gray limestone reflected sunlight almost like a mirror. Bodies were sticky and ripe with sweat. Everyone worked more slowly, not expending energy too fast, stopping to drink often lest they faint from heat exhaustion or dehydration. This was summer in the quarry, and it was murderously hard on both man and beast.

It was Saturday, August seventh. Nathan and Benjamin had last seen duty in the quarry on the twenty-sixth of July, which meant that they were actually a couple of days overdue for their "tithed" labor. It didn't always work out at exactly one day out of ten, but the building committee encouraged the brethren to come as close as possible so it would be easier to keep records.

Today Matthew and Derek were also there taking their tithing day as well. On seeing the four of them together, the quarry foreman put them on the task of cutting into blocks the massive slab of stone blasted out the previous evening. The slab was three to four feet high, with about the same thickness, and was fifteen to twenty feet long. Now the task was to cut it into equal-sized blocks.

Limestone is a fairly soft stone and more easily worked than granite or marble, but it was still back-breaking labor. Up and down the sides and across the top of the slab, a series of holes had to be "drilled" in a precise line about nine to twelve inches apart. This was done by using a point drill—a chisel-like piece of steel with a square point that had four cutting edges. It took two men working together. One would hold the point drill in place while the other struck it with one of the big eight-pound jack sledges, or "double jacks." After each blow of the hammer, the one holding the drill would turn it about a half turn so that the cutting edges were in a different position. An experienced team of drillers could cut a hole three to four inches deep about every ten to fifteen minutes.

At the moment, Derek and Matthew were taking their turn on the hammers, while Benjamin and Nathan held the drills. The one turning the drill bit never looked up to watch the hammer blows coming. Seeing an eight-pound hammerhead coming down at full force to hit a drill head less than an inch in diameter which was being held by one's hands just below the strike point tended to make one flinch. And with an eight-pound hammerhead coming down at full force in a steady, rhythmic cadence, flinching was not at all a wise thing to do. *Wham!* Turn. *Wham!* Turn. The pattern became so habitual that one didn't even think about it.

They were working on the last two holes on the top of the great slab—Benjamin with Derek, and Nathan with Matthew—directly across from one another, so Benjamin was looking right into Nathan's eyes. But when he spoke, he spoke to Derek.

"You sure love that farm, don't you?"

Wham! Turn. *Wham!* "Sure do."

Benjamin held up his hand and Derek let the hammer swing down to the floor of the quarry, straightening. Matthew, seeing that, did the same, reaching up to wipe at his brow with the back of his sleeve. Benjamin and Nathan reached for the "spoons."

Drilling a three-quarter-inch-wide hole into solid rock necessarily produced quite a bit of limestone chips and dust. When a hole was being drilled horizontally into the side of the rock slab, the debris emptied itself out and the holes were kept clear. But the top holes, those going down vertically into the rock, didn't work that way. After a minute or two of hammering, the hole would begin to fill with debris, which would cushion the bite of the drill and slow the cutting efficiency. Thus, every two or three minutes they had to clean out the holes by using a device called a spoon. This was nothing more than a long, thin rod with a tiny scoop fashioned on one end.

Benjamin pulled out the first spoonful of dust and chips and threw it aside. He reached across and nudged Nathan with his free hand. "Derek sure loves farming, Nathan. Have you noticed that?"

"Uh-huh," Nathan murmured, concentrating on spooning out his own hole.

"And Carl. Have you watched him down at that brickyard? I've never seen a man so happy. Have you?"

"No," Matthew answered for Nathan. "He loves it down there."

There was another nudge from Benjamin. "You notice that, Nathan?"

Now all Benjamin got was a grunt in response. He took that to be an affirmative answer.

"And Joshua? What do you think, Derek? You think Joshua likes being a businessman?"

Derek had taken off his hat and was mopping his forehead with a large handkerchief. He stopped, looking down at his father-in-law as he realized this was more than just idle chatter. "He certainly does," he said cautiously.

Nathan also sensed something behind all this and was giving his father a quizzical look. Benjamin kept right on spooning as if they weren't there. With three more scoops he was finished and set the spoon aside. After a moment, when he said nothing more, Nathan started his spooning again, finishing after a few moments.

As the two younger men reached for their hammers, Benjamin looked at Matthew. "How are things at the shop with you and Brigham?" he asked casually.

Like the others, Matthew knew there was something going on in his father's mind. "Good," he said with a tentative grin.

Benjamin looked positively innocent. "I was just telling your mother last night, I said, 'You know, that Matthew is as happy as a meadowlark in a field of sunflowers. He sure does love that woodworking shop.' That's what I told her."

There was a long silence; then Nathan laid his spoon down slowly. "All right, Pa, what are you getting at?"

Benjamin looked hurt. "Getting at?"

"You want us to stand up and sing a hymn or something?"

"My, aren't you the testy one."

Nathan was feigning irritation, but actually he was amused. "Well?"

"Well what?"

"You know what. Derek's happy. Carl's happy. Joshua's ecstatic. Matthew's singing in the sunflowers."

"And Nathan's a storekeeper," Benjamin cut in quickly.

"Is that a sin?"

"No, not at all. An honorable profession. If . . ." He let it hang there, unfinished.

Nathan grinned up at Derek. This was Pa, through and through. Having something on his mind but never coming at it straight on, just nibbling around it, moving in on it a blade at a time, until the next thing you knew he was standing squarely in the patch of grass where he wanted to be and there was no budging him off of it. "If what, Pa?"

Benjamin shrugged and picked up the drill bit. He stuck it in the hole and eyed the mark on it. "I'd say we need about another quarter of an inch." He reached out with both hands again and held the chisel bit firm.

Nathan sighed and picked up his bit. In a moment, the steady hammering was under way again. Two minutes later they stopped to spoon once more, and this time Nathan measured the depth of the hole. "That's got it," he said.

They all straightened, and the hammers were again set aside for the moment. Matthew turned to the bucket of slips and wedges a few feet away. He picked it up and brought it over.

Once the rock slab was blasted off the rock face, blasting powder could no longer be used on the slab. Even light charges tended to split the rock in unpredictable ways. This is where the stonecutters came in. Using a simple but ingenious device, they could cut even huge slabs of stone cleanly. That is where the slips and wedges—also called "feathers" and "plugs"—came in. The slip looked like a steel tent peg. Only one side was smooth and flat while the rest was round. The top of the slip was curled over a little to provide a striking surface, creating its resemblance to a tent peg. It also looked somewhat like a feather from the side—thus its other name. Two slips were put into the hole so as to make a V-shape, with the flat sides facing each other. Then the plug, or wedge, was tapped into the V until it was firmly locked, with its head protruding enough to be struck with a hammer. With each blow, the wedge was driven deeper into the slips, forcing them apart and exerting pressure on the rock. As the stonecutters did this in sequence along a straight line of holes, constantly increasing pressure was applied until the rock split cleanly into two pieces.

Now, with the feathers and plugs in every hole, the three Steed men and Derek all got sledgehammers. Derek took the front face, Matthew the back. Benjamin and Nathan worked the top. Carefully, not striking with their full strength, but in precise rotation, they moved along the line of holes. On the fourth series, there was a sharp *crack* and the block split cleanly off the larger slab.

Setting his hammer down, Benjamin leaned over to examine the break. Then he straightened, nodding in satisfaction. "Clean as if we'd used a saw."

Nathan nodded. That was a slight exaggeration, but it certainly wouldn't take much work for the stonemasons to shape the rock down for its final placement in the foundation of the temple.

They moved over to the edge of the quarry where there was a large barrel of drinking water beneath the shade of a tree. As they did so, another team moved in behind them. This second team would lift the block enough to get rollers beneath it, then move it to where the boom crane could lift it onto a wagon.

After drinking deeply, they each dipped their bandannas into a bucket of water set aside for this very purpose and began to wipe the dust and sweat from their faces. Benjamin sat down and the others followed suit. It would take the other men a few minutes to get the block out of their way, so they had a brief respite. Then they would start drilling another line of holes for the next block.

Nathan lay back on the softer soil, pulling his hat down over his face. Benjamin watched him for a moment, then looked at Derek. "Speaking of loving to farm, Derek, how do you think Nathan feels about being a storekeeper?"

Nathan pushed his hat up with his thumb just enough to glare at his father. "I don't mind it," he said.

"That's a good answer, don't you think?" Benjamin said, still talking to Derek as if Nathan weren't there. "He doesn't *mind* it."

"Well, I don't."

"That's nice."

Derek and Matthew smiled at each other. There was no question that Nathan was the target of whatever it was Benjamin was driving at, and they were glad to be only observers. As for Nathan, he knew when he was licked. He sat up again. "All right, so it's not all that wonderful." Then he grew instantly serious. "Do you know what it is, Pa? I think it was handling the store for Lydia's father before he died. I know it wasn't for that long, but there at the last, when he was really sick, it was like it was my store. And with every passing day I felt more and more trapped, like it was closing in on me."

He turned, looking toward the slab, finding a better analogy. "It was like I was the rock and the store was the feather and plugs. Every day was one more blow with the hammer until I thought I was going to split wide open."

Benjamin smiled at Matthew and Derek sardonically. "This is why he doesn't really mind it," he observed.

"Well, having our own store isn't that bad," Nathan admitted begrudgingly. "In fact, I really don't mind the supply side of it—finding the buyers and getting the merchandise we need, working with Joshua to get it shipped in." He sighed. "But standing behind that counter all day. Keeping the books. Taking inventory." He rolled his eyes. "Oh, my. Taking inventory. I'd just as soon be dragged through a corral."

Benjamin nodded. "I knew something was wrong when you were excited about spending the day at the quarry."

Nathan looked at him sharply, then had no choice but to laugh. It was true. Nathan really had welcomed the opportunity to break away from the store. That was pretty desperate.

There was no further response from his father, and after almost a full minute, Nathan thought Benjamin had made his point and forgotten about it. Nathan lay back down, and almost immediately learned that he should have known better.

"You been paying attention to what's happening to the price of building lots lately?"

Surprised a little, Nathan shook his head. "Not really."

"Not so much in town, because Joseph and the Brethren are controlling the sale of land here so our people are not taken advantage of. But outside of town? Or in the surrounding settlements?"

"No, I haven't been following that at all."

"Remember Kirtland?"

Turning fully around to face his father now, Nathan nodded

soberly. When a land speculation craze hit the United States in the spring of 1837, land prices went berserk. Lots doubled overnight, then doubled again. Paper fortunes were made—and lost. It had been a major factor in the great apostasy that had nearly ripped the Church apart back then. Yes, Nathan remembered it well. Derek, having heard all about those events after his arrival in America, was nodding too. Matthew had been only sixteen at that time, and while he was aware of what they were talking about, he hadn't been that much into the crisis.

"It's nothing like that," Benjamin went on. "At least not yet."

"Good."

"But with hundreds still coming in every month—from the East, from the South, all the British Saints—the pressure for good land is mounting."

Nathan merely nodded again. He didn't know where this was all leading to, but he knew that now they were getting to the reason his father had started this whole line of conversation in the first place.

"A couple of people with the right experience and a good head on their shoulders could probably make a living developing land, and not be scalping their brothers and sisters in the process."

Ahhh! Benjamin Steed had been a farmer in Palmyra. He had made a decent profit when he sold out and brought Mary Ann to Kirtland. He bought another farm in Kirtland, but soon left it for Nathan to work while he turned his attention to land development. He had loved it, and was angered when people used land speculation to ruin everything. And now Nathan understood all the questions. Benjamin wanted to do something that he loved again.

And then it hit Nathan and it hit him hard. Benjamin was offering him a chance to do something he loved as well.

"But you are helping Joseph and the city council with lots here, aren't you?" Derek asked, before Nathan could speak.

"Yes. But mostly I'm just counseling with them." He turned

and looked at Nathan steadily now. "What I'm talking about is buying land. Getting it developed. Then selling it back to people at a fair price. Maybe even become a force in stopping others from letting things run wild again."

Nathan was surprised at the sudden excitement racing through him. Now *this* was something a man could take pride in, use his talents for, sink his teeth into. This was not sitting behind some musty counter filled with bonnets and corsets and pantaloons. He leaned forward. "I agree," he said. "A man could get to love something like that."

Benjamin was pleased but didn't want to show it. "We'd need capital."

Nathan considered that for a moment. It would take quite a bit of capital. "Joshua?" he finally asked.

There was a quick shake of the head.

Momentarily surprised, Nathan started to ask why, but then almost immediately he understood. Joshua would do it. And be glad for it. They both knew that. But Joshua had helped the family enough and now they were all prospering because of that. It was time to go it on their own. Not be beholden to Joshua's generosity.

"I was thinking that we might want to go down to Springfield. We've got my cabin and yours, if Lydia would agree. I think we could get enough of a mortgage to start buying a couple of pieces of land I've got my eye on."

"We could use our part in the store too," Nathan said eagerly. "I know Lydia will agree. I don't know if she knows how I feel, but—"

"She knows!" Benjamin said shortly, cutting him off.

"Oh," Nathan replied, a little crestfallen. "Has she talked to you?"

Before Benjamin could reply there was a shout from behind them.

"Hey! Nathan Steed!"

Nathan swung around to see who was calling. It was the foreman. He was pointing up to the crest of the quarry where a small figure was waving his arms back and forth. "Isn't that your son?" he called.

Nathan stood, lifting a hand to shade his eyes. It was. It was young Joshua. He looked toward the foreman. "Yes, it is," he called back. "Thank you."

Benjamin was up too, looking suddenly worried.

"I'll be right back." Nathan broke into a trot, crossing the quarry to reach the path that led to the small ridge above them. Breathing heavily, he slowed as he came to his son. "What is it, Joshua? What's the matter?"

Young Joshua looked up at his father, his face grave. "Mama said I'd better come tell you, Papa. Brother Don Carlos Smith died early this morning."

"Oh, no!"

"We just heard," Joshua went on. "Mama wants you and Grandpa to quit an hour early so you can go over and pay your respects."

Nathan's shoulders lifted and fell. Joseph always came by the quarry, usually first thing in the morning. He hadn't come today. Now Nathan understood why. He laid a hand on his son's shoulder. "All right, Joshua. Thank you for coming. Tell Mama we'll be home by five o'clock."

I n the end, it was decided that only Nathan, Lydia, Benjamin, and Mary Ann would go to pay their respects to the Smith family that evening. Even though it would be the Sabbath tomorrow, the Smiths had decided to have the funeral following the morning worship services. There would be time enough then for the rest of the Steed family to offer their respects.

They stopped first at the home of Don Carlos Smith to give their condolences to Agnes, thirty years old and now widowed with three small children. As it turned out, all the Smith women—Mother Smith and all of her daughters and daughters-in-law—were there. So Lydia and Mary Ann simply stayed there while Nathan and Benjamin went to see Joseph.

When they reached the Homestead, Hyrum was there with the Prophet, and so was George Albert Smith, or George A., as everyone called him. George A. was cousin to the Smiths and, being of about the same age, had been especially close to Don

Carlos. In fact, Don Carlos had performed the marriage of George A. to Bathsheba Bigler just two weeks before.

The three Smiths were out in the yard, taking advantage of the coolness of the night air, and warmly welcomed their visitors. They sat out on the grass, touched by the lamplight from the windows. All of Joseph's children were asleep except for young Joseph, who would be nine in a few months. He sat beside his father, content to listen to the adults without speaking, somehow sure that if he continued to hold his father's hand, it would help to comfort his father in his loss. Quite naturally, the conversation focused on the man for whom the family and the city now mourned. In addition to being Joseph's brother, Don Carlos Smith had been editor of the *Times and Seasons*. He was well known to the Saints, and news of his death had spread a pall over Nauvoo.

Joseph's face was somber but filled more with pride than with sorrow as he spoke of him. "Almost everyone knows that my brother Samuel was the first called missionary in the Church," he said, not really speaking to any one of them in particular, "but most people don't know that Don Carlos also went out to preach just a short time later." He looked at his brother. "Do you remember, Hyrum? We ordained him to the priesthood when he was only fourteen."

"I remember it well," Hyrum answered. "He was the one who convinced that Baptist preacher that the Church had been restored."

Joseph smiled, warmed by the memory. "Yes." He turned toward Benjamin and Nathan. "Father went to St. Lawrence County in New York to see my grandfather Asael Smith. Let's see, that would have been in August of 1830, so just four months after the Church was organized. Don Carlos had only turned fourteen in March of that year, but he went with my father. From the very beginning, he knew the work was true. And he was absolutely fearless in wanting to bear testimony of the work. Can you imagine a fourteen-year-old bearing witness to a licensed Baptist minister and converting him?"

"I can imagine that easily of Don Carlos," George A. said slowly. "Remember that experience on the boat?"

"Yes, yes," Joseph said quickly. "That's another great example of his courage."

"I guess I don't know about that," Benjamin broke in. "What happened?"

"You were there, George A.," Hyrum said. "You tell them."

George A. leaned back, his eyes half closing. "We—meaning me, Don Carlos, and two other brethren—were heading for Tennessee and Kentucky to see if we could raise some funds for the Church. This would have been in September 1838, right at the height of the tension in Missouri. Well, we got on a riverboat down on the Missouri River and then found to our dismay that it was filled with a whole group of men from Jackson County— Moses Wilson, Samuel Lucas, Colonel Thompson." There was a flash of anger now in his eyes. "A viler group of black hearts would be hard to find."

He paused, totally lost in his memories now. "They were cursing the Mormons up one side and down the other. We were forced to listen to the most hideous oaths and threats. Then somehow, they learned we were Mormons. Wilson was especially ugly. He got a whole big crowd around us, then started in. He was swearing and cussing, railing on about how terrible the Mormons were. He was taunting us, trying to goad us into doing something so they'd have some excuse to take action against us."

Young Joseph's eyes were large and round now. "What happened?"

George A.'s voice was very soft now. "Well, Wilson started boasting about how he and some others dragged our people out of their cabins and whipped them senseless with hickory withes. He was swearing and damning old Joe Smith, promising he would send him and all of us to hell if given half a chance. There was a large crowd all watching and listening. I didn't know what to do. It was terrible. And very dangerous."

He paused, then looked toward Benjamin and Nathan, speaking to them now too. "Suddenly Don Carlos stepped forward. I was stunned. Gentle, quiet Don Carlos. He stepped right up to Wilson and looked him squarely in the face. Wilson was shocked too. He didn't expect any response from us. Don Carlos told him he was Joseph Smith's brother and didn't appreciate his words against him."

"Just like that?" Nathan said in amazement.

"Just like that," George A. answered. " 'General,' Don Carlos said, perfectly calm, 'you are neither a republican nor a gentleman. You are but a savage without a single principle of honor or humanity.' "

"No!" Benjamin breathed.

"Yes!" George A. said emphatically. "There he stood, a twenty-two-year-old lad, eye to eye with this murderous Missourian."

"What happened?" Nathan asked in wonder.

"Well, Wilson went red as an overripe tomato. He was in a rage, as you can imagine. He had a pistol strapped beneath the skirts of his coat, and he put his hand on the butt of it, shouting and blustering and saying he would not stand for such talk from any blankety-blank Mormon. I happened to be standing next to Wilson and prepared myself to bump him slightly should he draw his weapon."

They all chuckled at that. George A. weighed somewhere around two hundred and fifty pounds. It wasn't hard to picture Moses Wilson sailing into the river had George A. chosen to "bump" the man.

"Fortunately," George A. went on, "General David Atchison was on board as well. As you know, he was well respected by everyone. He leaped up and, putting a hand on Don Carlos's shoulder, said loudly, 'I'll be blankety-blank if Smith ain't right in this matter.' Others then spoke up as well, expressing their shock that Wilson could brag so openly about such vile deeds. That took all the bluster out of the general in an instant. He was beaten and left the group totally defeated."

They all fell silent, thinking about what that said about the courage of Don Carlos Smith. Finally Joseph stirred. "Now I think you can see why Emma and I chose to name our youngest son after this man. It is a name that he can look up to for the rest of his life."

"Yes," Hyrum murmured, "and thank heavens that you did. Now we will have another little Don Carlos to remind us of the man we have lost this day."

Will Steed was sharply disappointed that Joseph had chosen not to preach this morning. Will loved the Sabbath meetings in the grove just to the west of the temple. He enjoyed the association with the Saints. He enjoyed singing out with full voice along with two or three thousand others. But he especially loved to hear the Prophet speak. Will was often hammered with questions by his father about the Church. Joshua was not directly confrontational, but he would slip in little comments here and there that would sow seeds of doubt. That was part of the tumult Will was in about the Church. But when he came to hear Joseph, the tumult seemed to calm. He would gain a surety of feeling and purpose that would fortify him for another week with his father.

It wasn't a surprise that Joseph didn't take the lead today. There were still the funeral services for Don Carlos to follow this meeting, but nevertheless Will was disappointed. And part of that disappointment was for Carl Rogers. Usually all the Steeds went to worship services except for Joshua and Carl. But this morning Carl had surprised them all by coming out of the house with Melissa and the children. Sensing their reaction, he offhandedly explained that while he hadn't personally known Don Carlos, he felt it only right to pay honor to the Smith family. And if he was going for the funeral, he may as well go for the worship services too.

But instead of Brother Joseph they got Brother William Clark, which proved to be a disastrous substitution. Perhaps the man meant well, but this was not a speech, it was a harangue. He launched a slashing attack against the current moral condition of the Saints. The Latter-day Saints were not living up to the expectations of the Lord. They were not demonstrating appropriate sanctity in their daily lives. Of all peoples, the Mormons were expected to be the most holy, the most righteous, the most solemn, the most pious. Instead they were frivolous, unholy, given to light-mindedness. They were clearly in want of more holy living. They were not temperate enough in their living.

That had been nearly two hours ago now. Will wanted to groan. His shoulder ached and his face hurt. His ribs were squeezing his lungs. And this was the last thing Will needed. Worse, it was the last thing Carl needed. But on and on Clark went, the condemnations rolling off his tongue like the beat of some discordant drum. It became clear enough what he meant by temperance. They were indulging in ungodly pursuits like dancing and games and parties that lasted into the late evening hours. They were not showing the solemn piety expected of true believers. They were even laughing on the Sabbath!

Two hours! Will felt as if he had been pummeled by the ugly typesetter in Warsaw all over again.

And then at last, there was one last passionate burst and Clark sat down. One could feel the relief sweep across the congregation, as tangible as if a sudden fresh breeze had sprung up. The heads came up. The children stopped whatever they were doing and turned to the front as Joseph slowly stood. That alone was a surprise, for Hyrum had been conducting the meeting. It had been two full hours now. Would Joseph simply close the meeting, or would there be something more?

Joseph walked slowly to the spot where William Clark had stood to rail at them. He turned, noting that every eye was upon him. His eyes were grave, his demeanor troubled. For a long moment, he let his gaze move across the assembly, finally stopping on the face of the previous speaker.

"Elder Clark," he began in a loud voice, so as to make it carry across the crowd. "Thank you for addressing us. You have spoken your sentiments clearly and forcefully." Now his eyes left Clark and began to move from face to face. "I know it is time to close the meeting, but I am compelled to say a few additional words."

Good! Will's spirit soared with hope. Maybe this could be salvaged somewhat after all.

"I wish to give no offense to Brother Clark," Joseph began, speaking slowly, obviously choosing his words with care, "but I feel that I must reprove him for the things he has said and the way in which he said them."

Oh my, Will thought, glancing at Carl, whose boredom was now replaced with complete attentiveness.

"The Spirit that he has demonstrated," Joseph went on, "is pharisaical and hypocritical, and he has not edified the people. His accusations that we are not living as holy a life as we should, that we as a people are not showing sufficient sanctity or solemnity, and his call for temperance in such extremes as he has outlined are not in keeping with the spirit of the gospel of Christ. It is a reflection of the rigid sectarian style that we find exhibited in so many religions today."

Ouch! Will craned his neck, trying to see Clark, who was on the front row. A murmur of surprise and shock was passing through the crowd. Everyone had been expecting Joseph to say something to smooth things a little, so as not to let the meeting end on such a jarring note. But this was a direct and stinging rebuke. Suddenly Will felt sorry for the man. And then the tiniest of movements caught Will's eye. He turned. Carl Rogers was nodding his head. It was ever so slight, but he was nodding in agreement.

And then Will understood. Which was more important? To protect the feelings of a man who, though well meaning, was clearly in error, or to make it clear that this did not represent the teachings of the Church of Jesus Christ?

Joseph went on, calmly but firmly. "Brethren and sisters, Brother Clark felt that to move us forward in the execution of our duty he needed to accuse us of being lax in that duty. This is not surprising, for Brother Clark, like many of you, comes out of Christian sectarianism, where this is the normal approach to getting people to repent."

His voice rose sharply now. "But I say to you, this is not

pleasing to the Lord. In the Revelation of John, twelfth chapter, tenth verse, we learn that Satan is called the 'accuser of the brethren.' Before the foundation of the world, there was war in heaven, and Lucifer accused his brethren both day and night. That is one of the reasons he was cast out of heaven.

"I solemnly charge you this day that you do not follow the example of the adversary in accusing one another. If we do not accuse each other, God will not accuse us. If you will follow the revelations and instructions which God gives you through me, and if you have no accuser, you will enter heaven. If you will not accuse me, I will not accuse you. If you will throw a cloak of charity over my sins, I will over yours—for charity covereth a multitude of sins.

"I should like to instruct you further in these qualities that Brother Clark has mentioned—temperance, faith, virtue, charity, and truth—and teach you what they really are and how they are viewed by God. What many people call sin is not sin in the eyes of God, and we must be careful that we do not accuse people of being sinful when they are not. One of my purposes as God's servant is to break down superstition and error."

It was amazing to Will. In a matter of moments the whole tenor of the meeting had changed. The spirit of oppressiveness and discouragement was gone now. Joseph spoke without bombast or railing accusations, and the effect was so dramatically different from what had prevailed at the meeting before. He could feel his own spirits lifting, and he could tell that the vast assembly was feeling the same.

"Brothers and sisters," Joseph cried, "there is an important truth that you must understand. Religion was not meant to beat down and oppress. True religion should lift people and make them happy. You see, happiness is the object and design of our existence." He stopped. "Let me say that again. *Happiness is the object and design of our existence*, and happiness will be the end thereof if we pursue the path that leads to it. As father Lehi taught us in the Book of Mormon, 'Adam fell, that men might be; and men are, that they might have joy.' And as the Savior said, 'I am come that men might have life, and that they might have it more abundantly.'"

The congregation was watching him raptly, hanging on his words.

"Think about that, my brothers and sisters. Men are that they might have joy. We are meant to have an abundant life. Religion is not meant to knock a man down and make him miserable. If we follow the path that God has set, we shall have happiness and joy. That path is virtue, uprightness, faithfulness, holiness, and keeping all the commandments of God. It is not trying to be overly pious, overly solemn. Nor is it to call something sin if God has not labeled it as sin. Everything God gives us is lawful and right, and it is proper that we should enjoy his gifts and blessings whenever and wherever he is disposed to bestow them upon us. God never has, nor will he ever institute an ordinance or give a commandment to his people that is not calculated in its nature to promote the happiness which he has designed, and which will not end in the greatest amount of good and glory to his children."

He stopped again, taking out his handkerchief to wipe his brow. It was nearly noon now, and getting very warm, even in the shade of the grove. Joseph wore a long coat, as he usually did when preaching to the people. Will could imagine how warm it must be for him.

The Prophet returned the handkerchief to his pocket, then smiled at the people. He turned again to look at William Clark, and now there was nothing but kindness in his eyes and in his voice. "My brothers and sisters, let us preach faith and hope and temperance, but in the way that God has ordained, for therein lies the path to happiness. Let us not accuse one another of sin but leave such things in the hand of the priesthood or in the hands of God." He stopped, weary now. "We shall sing a hymn in closing and then ask Brother Derek Ingalls to close our meeting with prayer. Those of you wishing to pay your respects to Brother Don Carlos Smith, who passed away yesterday morning, may stay for the funeral services in his behalf, which will start one half hour from now."

———•———

Because of the pleasantness of the morning, the Steeds had chosen to walk to the grove rather than hitch up the buckboards and wagons. Now as they moved slowly back down the hill toward the main part of Nauvoo, it was past two o'clock, and the heat was stifling. They were strung out in clusters of varying size. The children were in front, chattering happily as they darted back and forth, grateful to be free after almost four hours of meetings. Benjamin and Mary Ann brought up the rear, deep in conversation with Caroline and Jessica. Nathan and Lydia, Matthew and Jennifer Jo, and Melissa were walking together, reviewing the startling turn of events at the worship service. Carl, directly behind them, was listening but not participating. He had Sarah, his youngest, up on his shoulders and was slightly behind them. Seeing an opportunity, Will moved up beside him. "Hello, Carl."

He looked around, then smiled. "Hello, Will."

"Wanna be with Savannah," Sarah said, twisting on her father's shoulders.

"All right." Carl swung her down and she was off to join the others. Will slowed his step a little, creating some distance between the two of them and the others. Carl naturally moved back to walk beside him. The two of them walked for a few moments, neither one speaking. Then Will cleared his throat. "What did you think of today?" he ventured.

Carl gave him a quick look, then grinned. "Probably exactly what you did."

"What?"

"Thank heavens Joseph had the courage to let us know that Mr. Clark didn't represent his feelings."

Will grinned. "Yeah, exactly."

"As you know, Will, I'm not much of one for formalized religion. I'm not sure a man needs a church to show him how to be a good Christian. But . . ." He turned to look at Will. "But if I had to choose a church, I think I'd like Joseph Smith at the head of it. I find him to be immensely practical and very much against things that I find to be quite ridiculous."

"Me too," Will said, not hiding his surprise at Carl's directness.

Melissa looked over her shoulder and, seeing them talking, slowed her step, leaving the others in order to join her husband and Will. "How are you doing, Will?" she asked.

"I'm fine."

"Good." Melissa stepped between them and slipped an arm through both of theirs. Will felt a sudden affection move through him. He got along very well with all of his aunts, but Melissa had a special way of making him feel totally comfortable. She viewed him no differently than any adult in the family and treated him accordingly.

"So," Carl asked, surprising them both, "do you think you've found your church, Will?"

Caught off guard, Will stammered for a moment; then he decided to be as direct as Carl had been. "I think so, but I'm not completely sure yet. I suppose that if I could do it right now, I would be baptized." His countenance fell a little. "But by tomorrow . . . ? I don't know."

If he had been surprised by Carl's question, now he was shocked by his next comment. "It's not your pa's decision, you know."

Melissa's head came around too, and she was staring at him just as Will was.

"The important thing, Will," he said slowly, "is that it be your answer. Not your father's. Not your mother's. Not Jenny's. Not Joseph Smith's." He pulled on his wife's arm playfully. "Not even Melissa's. *Your* answer, Will. Then, and only then, will you know what to do."

Matthew watched Brigham planing down the large plank that would eventually become a mantelpiece for a fireplace. He loved to watch Brigham's hands as they almost caressed the wood, Brigham stopping from time to time to rub his palm along the grain to see if it was responding properly. The reddish hair was frosted with sawdust, and there were wood chips dotted across the leather carpenter's apron. The blue-gray eyes were narrowed in concentration.

"How was the meeting yesterday?"

Brigham glanced up only for a moment. "Good. Very interesting, as a matter of fact."

"Oh, really." Matthew didn't ask more. He always loved it when Brigham reported on what happened in the meetings the Twelve held with the Prophet, but he never felt comfortable doing more than just making a gentle inquiry. He didn't want to pry.

"Yes." Brigham bent over and blew hard on the wood, sending a puff of sawdust flying outward. "He spent all day with us."

"It was no problem," Matthew said hastily, not wanting Brigham to think that's why he had asked. "I just worked on that cabinet for Sister Buckmiller all day."

"And it's looking real good, Matthew. You've got the touch, all right."

"Thank you." He waited for a moment. Then, realizing that Brigham, in his concentration, had forgotten what he had started to say, Matthew cleared his throat. "So?"

Now Brigham laughed. "They say the first sign of old age is when your memory goes." Then he sobered. "It was interesting. There were just the five of us there yesterday—me, Heber, John Taylor, George A., and Orson Pratt. But Joseph was very somber. Part of that, of course, is that it was just two days after the funeral. But I also think he's feeling the weight of the Church on his shoulders more and more."

"Well, as fast as it's growing, that's no wonder."

"Yes, that's part of it. But . . . I don't know, it's almost as if he's—" He stopped, looking up at nothing. Then he shook his head. "I don't know. But anyway, he told us that he wants the Twelve to take the burden of the Church here in Nauvoo upon ourselves. As the Twelve, we are to stand beside him in administering in Church affairs."

"Hmm," Matthew responded. "That's interesting."

"Yes, very interesting. He wants us to oversee the Church lands, either apportioning it out or selling it, as the case may be. And the primary responsibility for getting incoming Saints settled here will now be on our shoulders."

"That's good, isn't it? I mean, maybe not for you, but for Joseph."

"Exactly. Joseph needs to see to the ministry. He can't even find time to work on the translation of the scrolls of Abraham. He is so filled with new ideas, new doctrine to reveal to us, new insights into what we already have. And he can barely get to it. Every day people line up on his doorstep, sometimes with the most trivial of problems. The business of running the city, being the commanding general of the Nauvoo Legion, trying to get his new store built so he and Emma will have a reliable source of income—it's a wonder he gets anything done."

"As President of the Twelve, being given such responsibility to help in Church affairs must seem a little daunting to you though, doesn't it?"

"Oh, yes," Brigham said. He laid down the plane and leaned back against the bench top. "I find it very daunting. I am unlearned and unschooled."

"Not in the ways of the Lord, you're not," Matthew said quickly. "Look at the experience you had in England. It was as if you were President of the Church there. And Joseph had full confidence in you and the rest of the Twelve."

"Yes," Brigham mused. "That was a wonderful experience."

They were both quiet now, remembering their mission to England. Then Brigham straightened. He reached around behind his back and undid his apron. "Come on," he suggested, "let's go across the street and get a dipperful of water out of Sister Parson's well. It's so much better than drinking out of that old bucket here."

Matthew followed him out and across the street. The Parsons had one of the best wells in this part of town and Sister Parson had invited them to partake of its cooling waters at any time. Brigham dropped in the bucket and then reeled it up, handing Matthew the first dipperful. Then Brigham drank deeply, his eyes nearly closed with the pleasure of it.

"May I ask you a question, Brigham?"

"Of course."

"If it is inappropriate, you can tell me."

There was a quick, mischievous grin. "I will."

"Well, a minute ago you said Joseph has new doctrines for us. Related to that, I've been wondering about something Lydia told me. She said at a Sabbath meeting last spring, before we all returned from England, Joseph was speaking on the restoration of all things in this last dispensation. He made reference to the patriarchal order, when men such as Abraham and Jacob had more than one wife."

There was a sudden guardedness now in the Apostle's eyes. "Yes?"

"From what Lydia said, he implied that someday that practice would be restored again."

Matthew was concentrating on making sure he remembered how Lydia had said it, and he didn't notice the change in Brigham's expression. "I guess it caused quite a stir among the congregation, according to her. In the afternoon meeting, Joseph said he deemed it wisdom to modify his statement. He said perhaps the Spirit's whisperings had made the fulfillment of that restoration seem nearer than it was."

"Perhaps," Brigham said noncommittally. Then he dropped the dipper back in the bucket and made as though he was going to start back across the street.

"Do you think that's really true, Brigham? Do you think there would ever be a time when God would ask us to . . ." He faltered. "I mean, when he would expect men to . . . I don't know. Take more than one wife, I guess."

"Let me ask you a question, Matthew."

"All right."

"You mentioned that Abraham and Jacob had more than one wife."

"Yes."

"Do you think they were men of God?"

"Well, yes, but—"

Brigham laughed and started away, motioning for Matthew to follow. "No buts. Either they were or they weren't." He laughed again. "But that's far too heavy a subject for a young lad who has work aplenty to do on a summer day."

"Yes, but—"

Brigham waved him to silence. "There is no such word as *yesbut* in the English language."

He was smiling and half teasing, but Matthew also sensed that there was another message behind the lightness. Brigham was telling him he had asked an inappropriate question.

"Sorry," he said sheepishly.

"I'll have to talk to Jennifer about that, see if she can't teach you some new vocabulary."

And then, as they walked back across the street together and approached their little shop, Brigham stopped. He turned and looked Matthew squarely in the eyes. "You just remember this one lesson, Matthew Steed. If the Lord were ever to require such a thing of us, he would let us know, wouldn't he?"

"I suppose. Yes, of course."

"And he would do it through his prophet. You just remember that, Matthew Steed. Joseph Smith is a prophet of God. If you ever start feeling doubts, you just hold on to that fact, tight as you can hang on, and you'll be all right."

Chapter Notes

Don Carlos Smith was ten years younger than the Prophet Joseph. He died, probably of pneumonia, on 7 August 1841. He was a member of the Nauvoo City Council and a brigadier general in the Nauvoo Legion, and was the first editor of the *Times and Seasons,* putting out thirty-one issues of the same before his death. The story told by George A. Smith about the confrontation with General Wilson comes from Don Carlos's own journal account (see *HC* 4:394–95). Of him, the Prophet wrote, "My youngest brother, Don Carlos Smith, . . . was one of the first to receive my testimony, and was ordained to the Priesthood when only 14 years of age. . . . He was universally beloved by the Saints." (*HC* 4:393, 399.)

The sermon delivered by William O. Clark and Joseph's response to that sermon take place here in August of 1841, about three months earlier than they actually happened (see *HC* 4:445). Though some details of Joseph's talk are given in his history, other parts of it are only summarized there. The author sought things that Joseph said on these themes at about the same time period. The "happiness is the object and design of our existence" portion comes from a letter that was written by Joseph probably sometime in early 1842 (see Joseph Smith, *The Personal Writings of Joseph Smith*, comp. and ed. Dean C. Jessee [Salt Lake City: Deseret Book Co. 1984], pp. 507–9; also *HC* 5:134–35).

One cannot help but wonder how William Clark responded to such a public and pointed rebuke. Joseph's history does not say in the entry for that day. But two later references to Clark in historical sources are interesting. Under date of 9 March 1843, Joseph notes in his history, "William O. Clark gave me a load of corn, and Sanford Porter gave me a hog" (*HC* 5:300). It is also reported that Clark, a seventy, served a mission in Iowa and Illinois in 1844 (see Joseph Smith, *The Words of Joseph Smith*, comp. and ed. Andrew F. Ehat and Lyndon W. Cook [Provo, Utah: Religious Studies Center, Brigham Young University, 1980], p. 99). Both references would indicate that Clark did not allow the correction to turn him from the Church.

In his journal entry for 10 August 1841, Joseph says that he spent the day in council with five of the Apostles (not all of the Twelve were in Nauvoo at the time) and requested them to take the burden of the business of the Church in Nauvoo from him (see *HC* 4:400).

There is some evidence that Joseph began teaching the Twelve the doctrine of plural marriage shortly after their return from England (see *American Moses*, pp. 100–101). Heber C. Kimball's daughter records Joseph's early attempt to teach the doctrine to the Saints and the resulting dismay which was felt by the Saints (see *LHCK*, p. 328).

It was a glorious Sabbath day morning, the fifteenth of August. Lydia had risen early and fixed breakfast for her family. Then, with Nathan's encouragement, she left him to go for a morning walk. This had become the pattern, him cheerfully giving her this time to be alone while he would clean up the dishes, maybe read the children a story or two, and then start to get them ready for the worship services that would begin at ten. As usual, she had not paid much attention to the time, and now was hurrying back.

She was moving up Granger Street, still about two blocks from Steed Row, when she saw a figure coming toward her. She slowed her step, peering more closely in the bright sunshine. It was a small person, more of a child's height, but then Lydia could see it was an older woman. She wore a sunbonnet and had a white shawl around her shoulders.

Suddenly the woman saw her and began waving her arms. "Lydia! Lydia!"

Surprised, Lydia recognized the voice immediately. It was Mother Smith, Joseph's mother. Obviously she had been to the house and was now headed back to Joseph's, where she was living since her husband had died. Lydia increased her step again, raising her own arm to acknowledge that she recognized her. "Yes, Mother Smith. I'm coming."

Lydia smiled to herself. She had been right. It was a person of a child's height, just not of a child's age. Lucy Mack Smith was about four feet eleven inches tall. She was thin of frame and on first appearance seemed frail and vulnerable. But anyone who knew her knew better than to suggest in her presence that she was frail. Mother Smith—as virtually everyone, including her own family, called her—had been born on the eighth day of July in the year 1775. Five weeks ago she had celebrated her sixty-sixth birthday. The Latter-day Saints streamed to her door to express their love and admiration for this remarkable woman, mother of the Prophet. She was as tough and resilient as a lot of men twice her size and half her age. She was a woman of indomitable faith, unflagging good cheer, and endless energy. And she had played an enormous role in Lydia's own life.

She and Nathan had been in the group Mother Smith led from New York to Ohio via the Erie Canal. That had been in the spring of 1831 while Lydia was pregnant with young Joshua. Lydia had been standing by Mother Smith's side when she called on the people to have faith so they could get out of the icebound Buffalo Harbor. Almost in an instant, the ice had split open, and the ship had gone through. It was a lesson in faith Lydia sometimes neglected but never forgot.

"Oh, Lydia, I'm so glad I found you," Joseph's mother said as they closed the last of the distance between them.

Lydia saw the weariness and the sorrow that lined her face and felt quick alarm. "Mother Smith, what is it? What's the trouble?"

"You didn't stop by Emma's as you came by?"

"No. I was just out walking."

"Then you don't know?" Mother Smith whispered.

"Don't know what?"

"About Don Carlos."

That really surprised Lydia. "Well, yes, but . . ." She was fumbling in her confusion. She and Nathan had been at the funeral the previous Sabbath. In fact, Lydia had spoken with Mother Smith personally to console her over the loss of her son. Had she so soon forgotten all that? "I was to the funeral, Mother Smith, remember?"

Lucy gave her a puzzled look. "The funeral? But the funeral won't be until tomorrow. How could—" Then it dawned on her. "Lydia, I'm not talking about my Don Carlos. I'm talking about Emma's Don Carlos. I'm talking about my grandson."

A chill shot through Lydia, and she felt her knees go weak. "Emma's Don Carlos? I knew he was ill, but—" *Oh, dear Lord. Not another of Emma's children. Oh, please! No!*

There were full tears now in those wise, mature eyes that had seen and suffered so much. "Last night he took a turn for the worse, and then this morning . . ." She couldn't bear to say it.

There was a great hollowness inside Lydia. Don Carlos had celebrated his first birthday just two months before. For any child, fourteen months was a delightful stage of development. Children at that age were walking and talking. They loved life; they loved people and gave that love without reserve. And Don Carlos had been such a precious little boy, so loved by his father, and so dearly treasured by Emma. Suddenly Lydia's vision blurred and she swayed, feeling the pain lance through her. "Oh, Mother Smith," she said softly.

"Joseph sent Julia round to tell you, but Nathan said you had gone walking. Could you come, Lydia? You and Emma have always been such dear friends." There was a momentary hesitation. "And with you having lost your own baby, Joseph thought you could be of special comfort to her."

She nodded numbly. "I'm so sorry, Mother Smith."

Lucy Mack Smith's hands were trembling slightly. "Go," she said softly. "Go to Emma. She needs you."

———•———

They walked slowly, shoulder to shoulder, neither one speaking. Lydia sensed that Emma didn't need words right now—not words of comfort or condolence, not words of encouragement, not promises of the resurrection or talk of her child being with God. When she was ready for words, she would let it be known. And so they walked, communing in a way that only women seem to achieve with one another.

Lydia had stayed at Joseph and Emma's house through the rest of the morning and all of the afternoon. Joseph didn't go to worship services, and for a time it was mostly the family coming to see the bereaved parents. But once worship services were concluded, the house was thronged, of course. Family, friends, neighbors, well-wishers. Word of the tragedy spread quickly. Joseph was their beloved leader and prophet. His loss was a community loss, and the expressions were numerous, well meant, and never-ending. But Lydia sensed that all of that only made the day more difficult for Emma. Part of Emma's burden in life had been to shoulder the task, whether welcomed or not, of accepting the public adulation and obligation that encircled her husband. Privacy was something rarely found and therefore all the more to be treasured.

She bore up bravely, fighting back the tears as she accepted the condolences. But it was difficult for her, and her responses were wooden and forced. It didn't help that Emma was pregnant again, in her third or fourth month. Not many knew that. But Lydia knew, and as she watched Emma through the afternoon, she saw that her friend became more and more distant and withdrawn. The circles around her eyes deepened; her handshake became limp and lifeless.

Lydia finally went to Joseph. A few whispered words were enough. This was why he had sent for Lydia. He knew that she, of all of Emma's friends, would be sensitive to her needs. "Take her," he said. "I'll stay and talk with the people."

Emma had protested, of course. She took her role seriously

and wore it well. There was no question why the Lord had brought these two together. Emma was a prophet's wife—gracious, intelligent, patient, sharing. But there were limits, and this day had brought her up against them, and so the protests were feeble and easily pushed aside. And now they were alone and walking slowly together.

The ache Lydia felt for Emma was so deep it almost made it difficult for her to walk. Tomorrow Emma Smith would bury her fifth child. Her firstborn lay in a small graveyard near the banks of the Susquehanna River in Pennsylvania. That had been back in 1828, before the Church was organized, while Joseph was still translating the Book of Mormon. Emma had come very near to dying herself, according to Joseph, and was nursed back to health only after a long time.

Her second pregnancy only repeated and deepened the tragedy. This time she bore twins. Again, within hours, they both died. Fortunately there had been the Murdock twins, given to Joseph and Emma a day or so later. That helped immensely to fill the void. But tragedy wasn't through with Emma Smith yet. One of those twins died after a mob broke into the house where Emma and Joseph were staying. The men dragged Joseph out into the night. In the terror of the moment, no one noticed that the door had been left wide open. Still recovering from the measles, the little boy, just eleven months old, caught pneumonia and died a few days later.

Now tomorrow, little Don Carlos would be laid to rest. This one was, perhaps, more bitter than all the rest because of his age. Emma had been able to keep him for so long. He was walking now, and saying "Papa," and pulling down or knocking off or dropping everything in the house that wasn't either nailed down or too heavy for him to move.

There were few women—be they mothers or not, be they married or not—who did not naturally and keenly feel the loss of another woman's child. But that was not the same as having actually experienced that loss. Lydia was behind Emma in numbers, but she too had lost a baby at birth—born in a cabin on the

Isaac Morley farm on the outskirts of Kirtland. And two years ago, her little Nathan, as precious and endearing as Don Carlos, had been taken from her. He had been not quite four at his death.

That was part of the ache Lydia was feeling now. Her son would have been five now, six in October. She could close her eyes and picture him with perfect clarity—not as he was at his death, but as he would be now. He would look all the more like his papa, with the same grave eyes and quiet demeanor, the same fair hair that always seemed to escape containment. He would have that tiny little smile that made her want to laugh and cry and hold him tightly all at the same time.

Yes, she thought, Lydia McBride Steed might not be able to fathom the breadth of Emma Smith's sorrow, but she fully understood its depth.

Without being aware of it, she slipped her arm through Emma's and pressed it lightly, just to let her know she was there. Emma returned the pressure, ever so slightly, and then the two women walked on in silence.

Mary Ann stood and tapped her fork on the side of her tin mug. "The Steed family women's council will now come to order," she called.

It took a moment or two because they were all chattering away in the various small groups, but the first to hear her started shushing the others and the talk quickly died. All eyes turned to Mary Ann, and she could see the curiosity on their faces. She smiled, pleased with her little surprise.

It was the afternoon of September eleventh, the second Saturday of the month. They were gathered outside in Lydia's backyard, seated in chairs and on benches and stools brought from all of the nearby houses. Normally, the monthly meetings of the Steed family "women's council" were held on Sunday evenings inside one of their houses, but today was different. And that accounted for the feeling of expectancy in the air. When Mary

Ann sent out word of the change, more than one had wanted to know why. But she would only give them an enigmatic smile and say, "Oh, you'll see."

The oppressive heat of August had finally broken the week before when a line of thunderstorms rolled out of Iowa Territory and crossed Illinois for three or four days, cooling the air and the land. Now the days were uncommonly pleasant, and the nights cool enough that light covers were put on the beds again.

There were eleven of them in all—nine Steeds or Steed family members and the two Pottsworths. Anyone twelve and older was considered a woman for purposes of the council, so Kathryn McIntire, fifteen, and Caroline's Olivia, thirteen, were there as well.

As Mary Ann looked around at their faces, her heart warmed with the knowledge that this was her family and that they were all here beside her. Then she had a sudden thought. "I think this is a first for us," she said.

Caroline, who sat just behind her, said, "A first? In what way?"

Mary Ann laughed. "No babies."

For a moment they were startled by that, looking around to be sure. Then they smiled too. She was right. They always left the children home for these meetings, but usually there was at least one baby in arms who was too small to be left home by his or her mother. This afternoon, there was not one. Caroline's Charles was now nineteen months old and in the process of being weaned. Rebecca's Christopher was two. Even Lydia's little Josiah, the youngest of the whole clan, was almost nine months old now. He was still nursing, but Lydia had fed him just before coming out, then left him with Nathan and the children.

Kathryn leaned over and nudged her sister with her elbow. "Bet that doesn't last for long," she said, loud enough for all to hear.

Jennifer Jo blushed deeply. She and Matthew had been married just seven weeks now. Still coloring, she smiled shyly at the faces around her. "I hope not."

Mary Ann nodded. "We hope not too." She looked around, the thought expanding. "And I'll bet you're not alone either."

She was looking at Rebecca, who likewise colored now. Derek had been home from England for over two months, and Mary Ann fully expected that the two of them would be making an announcement soon. And Melissa's Sarah was almost three now, and Mary Ann knew that Melissa and Carl were talking about having another one. And that would be just fine, she thought.

"Well," she went on, getting down to business. "I know you are all wondering why the change in our meeting time and day." She let her eyes sweep from face to face. When she got to Jennifer Jo and Kathryn, she stopped. "Are you two ready?" They nodded back, and then to everyone's surprise, they stood up and left, walking around the house quickly.

"As you know," Mary Ann continued, ignoring the questioning looks, "we had the first meeting of our women's council last December, shortly after we celebrated our first Thanksgiving. We determined then that we could best show our thanks to God by serving others in greater need than ourselves." She smiled softly. "It's what Father Steed calls being thankful with your hands as well as your hearts."

She paused for a moment, but no one spoke. "We adjourned for the summer because it is a busy time for all of us and also it is a time when the poor are more able to care for their needs. But September is upon us now. The harvest is all but over. The first frost will be here in a few weeks. And—"

"Thank heavens," Abigail Pottsworth breathed. That brought a laugh from everyone. The English Saints had found the heat of Nauvoo almost unbearable, making them "melt down into little puddles of fat and flesh," as Sister Pottsworth put it. Even the Twelve, after a year in England's climate, had found it quite a readjustment, and Brigham had written a letter back to Great Britain warning those who were coming to prepare for a "roasting."

"While Sister Pottsworth is anxious for winter to arrive," Mary Ann went on, "we all know that once it comes, those who are less fortunate than ourselves will find the cold very challenging. They will need quilts, mittens, stockings, blankets, and coats. We have made such things in the past and I think we are agreed that this is probably the best thing we can do."

"Are we going to choose families again, Mother Steed?" Jessica asked. "I have some names if we are."

"We are," Mary Ann responded. "Actually, I want each of us to start praying about the matter. Only the Lord will know who is really in need and how we can best help them. But—" She held up one hand, enjoying her surprise again. "But that is not our purpose today. We shall do that in our next meeting. No, today is a working meeting. We felt it best to start right out doing something."

"So that's why we moved to Saturday?" Lydia spoke up.

"That's right. And to do that, I suggest we adjourn this meeting and move to the large drying shed at the brickyard of Carl and Melissa Rogers."

That brought Melissa's head up in surprise. "Our shed?"

Mary Ann laughed merrily. "Yes. Jennifer Jo and Kathryn have a surprise for us there. They swore Carl to secrecy so as not to spoil it, even for you." She waved in the general direction they were going. "We shall reconvene in five minutes at the drying shed."

⸻ ◆ ⸻

The two McIntire sisters were actually waiting for them just outside the shed. When they saw them approaching, Kathryn quickly shut the door and stood in front of it. As the women all gathered, they were buzzing with excitement and questions.

"Surely we're not going to be making bricks for the poor," Lydia said to Jessica.

Jessica just shrugged. "Kathryn hasn't told me a word about this. I don't know what they're up to."

Mary Ann merely smiled, waited until they were all there, and then turned to the two girls. "All right. We're in your hands."

Though Jennifer Jo's hair was a light brown and Kathryn's almost jet black, and though there was four years' difference in their ages, and though Kathryn did not have Jennifer Jo's sprinkling of freckles across her nose and cheeks, there was no mistaking the fact that these two were sisters. Both had wide blue eyes half-hidden beneath thick dark lashes. Both had the same fair skin. Both of their noses had that little upturn on the end that Matthew loved to tease Jennifer Jo about. Both had the same rich, full mouth and even white teeth. Their voices sounded quite similar, and when they laughed, one almost had to turn to see which of the two it was making the sound.

With their audience before them, they looked at each other, both suddenly a little embarrassed by all the attention. Kathryn motioned for Jennifer Jo to speak, but she shook her head. "It was your idea originally," she answered. "You tell them."

"All right." Kathryn turned back to the others. "Well, actually, we want to show you something as much as tell you something. That's why we've come here. But first, I need to explain a few things." She took a quick breath, then plunged in. "When it comes to fabric, England is best known for its great cotton mills. Derek, Jenny, Peter, Sister Pottsworth—they were all part of that. But in other parts of the British Isles, there are other fabrics which are equally common there. For example, in Scotland, where it is often colder and windier than in England, the most common material is—" She stopped, inviting them to answer.

"Wool!" Sister Pottsworth exclaimed. "The Scots are famous for their woolens."

"Aye," Kathryn agreed. "And what about the Irish?"

"Their linens," Jenny Pottsworth answered just as promptly.

"Aye," Kathryn said again. "Even in America, Irish linen is well known." She turned to Jennifer Jo, motioning for her to continue.

"While wool keeps a person very warm," Jennifer Jo explained, "it can be quite uncomfortable on the bare skin, and it wears out quickly with heavy use. The Scots, who are renowned for their thriftiness, did not like that."

"On the other hand," Kathryn came in again, "linen wears well and is very cool. In the summer that is great, but in winter, one would certainly not want a linen coat."

"So," Jennifer Jo asked with a smile, "what is the solution?"

The others looked blank, but Sister Pottsworth spoke up again. "Linsey-woolsey."

"Yes," both sisters said together. Then Kathryn explained. "It is a combination of both materials. It has the warmth of wool, but the durability of linen. Here in America, what you call linsey-woolsey is a cheap, coarse material, but in Scotland and Ireland, this is not the case. It is of the highest quality and very valuable for winter clothing." She paused, letting that sink in a little before going on. "My sister and I talked to Mother Steed. We think that if we are going to make winter clothing for the poor, there isn't anything better we could make it from than from linsey-woolsey."

Sister Pottsworth clapped her hands together. "A wonderful idea. I had a coat back when Jenny was just a tot which was made from Scottish linsey. Warmest coat I ever had. It lasted for years."

Mary Ann found that too good an opportunity. "So if we wanted to really bless people who have to winter here in Nauvoo, we would make them coats of linsey-woolsey."

"But," Rebecca spoke up, "we don't have any of that kind of material."

Jennifer Jo clapped her hands. "Well, what if you had two humble Irish girls who would teach you how to make it?"

"And," Kathryn added, opening the door to the shed behind them, "a building generously donated by our own Carl Rogers in which to do it?"

Mary Ann laughed at the effect they had created. "Ladies, shall we?" And with a little flourish she gestured toward the open door.

"Come in, Will." Lydia tried to hide the surprise in her eyes as she stepped back, holding the door open wide. She held Josiah under one arm.

Will Steed came inside, taking off his hat. Though it was not quite eight o'clock, it was the thirteenth of September and the days were getting noticeably shorter now. It was already full dark outside.

"Do you have a minute, Aunt Lydia?" He looked around with just a trace of nervousness.

She smiled warmly at him. "Yes. Nathan and your grandfather went out east of town looking at some property. They took the older children with them and probably won't be back for another hour. So it's just me and the baby." She started for the parlor. "Come in and sit down."

He did so, following her into the sitting room, pleased that she was alone. He moved to the large overstuffed chair and dropped into it wearily. Lydia picked up a ball and a toy rattle for Josiah, then took a hard-backed chair directly across from Will. "Well, this is a pleasant surprise."

Will nodded. "I came to see you Saturday evening, but you were all still down at the brickyard."

"I'm sorry. We were having so much fun."

He nodded but didn't speak further.

Josiah threw his rattle down, then leaned out to get it. Lydia put him down and he crawled after it. Then she decided to lead out a little. "How are you, Will? Your face is all better now. How's the shoulder and the ribs?"

"Good. I hardly ever think of them anymore."

"I haven't seen you at the store much this past while."

He flushed, instantly catching her meaning. "Me and Pa have been traveling around quite a bit trying to get a full crew to go to Wisconsin. They're supposed to leave in about ten days, and he's getting concerned that he's still got only about half of what he needs."

"I know," Lydia said forlornly. "I'm already dreading Nathan being gone." She hesitated, then asked, "Are you going with your father?"

He scowled deeply. "He thinks I am."

"But you're not sure." It was a statement, not a question.

"Oh, I'm sure, all right," he snapped, speaking to the lamp across from him. "He just won't listen when I try to tell him."

Lydia sat back watching him, her eyes showing understanding but not approval. He saw that and reacted almost instantly. "What? You think I should go?"

She shook her head. "I didn't say that."

"But you were thinking it, weren't you?"

She sighed, wondering if it was really her place to say it. "Can I be honest with you, Will?"

"Of course." And he really did mean that.

"I know you want to stay here so you can be close to Jenny." She hesitated. "I know you're worried about Andrew Stokes."

His head came up and his eyes were flashing. "I don't give a hoot about Andrew Stokes."

Lydia just watched him steadily.

Finally, he dropped his eyes from hers. "All right, so I am worried about Andrew Stokes." Then the fire was back. "Wouldn't you be? You see the way Jenny gets all fluttery when he comes in the store. You know how everyone thinks he's so wonderful."

"Everyone thinks you're wonderful, Will."

"Yeah," he retorted, completely glum now. "Everyone except Jenny."

It was as if the baby sensed Will's sudden pain. He sat up, watched him with large grave eyes for a moment, then crawled over to him and held up his hands.

Will laughed, leaned down, and picked him up. In a moment, Will was bouncing him on his knee and Josiah was squealing in delight. "You have a wonderful way with children, Will," Lydia said. And then she took a quick breath. "Jenny is . . . Will, Jenny cares a great deal for you. You know that. It's just that she also cares a great deal for Andrew. Jenny doesn't know her own heart yet, Will. If you think you're hurt, think of poor Peter. Jenny just wants to be friends with him, like they've always been, but that's not what Peter wants, and he's just plain miserable."

"Yeah, I know." He stood and began walking with Josiah. "I know you're right, Aunt Lydia. About Jenny. But going to Wisconsin isn't going to help my cause any."

"Probably not. It may make things worse."

He winced a little with the bluntness of her response. "And you still think I ought to go?"

"I didn't say that," she repeated.

"Then what *are* you saying?"

"I'm saying that right now your relationship with your father is just as important—maybe even more important—than your relationship with Jenny Pottsworth."

His mouth opened slightly, but Lydia went on quickly now. "Will, I don't know whether or not you're going to get your answer about the Church. Or when. When you decide, you do what you have to do. But if you and your father are battling—about Jenny, about going to Wisconsin, about whatever it is that seems to be jarring the two of you—your being baptized certainly won't make it any easier."

"I don't care if it's easy or not," he blurted. "Pa won't even try to understand my feelings. Why should I worry about his?"

"I wasn't talking about it being easier for you, Will," she said softly.

He visibly flinched as the meaning of her words hit him. "Mama?" he asked in a whisper.

Lydia nodded slowly. She clasped her hands together, watching his eyes. She wanted to take him and hold him, he was so much like her little Josiah at that moment. At the same time, she wanted to take him by the shoulders and shake him hard. This was just what she had seen happen before—with Benjamin Steed and his oldest son.

Then Lydia had a thought. "Just a minute, Will." She stood and started toward the bedroom where she and Nathan slept. Josiah, seeing he was being deserted, yelped in protest and she came back and took him from Will. When she returned she had a copy of the Book of Mormon in her hand. She walked over and handed it to him. She remained standing, rocking back and forth slowly to keep Josiah happy.

He looked at it, then at her. He had one just like it. "What's this?" he said.

"That's the Book of Mormon Nathan gave to me before we

were married. It's the book that finally brought me into the Church."

He nodded. He had heard both Nathan and Lydia tell the story about how she had fought the idea of being a Mormon at first. That, in fact, was one of the reasons he had come to talk with her. Nathan, Matthew, Grandma Steed, Rebecca, Jennifer Jo—all of them had found it easy to accept the gospel. Grandpa Steed had struggled, but not in the same way Will was. He hadn't wanted to know, not at first. Then Joseph had finally won him over through friendship.

"Look at it!" she commanded.

He started to open it, but she shook her head. "No. At the outside."

He examined it more closely, turning it over. And there it was on the back. One corner had a dark brown stain in the leather. It marred the appearance of the book, making it look as though its owner were slovenly.

He touched it again, then looked up. "What is it?"

There was a faint smile. "Coffee grounds."

His eyebrows rose. And with that she told him the story, told him how bitterly she had resented Joseph Smith, how totally she was caught up in the wave of mockery and ridicule aimed at the boy from Palmyra. Then she fell in love with Nathan, and Joseph's mission became like a giant tree stump between them. They couldn't seem to get around it, and they could never go through it. Her voice grew quiet as she recounted Nathan's final, last-ditch attempt to get through to her by sending her a copy of the Book of Mormon with an accompanying letter of testimony. But it went to her father first, and her father—who harbored a deep and bitter animosity toward this new religious movement—threw it in the trash.

By the time she finished, Josiah had laid his head against her shoulder and fallen asleep. She walked across to Will and took the book from him, holding it in her free hand. She began to rub her thumb over the soiled cover. "Nathan has offered to buy me a new one, but I won't let him. I wouldn't take a hundred dollars for this."

Will slowly nodded. He thought he understood. He was wrong. She wasn't going to talk about her conversion at all.

She went back to her chair, set the book on the lamp table, and then sat down gently so as not to wake her son. "When my father died, Will, he still had strong feelings against the Mormons." Her voice was low and husky now, and her eyes were filled with tears. "But I was there, Will. I was back home. Nathan was there too, and my father loved him." There was a short, tearful laugh. "You can't know what a miracle that was. For years, he wouldn't even call Nathan by name. He just called him 'that farmer' or 'that farm boy.'"

Now Will smiled. "Pa always calls Jenny 'that English girl.'"

She laughed again, and shook her head. "It says so much about what they're feeling, doesn't it?"

"Yes."

"But, Will, that's what this coffee stain means to me now. You see, Nathan didn't much like my father either." She shook her head, remembering well some of the collisions between the two most important men in her life. "He was especially upset when they sent me away because I wanted to be a Mormon. But—" She stopped, very earnest now. "And this is what I want you to think about, Will. In spite of all his feelings about my father, Nathan went back to Palmyra with me. Twice!"

She smiled softly now, her eyes misting again. "You know how Nathan hates being a storekeeper."

Will couldn't help but chuckle at that as he nodded.

"In spite of all that, Nathan went back with me and he worked in my father's store. When my father got sick, he ran the store completely. Do you understand what I'm saying, Will?"

He looked away. "I . . . I think so."

"The Church can divide us from those we love, Will. Sometimes we have no choice in that, but it shouldn't stop us from loving them. If we let anger and contention dominate that relationship, how can we say we truly follow the Savior? My father hated the Church and he didn't like Nathan, but Nathan didn't let that determine how he would respond to my father."

She leaned her head against the baby's, letting the tears flow. Now her voice was barely audible. "And when my father died, he loved Nathan as though he were the son he always wanted. And if he ever, in the world of spirits, accepts the gospel and realizes how blind he was here, it will be because of Nathan, not because of me."

For a long time they both sat there, Lydia weeping quietly, Will withdrawn deeply into his own thoughts. Finally he stood. "Thank you, Aunt Lydia." There was a quick, regretful grin. "It wasn't what I wanted to hear."

She smiled through the tears. "I know," she whispered. "But then, you should never ask a McBride for an opinion unless you're willing to hear what you're not expecting."

"Thank you. Don't get up. You'll wake him. I'll show myself out."

She stood anyway. "Will, I want to ask a favor of you."

That surprised him. "What?"

"It's not something that has to happen now. Maybe when you get up there if you go."

"All right. What is it?"

"I want you to read something."

He looked forlorn. "I've already read that passage in Moroni a dozen times or more."

She laughed. Every Mormon in the world asked nonmembers to read the promise the angel Moroni had made to those who would read the Book of Mormon with an honest and sincere heart. "No. I want you to read a parable in the book of Luke."

"A parable?"

"Yes. It's not long, only the first few verses of chapter eighteen. It can be troublesome in a way. I want you to really think about it." She held his gaze. "Will you do it?"

"Will it give me my answer?" he shot back, challenging her in return.

She had to answer that honestly. "I don't know. But it might help you know how to get the answer."

———◆———

It was close to midnight when Joshua jerked up with a start. Caroline gave a low moan and turned over. Joshua cocked his head, wondering what had brought him out of so deep a sleep. Then it came again. There was a soft knock on their bedroom door.

He sat up completely, trying to shake the stupor from his mind. "Yes, who is it?"

"It's me. May I come in?"

Caroline sat up now too, pulling the covers up around her. "Will?"

The door opened and a dark figure stepped inside.

"Where have you been, son?" Joshua asked, feeling a quick jolt of concern.

"Out walking."

"*What?* Have you been with Jenny again?"

"No."

"What's wrong, Will?" Caroline asked, jabbing Joshua hard with her elbow.

"Nothing. I've just been thinking about things. And I've made a decision."

"What decision?" Joshua exclaimed, exasperation heavy in his voice.

"I'll be going with you to the pineries, Pa. I thought you ought to know that."

———

Chapter Notes

Don Carlos Smith, the youngest son of Joseph and Emma, died on 15 August 1841, just eight days following the death of his uncle and namesake (see HC 4:402). This was the fourth loss in the Smith family in eleven months. Joseph Smith, Sr., died in September 1840, never having fully recovered from the shock of the persecutions the family suffered in Missouri. Samuel Smith, another of Joseph's brothers, lost his wife, Mary, in January of

1841. She too had suffered permanent damage in 1838 after being compelled, with her children, to leave their home and being exposed to the inclement weather. Finally, there were the tandem deaths of the senior Don Carlos and his namesake.

Nor did that end it. Two weeks later, on 27 August 1841, Robert Blashel Thompson, husband of Mercy Fielding Thompson and brother-in-law to Hyrum Smith, died of pneumonia. Robert had served as the associate editor with Don Carlos Smith at the *Times and Seasons* and as a scribe to the Prophet. The Smith family counted Robert's death as another loss of one of their own. (See *HC* 4:411.) Finally, on 25 September of that same year, not even one month after Robert's death, Hyrum Smith, Hyrum's son, died at the age of seven years four months (see *HC* 4:418), making the sixth death in the Smith family in one year's time.

H e's back in the corral, Mrs. Steed. They're trying to get Elena into a harness."

"Elena?"

"Yes, ma'am. She's that little mare your husband took in on trade about a week ago."

"Oh. All right, thank you." Caroline started for the door.

The boy cleared his throat quickly. "Uh . . . Mrs. Steed, ma'am?"

She half turned. "Yes, George?"

"Uh, Elena is real skittish, ma'am. They're having a h—" He caught himself. "A heck of a time with her. Maybe it's . . . uh . . . maybe you'd like to wait here for Mr. Steed, ma'am."

She smiled sweetly at him. "Thank you for your concern, George. But I'll go quietly and not disturb them."

He started into his stammering drawl again, but she waved airily and walked out. The moment she left the building, she heard the battle going on behind the stables. A horse was snorting, then there came a sharp whinny. A moment later there was a heavy crash followed instantly by a burst of profanity. She slowed her step, glad that it wasn't Joshua's voice.

"Whoa, there! Settle down, girl!" This was Joshua, and she could hear him trying to keep his voice low and soothing. Another crash sounded, this one more like a hoof flashing back against a bucket or something. There was one short swear word—this time from Joshua—and the horse began to snort again.

As Caroline came around the front of the stable to where the corral was, she saw why they were swearing. The horse, a beautiful gray, was plunging backward, her head up, eyes wild. One man was just getting up from the ground. Another was circling around, a looped rope in one hand, trying to snare the horse's head. Joshua was on the halter rope, heels dug in, but being dragged along as though he were a child. His boots left deep furrows in the soft dirt of the corral.

"Get her head! Get her head!" Joshua shouted.

The man in the dirt leaped up and grabbed the rope to help Joshua hold her. The second man threw his rope but the mare saw it and jerked away, and the rope missed her completely. Whinnying wildly now, the mare backed into the corral fence, which was made of thick posts and cross beams lashed together with long strips of rawhide. The whole fence trembled, but it stopped her backward progress for just a moment. Joshua flung himself forward, leaving the other man to hold the rope. In three steps he was to the mare. He grabbed her ears, locking his arms around her neck as he did so, and lifting his feet off the ground so she carried his full weight. "Easy, girl!" he shouted as she jumped back with a startled snort. "Easy, Elena."

She tried to shake him off, but Joshua hung on doggedly. She reared up, her hooves flashing out, dragging the rope out of the other man's hands. One of the hooves caught Joshua in the back of his calf and Caroline heard him grunt with the pain. She nearly cried out, but cut it off with a hand to her mouth, knowing that it would only make things worse.

Freed now of the man on the rope, the mare was bucking wildly, trying to dislodge this terrible weight hanging on to her head. Joshua was swinging back and forth, like a clock's pendulum gone wild, but he wouldn't let go and finally his weight was too much for her. The bucking stopped, then the swinging of her body from side to side, and finally even the tossing of her head. She came to a halt, her head down, her nostrils flaring, her sides heaving. Joshua slowly straightened, not letting go. He reached out with one hand and began to rub her nose. "There now, girl. We're not trying to hurt you." He reached up and scratched at her ears. "See there? Nobody's gonna hurt my Elena now."

Slowly he let her go and stepped back. She turned her head to eye him warily, but she was too winded to fight anymore. Joshua turned and walked slowly back to the other two men. As he did so, his eyes lifted and he saw Caroline. There was a flicker of surprise, and a brief wave, but he didn't change course.

"What are we going to do?" the one man said. "We're short on teams." Then Caroline saw the harnessing lying on the ground near the fence. Just out the gate was a wagon waiting, with one horse already hitched in the traces.

"Go get Old Red," Joshua said. "Bring him in the corral."

"Yes, sir."

As the two of them headed for the wagon, Joshua came over to see Caroline. She saw that he was limping heavily but trying not to wince.

"Are you all right?"

"Yeah, I'm fine. What brings you here?"

"Lydia and I went to see Emma today. I needed to tell you something so I came by here on my way home."

"Oh."

"What's the matter with her?" Caroline said, looking at the horse now.

He turned too. "She's real high strung by nature," he said. "And this is still all new to her." There was a note of disgust in his voice. "Besides, I think that teamster was selling me a load of buffalo chips when he told me she was a good wagon horse."

"So what do you do?"

"I'll try one more thing. If that doesn't work, I'm going to have to sell her off again. We can't go through this every time we want to hitch her up."

Caroline felt sorry for the gray. She still stood where Joshua had left her, her head down, her belly still rising and falling.

"What did you have to tell me?"

It took Caroline a moment to come back to that. "Will stopped by the house on his way to get that load from the boat landing. He won't be home for supper. He's going to Jenny's."

There was an instant frown.

"Joshua," she reminded him, "he told us that last night. You leave for Wisconsin in two days. Tomorrow night we'll have the family dinner, so this is the last night he can be with her."

He blew out his breath in disgust. "Like some lovesick kid. Can't even leave her alone for one day."

Caroline sighed, not wanting to fight about that right here. "He just wanted you to know so that you wouldn't worry when he didn't make it back with the wagon. He said he'll bring the team in after supper."

"Don't know why he bothers to let me know anything," he muttered. "Nothing I say or do makes any difference."

Again Caroline let it pass. She was about to turn and go, when she saw that the two men had unhitched the other horse from the wagon and were bringing it into the corral. Joshua went up and gave Caroline a perfunctory kiss over the top rail. "I'll be home about six," he said, then turned to intersect the other two men.

Curious, Caroline decided to see what would happen next. She recognized this second horse they were bringing in. He had been in Joshua's stables for many years. For a long time, he had been called just Red, being sorrel in color. In the last few years he had become Old Red.

Still in most of his harnessing, Old Red came forward at a steady, plodding gait. Joshua reached out and took him by the strap of his bridle. He waved the other two men back, then started walking Old Red toward the mare.

Immediately her head came up and her ears lay back. Her eyes started to roll again. Speaking softly, moving slowly, Joshua made a wide circle so that when he started in toward Elena he was coming at her head on. Old Red lifted his head and snuffled quietly. Elena shook her head, as though still trying to clear the weight of Joshua, then snuffled back. Joshua stopped and waited for a moment, then moved forward again, even more cautiously than before. Elena was wary, but she stood her ground. Ever so slowly now, stepping back to walk beside Old Red and not in front of him, Joshua eased forward. In a moment the two horses were head to head.

They sniffed at each other for a moment, then dropped their heads so they were side by side. Gingerly, Joshua reached out again and began to rub behind Elena's ears. She shuddered slightly, as horses do, her flesh rippling back in little waves. Her tail was flicking back and forth, but steadily now, not in any kind of excitable pattern.

Joshua stood there, speaking so low that his voice was only a murmur. Caroline watched in amazement as Elena's head finally came up and her eyes were calm again. Joshua took her by the halter rope, and still holding on to Old Red's bridle, he began to walk the two horses, with him in between. Around the corral they went. Once. Twice. Old Red plodded along without hesitation. And soon Elena was doing the same.

After the third circuit, Joshua came to a stop next to where the harnessing lay on the ground. He motioned with his head for one of the men. The younger one came forward, moving slowly so as not to startle her again.

"Take their heads," Caroline heard Joshua say. Then he stepped around and picked up the bridle from the pile of harnessing. Almost in slow motion, he brought it back around to Elena's head. He held it out for her to smell. He rubbed it along the side of her face. Back and forth, talking gently all the time. And then almost before she realized it had happened, Caroline saw that he had slipped the bit between the mare's teeth and then had the bridle on over her head.

Old Red looked as if he were asleep on his feet. His eyes were half closed and his head half down. Elena would keep moving her head across to touch his for a moment. He would push back at her, then return to drowsing. In five minutes she was completely harnessed. Coming back around, Joshua took the horses and walked them out the gate and to the wagon. One more minute had them hitched up and the teamster drove the wagon out of the yard.

Joshua was a little surprised to see Caroline still there. He came back over to see her.

"I can't believe that was the same horse I saw when I first got here."

He laughed softly. "Don't give me the credit. That Old Red, he's like a wise old grandfather with a granddaughter going out with her first suitor. She just needs a steadying influence, that's all."

"Joshua?"

He didn't look up from reading his copy of the *Warsaw Signal*.

"Joshua!"

He lowered the paper slowly. "Caroline, I don't want to talk about it. All right?"

The "it" he referred to was the clash between him and Will that had happened half an hour before. Will hadn't gone straight to Jenny's house. Finishing early at the dock, he had decided to come home and wash up before going back to the Pottsworths'. Joshua couldn't bear to let him come and go without firing off at least one of his usual barbs. To everyone's surprise Will had shot to his feet, his eyes blazing—normally he just gritted his teeth or looked away. "I'm going to the pineries, Pa. We leave day after tomorrow. If you'd rather I didn't see Jenny tonight, that's fine. Find someone else to go north with you and I'll just see her after you've gone." And with that he had stomped out of the house.

Caroline just shook her head in weariness. "Actually, I don't want to talk about it either. Savannah wants you to come and kiss her good night."

"Oh!" Feeling rather foolish, he laid the paper on the table and stood up. As he walked past her and up the stairs, she didn't meet his eyes.

"Hi, Papa."

"Hello, sweetheart. Are you ready to go to sleep?"

"No." It was petulant and angry. "But Mama says I have to."

"That's right. It's after eight o'clock."

"But I'm a big girl now. I'm four years old now, you know. I'm almost five."

He laughed as he sat beside her on the bed. "You little wart. You're not going to be five for another"— he calculated quickly—"six months."

"Livvy doesn't have to go to bed when I do."

"And Livvy's almost fourteen. Baby Charles goes to bed at seven."

"I'm not a baby," she said.

He leaned over and kissed her on the forehead. "No, you're not, Savannah. You're Papa's great big girl."

"Then can I stay up just for a little while, Papa? Please?"

He shook his head. This was how it was with her. Every night was a major negotiation. When he gave an inch, she demanded five more. If he held firm, then she would settle for the inch. She had raised stalling to an art form. He stood up and pulled the sheet up around her neck. "Savannah, it's late. And Mama and I need to talk."

Her deep blue eyes were round as half-dollars, and almost black in the half light. "Is Will going to run away, Papa?"

Startled in spite of himself, he reared back a little. "No, Will is going north with Papa, but he's not running away."

"Why are you angry at Will, Papa?"

"I'm not—" That was a little hard to deny after what had happened. "Will and I just had a disagreement. We're not angry with one another anymore."

"Promise, Papa. Promise Will won't run away."

He hesitated for just a moment, then smiled at her. "I promise."

"I love Will so much, Papa."

Once again, he reached down and kissed her, this time on the cheek. "I know you do, Savannah. And Will loves you too. You just stop worrying. Everything is going to be fine."

She snuggled deeper into the covers, and he saw that she had her favorite doll in bed beside her.

"Good night, my little sweetheart."

He made it to the door before she spoke again. "Papa, I'm thirsty."

"She's already had a drink." Caroline's voice came up to him from the bottom of the stairs. "She's already been to the bathroom. She's blown her nose and fixed her dolly and I put lotion on her sore elbow. She *is* ready for bed."

"That's it, then," he said gruffly, trying not to smile. "Do you want me to shut your door?"

Savannah shot up to a sitting position. "No, Papa!" She hated to have her door closed.

"Then you lie down and go to sleep."

"Yes, Papa. Good night, Papa."

"Good night, Savannah."

When he came back down, Caroline was in the parlor, standing beside the table where he had laid his paper. As he came in, she looked up. "Why do you read this stuff?"

He came over to stand beside her, immediately on the defensive. "Thomas Sharp puts out a good paper."

"Thomas Sharp is a bitter anti-Mormon, and he uses his newspaper to sow hatred and bigotry. After what happened with Will that day, how can you bring it into the house and flaunt it before his face? That was why he was angry, you know. He thinks you do it just to spite him."

"Well, I don't," he snapped. "What do you want me to read? The *Times and Seasons*? Sorry, but I hear quite enough about the Church just living here without reading a whole newspaper devoted to it."

She let that go, knowing this would go nowhere. In two days he would be leaving her, and Will would go with him. She didn't want these last nights to be filled with contention. She turned and started away.

But Joshua was smarting now. First Will had lashed out at him, now his wife. "You think I'm wrong, don't you? About Jenny. Well, I'm telling you, Jenny Pottsworth is not the girl for my son, and the sooner he gets that into his head, the happier he'll be."

"Your son has the right to decide for himself which girl is right for him and which is not." She hadn't meant it to, but the "your son" came out with just the slightest touch of rebuke. Joshua winced inwardly at that. He had legally adopted Will and Olivia a few years ago, but both were from Caroline's first marriage. They were not his natural children, though now he never considered them anything but.

"Joshua," Caroline said, pleading now, "Will is going to the pineries with you. Don't you understand what that means for him? He doesn't want to go. He thinks he's going to lose Jenny. And maybe he will. But he's doing it for you. So can't you let him have this last night or two without trying to make him feel like a fool?"

"She's the one who's making him the fool. Everyone knows how she's throwing herself at that Stokes boy. Doesn't he have any pride at all?"

"I'm sorry, Joshua," she said. "I can't take this tonight. I'm going for a walk."

"Yeah, yeah!" he muttered. "I'm always the rotten father, aren't I? It doesn't matter what's best for Will. Let's not hurt his feelings. Let's not tell him the truth."

She swung around on him. Her voice was low and filled with anger. "I don't mind you telling him *the* truth, Joshua. But that's not enough for you. It's not just *the* truth you care about, it's *your* truth. What *you* think, is always the way it is. He can't be baptized because *you* don't like it. He can't like Jenny because *you* don't like her. He has to go to Wisconsin because *you* think it's best for him."

"Maybe so," he retorted hotly. "But mark my words, by spring he'll thank me for getting him away from her. I hope Jenny does marry Andrew Stokes. I hope she's four months with child by the time we come back. Maybe then he'll get her out of his head."

Caroline's chest rose and fell as she stared at him, not believing that he couldn't see that he had just proven her point. Then she took a deep breath, fighting for control. "Do you know something, Joshua?"

He was wary now. "No, what?"

"As I watched you today, with Elena and Old Red, I was amazed."

That surprised him. He hadn't expected this turn in the conversation.

She was staring at the floor now. "It's ironic, isn't it?"

"What?"

Now she looked up at him, and her eyes were glistening. "Joshua, you know your horses better than you do your own son." And with that, she turned and walked down the hallway and out into the night.

Lydia stood across the table, watching as Nathan toyed with the last of the meat on his plate. His eyes were down and it was obvious that his mind was a long way from anywhere on Granger Street.

She turned around, looking to where young Joshua and Emily were piling up the supper dishes at the sink. "Joshua, why don't you and Emily take Elizabeth Mary outside and play for a little before it gets dark."

Young Joshua's head came up sharply and he stared at his mother. Emily's eyes got big. "Really?" she said.

"Yes. The dishes can wait for a while. Go on, now."

"What about Josiah?" young Joshua asked.

Lydia looked around. The baby was in the high chair his Uncle Matthew had made for him when he was born. He was still eating the corn Lydia had cut from off the cob, concentrating intently as he tried to pick up each kernel with his fat little fingers. "He's fine. I'll watch him."

Nathan finally looked up, as if waking from sleep. At this particular Steed household, nothing happened after supper until the table was cleared, the dishes done, and everything put in its place. There were no exceptions. Young Joshua saw the puzzled look on his father's face and leaped into action before Nathan could contradict Lydia's order. "Come on, Lizzie. Emmy, you get Lizzie's sweater."

In hardly the time it took to take a full breath, they were out the door. Once they were gone, Lydia came over and sat across the table from her husband, stretching out to put her hand in his.

"What brought that on?" he asked.

"I'm ready to hear what you have to say."

He started a little, then almost immediately grinned. "Do you suppose we've been married too long?"

She laughed lightly. "No. Now I only know when something is on your mind. When I know *what* it is, then maybe we'll have been married too long."

"I think you already do."

"You're thinking about having to leave me in two more days."

"Yes, partly."

"What else?"

"About Will and Joshua."

She shook her head. "Caroline said Joshua just won't let it be."

"I know." He sighed. "I hate the thought of leaving, but I'm glad I'm going to be up there with them."

"I know," she agreed. "Now I'm beginning to wonder if I told Will the right thing when I told him he needed to go."

"You did," he answered firmly. "If he didn't go, I'm not sure Joshua would ever quite forgive him."

"But . . ."

He smiled again at her perceptiveness. "But this isn't just about Jenny. Joshua sees this as his chance to work on the other problem."

"What other problem?"

"Will wanting to be a Mormon."

She started to answer, then the impact of what he had just said sunk in and she stopped, nodding slowly.

"Joshua has openly said it to Carl. Get Will out away from all this Mormon influence and he'll come to his senses about that too."

"Especially with Joshua coaching him," she confirmed.

"That's right." He reached out and laid a hand on hers. "And it's not like that crew Joshua's hired are some of the world's more spiritual giants. Oh, there's a few good brethren among them, but the bigger share of them are teamsters or day laborers. And he's going to have to hire a lot of locals up there."

"You need to be there for Will, Nathan."

He nodded. "The closest of our camps will be only about a mile from where Joshua plans to cut timber. I'll get to see Will once or twice a week."

"Will is still struggling too much with his own doubts," she murmured. "He doesn't need Joshua hammering at him day after day with no one else to talk to." She was talking quickly now, not letting herself think about Nathan's leaving. "I'm glad you're going to be there."

She got up and walked around the table to him. Josiah, seeing her pass, raised his arms, but she just smiled at him. She pulled Nathan up to face her, then cuddled in against him, ignoring Josiah's protesting squawk. She buried her head against his chest, not wanting him to see the first of the tears that were starting to come. "I can hardly wait for Christmas," she said faintly.

———•———

The three-quarter moon was softly diffused through a high, thin layer of clouds, leaving the landscape muted and ghostly.

Will was glad for it. Though cool enough that Jenny wore a shawl, it was a perfect night. The moon had risen in the afternoon, looking like some transparent globe pasted up against the bright blue eastern sky. Now it was on the latter part of its journey, heading toward the western horizon, huge and golden and beautiful. It left a shimmering path across the river below them.

They were standing beneath a young hickory tree up on the bluffs, just a few rods off of the Nauvoo-Carthage Road. Will reached up and snapped off a small branch, then slowly began to strip the leaves into shreds and let them flutter to the ground.

"It's a beautiful moon tonight, isn't it?" he said, gazing out across the city below them.

"It's perfect. Just perfect."

"It'll be full in a few days. And then it will have to get full two more times before I get back to see you again."

"Don't, Will."

He turned to look at her.

"Let's talk about something else. Please."

"It won't make leaving you any easier," he growled huskily.

She turned and looked up at him. His eyes moved slowly across her face. Her skin was translucent in the pale light, looking like some gossamer veil. Now her hair was combed out and full, glinting like harvest wheat as it cascaded over her shoulders and down her back. Her lips were parted slightly, which only accented their full richness. Her eyes were large and dark and dizzying.

He stepped forward and took her by the shoulders. For several seconds they just looked at each other; then she tipped her head back just a fraction and slowly closed her eyes. Gingerly, hesitantly, Will bent his head and kissed her. Though he had kissed her a few times previously, now it was as if he had never kissed her before. The sweetness of it was almost startling to him, and he feared that once it ended he would not be able to recapture it in quite that same way ever again.

When he finally straightened, she did not open her eyes, or move her head. So he kissed her again. This time her arms came

up and went around his neck and she kissed him back. Her longing was as poignant as his. Her tenderness matched his own.
And he was proven wrong almost in an instant—the second was
far sweeter than the first.

Finally, he stepped back, a little dazed. "I . . ." He grinned,
shyly now. "That was nice."

"Yes," she murmured. She put her arms around his chest and
leaned against him. "Very nice."

He put his arms around her now as well. "I'm going to miss
you, Jenny Pottsworth."

"Then don't go," she said softly.

He looked down at her, a little taken aback. "What?"

She stepped back, her eyes wide open now and fierce with
intensity. "Don't go, Will."

"Jenny, I have to go. You know that."

"No!" she exploded. "Tell your father you have to stay. Don't
leave me."

"Jenny . . ."

"Do you want to leave me, Will?"

"You know I don't. It's all I can think about anymore."

"Then don't," she said, as though it were really that simple.

"I made a commitment to my father, Jenny. I can't back out
of it. Not in light of everything else."

"Everything else?" she cried. "What do you owe him? If it
weren't for him, you'd be baptized by now."

"No," he said slowly, "I'm not sure I would be. I—"

"Will, I know you love him. And rightly so. And that's
what's holding you back. If your father was a Mormon, you'd be
one by now."

He hadn't thought of it in quite that way, and finally he
bobbed his head once. "Maybe so, but talking about ifs doesn't
buy much in terms of making things better. I'm sorry, Jenny. I do
love Pa, and I've promised him that I'm going with him."

"Oh!" She whirled away, hugging herself as though suddenly
chilled. Now her voice was contrite. "I know, Will. I know. I'm
sorry. I promised myself I wouldn't make this harder."

"It's all right." He moved to her and put his arms around her waist from behind, pulling her against him, feeling the warmth of her body against his chest as she continued to keep her arms folded. But she leaned back against him, liking the feel of being in the circle of his protection.

They stood that way for several minutes, only moving enough to turn and face the river and the moon again. Finally, Jenny straightened a little. "Will?"

"Yes."

What she said next came out with considerable hesitancy. "When Matthew went to England, he . . . he asked Jennifer Jo if she would be promised to him."

He didn't release her, but now he was very still. "Yes, I know."

"I . . . Have you even thought about that?"

He let her go, turning her around to face him, suddenly and keenly feeling her vulnerability. "Yes, Jenny, I have. I have thought about it a great deal."

"And?"

"I'm not sure if that's what you want," he finally said, groping for words to express why he hadn't talked about it before. "I don't know if I could bear it if I asked you and you turned me down."

"And you think I would?"

"I thought you wouldn't marry someone who wasn't a Mormon."

"What if you promised me that you will be baptized?"

That took his breath away a little. It was a bargain, pure and simple, that she was offering him. It was more than he dared to hope for and, at the same time, more than he could comfortably commit to. "And if I did?" He spoke very quietly now. "Then would you agree to be promised to me?"

She tried to hold his gaze, but she couldn't and finally turned her head aside. "I'm not sure if I can bear to have you leave for six months, even if you do come home for a visit at Christmas."

His eyes were hooded now, and his face was grave. He was

glad she wasn't looking at him. "Suppose I promised you I would
be baptized, and I stayed home . . ."

"Oh, yes, Will," she cried, turning to face him again. She
went up and kissed him hard. "I would be promised to you this
very night."

It was the most curious sensation he had ever experienced.
A shaft of pure joy jolted through him, blazing through his being
and lighting it up like the first rays of the dawn. To think that
she would say yes if he asked her to marry him—it was more
than he could have hoped. But at the same time, the coldness
swept in as well—dark, permeating, total. She was asking the
two things of him that he could not give, not without compromising too much. Slowly he began to shake his head. He stepped
back. "I have to go, Jenny. I have to."

For what seemed like an eternity, she looked at him with
those enormous eyes. Then finally she nodded, and forced a
fleeting smile. "I understand."

"Do you?"

"Yes, Will. I really do." Now the smile broadened. It was
forced still, but it was her earnest effort to make him believe her.
Then before he could ask her any more questions, she slipped
her arm through his. "Come on," she said, with forced brightness. "It's too beautiful to stand around here moping. Let's walk."

They did, not talking much now, just being together.
Tomorrow night, the last night before their departure, Will and
Joshua and Nathan would be at the big family farewell dinner.
So this was Will and Jenny's last night together for a long time,
and they both knew it.

And now that you know I can't promise that I'll be baptized, and
that I have to go to Wisconsin, now what would you say if I asked you
to be promised to me? Would you say yes with the same excitement in
your voice that I heard a minute ago?

But Jenny didn't bring up the subject again, and Will didn't
have the courage to ask her that question unless she did. He
couldn't. Because he was afraid he already knew what her answer
would be.

On Wednesday, they caught the first morning steamboat headed upriver. There were well over a hundred men leaving, between Joshua's crew and the brethren called to the pineries by the Church. The temple was moving along well now. The Nauvoo House—the hotel that would not only be a place for entertaining the increasing number of important visitors to Nauvoo but also provide accommodations for Joseph and Emma's family—was under way as well. Lumber for these two projects, as well as for the burgeoning growth in the city, was a critical necessity.

All the Steeds were there to see their three men off. Joshua was ebullient. Although he would certainly miss Caroline and the children, this was a new adventure for him. Since the exploratory trip the previous winter, he had been anxious to get back and start cutting timber. If his projections were right—and in reality, they were most likely quite conservative—by spring he would make a small fortune. And he would share that with Will. At eighteen, his son would be a well-to-do businessman in his own right. Then he could have any young woman in the city, and not just be fawning over the Pottsworth girl.

Will was subdued, but not downcast. He and Jenny talked quietly off to one side until they heard the whistle, and the boat came around the great bend in the river. Then he gave her a quick kiss and went over to be with his mother and sisters.

The smaller of Nathan's children clung to him. Elizabeth Mary was crying. Emily was trying to be brave. Young Joshua stood tall, showing his papa that he could be the man of the house as they had discussed the night before. Lydia had vowed that she would not cry. But at the last minute, as the boat docked and the gangplank came down, the baby suddenly started to wail. Josiah could barely say "Papa," but somehow he knew Nathan was leaving. He held out his arms for his father and started to scream. And that broke down the last of Lydia's resolve and she began to cry too, shushing him and rocking him back and forth.

They watched and waved as the boat backed out away from the dock, then started forward again, paddles churning furiously, black smoke belching into the crisp morning air. Some of the people started moving away then, but the Steed family stayed until the boat rounded the curve of the river and disappeared behind the trees. Then they too started back toward Steed Row.

Grandpa Steed was carrying Josiah now. He was the only one who had been able to calm him down. Caroline handed Charles to Olivia, then moved swiftly up to walk beside Lydia. They looked at each other, eyes glistening. "It's only about ten or eleven weeks until they're back," Lydia said, trying to put a cheerful face on.

"I know," Caroline said, trying to smile through her tears. "But it already seems like a month." And then, surprising Lydia, she moved closer to her and put an arm through hers. "I'm so glad Nathan will be up there," she said quietly.

Lydia turned, squeezing her arm in hers. "I am too, Caroline."

They didn't say anything more then. They just walked on, their shoulders occasionally brushing as they moved back toward town to begin the months of life without their husbands.

Chapter Notes

Wisconsin Territory proved to be a great blessing for the Saints. Most of the nearby timber, which was scarce at best on the northern plains of Illinois, was gone by the time Nauvoo was settled. Though the growing brick indus-try and the stone quarries provided important building alternatives, lumber was still a critical need for an exploding population. On 22 September 1841, a group of brethren left Nauvoo to go upriver some five or six hundred miles to Wisconsin. There on the Black River they established a lumbering colony that eventually would provide an astonishing amount of lumber for their brethren and sisters back in Illinois. (See *In Old Nauvoo*, p. 26; Dennis Rowley, "The Mormon Experience in the Wisconsin Pineries, 1841–1845," *BYU Studies* 32 [Winter and Spring 1992]: 119–48.)

Jessica Griffith had first started teaching school in Haun's Mill and found great joy and satisfaction in it, as well as a passable livelihood for her and Rachel. When she married John Griffith, he had encouraged her to continue, even though he was making a sufficient living to support them. Then John was killed and Jessica was on her own again. So when they came to Nauvoo and Joshua had helped the family start their first houses, a schoolroom had been part of the plans for Jessica right from the beginning.

It was on the back of the house, with a separate entrance. It wasn't a large room, and the low ceilings made it seem even smaller. But she could fit enough benches for twenty students comfortably and could push that up by four or five more if she needed to. Currently she had eighteen pupils—ten girls and eight boys—ranging in age from eight to seventeen. There was one wall with shelves for the few books she had and for the lap slates. And Joshua had given her a small desk with three drawers for her personal papers. But her latest and proudest acquisition, purchased while she was in Warsaw looking for textbooks, was a four-by-four black chalkboard. It had been used before, but there was only one scratch and it had a tray for the chalk and eraser.

When the knock came—not at the side door but at the front of the house—Jessica was at that chalkboard, teaching the mysteries of adding and subtracting fractions. The students were laboriously copying the problems on their own slates, rubbing out the errors with the heels of their hands. So she ignored the knock. But as it grew louder and more persistent, the children would not. They kept turning their heads and giving her questioning looks. Finally, she motioned to Kathryn McIntire, who got up and slipped through the door that led into the main part of the house.

A minute later Kathryn returned, but she didn't go to her seat. She walked to Jessica. For the students, any focus on the blackboard was now gone. A little frustrated, Jessica stopped and turned to her foster daughter. "What is it, Kathryn?"

"It's a man. He insists on seeing you." And then before Jessica could ask the obvious question, she shrugged and added, "I've never seen him before."

Jessica frowned, looking toward the door. "Did you tell him I am in class?"

"Yes. He apologized but said it has to do with the school. He says he must see you."

Jessica sighed and handed the chalk to Kathryn. "All right."

As she left, she heard Kathryn rap sharply on the desk with a book to stop the tittering the interruption had created. She walked down the short hallway to the entry. He was standing just inside, hat in hand. He had been looking at the furniture in the parlor to his left, but at the sound of her footsteps, he turned. The first thing that caught her attention was how big he was. Jessica was a small woman, no more than five two or three, and this man looked six foot two or three, with broad shoulders and large hands. His hair was thinning—he was probably in his mid-thirties—but it was combed straight back so it didn't show as much. His clothing was plain but well kept. His shoes had been blacked recently and showed little dust.

"Yes?" she said, moving to face him.

"My name is Solomon Garrett."

"Jessica Griffith," she said. He extended his hand and she shook it. It was surprisingly gentle for as large as it was. Now that she was next to him, she saw that though he was broad through the chest and shoulders, he wasn't as tall as she first thought. He was no more than six feet. Maybe an inch or two less than that.

"I apologize for the interruption. I was hoping to arrive before you started class." She noted that his voice had a touch of a Southern accent—Virginia, or Kentucky, she guessed. Maybe Tennessee.

"That's all right," she said. "How may I help you?"

There was an embarrassed smile. "I wondered if I might attend your school today." He laughed at the reaction that triggered. "I guess I'd better explain before you answer."

"Won't you come in and sit down?" she asked, trying to hide her surprise. Attend school? Hadn't he seen her sign outside which specifically stated she was not accepting adults?

"I'm from Ramus. I assume you know where that is?"

"Vaguely," she admitted. "I've not been out that way."

"It's about twenty miles from here. It's northeast of Carthage about eight or nine miles."

She nodded. Ramus had been founded completely by Latter-day Saints and was now the largest settlement of Mormons outside of Nauvoo.

"I am employed by the common schools of Hancock County and am here as their representative."

In spite of herself, Jessica felt a little lurch. Public schools—or "common schools," as they were popularly called—were on the rise in Illinois and across America. She guessed that in a few years, they would be the norm and not the exception as they were now. Most of the schools in Nauvoo—and many other Illinois communities, for that matter—were subscription, or private, schools. In subscription schools, basically a teacher set up a school in his or her home, enrolling whoever might be interested and could pay the set price in cash or goods. But with the rapid growth of certain communities, the state and local governments were taking more of an interest in the education of their citizenry. There was talk of setting up standards for teachers and perhaps even making them pass qualifying examinations. As a saloon keeper's daughter, Jessica had never had much formal schooling. As an adult she taught herself to read and write, but she was afraid that might not count for much with an examining board.

He noted the shadow that crossed her face and smiled kindly. "Oh, this is nothing to be concerned about. We've just had reports of the excellent job you are doing here, and the board has asked me to observe your teaching to see if we might get some ideas."

"Oh." The relief was plain in her voice. "Why, of course. Won't you come in?"

She started down the hallway; he followed. "I won't disrupt your class?"

"You won't bother the students at all," she said with an easy laugh. "But the teacher might be a different matter."

Which showed that Jessica was still a little flustered, for the class totally disintegrated after she brought the stranger in, introduced him, and invited him to sit down. He sat awkwardly on a bench, his knees jutting up to almost eye level. But after a time, and after she gave them several of her most severe looks, the students settled down again and class continued.

———◆———

Tuesday, Nov. 9th, Nauvoo, Illinois

My dearest Nathan,

I know that I wrote you just a few days ago and that the two letters may arrive together, but three things have happened in the last few days that I felt I must tell you about. First, and most surprising, Jessica is gone! The whole family is still in a bit of a daze. Here is what happened.

About three weeks ago, Jessica had a visitor come to the school. His name was Solomon Garrett. He lives in Ramus out east of Carthage. Someone told him about Jessica's school and gave him such a glowing account of what she was doing that he decided to come and see for himself. Well, he sat through one day at the school. He didn't say much, just sat there and watched. When it was over, he thanked her and left. She thought it strange, but that was that. Then three days later he reappeared and asked Jessica if she would be willing to move to Ramus and be the schoolmistress of the new common school they are starting there. He has been hired by the county to supervise establishing common schools. Jessica was flabbergasted. At first she said no, but when he told her that the county would pay her an allowance for each student enrolled, it was just too wonderful to pass up. There will be three teachers. Jessica will be the head of the school and will also have a large class, so she will get about a dollar per day. After watching Kathryn help Jessica with the students, Mr. Garrett offered Kathryn a position too. Because she is still learning, she will get only about fifty cents a day, but between the two of them, that's a handsome wage indeed.

So Friday, she closed her school. There was much disappointment among the students, but Mr. Garrett—or I should say Brother Garrett, he is a Latter-day Saint—says the board insists on starting the school in Ramus this season. Saturday he came with a wagon and they packed up and moved to Ramus. As you can guess, there were many tears at her parting. The cousins will miss Rachel and the boys terribly. Jennifer Jo is especially distraught to know that she and Kathryn will be parted. And Jessica will be sorely missed. Thankfully, Ramus is only a day's ride away and we can see them from time to time. But this leaves "Steed Row" with an empty house now, and we are all a little saddened.

The second bit of news happened yesterday. At 5:00 p.m., we assembled at the temple site and there the baptismal font for the temple was dedicated. Oh, Nathan, how I wish you could have been here with us for that wonderful occasion. Brigham Young gave the dedicatory prayer, which was most sacred and appropriate to the occasion. In spite of colder weather, there was a large crowd. The font is so beautiful! I can hardly wait for Christmas when I can walk up on the bluff with you and we can see it together. A temporary roof and walls have been built around the font itself to keep out the weather until the upper floors of the temple are completed. The basin for the water is about four feet deep and on the outside is finished with panel work. Following the model used by King Solomon in Old Testament times, the font sits upon the backs of twelve oxen, four on each side, and two at each end. Joseph says these represent the twelve tribes of Israel. They are carved out of several layers of pine planking which have been glued together, and their features have been patterned after the finest-looking steer that could be found. The carving is of such quality that the wooden oxen are a striking likeness of the original. It is a work worthy of the Lord's house.

Now to the third, less happy matter. This morning I decided it was time to have a frank talk with Jenny P. It has been about seven weeks since your departure, and as yet she has not written Will a single letter. She says she cannot bring herself to write because she is torn in her feelings. I find that a poor reason. I think it will hurt Will more if she doesn't write, but I think Jenny hopes you will tell him what I say to you and spare her the task of doing it. I am disappointed with that, but am writing so you can tell him if you think it best. I feel that he needs to know before he comes down for Christmas. Caroline agrees that your judgment in the matter is to be trusted.

Jenny is a sweet girl and pure of heart but very confused at the moment. She says she truly loves Will, but as I watch her with Andrew Stokes, the confusion is only in her mind. Her heart is given to Andrew. He has asked her to be promised to him and presses her continually about the matter. She demurs only out of loyalty to Will—or is it guilt? She told Andrew that she will not give him an answer until Will is home at Christmas and she can talk to him. But Will's inability to get an answer about the Church only confuses her feelings for him all the more. Will may be tempted to return home to try and fix things, but tell him it will only make things worse.

Well, I shall close. I miss you, my darling, and count the days until Christmas. Each of the children make mention of you every night in their prayers. Elizabeth Mary last night asked Heavenly Father to be sure and not let any bears eat you. I'm not sure where she got that idea. I have said nothing about bears to her. I, of course, miss you most of all. I love you, my darling. Hurry back to us as quickly as possible.

All my love,
Lydia

By the way, will you ask Will if he has read the parable he and I talked about before he left? It is in Luke 18.

———•———

Lydia's letter to Nathan arrived in the Black River camp on Saturday, the twentieth of November. In the Mormon camp, worship services were held each Sabbath morning, and Will always went up to join them, ignoring the grousing it brought from his father. After worship services, Nathan took Will aside, walking out into the trees that surrounded the Mormon lumber camp.

"Will," he said, once they were alone, "I want to show you something."

"Yes?"

They stopped and Nathan fumbled inside his coat, then withdrew the letter. "This came yesterday. "

Will's eyes lit up and he grabbed for it.

Nathan snatched it away. "No, it's not from Jenny. It's from Lydia."

"Oh." There was sharp disappointment in Will's eyes. He reached for it again, this time without enthusiasm.

Nathan still held it back. "First, you've got to promise me something."

"What?"

"Promise me we'll talk before you go making any decisions. All right?"

"Talk about what?"

"Promise?"

Now he had Will's full attention. "What's in that letter?"

"Uh-uh. Not until you promise."

A little peeved, Will finally shrugged. "Sure. Why not?"

Nathan reached up and handed him the letter. "You can read the whole thing if you like."

Now Will was openly wary. He took the letter, walked a few steps, and leaned against a tree. Nathan found a stump and sat down, not watching him. For almost five minutes there was hardly a sound except for the soft rustle of the wind in the treetops above them. Nathan knew when Will got to the part about Jenny Pottsworth, because he could hear Will's breathing tighten, and once or twice there were almost inaudible grunts. He turned in time to see Will turn back one page and start that part over again.

Finally Will folded the letter back together again, then came and handed it to Nathan.

"Will, I—"

He raised his hand. "Can we talk some other time, Uncle Nathan? I think I'll just walk for a while."

"Will, I know—"

"I made you a promise, and I'll be keeping it. But I'd just like some time to think about it now. All right?"

"All right." Nathan put the letter away and stood up.

Will shoved his hands into the pockets of his coat, then turned and walked on down the path without another word.

"Maybe I'll come over and see you sometime this week."

One hand came up and waved, then went back into the pocket, and then he was gone.

———•———

Will and a "Scandie"—or Scandinavian—named Olaf Knutson watched Jean Claude Dubuque from the riverbank, waiting for direction from him. He was out in the middle of the logjam that blocked a third of the river's progress and kept snagging new logs and adding them to the pile as fast as they appeared. The three men had been upriver about half a mile, making the back cut on a huge pine tree, when word came that there was a jam in the river. There was never any question about who would go. "Frenchie," as everyone but Will called him, was the oldest and most experienced logger in camp and the acknowledged expert on breaking up logjams. He had an uncanny knack for finding the "key log," that log which hung up on a rock or a snag and caused everything behind it to become blocked. Until the key log was freed, the jam wouldn't move. Will and Olaf were only there to provide the muscle to help the Frenchman break it up.

For now they both waited while the older man assessed the situation. Both of them carried a pickaroon, an axlike tool but with a pointed head that was driven into a log so it could be "horsed" around by sheer muscle power. Will also carried a cant hook, a five-foot-long pole with a hinged steel hook on one end. This was used for the same purpose and was particularly useful in working with logs in the water.

Will brought the collar of his coat up around his face. There was a north wind blowing today, promising snow later tonight, and the air was biting cold. Both he and Ollie, as he called the Norwegian, wore thick beards to help ward off the cold. That was a new experience for Will. He had never let his beard grow, not even at sea. It came out dark and thick, like Joshua's, and made him look older than Ollie, even though the Scandie was twenty-one and Will was only seventeen. They wore thick coats, two pairs of pants over their long johns, and heavy woolen caps pulled down over their ears. The clouds from their breath whipped away almost instantly.

Many of the logs had a thin sheen of ice across the bark, which made what Jean Claude was doing all the more dangerous. But he wore hobnailed boots and seemed oblivious to the heightened risk. Will watched in amazement as he worked his way across the logs toward the front end of the jam. Though the man was in his fifties, he was as nimble as a tree squirrel. Short, wiry, tough as the whipsaws they used on the trees, the Frenchman seemed tireless. He too carried a cant hook and used it to help maintain his balance. If he stepped on a log which started to roll on him, he was off it in an instant and on to another.

Will heard the crunch of footsteps and turned around. To his astonishment, he saw Nathan coming toward them, walking swiftly. "Well, hello," Will said.

"Hello, Will."

"This is a surprise."

Nathan grinned from beneath his heavy wool cap. "Thought it would be. Where's your pa?"

"He's out cruising along Roaring Creek." To "cruise" was the lumberman's term for going through the forest and estimating where the best places to log would be. "Nathan, this is Olaf Knutson. Ollie, this is my uncle Nathan Steed."

"Yah and hello," Olaf said in a heavy accent as they shook hands.

"When you said you might come see me this week I didn't think it would be in the middle of the day."

Nathan shot him a quick look. "Just wanted to see how Will Steed was getting along."

Will grimaced. "Well, I haven't run off to Nauvoo, if that's what you mean."

"That's good," Nathan said, keeping his voice light.

Will's frown deepened. "To be honest, I've thought about it. First, I was hurt. Then I was devastated. Now I'm just plain mad. Not about her choosing Andrew over me. That's her choice, I guess. But why didn't she say something? Why didn't *she* have the courage to write and tell me? I'm sorry, but I don't accept her reasons."

He swung the pickaroon at a small tree beside him, burying the point two inches into the wood. "I think that was really rotten, to put it bluntly. So right now, I'm not inclined to even walk across the street to see Jenny Pottsworth, thank you."

Nathan nodded, deciding there was no sense pursuing that, not here with the other man. They could talk more at the noon mealtime. He turned and looked to where Jean Claude was bent over, peering into the heart of the jam. "This is a bad one," he commented.

Will turned too, glad for a chance to change the subject. "Yeah. Somebody should have caught this sooner, before we sent all those logs downriver this morning."

The Frenchman looked up at that moment and waved. If he was surprised to see Nathan there with the other two, he gave no sign. "I think I've got it. Will, Ollie, come on out. But be careful. Those logs are very treacherous."

"I don't have my spikes," Nathan called, "but I can work in close to shore."

"Good." Jean Claude called to Will again. "Give him the cant hook. You bring the pickaroon."

Like Jean Claude, both Will and Ollie wore calked boots— the loggers pronounced it "corked"—which gave them some bite into the wood of the logs. Will led the way, hopping cautiously from one log to another, staying on the front end of the jam where the logs were wedged in tightly and wouldn't roll on him. Ollie followed. In a moment, they stood beside the older man.

Jean Claude took Will's elbow in one hand and pointed with his cant hook. "There, that's the one." He reached in and tapped it.

The log the Frenchman was hitting lay almost at right angles to the current. Through the gaps between the logs, they could see the water rushing beneath their feet. It was hissing angrily. Will couldn't see the far end of the log because of the other logs which had piled up on top of it, but it was at least a thirty-footer, maybe more. And it was three feet thick at least. And there lay the problem. One end had caught on a rock. The log had swung sideways and hung up on a second rock. It was like dropping a thirty-foot-wide dam in the river. Immediately, several other logs slammed in against it, wedging tighter. Then the power of the current began forcing logs up and over and down and under, like jackstraws being tossed in the wind. The place where the three men stood, right near the front of the jam, was now four or five feet out of the water.

Jean Claude was shouting now over the roar of the river. "We're going to have to get these other logs off it or it'll never budge." He pointed. "We'll start with this top one. Will, you get on that end. Ollie, you take the middle."

The pickaroons and the cant hook dug into the uppermost log, another one that was about three feet thick and about twenty-four feet long. "Ready! One. Two. Three. Heave!" They laid their weight into it, and the log moved about a foot. It had to go up and over the end of another log, and so it was like moving close to a thousand pounds of dead weight straight uphill.

"One. Two. Three. *Heave!*"

Will's foot slipped on a patch of ice and he went down hard on one knee. He cried out as he felt the rough bark take off the skin, even through his pants. But the log moved another foot and a half. One end swung up and over the log beneath it. The Norwegian yanked his pickaroon free and gave the log a final shove with his boot. Like some great fish, it rolled slowly over the other logs and fell with a mighty splash into the river directly in front of the jam. It almost buried itself in the water, then surfaced again and slowly started to move away.

As the three of them worked the center of the jam, moving a second log and then a third, Nathan did what he could from where he was. His boots were not calked, so he stayed within a few feet of the bank. Should he slip, he would not be in too deep and be swept away. As much as he could, he shoved the smaller logs out into the current where they would clear the jam and not add any more pressure to it.

Out farther, the three men had moved all but the last log that had ridden up and over the key log. "All right," Jean Claude said, pausing for a moment to catch his breath. "Once we get this last one out, then we've got to relieve the pressure from behind it a little. But watch it. If it starts to break up, then—"

But the very thing about which he was warning them happened at that instant. There were several hundred tons of logs being driven by a swift current pushing against the key log. But now the weight holding that log down against the rocks was almost gone. With a sudden, violent lurch, one end of the key log broke free, turning vertical to the current. The logs started to crack and screech as they rubbed against each other, looking for new space to fill. The Frenchman's cant hook almost went flying as he lost his balance. But his agility was incredible, and with a yell he jumped to another log, steadying himself with the long tool in his hands.

"It's going!" he screamed. "Off! Off!"

Olaf Knutson didn't need to be warned. The key log had been a big one. When it gave way, it was as if a dam had just been blown and now the reservoir behind it rushed in to fill the vacuum. Suddenly everything was moving. The Norwegian went down to one knee, was up in an instant, and started for shore, frantically hopping from log to log. As he leaped from one big log to a smaller one—only two or three feet in diameter—the logs around that one started to move forward, feeling the tug of the unshackled current. The smaller log, with nothing to wedge it in, rolled under the sudden weight of the lumberjack. There was one sharp cry and Olaf Knutson plunged into the black water between the logs.

"No!" Will shouted. Jean Claude wheeled around at his shout. There was the flash of a hand clawing at the log, then other logs moved in to fill the newly opened space. In an instant, the logs were wedged in solid again.

"Get off! Get off!" the Frenchman screamed at Will. "I'll get Ollie." In three great leaps, Jean Claude was over to the spot where the Scandie had fallen, shoving at the logs beneath his feet in a rage, trying to open up another hole.

Frozen in horror, Will still clung to the handle of the picka-roon that he had buried in the log on which he was standing. He tried to pull it out but it wouldn't budge. As he reached down with both hands, suddenly the log beneath him heaved up as another log was shoved under it from behind. His left foot slipped, and as he scrambled for balance his right foot hit a thin crust of ice that sheeted one part of the tree. His feet shot out from under him, and he dropped hard. He gasped with shock as both legs were plunged into the icy water and pain shot through his tailbone. Two things saved him at that moment. First, he had dropped to the log like a man jumping astride a horse. Second, the pickaroon pulled free as he grabbed at it. Had it held and he been holding it, his weight would have been too high and the log would have rolled beneath him. As it was, as the log began to turn in the water, he fell forward, like a man clutching around a horse's neck, and threw his full weight in the opposite direction. Slowly his "mount" righted itself again.

"Will! Will!" Vaguely he was aware of Nathan's shouts off to his left somewhere. But he had no time to look. He had broken free from the jam now and the log was caught by the rushing current. Slowly it swung around, turning parallel to the shore. Will was now riding backwards downriver. Even if he could get to his feet, there was no longer a "floor" of logs for Will to use to get to shore.

"Will, watch out!"

He turned his head to see Nathan. He was on shore, running, pointing, screaming, waving frantically. Will couldn't make out what he was saying. Then beneath the water his foot, which was rapidly going numb with the cold, struck a rock. He jerked it away just before it was pulled beneath the log and crushed. Now he realized his danger. He was going through the worst of this narrow stretch of rapids. There were rocks everywhere around him, making great curls in the water. And the water was filled with logs, like huge battering rams coming at him on every side.

"Watch out! Behind you!"

He turned his head and gasped. One jagged black rock, two or three feet across, was big enough that it came six or eight inches out of the water. Around it, the current roared its fury at being blocked. And Will saw that his log was heading straight for it. Wildly, he started paddling, trying to pull the log out of its course. But he was too late. There was a sickening crash as the end of the log slammed into the rock. Will hung on, and for a moment he felt a quick burst of elation. He hadn't been thrown off. But then, as the current caught his end of the log and turned it sideways, the log started to slowly roll over. He threw his weight the other way again, but this time it was too late. The last thing Will saw before he was sucked beneath the water was Nathan racing along the bank, screaming hoarsely, tearing wildly at his heavy wool coat.

Gradually, Will was conscious of a deep, violent shaking all through his body. Then after a moment his brain came awake enough to realize that what he was feeling was his body's response to the cold. Cold enveloped him, invaded him, penetrated him, permeated his every body cell. He had never known such horrible, numbing, deadening cold before.

"We've got to get back to camp or we're all going to freeze."

He recognized the voice and the French accent, and opened his eyes. Jean Claude Dubuque was crouched over him, looking down into his face. When he saw Will's eyes open, his face softened. "Ah, *mon ami*," he said quietly. "How are you?"

"I am so cold," Will answered, barely able to speak through the terrible chattering of his teeth.

Jean Claude nodded grimly. Only then did Will realize someone was holding him in his arms. He looked up into Nathan's face and saw his uncle smiling down at him. "Hello, Will."

Will tried to sit up and felt Nathan's arm helping him do so. He looked back at Jean Claude. His hair was wet. There were tiny beads of ice on his neatly trimmed mustache and beard. His coat was soaking wet. Will looked up at Nathan. His hat was gone. His hair was wet and already visibly stiffening in the frigid air. Unlike most of the other men in the camps, Nathan continued to shave each day and wore no beard. His cheeks and chin were almost blue, his eyebrows frosted with ice. Unlike

On the Black River

Jean Claude, he had no coat. Like the Frenchman, his clothes were dripping wet. Then Will realized that Nathan's coat was covering his own body. And miraculously it was dry. And then he remembered Nathan running, and pulling off his coat.

"Did you get me out?" he asked weakly.

"He did, my friend," Jean Claude said. "You are very lucky to be alive."

Will's head jerked to one side. "Olaf?" he asked. "Where's Ollie?"

Nathan just shook his head.

Jean Claude looked away. "I could not get to him in time," he said, his voice barely a whisper.

"No," Will cried, shocked deeply.

"We must move swiftly," Jean Claude said to Nathan, taking one of Will's arms. "There is no time to delay. We must get moving, get our bodies working, or we shall all perish."

Wednesday, November 24th, Black River

My dearest Lydia,

This will be just a quick note. Due to some unusual and tragic circumstances which I will explain at some later date, a man was drowned this morning. Will nearly was too. Two men are going to take the man's body to La Crosse in the morning and will take this letter out with them.

Your letter about Jenny came Saturday. I showed it to Will the next day. I decided he had a right to know what was going on. It has been a difficult thing for him. He was determined to go home right away, but after what happened today he has had a change of heart. He is writing Jenny tonight to tell her to marry Andrew if that is what she wishes. Now, however, he has decided he won't go home at all, not even for Christmas. Perhaps I should have tried to talk him out of that decision, but, all things considered, I think it is for the best. Jenny can move on without being torn further. Please let Caroline know. Will wanted to write to her tonight too, but felt he must write Jenny. He said to tell his mother that he will send her a letter explaining everything in the next mail.

Joshua knows none of this yet. He has been gone from camp and won't be back until later tonight. Will wants me to be with him when he tells Joshua and so I am here in their camp tonight. I hope Joshua doesn't rejoice too openly over the matter. Will's heart is still very tender over all of this.

Here is the problem that creates. I think that it is best if I stay on here with Will rather than go home. Please, my darling, I know this will be disappointing news, but hear me out. I have talked this over with our leaders, and they have agreed to let me move over here to start working with Joshua's crew on the day that Joshua leaves to go home. While it will mean a loss of a man to them, our camp is very low on supplies and on the most meager of rations now. Joshua's camp is better supplied and so my coming over will be one less mouth for the other camp to worry about.

Joshua still plans to go home. He has some kind of pressing business in Nauvoo that cannot wait. He had planned to leave a Frenchman here in charge, but when he learns that Will is not going, he will undoubtedly leave him as foreman. This is a mistake. The men like Will, but he is not yet eighteen. He cannot begin to handle them. Some are very rough. But if I am here with Will and I let the men know that we view the Frenchman as the true foreman, things should be fine.

There is a good part to this. Once Joshua returns (about mid-January, I hope) and is back with Will, I will go home. And not just for a brief visit. I will stay there until spring and then come back only long enough to help them get the rafts of lumber downriver to Nauvoo. So while my not going home for Christmas is a disappointment, when I do return to Nauvoo, I will not have to leave again for almost three more months, and that will be wonderful.

I have so looked forward to being home with you and the family for Christmas, but when all is taken into consideration, I

think this is best. Kiss the children for me. Help Caroline understand that this is best for Will. It truly is.

Your loving husband,
Nathan

By the way, you were right. I was totally shocked with your news
about Jessica. And yet it is great news. The steady salary will be
a great boon to her.

Chapter Notes

It is a common misconception that Nauvoo was the only planned settlement for the Latter-day Saints at this time in Illinois and that all but a few of
the Saints lived there. In actuality, under Joseph's direction, there were seventeen planned communities of Saints in Hancock County, Illinois. Some, like
Ramus, were established totally by Latter-day Saints. There, Mormons made
up virtually the whole population. There were also missionary settlements—
that is, places where Mormons were sent to live among non-Mormon popu-
lations in hopes of having a positive influence on them for the Church. (See
S. Kent Brown, Donald Q. Cannon, and Richard H. Jackson, eds., *Historical
Atlas of Mormonism* [New York: Simon & Schuster, 1994], p. 56.)

We do not know at what point Ramus started a common school, but we
do know that it was during 1842 that the movement for local governments to
help fund common schools in Hancock County began in earnest (see *In Old
Nauvoo*, p. 238).

Payment for teaching was usually based on the number of students. A
husband noted that his wife received $1.50 per student per quarter, which was
a healthy supplement to their family income (see *Women of Nauvoo*, p. 58).
One woman received 877 mills (one mill being equal to one-tenth of a cent)
per student per one hundred days of teaching, or less than one cent per day
per student. Another teacher received four cents per student per day. (See *In
Old Nauvoo*, pp. 239–40; this book contains a whole chapter on schools in
Nauvoo during this time, pp. 237–52.)

Lydia's description of the temporary baptismal font, which was dedicated
on 8 November 1841, is drawn from a detailed account given in Joseph's history (see HC 4:446–47). Two weeks after its dedication, members of the Twelve
performed forty baptisms for the dead, the first done in the font (see HC 4:454).

Will you just stop grumping?" Caroline said, pulling Joshua's arm in against her. "We won't stay long."

"Caroline," Joshua replied, "you know I have to start back for Wisconsin in the morning. If I don't get the books at the stable straightened out before I go, they won't get done until April or May."

"Joshua, we owe it to Joseph and Emma to be there. With us owning a store, it will look like we're unhappy that Joseph is giving us competition."

"Don't be ridiculous. Nauvoo is growing so fast it could take two or three more stores and still be fine. Besides, Joseph will never notice whether we're there or not. I have got to get those books done."

"Well," she said, with just a touch of tartness in her voice, "you didn't seem too concerned about the books the other evening when John C. Bennett and some of his associates invited you over and you stayed until after midnight."

"That was business. We were talking about a possible partnership on—"

"This is business too," she said sweetly, but there was no mistaking the firmness in her voice. "We are going to welcome a fellow store owner to town."

Joshua opened his mouth, then shut it again. He knew when he wasn't going to win. "All right," he finally growled, "but we can only stay for a few minutes. Agreed?"

"Agreed."

When Joshua left for Wisconsin in September, Joseph's store was still in the first stages of its construction. He had been impressed with the size of the foundation—far larger than any normal country store—but thought little else about it. Now as they came south along Granger Street and approached Water Street, they could see the store directly ahead of them. There were several horses and half a dozen carriages drawn up out front. People were milling around outside. Joshua slowed his step, not hiding his surprise. It was a large building and made entirely of brick. There was a full second story and large windows.

"Well," he said with new respect, "that's quite the building. Joseph did this?"

"Yes, and Emma says Joseph hasn't spared any expense on the inside either. It will be the finest store in Hancock County."

"Good for him," Joshua said. And he meant it. "All right, let's get this over with."

———————◆•◆———————

The opening of the Prophet's store was *the* event in Nauvoo, at least for the moment. Inside the store it was controlled pandemonium. The store was packed with people. Joshua shot Caroline a pleading look, but she merely smiled, looking around. "Oh, Joshua, this is wonderful," she breathed.

He let his eyes follow hers and had to admit she was right. If you forgot about the crush of people, this was an impressive room. The ceilings were high—probably ten feet, he estimated. At the very back on the left side there was a small alcove which

"Wonderful. She and the children came over for a few days at Christmas. She's as happy as I've ever seen her."

"There is no one who deserves it more than she does."

Caroline looked around. "Joseph, this is incredible, what you've done here."

"It is, Joseph," Joshua agreed. "You've done yourself proud."

"Do you really think so?" Joseph said eagerly. "That means a lot coming from someone as astute as you, Joshua."

"I'm very impressed." Joshua made a face as he looked at the crowds. "Has it been like this all day?"

The Prophet laughed with pure pleasure. "From the moment we opened. Isn't it wonderful? Come, let me show you around."

———————

"Now, was that so bad?" Caroline said. They had reached the corner of Sidney Street where Joshua would leave her and turn west for his freight office.

"No," he admitted. "It was good that we went. Joseph is so pleased to show off what he's done."

"It's wonderful, isn't it?"

"I hope it does well for them."

She looked up at him quizzically. "With crowds like that, you're worried?"

"If you're selling things at a loss, the more customers you have, the worse off you are."

"Whatever made you say a thing like that?" Caroline asked, a little dismayed.

"Well, sometimes Joseph is too good-hearted," he said. "You remember what happened to his store in Kirtland. He basically didn't have the heart to say no to anyone and they cleaned him out. He admitted to me today that one of the reasons he's opened this one is so he can be of service to those in need."

"And is that so bad?"

"Not if you can afford it. What Joseph needs is a good business manager to run his temporal affairs so that he can devote his time to the Church. He'd prosper more that way."

Somehow it touched Caroline that he had that kind of concern. She slipped an arm through his, then glanced up at him. "Are you volunteering?" she asked, only half teasing.

He gave a short laugh. "Sure. That would give the devil a good laugh, wouldn't it? Old Joshua Steed in partnership with the Mormon prophet."

She cocked her head to one side. "Actually, if you want my opinion, I think the devil doesn't have much hope for old Joshua Steed anymore."

The door to the freight office opened and a man stepped inside, shaking the snow from off his coat and hat. Joshua looked up from the ledger book; then his eyes widened a little. "Well, John, good evening."

John C. Bennett, mayor of Nauvoo, smiled back at him. "Evening, Joshua. You're working late enough. Aren't you supposed to be leaving in the morning?"

Joshua laid the pen down. "Yes. That's why I'm here. I have got to get these books straightened out before I leave again." He shook his head ruefully. "I've got myself a good foreman here, but he just doesn't have a head for figures."

He stood and came around the desk, gesturing toward the two wooden chairs in the corner. "Sit down."

Bennett shut the door behind him and removed his hat and coat. He hung them up, then came and sat down across from Joshua. "I saw the light in the window and hoped it might be you. Do you have a moment that I could discuss a matter with you?"

Joshua shrugged. "If it doesn't take too long."

Bennett sat back, crossing his legs. "Heard your wife and boy would like to join the Church."

Joshua frowned, caught off guard by that. "Only my wife. My son has looked into it, but he can't make up his mind."

Bennett smiled benignly. "I suppose that wouldn't be your first choice for either one of them."

"Probably not," Joshua said warily. This was something he didn't discuss. Even he and Caroline had come to a silent truce on the matter.

Bennett was watching Joshua, looking as if he was weighing whether or not to say anything further. "I would guess that to a man like you, there are some things we believe in the Church that are downright troublesome."

"More than one," Joshua allowed carefully. Bennett was Assistant President to Joseph, almost the equivalent of being in the First Presidency. Surely he wasn't fool enough to try and proselyte Joshua Steed. Even Joseph knew better than to try that.

Bennett looked around, verifying that they were alone. "Actually, if you promise not to tell anyone, there are some things that bother me too."

That totally caught Joshua from the blind side. "Oh?" he said slowly.

"Yes." Bennett sighed. "I'm really quite concerned."

"Like what, for instance?"

Bennett's voice dropped to a conspiratorial whisper. "Spiritual wifery."

"Spiritual wifery?"

"Yes."

"What in the world is that?"

Again Bennett looked around. Then he got up and walked to the door. He pulled the curtain back a little and looked out, first in one direction, then the other. Joshua tried not to show his irritation. This was just a bit melodramatic. Bennett picked up his chair and moved it closer to Joshua. "You must swear to me that you won't tell anyone what I am about to tell."

Now Joshua didn't try to hide his annoyance. "How can I swear to something before I've heard what it is?"

"Point well taken," Bennett conceded. "But you must promise that you won't just banter this around. It will have serious consequences."

"I don't believe in bantering stuff around," Joshua said dryly.

That was signal enough. Bennett leaned forward, and Joshua saw a sudden cleverness come into his eyes. "You know about all the rumors and things that led to my . . . to my attempt to end my life?"

"I heard them," Joshua said bluntly. "I don't put much stock in rumors."

"As you know, then, I was accused of moral turpitude and immoral behavior with some of the finer ladies of the town."

"I told you, I don't put much stock in rumors."

"That's good, but a lot of other people do. My reputation was almost ruined. My physician's practice dropped by half." He sat back, measuring Joshua shrewdly. "In fact, your own sister was once my patient, but has never been back."

"My sister?"

"Yes, Rebecca."

"I didn't even know she had gone to see you."

"See there?" Bennett said triumphantly. "People are ashamed to admit they have any association with me."

Joshua was thoroughly irritated now. And he didn't have the patience for this. Not now. He wanted to be home with his family, and he couldn't do that until the books were done.

Bennett sensed his mood and stopped dallying. "What would your good wife say about the Church if she knew Joseph was teaching spiritual wifery?"

"What is spiritual wifery?" Joshua exploded. "Just come out with it, man. What are you talking about?"

"I'm talking about a man's right to have more than one wife."

"I—" He stopped as the words registered in his mind. "Say again?"

"That's right," Bennett retorted, pleased with the reaction he had finally triggered. "In the Old Testament, Abraham had more than one wife. Jacob had four wives, remember? Well, Joseph claims he has been told by the Lord that this was his law and that men today have to live that law again."

Joshua sat back slowly, studying the man very carefully now, feeling a swell of revulsion at what he was hearing. "I don't believe you," he finally said.

That didn't seem to faze Bennett in the least. "That's just it, Steed. No one does. I was accused of taking advantage of those poor women, but I was only practicing spiritual wifery. And I was doing it with the permission of the First Presidency, including Joseph himself."

"From what I hear, all you were doing was fancy talking those women into your lair."

"I thought you didn't put much stock in rumors," Bennett shot back, pleased to have tripped Joshua up. "I merely taught them the doctrine taught me by Joseph. If a woman is your spiritual wife—that is, if she is destined to be your wife in the hereafter—then there is no wrong in having relations with her now. She's your wife. How can you commit adultery with your own wife?"

Joshua remembered one particular vicious rumor, one that seemed to be more than just feathers in the wind. "And what if that woman already has a husband?" he asked, his voice hard and brittle now.

Bennett knew instantly what he was referring to. "You mean like Sarah Pratt?"

"That's exactly what I mean. Is it true that you were having relations with her?"

"Yes."

"While her husband was off in England?" He spat it out with complete contempt.

"Joseph granted her to me as my spiritual wife. It matters not whether she has been married to another. At least, that's what Joseph said."

"I don't believe you. I don't care for a lot of what Joseph says and does, but he's not an immoral man."

"That's just it, Joshua!" Bennett cried. "He doesn't believe it is immoral. And I didn't either. Not at first. Now . . ." He passed his hand before his eyes "Now I'm beginning to have doubts about my actions. Now I'm beginning to see that perhaps I have been guilty of a great sin. That's why I tried to end my life, Joshua."

Joshua was shaking his head. It was like having something dead in the barn. The smell of it was so terrible you didn't even want to go in and see what it was, let alone find it and drag it out for burial.

Bennett's eyes were filled with cunning now. "You don't believe me? Why don't you ask Sarah Pratt? Why don't you ask her about the night Joseph came to her and asked her to be *his* spiritual wife? She was shocked and horrified, and told him that she could never consider such a proposal from a married man. Joseph finally backed down. He made her promise not to say anything, lest Emma should find out about it."

For a long moment, Joshua considered that. Then he shook his head. "If Mrs. Pratt was so horrified about this spiritual wifery idea, then why did she take up with you?"

Bennett looked startled, realizing his error, but he recovered smoothly. "Because I was not already married."

"But she was!" Joshua exploded. "Come on, man. Your story doesn't make sense. And besides," he added, remembering something else Nathan had once told him, "I thought you *were* married, John. I heard that you left a wife and children back in Ohio."

That hit home. Bennett shot to his feet, clearly angry. "You can scoff all you want, Joshua Steed. I've come to you because I'm deeply troubled. I've come to help you keep your wife from making what could be a grave mistake. I can't go to those in the Church because in their minds Joseph can do no wrong. And because of what has happened, no one will believe me."

"That's a problem you've got, all right," Joshua cut in pointedly.

"I have other names," Bennett said, sniffing away Joshua's comment with disdain. "If you want to know the truth, go ask Melissa Schindle. Go talk with Martha Brotherton. They'll tell you tales that will show you what is going on all around you at this very moment."

Joshua suddenly stood, tired of it all. "John, listen. I must finish these books tonight, and then I must go home and pack. My son and my brother are up north trying to run a lumber camp and a sawmill for me. I need to get back up there and join them. I don't have the time to be out snooping around."

Bennett was cowed a little by the hardness in Joshua's eyes. "It doesn't have to be tonight, Steed. But if you're a wise man, when you return in the spring, you'll look into what I say."

"Fair enough. When I return, I shall do that. And if what you say is true, I shall join with you and every other honest and decent man in seeing that Joseph Smith is not only exposed but brought to trial before the courts of this land."

Bennett stood now too. "That's all I ask, Joshua. All I want is to make amends and—"

"But," Joshua cut in sharply, "if I find that you are lying, as you have been known to do, then know this, John. You shall rue the day that you came to me, for I shall run you out of this town with your tail between your legs."

Will pushed the Bible forward a little on the table in his small room. Kerosene was scarce in the camp, and so he had the lamp turned low. He was looking down at the eighteenth chapter of the Gospel of St. Luke, finally ready to keep a promise he had made to his Aunt Lydia almost four months ago. He had read it a couple of times before and gotten nothing out of it. Now he was ready to try and see why she had recommended it to him.

He hunched over the Bible and his lips began to move softly as he read to himself. "'And he spake a parable unto them to this end, that men ought always to pray, and not to faint; saying, There was in a city a judge, which feared not God, neither regarded man: and there was a widow in that city; and she came unto him, saying, Avenge me of mine adversary. And he would not for a while: but afterward he said within himself, Though I fear not God, nor regard man; yet because this widow troubleth me, I will avenge her, lest by her continual coming she weary me. And the Lord said, Hear what the unjust judge saith.'"

He stopped, his brows furrowed in concentration. This was what had happened before. What did this strange parable have to do with his finding an answer? He started over, reading it carefully through a second time.

A phrase caught his eye. "Men ought always to pray, and not to faint." He sat back, frowning a little. That was an odd thing to say. Men normally didn't faint while they were praying. Then, with a bit of a start, he remembered something. To "faint" had another meaning. It wasn't heard much in America anymore, but he had heard it while he was in England, and Jenny and her mother would sometimes use it still. To faint meant to quit or to give up. Even Derek had once said to him, "Don't faint on me, Will."

Was that it? Was Lydia telling him not to give up in his search for answers? His brow furrowed. But he *had* been praying. Since last January. That was a full year now. Then he shook his head. Maybe so, but in the last two months, he had fainted. He had all but quit searching.

He read again the description of the judge and the woman who came to him. There was no question but what the judge was a hard man. He wasn't motivated by any feelings about God, and he had no concerns for his fellowman. Will shook his head. He had met men like that. Some worked for his father right now. They weren't pleasant people to be around.

And then he saw something about the widow he had missed. There was no mention (not a very specific one, anyway) of what her problem was, what she wanted help on, but when the judge wouldn't listen to her—not surprising, considering his nature—she didn't give up. He straightened, suddenly understanding. She didn't *faint*. That was the lesson of the parable.

He read it again, slowly now. And then the words of the judge hit him. "He said within himself, Though I fear not God, nor regard man; yet because this widow troubleth me, I will avenge her, *lest by her continual coming she weary me.*"

He was suddenly amused. So this hard-hearted, merciless

judge had finally given in, not because it was the right thing to do, or not because he had the slightest feelings of pity for the woman, but because the woman was driving him to distraction. Like having a buzzing fly in a quiet room, or a particularly persistent gopher in the garden. One finally acted, not out of conscience or duty, but simply to rid oneself of the annoyance.

He sat back, his mouth pulling down. "And that's what I'm supposed to learn about prayer?" he asked of the lamp. "Do I have to pester God to the point that he finally gives in?"

Instantly he knew that wasn't right. Once again he read it slowly, carefully, forcing himself to think about the words. Lydia had said the parable was a little troublesome. A little? Was God like this unjust judge? And then a thought came into his mind. Years ago, when Will had been particularly troubled by a story in the Old Testament and kept challenging his mother about it, she had said simply this: "Will, if you read something in the scriptures that you don't understand, just remember, the problem is in you, not in the scriptures."

Will leaned back in his chair, staring out at nothing, letting his mind begin to push at the problem. It was like a knot in the rigging of a ship. Swollen with salt water, or stiff with ice, at first it looked as if it might be impossible to undo. But you just kept working at it, pushing here, prying there, pulling hard, then starting all over again. And eventually it gave way.

God was a caring being. He called himself Father. That surely said something, didn't it? He wasn't like the hard-hearted judge. So why would he demand that his children ask for something over and over before he responded? It wasn't just to make them grovel. That wasn't the kind of God he believed in. So why say a man must pray and not faint?

In his own way, Will was very methodical and precise. He liked to sort things out and have them neatly in their place. Like working a ship. If you left things lying around, the next thing you knew, someone would get hurt, or you were left empty-handed in a crisis. So he took up the pen and wrote down what had just occurred to him.

If a hard-hearted, unjust man will respond to someone who is persistent, won't a loving Father do so all the more?

Pleased that he had come to that on his own, he laid the pen aside and went back to the book. He read the parable yet again. "But wait a minute," he said aloud, remembering something he had read elsewhere. He couldn't remember exactly where it was, but he remembered the concept clearly. *God knows what we need before we even ask him.* The Savior had said that too. You didn't kneel down and ask the Father for something and have him say, "Oh, I didn't know that."

He picked up the pen and wrote quickly again.

God already knows what we need. Before we even ask! So why do we even have to ask at all?

He set the pen aside, pushed the paper away, even shoved the Bible back. Why had Lydia sent him to this odd little story? Why did she feel this would help him? And more important, Will *had* been asking. Why hadn't God answered him? Maybe in the past few weeks he hadn't been completely diligent, but before that he had. He had truly wanted an answer. Didn't God hear him? Didn't he care? He immediately shook that off. *No,* he thought, remembering his mother's counsel. *God isn't the problem here.*

"Ah!" he said softly as his head came up. Now he grabbed the pen and his hands literally flew across the paper.

If the problem is not with God, then the problem must be with <u>me</u>.

Now he was up, leaning over to stare at what he had written. *So what's wrong with me?* he asked himself. *Why can't I get an answer?* Had he stopped searching as a way of punishing Jenny? Was the Lord displeased with—

He stood bolt upright, staring across the room at nothing.

That was it! He shook his head, a little dazed by the stunning clarity of the thought that had just come to him. *That was it!* He let out his breath in a long sigh of amazement. *Of course!*

He sat back down at the table, and this time he wrote very slowly, wanting to remember exactly how it had come to him.

We do not pray to God over and over to change him. We pray over and over to change us!

He read it, and reread it.

His mind racing now, he took the blotter and carefully dabbed at what he had written. Now he understood. And it was not just the parable that he understood. He knew now what he had to do. With determination, he pushed his chair back and dropped to his knees.

———•———

Dawn was just coming when he found it. His back was stiff, his eyes blurred and burning from the dim lamplight. He had read from the Book of Mormon most of the night, but then, ten minutes ago, he had gone back to the Bible again. And then he stumbled across it, quite by accident.

It was in the seventh chapter of the Gospel of John. It was so simple, he read right over it at first. "If any man will do his will, he shall know of the doctrine, whether it be of God, or whether I speak of myself."

Through the weariness something suddenly clicked. He read it again. There it was. In one marvelous, clarifying instant of light, Will Steed had his answer. *If ye do his will, ye shall know!* He straightened, very slowly, feeling the weariness flee like a storm cloud before the sun. *Do! And then know!* He had been doing just the opposite. He wanted to know, and then he would do.

He read it again. And a fourth time. Then with a cry of joy, he shut the Bible and dropped to his knees again.

Chapter Notes

The store built by Joseph and Emma was on the corner of Water and Granger Streets, just one block west of Joseph's original home. It was finished sometime in December 1841, and opened for business on 5 January 1842. The descriptions of the interior come from a letter Joseph wrote to a friend (see HC 4:491–92). Now popularly known as the "Red Brick Store" because of its exterior, the upper floor had offices for Joseph and the First Presidency and became the "headquarters" of the Church for a time (see CHFT, p. 243). Today the store and the Homestead, Joseph and Emma's first Nauvoo home, are part of the properties owned by the Reorganized Church of Jesus Christ of Latter Day Saints.

Joseph Fielding returned to Nauvoo during the latter part of November 1841 after a four-year mission to England, including presiding there as mission president. On 28 November 1841 the Prophet met in council with the Twelve at Brigham Young's home to discuss various matters and to hear Fielding's report on the English mission. It was during this meeting that Joseph Smith made the following statement: "I told the brethren that the Book of Mormon was the most correct of any book on earth, and the keystone of our religion, and a man would get nearer to God by abiding by its precepts, than by any other book." (HC 4:461.)

Joshua arrived back at the Black River camp on Monday, January seventeenth, just before sundown. As he came into camp, it was sixteen degrees below zero, with a stiff wind blowing out of the north. It had been eleven days since he left Nauvoo and about six weeks since his departure from camp.

The men had just finished their supper as he arrived, and they poured out of the dining hall to greet him. It was not that they were so happy to see the owner and boss of the company, but rather that many of the crew had been hired from the Nauvoo area and knew that Joshua would bring letters and small packages from their families. So in spite of the cold, they swarmed around him and the big bag he'd brought with him.

Nathan gladly received the package and letter from Lydia, but unlike the others, he didn't immediately move off to be by himself while he opened it and read it. Instead, he stepped back, watching Will. Will pretended only casual interest, but every time Joshua reached down into the bag for the next letter or package, Will's eyes tracked his every movement. When the bag was emptied, Will had a letter from his mother and one from Olivia, on which Savannah had proudly written her name and little Charles had been encouraged to scribble, but nothing else. Without a word, he turned away.

Nathan stepped forward again. "Nothing from Jenny Pottsworth?" Nathan asked, just loud enough for Will to hear. Will turned back, fully aware what Nathan was doing, but still wanting to hear the answer for himself.

Joshua glanced at his son and then shook his head slowly. "Jenny and Andrew Stokes are officially engaged. They plan to marry next month and move across the river to Zarahemla."

Will faltered for an instant, and then his head bobbed once. "Good. That's what I told her to do." And with that, he turned and walked away.

As Joshua turned and went into the dining hall, he finally looked at his brother, who had followed him inside. "I'm sorry about Jenny, believe it or not. I'm not sorry that he's lost her, but I hate to see him hurting like this."

"I know."

"But it's for the best."

"Probably," Nathan agreed. "But that doesn't make swallowing it any easier." He gave Joshua a warning look. "And telling him it's for the best isn't what he needs right now."

"I know." And then Joshua surprised Nathan. "I'll be easy on him," he said slowly.

"Good."

Joshua turned back to face Nathan. "Well, I'm back. What are your plans?"

"Pack up and leave tomorrow."

"Don't blame you. Lydia is most anxious to see you."

"And I her."

"Nathan?"

"Yes?"

"Thank you."

"For what?"

"For staying here with Will. I know he needed someone. I'd have stayed if I'd thought I could help, but . . ." He sighed. "You were better for him. Anyway, thanks." His voice was suddenly tight as he tried not to show emotion. "And thanks for that day in the river. When I think how close we came to losing him, I . . ."

Nathan waved it away. "You know that I love Will like my own son, Joshua. You've got a fine boy there."

"I know. And when things settle in a little, I'll tell him so too." A little embarrassed that he should be that open, he cleared his throat. "Come on," he said gruffly. "Where's that food you're talking about?"

———●———

They lingered over the supper table, Joshua talking about the news of home, Nathan reporting on how things were in the camp. Joshua started to say something about John C. Bennett's visit, then changed his mind. He knew how Nathan would react to it, and until Joshua could verify or disprove it, there was no sense in stirring up the pot. After about half an hour, Will came back in and joined them.

"Guess what!" Nathan said.

"What?"

"Your father says that both Rebecca and Jennifer Jo are in the family way, due only a few weeks apart in the summer."

"Really?" That was the first genuine smile his father had seen on Will since his return.

"Isn't that great?" Joshua exclaimed. "Matthew is so excited. He just sits there and grins and grins at her."

"He'll make a wonderful father," Nathan volunteered. "All of the nieces and nephews adore him. In fact, from the time young Joshua was little, it's not ever been, 'Let's go to Grandma's house, or Grandpa's house.' It's been, 'Let's go to Uncle Matthew's house.' "

"And I'll bet Derek is tickled too, isn't he?" Will asked.

"Greatly," Joshua replied. "He's convinced it's another boy. Rebecca thinks it will be a girl. Derek doesn't really care, but another boy would be a great companion for Christopher."

They talked on, enjoying one another's company and the chance to sit back and visit before diving into the work again. But after another half an hour, Joshua stretched mightily, then yawned. "Sorry, but I've been on the road for eleven days. If you don't mind, I'll turn in."

"I'll see you before I leave," Nathan said.

"All right." He waved and left the small dining hall. Will watched him go and waited until the door closed behind him; then he looked at Nathan. "Did you say anything to Pa?"

Nathan looked up. "About what?"

"About my finding an answer."

Nathan shook his head. "I figured that's your place to do, Will."

He looked relieved. "I've been thinking about this a lot. I've decided not to say anything to Pa right now."

One eyebrow came up, but Nathan said nothing. He just waited.

"Since coming up here," Will began, speaking hesitantly, searching for the right words, "I don't know. Something special has happened between Pa and me. This thing with Jenny was driving a real wedge between us. But things have been much better now."

"Yes, they have," Nathan agreed.

"I . . . If I tell him that I've decided to become a Mormon, you know what will happen."

"Yeah," Nathan said glumly. There wasn't much question about that.

"I've decided I won't be baptized until Mother is baptized."

"Oh?"

"Yes. Once we get back, Mother and I can decide how to convince Pa that it's not going to hurt him if we join the Church. Together I think we can do it."

"Maybe," Nathan said slowly, not convinced, but not wanting to dash Will's hopes. "And if you can't convince him?"

There was a long silence; then Will answered, trying to say it firmly, but not quite putting the doubts out of his voice. "Then I'll not wait after that. The answer I got was that I had to live the gospel, then I would know. If I wait too long, I'll not be true to that."

"I see," Nathan said. "Are you going to tell your mother all this?"

"I've written her a long letter. Will you take it to her?"

"Of course." Caroline would be thrilled to know that her son had finally made his decision. She would also understand, better than anyone, what it would mean to Joshua.

"It's kind of ironic, isn't it?"

"What's that, Will?"

"Jenny wouldn't make any promises to me because I wasn't sure if I would ever be a Mormon. Now I'm sure, and it's too late."

"You didn't do this just for Jenny, Will."

"Oh, I know that," came the quick reply. "But . . ." And now there was no mistaking the wistful longing in his voice. "It's just ironic. That's all."

———•———

It was one of those glorious snows, with not even a wisp of a breeze. The huge flakes floated down like the finest of goose down, so gently and so slowly. At first only one or two came drifting down, but then the skies opened and they came in prodigious numbers. The ground was covered immediately, and in two hours there was a full four inches covering everything in the virgin mantle of white.

It was a perfect snow for making a snowman, or having a snowball fight. It was the second day of February, and the deep cold of the previous weeks had been broken by a brief January thaw. The temperature was just above freezing, so the snow packed easily and clung together just right. All over the city, tiny laborers grunted and called and pushed and shoved balls of snow together. Much effort went into the creation of snow people. Much also went into the making of snow forts and the creation of formidable arsenals. And all across the city, little boys—some in their thirties and forties—succumbed to the age-old temptation to go to war, laughing and squealing and crying foul when hit with the flying missiles.

On Steed Row it was no different. All of the cousins were out now, except the babies. They picked the backyard behind Jessica's house, because with no one living there now, the entire yard was unspoiled. There were eleven children in all, ranging in age from Olivia, who at fourteen was the oldest, to Caroline's little Charles, nearly two now, who waddled around in his snow clothes, barely able to bend over and pick up a handful of snow. Mary Ann, Lydia, Caroline, Rebecca, Melissa, and Jennifer Jo were all there to watch and supervise.

They were just finishing the heads on a snow family when a large snowball came hurtling over the fence and splattered on the ground just behind Emily and Olivia. They jumped, swinging around to see where it had come from. On the north side of Jessica's lot, along Mulholland Street, there was a slat fence. The slats were close enough together that they mostly hid anyone from view. Now, from behind the fence, another snowball was thrown. This one was lobbed up high, giving the children plenty of time to dart away, screeching in warning, before it too hit the ground with a solid whack.

Now all thoughts of the snow family were forgotten. Everyone, children and adults, turned to see who their assailant was. They could see a figure moving behind the fence, but there was no way to identify who it was. Young Joshua, always the daring one, armed himself and moved cautiously forward. As he approached the fence, a tall figure reared up, growling fiercely. He had a scarf wrapped around his face to hide his identity. There were squeals and screams and the children broke ranks and fled. Except for Joshua. He blanched a little, but held his ground, peering at the stranger, trying to see who it was. The man moved to the gate and entered the yard. Still not intimidated, Joshua rushed the man, hurling his snowball with all his might. It caught the man squarely in the chest. There was an agonized cry; then the man staggered back, clutching at himself as though hit by a cannonball. Gasping and wheezing, he sank slowly to the earth and rolled over, one leg shaking spasmodically in a last death rattle.

"I got him! I got him!" Joshua yelled. He scooped another handful of snow up and threw that at the downed man as well. That did it. The others charged in, pelting the writhing figure with a hail of snowballs. The man rolled away, then sprung to a crouch, his back to them, holding his arms up over his head to ward off the missiles. "I surrender! I surrender!" he yelled.

Melissa stepped up beside her mother, laughing. "Who is it?" she asked.

Mary Ann smiled, watching the children swarm the man under. "It's Brother Joseph. Who else?"

Suddenly with a roar, the "mortally wounded" came to life again. He snatched Elizabeth Mary under one arm and little Christopher under the other. "The snow monster has got you now," he cackled. "Back to the cave and I'll have you for dinner."

That brought a new wave of piercing screams, and the others rushed in to free their comrades. Just then, Savannah, who had broken free from the melee, came running up to the women. Tendrils of red hair poked out from beneath her stocking cap. Her nose and cheeks were as red as if she had put rouge on them. Her deep blue eyes danced with excitement. She had dumped a handful of snow into Joseph's face while the others had him down, and then thought it best to retreat from the fray before retaliation was forthcoming.

"Go get him, Savannah," Rebecca urged. "Go get Joseph."

"No," she said, her eyes wide with concern. "He said he's going to eat me."

Caroline reached down and poked the hair back in beneath the cap. "Well, if you don't help, he's going to eat Christopher."

That was enough. Off she went, running as fast as her little feet could move.

Finally, puffing like a winded horse, Joseph extracted himself from the children and, retreating under a barrage of snowballs, came over to join the women. The children closed in, hands filled with snowballs, but hesitant to throw when their mothers were in the line of fire.

"All right, children," Mary Ann said, holding up her hands. "Let's give Brother Joseph a rest for a moment." Reluctantly they retreated, waiting to see if he might return.

Chuckling, Joseph looked around the yard. "What a glorious day. I wish I dared bring Emma out into it."

"How is she, Joseph?" Mary Ann asked.

He laughed. "More than ready to have this baby, I think."

"Is it close, do you think?" Lydia inquired.

"Mother Smith and the midwife are guessing it will come within the week."

"Will you let us know when it's time, Joseph?" Lydia asked. "I'd like to be there to help."

Joseph reached out and touched her arm gratefully. "Actually, that's why I came by. I was hoping that you could. You're such a steadying influence for Emma."

Something in the way he said that raised Mary Ann's concerns. "Is everything all right, Joseph?"

"Oh, yes, I think so. It's just that . . ."

"We understand," Lydia said, remembering Emma's anguish at the loss of Don Carlos. She had still not fully recovered. "Just send one of the children. I'll come immediately and—" Lydia's mouth suddenly opened and she stared at something behind Joseph.

They all turned. A man had just stepped through the gate of the slat fence. He was bundled up against the cold, and his hat hid much of his face. When he saw that he had been seen, he raised one hand and swept the hat off. Lydia gasped. "Nathan?"

"Oh my word," Mary Ann whispered.

With a cry of joy, Lydia was off the porch and running hard across the snow. "Joshua! Emily! Lizzie! Look! Papa's home! Papa's home!"

———•———

They left the house just as it was getting light, bundled up in their winter coats and scarfs, their feet crunching softly in the snow that had fallen throughout the night. Lydia left a note for young Joshua telling him they would be back in an hour or so and to get some breakfast for the children. They had tried to find time together the previous evening, but it was not to be. The children needed to be with him. The family came over. And finally when they were alone, Nathan was exhausted. So this would be Lydia's time alone with Nathan, and she wanted it to be undisturbed.

Now they climbed the gentle slope that led to the top of the bluffs and the temple site. They walked slowly, savoring their time together. There was nothing profound in their conversation. Lydia was just catching him up on all the news she hadn't been able to put in her letters.

"Tell me more about Jessica," he said. "Is she happy over there in Ramus?"

"She should be."

"Why's that?"

"Well, first it is a grand opportunity for her. The school is doing very well and she gets a regular salary." She smiled up at him. "But more important, I think something might just come of this."

He looked puzzled. "What do you mean?"

"Solomon Garrett."

"Who is Solomon— Oh, he's the man who offered her the position?"

"Yes." Her eyes were dancing with excitement now. "He isn't married, you know."

He pulled up short at that. "He's not? You never told me that."

"No. He was married to a woman in Kentucky, but they were never able to have children. She died of smallpox several years ago and he's never remarried."

"Well, well," Nathan said, really surprised at that bit of news. If Joshua knew about this, he hadn't bothered to share it. *How like a man*, Nathan thought. "And you think . . ."

Lydia nodded. "Solomon brought her over for Christmas. He's a good man. Very kind and gentle. Very strong in his testimony of the Church. Rachel and the other children think he's wonderful."

"Has he . . . you know, said anything to Jessica?"

She shook her head quickly. "Of course not. It's only been three months since they met." She went suddenly stern. "And you're not to say anything to anyone else either. But one night when we were alone with her, all of us ganged up on Jessica. You know her. She won't speculate, but down deep, she thinks it just might work. Kathryn told us he comes over to their house two or three times a week."

"Well, I can't think of anything more wonderful," Nathan said with deep pleasure. "There's no one who deserves it more."

Suddenly he stopped, his head coming up. They had just crested the top of the bluffs, and the temple site was only a block ahead of them. "Oh, my," Nathan said in a low voice. "They've really been making progress, haven't they?"

When he had left for Wisconsin, the temple site had been one huge hole in the ground. They had still been completing the final courses of stone that would bring the foundation walls just above ground level. Now there was no more hole. The basement walls were completed and the trenches around them filled in. A temporary floor had been laid over the basement rooms, and the snow from the day before had covered it completely. The temple was now like a huge slab, sticking a few inches out of the ground, but perfectly flat on the top of it. And where there had been only two small wooden cranes on the site before, now there were three additional ones—tall ones, high enough to reach the upper floors. Between the three of them, they would be able to lift stones into place about anywhere on the walls. Nathan was impressed.

Lydia tugged on his arm. "Come on, I want you to see the baptismal font."

"You think it will be open this early?"

"I hope so." But when they went down the stairs to the front room, they saw that the door was locked. Disappointed, Lydia looked around. "Let's see if anyone is here yet." She immediately started for the small shack that served as the construction office. To their good fortune, this door was unlocked and slightly ajar. Lydia knocked and it immediately opened. Inside was William Weeks, temple architect.

"Oh, Brother Weeks," she said. "Good morning."

"Ah, Sister Steed, good morning to you—" He stopped, peering more closely. "Brother Nathan? I say, is that you?"

Nathan reached him and stuck out his hand. "It is, Brother Weeks. I'm just back yesterday from the Pine Woods."

"Well, I'll be." He shook Nathan's hand vigorously. "Welcome home." His New England accent was sharp and easily recognizable. "We received word that you would be coming home early. Is it true? Are the reports from the north as good as they say?"

"Yes," Nathan answered immediately. "Our camp was a little slower getting started than my brother's, given all the problems with that rundown mill we bought half-interest in, but it's fairly humming right now. Our brethren up there think we'll have eighty to ninety thousand board feet for you by summer."

"That's marvelous!" the architect boomed. "We can't put in the permanent flooring over the basement until we get that wood here, so that is good news."

"You've made great progress in spite of that," Nathan said.

"Yes. It's coming along very nicely." Then he brightened. "I have the plans right here. Would you care to see them?"

"Oh, yes!" Lydia exclaimed.

Weeks stepped back, inviting them inside. The shack was crowded and cluttered with tools and sheets of paper with diagrams and sketches on them. The plans were unrolled across a drafting table with a T square on them. He pushed that aside and pulled back the cover sheet, then two more that showed the plan for the basement level. "Let's skip the basement for now." He was to the third sheet now, and smoothed it out. "This is the main floor."

"Ah," Nathan breathed as he and Lydia bent over it. It was titled, "Grand Hall for the Assemblage and Worship of the People."

"It's very much like the Kirtland Temple, I'm told," said Weeks.

"It is," Nathan nodded. Weeks was a relatively new convert, a builder and architect originally from the eastern part of the United States. He had known nothing about the Church during the Kirtland years, but there was no mistaking the similarities between the two temple designs. All but the entryway of the main floor was given over to a large assembly room filled with rows and rows of benches. A neatly penciled note said these would be moveable so they could be turned to face either direction. That was the same as in the Kirtland Temple and for the same reason. Each end of the room was filled with the priesthood pulpits—Melchizedek on the west and Aaronic on the east. Thus, depending on which quorums were presiding, the congregation, by turning the benches, could face either pulpit.

"I'm estimating the hall will seat about thirty-five hundred," Weeks said.

"Thirty-five hundred!" Nathan echoed. "The Kirtland Temple didn't seat even a thousand."

"Around nine hundred," Weeks said. "At least that's what Joseph tells me." He pulled back the next three sheets, one after the other, commenting only briefly. The second floor had another large assembly room. The attic floor also had a central meeting hall, but it was smaller and there were several rooms off to each side. "Offices for the leaders of the Church," he explained, "and rooms for ordinance work."

"Ordinance work?" Lydia asked.

He shrugged. "Yes. Joseph hasn't said what those ordinances

are to be, but I've put them in." He reached for the next page, but hesitated for a moment before pulling it back. "Now, here's what I want to show you." With a bit of a flourish, he turned that page over.

"Oh!" Lydia said with a soft gasp of amazement.

"Oh yes!" Nathan said.

What they were looking at was the side elevation, the drawing of the building as it would look to someone standing outside looking from the south side. Weeks made no attempt to hide his satisfaction. "There it is," he said proudly. "What do you think?"

Nathan had heard Joseph speak of what the building would look like when it was finished, but it was one thing to hear it explained in words, it was quite another to see it visually represented. "It is magnificent," Nathan breathed. "Absolutely magnificent."

"Oh, yes," Lydia agreed.

The main part of the building was a large rectangle with windows in neat rows along it. On the top of the one end of the building—the front end—there was an additional third of a story above the roof line. From the center of that rose a gracefully rounded and tiered steeple which towered high above the rest of the building. This additional section and steeple robbed the building of any sense of squarishness and made the whole effect quite delightful.

"Are these pillars?" Nathan asked, pointing to the main bulk of the building. Evenly spaced along the full side were what looked like pillars of a Greek temple.

"Actually, they're called *pilasters*," Weeks said, proud to show off what he thought was one of his finest ideas. "A pilaster is kind of an imitation column, but it's only decorative. They help break up the flat expanse of that huge side wall."

"They're beautiful," Lydia said. "And what are these?" She was pointing to the base of one of the pilasters. There was a figure there, as well as on all the others, which looked like a crescent moon tipped on its face.

"Those are moon stones."

Both husband and wife looked at him in surprise. "Moon stones?" Nathan echoed.

"Yes." Weeks touched the drawing where the capital, or top, of each pilaster had another figure. "And these are sun stones. I'm not sure exactly what they'll look like when they're actually carved into the stone, but right now, they'll be a sun disk, with rays coming out the top. And here"—he touched figures of stars that were above each pilaster—"these are star stones."

"But . . ." Lydia was puzzled. "Why the moon, the sun, and the stars?"

Weeks chuckled. "Because Joseph asked for them." And then before they could comment on that, he sobered again. "Think about it for a minute. The stars, the moon, the sun—does that remind you of something?"

"The three degrees of glory," Nathan said with a sudden jolt of insight.

"Ah, yes," Lydia said, understanding immediately. One of the great revelations Joseph had received back in the early years of the Church taught that there were different degrees of glory in the afterlife and not just a simple heaven or hell. The Lord compared the glory of each degree, or place of dwelling, to various heavenly bodies—the celestial, or highest, kingdom being like the sun, the terrestrial like the moon, and the telestial, or lowest, like the glory of the stars. "What a wonderful reminder," she said.

Chapter Notes

The description of the Nauvoo Temple and its design both inside and out is factual (see *Encyclopedia of Mormonism*, s.v. "Nauvoo Temple").

Brother Ingalls?"

Peter turned from his typesetting table to face the clerk who had just stuck his head in the door of the room. "Yes?"

"You're wanted in the editor's office."

"All right. Let me finish setting this line and I'll be right there."

The clerk nodded and was gone. Peter pulled the letters and spaces down for the last few words, tapped them firmly into place, let his eye run along the line of type to check the spelling, and then set it down. Though it was in reverse, he had plenty of practice reading things backwards now, and he saw that he had made no mistakes. He wiped his hands on his apron, took it off and hung it on the hook on the wall, and started toward Ebenezer Robinson's office.

He stopped for a moment to check his reflection in the glass of the window, seeing that, as usual, one lock of hair had slipped down over his forehead. He brushed it back, wet his fingers with his tongue, and tried to plaster it back into place. Peter Ingalls would celebrate his eighteenth birthday in three more months. Unlike Derek, who was stocky and heavily built, Peter was more slight of body and narrow of shoulders. Bending over the type-setting cases day after day hadn't done a lot to broaden them either. His large blue eyes were usually thoughtful and inquisi-tive. His features, a legacy from his long-deceased mother, made him look younger than he really was. He made one more attempt to control the errant shock of hair, then gave it up and went on.

To his surprise, it was not Ebenezer Robinson who was wait-ing for him, however. Instead it was two members of the Council of the Twelve, Elders John Taylor and Wilford Woodruff.

Elder Taylor smiled at the sudden bewilderment on Peter's face. "It's all right, Peter. Come in and sit down."

Wilford Woodruff rose and shook his hand. "Come in, Brother Ingalls, come in."

Peter moved over to the proffered chair and sat down slowly. Brother Robinson was nowhere to be seen. Joseph's brother, Don Carlos Smith, had been the first editor of the Church's news-paper in Nauvoo up until his death the previous August. His assistant editor, Robert B. Thompson, had died a few weeks later. At that point, Ebenezer Robinson—who, since 1839, had been Don Carlos's business partner in the printing establishment that, among other things, published the *Times and Seasons*— became sole owner of the print shop and editor of the paper. There had been rumors in the past month or two about a change. Peter knew that Brother Joseph had been negotiating with Robinson to step down as editor of the Church's newspaper and sell the printing business to Willard Richards. But, as far as Peter knew, nothing had come of it as yet.

Elder Taylor waited until he was settled and Elder Woodruff had come back to take the seat beside the desk. Then he smiled warmly. "Are you still reading, Peter?"

Peter nodded immediately, knowing exactly what he had ref-erence to. "Yes, sir, I am. Every chance I get."

Woodruff nodded. "John has told me how you've read about every book in his library, starting back in Far West. That's wonderful," he concluded. "As the revelations say, we should seek learning out of the best books."

"Yes, I firmly believe that," Peter responded, still not sure what was happening here.

Taylor began rummaging through some papers on the desk, his head down. Woodruff watched him, seeming to know what he was looking for. Peter's eyes moved back and forth between the two men; he was feeling just a little bewildered.

Wilford Woodruff was the shorter of the two Apostles, being probably no more than five feet seven or eight inches. Peter had heard that in his younger years Wilford had been a miller. That would account for his powerful build. Throughout Nauvoo, Brother Woodruff was known for being able to outwork most of the men around him. But it was his eyes that caught Peter's attention. They were light blue, almost translucent, and they were the most piercing eyes he had ever seen. It was as if one glance from them and you felt revealed completely. He wore a Greek-style beard that ran from ear to ear beneath his jaw and chin but left his face clean shaven. The beard emphasized the fact that his cheekbones were high and prominent, almost making his face look gaunt. It made him seem stern and fierce-looking, but Peter knew this was deceiving. In addition to his reputation as a hard worker, Wilford Woodruff was renowned for his gentle temperament and naturally cheerful disposition. Derek, who had spent so much time with him during those miraculous missionary days in England, described him as being totally free of jealousy and as having a natural trust of others. He dressed simply and lived simply. Joseph called him "Wilford the Faithful."

John Taylor was a distinct contrast to his companion. They were nearly the same age—Taylor was about thirty-four, Woodruff two years older than that—but there the similarity ended. John Taylor was almost six feet tall. He had been born in England and immigrated to Canada when he was about twenty. He there married another English immigrant—Leonora Cannon.

Peter knew that though he was a skilled cabinetmaker and wood turner, John Taylor loved literature and books. He spoke slowly, choosing his words with care. His British accent had softened little in his years in North America, and this, coupled with prematurely silvered hair, gave him a regal bearing. *Dignity* and *grace* and *courage*—those were the words that came to Peter's mind when he thought of John Taylor. During the dark days of Kirtland, John Taylor had been absolutely fearless in defending the Church and the Prophet from the attacks of the dissenters. Peter admired him greatly and had felt a close affinity to him from that day he had first brought the books to him.

Brother Taylor found the paper he was looking for. He scanned it quickly, then looked up. "Well, Peter, some changes are going on that we wanted to talk to you about."

"All right."

He handed the paper across to him. "This is a revelation received by Brother Joseph just a week ago. It has to do with the newspaper here."

Peter reached over and took the paper and sat back. Centered over the few lines of writing was one word: *Revelation*. Then he began to read. As he did so, his eyes widened slightly.

> Verily thus saith the Lord unto you, my servant Joseph, go and say unto the Twelve, that it is my will to have them take in hand the editorial department of the *Times and Seasons*, according to that manifestation which shall be given unto them by the power of my Holy Spirit in the midst of their counsel, saith the Lord. Amen.

He read it again, more slowly this time. Finally he looked up and handed it back.

"That was given a week ago today," Brother Taylor explained.

"Yes, sir."

"Well, as of yesterday, Brother Woodruff has been asked to superintend the printing office and I to take over the management of the editorial department of the *Times and Seasons*."

"Really?" Peter said eagerly. That was wonderful news. He had enjoyed working for Ebenezer, but to work directly under John Taylor, that would be a privilege indeed.

Brother Woodruff spoke up now. "This morning, we closed the contract with Brother Robinson for the purchase of the printing office, the newspaper, the bookbindery, the paper fixtures, and the stereotype foundry."

Peter was a little dazed. This would surely mean significant changes. He looked at John Taylor. "It will be a pleasure to work with you, sir. You shall have my complete support."

The Apostle nodded, pleased with that. "Thank you." Then there was a slow smile. "But actually, we were hoping for something a little more than that."

"What?" Peter responded immediately. "I am ready to do whatever you ask."

"Good. As things stand right now, it's possible that Brother Joseph may step in as editor-in-chief of the paper. That hasn't been decided for sure yet. But regardless, I have been assigned to take an active role in the editorial department. If Joseph indeed takes over as editor, I will be the associate editor." He paused, looking intently at Peter. "How about becoming my editorial assistant?"

Peter gasped softly, and both Taylor and Woodruff chuckled at that.

"Do I take that as a yes or a no answer?" Taylor teased.

"Do you mean that, sir?"

"Of course I mean it."

"I . . . I would be truly honored to work with you, Elder Taylor. And for you, Elder Woodruff."

"Until we receive any different instructions from Brother Joseph," explained Brother Taylor, "we can be making some plans. I would like you to begin thinking about editorials that need to be written, issues that we should bring to the fore. I'll ask that you read and do a preliminary edit on all the articles submitted for publication before sending them on to me." He leaned back, quite sober now. "As you know, Brother Joseph has placed more and more responsibility on the shoulders of the Twelve. Brother Brigham, as President of the Quorum, is taking that charge very seriously. There will be times when both Elder Woodruff and I are out of the office, due to the call of our apostolic duties. We need someone who can keep things moving along during such absences."

Peter's mind was reeling. "But . . ." Finally, he just gulped a little, then nodded. "I am honored that you would feel that much confidence in me."

Woodruff stood. "Then it's done?" he asked Peter.

"Yes, sir. Thank you, sir." Peter stood now too, as did John Taylor. They all three came together in front of the editor's large desk. They shook hands all around. "I will await your instructions," Peter said.

Lydia Steed was the only person at the Homestead who was not a member of the extended family of Lucy Mack Smith, which said a lot about the depth of the friendship between her and Emma. With the exception of a daughter and a daughter-in-law who lived in Plymouth, a settlement about thirty-five miles southeast of Nauvoo, all the other Smith women had come to help. Lucy Mack was there, of course, supervising all the others in her tireless way. Emma's children had been sent over to Hyrum and Mary's house, where Mercy Thompson, Mary's sister, was watching them along with her own and Mary's children.

The only men at the house were Joseph and Hyrum. The other Smith brothers were taking turns at the store so that Joseph could be here with Emma. The two brothers had fetched water or wood when necessary throughout the morning, but by midafternoon Mother Smith had grown tired of Joseph's hovering and sent him and Hyrum outside.

The kitchen had been crowded for most of the morning. The women worked shoulder to shoulder, boiling water, preparing clean sheets and towels, and cooking the food for the crowds that would surely come in the next few days to congratulate

Joseph and Emma on their good fortune. But as the day wore on, things got done, food was finished and put aside, everything was washed and in readiness. By two p.m., except for Mother Smith and Hyrum's wife, Mary, who were in Emma's bedroom with the midwife, the rest of the women were sitting around the kitchen or the adjoining parlor talking quietly.

When they heard the door above them open and then the sound of footsteps on the stairs, the room went instantly quiet and every head turned to the hallway. Mother Smith appeared. She stopped, surveying the room, then smiled. "We're down to about three minutes apart now. It shouldn't be long. Agnes, can you be sure the water is still boiling?"

The widow of Don Carlos Smith nodded and stood immediately. Mother Smith looked at Lydia. "Why don't you go out and let the boys know how things are coming."

"All right." Lydia stood and went to the coatrack by the door. She took down her coat and scarf and put them on. Young Lucy—as everyone still called her, even though she was twenty years old and married now—came over and did the same. "I'll go too," she said. "I can't stand just sitting here waiting anymore."

Lydia smiled at her. Lucy was Joseph's youngest sister, and Lydia had always liked her a great deal. "Me too. I'm glad for anything to keep my mind occupied."

The two "boys," as Mother Smith still called them, were standing out by the springhouse, which was on the south side of the home, near the river's edge. Even though it was February sixth, it was a relatively pleasant day outside. The snow from a few days previous was all but gone. The temperature was in the low forties. As the door opened, both of the brothers turned around. Joseph started toward the women, his face anxious.

Lydia shook her head. "Nothing yet," she called.

As Lydia and young Lucy went down the step and out to join Joseph and Hyrum, Joseph's shoulders lifted and fell. "And Emma?" he asked.

"Mama says things are progressing nicely," Lucy answered. "How are you two doing?"

Hyrum smiled. "Joseph and I are solving all the problems of the kingdom."

"Well, that's good, then, isn't it?" Lydia laughed.

Joseph gave her a wry look. "Now all that's left is to make it come to pass."

Lucy slipped an arm through Joseph's. "And what wonderful things have you decided?"

"Actually," Hyrum answered, "Joseph was telling me the latest about Brother Hyde."

"Orson Hyde?" Lydia asked. "Have you heard from him again?"

"Yes, I have received two letters in recent weeks. He has reached Jerusalem, dedicated the land for the return of the Jews—just as he saw himself doing in vision—and now is on his way home again." A frown momentarily crossed his face. "Well, actually, at his last writing he was in quarantine at Trieste in Italy, but he expected to be released soon."

Lydia was nodding. "I remember now. He spoke of his vision in conference, didn't he?"

"Yes," Hyrum said. "He saw London, Amsterdam, Constantinople, and Jerusalem. The Spirit spoke quite directly to him as he saw the peoples in those various cities. 'Here are many of the children of Abraham,' it said, 'whom I will gather to the land I gave to their fathers, and here also is the field of your labor.' And he saw himself in Jerusalem, standing on the top of a mount, with pen and ink, writing out a prayer of dedication."

"And from what he wrote in his letter, that is exactly how it happened," Joseph went on. "It is a great thing he has done."

"Yes," Lydia said. She couldn't think of anything else that would say it better than that. "Yes, it is," she repeated.

"And how glad we are that you are here, Lydia. I am so appreciative of your coming."

She looked up at him in surprise. "I wouldn't miss this for anything, Joseph. You know how I feel about Emma."

"I know. And I know how she feels about you. She wanted you to be here for her."

"It's been difficult for her these last few months."

Joseph was very sober. "I worry about her."

Lucy spoke up. "We all try to get her to take it easy, but you know Emma. She's always up and doing something, even when she ought to be resting."

"And unfortunately," Hyrum added, speaking to Joseph, "at your house there is always something to keep her up and doing it."

Joseph blew out his breath in discouragement. "I know. It seems like there's hardly a meal when we don't have someone at our table. People coming and going all the time. And I fear they don't pay much attention to the time."

Lydia nodded. Just a few weeks before, Joseph and Emma had taken four additional children into their home. A family by the name of Walker, who had been faithful members of the Church since the early days of Kirtland, and who had ten children, had lost their mother. Joseph and Emma immediately volunteered to take in the four oldest children for a time to help the grieving father cope with his loss.

"But that's why everyone loves her, Joseph."

He smiled, somewhat sadly. "I know, Lydia. But it is very difficult for her."

He turned and put an arm around his sister. "Well, shall we go in? I'm not sure that we can be of any use in there, but I want to be close for Emma when the time comes."

———◆———

When Lucy Mack appeared at the door, everyone looked up. The instant they saw the look on Lucy Mack Smith's face, they knew.

Joseph shot to his feet, his face twisting in horror. "No!"

Mother Smith looked exhausted. One hand passed over her eyes as she nodded dumbly.

"Oh, please, no!" Joseph cried.

Mary Smith and Hyrum were up now too. Every other person was frozen in place. Lydia felt as though someone had wrenched her stomach in a violent twist. *Not again! Not another loss for Emma. Especially not now.*

Great tears welled up in the eyes of Joseph's mother and her face crumpled. "It's a silent child," she whispered. "A little boy. He never took a breath. You'd better go to her, Joseph."

During the time that Nathan was in Wisconsin, Benjamin found a twenty-five-acre parcel of land just east of town and secured it with a hundred dollars earnest money. He had corresponded with two major banks in the state capital and arranged possible financing, but they would not finalize such a major transaction through the mail.

On Saturday, February nineteenth, Nathan and Benjamin left for the capital city. About a hundred and twenty miles southeast of Nauvoo, Springfield was approached by well-traveled roads; but a three-day thaw, followed by only mildly cold weather, had left the prairie highways a morass of mud and hub-deep ruts. It was a bone-jarring, teeth-rattling trip with delays and detours, and by the time they reached the city on the fourth day they were totally exhausted.

After a decent night in a small hotel near the state capitol building, Benjamin and Nathan were ready to start the business for which they had come. They spent most of that day at the two banks with whom they were dealing. Though they had good collateral, their being from Nauvoo made the bankers a little nervous and neither was willing to lend the full amount they needed. Thus both banks were brought in on the arrangements. With sample contracts in hand, Benjamin decided they should have some legal counsel before actually signing the papers. They asked for a recommendation for a local lawyer from one of the bankers and readily got one, but Benjamin was leery. He suspected that the recommended law firm probably did considerable work for the bank and would be inclined to favor the bank in any counsel they gave. At the hotel that night, Benjamin and Nathan asked the proprietor for his recommendation. He confirmed their suspicions, and suggested the small but independent firm of Logan and Lincoln. "Stephen T. Logan is one of the greatest lawyers to ever practice law in Illinois," the man affirmed solemnly, "but if it were me, I'd go for the junior partner. He gives legal advice for a reasonable fee. And he'll tell you straight out if there're problems you need to look out for."

"Sounds like exactly what we need," Nathan observed.

"Yep," the hotelier nodded. "Don't let his looks fool you. Mr. Lincoln ain't much to look on, but he's got a gift for knowing what matters and for saying things in a way that even a jury of twelve unschooled farm folk can understand. Not that you're expecting any problems with this, but if it ever has to go to court, you'll want Lincoln in the chair beside you." He laughed. "Besides that, he's one of the best darned storytellers in all of Illinois."

Benjamin agreed that Mr. Lincoln sounded like what they were looking for, and the next day they went down to the small offices of Logan and Lincoln, attorneys at law. The man had been right. Lincoln was a man to bring you up short when you first looked at him. He was tall and lanky, still carrying himself like a gangly teenaged boy outgrowing his own body, and his movements were slow and deliberate. Gray eyes peered out from beneath heavy brows above a large nose, a firm mouth, and a prominent chin. His expression seemed to carry an air of eternal sadness about it—until he smiled; then the eyes literally danced with inner amusement and the mouth broke into a generous grin.

They spent only half an hour with him. He looked over their contracts, made three or four minor suggestions, and charged them a dollar. As they stood and moved toward the door, Mr. Lincoln came out from around his desk and joined them. "Did Noah warn you about my being a strange-looking duck?" he asked with a droll smile.

"Noah?" Benjamin asked, taken aback a little by the directness of the question.

"Yes, Noah Goodson, the proprietor at the hotel. Usually he also tells people how strange I look."

Nathan laughed in spite of himself. "Yes, he did, as a matter of fact."

"Well," Lincoln drawled, "it'd be a little harder to swallow if it weren't so true." He chuckled, and it was a deep rumbling sound down inside his chest. "In fact, one time, while I was out riding circuit, I was just sitting down for supper in a small country inn. A man came up to me, staring at my face. Then suddenly he pulled out a pistol and pointed it right at my head.

" 'Beggin' your pardon, sir,' he said, obviously in great distress, 'but I've always told myself if I ever found a man who was uglier than me, I'd shoot the poor fellow and put him out of his misery.' "

Benjamin was staring at him, not sure if Lincoln was serious or not. "What did you do?"

Lincoln seemed totally dejected. "Well, I looked him up and down real slow, and then I said, 'Sir, if I really am uglier than you, you go ahead and shoot, because life ain't worth living.' "

Both Nathan and Benjamin exploded with laughter. After a moment, Lincoln, now smiling, reached out and shook both their hands. "Gentlemen, thank you for your business and good luck with your land investments."

They left and returned to the hotel and told Noah Goodson the story. The hotel keeper roared even more loudly than they had. That afternoon they went back to the two banks, signed the amended contracts, and received the notes for the necessary funds. The following morning, they were back on the road west.

Chapter Notes

The revelation concerning the Twelve's taking part in the running of the *Times and Seasons* was given on 28 January 1842 (see HC 4:503). Joseph then appointed Wilford Woodruff and John Taylor in the positions mentioned (see *HC* 4:513–14).

Orson Hyde left Nauvoo on 15 April 1840 and did not return until almost three years later on 7 December 1842. He worked, preached, wrote, and published on three continents. He journeyed over twenty thousand miles under difficult and sometimes perilous circumstances. It was one of the longest and most significant missions in the early history of the Church, one that rivals in many ways the missionary journeys of the Apostle Paul. (See *CHFT*, pp. 235–38.)

On 6 February 1842, Emma gave birth to her eighth child (see J. Christopher Conkling, *A Joseph Smith Chronology* [Salt Lake City: Deseret Book Co., 1979], p. 161). It was a stillborn son. It was the fourth child to die at birth or within hours of it, and the sixth child (including one of the adopted twins and Don Carlos) that she lost in death.

Mary Ann watched the women of the family file into Caroline's parlor, their cheeks red from the cold air outside. There were four missing from the original council—Jessica was in Ramus now with Kathryn. Jenny Pottsworth had stopped coming after she announced formally that she and Andrew Stokes were promised, and her mother gradually stopped coming after that. Finally, as Rebecca and Melissa came in together and found a place on the long sofa beside Olivia, Mary Ann stood. Immediately the chatter of conversation died away and all eyes turned to her.

"Thank you for coming on such short notice. I know that meeting on an evening other than the Sabbath day is not convenient, but something has come up. I felt like we needed to decide on it immediately rather than delay."

That interested them all and now every eye focused intently on her.

"As you know, winter is almost gone. Our linsey-woolsey

project has been very successful. The families we chose to help have been benefitted by all of your work. Several have expressed their deep thanks to me, as I am sure they have to some of you as well."

Several heads nodded in confirmation of that.

"With the coming of spring, the needs of those families will diminish and our work will be mostly finished for a time. Yesterday I was feeling a little saddened by that thought. But then this afternoon I happened to meet Sarah Kimball down at the post office. Do you all know Sister Kimball?"

Most nodded, but Melissa shook her head.

"They own the store down near the steamboat landing," Caroline spoke up. "Hiram isn't a member of the Church."

"Oh, yes," Melissa answered.

Lydia nodded. Hiram Kimball's store was one of the most prosperous in Nauvoo, and he owned other properties as well. He was a well-to-do businessman and his wife was a cultured, gracious woman. She was a member of the Church, he was not. Much like Carl Rogers, Hiram Kimball was friendly to both the Church and its members, but just didn't seem interested in becoming a Mormon himself. But Sarah was a faithful woman of strong commitment to the Church.

"Well," Mary Ann went on, "Sarah told me that the other day she was talking to Margaret Cook, a young woman who does seamstress work for her. Somehow the topic turned to the idea of sewing some shirts for the temple workmen. As you know, the workmen get paid in tithing scrip or other goods, but there just haven't been any clothes donated. Sister Cook said that she'd really like to do that, but said she had no material and no means for furnishing any to make clothing. Sarah said she'd be happy to furnish the material but was not very good at sewing."

"That's a wonderful idea," Rebecca spoke up. "Working on the building is very hard on clothing. I can't believe what happens to Derek's trousers while he's in the quarry, and he's there about every tenth day."

"That's right," Mary Ann said. "Well, as Sister Kimball and

Sister Cook talked about it, they got the idea that there might be other women interested in helping as well. Sarah has known about what we are doing. She and I have talked about it several times. When I told her about our linsey-woolsey project she got very excited. That would be just the solution for getting the material they need."

"And it would be really good material for wintertime work," Jennifer Jo spoke up.

"Yes. We'll also try to find some cotton material to make summertime shirts as well. Anyway, I told her that I would call our council together and see if you wanted to join our efforts with theirs. What do you think?"

Several started to speak at once, but it was evident what their inclination was. In five minutes, Mary Ann had her decision. "Good," she declared. "That pleases me. I'll see Sarah in the morning and tell her we are with her on this."

———◆———

Benjamin had the side of his face pressed against the cow's flank, leaning into her as his hands moved up and down, squeezing, releasing, squeezing, releasing. The milk from the cow's udder shot in rhythmic streams into the bucket of milk, raising a thick froth on the surface. The bucket was nearly two-thirds full now and the udder considerably reduced in size.

"Grandpa Steed! Grandpa Steed!"

He straightened, his hands not slowing at all, and peered around the cow's rump, watchful that she not swish her tail and catch him in the face. "I'm in the barn," he called.

A moment later, Peter Ingalls came dashing through the side door.

As Peter came slowly forward, Benjamin saw that he carried what appeared to be a newspaper. He was wheezing heavily. "Hello, Grandpa Steed," he managed between gasps for breath.

"My goodness, what did you do, run all the way home?"

Peter moved around and leaned against the side of the stable, still puffing. "Yes, all the way."

"Is there anything wrong?"

He shook his head, then waved the newspaper he held in his hand in Benjamin's direction. "I've got a copy of today's edition of the paper. Brother Taylor said I could bring it home and show you."

"Oh?" Benjamin replied. Peter loved his work at the printing office and would always bring a copy of the *Times and Seasons* home with him after it had been printed. But that was usually the day after it was sent out to the Saints. This was the first time he had brought one home early.

"By the way, how was Springfield?"

"Fine. We got what we were looking for. We just got back last night."

"Good." Peter waved the paper again. "Oh, Grandpa Steed, this is the most marvelous edition. I couldn't wait to show you and the family."

Benjamin nodded, then looked down. The streams of milk were considerably thinner now. "I'm almost done. Let me just strip her out and I'll be in."

Peter nodded, his breathing finally more controlled. "Can you bring Grandma over to our house? I'll tell Nathan and Lydia. I want them to hear this too. This is exciting, Grandpa."

"All right. I'll get Mother Steed and we'll be there in a few minutes."

⸺•⸺

It took almost a full ten minutes before the door opened and Lydia and Nathan came in behind Benjamin and Mary Ann. Young Joshua was with them.

"Good," Peter exclaimed with great relief. "They're here."

"Come in, everyone," Derek invited. "Find a seat. Peter is going to burst a blood vessel if we don't let him get started."

They moved in and found chairs, settling in. Peter stood immediately. He reached to the table behind him and retrieved the newspaper. He held it up. "This is today's edition of the *Times and Seasons*." He pointed to just below the masthead.

"See? March first, 1842." Then his face fell and he held the paper back down at his side. "But actually it won't be ready to print until at least tomorrow, maybe the day after. It's taken longer to get it ready than we originally planned."

Young Joshua turned to his mother in puzzlement. "How can it be today's paper if it comes out tomorrow?" he asked.

Peter laughed. "We typeset the paper today, Joshua. This is just one of the first copies we ran to check it for errors. Brother Joseph still wants to check it too." As Elder Taylor had indicated to Peter might happen, Joseph had indeed stepped in recently as editor of the paper. That meant John Taylor was Joseph's assistant editor, and Peter worked directly with Elder Taylor as *his* assistant. "Joseph has two major articles in this edition," Peter continued. "And that's what I'm so excited about. They take up almost half the paper."

Nathan was dutifully impressed. "That's a little unusual, isn't it?"

"Yes."

"What kinds of things did he give you?" Benjamin asked, smiling at Peter's excitement.

Peter sobered now. He had spent all day checking the spelling and punctuation and helping set the type. But through the tediousness of the editing and typesetting, Peter's excitement had only grown. What he had read lit a fire inside him, and he had been thrilled when Brother Taylor agreed to let him bring a copy home to show his family.

"Well," he said proudly, "I think you all know about the Egyptian mummies Joseph purchased while we were still back in Kirtland."

"Yes," Benjamin said, "and the papyrus scrolls that were with them."

"Pap . . . Pap-eye . . . ," young Joshua started.

"Papyrus," Mary Ann smiled. "It's a kind of paper that the Egyptians made." Suddenly her head came up and her eyes widened. "Has Joseph finished the translation?"

"No," Peter said exuberantly, "but he's finished a major part of it and has decided to begin publishing it for the Church. It's called the book of Abraham."

"Well, I'll be," Mary Ann said. "After all this time, he's finally been able to do it."

Peter held the paper up again for all to see. On the front page there was a strange black-and-white line drawing above a numbered list. The drawing showed a man lying on a table, with another man standing beside him with an upraised knife. There were also other strange figures above and below the two men. "Look, here's a picture taken from the papyrus. Joseph had Reuben Hedlock do some woodcuts, copying right from the actual record. There are others too that will appear in later editions."

They all leaned forward, peering at the picture. Young Joshua spoke first. "What is it, Peter? It looks like that man has a knife."

Peter moved closer, holding the illustration out so that they could see it better. "Joseph is calling these pictures facsimiles." He looked around at them. "A facsimile is just a copy of something. This one is a picture of Abraham lying on an altar. The man standing beside him is a priest of one of the false gods. You're right, Joshua, he does have a knife. He's trying to sacrifice Abraham to this false god."

"How do you know that?" Nathan inquired.

"Because Joseph has printed a key for the picture, see? It's printed right here below the facsimile. On the pages that follow, the text tells us that Abraham's father was an idolater. He was willing to offer Abraham to be sacrificed so as to appease the false gods."

"Are you sure you're not talking about Abraham sacrificing Isaac?" Rebecca asked. She had never heard anything about Abraham being sacrificed by his father.

"No. This is something that the Bible doesn't tell us. It's Abraham, all right." He reached around with one hand and touched the upper corner of the drawing where there was a small figure. "See this bird here? If you read the key below, it says that bird represents the angel of the Lord. The record says that God delivered Abraham."

Peter looked around, pleased with the reaction he had created. "Isn't it wonderful? It's just like scripture. Imagine, having the writings of Abraham himself from almost four thousand years ago!"

"That is marvelous," Derek agreed. "You say this is only part of the translation?"

"Yes. It's too long to do in one edition. Also, Joseph is still finishing making us a copy. We'll publish more of it in the next issue."

"Well," Benjamin said, speaking for all of them. "That really is something, Peter. Read some of it to us."

"In a minute, but let me tell you about the other thing Joseph gave us. It's pretty exciting too."

"What is it?" Rebecca asked.

"Well, a few days ago, Joseph got a letter from a Mr. John Wentworth, who is the editor and proprietor of the *Chicago Democrat*. That's a newspaper," he added for young Joshua's benefit. "This Mr. Wentworth asked Joseph for a brief summary of his religious experiences and the history of the Church. Mr. Wentworth said he was making the request in behalf of a friend of his, a Mr. George Barstow, who's writing a history of New Hampshire. Anyway, Joseph wrote Wentworth a long letter back and told him his friend Barstow could publish it as long as he doesn't change it or add things to it."

"And this is in the paper too?" Mary Ann spoke up.

"Yes," Peter said excitedly. "Since it is a summary of how Joseph came to be called of God and the rise of the Church in these latter days, he felt that it might be of interest to the Saints as well."

"I should say," Nathan murmured.

Peter looked at Nathan and Lydia now. "I know that you have known Joseph from the beginning and have heard him tell these stories, about how he first saw God and Christ in the trees near his home, and how Moroni came, but I never have. Oh,

I've heard him make reference to them, of course, and bear testimony to the truthfulness of those happenings, but I've not ever heard him personally talk about how it happened and what it was like."

"And that's what he does in this letter?" Lydia asked, leaning forward.

"Yes, in great detail. In fact, I got so engrossed in reading it, I forgot I was supposed to be preparing it for publication. Brother Taylor had to call me back to my work."

"Read some of it to us," Mary Ann exclaimed. "I want to hear it too."

He grinned, pleased that his hoped-for response was forthcoming. "I will, but first there's something else. Right at the end of the letter, Joseph talks about what we believe as a church. He summarizes our beliefs in thirteen statements, or declarations. They are simple, but as I read them over and over, I was so impressed. I just kept thinking to myself, Yes! That's what we believe."

He searched through the newspaper for a moment. "Let me just give you a couple of examples. The first one talks about how we believe in God the Eternal Father and in Jesus and the Holy Ghost. That wouldn't come as a surprise to most other churches. But listen to this. 'We believe that men will be punished for their own sins and not for Adam's transgression.' "

He stopped to let them consider that. Nathan slowly nodded. "So much for how people think about original sin."

"What's that, Papa?" young Joshua asked.

"Some churches think that because Adam and Eve did wrong, all of mankind are evil. In other words, all mankind is being punished for what Adam and Eve did."

"Here's another," Peter went on. " 'We believe that a man must be called of God by "prophecy, and by laying on of hands" by those who are in authority to preach the gospel and administer in the ordinances thereof.' And another, 'We believe in the same organization that existed in the primitive church, viz: apostles, prophets, pastors, teachers, evangelists, etc.' "

"Well, that says it straight out, doesn't it?" Derek said.

Peter went right on, getting excited all over again. " 'We believe in the gift of tongues, prophecy, revelation, visions, healing, interpretation of tongues, etc.' " His eyes skipped down a few lines. " 'We believe all that God has revealed, all that he does now reveal, and we believe that he will yet reveal many great and important things pertaining to the kingdom of God. We believe in the literal gathering of Israel and in the restoration of the Ten Tribes. That Zion will be built upon this continent. That Christ will reign personally upon the earth, and that the earth will be renewed and receive its paradisaic glory.' "

He stopped, a little breathless again. "See what I mean? They are so clear and so plain. But here's my favorite part of this whole issue. Listen to this."

He found his place but looked at the family members around him. "A little bit earlier in the letter, Joseph talks about how the gospel is spreading around the world. Now listen to this." His eyes dropped to the paper and he began to read. " 'Our missionaries are going forth to different nations, and in Germany, Palestine, New Holland, the East Indies, and other places, the standard of truth has been erected: no unhallowed hand can stop the work from progressing, persecutions may rage, mobs may combine, armies may assemble, calumny may defame, but the truth of God will go forth boldly, nobly, and independent till it has penetrated every continent, visited every clime, swept every country, and sounded in every ear, till the purposes of God shall be accomplished and the great Jehovah shall say the work is done.' "

He stopped. The room was hushed as the impact of the words settled upon them. All were greatly sobered. Images of Kirtland and Jackson County, Far West and Haun's Mill, filled their minds.

"Read it again," Nathan demanded.

" 'Our missionaries are—' "

"No, further on. Where he talks about no unhallowed hand."

Peter nodded, found the place, and started again. " 'No

unhallowed hand can stop the work from progressing—' " He looked up.

"Yes, there. Only more slowly."

Peter obeyed and began one more time. " 'The standard of truth has been erected: no unhallowed hand can stop the work.' " He paused again to see if that was what Nathan was after.

"Yes! Go on!"

" 'Persecutions may rage, mobs may combine, armies may assemble, calumny may defame, but—' "

"Wait! Is calumny what I think it is?"

Peter smiled. "What do you think it is?"

"Slander."

"Yes. Calumny means to spread false information about a person's character." He waited for a moment, but Nathan only nodded and so he continued. " 'But the truth of God will go forth boldly, nobly, and independent till it has penetrated every continent, visited every clime, swept every country, and sounded in every ear, till the purposes of God shall be accomplished and the great Jehovah shall say the work is done.' "

"What a glorious statement," Lydia said. "It is so beautifully put."

Now Nathan looked up. "You know what I was thinking as Peter read that?"

They shook their heads.

"Didn't any names come to your mind as he read? Names like Simonds Ryder. Sampson Avard. Lilburn W. Boggs. General Samuel Lucas."

"General Moses Wilson," Mary Ann added quietly. Here was a roll call of unhallowed hands that had made every effort to stop the work, all to no avail. In fact, as you walked through Nauvoo today it was clear that, if anything, their opposition had only strengthened the Church.

"And what about those who didn't oppose us so much as they simply didn't stay faithful?" Benjamin said, equally sobered now. "What about Martin Harris? Oliver Cowdery? The Whitmer brothers? William McLellin? Where are they now?"

"Thomas B. Marsh," Derek added. "He was President of the Twelve."

There was a deep silence in the room. Then Benjamin looked up. "The only real question is, when the great day of Jehovah comes, when the purposes of God are accomplished, which side of the ledger will our names be on? That's all that really matters, isn't it?"

When Nathan came back into the kitchen from kissing the children good night, Lydia had a bolt of linsey-woolsey cloth spread across the table and was measuring it carefully with a string. Satisfied that it was the right size, she picked up the scissors and began to cut down the one side of it. He came over and stood beside her for a moment, watching her work. This was part of the ongoing work of the Steed family women's council to help needy families. Then he leaned over and put his arms around her, pulling her back against him. "Mmm," he murmured, "it's so good to be back home again."

"You'd think you had only just gotten here," she teased.

"Well, it's only been three days since we got back from Springfield."

"I know. I wasn't complaining."

He looked down at the shirt. "Who is this for?" he asked.

She gave him a whimsical glance. "Maybe you."

"Me? I thought this was something you were doing for the families you're helping."

"Not anymore," she answered, enjoying her little joke.

"I don't understand."

"Well, I haven't told you. There's been a change." She explained quickly about Sarah Kimball and the project of making clothes for the temple workmen. "So," she said, "it really isn't for you, unless you decide to become a full-time worker on the temple."

"That's a wonderful idea," he said, really meaning it. "And what does Hiram Kimball think of all this?"

"He seems to be pleased with what we are doing. He has even donated several bolts of cotton cloth to make some lighter summer clothing. He's a good man."

"He's given more than cloth. Haven't you heard about Sarah's bargain with him?"

"Bargain? No, what bargain?"

"This is delightful. Joseph was telling me about this. It's probably the most unusual way I've heard of for raising money for the Lord's house."

She laid the scissors down and sat back, curious now.

"When Sarah had her last child, according to Joseph, a few days after he was born, Hiram was at Sarah's bedside, holding the baby and admiring his new son. Sarah watched him for a few moments, then said, 'Hiram, what do you think a son like that is worth?' Hiram was surprised by the question, but answered, 'Oh, a great deal, I should think.' 'How much?' Sarah persisted. 'Would you say he is worth a thousand dollars?' "

Nathan was chuckling now even as he told her the story. " 'Yes,' Hiram agreed, 'I would say he is worth at least a thousand dollars.' 'Good,' said Sarah, 'then my half of his worth would be five hundred dollars. I would like to give my half to the temple fund.' "

Lydia clapped her hands. "Really? Did she really say that?"

"She did. She caught him in her trap that easily. But that's not the end of the story. A few days later, when Hiram saw Brother Joseph, he told the Prophet what had happened. Joseph was delighted. 'I accept all such donations,' Joseph promptly said, 'and from this day forth, the record for that boy shall be marked, *Church property*.' "

Lydia was laughing merrily now. "And what did Hiram say to that?"

"Joseph was joking, of course, but he told Hiram that he had two options. One, he could either pay five hundred dollars to the Church and retain possession of his son, or two, he could receive five hundred dollars and turn the boy over to Joseph as the Trustee and Trust for the Church."

"So what did Hiram do?"

Now Nathan grew more serious. "Well, believe it or not, Joseph said he deeded a piece of property to the Church which was easily worth the five hundred dollars if not more. I guess that says what kind of man he is as much as anything, doesn't it?"

"I should say. And his wife is of that same character. Sarah has gotten so excited about the number of women who want to help with this project, she's started to talk about forming a ladies' society. There is going to be a meeting at her home day after tomorrow. She's talking about electing officers, drawing up a constitution and everything."

"Hmm," Nathan said, surprised at that.

She frowned. "Did that little 'hmm' mean you think that it is a good or bad idea?"

"Oh, I think it's a great idea."

"Good. I want to go to the meeting."

Chapter Notes

The ninth number of volume 3 of the *Times and Seasons* was a highly significant issue of the Church's newspaper. It is dated 1 March 1842, although it was probably not actually published until two or three days later (see *HC* 4:542, footnote). From that issue eventually two things became canonized scripture and are now part of the Pearl of Great Price: the book of Abraham and the Articles of Faith. The famous statement about the work of God going forward is from the same letter that contains the Articles of Faith (see *HC* 4:535–41).

Though no specific date is given for when it took place, the account of Sarah and Hiram Kimball's "temple donation" is accurate (see *Women of Nauvoo*, p. 148).

As he and Lydia rounded the corner of Water and Main Street and moved toward the front gate to the Homestead, Nathan looked across the street a little farther to the south. It appeared that the foundations of the Nauvoo House were in place now. He stopped for a moment. "That is going to be some building," he said.

"Yes, it is," Lydia agreed. It was going to be a large brick building, L-shaped, with one wing parallel to the street and the other facing the river, and would have almost eighty rooms. She slipped an arm through her husband's. "I've always found it interesting that the Lord would tell Joseph to build a hotel at the same time he told him to build a temple."

Nathan's head bobbed up and down. He had thought the same thing on several occasions. "But when you think about it, it makes sense. The Lord doesn't want his people to be cloistered away from the world. How did he say it in the revelation? 'Let there be a delightful habitation for man, and a place of rest for the weary traveler.'"

"Something like that. But aside from that, it's a practical thing too. Joseph and Emma are constantly entertaining visitors. They've always got someone staying with them."

"Oh, I know," he agreed.

"Well, it is going to be beautiful. And the view from the top floors will be magnificent."

It would, Nathan thought. The Nauvoo House was going up right at the south end of Main Street, just a few rods from the river's edge. Already plans were under way for turning the small boat dock there into a second full riverboat landing to match the one on the north side of the city. And to have a grand hotel right at the landing, that made good business sense.

"Well," she said, giving his arm a slight tug, "speaking of visitors, it's a pleasant morning. Let's see if Joseph and Emma are home to receive some guests right now."

As they went through the side gate and came around to the south of the Homestead, they found two boys playing in what was left of the snow on the grass. Lydia's face immediately was wreathed in smiles. "Well, what have we here? Two young Joseph Smiths, I think."

The two boys looked up, then straightened. The nearest was Joseph Smith III, Joseph's son and namesake. He had turned nine in November and was in that time of his life where he was shooting up so quickly that his arms were always too long for the sleeves of his coat, and his legs too long for his trousers. He had Emma's dark hair and eyes but Joseph's open, pleasant features. He was a cheerful boy and a joy to both of his parents.

His head bobbed quickly. "Morning, Sister Steed. Good morning, Brother Steed."

"Hello, Joseph," Nathan smiled.

"And good morning to you too, young Joseph F.," Lydia said.

The second boy was only three and a half years old and about half his cousin's size. He stepped up behind Joseph III and peeked out bashfully from around his arm.

Joseph Fielding Smith—or Joseph F., as virtually everyone called him to distinguish him from the other two Josephs in the family—had not been named for his uncle Joseph Smith, but for his uncle Joseph Fielding, his mother's brother. He was the first child born to Hyrum Smith and Mary Fielding, who were married in 1837 after Hyrum's first wife had died. Except for their size, the two boys could have been brothers, almost twins, which wasn't too surprising considering how much alike their fathers were.

Joseph III nudged his younger cousin. "Say hello to Sister Steed, Joseph F."

"Morning, ma'am," came the murmured reply.

Lydia smiled at his shyness. She knew that when he wasn't around strangers, he was a rollicking lad who talked almost non-stop. Here was a young boy who almost hadn't made it past infancy. Born in the fall of 1838 during the final tragic days of Far West, his father wasn't even present for his birth. He and Joseph had been dragged off to prison by a mob. A few days later, the boy had nearly been killed when some of the mobbers broke into Mary's house looking for Hyrum's papers. As they ransacked the home, a mattress was thrown over the tiny baby lying on a bed. When the problem was finally discovered, the family thought the child had suffocated, but he had proved too hardy for that.

Lydia smiled at the older boy. "Are you taking care of Joseph F. today?"

He nodded, looking proud. "Aunt Mary is helping out at the store. Julia's staying with the other children, but I've got Joseph F."

"Good for you," Nathan said. "Are your father and mother home, Joseph?"

"Mama's home," he said. "Father has gone to get Mary."

Lydia nearly said, "*Aunt* Mary." It was expected that nieces and nephews always address their aunts and uncles by title, but she decided that it was not her place to correct him.

Joseph III left his cousin and ran to the front door. He opened it and stuck his head inside and hollered. "Mama! Your friend Sister Steed is here. And her husband."

There was a sound from inside as they walked over to the

small doorstep. In a moment, Emma appeared. When she saw them, her face broke into a wide and genuine smile. "Lydia! How good to see you." She opened the door wider. "Nathan, how wonderful. Come in, come in."

"We were just out walking and thought we'd stop and say hello. Is this a bad time?"

"No, no!" There was real pleasure in her voice. "It's so good to see you. Please come in. Joseph should be back in a moment or two."

As they stepped inside, Lydia took both of Emma's hands in hers. "How are you, Emma?"

Emma nodded slowly. "I'm all right."

"Really?"

"Yes. I'm feeling better every day now."

Nathan watched her as they continued to talk. Her voice was strong, but her appearance was still enough to give serious concern. In three more days it would be a full month since she had lost the baby. He and Lydia had gone to visit her a few days after that, and he had been shocked by her appearance. She was much better now, but she still looked haggard and drawn. Her face was pale, and there were dark circles under her eyes.

"Come in and sit down. Joseph has just gone to get Mary. He should be back in a few minutes." There was a moment's hesitation, and then even more earnestly, she finished. "It's so good to see you."

As they sat down on the sofa together, Emma took a large overstuffed chair across from them. She looked at Nathan. "You know that you have an angel of a wife here, don't you?"

He smiled. "I do. I was very fortunate to get her to marry me."

Emma smiled. "And how is Mother Steed?"

Nathan answered that question, and then Lydia began asking after Emma's children. They were still discussing family when a sound in the adjoining room brought their heads around. The door opened and then shut again.

"Is that you, Joseph?" Emma called.

"Yes, dear."

"We're in here. Lydia and Nathan are here."

A moment later Joseph appeared at the entry to the parlor. "Well, well," he boomed, "this is a pleasant surprise." He still had his coat on, but, to Lydia's surprise, in his arms he carried a baby, all wrapped up in a small quilt.

"Hello, Joseph," Lydia said. Nathan stood and came over to shake his hand.

"Here," Joseph said to him, "you take Mary until I get my coat off."

Lydia's eyes widened. *This* was Mary?

Nathan took the bundle carefully from Joseph, cradling it in both hands. Joseph made no move to remove his heavy coat. Instead he leaned over and pulled the quilt back away from the baby's face. Nathan smiled down at what he saw. The baby was tiny, no more than a few weeks old. Her eyes, a deep blue, were open wide, as if she had been waiting for the covering to be removed. There was just a brush of short black hair, as fine as the down from a baby duckling.

"There you go," Joseph cooed. "There's my little Mary." He reached down and touched her cheek with the back of one finger. "You're such a good girl." He reached into the quilt and picked her up, leaving the blanket in Nathan's hands.

"Shall we go see Aunt Emma?"

"Oh, yes," Emma said, "come see Emma, you little darling."

As Joseph moved across the room he stopped in front of Lydia, holding up the baby so that she looked at Lydia. "And this is Lydia Steed, young lady. She is a dear friend of our family."

When he saw Lydia's expression he laughed. "This is Mary McIntire, Sister Steed. She has consented to spend the day with Joseph and Emma, just as she does every day now."

Lydia watched Emma as Joseph took the baby to her. She was totally puzzled. "When young Joseph said you had gone to get Mary, I assumed he was talking about his Aunt Mary."

"Oh no," Emma said, taking the baby from Joseph and cuddling her in her arms. "He went to get our little Mary."

Joseph stepped back, still looking at Emma. "Before I take my coat off, I think I'll bring in some more wood."

"I'll go with you," Nathan said.

Joseph nodded and the two of them went outside again.

Emma was singing softly to the baby now, rocking it back and forth. The tiredness in her eyes was gone and her face was radiant. Lydia watched in amazement, not understanding exactly what was happening here.

Emma seemed to sense her bewilderment. "It's Joseph's idea," she explained. "This is one of the McIntire twins. Sister McIntire just lives a few blocks from here. Joseph gets little Mary each morning and brings her to me for the day."

"She's a twin?" Lydia asked.

"Yes, she and her sister Sarah are as alike as two peas lying side by side in a pod." Emma laughed, and it was filled with joy. "In fact, yesterday morning, when Joseph went to get Mary, Sister McIntire gave Sarah to Joseph by mistake. They're that much alike. But the moment Joseph picked her up, he knew. 'I'm sorry, Sister McIntire,' he said, 'but this is not my little Mary.' Sister McIntire was a little embarrassed, actually, that she had made the mistake."

"I don't understand," Lydia said. "Joseph gets her every day?"

Emma nodded and smiled. The baby's eyes were getting heavy, and Emma slowed the rocking into a gentle swaying motion. She hummed softly for another minute or two until Mary was asleep; then she looked toward Lydia. "When my baby was born a silent baby, I was devastated, as you know, especially after losing my little Don Carlos too. I so wanted another . . ." She had to stop and look away.

"I know," Lydia said. "I know."

"Well, Joseph decided I needed another baby to help comfort me. Sister McIntire had given birth to these adorable twin girls a little before my baby was born. Joseph went to her and asked if he could borrow one of them each day for a while, to help me through this."

Lydia sat back, understanding now.

"Well, as you can imagine, Sister McIntire was somewhat reluctant about the matter, but Joseph promised that he would bring her back each afternoon and that we would never keep her overnight. So she finally relented."

"What a wonderful idea."

"Oh, yes. She is such a little beauty. And so good. She hardly ever cries."

"It has been good for you, Emma. I can see it in your face."

"I know. I really am feeling much better now."

"I'll bet it's good for Joseph too."

"Yes," Emma agreed with some sadness. "Joseph is much stronger than I am, but losing little Don Carlos was very difficult for him too. And then when we lost the baby as well, it was very hard for both of us. And he loves this little one like she was his own."

"I could see that when he came in," Lydia replied.

"In fact, a few days ago we got Sister McIntire a little upset. Joseph always picks Mary up at the same time each morning and takes her back the same time each afternoon. I thought he had gone to take her home, but then there was a knock on the door and when I went down it was Sister McIntire, wondering where her baby was. A little concerned, I went into the back room. There was Joseph. He had Mary on his knee, trotting her and singing to her, trying to quiet her. She had started to fret just as he was getting ready to leave, and he couldn't bear to cover her face when she was crying."

"And I'll bet Sister McIntire forgave him immediately, didn't she?"

"She did." Emma's voice got a little wistful. "Joseph has been wonderful in this whole thing, but . . ." Her voice trailed off and she looked away.

As Lydia was thinking what to say to that, the door opened and Joseph and Nathan came back in. In a moment they were in with the two wives and the conversation turned to other things.

Nathan was playing "horse" with his children. Elizabeth Mary, who would be four in May, was "in the saddle" squealing with delight every time the horse lurched this way or that. Josiah—who celebrated his first birthday in January by turning from a chair and taking his first three steps—toddled after them. He giggled and screeched, hanging on to the "reins"—a loose end of Papa's suspenders—and urging him on.

When the door opened and Lydia and Mary Ann stepped in, Nathan didn't even hear them. It was Josiah's cry of "Mama" that let him know they had company. Laughing, he reached around and helped Lizzie dismount, then stood up.

Lydia looked around. "Joshua and Emily aren't home yet?"

"No, but you're back sooner than I expected. It's not yet three. How was the meeting?"

Mary Ann slipped off her bonnet. Spring was definitely showing its face for the first time, but it was still cold enough to warrant bundling up. "It was wonderful," she said. "Sarah is such a fine woman."

"Such a doer," Lydia agreed. She reached down and scooped Josiah up, kissing him soundly. "Did you miss Mama?" she cooed.

Nathan looked offended. "I beg your pardon. I don't think he even realized you were gone."

She walked to Nathan and kissed him quickly on the cheek. "I'm sure he didn't," she laughed.

"I wanna play horse more, Papa," Elizabeth Mary said.

"In a while," he replied. "Papa needs to talk to Mama and Grandma for a minute." He turned back to his mother. "So what are you?"

She looked blank.

"Lydia said you were going to elect officers and everything for your ladies' society today. I just assumed my mother would be president or something."

Mary Ann poked at him playfully. "Oh, we didn't do anything like that. Today we just talked about what we wanted the society to be."

"What are you going to call it?"

Lydia set Josiah down and began to remove her coat. "We're not sure yet. Probably just the Ladies' Society. Eliza Snow is going to write some bylaws up and also draft a constitution to be presented for approval at our next meeting."

"Hmm," Nathan said, nodding.

Lydia laughed and looked at her mother-in-law. "That little 'hmm' of Nathan's means he approves."

Mary Ann laughed too. "I know. He first started using it when he was about Josiah's age."

"Why use a bunch of words when an effective murmur will do the trick?" he asked. "So when is the next meeting of your Ladies' Society?"

"We're not sure," Lydia said. "Eliza will work on the constitution, and then when she's ready, Sarah will call us back together."

"Hmm," he said again, winning him a pitying look from both his mother and his wife.

Jean Claude Marque, now Jean Claude Dubuque, had wise gray eyes hidden beneath heavy eyebrows that had once been black but now were peppered with gray. The wrinkles around the corners of his eyes were deep and made it seem as if he were in a perpetual squint against a bright sun glaring off the snow. Before coming to North America as a young adult, he had been one of eleven children in a family of poor farmers in the Alsace-Lorraine region of northeastern France. When a French Canadian timber baron advertised in the Old Country for young men willing to work two years in the forests of North America for free passage across the ocean, Jean Claude and two of his brothers signed on. But at the end of the two years, as was the case in many lumber camps, not only did the brothers have no money saved, they were deeply in debt to the owner, or rather to the store owned by the owner.

The youngest of the three brothers was killed when a saw blade in the mill hit a frozen gnarl in the wood and shattered, spraying metal like cannon shot. Shortly after midnight of the day following his burial, Jean Claude and his other brother quietly slipped away, taking only what they could carry, and leaving a burdensome debt that could never be erased. Arguing over what direction to take, they finally split. His brother turned east, determined to return to France. Instead, he made his way down the St. Lawrence River and ended up in New Scotland, or Nova Scotia, working the cod boats. There he married a stout English girl and eventually raised seven strapping fishermen sons.

Jean Claude realized that while his family's specific situation back in France had been intolerable, he had no desire to return to the life of a farmer. Lumbering was what he loved. Fearful that the long arm of the wealthy lumberman extended throughout Canada, he stowed away on a boat, crossed Lake Superior, and entered the territory of the United States of America. Changing his last name to Dubuque, after a childhood friend, he joined one of the lumber camps working the St. Croix River valley of Michigan Territory (a valley which eventually became part of Wisconsin Territory). As the need for good lumber soared and forests became depleted, he moved from place to place, eventually ending up at La Crosse. It was there that someone had pointed him out to Joshua Steed and he signed on for the new mill on the Black River.

It was the best deal he had yet made. He found Steed to be a hard-driving boss, but fair. Most important, when Joshua Steed found help he liked, he rewarded them well. Jean Claude was now the highest paid employee of the Steed and Son Timber and Lumber Company. And better than that, in Will, Dubuque had found a protégé and a young friend, filling the place of the son he had never had. It had proven to be a profitable choice for him all around.

He thought about all of that as he sat on the stool outside Joshua's office waiting to answer Joshua's summons. The door opened and the cook came out, Joshua just behind him. Joshua was still talking to him. "Get me that list of what you need and

I'll send it down to La Crosse. We may even be able to get some things sent up from Prairie du Chien."

"And you want me to plan enough to get us through the first of June?"

"Yes. At that point, we'll know better how many are staying on."

"All right." The cook nodded briefly to Jean Claude as he passed.

Joshua came forward, hand extended. "Ah, Frenchie. There you are. Come in."

They moved into the office and sat down, Joshua at the rough table that served him as a desk, the Frenchman directly across from him. "How is the work coming?"

"Very good," Jean Claude reported. "I think we can have another fifteen or twenty thousand feet cut before we start downriver."

"We only have another week," Joshua reminded him.

He shrugged that aside. "We can easily cut five thousand feet a day, and we've got enough logs backed up that you won't run short."

"Good." Joshua slapped his desk in satisfaction. "It's been a good year, Frenchie. A good year."

"Yes. Very good."

Joshua watched him narrowly for a moment, then smiled. "I don't like to beat around the bush, Frenchie, so let me get right to what I'm thinking."

"All right." Jean Claude, who was a man of few words himself, liked Joshua for that.

"You need to understand how I work. It has been the pattern in all of my endeavors. I hire the best men I can find, then watch them work. You can't always tell a good man by just looking at him, but you can sure get an idea of what kind of man he is while watching him work."

"I agree. It is the measure of a man."

"Yes. Well said. Once I find a man that I can trust, I move him up to a position of responsibility. As you know, my son has been assigned to be foreman of the camp."

"Will is a fine young man, Monsieur Steed. He learns very quickly and is a diligent worker."

"Thank you. I've been pleased with what he's done. But don't think that I am so blind to things that I do not know that it is you who has really kept the camp together."

Jean Claude did not dispute that. But, pleased at the acknowledgment, he inclined his head for a moment. "Thank you. The title is not important. You have been most generous in compensating me for my efforts."

"I think the title *is* important," Joshua said, "and I'd like to announce to the crew before we leave that you are foreman of the camp."

"Ah," he said softly. "Thank you. That is most kind."

"That means that once you get back up here you'll be in charge throughout the summer. I'm not coming back up here before October. And even then, I don't plan to stay. You'll be totally in charge, have full power to make decisions. Keep as many men on as you think is necessary. Order what you need. You do whatever it takes. By the time snow flies again next winter, I want two shifts running at the sawmill."

"Yes, monsieur. That is the way to plan. Too many come up just before the cutting season and start their preparations then. This way is better."

"Jean Claude," Joshua said, calling him by his formal name for the first time, "if you prove yourself this next season, come a year from now I'll make you a full partner. You, me, and Will."

Now Jean Claude was dumbfounded. A full partner? An owner? He had never made the mistake of allowing himself to get into financial bondage again, but over the years he had saved little of his earnings. Some of them went back to France; most of it was consumed just living. "Ah, monsieur."

"Joshua," Joshua corrected him firmly. "From now on, it's just Joshua. All right?"

"Yes, m— Joshua. But this is far too generous."

"It's how I work, Jean Claude. So far it's not ever proven me wrong." Then before Jean Claude could protest further, he changed the subject. "Now, there's one other thing."

"Yes?"

"I know I need an experienced man to stay in camp, but I'm also very worried about getting those rafts downriver. I'd like you to come with us to Nauvoo."

His eyes widened. "But—"

"You can come back up immediately thereafter. I think the Swede can oversee the camp for that long, don't you?"

"Yes, of course. But Joshua, this is wonderful. Will has told me so much about Nauvoo, how beautiful a city it is."

"Yes, it is."

"I have wanted to go, but did not dare to ask."

"Then it's done," Joshua grinned. "Let's call it settled."

"Ah," Jean Claude sighed, still unable to believe his good fortune. "Will has told me so much about your church and your Joseph Smith." He pronounced it Yo-sef Smeeth. "I never dreamed that I might actually have the chance to meet him."

Joshua's eyes were suddenly hooded, but in his enthusiasm Jean Claude did not notice the change. "The Mormons in the other camps? I have been much impressed. They are inexperienced lumberjacks, but good men. And they care for one another. That is a strange thing in a lumber camp."

"Will's been talking to you about the Mormons?" Joshua asked, with forced casualness.

"Ah, yes, we have talked about it many nights." He looked suddenly ashamed. "My family in France, we were all Roman Catholics, of course. Alsace-Lorraine is strong Catholic country. But since coming to North America, I fear I have not paid much attention to religion. It has been heavy on my mind these past few years. And this church of yours sounds very interesting."

"I'm not a Mormon," Joshua said shortly.

"Of course, I know that. I didn't mean to suggest . . ."

Joshua waved that off, leaning forward, deliberately keeping his voice level. "Will isn't either. Did he tell you that?"

"But of course. But now that he has decided, he will become one after you return to Nauvoo, no?"

"He's decided?" Joshua asked slowly.

Something in Joshua's eyes must have alerted Jean Claude, for the Frenchman was suddenly guarded. "He has not told you this?"

Joshua started to shake his head, and then snapped his fingers. "Oh, yes. He came to a decision while I was gone, I think."

Jean Claude was immediately relieved. "Yes, it happened just before you returned from Nauvoo."

Joshua stared at him. He had gone down to La Crosse a week ago. The thought had occurred to Joshua that maybe Will's decision had come then. They were in a wild race to finish getting the trees they had downed to the mill and ready for the raft. There had hardly been time for him and Will to talk at all. But if Will's decision had been made while Joshua was in Nauvoo, that was at least two months ago now. *Two months!*

He was aware of Jean Claude's puzzled expression now. He smiled to cover the tightness in his stomach. "Did my brother talk to you about the Church while he was here? He *is* a Mormon."

"Nathan? No, not at all."

"And Will? He's not been trying to force this religion stuff on you, has he?"

There was a short bark of laughter. "Ah, no. Just the opposite. I am the one asking questions all the time."

Joshua stood abruptly. "Well, I won't keep you." He reached across the table and shook the Frenchman's hand. "Then the foreman thing is settled?"

"Yes, Joshua. And thank you."

"No, thank *you*, Jean Claude."

Jean Claude gave a curt nod and turned on his heel. As he reached the door, Joshua called after him. "By the way, I need to talk to Will. Where is he right now, do you know?"

"He's about half a mile up Roaring Creek cutting timber with the Webster brothers."

"All right. I'll send someone for him if I need him."

Jean Claude went outside, stopping to breathe deeply in the spring air. As he rounded the corner of the building out of sight of the window to Joshua's office, he slammed the palm of his hand against his forehead. "*Quel dommage!*" he exclaimed. "Ah, Will, *mon ami*, my friend, my friend. What have I done?"

———◆———

Will was surprised to see his father striding toward them through the trees. He was making the undercut on a smaller tree, working alone while the two brothers were a dozen or so yards away, working together on a much bigger tree.

Will lowered his ax and waved. "Pa! I'm over here."

Joshua turned in midstride, making a straight line for Will.

"This is a surprise," Will said, pulling a large bandanna from his pocket and wiping his forehead.

There was the briefest of nods, and then Joshua turned toward the other two men. "Hey, you two." They were working on the back cut with a two-man saw. They stopped and looked in Joshua and Will's direction. "I've got to borrow Will for a while. When you finish with that one, take this one down too."

The older brother waved and they went right back to sawing.

Stepping away from his tree, Will shouldered his ax. "What is it, Pa?"

Joshua jerked his head and started off without a word. Puzzled by the cold abruptness of his manner, Will followed. They moved silently through the trees for almost five minutes, going deeper into the forest. When they were clearly out of earshot of the other men, Joshua stopped and turned. As Will came up, he saw the planted feet, the rigid jawline, the crackling eyes. He lowered the ax and set it against the nearest tree, then straightened slowly, looking squarely at his father. "Care to tell me what this is all about?" he asked quietly.

For several seconds, there was no response. But Will could see that his father was breathing deeply, fighting for control. Then it came. "Would *you* care to tell *me* about your decision to join the Church?"

It was as if Will had just plummeted over Black River Falls in a canoe. He just stared at his father, stupefied.

"I see," Joshua said after a moment. "And did Nathan baptize you too while I was safely out of the camp?"

"Nathan?" Will shook his head. "I haven't been baptized yet, Pa, I—" And then he understood. "You think it was Nathan who convinced me?"

It didn't even register. Joshua went on, his voice rising sharply now. He was almost raving. "I leave you two alone for a few weeks so I can go see to things at home and what happens? No wonder Nathan was so eager to come over to our camp and stay with you."

"It wasn't Nathan, Pa." Will was feeling a little dizzy now, still reeling from the suddenness of the realization that his father knew, and rapidly sensing that he had made a terrible mistake in not telling him before.

"Right!" It came out with heavy sarcasm. "And it wasn't your mother who encouraged you. And it wasn't Grandpa Steed who got his licks in every chance he got. Oh, no! It wasn't anything like that, was it?"

That cut deep and Will lashed back. He laughed softly, sadly, derisively. "It's always that, isn't it, Pa?"

"What?"

"It's always somebody else's fault, isn't it? It never occurs to you that I might do this completely on my own."

"Yeah. And I suppose Jenny had nothing to do with it either."

Will stopped in surprise. "Jenny?" Then his mouth pulled back into a tight line. "Jenny who, Pa?" he asked.

Joshua looked at him as if he were daft. "Jenny Pottsworth, who else?"

"It's not Pottsworth anymore, Pa. If you remember, it's now

Jenny Stokes." Then he was very tired. "No, Pa. Not Jenny. Not Nathan. Not Mama. Me! Just me! Sorry that you don't think I'm capable of that, but it's only me."

Joshua's head swung up and his eyes were blazing. "Don't you get smart with me, mister."

"Oh," Will flung right back at him, "so it's mister now, is it? Now that I've decided to become a Mormon, it's no longer Will or son. Now it's mister."

"A son of mine would have the courage and the integrity to come to me and tell me about this before I learned it from some-one else."

"Pa, I wanted to tell you, but things were going so well up here for us, I thought—"

"No!" Joshua shouted. "You didn't think! You didn't care." He flung one hand out. "You didn't care enough to even face me and tell me the truth. And now you're trying to sell your bag of beliefs to Jean Claude. Well, I won't have it, Will. Do you hear me? I won't have it!"

"Jean Claude?" Will repeated dumbly.

"Yeah, that's right. He let it slip. Let it slip that you've been feeding him all this tripe about Nauvoo and Joseph Smith."

"I've answered questions that he has, that's all."

There was an explosion of total disgust. "Don't, Will! Save your excuses for Nathan and the family. Personally, I'm sick of all the lying and the deceit."

Joshua spun around and started away, took only three steps, then whirled back again. "Well, I was planning on taking Frenchie south with us on the rafts, but not now, I'll tell you. Not now."

The sickness in Will was shoved aside by flaring, white-hot anger. "It must be a terrible burden for you," he shot back, "pro-tecting all the world from the evil influences of Mormonism."

That hit home and Joshua rose up to his full height, his jaw jutting out. But Will rode right on, giving his emotions full spur now and the devil with the outcome. "You want to know why I didn't tell you?" he cried. "Because I knew it would be just like this. It doesn't matter what I believe. It doesn't matter that I found that answer totally on my own. No, you can't accept that. Being a Mormon is something so awful that you can't face it. And so yes, I was afraid to tell you. You had me cowed, just like you have Mama cowed."

Joshua came stalking back, his fists clenching and unclenching, his eyes dark with fury. Will tensed, sure he was coming to strike him. In spite of his desire to stand his ground, he fell back a step in the face of what was coming.

"Cowed!" Joshua roared. "I've told your mother she can be baptized any time she chooses. She's the one who says she's going to wait."

Will hooted right into his face. "Only a dolt could be that blind."

Joshua's left hand shot forward, grabbing the front of Will's jacket. The other hand cocked back, fist doubled.

Now Will didn't flinch. "Is that what you did to Jessica when she wouldn't cheat for you at poker, Pa?"

Joshua froze, the fury suddenly laced with pain.

Will leaned forward, sticking his face out, daring Joshua to strike it. "Or maybe you ought to take a bullwhip to me like you let someone do to Nathan," he said contemptuously. "That's another way of handling things, isn't it?"

The fist dropped, the hand released his coat. Joshua stepped back, staring at his son—staring through his son—his eyes filled with a look Will had never seen before.

"You know not of what you speak," Joshua said in a hoarse whisper.

"Oh?" Will said, close to tears now. "You told me, Pa. Remember? That day when the other kids beat me up in school, you told me about Jessica. You told me about turning your back on Rachel." His voice strangled now, and what followed was half a sob. "She was your baby, Pa."

"That was a long time ago," came the reply, in a voice that sounded far away.

"Was it? Then why don't you do something for Rachel now? You act like she isn't even your child. You finally let her be first with the daguerreotype, but only because I said something to you. You give Savannah and Olivia all those beautiful things every time you come back from a trip. Why don't you ever, ever do something for Rachel?"

Joshua turned away from him, as though Will were no longer there. "We'll be starting to put the rafts together tomorrow," he said in a dull voice. "I want you to help Jean Claude with that."

Will stared at him in amazement. "What?"

He stopped, but didn't turn. "I've changed my mind. Jean Claude will be going with us to Nauvoo. We need his experience, taking all that lumber down the Mississippi."

He started on again, moving into the trees. "Pa!" Will shouted, crying now in rage and frustration. He didn't slow his step. "Pa, when we get back, I'm going back to sea again."

There was a moment's hesitation, and then he strode on, disappearing from Will's view.

———•———

Black River, Wisconsin—Sunday, 6th March

Dear Nathan,

This will be just a quick note, but I thought I'd better write it now so it will reach you in time for you to alter your plans. The cutting of timber continues to go well here in the camp. Jean Claude is guessing that the Mississippi should be clear enough to raft on by the 2nd or 3rd week of April. We plan to start sending the smaller rafts downriver to La Crosse around the 5th of April. That should take about a week. Then at La Crosse we'll tie them together into one big raft that we can take down the Mississippi.

But what I wanted to say to you was that I think it is not necessary for you to come back up here to help us. I know we talked earlier about needing your help, but I've asked Jean

Claude to accompany us and we should be fine. You have been away from your family enough for one season. We'll see you when we arrive in Nauvoo.

Joshua

Joshua laid down the pen and sat back. He read the letter again, picked up the pen, leaned over to make an addition, then changed his mind. Instead, he blew on it until the ink was dry, then folded it and wrote Nathan's name and address on the outside. He took the candle and tipped it so that a drop of wax sealed the fold shut. Then he tossed that letter aside and took another sheet.

The second letter was considerably longer than the first, taking almost two full sheets. When he finished, he read it over, scratched out a duplicate word, and corrected the spelling on another by writing over it twice. When the ink was dry, he folded the two sheets together and sealed them shut with another splotch of candle wax. He picked up the pen again and wrote the address in bold letters:

John C. Bennett, Mayor
Nauvoo, Hancock County, Illinois

———————

Alpheus Cutler, the foreman of the Mormon lumber operations on the Black River, was surprised when he opened the door and saw Will Steed standing there.

"Hello, Brother Cutler."

"Well, good evening, Will. We missed you at worship services today."

"I know. I . . ." He looked away momentarily. "I may not be able to come again before we leave. Things are getting pretty hectic for us."

"Us too. That's too bad. Is there something you need?"

Will stuck his hand into his coat and withdrew a letter. It

was one sheet, folded over and with the address written on the outside of it. "Could you see that this goes out with the next mail sled?" He reached into his trouser pocket and brought out some coins.

Cutler took the letter without comment, but was looking at Will strangely. The mail and supply sled from La Crosse would go through the Steed camp before it came here. Will could give it directly to them. But he kept his face expressionless. "Sure," was all he said.

Will dumped the coins into his hand. "I don't want my father to know about this," he said evenly.

So that was it! Cutler nodded. He didn't know Joshua Steed well at all, but he knew about his feelings toward the Mormons. "I understand."

"Thank you." Will turned and walked away.

The Mormon high priest watched him go, then looked down at the letter. It was addressed to Nathan Steed on Granger Street in Nauvoo, Illinois.

Chapter Notes

Joseph F. Smith, the firstborn son of Mary Fielding and Hyrum Smith, went on to become the sixth President of The Church of Jesus Christ of Latter-day Saints.

Joseph's "borrowing" of a baby, his ability to distinguish between the identical twin girls, and his caring for little Mary when she was fretting are all true. According to those who knew about this, he kept bringing Mary McIntire to his home until Emma could be comforted. (See Preston Nibley, *Joseph Smith, the Prophet* [Salt Lake City: Deseret News Press, 1946], pp. 378–79.)

A meeting was held in early March at the Sarah Kimball home to propose that a ladies' society be formed. Eliza Snow was given the task of drafting the bylaws and a constitution. (See *Women of Covenant*, pp. 26–27.)

The hastily called meeting finally ended up at Caroline's because Charles had just gotten up from his nap and was still a little crabby. Melissa was over at the brickyard help-ing Carl with some paperwork, but all the rest were there. Jennifer Jo and Rebecca, both awkward now in their coming motherhood, sat on chairs. Most of the rest stood. The chil-dren—except for Charles—were allowed to play outside under the care of the older ones.

Mary Ann looked at the eager faces and smiled. "I just talked with Sarah Kimball."

"And we are ready to form the Ladies' Society?" Jennifer Jo asked eagerly.

"Well, as you know, in our last meeting Sister Eliza Snow was given the assignment to draft a constitution and a set of bylaws for us. She did that, but decided to let Joseph look at what she had written first to see if he had any suggestions."

Caroline cut in now. "And what did he say?"

"He didn't like it."

There was a moment of stunned silence, then a chorus of disappointed groans. Mary Ann smiled. She was enjoying this. "Well, that's not really true. Actually, he said it was the best constitution for such an organization that he had yet seen."

Rebecca was relieved. "Really? He really thought that?"

Mary Ann sighed. "Yes, but he doesn't want us going ahead with our organization."

Down they plunged again. "No," Caroline cried. "Why not?"

Mary Ann was milking the moment for its maximum worth. "Because he thinks our constitution and our bylaws are not appropriate to the purposes of the Church as a whole."

The effect of that news was devastating. "But we were doing this to help others," Lydia said, clearly bewildered by this turn of events.

"Did he say what specifically was inappropriate?" Caroline asked, equally dismayed.

"No, he didn't," Mary Ann said. She paused, and now an elfish little smile stole across her face. "But what he did do was tell Eliza to come back to the group and see if we could meet at his store on Thursday afternoon next."

Their heads came up, and for a moment they weren't sure whether to believe her or not. Mary Ann nodded, her eyes beaming now. "Yes. Joseph said that he wants to meet with us and provide us with something much better than a written constitution."

That took a moment to sink in. She looked around from face to face, smiling broadly now. "He said that he wants to organize the women of the Church under the priesthood, after the pattern of the priesthood."

Rebecca was the first to speak after several seconds of silence. "You mean that . . ." She stopped, groping. "We'll be a part of the Church?"

"Yes," Mary Ann exulted. "Think of that. This won't be just another benevolent society. It won't be just us and Sarah and her friends. It will be part of the Church, for all the sisters. And the Prophet is going to organize it."

There were only four members of the Steed family women's council who came to Joseph's red brick store on Thursday, March seventeenth, 1842. Abigail Pottsworth felt that she could not take time away from work. Jenny Pottsworth was married and had moved across the river. Caroline and Olivia demurred—over Lydia's vigorous protest—fearing that their not yet being members of the Church might make their presence awkward. Kathryn McIntire and Jessica Griffith were no longer in Nauvoo. And Jennifer Jo had taken ill two days before and was feeling very weak. With her being in the family way, she and Matthew decided it wasn't wise for her to leave her bed. So it was only Mary Ann, Lydia, Melissa, and Rebecca who represented the family here.

They sat near one side of the lodge room on the second floor of the store. When they arrived, there were already nearly a dozen women there. Sarah Kimball was there, of course, accompanied by Margaret Cook, the seamstress who had first suggested to Sarah the idea of sewing clothes for the temple workers. Eliza Snow stood near the door, talking with Elizabeth Ann Whitney, wife of Newel K. Whitney, the second man called as bishop in this dispensation. Nancy Rigdon, one of Sidney's unmarried daughters, sat beside her sister, Athalia Robinson, wife of George Robinson, former Church recorder. Though Mary Ann recognized most of the women present, some she knew only as passing acquaintances. Most were married, but there were two teenaged girls, two widows, and others, like Eliza Snow, who had not as yet married.

Just then, the door opened and two more women came in accompanied by Elder John Taylor. The first woman was Elder Taylor's wife, Leonora. The second was also a wife of one of the Apostles. Bathsheba Bigler had married George A. Smith shortly after his return from England the previous summer. She was not yet twenty and was vivacious and full of life. Mary Ann liked her very much. The newcomers greeted Eliza and Sister Whitney at the door and the Taylors stopped to talk with them. Bathsheba saw the empty chair beside Lydia and immediately came across the room towards them, nodding at others she knew.

"Hello, Lydia," she said as she sat down. She reached across and squeezed Mary Ann's hand. "Mother Steed." She nodded to Rebecca and Melissa. "Joseph and Willard Richards are just downstairs. They'll be here in a moment. Emma's with Joseph."

"Oh, good!" Lydia exclaimed. "I know she very much wanted to come. I'm glad she's feeling up to it."

"She looks much better," Bathsheba said.

As they nodded, pleased with the news, the door to the room opened and the Prophet entered, followed by Emma and Willard Richards. Immediately the conversation in the room dropped off. Leonora Taylor, Eliza Snow, Elizabeth Ann Whitney, and Sarah Kimball all moved in to greet Emma. Joseph stepped back, conferring quietly with Elder Richards and Elder Taylor for a moment. Finally, Emma finished and Joseph escorted her to her seat.

To Mary Ann's surprise, after an invocation, Joseph made a few introductory remarks, then asked the sisters to discuss what kind of organization they had in mind. Instantly, hands shot up. He simply nodded, encouraging them to speak. "We have talked about this being a benevolent society, like other such societies in America," Sister Robinson said. "This was how the whole idea got started."

"Yes," Melissa spoke up. "We should have as our primary goal serving others."

"But I think we need to be different than other organizations," Lydia said. "They have noble goals for the most part, but they aren't working from a gospel perspective."

Sarah Kimball raised her hand. All eyes turned to her. "As many of you know, I lived in Utica, New York, for a time. It is one of the centers of the women's benevolent movement. As Lydia says, those organizations have become a wonderful and powerful force for good throughout America, but there have also been serious abuses."

A sister that Mary Ann knew only as Sister Cowles was nodding vigorously. "Where I came from, some of the funds were used to buy personal clothing and house furnishings for some of the members."

"We've got to be different from the world," someone else said from behind her. There was a murmur of assent that followed that.

"Sister Eliza," Joseph said, seeing that Eliza Snow's hand was up. She stood, turning to face her sisters in the gospel. "I move that the popular institutions of the day should not be our guide. I think that as daughters of Zion, we should set an example to all the world, rather than confining ourselves to the course which others have heretofore pursued."

"Second the motion," Melissa cried.

The room buzzed with agreement now. "Yes," several called out. "Let's have our own organization," said one. "Let's not do what everyone else is doing," agreed another. "Vote!" several cried.

Eliza turned to Joseph with a questioning look. "I think you should follow parliamentary procedures," he said. "We have a motion and it has been seconded. All in favor?" Every hand went up.

Following the vote, Sarah Kimball raised her hand to speak again. "I move that all of those present be accepted as members of this new organization in full fellowship."

Mary Ann spoke up now. "We have some who wished to be here today but could not. I would like to amend the motion to include them as well."

"Yes," Sarah agreed instantly. "Who are they?"

Mary Ann mentioned Jennifer Jo and Sister Pottsworth. Sarah had a neighbor. Another's sister was ill. When they finished they had seven additional names. Joseph called for a vote. "All in favor of accepting those so named plus those present as members in full fellowship?"

Again it was unanimous. Willard Richards—who, as one of his assignments as an Apostle, served as scribe and recorder for Joseph—was writing furiously to get it all down.

Joseph looked around. The room went very still. "This is as it should be, my dear sisters. As I said to Sister Eliza a few days ago, you are not to be organized after the pattern of what the world is doing. I see the purpose of this organization as becoming a Society of Sisters that provokes the brethren to good works in looking to the wants of the poor. I want you to search after objects of charity and administer to their wants. Correct the morals and strengthen the virtues of the community and save the elders the trouble of having to rebuke. I see you giving time to such duties and also to teaching."

Lydia leaned over to Rebecca. "A Society of Sisters. I like that."

Rebecca nodded. "Yes, very much."

"We have something much better for you than what the world has set as the pattern," Joseph continued. "We are going to organize you after the pattern of the priesthood. As you know, the revelations require that priesthood quorums be organized with a president and two counselors. As you prepare now to go to work, I recommend you organize yourselves in like manner. I would suggest that you elect a president and that she in turn select two among your number to be her counselors to assist her in the duties of her office."

He let them consider that for a moment before he asked, "Are there any nominations for president?"

Elizabeth Ann Whitney's hand was up instantly.

"Yes, Sister Whitney."

"I nominate Sister Emma Smith to be our president."

Emma whirled around in surprise, but Joseph was nodding, obviously deeply pleased. "We have the name of Emma Smith in nomination," he said, smiling down at his wife. "Are there other nominations?"

There were none. Everyone was smiling at Emma now, feeling the rightness of that choice.

"All in favor, then."

Every female's hand in the room went up.

Joseph motioned for Emma to come up and stand beside

him. "The election has been unanimously sustained. Do you accept?"

She nodded in dazed bewilderment. "I . . . yes, I am highly honored. Of course. I would be deeply honored to serve as your president."

He put an arm around her, pulling her softly against him. "Are you prepared to select your counselors, or would you like a few minutes to think about it?"

To his surprise, she looked around the room and then shook her head. "I don't need more time. I would like to select Elizabeth Ann Whitney as my first counselor."

There was a soft chorus of "aahs" at that and numerous heads bobbed up and down. Elizabeth Ann—or Mother Whitney, as many affectionately called her—was a woman of great faith and spirituality. The mother of seven children, one only recently born, she was not only beloved by all who knew her but greatly respected as well. Blushing deeply, she looked at Emma with tears in her eyes. "I would be honored, Emma. Thank you."

"And for the other?" Joseph asked.

Emma turned. "I select Sarah Cleveland," she said, smiling at a woman on the second row.

Mary Ann wanted to clap her hands at that. Sarah Cleveland was probably the oldest person in the room next to Mary Ann. She was also one of the kindest and had one of the purest hearts of anyone Mary Ann knew. Like Sarah Kimball's husband, Hiram, her husband was a well-to-do merchant in Nauvoo who was not a member of the Church. But, like Hiram, he was also a good friend to the Church. And then Mary Ann remembered something that at least partially explained Emma's choice. When Emma had fled Missouri with her children, Joseph had still been in Liberty Jail. Crossing the frozen Mississippi with children clinging to her skirts or in her arms, Emma had finally reached Quincy. There it had been the Clevelands who took Emma and her children in and cared for them. She had still been with the Clevelands when Joseph and Hyrum finally escaped and returned to the Saints.

Joseph was nodding too, and was probably thinking the same thoughts as Mary Ann. He whispered something in Emma's ear, then kissed her on the cheek. She smiled back at him, then returned to her chair.

"You have heard the names of Elizabeth Ann Whitney and Sarah Cleveland proposed as counselors. Those in favor?" There was no need to call for any opposing votes. Again it was clearly unanimous.

"You now have a president and two counselors to lead you," Joseph said to the group. "I commend Emma for her selection of counselors. I know both of these sisters very well and heartily concur in the choice." He turned and walked to a small table near the front of the room where copies of the Bible, the Book of Mormon, and the Doctrine and Covenants all sat on one end. He picked up the copy of the Doctrine and Covenants, then turned back to them.

"I need not tell you how I feel about your choice of my dear Emma to be your president. I may be a little prejudiced in this matter"—he stopped as the laughter rippled across the room— "but I think you will agree with me that she is a woman who has a unique standing in the Church. She has been at my side from the very beginning of the Restoration. She has endured loss and privation, ridicule and persecution. She has never wavered—not when I have been gone from her for long periods, not when we have had to have bodyguards sleep at the foot of our bed, not when we have been driven from state to state."

His voice caught now and he had to stop for a moment. "This woman has watched me be torn from her very arms, and from those of my children, and dragged off to what seemed like certain execution and she did not falter. She carried the precious manuscripts under her skirts as she and my children fled from the lawless rabble that ruled western Missouri. She has not stumbled. She has not fallen. Even now she stands by my side."

The sound of sniffing could be heard now, and Emma's eyes were moist as Joseph gave his tribute. He opened the book in his hands. "Just a few months after the Church was organized, I was privileged to receive a revelation from the Lord which was directed to Emma. I would like to read you something from that revelation now, for it is most appropriate in light of what has just transpired."

Looking down, he turned a few pages, found his place, then raised the book higher, "'Hearken unto the voice of the Lord your God, while I speak unto you, Emma Smith, my daughter. . . . Behold thy sins are forgiven thee'"—his voice rose sharply to emphasize the next phrase—"'and *thou art an elect lady*, whom I have called.'"

He lowered the book. "Shortly after that revelation was given, I laid my hands on Emma's head and set her apart to become an elect lady, to expound the scriptures to all, and to teach the female part of our community. On this day, you have raised your hands and *elected* Emma to preside over you."

He paused for a moment to let the import of what he had just said sink in. "This day, a prophecy, which was given almost twelve years ago now, is fulfilled."

Now his eyes came back to his wife, and Joseph spoke with great tenderness. "As we have said, this organization will have as its primary purpose the doing of good to those in need. Is there any better than Emma Smith to lead you in that endeavor? If you were to walk a block to the east of here, to the little house we all know as the Homestead—our home—you would find we have several others living with us at the moment. Many of you remember those terrible days in the summer of 1839, when every room in our house, when practically every square inch of grass around our house, was covered with the sick and the dying. And who ministered to them? Emma Smith.

"A few years ago, Emma once said something like the following to me: 'Joseph, I desire to be a blessing to all who may in any wise need anything at my hands.'" Now he had to stop and look down. He was blinking rapidly. Finally he reached up and brushed at the corners of his eyes with the back of his finger. "If there was ever a woman who deserved to preside over the organization we are putting into place this day, it is my beloved wife, Emma Smith."

Emma was weeping openly now, and so were most of the women in the room. Mary Ann could barely see Emma through her own tears. Beside her, Lydia and Bathsheba Smith were holding one another's hands. Rebecca was wiping at her eyes with her handkerchief. Melissa just let the tears stream down her cheeks.

Joseph looked up again at Emma, started to speak once more, but couldn't. He finally motioned for John Taylor to come up and join him. As he did so, the Prophet took a breath, then another, trying to regain his composure. "As I said," he finally managed, "some years ago I laid hands on Emma and set her apart to this calling. I'd like Brother Taylor to now give Emma a blessing and then ordain Sisters Whitney and Cleveland to their callings."

The blessings given to Emma and her two counselors were simple but filled with beautiful promises and gentle admonitions about fulfilling their duty. When he was finished and Sarah Cleveland had returned to her seat, the Apostle looked around. "Sisters, we have referred to what has just happened as an ordination, and so it is in a way. But this should not be confused with priesthood ordinations where priesthood power is given. Rather this is a setting apart to an office and calling by the hands of the priesthood. The blessings are real and will be ratified as these sisters fulfill their callings faithfully." And with that, he too sat down.

Three additional officers were selected—Elvira Cowles was chosen to be treasurer, Eliza Snow as secretary, and Phebe Wheeler as assistant secretary. Mary Ann didn't know the other two that well, but she couldn't help but nod at the choice of Eliza. She was an accomplished writer and a gifted poet. Many of her poems had been published throughout Illinois, and she was now referred to as "Zion's poetess." It was also interesting to Mary Ann that Eliza and Sister Cowles were not married and that Sister Wheeler was a widow. *Good!* she thought. This would tell the sisters that this was an organization of sisters, not just of wives.

Joseph next arose and spent some time teaching the sisters the rules of proper parliamentary procedures. This was the way to allow for discussion and even dissent in an orderly and amiable fashion, he told them. This would be important as they met and worked out how their society was to operate. Then Joseph gave them an opportunity to practice the principles he had just taught them. "Emma," he said, "I think it is appropriate that the first item of business for your new organization is to decide upon a name. As its president, the meeting is now yours."

Emma stood and came to the front. She stood quietly for a moment, just looking around at the sisters before her. Lydia watched her closely. There was still some evidence of what she had been through in the past six months, but this was more like the old Emma. Her face, for so long pale and drawn, was filled with color again. Her jet black hair hung in shining ringlets. The dark brown eyes were clear and wide, though they were still glistening from the emotions of the moment. Lydia felt a great surge of affection for this beautiful woman who stood before them now. Aside from being a wonderful friend, she was all that the "first lady" of the Church should be—kind, generous, giving, patient, gracious, articulate. It was little wonder that every hand had come up so swiftly to sustain her election as president.

As Emma began to speak, her voice trembled a little and she clasped her hands together to keep them steady as well. "My heart is full," she finally began. "This is such an honor to be so elected by you wonderful sisters." She glanced at Joseph and her mouth softened into a smile. "And to know that some twelve years ago, the Lord foresaw this day. I am truly humbled."

She took a deep breath, then became more businesslike. "Now, as to a name for our society."

Rebecca leaned over. "I like Society of Sisters," she whispered to Lydia.

Lydia nodded; then they both turned back to listen.

"I will express my feelings," said Emma, "and then we will hear suggestions from the floor." She took another breath, collecting her thoughts. "I feel very strongly that we should not be called after other societies of the world, especially when some of them have such a tarnished reputation. Those are my feelings, but I wish now to hear yours."

Sarah Cleveland's hand came up immediately.

"Sister Cleveland."

"What we are hoping to do is to provide relief for the poor and those in need. Therefore I would like to suggest that we call ourselves 'The Nauvoo Female Relief Society.'"

That brought a ripple of response from the sisters. John Taylor raised his hand. Emma nodded in his direction. "I agree that helping others will be the aim of this society, but it seems to me that *benevolent* is a better word than *relief*. Benevolence suggests charity and caring. I know that other societies have used that name, but it is still a noble word."

"But it is too much used by the rest of the world," Lydia spoke up. Then, a little embarrassed by her spontaneity, she raised her hand. Emma smiled and nodded for her to continue. "It is a good word, but if we make it part of our name, it will suggest to everyone that we are just another benevolent society. And I don't think we are."

Several around the room nodded at that, and Lydia was pleased to see that after a moment, John Taylor nodded too.

Now Eliza Snow's hand was up.

"Sister Eliza."

She stood. Now that she was secretary, she too was making a record of the proceedings and she had the papers and pen clutched in one hand. "I agree that *benevolent* is a tainted word and that we should not use it. On the other hand, *relief* seems too limited in my mind. *Relief* seems to suggest that we rise to meet the needs of people on some extraordinary occasions only. I think what we are after is meeting the more common occurrences of needs."

"I agree with that," Emma said quickly. "I agree that we do

not want people to think we are simply responding to great crises around us. But then, we are going to do something extraordinary too. When a boat is stuck on the rapids, with a multitude of Mormons on board, we shall consider that a loud call for relief. We expect extraordinary occasions and pressing calls for help. But at the same time, we must not ignore the commonplace needs. We must be observant and aware of what is right around us, perhaps even next door. Take, for example, Philindia Myrick, who is with us here today. She lives right among us, and yet she is in need. Her husband was martyred at Haun's Mill. Philindia is an industrious woman; she performs her work well, doing excellent needlework. But she has three children to support and care for. Think what a relief it would be to her if we in this society not only used her services when possible but also recommended to others the patronage of her needlework."

She stopped and smiled warmly at Philindia Myrick. Sister Myrick looked a little uncomfortable, but it was clear that she also appreciated Emma's concern and her suggestions.

Emma looked around at the others. Her words had had an effect, and she saw no more hands. "Unless there is further discussion, I then move that we call our organization, as recommended by Sister Cleveland, 'The Nauvoo Female Relief Society.'"

Again Eliza Snow's hand shot up. There was a quick, embarrassed smile. "I guess this is just the poet in me, but if we changed that slightly to be 'The Female Relief Society of Nauvoo,' it has a little better ring to it."

Emma smiled. "I agree. The motion is amended to read, 'The Female Relief Society of Nauvoo.' All in favor?"

She looked around, her face infused with pleasure. "Let it be shown that the motion has been passed unanimously."

Joseph stood and came to her. He slipped an arm around her waist. "This is wonderful, sisters. I now declare this society organized with president and counselors according to proper parliamentary procedures." He reached inside his coat pocket, giving his wife a huge grin. "From henceforth, all I have to give to the poor I shall give to this society so that it can be administered properly."

He extracted a five-dollar gold piece from a small purse. "Let me be the first to contribute to this wonderful cause." He handed the money to Emma and then gave her a solid kiss. That brought the women to their feet, and the room filled with the sound of enthusiastic applause.

Chapter Notes

The natural progression from various informal women's service movements to the sewing society for workmen's temple clothes proposed by Sarah Kimball led to the drafting of a constitution and bylaws as mentioned here. The intent was to organize a "ladies' society." Joseph's reaction to that draft led to the meeting in the Red Brick Store on 17 March 1842. Excellent minutes were kept of that meeting and we have extensive detail of what transpired. Wherever possible, the words found here are those actually spoken by those present or follow closely the summary of what was said. (See *Women of Covenant*, pp. 26–31, which offers a detailed and excellent treatment on the founding of the Relief Society.) In the original meeting there were twenty women listed as attending. Later, the names of Nancy Rigdon and Athalia Rigdon Robinson, daughters of Sidney Rigdon, were crossed out, probably because of their dissent and the fact that they eventually left Nauvoo. For this reason, later sources often say there were only eighteen present on the day of the organization. (See *Women of Covenant*, p. 444 n. 15.)

John Taylor's explanation that the sisters' "ordinations" were not priesthood ordinations but instances of what we now call being "set apart" was actually not given until much later (see *Woman's Exponent* 9 [1 September 1880]: 53–54). It is added here for clarity.

Elvira Cowles is listed as Cole in Joseph's history (see HC 4:567).

After several weeks of wet and cold, the last week of March saw spring come in its full power. The days dawned bright and clear, and the sun warmed the long-dormant earth. A frost of green began to cover the fields and hillsides. Suddenly there were songbirds again. The temperature soared into the sixties, which, after months of winter, felt like the heat of full summer. People came out of their houses in droves. Women sat on the porches with babies on their laps and toddlers playing nearby. The older children were like prisoners on a chain gang suddenly cut loose from their bonds. They roamed the city, rolling metal hoops, playing "run, sheepie, run" or "red rover." They flowed into the vacant lots for games of stickball. There was hardly a flat, open spot of ground that didn't have either a ring of boys around a marbles circle or a scattering of girls jumping their way through the hopscotch pads scratched into the ground.

It was young Joshua who saw them first. He and a group of other boys, ranging in age from seven to twelve, went to a large field on the eastern outskirts of the city. It had been plowed the previous fall, and while the winter's moisture had smoothed the ground considerably, there were still clods aplenty for a rousing game of "war." He and four others were huddled together, plotting their next attack, when a shout brought them up. "Joshua! Joshua!"

Just to the south of their battlefield lay the intersection of Parley Street and Carthage Road, the main road that led to the county seat and on to the east. It was a busy thoroughfare, and wagons and carriages had been passing back and forth most of the afternoon. But in the wagon now approaching from the east, Joshua saw two boys. They were on their feet waving and hollering. He stared for a moment, squinting, and then the clod of dirt he was holding dropped from his hand. "Luke? Mark?" He turned to Carl and David Rogers, his two cousins. "Look!" he cried. "It's Aunt Jessica and the boys."

With a whoop they were off, racing, shouting, jumping, waving to greet those in the wagon, who were doing exactly the same thing.

———◆———

"Nathan, I don't think you've ever met Mr. Garrett."

Nathan stepped forward, his hand outstretched. "No, I haven't." They gripped each other's hands firmly. "Solomon, I've heard a lot about you. It's good to meet you at last."

"My pleasure." Solomon stepped back, looking down at Jessica. Jessica was only about five foot three inches tall and he was close to six feet. But he was broad through the shoulders and solidly built, which only emphasized her slenderness. He smiled at her. "I guess that leaves only Joshua and Will that I haven't met."

"Now, you know that you are expected to have everyone's name memorized and recognize them on sight, don't you?" Lydia asked with a teasing smile.

Rachel sang out before he could answer. "We've been practicing all the way here."

They all laughed as Solomon Garrett colored. "That was supposed to be our secret, Rachel," he said with mock severity.

She just giggled.

Jessica poked at him with an elbow. "I told him that he had to be able to name every person in the family, tell who belonged to whom, and know what things he can or can't talk about with certain ones of us."

He gave them a crooked grin. "Don't talk religion around Joshua. Don't ask Will about Jenny Pottsworth. Don't ever tell Carl you're thinking of building a frame house."

Carl hooted at that. "That's right. What man in his right mind would consider building a house of wood?"

Jessica was beaming. "See? He's a good pupil, don't you think?"

As the laughter again rippled through the family, Nathan shot a quick glance at Lydia. One eyebrow was up in amazement. She read his meaning instantly, for exactly the same thought had crossed her mind. Jessica was teasing this big, gentle man beside her. They were bantering with each other. This from the woman who even among the family was the one who was most content to sit back and listen to the conversation around her.

Over the years, Jessica had become a very different woman from the one Nathan had met so many years ago on his first trip to Missouri. On that day, she still bore the bruises from Joshua's fit of rage. She had seemed so frightened, so timid and vulnerable then. And he had thought her plain. How wrong he had been. She was quiet, often content to just sit and listen to those around her, but there was a core of strength in her that amazed him. She still wore her brown hair straight and cut square at the neck, but her face had filled out with age and motherhood, and her features were intelligent and open. As he looked at her now, glowing as she watched Solomon Garrett, she was beautiful, and Nathan had to fight the temptation to sweep her up in his arms and hold her tight and say, "Thank you for being a part of our lives."

Someone else must have noticed that glow too, because once the laughter died again, Benjamin looked up at Solomon. "So, do you two have any announcements you would like to make?"

There was a stunned silence for a split second; then a kind of collective gasp went up from the family. Jessica nearly choked, and went instantly beet red. Solomon Garrett was only a shade or two behind her.

"Benjamin!" Mary Ann cried, whirling on him. She slapped at his arm. "For heaven's sake!"

He looked at her in surprise. "What?"

Nathan tried to stifle a smile. Caroline was openly chortling. Derek and Rebecca still looked shocked, as did Matthew and Jennifer Jo.

"Oh, you!" Mary Ann said disgustedly.

"What's the matter?" he persisted. "It's what we all want to know, isn't it? Just because I'm the only one with the courage to ask it."

"Not courage," she retorted, "gall!"

Kathryn McIntire sided with him against her foster mother. "Grandpa's right. They do have something to say."

Jessica turned to her, mouth open in a cry of betrayal.

"Well, you do!" she laughed, darting away as Jessica made a lunge for her.

"But I thought we would at least get inside the house first," Jessica said, laughing in spite of her embarrassment.

Solomon moved over to stand beside her and took her hand. "Yes, we do have something to say. It's not an announcement. Not yet. But it's something."

That brought an instant hush to the group. He turned and looked down at her, asking her with his eyes if it was all right to proceed. As she looked up into his face, he needn't have said anything. That look alone revealed more than he could say, but she nodded for him to go on anyway.

"Last Sunday evening," Solomon began, still looking at Jessica, "I proposed marriage to this wonderful woman here."

"Oh, Jessica!" Lydia cried. Rebecca clapped her hands together in an expression of pure joy. Mary Ann's hand came to her mouth and there were sudden tears in her eyes.

"She hasn't given me a final answer yet," Solomon started, "but—"

"She will," Benjamin cut in. "We'll see that she says yes before you leave here."

Mary Ann swung around, genuinely shocked now. "*Benjamin Steed!*" she exclaimed.

Benjamin simply ignored her. "Jessica may not know her mind yet, but we are all certainly rooting for you, Solomon."

Jessica was just staring at Benjamin, too dumbfounded to even blush now.

Brushing aside Mary Ann's withering look, Benjamin walked over to Jessica. He took her in his arms in a big hug, burying his face into her hair. "Jessica," he whispered into her ear, "you know that we count you as if you were our own flesh and blood, don't you?"

He felt her head bob up and down against his.

"We have been praying ever since you lost John at Haun's Mill that you would find happiness again."

She pulled back enough to look into his eyes. "You have?" she whispered.

"Every day." He jerked his head in the direction of the tall man behind him. "This is the answer, Jessica."

Now her eyes were wide with wonder and glistening with happiness. "Do you really think so?" she murmured. She was aware that the family was following very closely this quiet inter-change.

"No, I don't think so. I *know* so."

She pulled back even farther. Solomon had taken a step toward them, just beginning to sense what was happening. "But how?" she asked.

"I just know," answered Benjamin. "And in your heart you know it too. I know why you're a little afraid. But if you know it and I know it, don't keep this poor man in pain any longer. Just tell him yes."

Her eyes were suddenly brimming with tears. She turned to Mary Ann, who was close enough that she had heard every word. Mary Ann was no longer wanting to clap a hand over Benjamin's mouth. She nodded solemnly. "Grandpa's right."

Jessica turned back to Benjamin. Seeing the consternation he had caused only made him chuckle. "Are you ready?" he asked.

She almost fell back a step. "You mean right now?"

"Of course."

Solomon Garrett was hanging on every word, his head cocked forward a little, hardly daring to believe what was happening.

Suddenly, Jessica laughed, then threw her arms around Benjamin's neck. "Oh, Grandpa Steed," she cried. "I love you."

He was going to make some clever quip, but his voice betrayed him. "And we love you, Jessica," was all he could manage. "Very much."

She let him go and turned to Solomon. She took two steps forward. He did the same. And then her face softened. "Yes," she said.

He stared at her for a moment, and then he whirled toward Nathan. "She said yes."

"That's what I heard," Nathan laughed.

He swung back around, disbelief twisting his face again. "Really?"

"Yes."

It was Carl who broke the spell. He turned to Melissa and, loud enough for everyone to hear, said, "Remind me to talk to your father about becoming one of my salesmen down at the brickyard."

As the family erupted with wild joviality, Solomon covered the last two steps between him and Jessica and swept her up in his arms. The women rushed in right behind him and nearly swarmed them both under.

Mary Ann did not join them. Instead she walked over and slipped an arm through Benjamin's. "You really are quite hopeless, aren't you?"

"Hopelessly hopeless," he admitted cheerfully.

Then she gave him a strange look. "Did you really know?"

He nodded. "At Christmas. I was just waiting until Jessica knew too."

———◆———

It took about five minutes for the congratulations and the hugs and the handshakes to be concluded, but finally the family started moving into the house. As they did so, Peter hung back. Kathryn and Jennifer Jo were still near the back of the group, holding hands and both talking like competing squirrels. It had been almost three full months since the sisters had last seen each other, and they were holding hands and talking with great animation.

Matthew, seeing Peter, came over to stand beside him. "Kathryn looks good, doesn't she?"

"She looks wonderful," Peter said, just a touch too eagerly.

Matthew gave him a sideways look.

"I've missed her since she moved to Ramus," Peter said, a little self-consciously. "We've been good friends."

"Yes," Matthew said. He took Peter by the shoulder. "Well, let's go say hello, then."

As they moved forward, Kathryn glanced in their direction and the smile on her face slowly faded. She half turned to face them.

"Hello, Kathryn."

"Hello, Peter." It was said with cool detachment, as though she were being introduced to a passerby.

"It's good to see you again. How do you like being a teacher?"

"I'm not a teacher, just an assistant teacher."

"Oh, but still—"

She cut him off with clipped precision. "It's all right, I guess." Then she looked at Jennifer Jo. "I suppose we'd better go in and help Grandma Steed." She turned and flounced away, chin high, head forward, leaving Peter standing there feeling utterly foolish and Matthew looking like he had just witnessed an innocent bystander get hit by a wagon.

When they reached the door, Jennifer Jo took her sister's elbow. "Kathryn Marie McIntire," she said in a fierce whisper. "That was absolutely shameful. He was just trying to say hello."

"Yes," Kathryn hissed. "Now that Jenny's married, I'm finally on his list of people to be nice to."

"That's not fair, and you know it."

Kathryn opened the door and just tossed her head, then went inside.

Jennifer Jo stood there for a moment, staring after her. "Oh my," she finally murmured to herself, "he really did hurt you, didn't he?"

———————•—•———————

"Three letters today, Brother and Sister Steed." Sidney Rigdon, postmaster of Nauvoo, turned around to the row of pigeonholes behind him. "Two from Wisconsin, both for Nathan. One from Palmyra. I assume that's your mother, Lydia." He pulled them out and handed them to Nathan and Lydia.

"Thank you, Sidney," Nathan said.

As they walked outside, Nathan handed Lydia her letter, then looked at his two. He frowned. The top one was from Joshua. He had been expecting it for over a week. If Nathan was going to make it back north in time to help with the rafts, he would have to be going soon. It was already the twenty-sixth of March. He slipped his finger under the fold and broke the small seal. Lydia waited before opening hers, knowing what was coming and already dreading it.

As Nathan quickly read the letter from Joshua, his eyes widened. "Well, well!"

"What?" she asked.

He handed it to her and she read it. She turned to look up at him, her eyes as wide as his. "You don't have to go?"

"That's what he says. And I'm sure inclined not to argue about it."

"But that's wonderful, Nathan! Your father is going to be

pleased too. He's been worried about having you leave just when you're getting the land all surveyed and ready to sell."

"I know. I can't believe it."

"Is the second letter from him too?"

He looked at it. "No, it's from Will."

"Let's sit down," Lydia suggested. "You can read Will's while I read Mother's."

They found an empty bench in front of a dress shop and sat down. Halfway through his letter, Nathan had to stop and look away, feeling a great emptiness in the pit of his stomach. He looked at Lydia, but she was engrossed in her mother's letter and he decided to finish reading before letting her know. So he continued, his face growing more and more grave, the sickness within deepening with every sentence. When Lydia finally finished and started folding her letter again, Nathan spoke. "How's your mother?"

"She's fine. In fact, she sounds quite good."

"I'm glad."

"What does Will have to say?" And then she saw his face. "What?"

He handed this letter over to her too, not trusting himself to read it aloud to her. She began to read. First her eyebrows lifted in surprise, then she recoiled. "Oh no!" she exclaimed. Then after a moment, "No!" Still reading, she started to shake her head, one hand coming up to cover her mouth, as though she too were going to be sick. She glanced up at him once. "Oh, Nathan."

He nodded grimly.

When she finally finished, she let it drop to her lap. "This is terrible, Nathan."

"I can't believe it." Then suddenly his head came up. "*That's* why Joshua doesn't want me going up."

Her eyes narrowed a little. "You think so?"

He groped for Joshua's letter, opened it, and read the date. He folded it up again. "Both letters are written on the same day, which according to Will is the day after the fight between them."

"Oh, Nathan! What Will said to him about Jessica and

Rachel . . ." She wanted to cry, and surprisingly it was as much for Joshua as for Will.

Nathan reached out and took her hand. He was quiet for almost half a minute before he spoke. "They were both hurt, and so they struck back where they could inflict the most damage." The bleakness swept over him like a chill wind. "But I think Will has done the greater damage."

"So what do we do?"

He tipped his head back, rubbing his fingers against his temples, not sure even how to begin to formulate an answer to that. And then Lydia so startled him that he jerked forward again.

"You've got to go," she said simply.

He stared at her. "You read what Will said. Joshua thinks I am responsible for what happened. That's why he's saying don't come." But then instantly he nodded. "Yes. You're right." The euphoria of a few minutes before was totally dashed now. "I'll leave tomorrow."

He stood to face her, gathering her in his arms. Then suddenly he had another thought. "No, tomorrow's too late. Will said he's not going to run away from this, that he'll stay on until I get back up there. But I'm not sure how long that will last. If there's another blowup between them . . ."

Now his mind was racing. "I'll go to Joshua's stables and take one of his horses. We can either bring it back with us or leave it as one of the draft animals. If I ride hard, sleep only when I have to, I think I can make it in seven or eight days."

"Yes," she said, with fierce determination. "Yes, the sooner you're there, the better."

As Carlton Rogers backed out of the office at the brickyard and closed the door, a figure out near the low picket fence that separated the yard from the street straightened. "Mr. Rogers?"

Carl turned. It was almost seven p.m. and nearly full dark. The night was clear and there was a quarter moon, but Carl couldn't see clearly who it was. "Yes?"

"May I have a word with you?" The figure came forward swiftly.

Carl, hand still on the door latch, stiffened just a little. It was the mayor of Nauvoo, Mr. John C. Bennett. Carl's hand dropped to his side and he turned to face the man as he joined him on the narrow porch. "Evening," Carl grunted.

If Bennett noted the lack of cordiality, he gave no sign. Instead, he plunged right into the matter at hand. "Carl, I have—" He stopped, unctuous now. "May I call you Carl? I know so many of the rest of your family, I feel like I know you as well."

Carl nodded. They had met before at some general functions, but Bennett's fawning amiability was highly distasteful to him.

"I have a letter from your brother-in-law in Wisconsin."

"From Joshua?" Carl said in surprise.

"Yes. This is a matter of the utmost urgency." He gestured toward the closed door. "May we speak inside, please?"

When Lydia opened the door of her home about an hour later, she was surprised to see Carl standing there, hat in hand. "Evening," Carl said.

"Why, Carl, good evening. Come in."

He shook his head. "Thank you, but no. I was wondering if I could borrow your husband for a time."

"But didn't you hear? Nathan left for Wisconsin this afternoon."

"Wisconsin? But I was just talking to him yesterday. He said he wasn't sure when he would be leaving."

"You haven't talked to Melissa?"

"No. I was working late at the brickyard. I . . . Something came up and I came straight here."

"You'd better come in," she said, stepping back.

Ten minutes later when Carl left the house again, he walked away very slowly. "Oh, Joshua," he finally muttered, looking up at the sky, "what have you done?"

Late into the night and on into the early hours of the morning, Carlton Rogers lay awake beside his sleeping wife, staring up
at the ceiling in the darkness. Finally around three a.m., he fell
into a fitful sleep. When Melissa awoke about six-thirty, she was
amazed to find her husband still in bed beside her. Carl was
always up by five or five-thirty, winter or summer. He would slip
out of bed, dress, and go out into the main part of the house to
read or work on the books or just putter until she finally crossed
that long, long bridge between death and life and pulled herself
out of bed.

She went up on one elbow and stared down at him. It was
enough. He stirred, groaned softly, then cracked one eye open
and peered at her.

"Are you all right?" she asked.

He groaned again and turned over. "I didn't sleep very well."

She lay back down and snuggled up against him. He lifted
one arm and drew her to him. "You're working too hard at the
yard, honey," she said chidingly. "You were there until late last
night. You've been going early every day."

He reached up and put a finger to her lips. "Melissa, there's
something I need to talk to you about."

She reached up to pull his hand away, but just then they
heard Sarah start to cry down the hall. Melissa turned, sighing.
"Let me see to her. I'll be back."

He reached out and caught her hand. "This is really important, Melissa. Can you get breakfast for the children while I
shave and dress? Then we can maybe go for a walk, leave the
children with young Carl."

She gave him a strange look, then finally nodded. "All right."

Carl waited until they were clear away from the house before
he began. By then, Melissa's curiosity was spilling over into open
impatience. "John C. Bennett came to see me last night," he said
without preamble.

She stopped dead, as though he had struck her with the flat side of a brick mold. "Oh?" she finally said.

"Yeah. He told me some things that are pretty disturbing."

This time there was an open snort of disgust. "What did he do? Tell you about his private life?"

He gave her a sharp look. The sarcasm surprised him. By nature Melissa was one of the most tolerant people he knew. She abhorred talking about people in any kind of a negative way. It was one of the things he most loved about her.

His feelings must have shown in his face, because she turned just a bit defensive. "Well, there are some things I know that you don't. Someday I'll tell you about Rebecca's experience with that man."

His eyebrows knitted together and there was a sudden hardness to his face. "Rebecca?"

"Yes."

"Tell me now."

"No, I want to hear what—"

"Tell me now, Melissa. This is important."

So she did. She told about Rebecca's visit to the office of John C. Bennett and what happened there.

"Did she tell anyone else besides you?"

"She told Lydia. Lydia told Nathan. Nathan told Joseph. Why, Carl? What is going on? What did Bennett want with you?"

And so he told her. He told her about Joshua's letter and how he had specifically asked Bennett to come to Carl and tell him the same story he had told Joshua in January. Carl wasn't a member of the Church, Joshua said, but he wasn't a Mormon-hater either. He would be fair-minded about this. There wasn't time to wait until Joshua returned to investigate Bennett's charges. Someone had to look into them now.

Melissa's mouth was open in disbelief. "And Bennett wants you to . . . ?" She erupted, throwing up her hands. "And just what charges are you supposed to look into?"

So he told her that too. He outlined Bennett's accusations

against Joseph and the other leaders of the Church, holding back on some of Bennett's specific language, totally skipping other things he had said, not willing to have them fall on his wife's ears. Now her anger turned to horror. "Oh, that man! Carl, he is an evil, vile person."

"He swears there are others who will back him up in this. Men and women who will testify to what is happening. That's what he's asking me to do. Just to listen."

Suddenly, Carl swore softly and kicked at the dirt, completely startling his wife. "What is Joshua thinking, for heaven's sake?"

"You're not going to do it, are you, Carl?" Melissa cried in dismay. "You're not going to listen to those people. You know what they'll be. They'll be people who will say exactly what Bennett wants them to say."

Carl watched the emotions playing across his wife's face, and then spoke softly but earnestly. "Melissa, I've been awake most of the night thinking about this. So listen to me, and listen to me very carefully. I need you to hear what I'm saying."

"If you're saying that for one minute you're going to help out in this, I don't want to listen, Carl. I can't listen to that."

"You have to listen!" he said sharply.

Finally, she nodded, not looking at him.

"You know about what happened between Will and Joshua. Lydia told me that she let you read Will's letter."

"Yes."

"That's what triggered Joshua's letter to Bennett, Melissa. Think about that for a minute. Joshua knew all of this back in January, but he's ignored it until now. Why? Oh, he may have thought he would look into it when he got back, but he did nothing. Not until now. Why?"

Now she *was* listening. And thinking. "Because," she slowly ventured, "he feels like he's losing his whole family to the Church and he's looking for something that will help him stop that."

"Yes!" He gripped her arm. "And if we just brush this aside, pretend that it's not happening, or say that there's nothing to any of it, what is Joshua going to say?"

She began to nod, concern pulling at the corners of her eyes. "He'll be all the more bitter."

Carl swung away, throwing his hands up into the air. "I don't want any part of this. Even being around the man makes me feel like I need to spit something dirty out of my mouth. But we've no choice now." He sighed, very tired now. "If we're not careful, Melissa, this could tear your family apart again. I mean, it could totally tear them apart all over again."

Chapter Twenty

It was on the afternoon of April first, his sixth day out, that Nathan topped a bluff overlooking the frontier outpost of Prairie du Chien and Fort Crawford, which lay at the confluence of the Wisconsin and Mississippi Rivers. He reined in the horse, stopping for a moment to look at the scene before him. He had told himself he would stop at Prairie du Chien and pamper himself with the luxury of a bed, a bath, and a barber, and in that order. He was a sorry-looking sight. Three of the six days had seen heavy rains. He had slept in barns and sheds a couple of nights, under trees or out in the open for the rest. His face was covered with six days' beard, which itched to the point of driving him mad. His horse was filthy and nearly spent. It was time for a rest, before he pressed on for the last leg of the trip.

Suddenly, he stood in the stirrup, leaning forward. He rubbed his eyes, and peered more closely at the muddy brown river below him. He was absolutely thunderstruck. There in the river, tied up about a quarter of a mile downstream from the town, was a lumber raft. All through the winter, Nathan had listened to the experienced men talk about getting the lumber downriver. They bragged about the size of the rafts and about what life on them was like, but Nathan had put that down to the typical tendency of lumberjacks to boast and exaggerate. Now, as he stared in openmouthed amazement, he believed them. He had been prepared for something quite remarkable, but this?

The raft—or rather, the three separate rafts, hooked together loosely, like the skeleton of some gigantic serpent—was easily three hundred feet long, and a hundred wide. Close to an acre in total area if it was a foot, he decided. He shook his head. His mind would not accept what his eyes were telling him. How did you take something like that down the Mississippi? How did you even steer such a monster?

He sat there for almost a minute, trying to comprehend what it must have taken to put that thing together, but then the weariness caught up with him and he finally rode on. But as he started down the hill toward the town, he made a decision. As anxious as he was to reach his destination, he decided he wouldn't leave first thing in the morning after all. This he had to see for himself.

———•———

Nathan had to smile as he saw the man kneeling at the river's edge scrubbing out a shirt in the muddy water. The Mississippi was running high with the first of the spring runoff, and the water was a thick chocolate brown. He wondered if the shirt had been white to begin with. It certainly wouldn't be after the man was done. And evidently this was his only shirt, for his suspenders were down and he wore no other shirt over his long johns.

At the sound of Nathan's footsteps, he looked up. His hair was long but clean, his thick beard almost as red as his underwear. His eyes were surprisingly blue.

"Mornin'," Nathan called.

The man nodded.

"Could you tell me who's in charge of the raft here?"

The man sat back on his heels and started to wring out the shirt. "Why do you ask?" It wasn't said with any rancor, but there was a touch of wariness in the eyes. Nathan detected a clear Irish brogue in the man's voice.

"I'm headed back up to a lumber camp on the Black River to help my brother bring a raft down." He turned and surveyed the expanse of huge craft before him. "All winter long the men kept talking about how big one of these would be. I didn't believe them."

"Which camp?" the man asked, noticeably more amiable at the suggestion that Nathan might be a fellow lumberman.

"Joshua Steed's the owner. Frenchie Dubuque's the foreman."

"Ah," he said, smiling now. "Frenchie and I cut Norwegian pine up farther north a few years back." He shook out the shirt and then came over, sticking out his other hand. "Patrick McDonnell. I'm in charge here."

His grip was solid and powerful. Nathan would have hated to arm wrestle this man. "Nathan Steed. Would you mind if I looked around? This is fascinating."

"Come on," was the quick reply, "I'll show you."

As they moved to two boards that served as a gangplank, Nathan peered at the side of the raft. Some rafts were made of logs, but this was all sawn lumber, thick planks cut in a mill, just like what Joshua planned to do. He counted quickly. The raft was ten planks thick and the planks were two-by-twelves, so that made the deck of the raft about twenty inches above the waterline.

Nathan pointed. "How many more planks are below the waterline?"

McDonnell shrugged. "About that many more, I suppose. Frenchie will know this, but you've got to be careful you don't make your platform too thick or your draft will be too deep." He swore amiably. "And believe me, getting this little boat unstuck from a sandbar is no picnic."

"I can believe that," Nathan said. "How in the world do you steer this thing?"

"Come on, I'll show you." As they went aboard the raft, Nathan noted that two temporary shacks had been built on this section.

Another man, cooking something over a small fire in a brazier near one of the shacks, watched them curiously but said nothing. The Irishman moved to the front center of the lead section. There a huge oarlock and a massive oar had been attached to the raft. The oar was tipped down so that the blade was up and out of the water, and Nathan could see the oar's whole length. The blade itself was three to four feet long, and the handle another fifteen or sixteen, making the whole thing a good twenty feet long.

McDonnell laid out his shirt on the deck to dry, then moved to the oar. "These oars are used for basic maneuvering in the current. In shallower water we also use long poles." He turned and pointed. "There's an oar at the front and rear of each section. One or two men are at each oar. You just work together."

Nathan whistled softly. "And it really works?"

"Well, you gotta know what you're doing. And you have to remember that you can't turn this thing like a carriage."

"So you live right on the boat?" Nathan asked, turning to look at the two hastily constructed wooden shacks behind them.

"Well, kind of. We sleep out on the deck unless the weather's bad. Some always prefer to sleep on shore. The smaller shack is the cook shack. But the same thing holds true there too. If the weather's good we cook on deck or on shore."

"You tie up every night, then?"

"Oh, yes," McDonnell said. "You'll not be wanting to float this thing down the river when you can't see what's ahead of you."

"How big a crew does it take to run this?"

"We've got four men for each platform section, plus a cook."

Nathan moved to where long lateral boards, spaced at about eight-foot intervals, tied the whole platform together. He dropped to one knee to examine the system more carefully. At three-foot intervals all along the lateral boards, holes had been drilled and long steel pins driven into them.

He looked up at McDonnell, who had come to stand beside him. "The pins go all the way through?"

"Have to, otherwise the bottom layers would shift on you. Ever seen a raft auger?"

"No."

"It's just a very long brace and bit." He demonstrated with his hand. "The bit is about five feet long, and the brace is about here." His hands were at chest height. They started turning, as though he were drilling a hole. "You just drill straight through the whole lot, then drive the pins all the way through."

Nathan straightened. It was incredible. There was no other word for it. Even now, standing right on top of it, he could hardly believe what he was seeing. But what a savings of manpower. "Can you imagine trying to haul this much lumber six hundred miles by wagon?"

McDonnell laughed shortly. "You can try that if you like. Me, I'll stay with the river rafts."

By the time Will had been in bed for two hours he was into the deepest part of his sleep. The first three knocks on the door had no effect. Then, as the sound continued more loudly than before, it finally penetrated his consciousness. With a groan he finally opened his eyes. He threw the covers back and swung out of bed. Rubbing at his eyes, he stopped at the small table by the window and peered at his clock in the dim moonlight coming through the window. It was five minutes after eleven. He moaned. What idiot was out and about at this hour?

When he opened the door and saw Nathan standing there in the darkness, he just stared dumbly at him.

Nathan grinned. "Sorry, Will. Were you asleep?"

"Nathan?"

"Yes, Will. It's your uncle. Remember me? I'm back."

"But I thought . . ."

Nathan pushed his way inside, not waiting for an invitation, and set his bag down on the floor. "I know. You didn't think I was coming, did you?"

"No. Pa said he wrote you."

"He did. And I got it. I also got your letter. I decided it was best that I be here."

Will was awake now, though still a little dazed by the sight of his uncle standing there before him. Then he spontaneously reached out and hugged Nathan. "I'm glad."

"Me too. How are things?" Nathan asked quietly.

Will shrugged, shutting the door now. "All right, I suppose. I tried to apologize once and he just brushed it off. Said it wasn't that important, to just forget about it."

Nathan grunted. "Just like he has forgotten it, right?"

"Yeah," Will responded glumly. "We talk when we have to, but that's about all. And even then it's only about the business here." He tried a smile. "But I'm still here. That's something, isn't it?"

Nathan nodded. He pulled out one of the two simple chairs in front of the table and sat down. "I know this is not the best time, Will, that you need your sleep, but I don't know what's going to happen once your father knows I'm here. Maybe he won't let me stay."

Will took the other chair and sat down across from him. He considered lighting the lamp, but decided against it. They could see each other well enough in the moonlight through the window. "All right. But if you're going to tell me that what I did was stupid, you may as well save your breath. I know that. I've kicked myself a hundred times for losing my temper."

"You're not the only one at fault here," Nathan answered. "And it's not just you and your decision to be baptized that caused it. This whole thing with your mother and . . . well, I don't need to tell you all that."

"I know."

Nathan shook his head slowly. "You know part of it, Will,

but there are some other things you need to hear. I'm glad you told me what you said to your father about Jessica and Rachel."

"I shouldn't have said those things to him," Will cut in morosely. Then suddenly he flared. "But darn it, Nathan! Jessica used to be his wife. Rachel *is* his child. It's not right that he just pretend that she's not."

"Will, I want you to listen for a minute. You may not agree with it. I'm not even sure I do. But that doesn't matter. What's important is that you see into your father's heart."

"Yes." Will sat back, his demeanor very subdued.

"Good." Nathan took a deep breath, then let it out in a long, weary sigh. "I'm not going to go into all of what happened in the past. You already know that. I think you also understand that when your father was reunited with the family it created a very awkward situation between him and Jessica and Rachel."

"Yes. I know all that, but—"

Nathan's hand came up, cutting him off. "Maybe it wasn't the best choice. I've asked myself many times what I would do. I'm not sure. But his choice was not made out of selfishness or because he didn't care, Will. That's all I'm trying to help you see. You may fault him on his wisdom, but you can't fault him on his intentions.

"Did you know that your father risked his life to go into Haun's Mill and get Jessica and Rachel out?"

"I knew he went in, but he had the militia with him."

"The militia had specific orders not to help the Saints in any way. Your pa was under the gravest of danger when he disobeyed that order. Did you know that your father paid for Jessica's house here in Nauvoo?"

"Yes, but he helped everybody else too."

"That's right, but he didn't just *help* Jessica, Will. He paid for it. The rest of us have tried to pay at least some of that back. He wouldn't let Jessica pay him anything."

Nathan bored in relentlessly now. "Did you know that some of the money from Jessica's students came from your father?"

Will's head came up. "What?"

"That's right. Joshua hired some men at the freight yard specifically with the understanding that with the wages he paid them they would enroll their children in her school. It was a way of getting cash to her without making her feel like she was on charity."

One hand came up and Will began to rub slowly at his eyes. "No, I didn't know that," he said softly.

"And there's one other thing. I just learned this a few days before I left to come here. Jessica's engaged to be married again."

"No!" Will exclaimed. "Really?"

Nathan nodded, watching him steadily now.

"To whom?"

"To Solomon Garrett."

"That schoolteacher guy who asked her to come to Ramus?"

"The same."

"But that's wonderful!"

"Yes, it is, Will. And do you remember how that whole thing came about? Somebody told Garrett about Jessica and he came over to watch her teach. He was so impressed, he offered her that position in Ramus."

"Yes, Mother told me all about that."

Nathan was silent for a moment; then very quietly he asked, "Would you care to guess who it was that told Solomon Garrett that he ought to come and see Jessica Griffith's school?"

"Who?" Will started, then suddenly he reared back. "No!" he said again.

Nathan nodded slowly. "I'm not positive, but when I asked Solomon who had told him about Jessica's school, he said that a teamster was passing through Ramus and delivered an anonymous letter to him telling him all about her. He can't remember the name of the teamster, but he remembers the name of the freight company."

"Pa's?" Will asked in a whisper.

"Exactly."

Now Will dropped his head into his hands. "And I said those horrible things about him not caring."

Nathan reached across and laid a hand on his shoulder. "What's done is done, Will. But I felt that if you understood, if you knew what had been in his heart, whether you agree that it was right or not, it would be a first step to making things right again."

Will looked up in anguish. "What do I say to him?"

"Nothing. Not yet. When the time is right, just understanding him will help you know what to do."

Nathan stood. "Now, let's go to bed. I'm exhausted. You're exhausted. And there's still your father to deal with in the morning. And I don't think he's going to be very happy to see me."

When Joshua looked up and saw Nathan and Will entering the dining room together, he nearly dropped his fork. But there wasn't much of a chance to do any more than that. Nathan had been well liked during his stay in Joshua's camp, and he was warmly greeted by the crew. Jean Claude and Will eventually brought him over to sit across the table from Joshua, who smiled with forced warmth. "This is a surprise," he said. "Didn't you get my letter?"

"Yeah, it came an hour or two before I left. But I was all packed by then, so . . ." He smiled. "So here I am."

Frenchie clapped Nathan on the shoulder. "Well, we could have done it without you, but it's always good to have another man on rafts as big as we're going to have."

"Oh," Nathan said, turning to look at the camp foreman, "that reminds me. I bring you greetings from Patrick McDonnell."

"McDonnell!" the Frenchman cried. "Where did you meet that old bundle of gristle?"

And they were off as Nathan began to tell them about his experience in Prairie du Chien. After listening for a few moments, Joshua finished the last of his cup of coffee and stood. Nathan glanced up at him but Joshua didn't return his look. He moved to the door and started out. Then he paused, turning his head. "We've got some rafts to build, men," he said. "Let's not be spending the morning chawing on a piece of rawhide."

Ten minutes later the door to Joshua's office opened and Nathan stepped inside. Joshua didn't seem at all surprised and finished making an entry in the journal that kept the daily record of cuttings before he looked up. "You really did take me by surprise, little brother."

"I thought I would." Nathan came over and sat down on a chair beside him.

"If you got my letter, why did you still come?"

Nathan had expected that to be one of the first questions he would be asked and he had thought about it all the way up. There was only danger in trying to play games with Joshua in this matter, so he answered honestly. "I also got a letter from Will that same day. He told me everything. Then I knew why you were telling me not to come."

Joshua sat back, putting the tips of his fingers together and making a steeple with his hands. "So," he mused, "you jumped on a horse and came up to save us from each other?"

"Something like that," Nathan smiled.

There was no answering smile, not even a grunt.

"Joshua, I—"

"You're not needed, Nathan. This is none of your affair."

"Oh, I see," Nathan said. He had thought through this conversation too, so with just a touch of asperity in his voice he went on quickly. "If your boy falls in the river you want me to be there. Any other problem, it's none of my affair."

If the shot hit its mark, Joshua gave no sign.

"I'm not here to take sides against you, Joshua, in spite of what you think. I'm here to—"

"What time did you get in last night?" Joshua cut in bluntly.

"About eleven."

"Why didn't you come and wake me up?"

Nathan shrugged. "It was late. When I was here before, I

always slept with Will. I thought waking you could wait till morning."

"So you two lay awake all night talking religion and moaning about Will's wicked father."

Nathan slowly shook his head. "Wrong on both counts. Actually, I don't think the subject of religion was even mentioned."

"You didn't talk at all about his decision to become a Mormon?"

"Not a word."

Joshua's eyes were dark and brooding and there was no mistaking the suspicion in them. Nathan went on evenly. "Nor did we spend the night rehashing your battle."

"So you just came in, shook hands, said your prayers, and went to bed." Now the derision was open and contemptuous. "Or maybe you discussed the going price of lumber down south, eh?"

"No, we talked for about ten minutes. We talked about the family. I told him the news."

"What news?"

"Solomon Garrett has asked Jessica to marry him. With a little help from Father Steed, Jessica accepted."

For the first time there was a softening. "Really?"

"Yes. We're all very pleased. She seems very happy."

"That is good news." Then immediately the stiffness was back. "Does Caroline know about this whole thing between Will and me?"

"Yes. Will asked me to give his letter to her after I finished reading it."

Joshua shook his head, staring at the table top. "Welcome home," he muttered to no one in particular.

"You might be surprised."

Suddenly Joshua sat straight up. "Did Carl talk to you before you left?"

Nathan gave him a quizzical look. "Well, I didn't see Carl on the day I left, but he was at the family dinner three nights before where we honored Solomon and Jessica."

"But he didn't say anything about—" He caught himself and shook his head. "Never mind. If he had, you'd know what I was talking about."

"What?"

"It's nothing. It can wait until we get back to Nauvoo."

Nathan saw a chance to move to safer ground. "Which is how soon?"

Joshua shrugged. "The river's running high right now, which will save us lots of grief with the rapids. Jean Claude figures it will take about ten rafts to get it all down to La Crosse. Then we'll put them together into three or four platforms there. We've got four of the ten done, another one nearly so. We're hoping we can be on our way by next Monday."

"Monday! That's great. Then I got here just in time."

Joshua stood. "Let's go take a look."

Nathan stood too. Joshua started around him, then stopped and gave him a warning glare. "I appreciate you coming back up to help, Nathan. I do. But this isn't the time for meddling. Will and I are going to have to work this out between us, but we need to do it in our own way. Understood?"

"Understood. I didn't come up here to take over your role as father, Joshua."

"Good," he grunted. "I wasn't looking for a replacement."

They walked out together and started down the path that led to the sawmill. Nathan watched his brother out of the corner of his eye, but if Joshua was aware of the scrutiny he didn't show any sign of it. As they approached the clearing where the sawmill had been constructed, Nathan steeled himself and spoke. "Joshua?"

There was a murmured grunt.

"There's something you need to consider."

There was a sudden icy glint in Joshua's eyes. Nathan flinched a little, knowing this wasn't going to lessen the strain between them but knowing also that it needed saying. "You say you're not looking for someone to replace you as Will's father."

"That's right." It came out in clipped, hard words. "So don't you be volunteering."

"Then maybe you'd better ask yourself why it is that Will shares his innermost feelings with me and with Jean Claude but not you. You don't know what he thinks about Jenny. You don't know why he decided to join the Church. You don't know what he's feeling about you. In other words, you have no idea what's in that boy's heart, Joshua, and that's part of being his father too."

Joshua stopped, the fury rising in his eyes.

Nathan met it calmly. "Sorry, big brother. But that's something you need to think about, like it or not." And with that, he turned and walked on, leaving Joshua to stare balefully after him.

Chapter Notes

The great rafts of logs or lumber shipped to growing markets for building materials via the rivers of America are one of the little known aspects of our heritage. Masts and spars for the shipbuilding industry were a major export from the New England states, and people from those states perfected many of the rafting techniques described here. It is reported that along the Delaware River, which flowed out of the Catskills in New York State into Delaware Bay, there were as many as a thousand rafts going downriver each spring and summer. Huge rafts carrying as much as 150,000 board feet of lumber in a single chain became a common sight along the Mississippi as well during the early 1840s. The Wisconsin pineries—or "the Pine Woods," as the Saints often called them—became a major self-support effort of the Nauvoo Saints and proved to be a valuable source of lumber for the temple, the Nauvoo House, and other construction needs in the burgeoning city. (See Eric Sloane, *A Museum of Early American Tools* [New York: Ballantine Books, 1964], pp. 42–45; Dennis Rowley, "The Mormon Experience in the Wisconsin Pineries, 1841–1845," *BYU Studies* 32 [Winter and Spring 1992]: 136–37.)

I'll be working at the quarry today."

Melissa, at the stove, turned around slowly, the surprise obvious on her face.

Carl's head was down and he was working on cutting his ham and eggs with studied intensity. "Your father mentioned they're behind on getting the rock up to the temple site because they don't have enough teams."

"I thought you were taking that load of bricks out to the Morley settlement this morning."

He popped a generous forkful of ham, eggs, and fried potatoes into his mouth and began to chew. "That can wait until tomorrow, I reckon."

Melissa pushed the pan back to a cooler part of the stove and came over to sit across the table from him. "Did Papa ask you if you'd help out?"

"No, he just mentioned in passing that they were short."

"I see," she responded. She hadn't thought her family would make that request of him, and so it pleased her all the more that he was doing this on his own.

"Melissa?"

"Yes?"

"I do want to help out at the quarry. That's my main reason for going, but it may give me a chance to talk to people too."

She gave him a quizzical look; then a moment later she understood. He meant that he would talk to people concerning John Bennett and his wild stories. "I think that's good, Carl. Are you ever going to tell me what you're learning?" She had bitten her tongue more than once, trying to be patient until he felt it was right.

He sighed heavily. "Yes, of course. And I'll tell you now if you want. But I don't have all the answers. I'd really like to wait until I do. That is, if you're sure you want to hear it."

"Why wouldn't I?"

"It's not pleasant stuff. It's ugly, twisted, vicious. It's like taking poison for your mind."

Melissa nodded. And what was this doing to her husband's feelings about the Church? After all, Joshua wasn't the only one who needed worrying about. "I'm sure some of this is coming from our enemies. Is there any danger in hearing only one side of the story?"

There was a moment's silence, then a touch of reproof in his voice. "Joshua sent Bennett to me because Joshua thinks I will be fair-minded. Do you think I am a fair-minded man, Melissa?"

She was instantly contrite. She came over and stood beside him. "Yes, of course. I'm sorry, Carl." She bent over and kissed him on his forehead. "I have complete faith in you. And I'm glad you'll be talking to people at the quarry too."

He finished the last piece of ham, then stood up. "Kiss the children for me when they wake up."

"I will."

———•———

"Well, well. Good morning, Carl."

"Good morning, Israel."

"Where you off to this morning?"

Trying to appear nonchalant, Carl clucked softly to his team, pulling on the reins. He turned them off the road and pulled them in alongside Israel Barlow's wagon and team. "To be honest, I heard you might need some help hauling rock. I've got a free day, so here I am."

Israel gave him a long, appraising look, then smiled. "That's right decent of you to do that. We are running quite a bit behind."

"Then what are you doing sitting up here?" Carl asked chidingly. "Why aren't you down in the quarry loading up?" They were up on the bluff above the stone quarry. Some of the bluffs lining the river were made of limestone. The quarry was being cut into the face of one of those bluffs. Across the road and about fifteen yards beyond, the ground sloped and then suddenly disappeared. That was the edge of the quarry. About thirty feet below that was where the men were blasting and cutting the great stone blocks for the temple walls.

Barlow ignored the good-natured dig. "You're so anxious, you drive on down there. About the time you get your team backed into place, they'll set off that black powder and then you'll have your hands full."

"Oh," Carl said meekly. "So that's it. How soon?"

"About ten more minutes, they said. And that was five or six minutes ago. They're the ones who suggested it might be well to wait up here."

Carl nodded and set the brake lever. Then he stood and jumped off the wagon. Barlow's two horses, a finely matched team of black mares, jumped at the sudden movement. The near one snorted and started prancing nervously in the traces. Barlow grabbed the reins and pulled them in. "Whoa there, girls. Whoa! Settle down."

Snorting and blowing, gradually they calmed again.

"I see they're full of vinegar this morning, as usual," Carl said, admiring the two animals. The two of them looked almost like twins, though they had been foaled by different mothers. Black, with white stockings and with white blazes down their faces. They were a handsome team. But they had always been high-spirited and more than a touch jittery.

"They'll settle in, once they pull a couple of loads of stone back up this road and on to the temple grounds." Barlow stood and swung down from the wagon seat as well. He came around and took the bridle of the more nervous animal. "You may want to hold the heads of your team," he said, looking at Carl's heavier pair of draft horses. "The blasting always seems to spook 'em."

Carl laughed. His two—a roan and a bay—were a good working team, but they weren't much to look at. And right now their heads were down and their eyes half-lidded. "If I'm lucky it'll wake 'em up."

But as Barlow chuckled, Carl went around anyway to take the bridle of the near horse. The two men stood that way for a minute or two, looking over in the direction of the quarry, and then Carl decided to take advantage of the opportunity. "Can I ask you a question, Israel?"

"Sure."

He hesitated a moment, anxious not to offend this good man. And yet he knew Israel well and felt that he could ask him things he wouldn't feel comfortable asking other Church members. "I don't cotton much to gossip. Never had much patience for it."

"Wish more were like that," Barlow said, obviously surprised by that opening line.

"But I've just got to ask this."

Barlow guessed what he was going to ask. "No, Carl. There's no truth to those crazy stories about Joseph and Hyrum and the Twelve. None whatsoever."

Carl smiled briefly. Israel was a shrewd man, you had to give him that. "Then why isn't Joseph or any of the other leaders saying anything? Is Joseph aware of what's going on? Or the Twelve?"

There was a long silence, then finally a slow nod. "Oh, yes, they are very aware of it."

"You know how I feel about the Church, Israel, so what I'm about to say I say as a friend."

"And I'll take it as coming from a friend."

He reached up and started rubbing the muzzle of his horse. "There have been no public denials, no outward action. John C. Bennett—" Carl shook his head. "He's Assistant President of the Church, Israel. It looks like Joseph is either protecting him or is looking the other way."

"Carl, let me say something. Maybe it will help."

"All right."

"First of all, you need to understand something about how the Church works."

"I'm listening."

"In the revelations given to Joseph, the Lord set up ways for the Church to govern itself and cleanse itself of iniquity. In some ways, that system is similar to civil court systems. You appear before a tribunal, witnesses can be called, testimony heard, and if you disagree with the verdict, there is a way to appeal to a higher court, if you wish."

"Yes, Melissa has told me a little about this."

"But in the Church, just like in other courts, you can't simply act on hearsay, especially if someone is denying the accusations. You have to look into it, find out what is true. That's the first point. The second point is that the Lord specifically said these things are not to be done before the world. In other words, the proceedings are confidential. If the decision is that a person has fellowship withdrawn or is excommunicated, then that will be made known, but until then, the proceedings are confidential. This protects the innocent from being victimized by every rumor or wild accusation."

Carl grunted, considering that. "Then let me just ask you straight out. Is the Church trying to deal with this whole thing with John C. Bennett or is it simply being ignored because it is too embarrassing?"

Barlow just looked at him steadily.

"I'm not asking you to break any confidences, Israel. Just tell me this much. Is it being looked into?"

Barlow nodded slowly and solemnly.

"All right," Carl said, glad to hear that. "But I think Joseph is foolish if he doesn't publicly do something to counteract the stories."

"Why don't you come to the conference tomorrow? You might hear some things that will interest you."

Carl knew about that. Tomorrow was April sixth, the twelfth anniversary of the Church's founding. There would be three days of conference as part of that. "I've got to take a load of brick down to Yelrome. That'll take a couple of days, so I won't be back until Thursday afternoon."

"Then when you get home, ask Melissa if anything happened."

Carl leaned forward a little. "You think there will be something said?"

Before Israel could answer that, from behind them there was a tremendous *carrumph!* The earth shook beneath their feet. Carl's team jerked up, thoroughly startled, but he had a firm grip and that was that. Barlow's team was another thing entirely. The smaller of the mares jumped violently, nearly jerking Barlow off his feet.

"Whoa, girl! Whoa!" She whinnied wildly, panicking the second horse. They tried to bolt, nearly yanking Barlow off his feet, but he was hanging on to both bridles now. "Steady, girls! Steady!" he soothed, not giving them an inch of slack. Gradually his quiet firmness, the steady hand, and the soothing tones did the job. The blacks settled down again, though the far one was looking around with nervous jerks of her head.

Barlow patted them both a couple of times, then walked around to the wagon. "Well, I think that was our call to go to work."

———◆———

There wasn't a lot of turning room within the quarry itself, so the drivers wheeled around at the entrance, then backed the wagons to the spot where the big jib crane could lower the blocks of stones onto the wagons. Backing a team was always a bit tricky, and Carl watched Israel Barlow with admiration as he went in first.

The two black mares were almost dancing as he swung the wagon around and then started them backing up. He spoke softly, gently, as if he were talking to small children, coaxing, cajoling, imploring. He barely had to touch the reins.

"He does have a way with them, doesn't he?"

Carl turned in surprise to see Joseph Smith standing beside his wagon. He was dressed in workman's coveralls, wore a bandanna around his neck, and had work gloves stuffed in one pocket. He had come to spend a day at the quarry with his brethren. Carl turned back toward Barlow. "He certainly does. It's amazing to watch him."

Barlow finally had the wagon where it needed to be. "Whoa!" he called to his team. "Whoa, girls. Stand steady, now."

"We're beholden to you, Carl," Joseph said.

As Carl turned back to him, Joseph's eyes—blue as a spring sky—assessed Carl with disarming directness. Embarrassed, Carl tried to shrug it away. "Benjamin said something about you being short of wagons."

"It was mighty kind of you to pay heed," Joseph said, smiling now. "It seems like the Steed family are always putting us Smiths in their debt. Thank you."

"Glad to be of service."

Joseph moved away, going over to Barlow's wagon. He stopped at the head of the team, rubbing the nose of the near mare. "Morning, Israel."

"Mornin', Brother Joseph."

"Fine mornin' for hauling stone, no?"

"Indeed," Israel agreed. "Shouldn't be too hot today."

With a nod and a wave, Joseph started away, heading toward the quarry foreman. Then suddenly he stopped and turned back. "Israel?"

Barlow was just climbing down. He turned. "Yes, Brother Joseph?"

"On your way back from this trip, why don't you stop and get yourself a buggy whip for that team of yours?"

Israel stopped in midair, hanging from the wagon seat. "What was that?" he said.

Joseph smiled. Carl leaned forward, suddenly intent on this interchange. If anyone else had dared suggest such a thing, Israel would have taken his head off.

"Once you get that first block off-loaded, why don't you swing around in town and get yourself a whip."

Barlow slowly lowered himself to the ground. "But Joseph, you know I never use a whip with my team."

There was a quick nod, and then the smile broadened slowly. "Israel, why don't you stop in town on your way back and get yourself a buggy whip."

There was a long pause, and then, "Yes, Joseph."

Carl just stared as Joseph walked away. Israel Barlow watched him for several seconds, then swung around. He saw Carl and stopped. There was no expression on his face. He went to hold the heads of his horses as the men on the crane began cranking the first block of stone around into position.

———◆———

It was almost ten by the time Carl came back along the road that led above the stone quarry, headed back for his second load. As his wagon approached the quarry itself, Carl grinned. Two more wagons and teams had joined the work force now, and they were down below, waiting to be loaded, so Israel Barlow had pulled his wagon off the road at the same spot where they had talked earlier. The team was facing a small clump of trees, waiting for their turn. Even from this distance, Carl could see the slender shape of a buggy whip standing in the holder beside the wagon seat.

Pulling on the reins, Carl swung his team to the right, bringing them right in alongside Barlow's. "You made good time, what with going into town." He said it with a straight face.

There was a low grunt, noncommittal and expressionless.

"I'm sorry," Carl said, "but isn't this the man who brags all over town that he will never use a whip on his animals, the man who says that all he has to do is speak to his horses and they'll pull their hearts out for him?"

There was no mistaking the man's embarrassment. "It is the same."

Carl made no effort to hide his astonishment now. "Joseph makes one offhand comment, and you go and buy you a whip?"

"It wasn't just an offhand comment."

"He was making conversation, Israel. Teasing you a little, like the rest of us do."

Barlow's face was leathery and sunburned. The eyes seemed to be in a perpetual squint, a common trait of farmers and wagoners. He removed the hat and wiped at the dampness of his forehead. "I know this is something that you may not understand, good friend, but I believe Joseph Smith is a prophet of God. And when a prophet suggests that I ought to have a whip for my team, I'm going to get me a whip for my team."

Carl pushed back the smile that was fighting to surface. He didn't want to offend the man. He thought too much of him. "And so are you using it?" he asked.

There was a quick, emphatic shake of the head. "Not so far."

Carl couldn't help it. "Oh?" he said sagely.

"Look," Barlow growled, obviously chaffing. "He didn't tell me I had to use it, only that I should get one."

"Oh," Carl said again. "I see." And with that, he got down and busied himself with checking the harnessing on his own team, not wanting to embarrass the man further.

A few minutes later one of the wagons rumbled by, loaded

with one massive block. Carl climbed back up in the wagon, standing so that he could see down below. The second wagon was beneath the crane and the workers were winching the block up in preparation for loading. Barlow was also looking in that direction. "Looks like they're about ready for us," he said.

Carl nodded, and dropped to his seat. "You go first. I'll follow."

Israel sat down, released the brake lever, then took the reins in his hand. He snapped them softly over the backs of his team, pulling back on them. "All right, girls. Back it up. Here we go."

As they started moving, Carl watched. Those two mares didn't like backing up, he could see that. Their heads were snapping up and down. The one's ears were laid back flat against her head. Israel paid that no mind. He just kept talking to them in a low voice.

Then around the corner, from the same direction Carl had come a few minutes before, a buckboard appeared, coming at a trot. A man and a woman were inside, either headed for town or coming out to watch the work at the quarry. The light buggy clattered noisily on the hard packed road.

The nearest mare of Barlow's team swung her head around sharply, eyes bulging. "Whoa!" Israel said, raising his voice some. The team was still backing and the wagon was onto the road. But even though Israel was pulling on the reins now, trying to turn the horses, they weren't turning for him and the wagon was headed straight for the edge of the cliff overlooking the quarry. "Come on, girls," he cried, for the first time with sharpness to his voice. "Turn around there, now." He yanked on the left reins, trying to turn the horses' heads. But this only panicked the team further. The one whinnied wildly and reared, kicking back at the traces.

Carl was on his feet now, waving off the approaching buggy. Barlow's wagon was across the road now and was still going straight back. Another ten or fifteen yards beyond that lay the lip of the quarry. Worse, the ground began to fall off sharply right near the edge. "Israel, watch the cliff!" he shouted.

Barlow turned around and saw the danger. He slapped the

reins hard across the backs of his team. "Giddyap!" he yelled. The blacks did not respond. They were blindly fighting to be clear. Their necks were arched, yanking at the harnessing. Their nostrils were flaring, their breath whistling.

The buckboard driver, seeing what was happening, pulled his horse up sharply. But it was too late. The horses had finally stopped backing under Barlow's urgent commands, but the wagon was on the down slope now, just ten or fifteen feet from the edge of the cliff. Its weight started dragging them back. They began to paw the ground, trying to stop themselves, but it was no use.

In one leap Carl was off his wagon and running, but there was no way he could reach them in time. "Jump, Israel!" he screamed.

And then it happened. Israel Barlow was on his feet, flailing at his team with the reins, shouting hoarsely at them. In one instant, his hand shot out. He grabbed the buggy whip waiting in its holder. *Crack!* The tip of the whip caught the near horse square on the left flank. It jumped violently, smacking into the harnessing with an audible pop. *Crack!* The second snap of the whip was an inch above the second horse's ears. "Go!" Barlow bellowed. "Giddyap, there! Go!"

The whip was a blur, sometimes popping in midair, other times lying across the horses' flesh. This was a team not used to the lash, and they lunged forward in stunned surprise. Clods of dirt flew from the clawing hooves. Barlow was slammed back down into his seat, and nearly somersaulted backwards into the wagon bed. But he hung on as the wagon leaped ahead and was back out into the road again.

He let the horses run for twenty or thirty yards before he pulled them up. Carl was running hard after them, and as they stopped he slowed his step, coming up behind the team carefully. He took the bit of the closest mare. "There, girl," he soothed. "Whoa!" He rubbed her nose, then behind her ears, all the time speaking softly to her. He stepped to the other and did the same.

When they calmed enough so that Carl knew they weren't

"What did he say?"

"He said there was a story going around about him and members of the Twelve."

Carl sat up straighter now. "Yes?"

"Have you heard anything like that?" she asked.

For a moment he wasn't sure how to answer, but finally he nodded. "About how Brigham Young and Heber C. Kimball and others locked one of the women in her room for several days and wouldn't let her out until she agreed to being a dual wife?"

Melissa was amazed. "You knew about that?"

He sighed wearily. "Melissa, you wouldn't believe all that I've heard."

"Hyrum said that this story was common gossip lately, but judging from the reaction of the congregation, including most of my family, many hadn't heard it."

"*Most* of the family?" he repeated.

"Yes, my father admitted that he had heard it, but he hadn't even told Mama about it."

"And what did Hyrum say about this story?"

"He said that it was nothing but lies, that there was no truth to it whatsoever."

"Well, it's about time," he murmured.

"It's about time what?"

He shook his head. "Anything else?"

"The moment he sat down, Joseph stood up. He went right on from where Hyrum left off and then he gave us a pretty good dressing-down for believing and conversing about such fantastic stories and rumors as that."

"But he publicly said the story was false?"

"Yes, he did. Father says he's going to say more at Sunday worship services."

Carl nodded absently. "What time will that be?"

Her eyes were wide. "Ten o'clock. Do you want to go?"

He seemed surprised. "But of course."

Chapter Notes

Though a few details have been added for purposes of the novel, the story of Joseph's counsel to Israel Barlow about a whip and what followed shortly thereafter is found in Barlow's life history (see Ora Haven Barlow, *The Israel Barlow Story and Mormon Mores* [Salt Lake City: Ora H. Barlow, 1968], pp. 195–96).

At the general conference in April 1842, Hyrum and Joseph did both speak in condemnation of the stories that were being spread around Nauvoo at the time (see *HC* 4:585–86).

Ⅰf the family was surprised to see Carl come out of the house with Melissa and the children on Sunday morning, none of them gave the slightest sign. Melissa glowed inwardly at that. It would only have embarrassed him, so they simply took it without comment. They were so good to him. So good *for* him.

"How was Yelrome?" Benjamin asked.

"Good. Father Morley said to give you his best regards. Especially to Nathan and Lydia."

Jennifer Jo leaned toward Matthew. "Why especially them?"

"When they first moved to Kirtland, they lived out on the Morley farm. They know the Morleys very well."

"Oh."

"I hope Joseph is at the meeting this morning," Derek spoke up. "He still didn't look very well to me even yesterday."

"I hope so too," Carl said, causing the rest of the family to give each other surprised looks.

———•◦•———

If Joseph was sick, he gave no sign of it. When Hyrum turned the pulpit over to him he strode up there with great decisiveness. His countenance was somber but he seemed filled with energy. He let his eyes sweep across the group gathered beneath the newly budding leaves in the branches overhead. This was his style, this looking at his audience, but usually his face held a smile and his eyes were filled with appreciation and affection for his people. Today his face was grave and his eyes piercing in their intensity.

"Brothers and sisters, I have but a few remarks to make this day, but I shall be direct. The times demand it. I shall speak with the authority of the priesthood and in the name of the Lord God. My words shall prove to be the savor of life unto those who love life, or of death unto those who love death."

His voice was strong and filled with ringing power. He spoke effortlessly, yet his voice carried as clearly to the people at the very rear of the congregation as it did to those at his feet. Carl was fascinated. Melissa's report of what Joseph and Hyrum had said at the conference had piqued his curiosity. He wanted to know if Joseph was going to say more on that theme. Now he had his answer.

"Notwithstanding this congregation profess to be Saints, yet I stand here in the midst of all kinds of characters and classes of men."

John C. Bennett was sitting on the second row. Carl saw his head jerk up to stare at the Prophet, then drop as the scalding gaze swept across him. "I tell you in the name of the Lord, if you wish to go where God is, you must be like God. You must possess the principles which God possesses, for if we are not drawing towards God in principle, we are going from him and drawing towards the devil."

It was as if the words were smoking even as they came out of his mouth. The rest of the family would later say that he had the power of God on him. Carl didn't choose to put it into words.

He just felt the words slamming into the people around him, including some of those for whom they were precisely and specifically intended, and he exulted in it. This was what he had hoped for when he told Melissa he was going to the meeting.

"Yes," Joseph thundered, "I am standing in the midst of all kinds of people at this very moment. Search your hearts, and see if you are like God. I have searched mine, and feel to repent of all my sins."

He paused, not for breath, but to let them brace for his next words. "We have thieves among us. We who are supposed to be Saints have adulterers, liars, and hypocrites in our midst. If God should speak from heaven this very moment, he would command you not to steal. He would command you not to commit adultery, not to covet, nor deceive. He would say to you, my beloved brothers and sisters, be faithful over a few things and you will be rewarded in many things. Do you not understand that as far as we degenerate from God in this life, we descend to the devil and lose knowledge? And without knowledge we cannot be saved. When our hearts are filled with evil and we are studying evil, there is no room in our hearts for good, or for studying good.

"Do you hear me?" His question rang through the grove like a trumpet call. "Do you understand what I am saying to you? Is not God good? Then you be good. Is not God faithful? Then you be faithful. Peter speaks of becoming partakers of the divine nature. And how do we do that? We add to our faith virtue, to our virtue knowledge, and we seek for every good thing. *Every good thing.* And we shun the evil."

He stopped again. There wasn't a sound in the grove now. Even the birds which had been chirping steadily in the background seemed to have quieted. He looked around, his gaze sweeping like a great broom. Eyes were dropping everywhere, chins ducking down to avoid those blazing eyes that were filled with fire now.

"I declare unto you this day in the name of the Lord that the Church must be cleansed. I proclaim against all iniquity. I pronounce a curse on adulterers. I pronounce a curse on fornicators and every other unvirtuous person." Now there was a coldness that caused a little shiver to run up and down Carl's back. "I pronounce a curse on all of those who have made use of my name to carry on their iniquitous designs."

———•———

Melissa deliberately lagged behind the rest of the family. Carl was speaking to Benjamin about the land development and what they would do once Nathan returned. But when they finished, he dropped back to walk beside her.

"Well," she said quietly, "what did you think?"

He didn't have to ask her what she had reference to. "I think," he said very slowly and very thoughtfully, "I think that today the swords were drawn. The battle has been joined. Now we shall see much more clearly where the opposing lines are placed."

———•———

Jessica Griffith lay flat on her back, letting the patchwork of sunshine and shade play across her face. Her daughter, Rachel, and her foster daughter, Kathryn McIntire, sat beside her. Out in the sunshine, in an open field thick with the lush grass of springtime, her three sons—actually, two stepsons and a son—romped with wild abandon. Luke, who was nine and a half now, and Mark, who was seven, were pretending to be frightened townspeople. Little John Benjamin, who had just turned four a month ago, was in one of his doggy stages. He was on all fours, barking and attempting to snarl and growl. Thankfully, Luke and Mark acted as though he were terribly fierce. They shrieked and darted away. Then Luke "stumbled" and in a moment the dog was on him. He didn't go for the throat, as one might expect of a more threatening beast, but rather in moments he had Luke convulsed with laughter as he kept saying over and over, "I eat your tummy," and went for the abdomen.

Watching the boys play, Rachel shook her head, but not without affection. "Doesn't he ever get tired of that?"

Jessica lifted her head. "I don't think so."

Rachel, who was the one child Jessica had borne for Joshua Steed before they had divorced, was not quite a year older than Luke. She had turned ten in January. She had always been of a more sober nature, thoughtful, reflective, contemplative. It had been a great blessing to her when Jessica had married John Griffith and Rachel acquired a new father and two brothers. The boys were normal boys. They teased her and dragged her into their play, whether she was of a mind to join them or not. Over the past five years, any thoughts that they weren't full brothers and sisters had long disappeared. Kathryn McIntire was purely a foster daughter to Jessica, but the same was true with her; since moving in with Jessica and helping with the school, and particularly since they had moved to Ramus, she had become a full-fledged member of the family as well.

They were east of Ramus out on the open prairie. Since it was a beautiful spring day, school was out, and Solomon was engaged in a meeting, they had decided to have a picnic. Borrowing Solomon's buckboard and horse, they drove east of town, following a little-used dirt track that led past one or two isolated homesteads. About two miles out, Rachel had spied the creek and made the suggestion. "Let's follow the creek and look for blackberry bushes. Then when the berries are ripe, we'll already know where to come."

That sounded like a grand exploration to the boys and the decision was made. They unhitched the horse from the buckboard and put the hobbles on it, which would allow it to graze while they were gone. They took the picnic basket and started upstream, sometimes moving along the tree line looking for blackberry bushes, sometimes moving out into the open prairie when the undergrowth grew too thick. It had been leisurely and enjoyable. Eventually they found a stretch of blackberry bushes that was thick and several hundred yards long, and they knew their search had paid off. In celebration, that was where they spread out their picnic and ate lunch. Now it was time to lie back, let the boys play, and be simply and wonderfully lazy.

"I can hardly wait until we can come back and pick berries," Rachel said. "I'll bet no one even knows about this place. We'll have them all to ourselves."

"Yes," Kathryn agreed. "Maybe we could get the whole family to come and go with us."

Rachel sat up straight, her face infused with excitement. "Oh, yes, Mama! Could we do that? Do you think they'd come?"

"I'll bet they would," answered Jessica. "The promise of blackberry jam is a pretty strong invitation."

Rachel rubbed her hands together. "Let's do it. Can I write Grandma as soon as we get home?"

Jessica smiled at her daughter. It wasn't very often that Rachel got this excited. "Yes, of course. I think it is a wonderful idea." She sighed and sat up straight. "Well, I suppose we ought to think about starting back."

"Oh, no, Jessica," Kathryn cried. "This has been so wonderful today. Let's not go back yet."

Jessica yawned and stretched. "All right, if you absolutely insist." And with that, she lay back down and closed her eyes. "Just carry me to the wagon when it's time to go."

They lay there for nearly ten minutes, talking quietly, giggling at times like three-year-olds. Then Jessica stopped, coming up on one elbow and holding up her hand. Off to the west there was a low rumbling sound. She turned, then stood to see better. The sky above them had some high thin clouds but was still mostly clear and bright blue. But way out to the west, low in the sky, there was a line of clouds across the horizon. The tops were towering castles of white, beautiful against the blue. But their bottoms were almost black, and even as she watched, she saw the far-off glimmer of sheet lightning rippling beneath the gray undersurface.

She looked dejected. "Looks like there is a storm coming. We'd better pack up and head back."

They were into the middle of April now, which was still a little early for the spring thunderstorm season, but it wouldn't be unheard of at this time. She also knew how quickly such storms could roll in and cover the sky. "Boys!" she called. "There's a storm coming. Time to go." She ignored the cries of disappointment and the painful groans. "Come on. Help us gather things together."

"I don't want to go yet, Mama," Rachel said, even as she began folding up the quilt they had been reclining on.

"I know, Rachel. It's been a wonderful day, hasn't it?"

"We've got to be sure to remember how to get here, Rachel," Kathryn said. "I think your suggestion about having the whole family come out here to pick blackberries is a great idea."

———————

They had moved upstream at such a leisurely pace that Jessica had not realized how far from the buckboard they had come. Going up they had carried the full picnic basket and the quilt. Now, though the basket was empty, the boys were tired and finally Jessica and Kathryn had to take turns carrying Johnny. That slowed their progress even more.

By the time they finally came in sight of the buckboard, it had taken them nearly an hour, and the weather had deteriorated dramatically. The line of clouds was moving swiftly eastward. The sun was gone and the wind was blowing stiffly from out of the west, bending the grass and powering its way through the trees along the creek line.

"Where's Susie, Mama?"

Jessica turned and felt her heart drop a little. The buckboard was right where they had left it, but Susie, Solomon's mare, was nowhere to be seen. She forced a smile. "Oh, she's somewhere nearby, probably in the trees. With the hobbles, she can't be too far away. Luke, you and Rachel take Johnny to the buckboard. Mark, you carry the basket and the quilt." She glanced up worriedly. "If it starts to rain, just crawl beneath the buckboard. Kathryn and I will go find Susie." She handed Johnny to Rachel as the sky rumbled ominously above them.

Kathryn shook her head. "No, Jessica. You stay with the children. I'll go find her." She tried to sound optimistic. "She's probably in the trees."

Jessica nodded. The air had that heavy, oppressive feel that signaled this could be a real storm. And when it broke, it was going to be frightening to the children. "All right. Hurry."

Off to their left, a jagged tongue of fire lanced downward. Kathryn winced, but instinctively started to count. For every five seconds, the lightning strike was about one mile away. One, two, three, four—*crack!* She jumped. *That was close!*

"Hurry, Kathryn!"

She nodded and darted away.

"Mama. I scared!" Johnny wiggled out of Rachel's arms and hurled himself at his mother's legs.

She scooped him up. "Under the buckboard. Luke, put the basket in the wagon. Keep the quilt with us so it doesn't get wet."

Even as she spoke the first huge raindrops came slicing out of the sky at a forty-five-degree angle. One drop hit Jessica's arm, stinging like a pebble flung from a boy's slingshot. "Quickly now," she called. "Here it comes."

As Rachel and the two older boys dived beneath the small wagon, there was another flash, followed almost instantly by a shattering blast of sound. The air shook and the wagon rattled. Jessica let out an involuntary cry. Luke and Mark, who were trying to be brave, grabbed each other, hollering. Little Johnny screamed and clapped his hands over his ears. Jessica shook her head, momentarily stunned. She lowered Johnny to the ground and gave him a shove. "Under the wagon, Johnny. Quick."

And then it was as though that last shaft of lighting had punched upward, piercing the underbelly of some massive celestial reservoir. In one instant the huge raindrops came pelting downward, melded into a shimmering sheet, torrents so heavy that the trees lining the creek disappeared as though in a fog. With a cry of dismay, Jessica rolled beneath the wagon, already soaked clear through her clothing.

She raised her head, pawing at the hair plastered across her eyes, her head turning back and forth, trying to see through the curtain of rain that pounded down around them on all four sides now. "Kathryn!" She screamed it out. She couldn't see her. She grabbed at the hem of her dress and wiped her eyes. "Kathryn! Forget the horse! Come back."

"There she is, Mama!"

Jessica turned to look where Rachel was pointing. For a moment she saw nothing; then she saw the huddled figure, half-hidden in the grass that undulated like the roiling sea. She was forty or fifty yards away.

"*Kathryn!*"

Jessica saw her head turn. She seemed almost confused. Rain nearly obscured her. Then it cleared again. Jessica waved frantically at her. "Come back! Come back!"

There was a nod, and then she was up and running, head down, one hand up to shield her eyes from the downpour. Jessica peered at her more closely. She was carrying something in her other hand. It bounced and danced crazily alongside her body.

As Kathryn cut her distance to the wagon in half, she suddenly stopped. Straightening, she held up whatever it was she was carrying. She shouted something at Jessica.

"What?" Jessica cupped her hands to make herself heard above the roar of the wind and the pounding of the rain on the wood above her head.

"The horse is gone!"

And then Jessica saw what it was Kathryn was holding. She had the hobbles—two bands of iron held together by a short chain. She held them high in the air, waving them back and forth. Both bands were unclasped. And then Jessica knew what had happened. She wasn't used to hobbles, wasn't sure exactly

how the fasteners went into the clasps to lock the bands fast
around the shank of each front leg. Solomon had showed her
how to do it, but Susie kept moving away from her, anxious to
graze on the thick grass. It was far more difficult than Solomon
had said it would be. Now she knew she hadn't done it right.

"It's all right, Kathryn," she shouted back. "Come on!"

Kathryn started moving again, letting the hobbles drop to
her side. The wind was howling, tearing at her dress even though
it was heavy with wetness.

When the bolt of lightning struck, it hit the ground not
twenty feet off to Kathryn's right.

Blinding! Deafening! Shattering! Those were the words that
were normally used to describe such a phenomenon, but none of
those were even marginally adequate for the force of the strike.
Jessica had been up on all fours as she shouted at Kathryn, the
top of her head just touching the underside of the buckboard's
bed. The concussion slammed her backwards, so that she cracked
her head hard against the rear axle. With a cry of pain, she rolled
on the ground, knocked momentarily senseless. Dimly, as if in a
different room, she was aware that Johnny had bounced away
from her like a small ball. Now he was screaming hysterically.
Someone was sobbing. She turned her head, and even as she saw
Rachel clinging to Luke and Mark, she winced with pain. She
reached up and touched the side of her head. When she brought
her hand back down, the fingers were bright red. She stared at
them, not comprehending.

Gradually, her head and vision began to clear and she realized the blow had split open the scalp. Reaching up again, this
time more gingerly, she probed. It wasn't that bad. Less than an
inch long. And while it was bleeding freely, it wasn't that deep.

And then in a flash, almost as stunning as the lightning,
memory returned. She jerked around wildly. "Kathryn!"

Where Kathryn had been there was nothing, just the blinding rain and smoke. The smoke startled her, and then she saw
that there was a large black ring where the grass was scorched
and still smoking even as the rain extinguished any flames.

Scrambling like a crab, she was out from beneath the buckboard and hobbling across the meadow, as if staying in a crouch would somehow make her a smaller target for another strike.

A hundred yards behind her, the lightning hit in the tree line, and the earth trembled beneath her. There was a sharp tearing sound as the top half of a cottonwood tree sheared off and crashed to the ground.

"Mama!"

Jessica instinctively ducked, slowing only long enough to shout back over her shoulder. "Stay there!"

And then she saw Kathryn. She was flat on her back, sprawled grotesquely on the scorched earth like a child's doll thrown down in a fit of anger. Her arms were flung out above her head, one leg twisted crazily beneath her. Her shoes were gone. That registered oddly in Jessica's mind. She had been wearing shoes, but now they were gone. And then she saw one of them a short distance away, black, twisted, and still smoking.

"Kathryn!" She ran to her and dropped to her knees in the muddy soil, feeling the rain slashing at her back. "Kathryn!" She put her arms beneath the girl's shoulders and lifted her up. There was a soft moan, then silence.

"Oh, Lord, help me!" Jessica sobbed. She straightened Kathryn's arms and legs, then tried to lift her. She was dead weight. Dazed and half in shock herself, Jessica found it beyond her. Frantic now, blood streaming down one cheek, crying, sobbing, cursing the storm, cringing down against another possible strike, Jessica got beneath Kathryn's shoulders and tried to drag her back toward the buckboard. But it was too much. Kathryn didn't budge.

"I'll help you, Mama!" Luke was suddenly by her side, taking part of the load from her.

"No, Luke! Go back."

He ignored her, pulling hard, and grunting with the effort. And then Rachel and Mark were there too, their faces filled with terror, but determined to help. Mark clutched a handful of dress and pulled. Rachel grabbed one of Kathryn's hands. It was enough. Kathryn's body moved, and in a stumbling, halting scramble, they dragged the still form back to their makeshift shelter.

Beneath the buckboard, Johnny huddled in a tight ball, his face white, watching his family coming back to him, too terrified now for crying. Jessica reached out and touched his face. "It's all right, Johnny. Mama's safe now. It's all right."

And then she left the task of comforting John to Rachel. Ignoring the warm stickiness on the side of her head, she sat down beside Kathryn and gathered her up in her arms. "Oh, Kathryn," she whispered. "My dear Kathryn."

———•———

Solomon was the first to see the buckboard. He went up in the stirrups, staring for a moment, then shouted it out. "There!"

The men were scattered in a line, stretching clear to the trees. Some were on the other side of the creek, beyond the trees and out of sight. Solomon lifted his rifle and fired off a single shot, then spurred his horse.

At the sound of the shot, Jessica jerked up with a start, looking around wildly. The children came awake with a cry of alarm. Johnny started to wail almost instantly. On Jessica's lap, Kathryn didn't stir. And then Luke was out from beneath the buckboard and shouting, jumping up and down. "It's Solomon, Mama! They found us."

Carefully, letting Kathryn's head lower to the grass, Jessica crawled out and stood up beside her son. With a gasp, she felt her knees buckle, and she groped blindly for the side of the buckboard to steady herself. Her body was numb from sitting in a cramped position for almost three hours now, and the circulation in her legs had been cut off. But tears were streaming down her face as the horseman came thundering toward her. She laid a hand on her son's shoulder. "I told you Susie would go home. I told you they would come. I told you."

———•———

"Can you move your fingers?"

After what seemed like an eternity, Kathryn felt the command go down to her hands. There was a tiny movement in one finger.

"Wonderful! Can you move your hand?"

Concentrating hard now, Kathryn tried to raise her hand and do a little wave, let them know that everything was going to be all right.

"Can you move your hand at all, Kathryn?"

She tried again, fighting in her mind to make it happen. Sudden, hot tears spilled over and trickled down her cheeks. "I can't!"

The covers were pulled back from her legs and her night-gown was lifted slightly. Jessica rubbed her toes. "Can you feel this?"

"Yes."

Jessica didn't have to ask. More fiercely than anything she had tried since awakening, Kathryn willed her toes to wiggle back and forth. Nothing! The burning in her eyes was so intense she had to close them. "I can't!" she gasped.

"It's all right," Jennifer Jo said, leaning down to lay her cheek alongside her sister's. "You're awake, Kathryn. That's all that matters for right now."

She tried to move her arm. Nothing. Lift her leg. Nothing. "I can't move," Kathryn said, wanting to scream it out, wanting to throw her arms around her sister and cling to her with frantic desperation. But all she could do was croak it out as the hot tears burned her cheeks. "I can't move, Jenny. I can't move."

Chapter Notes

On 10 April 1842, two days following the general conference, Joseph preached at a grove near the temple site. In his history he described his address thus: "I preached in the Grove, and pronounced a curse upon all adulterers, and fornicators, and unvirtuous persons, and those who have made use of my name to carry on their iniquitous designs." Wilford Woodruff, renowned for his meticulously kept journal, wrote, "Joseph the Seer arose in the power of God; reproved and rebuked wickedness before the people, in the name of the Lord God." (HC 4:587–88.) It was Elder Woodruff who gave us a detailed report of the words Joseph spoke that day.

Jennifer Jo McIntire Steed tiptoed quietly up to Kathryn's bedside. Kathryn kept her eyes closed, pretending sleep, knowing who it was from the sound of the footsteps and the rustling of the dress. Kathryn was doing this kind of thing now, amazed at how quickly her other senses were developing. It had been only a week since she had regained consciousness, but she was discovering many things about herself that quite surprised her.

She could sense Jennifer Jo leaning over her, peering at her face to see if she was awake. When Jennifer Jo started to pull back, Kathryn let a tiny smile move around the corners of her mouth. "Good afternoon, Jennifer Jo."

"Oh, you!" her sister scolded with mock severity. "You're always doing that to me. How do you know for sure who I am?"

"It's easy," she said. "Your shoes squeak."

"They do not!"

"Yes, they do," Kathryn said solemnly. "Not bad, but they do.

And Matthew's boots have a little scrinchy sound. And Grandpa Steed's are—"

"Scrinchy?" Jennifer Jo feigned incredulousness. "Is that what you do all day, lie here and make up new words?"

"That and wait for my sister to try and sneak up on me."

Jennifer Jo leaned down and kissed her on the cheek. "How are you doing?"

"Good. It's been a good day. Lydia was here. Grandma Steed came over and read to me for a while. And the kids were here too. They are so darling. I only wish I could reach out and hug them. What did the doctor tell you?"

She rubbed her dress where the roundness of her stomach pushed against the material. "He thinks I'm going to have a baby."

Kathryn nodded gravely. "Have you told Matthew?"

Jennifer Jo giggled. "No, I thought I'd just wait until next month and surprise him."

"A month?" Kathryn cried happily. "Is it really down to only a month now?"

"That's about it. And I'm glad. Matthew is driving me to a frazzle. He'll barely let me lift a dish out of the cupboard."

"That's good. He's good for you."

Jennifer Jo's face broke into a smile soft with affection. "I know. He's so excited to be a papa." Then she straightened. "So, are you up to any more company?"

"Well, it's a busy schedule, but I suppose I could squeeze someone in. Who is it?"

"Peter's outside."

Instantly Kathryn's mouth pulled down into a sharp frown. She swung her head back and forth on the pillow. "I don't want to see him."

"Kathryn McIntire!"

"Well, I don't. Tell him I'm asleep or something." She quickly closed her eyes. "I am quite tired."

"Every time he comes over you're asleep. I think he's beginning to get a little suspicious."

"I won't see him, Jennifer. I don't need his sympathy."

"It's more than that, and you know it."

"Do I? He barely knew I was alive before all this happened. Now he's feeling guilty. That's all."

"He's been over to see you at least once every day, and you always have some excuse."

"Oh," Kathryn said sarcastically, "once a day even. How nice!" Then at the look which that won her, she relented a little. "Oh, I know, Jennifer. Aren't I awful? But . . . I don't want his sympathy, Jennifer. I don't!"

Jennifer Jo sat down on the edge of the bed beside her. "Do you know what I think?"

"No, and I don't want to," Kathryn said petulantly. She knew she was in for a lecture.

Her protest made no difference to her sister, who was trying hard not to smile. In a way this was wonderful, for this was much more like the girl they had known before the accident. "I think you're being absolutely shameful. And if you weren't in this condition, I'd put you over my knee and spank you a good one."

Kathryn giggled in spite of herself. "But I am in this condition, and if you tried something like that, people would think you were horrid."

Jennifer Jo smiled, then got immediately serious again. "I'm bringing him in, Kathryn." She stood.

"I don't want him to see me like this," Kathryn admitted in a small voice. "I must look awful."

Jennifer Jo reached in her pocket and whipped out a hair-brush. "I knew you'd say that, so I came prepared. Do you want me to have Matthew come and help prop you up with some pillows? He's right outside."

After a long pause, Kathryn finally nodded. "Yes, that would be better."

"Good." Jennifer Jo leaned over and began brushing her hair.

"You really are quite the tyrant, you know," Kathryn grumbled. "Has Matthew discovered that about you yet?"

"No." She shook the brush in Kathryn's face, looking very

stern. "And don't you tell him, either. He still thinks I'm adorable and wonderful and gentle and kind."

Kathryn wanted so much to reach out and touch that wonderful face that hovered above her. But she couldn't, no matter how fiercely she willed it, so all she could do was to say softly, "Then I promise not to give away your secret."

———•———

Matthew and Jennifer Jo left immediately, backing out of the room to leave Peter standing there in front of her with obvious awkwardness. As Jennifer started to close the door, she raised her hand, shaking her finger at Kathryn in warning, just as she had done earlier with the hairbrush. "Be good," she mouthed silently.

The door shut, and still Peter didn't move. "Please sit down, Peter," she said. "I won't bite you." There was a wry smile. "Actually, I couldn't anyway, not unless you come close enough."

Peter was obviously embarrassed by the direct reference to her condition. He came over slowly and sat down on the chair beside her. "How are you, Kathryn?" he finally mumbled.

"Well, doing the cleaning and the laundry today has really tired me out, but I'll be fine tomorrow."

He blushed deeply, thinking he had asked the wrong question. She laughed lightly. "Peter, it's all right. What happened has happened. If being all sad-faced and gloomy about it would make it go away, then I'd be the sorriest-acting female in forty-nine counties. But it won't change a thing. So it's all right to talk about it."

"I'm so sorry about what happened, Kathryn. It must be very difficult."

More terrible and difficult than you could ever, in your wildest imaginings, begin to comprehend. But she only smiled again. "Oh, it has its advantages. Everyone waiting on you hand and foot. Never having to do any work. People coming to see you. Even Peter Ingalls."

She thought he was going to faint with that much blood rushing to his face, and she remembered her sister's pointing finger. "I'm sorry, Peter. I don't mean to tease you. How are things at the printing office?"

He clutched for that like a man in a flood reaching for a passing log. "Fine," he blurted. "I'm having the best time now with Elder Taylor. And Brother Joseph is often there working with us. It's wonderful."

"That would be wonderful. How do you—" She suddenly stopped, turning to look at him. "Oh, Peter. Can you scratch my nose please?"

He started momentarily, then leaned forward. Gently, tentatively, he reached out and rubbed the tip of her nose.

"Up a little. Oh, yes, there. Harder." And then after a moment, she sighed. "That's good, thank you."

He was staring at her, his eyes quite filled with sadness. "I never thought about what that must be like."

She shook her head. "When there's no one around when I get an itch, sometimes I think I'll go mad."

He nodded, suddenly awkward again, and for some inexplicable reason, it angered her. She knew why he was embarrassed, even understood why it was difficult for him to face her like this. And had the situation been reversed, she knew that she would likely do exactly the same thing. But she didn't need his pity.

"Thank you for coming, Peter."

It came out so abruptly that he jerked up a little.

"It was very nice of you. Thank you."

He stumbled to his feet, not meeting her eyes. "I wanted to. I tried before and you—"

"I know. I'm sorry. It was really very nice of you, but I'm getting quite tired now."

"I understand. Well . . ." He lifted a hand. "Can I come see you again?"

She cut off her retort before it could clear her tongue, then finally nodded slightly. "I suppose."

He started to turn, then swung back, remembering. "Oh, I . . . I brought you something." He reached into his pocket and brought out a folded sheet of foolscap. He started to hand it to her, then realized his mistake. She wouldn't be reaching out for it. "I . . . It's a poem I wrote for you." Then almost in a panic, he dropped it on the coverlet and fled from the room. "Good-bye, Kathryn."

She watched the door close behind him, then slowly closed her eyes. "Good-bye, Peter."

It was not thirty seconds later that the door opened and Jennifer Jo came back in. She had a reproving look on her face, but when she saw Kathryn's expression, she changed it to a quick smile. "Well," she said brightly, "that was nice of him to come."

"Yes, I suppose it was."

She ignored that, spying the sheet of paper. "Hello, what's this?"

"It's a poem."

"For you?"

"Who knows?" she replied caustically. "Maybe it's one of his old castoffs that he wrote for Jenny."

Jennifer Jo frowned at her, but let it pass. She picked up the paper. "Did he read it to you?"

Kathryn moved her head back and forth against the pillow.

Jennifer started to reply to that, then took a quick breath instead, obviously trying to hold her patience. "Would you like me to read it?"

"No," she retorted. "Just leave it there on the chair. I'll get up and read it when I have more time."

Her sister watched her steadily for several moments, then put the paper back down again. "All right. When you need me, just call." She turned on her heel and started for the door.

"Jennifer!"

She stopped, turning to look at Kathryn over her shoulder.

"I'm sorry. Forgive me for being such a shrew."

Jennifer Jo gave one quick bob of her head and returned, acting as if nothing had happened. She picked up the paper, opened it as she sat down beside Kathryn, and skimmed it quickly.

Suddenly there was a shimmering in her eyes. Her lips pressed together as she read it again, more slowly now. Then her hand dropped and she turned her head quickly away.

Kathryn was astonished by her reaction. "What?" she asked softly. "What is it?"

She spoke to the opposite wall. "I don't know if I can read it out loud, Kathryn."

That was the last thing Kathryn had expected. Now any thoughts of anger toward Peter were forgotten. "What does it say? Read it to me, Jenny. Please."

She saw her sister's shoulders lift and fall. Her eyes were swimming, and Kathryn saw that the hand which held the paper was trembling slightly.

There was another moment as Jennifer Jo tried to collect herself; then she looked down. "He has titled it simply, 'Flight.'" She began to read in a low, husky voice.

> The bird in me flew free—
> Over forest, over sea—
> Rejoicing in the open sky;
> Gliding through the endless, boundless space.
>
> The hunter's net unseen—
> Blocking passage, snaring wing—
> Disdainful of unfettered flight;
> Clutching me within its cold embrace.
>
> A rusting cage now home—
> No more forest, no more foam—
> Confining more than death itself;
> Drooping down, my wings and heart debased.
>
> But spirit deep within—
> Unrestricted, lifts again—
> Refuses to surrender joy;
> Starts to seek alternatives to flight.

What bars of earthly form—
Steel or iron, wind or storm—
Can bind to earth my boundless heart;
Stopping me from pushing back the night?

My freedom lies within—
Only sorrow, only sin—
Can clip my inner wings;
And bind me tight.

Shackles of my own
Are all that stay my flight.

For several moments, there was silence in the room. Then Kathryn, her own voice tremulous and strained, spoke. "Will you read it again for me, Jenny? Very slowly this time."

———•———

Generally, each Thursday afternoon at two o'clock the Female Relief Society of Nauvoo gathered in the meeting room on the upper floor of Joseph's red brick store on Water Street and there met under the direction of Emma Smith and her counselors.

So it was that on the afternoon of April twenty-eighth, six women of the Steed family—Mary Ann, Lydia, Caroline, Melissa, Rebecca, and Jennifer Jo—climbed the stairs to the upper floor of the Red Brick Store. Mary Ann had asked about having Caroline become a member and was assured that was fine. Everyone knew she was a member in all but name only. They were greeted warmly at the door by the presidency, with Caroline and Olivia receiving a special welcome. As they moved inside, Mary Ann was surprised to see Joseph at the front of the room. He had his head down reading in his Bible and did not look up. "This is marvelous," she whispered to Caroline. "I think Joseph is going to address us."

"Oh, good," Olivia whispered back. "I love to hear Joseph speak."

After the song and prayer and general business were concluded, Emma stood again. "As you can see, we have our prophet
with us today. It is an honor and a privilege to have him take this
time with our society. He has consented to speak to us on some
matters related to the priesthood, particularly as they apply to us
as women. President Smith."

Joseph rose, and as Emma passed him to sit down, he reached
out and kissed her quickly on the cheek. "Thank you, Sister
President," he said loudly.

An appreciative ripple of laughter flooded the room as
Emma, pleased but embarrassed, inclined her head in acknowledgment.

Now Joseph's demeanor brightened all the more. "What a
grand sight this is! Your society is growing in size, and already
there are reports of your good service. The Lord is pleased, sisters. He is very pleased."

He turned and picked up the Bible sitting on the table.
When he faced them again, his demeanor sobered somewhat.
"As Emma has indicated, I wish to talk to you today about the
priesthood, showing you how the sisters can come into possession of the privileges, blessings, and gifts of the priesthood. Also
I wish to say a word or two about the gifts of the Spirit and how
you might attain to those gifts in your own life."

He opened the Bible to where he already had inserted a slip
of paper. "I should like to call your attention to the twelfth chapter of the book of First Corinthians wherein the Apostle Paul
says, 'Now concerning spiritual gifts, I would not have you ignorant.' That is my desire as well. I would not have you ignorant.
Paul also tells us that the Church is like a body and that every
member of the body is needed."

He closed the Bible and set it back on the table. "Now, sisters,
what Paul is teaching here is the necessity of every individual acting in the sphere allotted him or her, and filling the several offices

to which they are appointed. It seems to be part of human nature to consider the lower offices in the Church dishonorable or at least as having less honor. Many look with jealous eyes upon the standing of others who are called to preside over them. It is folly and nonsense of the human heart for a person to be aspiring to other stations than those to which they are appointed of God. It is far better for individuals to magnify their respective callings, and wait patiently till God shall say to them, 'Come up higher.' "

He smiled, but it was without mirth. "Now, you may be wondering, 'Why is Brother Joseph making these remarks?' I will tell you. I have learned that there are some foolish things circulating in this society already. I understand that in previous meetings some sisters who were ill had hands laid upon their heads and they were blessed to be healed."

Lydia and Melissa exchanged quick glances. At the end of the previous two meetings, women complaining of illness had requested a blessing at the hands of the presidency. Emma agreed to it, and she and her counselors anointed the afflicted individuals with oil, laid their hands on their heads, and blessed them to be healed. It had created no small stir among the women, and on the way home Lydia and Melissa had debated whether this was proper or not. Lydia thought that such an administration was strictly a priesthood ordinance. Melissa wasn't sure. What added fuel to the debate was that one of the sisters had made a remarkable recovery.

"There are those of your number," Joseph was saying, "who are critical, saying that such action is improper, that the presidency is not doing right in this matter. My first reaction to that is, if a person has been healed, should we not have common sympathies and rejoice in that, no matter the source of that healing?" Again he picked up the Bible. "Let me reason with you further." He turned the pages until he found what he was looking for. "This is the Savior's commission to the Apostles, as found in Mark, the sixteenth chapter, fifteenth through the eighteenth verses. 'Go ye into all the world, and preach the gospel to every creature. He that believeth and is baptized shall be saved; but he that believeth not shall be damned.'" Now he spoke with greater emphasis. "'*And these signs shall follow them that believe;* In my name shall they cast out devils; they shall speak with new tongues; they shall take up serpents; and if they drink any deadly thing, it shall not hurt them: *they shall lay hands on the sick,* and they shall recover.'

"Now do you understand, sisters? It says that these signs follow those—*whether male or female*—that believe, not just those who hold the priesthood. We are not talking about women taking upon themselves the priesthood. We are talking about women exercising faith! If the sisters should have faith to heal the sick, then let the rest hold their tongues and let everything roll on."

A shadow crossed Joseph's face now and he seemed suddenly weary. But when he went on, his voice was still firm and powerful. "I do not know that I shall have many opportunities of teaching you. You may not long have me to instruct you. Soon you may be left to yourselves," he went on, more quietly now. "The world has been much troubled by the instructions of Joseph Smith." He smiled sadly. "Well, ere they know it, they will no longer have me to teach them."

A pall had fallen over the room. Faces all around the room registered the shock at the bluntness of his words. It was as though he were saying farewell to them.

"Do not fear," he went on after a moment of looking down at his hands. "Soon I will deliver the keys of the priesthood to the Church, and you who are the faithful members of the Female Relief Society will receive those keys in connection with your husbands, that the Saints may know how to receive instruction for themselves. And this is good, for according to my prayers, though I know not how soon, God has appointed me elsewhere."

Jennifer Jo looked at Rebecca, clearly distressed and nearly in tears. Rebecca just shook her head. She could hardly believe what she had just heard.

But then, just as swiftly as the despondent mood had come upon him, it passed. Joseph's shoulders pulled back and his eyes cleared. He looked around at the assembly of sisters before him and his face softened with love for them. "I should like to exhort you sisters directly for a moment. Concentrate your faith and prayers for your husbands. Place confidence in them whom God has appointed for you to honor, and in those faithful men whom God has placed at the head of his church to lead his people. Arm and sustain them with your prayers; for the keys of the kingdom are about to be given to them, that they may be able to detect everything false. These keys shall be given to all the elders who shall prove their integrity in due season.

"Oh, my beloved sisters, this is a charitable society, and that is according to your natures. It is natural for females to have feelings of charity and benevolence. And you are now placed in a situation in which you can act according to those sympathies which God has planted in your bosoms. If you live up to these principles, how great and glorious will be your reward in the celestial kingdom! If you live up to your privileges, the angels cannot be restrained from being your associates."

Lydia straightened, feeling a chill run up and down her body. *The angels cannot be restrained from being your associates?* It shot through her like a jolt of fire.

"Females, if they are innocent, can come into the presence of God, for what is more pleasing to God than innocence? But you must be innocent, or you cannot come up before him. You need not be teasing your husbands because of their deeds, but let the weight of your innocence, kindness, and affection be felt. This is more mighty than a millstone hung about the neck; not war, not jangle, not contradiction, or dispute, but meekness, love, purity—these are the things that should magnify you in the eyes of all good men. When iniquity is purged out from the midst of the Saints, then the veil will be rent and the blessings of heaven will flow down—they will roll down over us like the mighty Mississippi River which lies just behind us."

Lydia felt as if she were being pummeled with the power of his words. Angels as associates. Coming into the presence of God. The veil rent! What greater promises were there than

"I Now Turn the Key in Your Behalf"

these? It was as though every cell in her body were being fed, enlightened, enlarged. She looked around and saw the rapture on the faces around her and knew that she was not alone in feeling it.

Joseph's shoulders drooped a little now, as if he had been drained of his strength. He let his eyes sweep across the group. No head was down, no eye was straying. He nodded in deep satisfaction. "Beware of self-righteousness. Be limited in the estimate of your own virtues and do not think yourselves more righteous than others. As you increase in innocence and virtue, as you increase in goodness, let your hearts expand, let them be enlarged towards others. You must be long-suffering, and bear with the faults and errors of mankind."

He sighed now and they all sensed he was moving toward a conclusion. "You will receive further instructions through the order of the priesthood which God has established, through the medium of those appointed to lead, guide, and direct the affairs of the Church in this last dispensation. I now turn the key in your behalf in the name of the Lord, and this society shall rejoice. Knowledge and intelligence shall flow down from this time henceforth. This is the beginning of better days to the poor and needy, who shall be made to rejoice, and they shall pour forth blessings on your heads. God bless you wonderful sisters. May he bless and sanctify your work and your desires. You have the keys to be part of the great work of God. Go forth and serve as only you can do."

And with that, he turned, walked back to the chair beside Emma, and sat down.

Chapter Notes

Joseph's address to the sixth meeting of the Female Relief Society of Nauvoo was recorded in great detail by Eliza Snow, the secretary to the organization. Many significant things he said are not included here. What is included are Joseph's words with only minor additions to clarify what he was saying. (See HC 4:602–7; *Women of Covenant*, pp. 43–50; Joseph Smith, *The Words of Joseph Smith*, comp. and ed. Andrew F. Ehat and Lyndon W. Cook [Provo, Utah: Religious Studies Center, Brigham Young University, 1980], pp. 114–19, 139–42.)

Two points require some additional explanation for modern readers. In reference to Joseph's comments about administering to the sick by females, the original minutes as kept by Eliza stated that Joseph said that the practice was in accordance with revelation. However, possibly concerned that the Prophet's remarks might be misinterpreted to mean that women were being given permission to officiate in a priesthood ordinance, Church historian and Apostle George A. Smith—who heard many of the Prophet's discourses and teachings, and was personally well acquainted with him—added clarifying comments to flesh out the minutes when the discourse was prepared for publication. The expansion (which points to D&C 42:43 as the revelation referred to by the Prophet) makes it clear that Joseph was speaking about the laying on of hands through faith and not a priesthood ordinance. (Compare HC 4:607 with *The Words of Joseph Smith*, pp. 119, 142.) Also, Elder Dallin H. Oaks has noted that during this discourse Joseph said that the time had not yet come that these things were put in their "proper order" and could not be until "the Temple is completed" (see HC 4:603; *The Words of Joseph Smith*, p. 115). Elder Oaks stated that once temples became more widely available to members, "'proper order' required that these and other sacred practices be confined within those temples." (Dallin H. Oaks, "The Relief Society and the Church," *Ensign* 22 [May 1992]: 36.)

The second item has to do with the Prophet's reference to the "keys of the kingdom." He said these would be given to the sisters through their husbands and would help the elders "detect everything false." Normally, today when we use that phrase "keys of the kingdom," we speak of priesthood keys. Here, Joseph almost certainly was making veiled reference to certain keys that would eventually be given in the temple endowment. The Sunday following the Relief Society meeting (1 May 1842), Joseph recorded: "I preached in the grove, on *the keys of the kingdom*, charity, etc. The keys are certain signs and words by which false spirits and personages may be detected from true, which cannot be revealed to the Elders till the Temple is completed. . . . There are signs in heaven, earth and hell; the Elders must know them all, to be endowed with power." (HC 4:608, emphasis added.) It was six days following the address to the Relief Society that Joseph gave the endowment for the first time (see HC 5:1–2).

Caroline was the only one in the Steed family store late on the afternoon of April twenty-eighth. She and Lydia had come here directly from the Relief Society meeting, but there hadn't been any customers in the last half hour and Lydia had gone back to watch their children. Nathan needed to go with his father out to their property. So Caroline was now straightening up the shelves, dusting off the glass lantern covers, sorting spools of thread by color, and generally doing the things that made for a well-kept store but which often had to wait for times such as these.

When the door opened she was on a stool, stretching on tip-toes with the feather duster to clean off the very top shelf, which was filled with some old metal pots. She halfway glanced around but saw only the dark shape of a man. "Be with you in a moment," she called.

There was a soft grunt of acknowledgment and the door shut behind him. There was one last pot just beyond her reach. She ought to have moved the stool to a better position, but decided she could try to reach the pot from where she was. Stretching to the utmost, she balanced on one foot, steadying herself with her free hand against the shelves, and tried to get it. It was still just a little too far.

"Could I help you reach that?" a deep voice asked.

She jerked up, nearly falling. With a little cry, she jumped clear, landing nimbly between the counter and the shelves. She whirled around to face him, her mouth agape. "Will?"

"Hello, Mama."

"Will Steed?" She took a step or two forward. The feather duster dropped from her hands and clattered to the floor totally unnoticed by her. "Is that really you?"

He reached up and rubbed the dark, thick beard with a chuckle. "Yep, it's me under all this."

"I can't believe—"

Will didn't wait for her to recover. In three running steps he made his way behind the counter and reached her, sweeping her up in his arms. "Mama!" was all he could say as he buried his face in against her shoulder.

———•———

"Will's home?" Lydia stared at Caroline, who was standing at the door. "You mean here? In Nauvoo? Now?"

"Yes," she cried.

"But . . . what about Nathan?"

"He's coming. But Will wants the whole family to come to the top of the quarry."

"To the top of the quarry? But why?"

"All he will say is we have to get everyone to the hill above the quarry as quickly as possible." Caroline had to stop for breath. She had run all the way from the store. "Will's gone for Derek. Olivia's gone for Mother and Father Steed. Your Joshua has gone for Matthew and Peter and Carl. Let's get everyone else. Will says we have to hurry."

It took them almost a full half hour to gather everyone and walk the several blocks to the small bluff that overlooked the stone quarry. Since Derek's farm was some blocks away, he and Will were the last to arrive. The family were waiting for Will, adults moving in to shake his hand or hug him tightly. The kids swarmed in behind them, dancing and crying out, laughing at the sight of Will with a beard.

"Where's Nathan?" Lydia blurted, the first chance she had to break in.

Will turned and looked north. The quarry bluff was high enough that the Mississippi's great arching curve could be seen in both directions. To the north it straightened out again, moving away in a northeasterly direction. From this vantage point they could see two or three miles up the river. Grinning like a kid with a ten-dollar gold piece, Will lifted an arm and pointed. "There!" he said.

The family turned, spreading out in a semicircle so they could see better. "Where?" Emily cried. "I don't see them."

"On the river. About a mile away now."

Benjamin squinted; then his eyes widened in surprise. "Oh my word!" he breathed. "Is that it?"

"Where, Grandpa? Where?" Savannah demanded. "I wanna see my papa."

Now the others were picking it out too. They had missed it at first because it was so long it looked almost like an island. "In the river," Derek exclaimed, as excited as one of the children. "It's that big raft."

"Big?" Benjamin said in awe. "That's not big. It's gigantic. Look at that thing!"

Caroline picked up Savannah and was pointing now too. "See there, Savannah? In the river. It's that great big boat. That's where Papa is."

"Would you look at that?" Matthew said. "It must be two hundred feet long if it's an inch. That's unbelievable."

"Actually," Will said modestly, "it's closer to three hundred feet. And that's only the first one. The second one is about half a mile behind it. See it?"

"I see it!" young Carl Rogers cried, jumping up and down.

"If the truth be known, Savannah," Will said, "it's that second one that Papa is on. And your papa too, Emily. I was on the first one with Jean Claude, the Frenchman."

"But how did you get here?" Carl broke in.

"I left camp early this morning and came overland. We talked about it and decided you needed to see it coming from up here first. You can't get quite the same perspective down close."

The great floating mass was coming steadily toward them, and now they could pick out the tiny figures moving across the top of it. Knowing those figures were actual men only added to the sense of the massiveness of the raft. Benjamin rubbed his chin. "I expected something pretty impressive, but this . . ." He just shook his head. "This is really something."

The welcome-home dinner at Joshua's house was filled with joviality and turned into an extended affair. It was frequently interrupted as friends and associates of Joshua and Nathan alike stopped by to welcome them home. At least, that was their ostensible purpose. In actuality, they came to ask questions and talk in awestruck tones about the great rafts of lumber they had brought down from the north. Their arrival had caused a city-wide stir in Nauvoo. By the time the two rafts tied up on the riverbank about a half mile north of the boat landing, a crowd had already gathered, and as word spread, there came a steady stream of people down to see this new wonder. The whole city was buzzing with talk of it.

So it was after dark before things in the house quieted down to the point where Carl could pull Nathan out on the back porch for a few moments. As they stepped into the darkness, Nathan breathed deeply, then sighed with great satisfaction. "It is good to be home, Carl. I loved the Pine Woods, but there's nothing quite the same as home."

"I know. And Lydia has missed you."

"I've missed her and the family."

"Nathan, I'm sorry to have to do this right now, but with Joshua leaving again in a day or two to go downriver, it just can't wait."

"What's the matter?"

"Didn't you see John C. Bennett here tonight?"

Nathan's mouth tightened. "Yes. I thought it was pretty rude of him to take Joshua outside to talk with him, even if it was only for a minute or two. I wonder what is so pressing that it couldn't wait."

Carl gave him a strange look. "But that's just it. Bennett probably heard that Joshua is leaving again too and he isn't waiting. So we can't either."

"Wait on what?" Nathan said, truly puzzled now.

Carl was a little exasperated. "You know what. I've done what Joshua asked me to—" Suddenly he stopped, his jaw dropping. "Didn't Joshua talk to you?"

"About what?" Now it was Nathan who was showing a little frustration.

"About Bennett."

"No. He's not said a word. What's this about?"

Carl looked away, lost in thought for a moment. "That changes everything," he said. Then suddenly he was all business. "All right. I heard Joshua tell Caroline that he's meeting with Bennett and some others tomorrow at ten. Joshua and I are meeting at noon. I want you there, but we need to talk first." He blew out his breath, disgusted at himself for not seeing this possibility. "I was so sure that he would have told you."

"Told me *what?*" Nathan exclaimed.

Carl shook his head. "It's much too complicated to even start telling you now. I'm sorry to do this to you so soon, Nathan, but can you come by the brickyard tomorrow morning? Say nine o'clock? Then I'll tell you everything."

"Carl! What is going on here?"

"Believe me, Nathan, there is not time to get into this tonight. I'll see you at nine in the morning. I think maybe you'd better bring your father."

Caroline watched from the bed as Joshua unbuttoned his shirt and tossed it across a chair. "You look tired," she said.

"I am. It's been a long two weeks coming down the river."

"Do you really have to leave again, Joshua? Jean Claude seems very competent. Couldn't he take the other raft down to St. Louis for you?"

He sat down and began tugging at his boots. "Maybe another time, but right now I've got nearly a hundred thousand feet of board lumber with no buyer. I'm not even sure anyone is expecting it. I sent a letter to Samuelson and hopefully he's working on it, but who knows what we'll be facing down there. I can't put that on Jean Claude's shoulders."

She nodded glumly. He had already explained that to her, but it was still a bitter disappointment. He would be gone another ten days at the minimum, maybe more. "Does it have to be right away?"

"Well, the crew's anxious for their money, but I told them we'd be here at least until Monday."

"Really?" Today was Thursday. That would give her a few days at least. "Well, that's not quite so bad. And you're not taking Will with you?"

He gave a quick shake of his head. "Will's been away from home long enough."

She sat up straighter, plumping the pillow behind her back. "How are you and he doing, Joshua?"

He lowered the first boot to the floor and then looked at her. "I assume Nathan gave you Will's letter about what happened up there between him and me."

"Yes."

"Well, that's passed. And don't let him give you any of that nonsense about going back to sea again. That's just his way of saying that he's hurting. Now that he's home again and Jenny's married, that will pass too."

Will it? It came out as an anguished cry within her, but her face remained impassive. She decided to change the subject. She reached up and touched his beard. "It's thick now."

He nodded, reaching up to stroke it too. "It's been almost six months."

"And Will, I hardly recognized him at first."

"It has its advantages in the cold up there, but now that it's warm, it's driving me crazy. I'm going to the barber tomorrow."

"Savannah will be glad. Did you hear what she said to me at dinner?"

"No, what?"

"She said you looked like a bear."

He laughed, lying down next to Caroline now. "And Olivia told me I looked like a wolverine. Nathan thinks it makes me look like a moose. I think it's time for it to come off."

She snuggled in against him, putting an arm across his chest. "It is so good to have you home again, Joshua. Don't go up there again, at least not for so long."

"I don't plan on it. That's what I'm hiring Jean Claude for."

"Good."

They both lapsed into silence for a minute, content to be close to each other. But finally Joshua spoke. He was staring up at the ceiling, and didn't turn to look at her. "Caroline, there's something I want to say."

She felt herself tense a little. His voice had become suddenly distant again. "What?" she asked.

"Will says he won't be baptized until you can be baptized with him."

"He told me that tonight." She hesitated. "I didn't put him up to that, Joshua."

He waved that away. "I know."

"My feelings haven't changed."

He brushed that aside too. "Caroline, there are some things happening here. Now that I'm back, I'm going to look into them."

"Oh?"

"Carl has been doing some checking too." He took a quick breath. "It could be something that might influence your feelings toward the Church. Will's too." She came up on one elbow to look at him in the darkness, but he rushed on. "Maybe it won't. It's still too early to say."

"What kinds of things, Joshua?"

"I don't want to say yet, not until I know for sure. But I'll tell you this much—if it pans out, it could change your decision and Will's too."

Caroline suddenly remembered things said in recent meetings. "If you are talking about the stories going around right now about Hyrum and Brigham Young and others locking that woman in her room, I already know about them. And I don't believe them."

"Hyrum?" That took him aback. "I haven't heard that."

"Well, it's trash," she said shortly. "So if that's what you're talking about, save your breath."

His mouth drew into a line. "It's not. But here's what I want to say. Promise me that you'll listen to whatever it is that turns up. When you've done that, if you still want to be baptized, I'll step aside."

There was a quick intake of breath.

"I mean it. If this doesn't change your mind, then you'll have my blessing. Will too."

"Not just your permission?" she whispered. "Because you've already given me that."

"No, not just my permission. You'll have my blessing. Fair enough?"

She lay back down slowly. "Why, Joshua?" she asked in wonder.

"I won't lie to you, Caroline. I think I'm going to win on this one. I think that what I'm going to have to tell you will end this infatuation with the Church and Joseph Smith and all that he teaches once and for all. But if not, then I'll stop fighting you. You have my word on it."

The door to Kathryn's bedroom opened slowly. It was about nine in the morning, but Jennifer Jo had not yet been in to draw her curtains and the room was semi-dim. She turned her head, expecting her sister, but was surprised to see the larger shape of a man step inside. Then the door shut behind him. For a moment she thought Matthew might have returned—she had heard him leave about an hour before—but this person was noticeably larger than Matthew. As he walked across the room, his face came more into the light. Her eyes widened. "Uncle Joshua?"

He moved over and took the chair beside her bed. "Hello again, Kathryn," he said softly, reaching out and taking her hand.

"Well, this is a surprise."

Matthew had carried her across the street the previous evening so she could be there for the welcome home for Nathan, Joshua, and Will. She had seen the shock in their eyes at her condition, but they had been warm and wonderful with her and she had enjoyed being out of the house immensely. She and Joshua had talked about what had happened, so seeing him here again so soon was a complete surprise to her.

"I can't believe you're finally home," she said. "It's been so long."

"It has," he agreed.

"I wish I could see the rafts. Everyone says they are amazing."

"They are." He squeezed her hand. "I just talked to Jennifer Jo and she has given me permission to bring a wagon here this afternoon at three o'clock. I'll have a bed in it and we'll just take you on down to the river so you can see those rafts, especially the big one before we take it on down to St. Louis."

"Would you?" she cried. "Oh, I would love that, Joshua."

"Then it's a date."

She smiled shyly at him. "All of my other suitors will be completely livid, but I accept."

He laughed right out loud. "Good enough." Then almost instantly he sobered. "Kathryn, I can't tell you what a shock it was to come home and find out what had happened to you. How are you doing?"

She wanted to force a smile and bravely say something like "Fine," or "Terrific," but something in his eyes wouldn't let her. Suddenly there were tears trickling down both of her cheeks. She turned away.

Joshua quickly reached in his pocket and brought out a handkerchief. With great tenderness he reached over and wiped her cheeks; then he blotted the cloth against her eyes.

"Thank you," she whispered.

He nodded, then leaned forward. "Jennifer Jo says I can only stay a few minutes. Will and Nathan will both be coming over too, and then with this trip this afternoon, she doesn't want you getting too tired."

"Oh, I won't get tired. I'll be so excited by this afternoon, maybe I'll just walk right outside to meet you."

He smiled, understanding what it cost her to say that. "So," he said again, "how *are* you doing?"

"Look at my hand," she said, under control again now.

He looked down to where her arm and hand lay in her lap. As he watched, she began to drum her fingers on the blanket. "I just did this last night for the first time."

Suddenly Joshua had to look away. "That's great," he finally said, his voice cracking just a little. "Just great." When he turned back, he was blinking quickly.

She smiled brightly, deeply touched and cheered that he would respond in such a manner. "It doesn't look like much, but then I never was a big one for overdoing myself."

"But you're doing it, Kathryn," he said, his voice low. "You're doing it."

"Yes," she said simply. "It was two weeks ago today. When I first woke up, I could barely move the tip of one finger."

"What about your feet?"

Now it was her reserve that broke. She turned her face toward the wall. "Nothing."

"I've come to ask you a question," he said, as if she were still looking at him.

She turned back slowly. "All right."

"Notice anything different about me?" he asked, smiling now.

That wasn't what she had expected and she was struck by the oddity of it, but she answered immediately. "Your beard."

His hand came up to his face. "No, no. That comes off this afternoon. What else?"

She looked at him again, letting her eyes go up and down his frame. "I don't know."

"Take a closer look." Now he was teasing her with his eyes.

Again she looked him up and down. After a moment, there was a slight shake of her head. "I'm sorry, Uncle Joshua. I don't notice anything."

"No cane," he said.

She looked at him for a second or two, not comprehending.

His smile broadened. "When was the last time you saw me using my cane?"

"I . . . I don't remember." She was still puzzled by this.

Now he took her hand in both of his. "Kathryn, you were there. It was in your mother's house in Missouri, just about three and a half years ago now. Remember? I had just regained consciousness. And then I learned that my one leg was paralyzed from that ball I took through the back."

Her eyes widened noticeably. "Yes," she breathed, seeing now what he was thinking.

"You were there when Matthew made me that awful, horrible crutch."

"Yes."

"You watched me hobble around your yard, dragging that no-good foot after me like it was a bag of wheat seed."

Tears were flowing again now, only not for the same reason. "I remember."

He stood up and bent down to kiss her forehead. "And now, Miss Kathryn McIntire, I don't even use a cane anymore. Haven't for more than a year." He reached down and punched softly at her chin. "So every time you start getting discouraged, you just remember your Uncle Joshua. No matter how long it takes, Kathryn, just remember. No more crutches. No more cane."

He took out his handkerchief and wiped her cheeks again as she smiled up at him. "Thank you," was all she was able to get out.

And then he said a most strange thing. "Why couldn't that stubborn son of mine have fallen in love with a young woman like you?"

Kathryn laughed in spite of herself. "Me and Will?" And then instantly her own eyes were teasing. "A Mormon? Why, Uncle Joshua, I am shocked."

He grinned. And then with a spontaneous move, he bent down and put his arms around her. "Promise not to tell," he whispered into her ear, "but in your case, I'd make an exception."

The doctor's office of John C. Bennett was on the back of his house. There was a walkway and a side door so that one did not have to go through the house to reach his office. The previous evening he had specifically warned Joshua not to stop at the front of the house but to use the side door. As Joshua passed the front entrance and came down the walkway he understood why. There was a nearby shed which blocked most of the view of this entrance from the street.

Joshua was not in a very pleasant mood as he reached the side door and knocked. After two weeks of sleeping on the ground or on the hardness of the raft's deck, he had expected that when he got into a real bed again he would simply float away in sleep. Instead, the soft feather mattress made him feel as if he were wrapped in a cocoon. And through the night he had numerous second thoughts about making his agreement with Caroline. He had meant it as a way to prepare her for the coming shock of what he would have to tell her. But she saw no threat at all, only a chance to lift his opposition to her being baptized. This morning he had come downstairs to find her singing and humming to herself as she prepared him breakfast.

He heard the sound of footsteps, then the door opened slightly. Through the narrow slit he saw part of the face of a man he didn't recognize. "Steed?" a guttural voice demanded.

"That's right," he growled right back.

The door opened and the man moved back. Joshua stepped inside and the man shut the door again quickly, locking it behind him. "Follow me."

He led him through the office and down a hallway that led into the main part of the house. John C. Bennett was standing at the end of it, waiting. "Ah, Joshua," he said. He came forward swiftly, holding out his hand. Joshua took it briefly, noting that even though the grip was firm and confident, the palm was slightly damp and quite cold. Was the man nervous? he wondered.

"Everyone else is here. Come in."

Joshua stepped in. There were three other men in the room, all standing now. Behind them, there were also three women seated in a small semicircle. As one of them looked up, he saw that her face was heavily veiled.

"Do you know everyone? You've met Robert Foster already." The man who had ushered him in stepped around and shook hands. "And these are the Higbee boys, Chauncey and Francis. You probably know their father, Judge Elias Higbee."

"How do you do, Mr. Steed."

As he shook each hand he looked the brothers squarely in the eye. "Your father is a man of integrity. As I recall, he's a good friend and confidant of Joseph Smith."

The younger of the two started and turned to Bennett, his small mouth twisting into a pout. "You said he could be trusted to be discreet."

Bennett just laughed, seeing that Joshua was toying with them. He turned to the third man. "And this is Gustavus Hills."

Joshua gave him a curt nod. Hills didn't move to shake hands with him.

"Come in and sit down, Joshua." Bennett turned to Foster. "Did you lock the door?"

"The outside one, yes."

"Shut this one too," he commanded. Joshua took the proffered chair. The others sat around the room but each where they could watch him.

"I'm sorry that we have to rush into this," Bennett said, "but when I got word that you would be leaving again Monday, I knew we could not delay any further."

Joshua inclined his head slightly to acknowledge that he understood.

"Have you talked to your brother-in-law?"

"No, not yet. I'm meeting him at noon."

"Good. He's been very thorough." There was a fleeting frown. "Perhaps too thorough. I fear that he has listened to those who would protect Joseph no matter what the cost."

"I trust Carl's objectivity in this."

"Oh, of course," Bennett said hastily. "He seems to be a fair-minded man."

"So," Joshua said, suddenly impatient. "Let's get on with it. What do you have?"

Bennett held out his hands in a gesture of frustration. "Knowing that our time is limited *and*"—he stressed the word with faint sarcasm—"that you had some doubts about the story that I told you in January, I have asked these people to come and confirm my accusations. These are eyewitnesses, Joshua. What they have to say is firsthand, not just hearsay."

Joshua kept his face impassive, but inside he felt great distaste. He respected Joseph Smith and considered him a friend now, though it had not always been that way. But he needed to hear this directly from those who were making the accusations. "Well, let's hear it, then."

"Mind you," Bennett continued, rubbing his hands in satisfaction, "this is testimony concerning only a small portion of what is happening among us. But with the time restrictions—"

"Yes, yes!" Joshua snapped.

"All right. When we talked in January, I admitted to you then that I had been indiscreet with some women, even one that was married, but that it came about because Joseph taught me that it was all right. You clearly doubted my word."

He looked to where the women were watching and nodded. One of them stood and came slowly forward. "Here is one of those women. I should like you to hear it from her own mouth."

"Who is this?" Joshua demanded.

The woman looked confused and turned to Bennett. He turned to Joshua. "I gave my word that she would not have to reveal herself."

Joshua considered that, saw her trembling hands. "All right," he said, "go on."

But it was Bennett who spoke. "Well, after this sister and I had . . . uh . . . consummated our relationship, Joseph came to me. He said he wanted her to become one of his seraglio and—"

"Seraglio?" Joshua cut in. "What's that?"

"His harem, his collection of wives. He determined that she would be one of his spiritual wives. He told me the Lord had given her to him and asked if I would intercede in his behalf."

Joshua leaned forward, his eyes narrowing. "And you were married?" he asked the woman.

She nodded. He noted that her fingers were twisting at her dress now. "My husband was gone at the time." When she spoke, her voice was still very soft and Joshua had to lean forward to hear her. "When Doctor Bennett told me what Joseph said, I thought he was lying. I said that unless I heard it from Joseph's own lips, I would not believe it. Doctor Bennett told me that Joseph's true motives would soon be revealed." There was a moment's hesitation. "And so they were. When John—uh, Doctor Bennett—refused to be his intermediary, Brother Joseph came directly to me."

"With the purpose of securing you as one of his wives?"

"Yes. He said that the Lord had revealed it to him. I was to be his spiritual wife."

"Just what does that mean?" Joshua asked. "Why *spiritual* wife?"

"It means that even though I was married in this life I was to be his wife in the next."

"Only in the next?"

She ducked her head. "Well, he said that we should act as husband and wife here, but that would all be in secret."

"And what did you say to that?" He wanted to be angry, but the quiet sorrow in the woman's voice held him back. He wasn't convinced yet, but he couldn't lash out at her as he had at Bennett.

"I was outraged. I told him I would consider no such thing."

Now he couldn't help it. "Even though you had succumbed to Mr. Bennett here before?"

Her head came up. "I was in error and I repented of that. I was determined that I would not fall again."

Now Bennett jumped in. "When he could not persuade her, Joseph came to me again. He begged me to represent his wishes to her. Finally, I relented. He was the Prophet, I decided, and so I must follow his wishes. So we came back to this sister's home."

She was nodding. "That only enraged me all the more. I told him he must immediately desist or I would tell my husband. At that point, the Prophet backed down. He begged me not to expose him, and I finally agreed to that if he would make no further advances toward me."

Bennett nodded and she backed away before Joshua could say anything more.

"That man must be brought to justice," Robert Foster burst out. "This is a crime of the most heinous sort, and we must act against it. The man has a wife already," he said bitterly. "Let him be satisfied with her."

"I don't need the dramatics," Joshua said tightly to Bennett. "What else?"

Bennett raised his hand and snapped his finger. Another of the women stood and came forth. She planted her feet, raised her veil, and stood defiantly before the two of them.

"Joshua, this is Melissa Schindle. Tell him your story, Melissa."

Her eyes were hard and cold and contemptuous. "There's not much to tell. Joseph Smith tried to take me to his bed. And I know personally of another woman with whom he was in bed."

Joshua felt sick. This was far worse than he had ever imagined. "What is this other woman's name?" he asked softly.

"I cannot say unless she gives her permission, but if you wish, I shall speak to her."

He shook his head. "No, not now."

Bennett motioned and the third woman came and stood beside Schindle. She too lifted her veil, but then she let it drop again. "My name is Martha Brotherton."

Joshua caught the accent. "Are you one of the British Saints?"

"Yes. My family and I came across on the same ship as Joseph Fielding last fall."

"All right."

"Martha has a little different story to tell," Bennett explained, "but it shows clearly that this isn't just limited to Joseph anymore. It is spreading among the leaders of the Church. Tell him, Sister Martha."

She started to twist her hands as she spoke, as if highly agitated, but her voice was flat and emotionless and had none of the hesitation that the first woman's had exhibited. "One night Heber C. Kimball and Brigham Young came for me. They asked if I would accompany them to a different house. This was at night. They were Apostles, members of the Twelve, and so I immediately agreed. I thought it might have something to do with my family, who are now staying down in Warsaw. But when we reached the house, they took me into a room and locked the door. Then they told me that the Prophet had received a special revelation from God permitting a man to have more than one wife. I laughed at them, thinking that surely they were joking. That angered them. They said this was the word of God and that I must submit."

"They wanted you to be one of *their* wives?" Joshua asked slowly. "So it wasn't for Joseph now?"

"That's right. When I realized they meant it and this wasn't just some kind of sick joke or some kind of test of my faith, I was angry. Like Sister—" She caught herself. "Like this other sister here, I couldn't believe what they were saying, so I told them to get out, to leave me alone." There was a derisive laugh. "They left, all right, but they locked me in the room. They just left me there. The next day they came back with some other Apostles and Hyrum Smith. They labored with me for hours trying to convince me that this principle was from God and that if I did not accept it I would be damned. I steadfastly refused. So again they left me. On the next day they finally brought Joseph himself in to try and convince me. He also told me it was from God and that I must accept."

"But you steadfastly refused?" Joshua asked with a faint touch of irony. Somehow this was a little too incredible.

She missed it entirely. "That's right," she exclaimed. "When they finally failed to sway me from my determination to do right, they made me swear that I wouldn't tell anyone, and finally let me go."

Robert Foster swore. "Isn't that enough for you, Steed? How many witnesses does it take?"

Joshua didn't even turn to look at him. He sat back in his chair, lost in thought. Brotherton and Schindle watched him for a moment; then when they saw he was done with them, they walked over to join the other sister. Bennett waved them away and the three of them quietly filed out of the room.

"Well?" he asked Joshua when the door closed again. "I told you I had others who would verify what I told you."

Joshua stood. His face was creased with deep lines as he considered what he had heard. "What I have listened to today is troubling, John. I can't deny that. And I have listened carefully. But I am not ready to make a decision about what to do. I want to talk with Carl and hear what he has to say."

They all stood now too. "He'll verify every word," Chauncey Higbee said. "He's interviewed these same good sisters and some of us as well."

"Then I shall speak with him." Joshua looked around at the circle of them. "As I said before, if this proves to be true, you shall have an ally in putting this terrible thing down. But I leave for St. Louis on Monday. Other than my hearing Carl's report, this will have to wait until I return." He looked at Bennett. "But I'll say it again, John. If this isn't true, it won't just be Joseph Smith you need to worry about."

"You must not tell Joseph," Bennett exclaimed. "Not yet. If he learns of what we are doing at this stage, he will make every effort to cover his tracks, make sure that no one can prove anything against him."

"If what you say is true," Joshua said sharply, "then it's far too late for that."

He turned and left them, wanting to get out of this dim and gloomy house with its terrible stories and depressing testimony. He did not go back down the hall and out through the offices. He went straight to the front door, unlocked it, and went outside.

When the door slammed shut again, Bennett turned to the others. "Well, I think we've got him."

Foster shook his head. "It's hard to tell. He's a crafty one, that's for sure."

"Don't worry," Bennett soothed them, "Steed's got an ax he wants sharpened here, and we're the grindstone."

"What ax?" Francis asked.

"His wife wants to join the Church and Steed violently opposes it. Now I hear that his son wants to do the same thing. This is exactly what he's looking for. Once they hear this, they'll never want to join the Church."

Gustavus Hills had been silent throughout the proceedings, brooding and sullen. Now his face showed a deep, silent fury. "We cannot depend on Joshua Steed or Carl Rogers in this matter. We must take action. When Joseph finds out what we are doing, and he surely will—we know that the high council is already sniffing around at his behest—then all hell is going to break loose in this town."

"Joseph has got to be stopped!" Foster exclaimed angrily. "This attempt to blame us for the problem has gone too far. He's got to be stopped before this whole thing breaks wide open."

Bennett looked around at them and smiled. But it was a smile filled with dry menace. His eyes were narrowed into slits and glittering like a serpent's. "Perhaps it is time that we take things into our own hands and make certain that Brother Joseph"—this came out with faint contempt—"is no longer able to make trouble for us."

"How!" Hills cried eagerly.

"One never knows," Bennett said archly, "but next week the Nauvoo Legion is going to stage a mock battle out on the green."

Foster's eyes widened and there was an instant gleam of pure joy. "A *mock* battle?"

"Yes, and with so many men running about with muskets and swords, one never knows when an accident might occur." The face smoothed and became calm. "Being a general in the Legion, I would have to make every effort to see that such accidents were avoided at all costs, of course."

Chauncey Higbee laughed right out loud. "Of course," he chortled. "At all costs."

———•———

When Joshua stepped inside the office at the brickyard he pulled up short. In addition to Carl, Nathan and Benjamin sat waiting for him. "What's this?" he said, caught completely off guard.

Carl looked at him steadily. "They know, Joshua. I've told them about your letter and about Bennett coming to me."

There was a flash of anger. "You had no right to do that, Carl, not until we talked at least."

"Oh?" Nathan retorted. "And what right did you have to try and keep this a secret from us?"

"I wasn't trying to keep it a secret, I just wanted to wait until—"

Benjamin raised a warning hand. "All right, that's enough.

This is not going to be an easy thing we're doing here today. Let's not make it any harder."

The two brothers, still glaring at each other, finally nodded. Joshua shut the door and sat down in the one empty chair.

The office of Carl's brickyard was small, and putting four chairs in it along with the small desk pretty well filled the space. The papers that normally cluttered the desk had been stacked on one corner and the rest was now clean. Carl sat behind the desk, his finger tracing circular patterns in the desktop. As Joshua settled into his chair, Carl looked across at him. "I haven't told them anything yet about what I've learned, Joshua. I felt like you needed to be here to hear that at the same time. But they do have a right to know about what's going on. This is bigger than any one of us."

Gradually the stiffness in Joshua's face smoothed, and then he nodded. "Yes, you're right, of course. I'm sorry."

"The important thing," Benjamin said, "is that we work together now."

"As long as we deal with it," Joshua warned. "I want to work this out, but I'll not be party to sweeping anything under the rug."

"Agreed," Nathan said. "But you don't sweep trash under the rug. You take it out and burn it."

"Let's just hear Carl, shall we?" Benjamin said quickly, feeling the testiness starting to rise again.

Carl came in quickly. "I'd like to have Joshua report on what happened at Bennett's house this morning first."

Joshua's head came up with a snap.

"We haven't been sneaking around spying on you," Carl assured him. "I heard you tell Caroline last night that you were going to see him today."

Joshua shrugged, settling down again. "All right. Bennett had brought people to back up his story. Four men, three women.

"Let me guess," Carl said. "Sarah Pratt? Martha Brotherton, Melissa Schindle?"

Joshua nodded. "One woman refused to identify herself—they were all veiled—but she was married."

"Very likely it's Orson Pratt's wife. She refused to identify herself to me too, but I'm almost positive that's who it was because of what she said. I'm surprised Nancy Rigdon wasn't there. She and Francis Higbee are courting now and she's very bitter. Well, anyway, tell them, Joshua."

And so Joshua told them. He didn't spare any detail, even though he saw his father's increasing gloom and Nathan's growing anger with every word. When he finished, he looked at Carl. "That's about it."

"Lies!" Nathan cried. "Lies of the blackest hue!"

Joshua sighed, the tiredness lining his face. "I hope so, Nathan. I truly hope so."

"You know Joseph," Nathan retorted hotly. "How can you even consider that he would do such a thing?"

"Nathan," Carl broke in firmly, "we're going to hear this out."

Nathan slumped back. "Yes. I'm sorry. Go on."

Carl turned to Joshua again. "You may have already heard that Joseph and Hyrum have publicly denied the locked-room story."

"Yes. Caroline mentioned that."

Carl leaned back now too, his face thoughtful. He brought his hands together, fingertip touching fingertip. "As I see it, this is the primary dilemma. Accusations have been made. Very serious accusations. On the one hand, we have eyewitness testimony saying the accusations are true. On the other, we have flat denials. So the question is, who's telling the truth?"

"Do you even have to ask?" Nathan asked bitterly.

"Yes, I think we do," Carl shot right back. "If they are lies, then wouldn't you want to expose them as such?" He didn't wait for Nathan's answer. "So, I asked myself, how does one determine which person is telling the truth and which isn't? That is the critical question. So let me tell you what I've learned first, then we'll talk about conclusions. But I need you to just listen first. All of you. All right?"

Nathan and Joshua looked at each other, then nodded.

"Good." He reached over to the stack of papers and took three or four sheets off the top. He looked a little sheepish. "I've made some notes. This got so complex I was having trouble keeping things straight. And I don't want you to think I have all the answers. There were some people I couldn't get access to. Others weren't very comfortable having a non-Mormon coming around asking very personal questions. I haven't tried to question any of the Church leaders directly."

He took a deep breath. "All right. It seems to me that the married woman's testimony is the most damning, so let me start there." He scanned a page, set it down, and then glanced at the second. "Here's why I think it's Sarah Pratt. Bennett admitted to me that he and Sarah Pratt were intimately involved with each other, but only after Joseph taught Bennett the doctrine of spiritual wifery. Well, that is Bennett's version. I think we all agree it would be to his benefit to show that he was duped, and if not innocent, then at least not totally to blame."

When no one responded to that, he plunged on. "Here is what I've learned. Bennett did live with Orson and Sarah Pratt for a time, after helping them build a small cabin. From the beginning, Sarah seems to have been totally taken with Mayor Bennett's considerable charms. In fact, his attractiveness to women seems to be a major factor through all of this. Be that as it may, evidently shortly after Orson's departure, the relationship between the two passed all bounds of propriety."

He consulted his notes. "Sarah moved in with a couple by the name of Stephen and Zeruiah Goddard. They were willing to talk with me, in fact quite eager to do so, because they know what Bennett is saying about this situation and they want the other side heard. Anyway, the Goddards said once she moved in with them, Bennett was there to see Sister Pratt 'as sure as the night came'—those are their words. At first he would stay until about nine p.m. Then it got later and later, sometimes until midnight. The Goddards became increasingly concerned. They said Mrs. Pratt and Bennett would sit close, their heads together, whispering continually and talking in low tones. Then one night, Mrs. Goddard came suddenly into the room where Sarah and the good doctor were. Though they were dressed, she found them in a most compromising situation. There was no question about whether this was just two friends talking. Later, highly incensed, Mrs. Goddard asked Bennett what Orson Pratt would think if he knew that Bennett was so fond of his wife. According to her, he just laughed and said he could pull the wool over Pratt's eyes any time."

"Does Orson know about any of this?" Nathan asked, feeling sick.

"I was told he has just learned about it. In fact, I have a theory about how Orson Pratt plays into all of this. I can't prove it, but I think it offers some possible answers."

"What?" Benjamin broke in.

"Let me establish the other thing first," Carl said. "Last summer when Bennett was nearly exposed and tried to take his life, I think Mrs. Pratt was the one who confessed to Joseph what was going on. I think she admitted that Bennett convinced her to submit to his advances by teaching the doctrine of spiritual wifery. Now, six months later, Bennett swears that he got the doctrine from Joseph himself and thus felt justified in teaching it to others. I think we have good evidence that this is a lie."

He turned to Nathan. "I think Joshua needs to hear what you told me this morning, about what happened last summer when you were in Joseph's home."

"I think Joshua also needs to know about Rebecca," Benjamin added.

Joshua's head jerked around. "Rebecca! What about Rebecca? She's not in on this in any way is she?"

Nathan told him quickly about Rebecca's visit and how she gave Nathan permission to tell Joseph. He recounted how he had gone looking for Joseph and ended up in his house that night when Joseph and Bennett came in. He described how Joseph was raging at the man for telling others that this doctrine was from him.

Joshua listened clear through. "Is there any chance Joseph was saying this just for your benefit?" he finally asked.

"He didn't know I was there!" Nathan shot back. "Emma's nephew and I were upstairs out of sight through the whole thing."

Joshua slowly nodded. "That's good to know." He looked at Carl. "I agree, I think that establishes that Bennett is lying about Joseph justifying all this."

Carl was pleased at his openness. "I think so too. So now, here is my theory about Sarah Pratt. Like I say, I can't prove it, but it's the only thing that explains all the facts for me. Sarah Pratt was a lonely, vulnerable young wife swept off her feet by the smooth talk and great charm of the handsome John C. Bennett. When he claimed that all of this was sanctioned by Joseph Smith, that was all the rationalization she needed to give in to what her heart desired anyway. So she submits to Bennett and they become involved immorally. Then her husband returns home. Rumors are flying fast and furious. Her husband doesn't want to believe any of this at first—would you?—but the evidence mounts. She knows that she can no longer hide the truth. But the truth is too damning for her. So how to make it not so terrible?"

"Tell the husband it's Joseph's doing," Benjamin answered quietly.

"Yes!" Carl exclaimed. "Oh, I think there is a good chance that Joseph went to her when he learned what was happening. And she was outraged, all right, but not because Joseph asked her to be his wife. I think it was because Joseph threatened to expose the two of them. So by twisting the account just a little, she becomes the innocent victim."

"And you don't think there is any truth to her accusations?" Joshua asked after a moment.

Carl sighed. "No, I don't, Joshua. Not one shred. I think she and Bennett have concocted the whole thing about Joseph to cover their own sins."

"And if you're wrong?"

"You can hang on and believe what you like, Joshua, but that's my conclusion. Remember, you have a mountain of evidence about Bennett that shows what kind of character he is. We know about his former life in Ohio—he was a wife beater, an adulterer, and a father who abandoned his children. He came to Nauvoo under false colors. We know that since coming here he has used his position as a women's doctor to seduce unsuspecting and vulnerable women. Though I am not absolutely certain, there is mounting evidence that he has tried to use his physician's skills to help certain women rid themselves of an unwanted child."

That even rocked Joshua. "You really mean that?"

"Yes. I haven't talked to the actual women, but this was told to me by friends or family members who would know. We also know that he is a frequent visitor to a brothel here in town and is probably one of the owners of the same."

"Brothel?" Benjamin echoed, genuinely shocked. "Here? Where?"

"Down by the river where it can serve the river traffic."

"I don't believe it," he said, thunderstruck.

"Believe it," Carl murmured darkly. "It's been kept very secret, but it's my understanding that this has now come to the attention of the city council and they will be acting on it very soon. I think you'll find that Bennett is behind it, at least to some degree." He turned back to Joshua. "So there is a man who swears he's telling the truth. And there is Joseph Smith who swears he is lying. Who am I supposed to believe? I don't think that's a hard question, Joshua."

There was a long silence, and finally Joshua nodded. "Agreed," he murmured.

Carl picked up his papers again. "I won't go through all of this, but here's a sampling of what I've found. Joshua told you which men were there today backing Bennett up. So let me tell you about them." He started to read off his notes now. "I have talked to four women, or to their families, who swear that Chauncey Higbee seduced them using the same lies Bennett did. I won't give you any names here, but one sister reported that

Higbee had gained his way with her five or six times, swearing that Bennett had sanctioned it as Assistant President of the Church. Another woman, a young widow, said Chauncey told her that she could never commit the sin of adultery because she was single. She submitted.

"Gustavus Hills is married," he went on grimly, "but I have a letter from a woman—she didn't want to talk to me personally— who says that Hills openly bragged to her that he was intimate with numerous women but that there was no sin in it as long as it was kept secret. She herself is with child by him. Hills obtained some medicine—I assume from Bennett—and tried to induce her to take it so she would lose the baby. When she refused to consider such a horrible thing, he begged her to leave town so that he would not be discovered."

As Nathan fumed, Joshua nodded slowly, feeling a growing anger welling up inside him. Bennett had set him up, and there would be a price for that.

Carl laid one page down and went to the next. "Melissa Schindle? She says that Joseph took her to his bed. It might be hard for her to remember who was in her bed, because I have sworn testimony from two men—neither are members—telling me that Melissa Schindle is one of those that will be out of work when Bennett's brothel is shut down."

"You're saying she's a harlot?" Joshua said, straightening.

"Yes. Very likely one of Bennett's employees. Which does bring the validity of her testimony into some question, I would say."

"One last thing," Carl said, tired now. "This whole story about Martha Brotherton and the locked room? She swears it's true. But men of known integrity—Heber Kimball, Brigham Young, Hyrum Smith—" He stopped and shook his head. "Hyrum Smith? Can you think of a more honest and decent man than that? Well, these men flatly deny it, saying the whole thing is a fabrication. So once again I am forced to ask, how do I decide what is the truth?" He sighed. "So let me tell you about Martha Brotherton."

"Who is she anyway?" Benjamin asked.

"She's an English girl," Joshua said. "She claims to have come over on the same ship with Mary Fielding Smith's brother last fall."

"That's right," Carl agreed. "I also had a man tell me he'd heard that Martha is another one of Bennett's harlots, but he finally admitted that was only common gossip. I didn't think that was sufficient. But I did go to Joseph Fielding, since he came in the company with them, to see if I could find out where the family is. No one here seemed to know."

Carl chuckled softly as he went on. "As soon as I mentioned the Brotherton name, Joseph Fielding just rolled his eyes. It seems that on the journey over they were a very troublesome family. When he tried to warn the Saints that they should not expect that there would be no tribulation once they arrived, that upset the Brothertons badly. Then as they came upriver from New Orleans, the riverboat crew filled their ears with horrible stories about the Mormons. By the time they reached Nauvoo, he said they were highly suspicious of anyone and everyone. They were terrified of meeting Joseph Smith because they were afraid he would demand money from them. So, after a short time, they moved to Warsaw."

"Ah, Warsaw," Nathan said sarcastically, "that seedbed of love and gospel harmony."

"All right," Joshua retorted tartly, "so Warsaw is a center of anti-Mormon sentiment, but just because a family doesn't find the Church all that wonderful doesn't automatically make them liars."

"Agreed," Carl said quickly. "And I wasn't suggesting the family was lying. I was just trying to learn more about Martha and her whereabouts. So I stopped at Warsaw on my way back from delivering a load of bricks one day and looked them up." There was a rueful chuckle. "They are right in the thick of that anti-Mormon crowd down there, and they didn't want to talk to me until I assured them I wasn't a Mormon. But here's what is interesting. They don't have much love for the Church, but when I asked them about this story Martha was telling around, they just laughed. Two of her sisters and a brother-in-law told me that Martha has been guilty of dishonesty in the past, that she is a known liar, and that she had recently been caught in a compromising situation with a young man. They were willing to sign an affidavit to that effect if I wanted. This is her own family, mind you! That's how they feel about Martha Brotherton." He set the papers aside now and sat back in his chair. "So there it is. That's what I've learned."

Finally, Nathan straightened. "Now are you convinced, Joshua?"

Joshua stared at Nathan for a long moment, then turned to his brother-in-law. "Are you convinced, Carl?"

"Of what?"

"That there is absolutely no truth to any of this? That Bennett is lying? That Sarah Pratt is lying? Brotherton? Schindle? All of it is lies?"

There was just a flicker of hesitation. "I am absolutely convinced that Bennett is lying. And the others. I cannot and I will not believe that Joseph is consorting with harlots nor that he is advocating that there is no sin in unrestrained relationships with the opposite sex."

Joshua sat back, digesting that. "I appreciate what you've done, Carl. This has been a lot of work, and not pleasant I'm sure."

"The question is, Joshua," Nathan said again, "are *you* convinced now?"

Joshua bent forward, rubbing his hands through his hair.

"*Are* you?" Nathan persisted.

Joshua didn't look up. "I trust Carl implicitly," he finally said. "If Carl says they are lying, then they are lying."

"So you'll let Caroline and Will be baptized now?"

Benjamin was not watching his two sons. He didn't see the look of resignation that crossed Joshua's face. Nor did he wait for his answer. He was watching Carl Rogers very closely now. Carl was staring at his hands, which were lying on the desk. His eyes seemed far away and troubled. "Carl?" Benjamin asked, very softly.

Joshua turned at the sound of his father's voice, grateful for a reprieve from having to answer Nathan's questions. Nathan turned too. Both of them saw Carl's head come up very slowly.

"Joshua asked you two questions, Carl," said Benjamin. "He asked if you thought Bennett was lying and you said yes, definitely. He also asked if you are convinced that there is absolutely no truth to any of this. Were you answering that question as well?"

For a long moment, Carl met Benjamin's gaze. There was pain in Carl's eyes and yet gratitude too. "No, not in the same way," he finally murmured.

Nathan's mouth flew open. "*What?*"

Joshua was staring now too. He was suddenly eager. "What's that supposed to mean?"

Benjamin shot them both a fierce look. "You two be quiet for a moment," he commanded curtly. Then he turned back around. "What is it, Carl?" he asked gently.

Carl had been debating how he was going to tell them. Benjamin had just solved that for him. He cleared his throat and looked at each one of them. He cleared it again and then began, speaking very softly. "I want to say this very carefully. I don't want Joshua to make more of it than what it is. And I don't want Nathan to make less of it than what it is."

"Go on," Benjamin said with an encouraging smile. "We all agreed that we are after the truth here."

"I have to be honest. Part of my hesitation is that I've not investigated this in the same way. For two reasons. First, I have been consumed with finding out about Bennett and his cohorts. It has taken my time, and frankly, it has taken far more of my energies than I ever expected. Second, I am an outsider. I'm not a member of the Church. As such, I cannot get the same access to people who would know about this as I could in the other matter."

"And thirdly?" Benjamin prodded.

Carl finally met his gaze square on. "Thirdly, I'm not sure I want to know."

"Why? Because it might be true?"

He swallowed once, looking bleak, then nodded. "That and because I think this could be very difficult for the family."

"If there's more, I want to hear it," Joshua snapped.

Benjamin swung on him. "Joshua, I mean it. You and Nathan stay out of this."

"Sorry," came the mumbled reply.

"If you have any reservations, Carl, any questions still in your mind, I think we need to hear those too. Then we can decide what to do about them."

Again the silence stretched out, heavy as a cloud of wood smoke in the room.

"Pa's right," Nathan finally broke in when Carl still hesitated. "Whether we like it or not, we need to hear what's bothering you."

"I concur," Joshua added.

"All right," said Carl. "Mind you, this is only a feeling, a suspicion. I've heard things that seem to confirm that suspicion, but that's all." His eyes searched theirs one by one. "I don't believe for one moment that Joseph is teaching that promiscuous relationships between the sexes is acceptable to God. Nor do I believe that he is whisking off young women and locking them into rooms." Again there was the hesitancy. Then he just shook his head. "But I do believe," he finished firmly, "that Joseph is teaching that a man may have more than one wife."

Chapter Notes

One of the difficult things in dealing with the tumultuous weeks in the spring of 1842 is separating truth from rumor, fact from speculation, evidence from innuendo and embellishment. Nauvoo was buzzing with the growing scandal surrounding John C. Bennett and his attempts to put the blame on the Prophet. There were charges and countercharges, accusations and counter-accusations. In this chapter, what happens when Joshua goes to Bennett's house and what Carl presents as the result of his investigation are based on known historical evidence. The testimony of the Goddard family about Sarah Pratt and John C. Bennett, the Brotherton family's comments about Martha, the declaration that Melissa Schindle was a harlot, the testimony of the women about Chauncey Higbee, the evidence that Bennett was likely running a brothel and also performed at least some abortions—all of these are drawn from carefully documented sources (see Danel W. Bachman, "A Study of the Mormon Practice of Plural Marriage Before the Death of Joseph Smith" [master's thesis, Purdue University, 1975], pp. 223–49; Andrew F. Smith, "The Saintly Scoundrel: The Life and Times of John Cook Bennett" [unpublished ms., Brooklyn, N.Y., 1994], pp. 119–24).

At Carl's quiet statement, Nathan rocked back. Joshua just gaped. Benjamin seemed only mildly surprised.

Carl was steadfast in his demeanor. "I know he has said things, even publicly, about the Old Testament patriarchs having more than one wife. He once even suggested this might be part of the restoration of all things. I wasn't there, but Melissa was. She said it created quite a furor."

"Is that true?" Joshua demanded of Nathan.

"Well, yes, he did make a statement like that in a conference once, but it was said in passing. He—"

Joshua dropped back in his chair, his face exultant. "So behind it all there really is something going on."

Carl flared at that. "That's what I mean, Joshua! That's the very thing I feared. You're so determined to find something—anything!—that will help you stop Caroline from being baptized, you already have your mind made up."

"That's not true," Joshua said, clearly stung by Carl's attack.

"Isn't it?" Nathan blurted. "We could all tell how disappointed you were when Carl proved Bennett's stories false. And these lies are no different."

"Nathan," Benjamin said, in a voice that brooked no contradiction, "you have just justified Carl's other fear. You have already made up your mind that there cannot be any truth to this."

"Do *you* think there's truth to it, Pa?" Nathan asked incredulously. "This is all part of the same pack of lies that Bennett is pandering around."

"Is it?" Carl asked quietly.

"Yes!"

"Maybe you'd better ask Joseph."

Nathan shot up, putting both hands on the desk. "Who is filling your head with that kind of stuff, Carl? Melissa Schindle? Martha Brotherton? Who? I want to know."

"Nathan!" Benjamin roared. "Sit down!"

The sound reverberated in the small room and shocked them all into silence. Nathan slowly sat back down. "Now," Benjamin finally said, "let's hear Carl out."

Carl seemed very reluctant now. "This is all very tentative." He looked at Nathan. "But this is not coming from Joseph's enemies."

"I'm going to Joseph with this," Nathan muttered. "This is not right."

"No you're not," Joshua exclaimed. "You'll just tip his hand. This stays just among us until we find out the truth here." There was a faint smirk. "Or is it you who is afraid to know the truth now?"

Benjamin sighed. "That's enough, Joshua."

"Why?" he flared. "I listened to the evidence against Bennett. And I *was* disappointed that his claims weren't true. But I accepted it! And now, when it looks like it might go the other way—"

"Suppose," Carl said, "someone started spreading vicious rumors about you, Joshua, and I learned about them. Would you want me to tip your hand?"

Joshua's mouth opened, but as he stared at Carl it finally shut again. Then he let out a muttered, "Yes."

"I would too."

"All right, then," Joshua went on, "how about this? Nathan can go to Joseph with the whole thing on Bennett. I told the man that if I found out he was lying to me, I'd do everything I could to bring him down. So take him down."

"I will," Nathan cried.

"But on this other, we say nothing until Carl looks into it some more." He gave Nathan a hard look. "And whatever he finds, we accept, whether we like it or not. Agreed?"

"It won't work," Carl answered. "I told you, I'm an outsider. If this is happening, it is known only in the tightest of circles. Church leaders only. They are not talking about it and most certainly not to some person who isn't even a member."

Joshua's disappointment showed on his face. There was no disputing the point. They all fell silent, mulling over how to get at a solution.

And then Nathan stunned them all. Still staring at the floor, he said quietly, "I will investigate this one."

Joshua spun around. Carl stared in disbelief. Even Benjamin was shocked speechless for a moment. And then he saw the wisdom of it. This was for Joshua. He began to nod. "Yes, that would work. Nathan knows the leaders well. He is a trusted friend of Joseph's. If there is truth in this, Nathan is the one to find it out."

"Nathan doesn't believe a word of it," Joshua snorted. "What kind of investigation will that be?"

Nathan was looking at the floor now. He didn't look up. "It will be as fair and as impartial as Carl's. That's what it will be. You have my word on it."

<hr />

Nathan and Benjamin found Joseph in his office above the store. They had gotten only a sentence or two into their report when Joseph held up his hand. "I'd like Hyrum to hear this. Can you wait?"

When they nodded he was up and gone. Ten minutes later he returned with his brother. Both looked grim. When they were seated, Joseph nodded to Nathan. "All right, start at the beginning again. Tell us everything."

For half an hour Nathan talked in a low voice, interrupted only when Benjamin added details Nathan had forgotten or when the two brothers fired questions at him. When Nathan finally finished, Joseph looked as though he had been whipped. He sat with his head in his hands. Hyrum was fuming. Benjamin decided it was time they leave it to them. "Is there anything more you want us to do, Joseph?" Benjamin asked.

It was as though he had to come back to them from a long way away. "What was that?"

Benjamin repeated his question. Joseph slowly shook his head. "No, not at present. Give us some time, brethren." He reached out and laid his hand on Benjamin's arm. "Will you tell Carl that we are deeply indebted to him? This is what we've needed. Exactly what we've needed."

"I will."

There was a deep, pained sigh, and he looked down at his hands. "We have been long patient with John C. Bennett. We have given him every opportunity to repent, to change his ways, and this is what he does."

Nathan waited half an hour before he finally saw Brigham come out of the door of the woodworking shop and start for home. Thankfully, Matthew did not come out with him. Nathan stepped out from behind the tree across the street and walked swiftly until he nearly caught up with him. Brigham, hearing his footsteps, turned, then stopped.

"Well, Brother Nathan. Good afternoon."

"Afternoon, Brigham."

Brigham gave him an odd look. "Just happening by?" he asked.

Nathan grinned. Brigham was pretty shrewd. He didn't miss

much. "No, actually I was waiting for you. Do you mind if I walk with you?"

Again there was that long searching look, then a brief nod. "Love to have your company." They started off again, walking slowly.

"How's Mary Ann?" Nathan asked. Like Nathan's mother, Brigham's wife was named Mary Ann.

"Fine."

"And the children?"

"The children are fine. Mary Ann's in a family way again."

"Really? Congratulations. This will be your sixth?"

"Seventh."

"Good. And she's feeling all right?"

There was a sardonic smile. "She's feeling fine. The children are fine. My cow's had a touch of the bloat, but she's better now. My horse is doing well. The roof leaks from time to time, but I plan to get at that this afternoon, as a matter of fact."

Nathan flushed.

Brigham laughed shortly. "Just come right out with it."

"All right. I'd like to ask you some questions."

Brigham glanced at him out of the corner of his eye. Brigham had stopped by the printing office earlier in the day to see John Taylor on a matter, and John had told him that Nathan Steed had been around asking questions. "To what end?" he finally asked.

Nathan decided that there was no being coy with Brigham Young. "There are rumors and stories floating about. You know my brother Joshua. Well, he's aware of these. He is greatly troubled and will use this to stop Caroline and Will from being baptized."

Brigham slowed his step until they were nearly stopped. "I appreciate your being honest with me, Nathan. Have you asked Joseph?"

Nathan flinched a little. "Uh . . . no. Not yet."

Brigham's round features softened. "I understand why you're doing this, Nathan." He laid an arm across his shoulder. "We can talk about it, but you need to know this. I can't and I won't speak for Joseph. There are some things you are going to have to ask him and him alone. Fair enough?"

"Yes, of course."

Brigham smiled, teasing him a little. "Now, just to stay on safe ground here, why don't I ask the questions."

Nathan had to laugh. In a way that would be a relief. "All right."

"We're agreed that the whole thing with John C. Bennett and his spiritual wifery is a fraud and that Joseph never gave him permission to teach any such doctrine? You have no question about that?"

"Absolutely not."

"Good. So what troubles you is whether or not Joseph is actually teaching that it is all right for a man to take more than one wife?"

"Yes," Nathan said emphatically. "Is he?"

"Do you agree that if God chose to restore that practice, he could do it?"

"Well, yes, but—"

"I didn't say he had, I'm just trying to clarify where you stand."

"Yes. I believe God could do it, of course. But I don't think he would, Brigham. Not anymore. It's . . . it just doesn't seem right. A man having more than one woman to love."

"Let me reason with you as Joseph reasoned with me. Are you a believer in the resurrection of men and women?"

"Of course."

"Do you believe that in the resurrection we will be much as we are now, only in a glorified state? That men and women, parents and children, will recognize one another there?"

"Yes, I believe that completely."

"And do you believe that in the resurrection we will have the same filial feelings toward each other, that parents will still love their children, that husbands and wives will love each other?"

Nathan considered that more carefully, but the answer was still the same. "Yes, I do."

"So, let me ask you this. You love Lydia and your children with complete love and devotion now?"

"Completely."

"Suppose Lydia were to die. Is it possible that you would remarry after a time?"

"Well, yes, I suppose."

"And do you think you could have the same tender feelings for and total devotion to that woman as you do with regard to Lydia now? And that if you had children with that woman, you would love them as you love your current children?"

Now Nathan sensed that he was being moved into a box and he answered more carefully. "Yes, I suppose that could be the case."

Brigham had turned very solemn. "Did you know that Mary Ann is not my first wife?"

Nathan started a little, then remembered. "Yes, I do remember that."

"I buried my beloved Miriam on a hillside in New York State. Do you think that because I truly love my Mary Ann now that it diminishes my former love for Miriam in any way?"

"No."

"All right, then. Now, let's come back to the resurrection. Everyone is dead now. Me, you, Lydia, my Mary Ann, this second wife of yours. We are all in heaven in the resurrection. Tell me what will happen there. If I am to have only one wife, what will happen to my Miriam and the two children we had together? Or if it is Miriam that I am given, then are Mary Ann and my current children to be sent away? Could you imagine sending your Lydia off and your children with her and saying, 'I'm terribly sorry, but I have a different wife now'?"

The logic was irrefutable, and Nathan had no choice but to shake his head. "No, of course not."

"Then you agree in principle at least that, since heaven is a pure and perfectly holy place and those who dwell there are in the presence of God and the angels, a man could have more than one wife at the same time and not have it be an evil thing?"

"Yes," Nathan said reluctantly, "I agree."

Brigham squeezed his shoulder and chuckled. "That was not much of an agreement, my friend."

"No," Nathan said earnestly, "I can see that for heaven. But here? To have two wives at the same time? I'm not sure that is the same thing. It would be terribly difficult, and I'm not sure that it could ever be right."

"So it's wrong on earth, but acceptable in heaven?"

"I know, I know," Nathan exclaimed. "What you say makes sense in a way, but . . . it just seems so wrong, Brigham. I can't believe God would ever require it of us."

They were stopped completely now, under the shade of a spreading oak tree. Brigham was silent, watching the anguish playing across Nathan's face. Finally, Nathan straightened, looking directly at the Apostle. "Has Joseph . . . ?" He stopped as Brigham cocked his head in warning.

"I can't and I won't speak for Joseph," he said.

"I know. I'm sorry. I understand."

"Good." Now Brigham smiled, the sternness gone as quickly as it had come. "Let me tell you a story, Nathan. Maybe you won't see how this is related to what we're talking about, but it is the same principle."

Nathan nodded glumly, still greatly distressed. Brigham hadn't answered anything directly, but he had as much as said it straight out and Nathan was shaken.

"In 1838, while we were in Missouri, Joseph and the brethren wished me to go among the branches of the Church and find out what surplus property the people had. I was to take that property under the law of consecration and forward it on to Far West for the building of the temple there."

Now Nathan was paying attention. "I remember that."

"Before I started, I asked brother Joseph, 'Tell me, who shall be the judge of what is surplus property?' Said he, 'Let them be the judges themselves, for I care not if they do not give a single dime. So far as I am concerned, I do not want anything they have. This is for the Lord.' That was good enough for me, so I went out to ask them for their surplus property as instructed."

"And did they give it to you?" Nathan asked.

"Well," Brigham said, a faint smile playing around the corners of his mouth now, "it was an interesting thing. When I talked with the people, I found them willing to do about as they were counseled. 'Do you accept the law of consecration?' I would ask. They would nod their heads and solemnly say, 'Amen, Brother Brigham.' 'Are you willing to give your surplus to the Lord?' 'Amen and amen, Brother Brigham.'"

Now his voice had turned sardonic. "But when I then asked them what surplus property they had, it was a very different matter. One would say, 'I have got so many hundred acres of land, and I have got so many boys, and I want each one of them to have eighty acres, therefore this is not surplus property.' Another would say, 'I have got so many girls, and I do not believe I shall be able to give them more than forty acres each.' Then I would point out that that would still leave about two or three hundred acres. 'Yes,' came the quick reply, 'but I have a brother-in-law coming on and he will depend on me for a living. My wife's nephew is coming of age and will be coming out here. He is poor and I shall have to furnish him a farm after he arrives here.'"

Nathan was smiling now, amused at the picture Brigham was drawing.

"Oh, some were disposed to do right with their surplus property and gave freely. But more commonly when you did find a man with a surplus cow he was willing to give, she was of the class that would kick a person's hat off, or knock your eyes out, or the wolves had eaten off her teats."

Nathan had been chuckling; now he guffawed right out loud.

"And you might find a man who had a horse that he considered surplus, but the animal had the ringbone, was broken-winded, spavined in both legs, had the pole evil at one end of the neck and a fistula at the other, and both knees sprung."

Nathan roared.

"You think I jest?" Brigham said, his eyes sparkling with amusement. "That is exactly how it happened." Then the humor receded. "I tell you, Nathan, there's a lesson in this. I wanted to see the people practice out of doors what they hypocritically professed before the Lord indoors. Oh, when their children are taken sick, or their wives, or husbands, how humble they then are. They send for the elders to pray for them. 'If you heal my wife,' they say to the Lord, 'then we'll give ourselves and all we have to thee.' And so the Lord makes them well by his power. But then what happens? They say, 'It is mine, and I will have it for myself.'"

It was as if Brigham suddenly remembered why he had started all of this in the first place. "Nathan, it's one thing to raise the hand to the square and say, 'Oh, yes, I believe Brother Joseph is our prophet. I believe the Lord speaks to him. Thank you, Lord, for Brother Joseph.' It is something else to say that same thing when the bullets are flying around your head, or when the bank collapses and you lose all your money, or when Joseph asks you to give up your surplus property, or when evil men spread terrible stories about Joseph. Or—" He leaned forward, peering into Nathan's eyes. "Or when Joseph tells us that the Lord has commanded us to do something that goes against everything we believe, everything we hold dear. Then—*then* is when you find out if a man is going to live his religion out of doors as well as in."

Brigham straightened again. "Anything further that you wish to know, you shall have to ask Joseph."

Joseph found Benjamin in the backyard, spading up his garden plot. He waved and came through the gate. "Morning, Brother Ben."

"Well, good morning, Joseph. What brings you by this way?"

"On my way to the quarry, then on up to the temple site."

"How do you keep it all going, Joseph?" Benjamin asked,

planting the shovel in the ground and then coming over to stand beside him.

"Keep all of what going?"

"Supervising the temple, running a store, being a father, translating, leading the Church? It seems like it never ends."

Joseph smiled gently. "Do you think I want it to end, Benjamin?"

That took him by surprise. "No, I guess not."

"It's a busy life, but I wouldn't trade any part of it. God is at the helm, and I'm pleased that he sees fit to use me as one of his instruments. It is a joy as well as a challenge."

"Of course," Benjamin said, a little chastened. Just the other night he had been having another one of his "walks through the valley of the shadow of death," as Mary Ann called them. But Joseph was right. Life could be challenging, but there was great joy in it as well.

Joseph clapped him on the shoulder. "But that's not why I came by. I've come to ask you if you can come to the store tomorrow."

"Of course. What time?"

"In the morning, say about ten?"

"Fine. Do you need me to bring anything?"

"No, but come prepared to spend a good part of the day."

One eyebrow came up and Joseph smiled. "I cannot say more, but come prepared to spend some time."

"All right."

A shadow passed across Joseph's face. "Ben, we have been friends for many years. You know how I feel about your family."

"I do, Joseph. And you know how we feel about you and yours."

"May I ask you a question?"

"Of course."

"Tell me about Nathan."

Benjamin couldn't hide the startled look that flashed in his eyes. "Nathan?"

"Yes. I sense he is troubled. I also know that he is asking

many questions of late. He's talked to John Taylor. He met with Brigham. George A. says he asked him if they could talk some time."

Joseph stopped, not bothering to ask the question. He didn't have to. Benjamin looked into his eyes and knew that he could not withhold what he knew. So he told him. Joseph already knew all about Bennett, so Benjamin told him the rest of what had transpired that day in Carl's office at the brickyard. He told him about Nathan's commitment to investigate the matter and have an answer by the time Joshua returned.

Joseph listened carefully, nodding from time to time. "That helps," was all he said when Benjamin finished.

"He'll work it through," Benjamin assured him.

Joseph didn't answer. He was looking past Benjamin now. "The Lord will test his people. And sometimes it seems like he tests us in ways we never expect."

"*Is* this a test?" Benjamin asked quietly.

Joseph looked at him for a long, searching moment. "I have learned this, Brother Ben. There are greater tests than mobs and persecutions. There are greater sacrifices than languishing for months in a jail."

Benjamin nodded slowly, not sure if that was the answer to his question or not.

"From the beginning," Joseph went on, "from the very first time I told Nathan about my experience in the grove, he believed. He's never wavered, never doubted. He's been one of the most loyal friends and associates I have had. Through it all he has never faltered."

"I know. He's like Mary Ann in that regard," Benjamin said.

"Yes. Your wife is another one. Well . . ." He sighed. "Don't try to stop him, Ben. Let him dig. Let him question and probe. Otherwise he shall never be satisfied."

Benjamin chose his words carefully now. "And what if what he finds shakes him, Joseph? He is so sure that this couldn't be possible. This could hit him very hard."

If Benjamin was hoping for reassurance he didn't get it. Joseph just shook his head. "I hope his roots are deep enough."

Benjamin's eyes widened. Now Joseph's eyes were filled with sorrow. "I had considered inviting Nathan tomorrow as well. Now . . . I think it better that we wait."

Joseph made as if to leave, but had a sudden thought. "Benjamin, I want you to sit down with Mary Ann tonight. Tell her everything. Even about Nathan."

"But—"

"I know that you agreed together that you would not talk about this to anyone else, but I want Mary Ann to know. You need her wise counsel, Benjamin. You need her great faith. No one else, but you tell Mary Ann."

"Yes, Joseph."

"Good. I'll see you in the morning. We'll meet upstairs in my private office."

Chapter Notes

While having Nathan and Benjamin Steed bring a report to Joseph about Bennett's activities is obviously not part of actual history, it was at exactly this time that Joseph seems to have learned about the full extent of what was happening. In his history the entry for 29 April 1842 reads: "A conspiracy against the peace of my household was made manifest, and it gave me some trouble to counteract the design of certain base individuals, and restore peace. The Lord makes manifest to me many things, which it is not wisdom for me to make public, until others can witness the proof of them." (*HC* 4:607–8.)

Brigham's reasoning about plural marriage in heaven and his comments on the law of consecration are drawn from his own writings and sermons (see *American Moses*, p. 101; *JD* 2:306–7).

B enjamin was surprised as he climbed the stairs to the upper floor of Joseph's store. Joseph was waiting at the door to his private office and greeted him warmly. When Joseph showed him in, there were only five others there in the small room— Brigham Young; Heber Kimball; William Law, Second Counselor in the First Presidency; William Marks, president of the Nauvoo Stake; and a man Benjamin didn't know.

"Benjamin," Joseph said, coming in right behind him, "this is General James Adams. General, this is Benjamin Steed."

The man was about the same age as Benjamin, perhaps a little older. He arose and they shook hands. "The general is from Springfield and will be with us only through today," said Joseph. And then to Adams, "Benjamin is a longtime friend and faithful member of the Church." He pulled a wry face. "He and I used to share the same jail cell."

Benjamin nodded. And in that same cell Joseph had once administered to him and saved his life, he thought. But he said nothing of that.

"Come in and sit down. The others should be here shortly."

Even as he spoke they heard footsteps on the stairs, and a moment later Hyrum was at the door. He was accompanied by Elder Willard Richards and two of the city's bishops—Bishop Newel K. Whitney and Bishop George Miller. As they shook hands all around and were introduced to General Adams, Joseph shut the door. Benjamin was surprised. Was this it? Here was the Prophet, one of his counselors, three Apostles, the Patriarch of the Church, a stake president, and two bishops. General Adams was obviously a member of the Church but he didn't know anything more about him. And then there was Benjamin Steed. He felt strange and out of place.

Joseph came and sat down at his writing table so that he was facing the group. He looked around at them and smiled warmly. His eyes were wide and filled with pleasure. "Brethren," he began, "welcome. I appreciate your coming. We are pleased to have Brother Adams with us."

The general nodded and murmured something in reply.

"The communications I have to make to this council today are of things spiritual. They are to be received only by the spiritually minded. The things which are about to be given to you, and which will eventually be given to the Church, are most assuredly governed by the principle of revelation. They are most sacred and are not to be discussed, except in general terms, outside of this room."

He hadn't asked them for assent on that, but he stopped and looked around the room. Each of the men nodded as the Prophet's eyes fell on them.

When he continued, it was with the greatest of solemnity. "Today, I shall be instructing you in the principles and order of the priesthood, attending to washings, anointings, endowments, and the communication of keys pertaining to the Aaronic Priesthood and so on to the highest order of the Melchizedek Priesthood.

"Brigham and Heber will remember that I spoke to the Twelve of an endowment in the fall of 1835, before the temple in Kirtland was dedicated. We had introduced the ordinance of the washing of feet, but I told them that the endowment about which they were so anxious could not be comprehended then, nor could Gabriel explain it to the understanding of darkened minds."

Brigham was nodding. "You told us that we must strive to be prepared in our hearts, to be faithful in all things, to be watchful and prayerful, and that if we did, we should sometime get a blessing worth remembering."

"Yes," Joseph said, pleased that he recalled it so clearly. "I then said something like this to the brethren there assembled: 'You need an endowment, brethren, in order that you may be prepared and able to overcome all things.' You also know that I introduced you in part to the ordinances of washing and anointing. This was preparatory to your receiving the full order of things."

He stopped and took a deep breath. The room was very still. Every eye was upon him. "Brethren, that time has now come. We are here today to set forth the order pertaining to the Ancient of Days. We are here to communicate all those plans and principles by which anyone is enabled to secure the fulness of those blessings which have been prepared for the Church, those things which are necessary if you are to come up and abide in the presence of Elohim in the eternal worlds."

His shoulders lifted and fell again, as if he had shrugged off a burden he had been carrying. He looked around at them and smiled. "Brethren, shall we begin?"

"It was glorious, Mary Ann. An ordinance of the most sublime beauty, and revelation of the most profound truths. Oh, I wish I were free to tell you about it."

"I know," she said wistfully, "so do I."

"It is a grand thing," he went on. "The endowment itself is richly symbolic of our journey through life and back into God's presence. And throughout, we were shown how to gain greater power and authority from God until we have all that is required to return to his presence."

She reached across the table and took both of his hands. "It sounds wonderful, Benjamin. I am envious."

His head shot up. "But I forgot to tell you that part. Joseph said this is not just for the brethren of the priesthood. In a short time he shall give the endowment to the women as well."

"Really?" Her eyes were suddenly shining. "Oh, Benjamin, that would be wonderful."

He leaned back, shaking his head. "I still do not understand why I was included."

Her eyes softened. "Because Joseph knows what you are and what you have to give."

He barely heard that. "And when I think that Nathan might have been there if not for his . . ." He blew out his breath. "I'm glad he doesn't know."

Mary Ann's mouth pulled down. "Lydia is troubled, Benjamin."

"She is?"

"Yes. Nathan is clearly distressed, but he won't say anything to her."

"That was our promise to each other."

"He came back from seeing Brother Brigham greatly agitated. But he would tell her nothing. Benjamin, it isn't right. She can help him. She needs to know. Melissa needs to know. She is worried sick about what Carl has been doing."

Benjamin rubbed a hand across his eyes. "You're right, of course. I will speak to Joseph. Ask him for his counsel."

He stopped, peering at her intently. "And what of you, Mary Ann? Now that you've had the day to ponder all of this, what do you think?"

"I am horrified at what John Bennett is up to."

"And what of the other?"

She looked down at her hands. When she spoke she didn't look up. "You think there's a chance it's true, don't you? You think Joseph has been told by the Lord to institute the practice of plural marriage, don't you?"

He finally nodded. "I think there is a very good chance that he has."

She bit her lip and looked away.

"And if he has?" he asked gently, putting his hand over hers now. "If it proves to be true, what then?"

Now her eyes met his and held them. "I don't know, Benjamin. I would be lying if I told you that I will not be greatly troubled if it proves to be true. Greatly troubled! But I've thought about it all day."

"And?"

"This is what I've come to. There are certain things I know with absolute certainty. I know that Joseph Smith saw the Father and the Son that day in 1820. I know that angels have come to him and restored the keys of the priesthood. I believe that Joseph still serves as God's prophet and his servant. I listened to him in that Relief Society meeting a few days ago. Oh, Benjamin, I wish you could have been there. He spoke with such power. He spoke like a prophet. We all felt it. It was as if we were on fire there for a time."

She took a quick breath, then with quiet resoluteness completed her thought. "The rest I don't understand. But I suppose that doesn't matter. I have decided that I will hang on to what I *do* understand and to what I *do* know. The rest is just going to have to work itself out."

———— ◆ ————

Lilburn W. Boggs, who served as governor of the state of Missouri from 1836 to 1840, was a Jackson County resident. He had been lieutenant governor when trouble broke out in the western part of the county between the old settlers and the new Mormon emigrants. Though he had deliberately kept a low profile during the hostilities, he had worked vigorously behind the scenes, encouraging the mob spirit, stoking the fires of hatred.

In 1836, he succeeded Daniel Dunklin as governor just in

time to see the same conflict start all over again. When the Mormon War broke out in the fall of 1838, the Saints found they had an implacable enemy in the governor's mansion in Jefferson City. He called out the militia and sent them north in strength. When wildly exaggerated reports of casualties in a skirmish between the Mormon forces and his own militia reached his ears, he issued the infamous order to his generals: "The Mormons must be driven from the state or exterminated." In less than a week, Haun's Mill had entered into the tragic history of the Latter-day Saints. Within a fortnight, Far West had been sacked, the Mormon leaders were in prison, and the shattered survivors were making plans for a spring exodus.

Some would say Boggs had done himself proud. Others suggested that he had carved himself a niche in the netherworld and was in for prolonged and exquisite torment there. If the prospect worried him, he gave little sign of it. No longer governor, and immersed in a bitterly contested race for a state senate seat, it is very unlikely that Boggs had the Mormons on his mind at all in the spring of 1842.

May sixth, 1842, had been a warm day in western Missouri. Clear and cloudless, it gave hint of the coming heat of summer. But it was evening now and many homes had their windows open to invite in the cooler air. At the Boggs home it was no different. The last of the light had gone and Boggs sat in a chair by his reading table. The lamp on the table cast his shadow on the window curtains in back of him. A slight breeze stirred them from time to time. In another room in the house, he could hear his young son moving around doing this or that.

His back was to the window and he never saw the dark form that suddenly appeared behind the sheer material. The form crouched down, peering over the sill into the lighted room. And then the curtain parted. The black snout of a pistol slipped through the opening. There was a moment's hesitation, then a shattering blast. The pistol was loaded with buckshot. Most of the shot sprayed wildly in the room, but three pieces of it caught Lilburn W. Boggs in the head. He slammed forward, the book he was reading crashing downward onto the table. Then his chair slowly twisted as he groaned and toppled sidewards to the floor.

A moment later, a young boy ran into the room to find his father in a pool of blood and the curtains stirring in the evening breeze.

———— ◦ ————

"Look," Emily cried, "there's Papa!" She started jumping up and down. "Papa! Papa!"

If Nathan heard, he gave no sign. Nor did Derek and Matthew, who rode beside him. But then, they were over a hundred yards away and there were some three or four thousand spectators lining the gentle slopes of the bluff overlooking the parade ground of the Nauvoo Legion. There were literally hundreds of children craning their necks to see their fathers, uncles, and brothers and shouting out when they finally spied them.

"Oh my!" Mary Ann said. "Isn't this grand?"

"Where's Grandpa?" Savannah said, tugging at her mother's dress. "I wanna see Grandpa."

Caroline handed Charles to Olivia, then picked her up. Savannah had turned five in March and was getting pretty big for Caroline to lift. Carl, seeing her struggle, came over. He already had Sarah, who was a year and a half younger than Savannah, astride one shoulder. He took Savannah and put her up on the other, so they were facing each other across his head. "Look," he said, pointing. "See up front there?"

Knowing that Rebecca and Jennifer Jo were both due to have their babies within the month, Carl and the older boys had come first thing this morning and set up a row of chairs. He had chosen carefully so that no one could get in front of them. Now Mary Ann, Rebecca, Jennifer Jo, Lydia, Caroline, and Melissa all had places to sit. Rebecca lifted her hand, pointing in the same direction. "See the band, Savannah? Where the music's coming from? That's the front. That's where Grandpa is."

The Nauvoo Legion band was at the north end of the field,

standing in formation, playing a rousing military march. They were surprisingly good and filled the air with a festive mood.

"You can't see him, Savannah," Mary Ann said, "but he's on Brother Joseph's staff. They're all there on the north side."

"Look behind the band," Rebecca suggested. "There's General Smith. See him? On the beautiful black horse."

"I see him!" Sarah cried. "I see Brother Joseph."

Young Joshua, standing just beside Carl, was pointing now too. "And that's Sister Emma on the horse right beside him."

"Well," Carl said, looking up at his niece, "Grandpa Steed is right in there somewhere."

"Who are *those* people?" Emily asked, pointing at the lines of men on the opposite end of the field from the band. And then she saw something else. "Are those guns?"

"Those are cannons," young Joshua said with a sniff.

"That's the artillery company on that end," Carl explained. "They are the ones who shoot the cannons, Emily."

The Legion had lined up on the parade field to form a long, hollow rectangle. The north end was for the dignitaries. Joseph, his small band of lifeguards, as they were called, his staff, and the officers' wives were gathered there along with the visiting guests. Directly in front of Joseph was the Nauvoo Legion band. In front of them, General John C. Bennett and his officers faced the rest of the troops. Bennett, as second in command, would be in charge of the parade and the sham battle.

Down the west side, over a hundred men on horseback were lined up in two rows facing into the rectangle. This was the Second Cohort of Cavalry. Facing them directly across the rectangle were two similar lines of horsemen. This was the First Cohort. The companies of infantry for both cohorts were massed in neatly aligned bodies behind the cavalry. The rectangle was closed on the south by the artillery company, with the three small cannon the state had recently sent them.

At this time in the history of the United States, state and local militia were the country's answer to the call to have a standing army. The federal army of full-time soldiers was less than ten thousand strong. But across the face of America there were nearly two million men in state and county militias. Most states required that all able-bodied white males between the ages of eighteen and forty or forty-five give at least six months of full-time service in the militia and then remain in the reserves. Preachers, Quakers, and others with acceptable reasons were exempt, but all others accepted service as a matter of course. In the Nauvoo Legion, nonmembers of the Church were not required to serve; thus Carl and Joshua were the only adult male Steeds not currently in the service.

There were no standard uniforms. Each of the enlisted men wore what they wore at home—homespun trousers, cotton shirts, boots, and various styles and colors of hats. Even the officers were not required to be in uniform, though most of them chose to be. But *uniform* was a misleading term, for there was no set costume and their dress ranged from the simple to the wildly flamboyant and spanned the rainbow in color.

Weapons were just as varied, if present at all. The state had also sent the Legion some two hundred rifles, and these were scattered among the two cohorts. Beyond that there weren't many others. The Missouri militia had disarmed the Mormons back in Far West, and money was too scarce for most to have replaced them. There were a few pistols and numerous swords. Some of the infantry carried old muskets, others long pikes with steel tips. A few even carried sticks on their shoulders so they could drill as though with real weapons.

But with all of that, they were still a stirring sight, Carl thought. There were now twenty-six companies in the Legion, about two thousand men. And to see the infantry lined up in formation and in front of them the lines of cavalry, over two hundred strong—as Mary Ann said, it was indeed grand.

"Are they really going to fight each other, Papa?" Sarah asked, running her fingers through Carl's hair.

"No, honey. They're going to have what they call a 'sham

battle.' That means they act like they are fighting so they can practice their drills and moves. They'll be drawing their swords and shooting off their guns, but only in the air. No one's going to be trying to hurt anyone else."

"You'd better hold your ears when it happens," Mary Ann teased them. "It's going to be very loud."

———•———

Had Carl been closer to the parade ground, down near the south end of the First Cohort, he might not have been so quick in reassuring his daughter. In the second row of horses, right on the far south end of the line, Robert Foster and the two Higbee brothers sat side by side. They each had a rifle in hand and wore a scabbard with a sword. Unlike most of the other men who were laughing and talking with great animation while they waited for things to begin, these three were grim and tight-lipped.

"Here he comes," Foster said, jerking his head toward the front end of the parade ground. Major General John C. Bennett was cantering down the line of the First Cohort, as if on an informal inspection.

General Wilson Law, commander of the First Cohort, saw him coming and stood in his stirrups, raising his sword high. "Ten-*shun!*" he yelled loudly. Instantly the men straightened. Those with rifles brought them up in front of them, held at the vertical in salute. Those with swords did the same. All the others raised their hands to their foreheads in salute.

Bennett raised his sword in salute, keeping his horse moving at a steady pace all the way down the line. When he reached the end, he wheeled around. "Very good, General Law," he shouted. "Are your men ready?"

"Yes, sir!" came the answering shout.

Bennett brought his horse around the end of the two rows of horsemen. As he came by Foster he gave him a hard questioning look. "Are you men ready?" he barked up the line. Others shouted out "Yes!" Foster merely nodded, fingering his rifle. "Good,"

Bennett grunted, and put spurs to his horse, running it along behind the First Cohort and joining General Smith at the north end.

"General Smith, sir!" he cried as he trotted up to where Joseph and his staff were waiting.

"Yes, General Bennett."

"The troops are ready for your command, sir."

"Good. Let us proceed."

"Sir? May I make a suggestion?"

Joseph had turned to watch as Emma moved away to join the other officers' wives, who would watch the battle from a safer distance. Some of his lifeguards rode with her and stayed by her side. He turned back. "Yes, General. What is it?"

"May I suggest that you take command of the First Cohort of Cavalry, sir. That way you can be right in the midst of the men to see how they do."

Benjamin was no longer of age to be in a militia, but he still served on Joseph's personal staff in the Legion. He was on foot, just two horses away from Joseph. He jerked up at Bennett's last words. That would put Joseph right in the middle of the melee. It was not unheard of that, in spite of the most careful precautions, people got hurt in these sham battles. Two thousand men firing off guns into the air, men engaged in mock sword fights, infantry jabbing here and there at make-believe opponents with their bayonets—Benjamin didn't like the idea of that at all. He wondered if he should speak.

But Hyrum had also stiffened in his saddle. Brigham and Heber and others of the Twelve were looking concerned. Hyrum kneed his horse and moved over right next to Joseph. He leaned over and there was a quick whispered exchange.

When Joseph straightened, he looked at Bennett. Any humor had gone out of his eyes now. "Thank you, General, but I think it best if we observe from this vantage point."

Momentary anger flickered in the mayor's eyes, but he forced a quick smile. "Then may I make another suggestion, sir. What if you took up station on the far end of the First Cohort, to the rear of them? That way you would not be in the thick of the fray but would still be in a much better position to observe."

"There is not room there for me and all of my staff," Joseph responded.

"Then leave your staff here," came the quick response. "I will personally escort you there and stay with you."

Now Captain Rockwood, commander of the lifeguards, was motioning for Joseph's attention. "Let me confer with my staff on the matter," Joseph said to Bennett. He reined his horse around, and he and Hyrum rode over to Rockwood.

"Don't do it, Joseph!" Hyrum said in a terse whisper. "He's up to something."

"Rockwood?"

The captain shook his head. "Foster and the Higbee boys are down on that end, General. I think you're better off to stay right here. Once things start popping, there's no way to keep it under control."

Now William Smith, Joseph's brother, leaned in. He had been close enough to hear what they were saying. "Do you really think someone would try to harm Joseph with all these people around?" he asked dubiously.

Rockwood didn't back down an inch. "One 'stray' bullet and who would know?"

"Joseph, don't do it," Hyrum said again.

Joseph looked from face to face. He was thoughtful, pensive. Then finally he shook his head. "The gentle breathings of the Spirit whisper that there is mischief in this sham battle," he said in a low voice. "And I think John C. Bennett is behind it. And if I am not wrong, time shall prove me right about his character."

He wheeled his horse around again. "Thank you very much, General Bennett," he called cheerfully, "but my staff still thinks my place is here at the head of the field with our guests and wives."

True anger twisted Bennett's features now. He muttered something under his breath, jerked on the reins, and rode back to his position directly in front of the band. Without waiting for a signal from Joseph, he raised his sword. "Let the battle begin."

It was a grand thing to behold as hundreds of men, with a mighty shout, put spurs to horses. Rifle and musket shots rang out. Puffs of smoke filled the spring air. Swords clanged against swords and men shouted in mock fury. Even the three cannons got into the act, firing off round after round of black powder, but with no cannon balls inside the breech. At first the great crowd was stunned by the seeming fury of it all, but then a thunderous cheer went up and down the line of people. The Nauvoo Legion was giving them a real show.

———•—•———

Benjamin picked up Joseph's plumed hat and carried it around the grandstand. Joseph was there, still in full uniform but minus his hat, bidding final farewell to their guests. Hyrum stood behind him waiting. Rockwood and his lifeguards were scattered here and there, but Benjamin saw with satisfaction that though they appeared to be relaxed and off duty, they were still watching the dispersing crowd with narrowed eyes and rifles at the ready.

When the entourage finally moved away, Benjamin stepped forward and handed Joseph the hat. "Ah, Benjamin, there it is. The general is complete again at last."

Benjamin smiled. "Emma said to tell you she would meet you at the house."

"All right."

He looked at Joseph. "Do you think—" He stopped, not sure if it was appropriate to ask.

"Yes?" Joseph encouraged him.

"Do you think Bennett had really planned something?"

Hyrum was listening nearby and nodded immediately. So did Captain Rockwood. Joseph just looked at him.

"I mean . . ." Benjamin couldn't keep the horror out of his voice. "We are talking about assassination here."

Joseph sighed, tucking his hat under one arm. "I'll say this much, Brother Ben. Let that man answer on the Day of Judgment when I stand before him and ask him this question:

'Why did you request me to command one of the cohorts, and also to take my position behind that cohort without my staff, during the sham battle, where my life would have been forfeit and no man would have known?' At the Judgment, he shall have no choice but to answer me that question, Benjamin. And then we shall know for certain."

Chapter Notes

On 4 May 1842, Joseph introduced the ordinance of the endowment to eight men. In the *History of the Church*, William Law and William Marks are not listed, probably because of their later apostasy. This was the first time in this dispensation that the full temple ordinance was given to others. (See HC 5:1–2; Joseph Smith, *The Papers of Joseph Smith*, ed. Dean C. Jessee, vol. 2, *Journal, 1832–1842* [Salt Lake City: Deseret Book Co., 1992], p. 380; see also HC 2:309.) In his history Joseph goes on to say that the next day General Adams departed for Springfield, but that the remainder of the council "continued their meeting at the same place, and myself and Brother Hyrum received in turn from the others, the same that I had communicated to them the day previous" (HC 5:2–3).

Though news of it would not reach Nauvoo for more than two weeks, ex-Governor Lilburn W. Boggs was shot as he sat in his house by an unknown assailant on 6 May 1842 (see HC 5:14). This would later prove to have lasting implications for Joseph and the Church.

The descriptions given of militia in general and the Nauvoo Legion in particular are accurate as to numbers, dress, weaponry, and so on (see *In Old Nauvoo*, p. 131).

The attempted assassination as depicted here is described by Joseph in his history (see HC 5:4–5). His comment about the "breathings of the Spirit" and the question that would be asked of Bennett at the Judgment come directly from his account. It should be remembered that while nothing public had been announced at this point, Joseph was by now fully aware of what Bennett was up to and was moving to take action against him. Whether Bennett knew that or not at this point is not clear.

T hey came quietly to the home of Benjamin and Mary Ann Steed. There were five of them—Nathan and Lydia, Carl and Melissa, and Caroline. They came separately, within minutes of each other. They each knocked softly at the front door rather than simply walking in as was their habit. That alone was proof that they sensed that this was not to be just another evening together at Grandma and Grandpa's. As Caroline arrived, the last of the five to do so, and Benjamin came into the parlor with her, he saw the surprise on their faces at who had been included in his unexpected invitation and who had been excluded. They were subdued and unusually reserved, though he could clearly see the questions in each one's eyes.

Benjamin had arranged the chairs so that there were two on one side of the sofa, one on the other. That put all five of them sitting together and facing Benjamin and Mary Ann, who had matching chairs side by side. Carl and Melissa were on the sofa, Caroline in the single chair, Nathan and Lydia in the double set.

Benjamin did not sit down. He stood beside Mary Ann, one hand resting lightly on her shoulder. "Thank you for coming. I know you have many questions, which we shall answer in a moment. This *is* a family council. It is limited to the seven of us for reasons you'll understand. To begin with, I'd like to take Carl and Nathan with me into the other room for a few minutes. Mother Steed will explain some things to the women while we are gone."

"But Pa!" Nathan exclaimed, guessing now what this was about.

Benjamin started away. "We'll meet in the kitchen."

Obviously agitated, Nathan stood and followed. Carl, his face impassive and unreadable, did the same. Benjamin went into the kitchen and, once Nathan and Carl had joined him, shut the door. Before Nathan could speak, he held up his hand. "I know what you're going to say, Nathan, and I want you to know that what I do tonight I do not do lightly."

"Are you telling them?" Nathan flung his head in the direction of the parlor.

"Yes, I am."

"Pa, we promised we wouldn't say anything to anyone else unless we all agreed to it."

Benjamin's head came up slowly. "There was a plan to assassinate Joseph yesterday at the Legion's parade and sham battle."

Nathan rocked back as though struck.

"What?" Carl cried.

He told them quietly, seeing the shock only deepen into total revulsion.

"And Bennett was behind it?" Nathan said in a hoarse voice.

There was a curt nod, and then Benjamin turned to Carl. "I don't think anything more will come of it. But this isn't something we can keep in a sack any longer. It could affect our wives and they have the right to know what is going on."

"Do they know about this, what happened yesterday?" Carl asked.

"No, and that is the one thing I'm not going to share with

them. Right now Bennett thinks that his plan was foiled, but he doesn't know that Joseph suspects him."

Nathan ran his fingers through his hair, thinking deeply. "You're right, this changes everything. But why bring Caroline? Joshua is going to see this as a real betrayal."

Benjamin dropped his second bombshell. "Joseph knows everything, Nathan."

Nathan had been looking toward the window. Now his head came around slowly. Carl was staring at Benjamin too.

"He knows that Nathan is looking into the plural marriage thing?" Carl asked in alarm.

"You told him?" Nathan exploded. "You told him that, Pa?"

"Nathan, Joseph is not a fool. You've been asking questions of the Twelve. You've been avoiding him. What did you think he would think?"

Nathan shook that off. "You didn't say he *suspects*, Pa. You said he *knows*."

Benjamin sighed. "That's right. I've told him everything."

Nathan reached him in three strides and grabbed his arm. "After we said we wouldn't? Don't you think I wanted to say something to him? Don't you think I've felt awful sneaking around behind his back?"

"Listen to me! This isn't something we can sit on any longer. Whatever happens now is going to profoundly influence Caroline. Joshua has no right to hide this from her and then spring it on her like a snare. Lydia is already sick with worry about you. You've been depressed, withdrawn, distant. She knows something is wrong, but she doesn't know what. Well, she has a right to know. The same with Melissa and Carl."

"I'm glad," Carl said quietly. "I've not felt good about this from the beginning."

"These are our wives," Benjamin said, pleading for understanding. "Not only do they have a right to know what is going on, but we need their counsel on this. I talked to Joseph and Hyrum about it. It was their suggestion that we hold this family council." He turned to the door again. "Now we've got a long night ahead of us, so let's get on with it."

He stepped through the door and walked down the hall to the parlor.

———•———

It was obvious that Mary Ann's news had cast a pall over the three women. Melissa stood as Carl came to her, and put her arms around him. "Oh, Carl," was all she said.

Benjamin sat down by Mary Ann and she reached out and took his hand, squeezing it gently. Lydia also took Nathan's hand, but she still seemed perplexed. She wasn't yet sure what all of this about Bennett had to do with Nathan's recent dark moodiness. Benjamin sighed, dreading having to add to their concern. But stalling wasn't a solution, so he jumped in, not willing to delay it with small talk. "Mary Ann has explained about Carl's investigation of Bennett. She hasn't told you the rest." He could see the change in their faces. They thought they had heard it all. "There's something else. Yes, Carl was satisfied that the whole sordid mess that Bennett described was nothing but lies, but—" He drew a quick breath. "But he learned that there was a good possibility that Joseph was teaching the doctrine of plural marriage."

It didn't register. All three of them looked blankly at him. "Plural marriage?" Caroline said, genuinely puzzled. "What do you mean by that?"

"That God authorizes a man to have more than one wife," Nathan said bleakly.

There was a collective gasp and simultaneously they recoiled in horror.

Carl was nodding. "I wasn't sure. I was just hearing things and—"

Nathan cut in sharply. "Pa, you talked with Joseph today. Did you ask him if it was true?"

"I did."

Now Nathan's eyes were filled with undiluted anguish. "And?"

"The answer is yes, Nathan."

Nathan dropped his head into his hands. "I knew it!" he cried. "They just kept hedging. No one would answer me directly. But they wouldn't deny it either."

"Knew what?" Lydia asked, reaching over to try and hold him. She turned to Benjamin in horror. "Are you saying . . . ?" Her eyes widened into great round circles. "You're not saying that it's true!"

He wasn't going to try and shield them on this. They had to know. "Yes, it is true."

Nathan was still shaking his head and mumbling to himself. "I knew it! I just knew it!" Then suddenly he snapped up. "Has Joseph already—?"

Benjamin said it very quietly, but firmly. "Yes."

It was as if he had been kicked. The air went out of him in a long whoosh. "No," he whispered.

Carl was aghast. "You don't mean . . ."

"Yes." The weariness made Benjamin's voice low and heavy. "Heber too."

"What?" Caroline cried. "What are you saying?"

"They have already married other women."

"Joseph?" Lydia cried.

"Yes. At least one, maybe more."

She was dazed. "Who?"

"I don't know. And I'm not sure that he's living with them as husband and wife. But they have been joined to him in eternal marriage."

Nathan was staring at the wall. "So there was some truth to it after all."

"To Bennett's lies?" Benjamin retorted in disgust. "Absolutely none. Joseph never gave Bennett any such licence. The man was acting totally out of his own depravity."

He leaned forward, earnest now, wanting Nathan most of all to understand. "Don't you see what's happening here, Nathan? From Satan's point of view, this is a brilliant strategy. Just as

Joseph is about to be told by the Lord that it is time for the principle of plural marriage to be restored, along comes John C. Bennett. He's smooth, he's handsome, he helps us get a charter, he's elected mayor. We are all a little agog that such a man has become one of us. And then he starts his work—silently, insidiously, treacherously. He starts teaching a corrupted form of the very doctrine that is about to be revealed. He's a man of influence and position. He's the Assistant President, of all things. There couldn't be a more destructive problem. It sows doubt, it raises questions, it has the whole city aflame with rumors. It is a brilliant stroke!"

He instantly shook his head. "No, not brilliant, for that implies light, and there is no light in Satan or his followers. But it is cunning to the highest degree." He paused, deeply depressed suddenly. "And we have not seen the end of this. Not by a long shot."

Melissa was still in shock. She was whispering something to Carl, and he just kept shaking his head.

Lydia looked ill. Her face was drawn and almost gray. "Does Emma know?" she asked in a small voice.

"Yes," answered Benjamin.

She felt like she couldn't get her breath. "And she . . . ?"

Benjamin's shoulders lifted and fell. "Joseph says she has accepted the doctrine, but not surprisingly she is having a difficult time with its application. But she has accepted the fact that—"

Lydia looked away, her hand to her mouth.

Benjamin looked around the circle. "I don't want to rush this. We need to talk about it as long as you want. But when you're ready, Brigham Young and Heber Kimball are waiting for us at Heber's house."

That brought all of their heads up with a jerk.

"Yes," he said. "Joseph thinks that we need to hear what they have to say. But not until you're ready. They'll wait as long as necessary."

He looked to Nathan. "And Joseph said to tell you that he

will be waiting for you. However long it takes, he'll be there when you're ready to talk with him."

———•———

In the end they only stayed at Benjamin's another fifteen minutes or so. Except for Benjamin and Mary Ann, they were all still a little dazed. There were a few questions, some comments that showed how deeply they had been affected, but mostly they just sat and stared at Benjamin, trying to comprehend what he was telling them. So eventually he led them out and they came to the home of Heber and Vilate Kimball.

But it was Brigham Young who met them at the door. As he ushered them into the sitting room, he spoke to Benjamin. "I apologize," he said, "my Mary Ann planned to come, but our little Brigham, Junior, has taken quite ill just since supper. Bad food, I suppose. And she felt it best to stay with him."

"We understand," Benjamin said.

In the sitting room, Heber and Vilate Kimball were waiting for them, seated side by side on a small divan. They both rose, Heber shaking hands with the men and the women, Vilate nodding to the men but taking only the women's hands.

Heber Kimball was a barrel-chested man. Though now a potter by trade, in his early years he had worked with his father as a blacksmith and he still had a blacksmith's arms and torso. Taller than Brigham by a couple of inches, he was considerably more stout. He liked to point out to people that he was the only person he knew whose chest measurements were the same from front to back as they were side to side. He and Brigham were of the same age, born only two weeks apart in the summer of 1801. They were approaching their forty-first birthdays, which made them four years older than Joseph. Heber was totally bald on the top of his head, but what remained on both sides was thick and wiry dark hair. He wore heavy sideburns down to the jawline.

Normally he was of a sunny disposition, always ready with a quip or a joke to make others smile, his piercing dark eyes quick to dance with humor. As he greeted them now and welcomed them to his home, there was little sign of that. His eyes were dark and troubled, his demeanor greatly subdued.

Vilate Murray Kimball was five years Heber's junior. Of Scottish descent, she was a lovely woman who carried herself with grace and poise. She was as dark haired as Heber and wore her hair parted down the middle and pulled to either side. This emphasized the fineness of her features, the bright, intelligent eyes, and the sensitive mouth. She was educated and literate. Lydia had seen some of the poems she had written and they were elegantly crafted. More sober by nature than Heber, she was nevertheless a pleasant and happy woman and greatly loved by those who knew her. But like her husband, tonight she was very quiet and deeply serious.

Brigham stood at the end of the room, waiting until all were seated. There was a brief, humorless smile. "Judging from what I see in the sisters' faces, I assume they know, Brother Benjamin."

"Yes."

"Good, then there's no need spending time on nonessentials." Now he spoke to all of them. "As you know, Joseph has not only given us permission to talk to you, he has requested that we help you understand better what is going on. And why. That is the most important—the why. I know this has come as disturbing news. I can see it in your eyes. You shall see that you are not alone in that reaction." He looked to his fellow Apostle. "I should like Heber and Vilate to tell you their story, but first I would like to make one or two points."

Heber nodded. Vilate did as well.

"On several occasions, the Lord has said that he will prove his people. He will test us to see if we are truly committed to keeping our covenants with him. In one of the revelations he says to us, 'I will have a pure people, saith the Lord, that will serve me in righteousness.' In another, he said that he will prove us in all things to see if we will serve him, even unto death. And if we cannot abide in our covenants even unto death, we are not worthy of him."

His eyes were fixed and looking above their heads now. "I do not fully understand why this is so, why the way has to be so hard, the required price so high. But it doesn't really matter whether I understand it or not. We have been tried by the sword and by the ball. We have been driven, mocked, spat upon, jailed, and slain. We have seen those who should have been our staunchest friends become our bitterest enemies. We have seen sickness and starvation. We have seen our children lie down with hollow bellies and raging with fever. We have been placed in the frying pan, and when that became unbearable, we were kicked into the fire."

He took a chair now and turned it around, leaning on the back of it as though it were a pulpit. His voice dropped to a low pitch, and it was filled with heaviness. "I thought we had seen it all. Jackson County. Kirtland. Haun's Mill. Far West." He shook his head. "How naive I was. How narrow my perspective was to think that we had been tested to the limits of our endurance. How little did I dream that there was something of far greater pain, far greater demands." His eyes bored into them in turn now, pinning them with his words. "If you do not see this in that light, then you will not understand what is happening."

He paused for a moment to see if there was any reaction, but there was none. So he plunged on. "Now, to something more practical. What we are going to discuss with you this evening, you are not free to discuss with others. Not even with others of your family." He looked directly at Caroline. "Not even with your husband."

She nodded slowly.

"This may be hard for you to understand. Some will say that Brother Joseph is trying to hide the truth. Some will say Brother Joseph is betraying his people. I will only say this. Joseph is not a coward." His voice was strong and challenging now. "He himself has said that no coward shall inherit the celestial kingdom. But caution is not cowardice. Especially when the Lord whispers, 'Be cautious. Give not this principle to the multitude as yet. Someday this doctrine shall be thundered from the housetops, but not yet. Reveal it only to those who can be trusted.

In the Home of Heber and Vilate Kimball

Reveal it only to those who have been proven, for there are those, even in high places, who seek your life.'"

Brigham let that sink in for a moment, pleased to see that they were suitably shocked. "Lest you think I am overly dramatic, there has already been a foiled attempt on Joseph's life."

Mary Ann rocked back. "What?"

"Yes."

"Here in Nauvoo?" Lydia asked, the horror twisting at her face.

"Yes, within the past week. I cannot say more than that. But I say it to impress upon your minds the importance of keeping confidences."

Now he turned to Carl. "I know, Brother Carl, that you are not a member and that we have no call upon your loyalty. But Brother Joseph is also keenly aware of what you have done these past few weeks. He is deeply grateful. It is at his specific request that you are asked to be here tonight."

Carl was deeply moved. Melissa, seeing this, slipped her arm through his and held him tightly as he spoke. "Tell Brother Joseph that I am honored by his trust, and assure him that it is not misplaced."

"He knew it would not be," Heber said.

Now Brigham turned to Caroline. "You are not a member either, but that is not by your choice. We know about your situation with your husband. We know that Joshua is looking for some way to break your determination to stay faithful. Therefore, Joseph felt that you needed to know it all, so you can choose for yourself."

It was Lydia who asked the question that was looming large in Caroline's mind. "If we cannot speak of what we learn here tonight, what does Caroline say to Joshua?"

"What do any of us say to Joshua?" Nathan exclaimed. "He knows about Joseph teaching the doctrine. He'll be home in a few days expecting an answer from me."

Brigham seemed unbothered by that. "What you have learned outside this room, you may share with him openly.

Joseph feels it is probably unwise to try and deflect him from his questions. But what Heber and Vilate are going to tell you now is not for him. It is not for anyone else. If you cannot commit to that kind of confidence now, then we shall ask you to withdraw."

There was silence in the room. No one moved. Brigham searched their faces and then nodded in satisfaction. "Then I suggest you proceed, Heber." And he moved to a chair and sat down.

For a long moment, the man with a blacksmith's body and an Apostle's heart stood silently. Then finally he straightened. He was looking at Vilate now, almost oblivious to the fact that there were others in the room. "Brother Brigham talked about the Lord testing us. In the revelations, he says that we must be tried even as Abraham was tried. And so it was with me. It was shortly after I returned from England last summer. Joseph immediately started revealing the principle of plural marriage to the Twelve. We were as stunned as you. We were every bit as sick at heart as you are at this very moment. It sounded like a thunderclap in our ears.

"It was then that Joseph took me aside. 'Brother Heber,' he said, 'the Lord has a special test for you.' 'What is it?' I said boldly, thinking that I was faithful and prepared to meet whatever demand my beloved prophet laid upon me."

He stopped, staring down at his hands now. Benjamin saw that they were trembling slightly even now as he went back in memory. "'Heber,' he said, 'the Lord requires that you give Vilate to me to be my wife.'"

The sharp intake of breath sounded loudly in the stillness of the room. Even Benjamin was gaping at Heber.

Heber took in a long breath, shaking his head. "I could scarcely believe my ears. At first I thought he was making a joke of this, though I saw no humor in such a horrible proposal. But he assured me that he was in earnest."

"But Vilate already belonged to another," Melissa cried. "She was another man's wife. Does the Lord justify that?"

Heber went on quietly without responding to her directly.

"My first thought, I am ashamed to admit to you now, was that Joseph had fallen. Surely God was not asking for such a heinous thing. Joseph's motives must be base and twisted. It was like a poisoned arrow shot through my heart. I was ready to spurn his proposition out of hand, without debate. But fortunately, reason prevailed. I have known Brother Joseph intimately for almost a decade. I have sat in council with him, been instructed by him, seen his face transformed by the light and power of God. I have never once doubted that Joseph is God's oracle. How could I do so now? And if that was so, then it was not Joseph who required my beloved Vilate, it was God himself. And how could I refuse?"

Everyone in the room was transfixed now. Hardly an eyelid fluttered as Heber's hands began to grip at the back of the chair, digging and twisting at the material. His voice had become hoarse and filled with pain. "I fled from his face. For three days I was gripped in the agonies of hell. I fasted. I prayed. I begged the Lord to comfort me. I felt as if my very heartstrings were sawn asunder. But at the end of those three days, I knew that I had no choice. I must submit to God's will. So with broken and bleeding heart, I led my beloved Vilate to Joseph. I placed her hand into his and told him that she was his to take as his wife."

Heber stopped, looking away. He reached up and brushed at the corner of one eye with the back of his hand. Lydia saw that Vilate's eyes were shining now too as she looked at her husband.

"As I placed her hand into his," Heber said, now stronger and more firmly than before, "Joseph broke down and wept like a child. He just sobbed. 'My dear Brother Heber,' he said, 'you have passed the test. You have proven yourself to be a child of Abraham, and like Abraham you have held nothing back, laying that which is most precious and dear to you on the altar for God's glory.'"

Heber's voice broke now, and he started to weep openly. "He swept me up in his embrace, crushing me to his bosom. 'Your sacrifice is accepted. This is proof enough of your devotion to your God. It is accounted unto you for righteousness.'"

He had to stop. Vilate stood and moved swiftly to stand

beside him. Though she was crying now too, her voice was still under control. "And then—" She sniffed back the tears. "Then he had us kneel there together before him. He placed my hand in Heber's, and there and then he sealed us together as man and wife for time and for all the eternities."

"And it was only a test?" Melissa said, crying as well. "Joseph didn't really want Vilate as his wife?"

"No," Heber said. He blew out his breath, fighting to regain control. He wiped at his eyes again. "I know not what it is like to have to offer a child to the Lord as Abraham did. But I will say this. Let me stand in the thickest of the battle, with balls whizzing past my head. Let me endure the sack of Far West all over again. Let me cross the wintry plains a thousand times. I will take them each or all together as a test rather than to face being asked to make such a sacrifice again."

Brigham stood. Vilate moved as though to sit down again, but he took her arm, holding her there with him. "Their story is not through and I want you to hear it all, but first, let me say this. In the minds of the wicked, this principle that Joseph has revealed will be seen as a license for a man to gratify his basest desires. We will be accused of seeking to warm our beds with more than one woman. And with men like John C. Bennett and others, this is how it *will* be.

"But to a man of God, nothing can be further from the truth. From the time I made my decision to join the Church and threw my lot in with the kingdom of God, I have tried to be obedient to whatever God asked of me. But when Joseph revealed this principle to the Twelve and said that we must live it, it was as if a stake had pierced my heart. It was the first time in my life that I desired the grave. For days, I longed for death. That, to me, was a far more pleasant prospect than having to go to my beloved Mary Ann and tell her what was required of us. When I saw a funeral, I felt a great envy for the corpse and longed to have it be my body in the coffin."

Nathan had been staring at the rug beneath their feet, listening but not wanting his face to betray what he was feeling.

Now he looked up. "Have you taken a second wife, Brother Brigham?"

The other day during their conversation, Brigham had carefully sidestepped Nathan's questions. Now he did not flinch. "Not yet." And then before the surprise and relief could register, he went on. "But it is about to happen. In a few weeks, I will be marrying Lucy Ann Decker Seeley. You may know her. She is a woman whose husband began to abuse her a few years back and then eventually abandoned her. He has since died. She has two children from that marriage."

"And Mary Ann knows of this?" Lydia asked, her own face filled with doubts.

"Yes," he said quietly. "I went to Mary Ann immediately after Joseph taught us the doctrine and we shared those difficult days together. She has now accepted it as I have. I have her consent to marry this woman. In fact, she will likely be present at the marriage, which Brother Joseph will perform for us."

Melissa couldn't bear it. She had to look away, sick at heart. Carl saw it and reached for her hand. His own face was unreadable.

"I think you'd better tell them the rest of the story, Heber," Brigham said, and then went and sat down again.

"Yes, but I think I shall let Vilate tell it from here." Heber smiled at her. "I shall fill in when I think it's necessary."

She nodded. The tears were gone now and she was totally composed. "Well, as Heber said, he passed the test and we were sealed together, which was a glorious thing for both of us. I thought we had been tested to the limit and it was over." There was a tiny, rueful smile. "But I was wrong. Vilate still needed proving.

"What I didn't know at the time was that after Joseph revealed the principle of plural marriage to them, Heber expected he would be called upon to live it and so he began considering whom he might take to wife. Two elderly spinster sisters by the name of Pitkin came to his mind. They were dear friends of mine, and he thought that this would cause me little, if any, unhappiness. But when Joseph finally said that it was time for him to act, he named another woman, an English woman, Sarah Noon. She is much closer to my own age."

"She came across on the ship with us when we returned from England," Heber broke in. "She was married to a drunkard over there who badly mistreated her. He came to America but then abandoned her and returned to England. Joseph said I was to marry her and provide for her and the children."

"Go on," Vilate said. "Tell them what happened next, then I'll tell them my part."

He nodded and continued. "I was shocked at that request, for I knew this would be much harder for Vilate to accept. This would be more than just a token marriage to two elderly sisters." He sighed. "So I delayed. Joseph came to me again, and again he told me I was to take Sarah Noon to wife. Still I did not act. I could not bear to deal with what it would mean to my beloved Vilate.

"Finally," he went on more slowly now, "Joseph came to me the third time. When he learned I had not obeyed, he was greatly disturbed. 'I command you in the name of the Lord, Heber,' he said. 'If you do not heed this commandment, you shall lose your apostleship and you will be damned.'

"I was stunned and knew that I could delay no longer. But then he shocked me even more deeply. Joseph told me that I could not divulge this information to anyone else, not even Vilate. He said he was in great danger, that there were even then false brethren who had crept like snakes into his bosom, and that I must keep it secret from everyone."

"Even Vilate?" Mary Ann echoed.

"Yes, even from me," Vilate answered for him. "I knew nothing of any of this, of course. I don't have to tell you how Heber loves the Prophet Joseph. He realized the situation fully and determined that he would not put Joseph's life in jeopardy in any way."

"But here was another great test of my faith," Heber came in again. "Vilate had been ever faithful to me, suffering great deprivation while I was in England, having to deal with sickness and the caring for the children. How could I do this to her? It would destroy her if she heard of this from some other source. I shrank from the thought of causing her any more unhappiness. Finally, I was so troubled, I went to Joseph. I told him that this was such a great trial of my faith that I feared I would falter and perhaps even completely fall. I begged Joseph to let me tell Vilate before proceeding further. He was full of sympathy and finally agreed to inquire of the Lord. But when he came back, the answer was like my death knell. 'Tell him to go and do as I have commanded,' the Lord said. 'If I see that there is any danger of his apostatizing, I will take him to myself.'"

Benjamin shook his head. He had come expecting these two brethren and their wives to explain the principles behind plural marriage. He had not expected anything like this.

Heber laughed in bitter irony. "That was comforting to me. 'If Heber is too weak, I'll take his life from him.'"

"Let me pick up the story from there," Vilate said.

He nodded and then went and sat down.

Vilate turned her attention now particularly to the women and began to speak to them. "Not surprisingly, I began to notice that something was wrong with Heber. He was highly distraught. He ate little and rarely slept. He would often walk the floor throughout the night and into the morning. I asked him what was wrong, and he would only evade my questions. Finally, growing more and more alarmed, I demanded to know what was troubling him. He was sick in body and was in a state of mental wretchedness. At times I would see him on his knees. He would weep like a child and wring his hands, beseeching the Lord to be merciful. What I didn't know was that he was begging the Lord to reveal this principle to me so that he would not have to break his vow of secrecy."

Vilate sat down now in the chair in front of her. She folded her hands in her lap, and took three quick breaths. "This is not easy for me to talk about, even now. But if you will bear with me . . ." She looked away, fighting for composure.

Finally, she turned back. For some reason, she was speaking directly to Caroline now. "When I found that it was useless to beseech Heber any longer, and being greatly distressed by his condition, I retired to my room. I remembered what Joseph had learned so many years before, that God has said, 'If any of you lack wisdom, let him ask of God, who giveth to all men liberally and upbraideth not.' I did not realize it at the time, but at that same moment, Heber was also on his knees, pleading for an answer in my behalf."

Now the tears came again, but her face was lustrous through them and her voice rose firmly. "While I was thus engaged, pleading with the Lord as one would plead for life itself, suddenly the vision of my mind was opened. It was as though a flood of light washed away the sorrow and the groveling things of this world. Before me, I saw the order of celestial marriage, in all of its beauty and glory."

She stopped, her voice breaking. Lydia was enraptured, watching her face. She was unaware that she too was weeping. Caroline and Melissa were riveted to her every word.

Vilate shook her head, willing the emotions to hold back for a little longer. "I saw what it meant to be sealed in the order of celestial marriage to Heber. I saw the glory and the honor and the exaltation that would be conferred upon me, and upon all women, if we could but accept it and stand by our husbands' sides. It was more glorious than words can describe and I was on fire with joy.

"And then . . ." She wiped at her eyes. She was looking only at Heber now, who also had started to weep again. "Then I was shown the woman Heber had taken to be his wife. I contemplated with similar joy the vast and boundless love and union which this order would bring about, as well as the increase of my husband's kingdoms and the power and glory that were being extended to the both of us throughout the eternities, worlds without end."

Heber took out a handkerchief and blew his nose. Brigham was blinking rapidly. Nathan and Carl were staring at her in

446

utter amazement. All the women in the room were weeping, including Melissa.

Vilate took a deep breath, wiping at the tears quickly. "I rose from my bedside and went to find Heber. He tells me now that when I appeared in his room, my countenance was gleaming with joy. 'Heber,' I said, 'the Lord has shown me what you were asked to keep from me.'"

Now a sob shuddered through her body. Heber was up in an instant and holding her against his shoulder, but she wasn't done and she wouldn't let him take her to her seat until she was. "I will not tell you that this is an easy thing to accept," she said haltingly, "nor that it has been without its trials and challenges since then. But I cannot doubt—" Her shoulders pulled back. "I *cannot* doubt that the order of plural marriage has been given by God, for the Lord revealed it to me through the glorious answer to my prayer."

Chapter Notes

The events recounted in this chapter come almost exclusively from Orson F. Whitney's biography of Heber C. Kimball. This source tells of the test with Vilate and of the agony it cost Heber. The experience Vilate had in getting her own witness was told by her eldest daughter Helen Mar and can be found in that same work. (See *LHCK*, pp. 321–27, 439–40.) Heber married Sarah Peak Noon sometime early in 1842.

Brigham's comments about desiring the grave come from his own words (see *JD* 3:266). Brigham was married to Lucy Ann Decker Seeley in June 1842 by the Prophet Joseph (see *American Moses*, p. 102).

It is the belief of Latter-day Saints that a person cannot achieve the highest degree of celestial glory in a single state (see D&C 131:1–4). *Celestial marriage* refers to a marriage in which a man and a woman are sealed together for both time and eternity by those holding appropriate priesthood keys. This is now done only in temples. However, since plural marriage was instituted at about the same time that Joseph began sealing husbands and wives together in celestial marriage, some early members assumed that these two were the same and that a man will someday have to have plural wives in order to be exalted. In a 1933 statement, the First Presidency of the Church specifically stated that celestial, or eternal, marriage and plural marriage are not synonymous terms and that it was incorrect to assume plural marriage is required for exaltation (see James R. Clark, ed., *Messages of the First Presidency*, 6 vols. [Salt Lake City: Bookcraft, 1965–75], 5:315–30).

Thus, as related here, Vilate Kimball saw two separate things in answer to her prayer. First, she was shown the glory and majesty that comes to a woman through celestial marriage. She then also saw that in plural marriage there could be eternal blessings as well.

Chapter Twenty-Nine

I . . ." Nathan looked down, rubbing his temples with the tip of his fingers. "I'm not ready for bed yet, Lydia. I think I'll walk for a little while."

They were on the porch. The house was dark and silent, which meant that young Joshua had gotten the children to bed and had finally gone to bed himself. She looked up at the full moon, which was high in the sky. It had been just coming over the eastern bluffs when they walked out of the door on the way to Benjamin and Mary Ann's. Now it was past midnight.

She reached out and took his hand. He barely noticed. "I'll walk with you, if you'd like."

He shook his head and she felt a little stab of pain. *I need to talk this through too, Nathan. Don't shut me out.* But instantly she bit it back. She was struggling, but it was nothing like the abyss Nathan had plunged into. She went up on tiptoes and kissed him lightly. "When you come in, will you wake me if I'm asleep?"

There was a brief nod in the darkness. He squeezed her hand once and then was gone.

———•———

Benjamin found him just after four a.m. He was nearly past the silent figure sitting in the rocking chair on the porch of the Steed Family Dry Goods and General Store, but then the rocker creaked and he saw the movement. Benjamin slowed his step, then stopped altogether.

"Nathan?"

"What are you doing out at this hour?"

"Just walking. And you?"

There was a soft grunt. "Just rocking."

"I like your way better. Mind if I join you?" In the shadows Benjamin thought he saw a shrug. He decided to go over anyway. There was a second wicker chair on the other end of the porch. He picked it up and came back to sit beside his son. "Not a good night for sleeping, is it?"

"Not really." There was a derisive laugh. "Do you think Carl is sleeping tonight?"

He shrugged. "It's hard to tell what Carl is thinking. He wasn't saying much. On the surface, at least, he seems less upset by it than Melissa. She is really struggling."

"Who isn't?" Nathan shot back.

Benjamin ignored that. "You heard about Carl's experience with Israel Barlow?"

"Yes, Lydia told me about it."

"Oddly enough, that really had an impact on him. He's a long ways from being ready to accept Joseph as the Prophet, but he certainly has a new respect for him."

"Enough respect that he'll accept Joseph's telling people to take more than one wife?"

"It all kind of comes down to that, doesn't it? Is Joseph speaking for God or isn't he?"

Nathan's head shot up. "Do you think he is, Pa? Do you think God requires this?"

Benjamin shot right back at him. "Are you ready to say that Joseph is a fallen prophet?"

"I—"

"Or that he's been deluded on this? That somehow he has made this terrible mistake?"

Nathan looked away.

"It's not a pleasant question, is it? But that is the fundamental issue here. It is for you. It is for me. It will be for Melissa, and for every other member of the Church when they learn about this. Is Joseph speaking for God on this or isn't he?"

Nathan finally swung back around. "Do you really think that Joshua is going to care one way or another?"

"Why is it that you always keep pushing this off onto Joshua's shoulders? Is that really all that is bothering you?"

"Maybe not, but your son will be home in the next two or three days. He's going to want some answers. And I promised to get them for him."

"So that's it? You were so sure there was nothing to any of this. Now you have to admit to Joshua that you were wrong. That will be tough, all right."

Nathan bristled at that. "You know it's more than that."

"We agreed we'd tell Joshua the truth."

"I can just hear me now. 'Oh yeah, Joshua, by the way, there is some slight truth to what you've been hearing. God has said it's all right to have more than one woman as your wife. No, of course it's not out of hand. Well, yes, Joseph has married someone else. And yes, Heber Kimball has, and soon Brigham Young will also. Maybe a few other brethren too. But don't be alarmed. At least they haven't asked for Caroline yet.'"

Nathan slammed a clenched fist down against the handle of the rocking chair. "He'll never let Caroline be baptized now. Assuming she even still wants to."

"Why wouldn't she?"

"Because she just might have a couple of questions of her own about this whole thing, Pa!" He threw up his hands. "Didn't that ever occur to you?"

"Nathan, I—"

"No, don't, Pa. I'm not up to a sermon tonight."

The tension was almost palpable, but when Benjamin spoke he kept his voice even and controlled. "No sermons, just one question."

There was a resigned sigh and he turned his head aside. "All right, go ahead."

"If Caroline asked you right now if she should be baptized, what would you tell her?"

He stared out into the darkness, not moving, giving no sign that he had heard.

Benjamin stood up and picked up his chair with a hard yank. "Never mind. As of a little while ago, Caroline has fewer questions about this than you do. Maybe you ought to go to her! Looks to me like it's *your* faith that needs the buttressing here."

He went back down the length of porch and set the chair back in its original position with a solid clunk. He could hear Nathan's angry breathing behind him. He didn't turn, just stepped off the porch and started away. But then he turned back.

"I'll tell you one other thing you don't want to hear, Nathan. You say you're afraid that once he hears all this, Joshua isn't going to let Caroline be baptized. Well, when he gets back, the first thing Joshua is going to do is start asking you questions. And if you haven't got this resolved in your own mind?" He shook his head. "You're going to be the worst thing that could happen to her."

When Caroline stumbled out of the bedroom shortly after eight o'clock, rumpled and bleary-eyed, Will and Olivia had the two younger children at the table feeding them breakfast. Charles, who had turned two in February, raised his arms for her. "Mama. Mama."

She moved over to him, bent down, and gave him a solid hug. That satisfied him and he went back to eating. She moved to Savannah and gave her a kiss. "Why didn't you come home last night, Mama?" she asked. "I waited for you."

Will laughed. "That means she stalled and wouldn't go to bed until after ten o'clock."

Caroline kissed her daughter again, smiling. "Mama was with Grandma and Grandpa until late." She moved to Olivia and took her hand. Then she looked at Will. "Thanks, you two, for taking care of them so well."

Will watched her closely. "What time *did* you get home? I was up until almost midnight."

"It was a little after that." She grimaced. "It was a short night for sleeping." Then she turned to ward off any more questions. "Savannah, Charles is almost done. Can you be my big girl and go help him get dressed?"

"Yes, Mama."

She sat quietly with Will and Olivia until Charles climbed down and Savannah took him upstairs. As soon as they heard the door shut, Will turned to her. "Is everything all right, Mama?"

"Everything is fine. We just had some things we had to talk about. Some serious things. It took a long time."

Olivia stood. "You want some breakfast, Mama?"

"No, I don't think so." She smiled at her daughter, pleased at what she saw. Olivia had turned fourteen in November and had become a young woman now. And she was a beautiful young woman. The little girlishness was nearly gone. She was poised and confident, an accomplished pianist, a voracious reader, the pride of her father's eye, and not only a daughter to Caroline now but a companion as well.

Olivia stood and began to clear the table. Caroline turned to Will. "I expect your father will be home today or tomorrow. Maybe the next day."

"I would guess tomorrow or the next day."

"He'll want to know what you're going to do, Will."

Olivia stopped, setting the plates she had in her hand back down again. She came around and sat beside her brother. "What are you going to do, Will?"

"I'm going to be baptized." He said it with quiet determination.

"But I thought you said you wanted to wait for Mama," Olivia blurted.

"I do."

Caroline reached out across the table and took both of their hands. "I think I am going to be baptized too."

Will grinned widely. "Really?"

Olivia was shocked. "You are?"

"Before your father left, he said that there were some things he had to tell me about the Church. He said that if I still wanted to be baptized after hearing about those things, he would not stand in the way anymore." She took a quick breath. "Well, I heard about those things last night and—" She held up her hand, staving off Olivia's question. "It's something I can't talk about with you yet. But I've heard them now, and I still want to be baptized."

Now she turned to Will, and concern pulled at her mouth and darkened her eyes. "What I heard last night will greatly upset your father. He may change his mind. I think he may try to stop you from going ahead, Will."

"I've waited long enough," he answered simply.

"I know. And even if it works out that I can't, you must go ahead. That was your answer from the Lord, Will. You have to follow that."

"Mama?"

She looked to Olivia.

"I want to be baptized with you."

Will snapped around in surprise. Caroline had expected no less. She knew that Olivia had read the Book of Mormon now. She was praying night and morning. They had talked much about it while Will and Joshua had been gone. "I know, Olivia," said Caroline.

"Will Papa let me?"

"I hope so." She turned back to Will. "There's something I want to say to both of you."

"All right."

"Do you remember when you got your answer, Will? Do you remember how you felt?"

"Yes, very well."

"That was the Spirit whispering to you, Will. That is how Heavenly Father speaks to us."

"I know."

"Heavenly Father told you that he wants you to become a member of his church. I want you to remember that, no matter what else happens—if your father tries to dissuade you, or if you hear things that upset you. Just remember the feeling you had and what it means."

Olivia's eyes were shining now with excitement. "I have the same feelings. I know it's true. Papa thinks it's just because all of the family and all of my friends are Mormons. But I know it's true, Mama. I do."

"That's wonderful, Olivia. That's how I feel inside too."

"But what if Papa won't believe me? What if he won't let me be baptized?"

Now Caroline squeezed both of their hands. "It will work out. Your papa made a bargain with me. It will work out."

———◆———

"I've never seen him like this, Mother Steed." Lydia bit her lip and began to draw circles on the table with her fingertip. "He wouldn't talk to me about it at all when he finally came back this morning. He says he's just got to work it out on his own. He left again right away. He wouldn't eat breakfast. He just left."

"So he doesn't know how you feel?"

She shook her head.

"And now that the morning's come, how do you feel, Lydia?"

"At peace."

That caught Mary Ann by surprise. "But last night you were still very troubled. You said you weren't sure what to think about all of this."

"Now I'm sure."

Mary Ann smiled and reached out a hand. "Why? What happened?"

Lydia took her mother-in-law's hand and held it. "This is so strange for me. Always it has been me who wavered. I was the one who thought Joseph was a religious crackpot back in Palmyra. Nathan never questioned but what Joseph was called of God. I'm the one who ran home to Mama when Nathan left on Zion's Camp. Nathan came to Palmyra and put me back together. I was the one who nearly fell apart spiritually when little Nathan died. Nathan never wavered. Now suddenly he's like a rag in the wind, and I'm the one who's at peace."

"But what made the difference?"

"Vilate." She smiled. "And Caroline."

Mary Ann understood the reference to Vilate. For the women especially, Vilate's testimony had carried a powerful impact. "Why Caroline?"

"Caroline came over for a while this morning. We talked a long time. And do you know what she said? This really hit me. This probably was the turning point for me."

"What?"

"We had been talking about what Vilate said, and I said something about how comforting it would be to have that kind of powerful witness for yourself that this was a true principle. Caroline just looked at me and said, 'Lydia, I believe Vilate's story. I don't have to have my own vision.'"

"Oh," Mary Ann murmured in soft surprise. "What a wonderful way to put it. 'I don't have to have my own vision.'"

"She's right. I've thought about it ever since then. I don't question in any way that Joseph is a prophet. I believe he still speaks for God. I had a strong witness of that in our last Relief Society meeting."

"Me too."

"So that's not it. My struggle is with what it will mean to have to live it, to have to share Nathan with . . ." She couldn't finish and looked away quickly. One hand went across her stomach. "It makes me sick just to think about it. It does. I get physically sick right here." She took a deep breath, then another, and then went on. "But if it comes to that, then I'll ask the Lord to give me the strength and the understanding. And until then, I don't need my own vision."

"You need to say that to Nathan."

"I will, if he ever comes home."

Mary Ann just nodded, feeling the pain for her son. Then her thoughts turned to another of her children. "Will you and Caroline go talk to Melissa?"

"Yes, we talked about that. This has hit her really hard."

"Melissa has a sweet and simple faith, Lydia. She always has. But she's not as strong as you and Caroline. You're at peace. Caroline is going to come through this with Joshua. But Melissa?" She shook her head sadly. "I don't know how she'll do. And Carl's not there—not in this—to stand by her. She needs to hear you and Caroline tell her how you feel."

"We'll go over sometime today."

"Thank you. It will be better coming from you."

"Do you know what's strange, Mother Steed?"

"What?"

Lydia had to steel herself again. "I told you how I feel about the possibility of having to share Nathan with another woman, but this morning, while I was nursing Josiah, I had a revelation of my own." She colored immediately. "Well, not a real revelation, but a thought."

"What?"

"I was thinking about Jessica. What if she had never met Solomon? What if she had to be a widow all the rest of her life? And suddenly, at that moment, I thought to myself, I would share Nathan with Jessica." Sudden tears sprang to her eyes. "I love her that much. If it meant that she wouldn't have to be alone for the rest of her life, I could share Nathan with Jessica."

Mary Ann was looking at her in wonder. "I had never thought of it in that way."

"I could share him with Jennifer Jo or Caroline if Matthew

or Joshua were to die. These women are the sisters I never had." She clung to Mary Ann's hands now. "And maybe that was *my* vision. And for now, that's enough."

————•————

"I'm not sure I want to talk about this anymore." Melissa stood up and went to where Sarah was playing with the new puppy Carl had brought home for her a few days before.

"Melissa—," Caroline started. They were at Melissa's house, having come just after lunch to visit and talk and strengthen.

"No, I really don't. It gets me too upset. I start to think about Carl taking another wife and it all starts welling up inside." Her bottom lip started to tremble, and she bent down quickly and picked up the pup. She held it to her breast, rubbing its ears back and forth, back and forth.

"But Melissa," Lydia pointed out, "you're not going to have to face that. Carl isn't a member. You heard what Brigham said last night. This isn't something a person just takes upon himself. Joseph is the only one who has the keys of this power. He chooses under the inspiration of the Lord. He would never ask a nonmember to do this."

"That's right," Caroline said emphatically. "I've got to make that clear to Joshua, too. This won't ever affect our marriage either, unless he and Carl were ever baptized, then—"

"I don't want Carl to be baptized!" It came out with a ferocity that shocked the other two. Melissa looked away, holding the dog so tightly that it began to whine. "Well, I don't," she whispered. "All this time I've been hoping that he would feel something toward the Church. Now . . ." She shook her head. "I'm not sure I ever want him too."

"Melissa, you can't mean that," said Lydia. "You're just upset."

"You're certainly right about that." She was near tears now. "I *am* upset, but if you think it's just that, that my feelings will change when things settle down, well, you're wrong. This is wrong, Lydia! This is terribly wrong."

Caroline watched Melissa with deep sadness. "And what is Carl feeling by now?"

"Well, as you saw, he didn't say much last night. But he's been brooding about it all night. He's very disturbed about it. "

"Does he think Joseph and Brigham and Heber are doing this because . . . ?" She couldn't bring herself to say it.

Melissa leaned down and handed the puppy back to her daughter. "No. He thinks they're sincere. He doesn't think it is out of lustful motives. But sincerity doesn't make it right. He doesn't believe it's from God, that's for sure. And he thinks it is a terrible mistake. 'This is going to bring down another Missouri on our heads.' He just kept saying that over and over. "

"But Melissa—"

Her hands came up. "Please. Not right now. I can't. Maybe later."

Caroline looked at Lydia, who finally nodded. They went to her and hugged her tightly, each in turn. "When you're ready," Lydia said, "we're here."

She reached out and took both of their hands. "I know." The tears were just below the surface again. "And I appreciate that. I'm sorry. I know I should be strong, but I just can't be." She looked away. "I can't."

Nathan hung back, deep in the shadows of a honeysuckle bush. He was barely aware of the touch of its trumpet-shaped flowers and the powerful fragrance that emanated from them. His feet were sore and the back of his legs ached abominably. But he was barely aware of that too. He had walked for miles out on the prairie, sometimes dropping to his knees, sometimes just standing there, staring at nothing. He had even curled up some-time during the afternoon and slept fitfully for an hour. But even then the voices in his mind kept shouting at him, pleading with him, taunting him.

He knew that Lydia would be deeply concerned. He hadn't been home as yet. He had circled around Water Street on the off chance that he might see Joseph, and found him just coming out of the store with members of the Twelve. He hung back, waiting for them to finish. Now four of them—Brigham, Heber, Wilford Woodruff, and John Taylor—all crossed Water Street and started north. Joseph, Hyrum, George A. Smith, and Willard Richards started moving toward him. He waited until they were just across from him and then stepped out. "Good evening," he said.

They leaned forward, peering through the darkness.

"It's me, Nathan Steed."

There was a soft murmur of surprise, and then he heard Hyrum say quietly, "I'll stop and tell Emma you'll be a while." The three of them moved on, murmuring greetings to Nathan as they passed, and in a moment there was just him and Joseph. Joseph gestured with his head back toward the store. "Shall we talk?"

———•———

They were in his private office. Joseph lit a lamp but kept the wick shortened so that there was just enough light to allow them to see each other. Nathan asked after Emma and how the store was doing, and they chatted aimlessly for several minutes. Then finally Joseph fell quiet.

Nathan watched him, seeing the concern on his face, and decided it was no use postponing it further. "Can we talk about it?" he asked tentatively.

There was a brief nod. "I've been hoping you would come."

"Pa said he told you about the situation with me and Carl and Joshua, how I am supposed to find out what is really true here."

There was a sad smile. "Benjamin said you were absolutely adamant in defending me, in saying there could be no truth to any of this."

"Yes. I was so sure."

"I understand, but you have to be careful that you don't try and speak for the Lord."

"I know. I can see that." There was silence again, but Joseph waited patiently.

Then Nathan spoke again. "Thank you for asking Brigham and Heber to speak with us. I know that is taking a great risk for you and . . ."

Joseph waved it away. "Your family—even the ones who are not members—are not a risk to me, Nathan."

"Even Joshua?" he asked.

Joseph smiled. "Even old blustery Joshua. He wants so badly to hate us. I'm sorry that we're making it so difficult for him."

"This could do it, Joseph. This thing with Will and Caroline has deeply upset him. And now he has just the weapon he's been looking for."

"Does he?" Joseph seemed unconcerned. "This may turn Joshua against the Church. I hope not." Then he shrugged. "Joshua will have to decide that. But it won't turn him into an enemy. Not anymore."

"I wish I could be so sure."

"Actually," Joseph said slowly, watching Nathan closely now, "it's Joshua's brother that I am more concerned about."

Nathan's eyes lowered and he said nothing for a moment. Again Joseph just waited. Finally it burst out of him. "I don't understand it, Joseph. I don't understand how God could ask such a thing. Not now. Not in our time. How can it be right? Do you know what the world is going to say when they learn all this?"

"That had crossed my mind," Joseph said with a droll smile. Then he sobered. "You don't have to understand it to believe it, Nathan."

"Why? Why can't I understand it? Am I expected to accept things blindly?"

"Is it blindness to accept something in faith, even when you don't fully understand it? Do you think Abraham fully understood why God asked him to sacrifice his son? He knew what the commandment was about killing and about human sacrifice. Don't you think he had many questions? So, did Abraham act blindly or in faith?"

Nathan hesitated, then blew out his breath in frustration. "I can't debate you out of the scriptures, Joseph. You know that."

"Is that what you think, Nathan?" he asked, the rebuke plain in his eyes. "That I'm looking for a debate?"

"No, it's just that . . ." He sat back, shaking his head. "I don't know anymore, Joseph. I don't know."

"So why are you here?"

"I want you to tell me."

"Tell you what?" Joseph asked softly. "That I'm a prophet? That God has spoken to me on this matter of having plural wives?"

"Yes!"

There was a slow smile. "I'm a prophet and God has spoken to me on this matter."

"Please, Joseph," Nathan said wearily. "Don't toy with me."

"Oh?" There was a bite to his voice now. "First I want to debate you. Now I'm toying with you?"

"I mean no offense, Joseph. You know that. But I'm trying to sort things out. I'm really confused."

Joseph watched him for almost a full minute, silently appraising him. Then he leaned back in his chair. "Let me tell you something, Nathan. In Liberty Jail, during those terrible, awful months away from my people, away from my family, away from all that was decent and good, I reached a point where I wondered what was happening. I was in the darkest despair. Why was God allowing this terrible tragedy to occur? We were his people, yet every day brought news of their suffering. Widows and children were starving."

Now there was real pain in Joseph's eyes as he stared beyond the dim glow of the lamp. "One day, my heart was filled with heaviness. I was discouraged and filled with concern. And so I cried out in the anguish of my despair. 'O God! Where art thou? Where is the pavilion that covereth thy hiding place?'" He began to rub his hands softly together. "I asked God why he wasn't acting in our behalf. Why had he stayed his hand from reaching out to us? How long was he going to allow us to suffer in this manner? He is the Lord Almighty! Well, why wasn't he unleashing some of that almighty power against our enemies? Those were the questions that were torn from my heart that day.

"Then in the sweetness of the Spirit, the Lord heard my cries and answered me." Now he finally looked at Nathan. "And do you know what, Nathan? He not only answered the questions I asked, he also answered the questions I should have asked. Well, maybe that's what you need, Nathan. Maybe he's waiting for you to ask different questions."

"Like what?"

He stood, surprising Nathan. "That is between you and God, and *you* must ask him that." He took a quick breath. "You have come tonight because you want me to still your doubts, Nathan. You want me to just hand you the answers. Even if I could, I'm not sure that I would."

"But why?" Nathan cried. "I need your help, Joseph."

"You're not ready for my help, Nathan."

Nathan didn't even look up. The words were too devastating.

"There are two things from the Old Testament that seem to apply here, Nathan. I share them with you in hopes that they might help you find your way through this. Do you remember Professor Seixas back in Kirtland?"

Nathan was caught off guard by that, but then nodded. "Yes, he taught Hebrew in the School of the Prophets."

"That's right. Here is a lesson he taught to me. When Elijah was having the contest with the prophets of Baal, to see who could call down the power of God, he asked the Israelites a question. He said, 'How long halt ye between two opinions?' Well, Professor Seixas told me that the phrase which is translated as 'halt ye between two opinions' comes from a Hebrew phrase which describes a bird hopping back and forth between two branches."

"And you think that's what I'm doing?"

"Do *you* think that's what you're doing?" Joseph shot right back. But then, without waiting for a response, he went on.

"The second thought comes from the book of Jeremiah. Jeremiah also asked a probing question. It comes from the twelfth chapter. He says something like this: 'If thou hast run with the footmen, and they have wearied thee, how canst thou contend with the horses?'"

Nathan shook his head. "I don't understand what that means."

"In battle, if you are in the infantry—that is, if you are a footman—and you are having difficulty contending with other infantry, what will happen when the chariots come? And what I'm telling you is this, Nathan—the time has come in the Church when we are facing chariots."

Now Joseph fell silent, letting Nathan digest that. Abruptly he blew out the lamp, signaling that the meeting was over. Surprised and a little bewildered, Nathan stood too. Without speaking they left the office, went down the stairs, through the store, and to the door. Joseph opened it and let him out, but he stayed there without following. As Nathan reached the bottom of the steps, he finally spoke. "Nathan?"

He turned, looking up at the Prophet.

"We need men who can run with the horses. There's no way you can do that when you're hopping back and forth between branches."

Nathan reeled a little at the slap of the words.

"When you decide which questions you really want to ask, then we'll talk again."

Lydia watched Nathan dress. He moved slowly, deliberately.

"Nathan. I think you need to eat something."

He shook his head and kept buttoning his shirt.

"Is it wise to fast this long?" she asked.

He just shook his head again. Then Lydia remembered something. When Joseph had asked for Vilate, Heber had gone three days without food or water, seeking an answer. This was starting Nathan's third day. Now she understood, though it did little to lessen her concern. He looked drawn and very tired. But there was also a change. She rose from the bed and went over to him, moving his hands away and doing the top buttons herself.

He watched her steadily, then took her face in his hands when she finished. "You're not going to give up on me, are you?"

She was astonished. "Is that what you think?"

"I would if it were me."

She shook her head emphatically. "You would only give up on yourself. You would never give up if this were me."

He thought about that and finally nodded. "Probably not."

"You didn't before. I have a Book of Mormon with coffee stains on it as proof of that." And then she reached up and kissed him softly. "The anger is gone."

That surprised him. "What do you mean by that?"

"I know that you haven't found what you're looking for, Nathan, but the anger is gone. I can feel it."

He considered that. "Yes," he finally said, half in wonder, "I guess it is." He sat down and began to pull on his boots. "What time did you need me at the store?"

"Caroline said she can cover it until eleven. Then that woman we hired last week will be coming in at one. But Nathan, I'll just go. I promised your mother I would go and look at some dress material with her, but that can wait."

He shook his head. "By eleven, I'll be tired of wandering out there, staring at the sky and wondering whatever happened to Nathan Steed." There was a wan smile. "No, really. I'll be there. This means a lot to Mother to have you there."

"Are you sure?"

He nodded, then stood. "I can't believe this has been so easy for you."

"I know. That's what I told your mother. Usually, it's the other way around."

"You really have no questions?"

"I have a hundred questions, but I have no doubts."

He shook his head, finding that difficult to contemplate.

The love Lydia felt for this man was suddenly like a great well of living water within her and the tears came unbidden. She put her arms around him and laid her head against his chest. "Maybe Heavenly Father knew that he couldn't have both of us down at the same time."

———•———

Jennifer Jo knocked softly, then opened the door. "Kathryn, you have company."

Kathryn was reading a book. It was propped up in a special stand which sat on her bed. Matthew had designed and built it for her at the woodworking shop. Lydia's daughter Emily was there to turn the pages and fetch anything that she might need.

Kathryn turned her head. "Who is it?"

"It's a surprise."

She looked at Emily, who would turn ten in a couple of months. "Surprise? Do you know anybody by that name?" she asked, acting puzzled.

Emily giggled as Kathryn turned back to Jennifer Jo. "Show him or her in, whichever the case may be."

That sent Emily off into peals of laughter, but Jennifer Jo just rolled her eyes. "I think you've been in bed too long."

As Jennifer Jo came to the bed, Kathryn grew more serious. "Really, Jennifer, who is it?"

"You'll see." She bent over and, to Kathryn's surprise, laid a towel over her eyes. "Lift your head." As Kathryn did so, she tied it behind her head, making a blindfold.

"What is this?" Kathryn asked.

"Never you mind." Jennifer Jo turned. "All right," she called. "You may come in now."

Kathryn cocked her head, trying to pick out individual sounds as three pairs of boots came clunking across her floor. But it was too muddled. "Who is it?" she called cheerfully. There was no answer, but suddenly she felt hands slip beneath her and lift her up. "Oh!" she gasped.

"Just hold still," Matthew said into her ear. "We've got you."

She felt herself carried across the room and then, more slowly, through the door. Then they crossed the main room and went outside. "Help! Emily! I'm being kidnaped."

She heard Emily laugh, and then, to her surprise, a lot of others joined in the laughter as well. "Careful, now," Matthew warned as they walked down the porch step.

Thoroughly intrigued now, Kathryn relaxed, letting herself be carried along, still wondering what it was they were doing and why the great mystery.

"Okay, we're going to sit you down now. Ready?"

They bent her at the waist and she felt her feet lowered. In a moment she felt the confines of a hard chair, with a cushion in the seat. Someone moved her arms so that they rested on the arms of the chair. Then they let her go. To her amazement, there were oohs and aahs and a sudden smattering of applause. Then, before she could consider what that meant, Jennifer Jo whipped off the blindfold.

She blinked at the brightness of the sunlight, seeing that it was the family gathered around her. They were smiling and looking at her with great pride. Emily came darting right around in front of her. "Yea!" she cried, clapping her hands. "How do you like it?"

"Like it?" Kathryn gasped as her chair began to move, gliding along smoothly, like a sleigh on hard-packed snow. She looked down now and saw that her chair had wheels. And they were turning. She was moving effortlessly down the walk, between the applauding family members. As they reached the front gate, the chair stopped. Arching her back, she turned to see who was behind her. There, grinning like two young schoolboys, were Peter Ingalls and Will Steed.

"Hello, Kathryn," they said in chorus.

"But . . . ," she started, totally bewildered now. "What is this?"

Jennifer Jo was suddenly kneeling at her side, smiling broadly. "It's a wheelchair, Kathryn. It's your very own wheelchair. Now you can go all around town if you like."

"A wheelchair?" she stammered, not fully understanding.

Now Peter was at her other side. "Yes. Matthew made it at his shop. It's just for you." He took hold of one of the large wooden wheels, which had metal bands around them as the tires. He rocked the chair back and forth. "See? It moves as easily as a feather."

She turned her head, searching for Matthew among the familiar faces. When she found him, her eyes were suddenly glistening. "You made this for me?"

In typical Matthew fashion, he blushed a little and shrugged. "Actually, it was Peter's idea. He showed me a picture from a New York catalog. The rest was easy."

She turned back, but Peter had moved behind her and now he said, "Matthew is the designer; I provide the horsepower; Will is the navigator."

Will bowed. "Would you care for a tour around town, Miss McIntire?"

"Oh, I would love one," Kathryn cried, hardly believing that this was happening.

"Then hold on tight," Will commanded. Then his face flamed as he realized his blunder. "Oh, I'm sorry, Kathryn."

She laughed in delight. "No, look." She flexed her fingers, then awkwardly clenched the two arms of her chair. "See? I *can* hold on. Off with you, good sirs."

With the applause and cheers of the family sounding in her ears, they navigated their way out the gate and started up Granger Street. The younger children ran alongside, laughing and clapping and calling to one another as though this were some grand parade. Kathryn laid her head back, letting the sun splash across her face, reveling in the sheer glory of it all.

———◆———

They had circled clear up around the stone quarry and were heading back toward Steed Row when they came past the family store. By then the children had tired and returned home and it was just the three of them—Kathryn in the chair, Will and Peter each taking turns pushing her. Suddenly the door to the store opened and Nathan came striding out. "Hey there!" he called. "Who is this beautiful young woman going past my door?"

"Hello, Uncle Nathan."

He came down to the street and Will let the chair roll to a stop. "Well," Nathan called, "I heard about this. What do you think of your new chariot?"

"Oh, Uncle Nathan, it's absolutely glorious. I feel like I'm free. I don't ever want to get back in that bed."

"Well, let's not overdo it on the first day, all right?" He walked around the chair, eyeing it up and down. "Very good," he said. "Matthew does good work."

"Isn't it beautiful?"

"How does it push?" he asked her two guides.

"Good," Will said.

"Better on hard-packed dirt than in loose dust," Peter added.

"But on the boardwalks it just flies," Kathryn cried. "I made them run with me."

Nathan leaned down and kissed her on the cheek. "That's wonderful, Kathryn."

She smiled at him, her eyes lustrous and wide. "Yes, it really is."

Nathan nodded, then looked at Will. "Say, Will, have you got a minute?" He grinned at Peter. "Think you could handle this young lady all by yourself?"

"Yes, sir," he barked.

Will started to follow, then turned and waved. "I'll catch you. Don't wait for me."

Peter moved along more slowly now, sensing that even though she was getting tired, Kathryn did not want this to end. She had laid her head back now, and her eyes were closed. They hadn't spoken for several minutes.

"Peter?"

"What?"

"I think you need to kiss the blarney stone."

"What?"

Her eyes opened and she laughed up at him. "The blarney stone."

"What in the world is that?"

"There's a castle in Blarney, which is near Cork, in Ireland." Without realizing it, she had slipped into a more pronounced Irish accent, sounding very much like her mother. "Legend has it that once the castle was threatened with attack from an enemy, but the nobleman saved it through his gift for talking and flattery."

"Oh?"

"Yes. In the inner tower—or the castle *keep*, as it is called—there is a large stone. It is said that if you kiss the blarney stone, you shall be blessed with the gift of sweet, persuasive eloquence." She smiled. "Not that I'm saying that you're not eloquent. Actually, you're very good with words. It's just that you are sure not very talkative today."

He blushed deeply. "I'm sorry, I thought you were resting and—"

She laughed merrily. "I shouldn't tease you so."

He smiled at her sheepishly. "I don't mind."

She kept her head tipped back so she could watch him. "Why aren't you at work?"

"Brother Taylor said to take whatever time I needed. I'll work later tonight."

"Thank you, Peter."

"Oh, you're welcome. This has been really fun for me."

"No. Thank you for the poem."

He started a little. "Oh."

"It was beautiful."

"I . . . I was afraid it might make you feel bad."

"Oh no! It made me remember that it's only my body that's crippled, not me."

He nodded, clearly pleased. That had been his hope.

"It's on my wall now," she said shyly.

"I saw it."

"You were one of the ones who carried me out?"

He grinned. "Yes."

She turned back to the front and smiled, wishing that she had known that then.

"Kathryn?"

"What?"

"Did you know that these wheels are big like this for a reason?"

She looked down to where the wheels were slowly turning. They *were* large. The tops of them were almost even with the arms of the chair. "No. Why are they so big?"

"So that when your arms get strong enough again, you can

turn the wheels yourself. Then you won't have to depend on anyone to take you out."

Her head dropped and she went very still. Peter's step slowed and then he stopped. He came around to where he could see her. He fell back a little. Tears were trickling down her cheek. Seeing him there, she sniffed quickly and jerked away.

"I'm sorry," he said in dismay.

Her head came back around. "Sorry?"

"Yes, for what I just said."

She shook her head, angry at herself for causing the misunderstanding. "Don't you realize *what* you just said?"

"No, what?"

"You said *when* my arms are strong enough, not *if* my arms get strong enough." Her voice was barely a whisper now. "Thank you, Peter."

———————

Nathan had been alone in the store and had some ledger books spread out across the counter. But he ignored those now and gestured toward the chairs in one corner. As the two of them settled in, Will watched his uncle with some curiosity. This was obviously going to be more than a brief question.

"Any word from your father?"

"Not yet. We expect him any time now. It's been ten days."

"I hope he got a good price for that lumber in St. Louis. You're about to become a well-to-do young businessman."

"Me? I'll get my wages, same as the rest of the men, but that's hardly enough to make me well-to-do."

Nathan was surprised at that. Joshua had told him that he considered Will a partner and would split the profits so that a generous share went to his son. But he clearly hadn't told that to his son. In light of all that had happened, Nathan decided it wasn't his place to say anything. "Have you ever seen Jenny Pottsworth since you got back?"

Will nodded, his eyes hooded. "She came over to the freight office one day last week."

"She did?" That was news.

"Yes. She was visiting with her mother. She came to apologize for how she had handled everything."

"That's good. Are she and Andrew happy?"

He shrugged. "That's what she said." He suddenly looked embarrassed. "I wouldn't say this to anyone else, Nathan, and you've got to promise you won't either."

He raised his hand, palm forward. "I promise."

"I think Jenny is sorry she didn't wait until I came home. By then I had made my decision to join the Church, but she was already married." Then he shook his head. "Ah, probably that's just my imagination. Wishful thinking."

"Lydia said the same thing."

"She did?"

"Yes. Jenny was over one day and spent a couple of hours at the store. Lydia said she had the definite impression that she had some regrets."

Will's shoulders lifted and fell again. "Well, she didn't wait and that's that."

"Are you sorry?"

He shook his head without the slightest hesitation.

"Not at all?" Nathan said in surprise.

Will nodded, thoughtful now. "It's funny, isn't it? There was a time when I thought the whole world had fallen in. Jenny was falling in love with Andrew. She wouldn't write to me. Then that letter of Lydia's came. I was ready to leave camp, throw everything over, run back here, and make everything right." There was a short, embarrassed laugh. "Or make a fool of myself, that's more what it really would have been.

"Anyway, then I took that ride on a log going down the river. Suddenly, that brought things back into perspective again. I was really being childish, wasn't I?"

"Maybe childlike," Nathan said softly. "But you're not a child anymore, Will. You've grown up."

"Thank you." His voice was suddenly husky. "And thank you

for pulling me out that day so I could live to see how really foolish I was."

"You would have done the same for me," Nathan murmured.
"You know that, don't you?"

Will considered that, remembering the swiftness of the
tragedy, remembering Nathan running along the riverbank,
screaming at him, tearing off his coat. "I don't know. I'd like to
think so."

"You would," he said flatly.

"Well, I know this. I'm sure glad it's not me who's married.
I'm not ready."

Nathan nodded absently. "With your father due back, have
you decided what you're going to do about being baptized?"

"I'm going to be baptized. I'm only waiting until he gets back
so I can tell him."

"I thought you wanted to wait for your mother."

"I do. She thinks she is going to go ahead."

Nathan leaned back, the amazement written across his face.
"Really?"

He nodded. "Don't you think she ought to?"

It was as if Will had stuck him with an ice pick. Nathan visibly jumped, remembering the words of his father that early
morning on the porch of the store.

Will gave him a searching look. "What is it, Nathan? What
is wrong?"

He let the question pass. "Your father will be furious if you
do."

"I know," Will said sadly. "But my other Father will be disappointed if I don't."

"What?" Nathan exclaimed. "What did you say?"

"Listen, Nathan. I got my answer up in camp that night. My
Heavenly Father told me very clearly what to do. Don't I owe
him something too?"

Nathan's eyes were wide and he leaned forward slowly. "Yes,
I suppose you do. And you're sure? You're really sure?"

"I should have been sure long before that. I mean, I'm the one who nearly sacrificed his life down at the *Warsaw Signal* office because they said something about the Church in the newspaper that I didn't like. But then I turn right around and can't make up my mind if the Church is true. I just kept going back and forth, back and forth. I couldn't make up my mind."

Nathan was looking at him strangely. "Like a bird hopping back and forth between two branches?"

Will's brow furrowed. "What?"

"You were kind of like a bird, hopping back and forth between two branches."

"Yes," he said. "That's a pretty good description. I had all these questions I wanted answered. Was the Church true? Was the Book of Mormon true? Should I be baptized? And I kept getting frustrated because I couldn't seem to get the answers. And finally the Lord simply said to me, 'Do and *then* you'll know.' And I knew that was the only answer I needed for now."

Nathan straightened slowly. "*Do* and then you'll *know?*" he repeated, looking puzzled.

"Yes. It comes from John, chapter seven, verse seventeen. The Savior said, 'If you do my will, you shall know of the doctrine.' So I'm going to be baptized. If Mother can join me, that will be wonderful. If not, I'm going ahead. If Father gives his permission, that will be wonderful. If not, I am going ahead."

Nathan had lowered his head and was staring at the floor.

"Do you think I'm wrong, Nathan?"

Nathan's head came up. It was clear he hadn't heard.

"Do you think I'm wrong to feel that way? Am I making a mistake by going ahead when I don't have all the answers?"

Again there was a strange, wondering look. Then Nathan smiled faintly. "*Do* and then you'll *know,*" he answered.

Will's mouth opened in surprise; then he grinned. "Yes. That's it, isn't it? I've got to keep remembering that. That is my answer."

Nathan jumped to his feet. "Will, could I get you to do me a great favor?"

"Sure. What?"

"Can you watch the store for me? We've got a new woman helping out now, but she won't be here for an hour. Could you take it just until then?"

Will was a little surprised by the sudden urgency in Nathan, but he nodded again. "Sure, I'd be happy to."

Nathan untied his apron, tore it off and tossed it onto a chair, then started for the door. He stopped. "What was that scripture again?"

"John seven seventeen."

"Thanks. You're wonderful, Will. You just pulled *me* out of the river." And out he went.

They found Joseph at the Homestead, working in his garden with Julia and young Joseph. While they were still half a block away, he looked up and saw them coming. He immediately left his work and came over to the fence and waited for them.

"Hello, Joseph."

"Nathan. Lydia."

Nathan took a quick breath, then wasn't sure what to say all of a sudden.

Joseph watched them steadily; then his mouth softened into a smile. "I'd like to change my clothes. Can you wait in my office upstairs at the store?"

"Of course."

Lydia looked up at Nathan. "I'll just wait for you here," she murmured.

Joseph gave her a stern look. "I wouldn't change my clothes just for Nathan," he said. "I'll meet *both* of you there in five minutes."

"I'm listening," Joseph said, sitting back and folding his hands together.

Nathan looked at Lydia, who smiled her encouragement. He

smiled back at her, squared his shoulders, and then looked at Joseph. "The other day, you talked about asking the right questions, asking the questions that the Lord would have me ask."

"Yes, one of the great lessons of Liberty Jail."

"I'm not sure if I've come far enough, but I'm not asking the same questions anymore."

"What were your questions, Nathan?"

He fumbled a little, finding this very difficult. "Oh, things like, Why is this happening? Is this really from God? Would God ask such a thing of us today?" He looked away, ashamed and yet not willing to hide it. "Has Joseph fallen? Has he been deceived?"

Joseph nodded solemnly. "And now?"

"Well, actually there was a middle level, another step. Yesterday, I started asking things like, If God did ask this of Joseph, why would he expect something so difficult? Why would he require a man or a woman to go against everything they have been taught? How could this possibly be pleasing to him?"

"And now?" Joseph asked again, very gently.

"There's just one question now. What does God want me to do?"

Joseph considered what that meant; then he leaned forward, his eyes pinning Nathan now. "And if I said that God wanted you to take another woman to be your wife?"

There was a long moment of silence as their eyes locked, but finally, Nathan bowed his head. "Then that is what I would do."

Joseph turned. "Lydia?"

Her eyes were glistening and the pupils were enormous and dark, like a cat's eyes in semidarkness. But she did not waver from his gaze. "We are ready to do whatever God asks of us, Joseph."

An audible sigh went through him and he sat back. "Ah, Nathan, I cannot tell you what that means to me. You have been like a rock all these years. And then, when you looked at me the other day as though I had betrayed everything you ever trusted in, it was as if a lance had pierced me through."

"I'm sorry, Joseph. I don't know what got into me. I was so angry. I—"

"But it's gone now?"

"Yes."

"So no more questions?"

Nathan thought of Lydia's words that morning and reached out and took her hand. "Lots of questions, but no more doubts."

That seemed to please Joseph. "I would worry if you did not," he growled good-naturedly. "I still have many, many questions."

"Really?" Lydia said. "Even you?"

"Even me. And I don't have all the answers either. But the important thing is, are your questions 'if' questions, or are they 'why' questions?"

"I'm not sure what you mean," Nathan responded.

"It's one thing to ask God *why* he does something, so we can better understand his will and purposes for us. It's quite another to question *if* something really is his will."

All three of them were silent for a few moments, thinking about the difference. Then Joseph turned to Nathan again. "The other day I told you to come back when you were ready to ask the right questions. And here you are."

"Yes. I'm ready to listen."

"All right. Let me say this first. I don't know all the whys of this. I think there is no question but what this is a test for us, individually and for the Church collectively. I understand Brigham already spoke to you of that, so I shall say nothing more. Second, there is no question that this will prove to be a blessing for some women." He looked at Lydia. "For you who are happily married to a good and righteous man, it will be a test and a sacrifice. But think of Sarah Noon, for example. Abandoned by her husband, left with two children, no means of support. Now Heber will care for her, provide her with safety and security."

Lydia nodded, thinking of the feelings she had had about Jessica. "I can see that."

"In the Book of Mormon, it says this practice is only acceptable when God desires *to raise up seed* unto himself. I know that the Church has a great destiny yet to fill. Maybe the Lord needs that kind of righteous posterity in the days ahead. Maybe there are other reasons as well. Remember, these are no more than the musings of an unlearned man trying to fathom the unfathomable mind of God. I give them to you only as food for thought."

Now his visage abruptly changed. "But," he said with sudden and deep solemnity, "there is one thing that you need to know with absolute certainty. We are living this principle because God requires it of us. It matters not whether there is any other reason at all. That is enough."

Nathan went to speak but Joseph rushed on. "I know that you do not dispute this any longer, Nathan, but I still must say it. I want you to hear just how clearly I know this is so."

He stood and walked to the window that looked out on the Mississippi River. "I first learned that this principle was going to be restored many years ago, when I was working on the translation of the Bible. When the Lord revealed it to me at that time, he said that it was not required that we live it yet but that he would reveal to me when that time had come. As the years passed, I knew that the time was coming when God would require it of us, but I kept pushing it back, not wanting to think about it.

"Then in the summer of 1840, the Lord said that it was time to prepare to live it. I can't tell you what feelings came over me. When the Twelve returned last summer, I was told to teach it to them. This caused me to feel the greatest of repugnance, Nathan. This is the greatest battle I have ever waged with myself. I know the voice of God, Nathan. I know it when he speaks. And I knew that he had spoken on this matter and told me to go forward, and not only to go forward with it, but that I myself must set the example.

"Oh, the feelings that swept over me. Not only did I have to do battle with my own hesitations, I knew full well what this would mean to our people. I knew what it would mean to the Gentile world." He passed a hand over his eyes. "As if they need another club with which to beat us."

Now he turned, his back to the window, his face in shadow. "I will not tell you of the sleepless nights, the endless pacing of the floor. How could I ask this of anyone? How could I tell

Emma? After all she has suffered and endured to stand at my side. Now this. But God had given the commandment. How could I withstand God?"

He began to pace back and forth across the room, his hands clenching, his mouth twisting as his mind took him back. "But even then I delayed. I could not bring myself to do it. I pleaded with the Lord to turn away this commandment, for I knew full well the trouble that would follow." He threw up his hands in despair. "But he would not."

Suddenly he stopped and turned to face them. His eyes seemed to be peering at them through deep water. "Three different times I had an angel come to me," he said in a hoarse whisper. "Three times he had to come and command me to follow the Lord's counsel. Can you imagine such a thing? An angel comes from the presence of God and directs me how to act, and I cannot obey."

He stopped, staring at them, seeing nothing. "The last time—" A shudder ran through his body. "The last time the angel had a drawn sword in his hand. He warned me that if I would not obey the command of God, my office would be taken from me and given to another—"

"No!" Lydia whispered.

"—and," he said in a great hollow voice, ". . . and he said that if I would not submit to God's will, he was commanded to slay me."

Nathan felt sick. He had been so caught up in his own personal hell that he had never even thought about what this must have meant to Joseph. He had been out bellowing and blowing, tramping around the prairies, shaking his fist at God, and he had never given even a moment's thought as to how Joseph was taking it. He felt hot tears of shame burn behind his eyelids.

Now Joseph's voice was calm and very soft. "Since that day, I have determined that I shall press forward, even if it shall cost me my life. It is the work of God. He has revealed this principle, and it is not my business to control or dictate it."

Suddenly Nathan's whole body began to tremble. A racking

sob was torn from his throat. He shook his head as he stared at Joseph in abject sorrow. "Oh, Joseph! Forgive me! Forgive me for doubting you. Forgive my blindness."

In a moment, Lydia was on her knees at Nathan's side, trying to put her arms around him, but he just huddled tighter into himself. "I've been such a fool," he cried. "Such a blind fool!"

Suddenly Joseph was standing before them. He reached out and laid a hand on Nathan's shoulder. "Forgive you for what, my friend? For struggling as I have struggled? For going through three days of agony like Brother Heber suffered? For longing for death as Brother Brigham did?"

He shook his head, and now took Nathan by the arms and lifted him up to face him. "Don't you think I understand, Nathan?"

With a great cry, Nathan threw his arms around Joseph, letting Joseph hold him tightly until gradually the shaking in his body began to subside. When Nathan finally straightened, brushing at his eyes with the back of his hand, Joseph turned to Lydia. He reached down and gave her a quick hug as well. "Thank you, Lydia. Your father-in-law told me about your quiet witness."

She was crying now and could only nod. She groped for Nathan's hand. Joseph now smiled. "You have come willing to accept whatever God asks of you."

"Yes," replied Nathan.

"Then hear what it is that you should do."

"Yes, Joseph."

"First, stand fast. You have come through the fire; now you are stronger. You will need that strength as you deal with Joshua and others who are troubled by this doctrine. You and Lydia can be pillars of strength to those who are faltering."

They were both nodding at that.

"Second, know this. The Lord does not at this time require that you enter this law." As there was a sharp intake of breath from Lydia, he smiled upon her. "Let your heart be at peace, dear Sister Lydia. For now, the Lord does not require that you share your husband with another woman. Maybe sometime in the future, but not at present."

She started to weep again and Nathan took her into his arms.

"Third, . . ." He paused, savoring the moment. "The Lord has accepted your offering of submission. Now it is his will that you be sealed as husband and wife for time and for all eternity."

"What?" Nathan cried. Then, incredulously, he remembered what Heber had said. After he had proven himself willing to sacrifice whatever God required, Joseph had sealed him and Vilate in the bonds of eternal marrige. Nathan hadn't dreamed there could be such a blessing for him, not after these days of darkness and doubting.

Joseph took Lydia's hand and placed it in Nathan's. Then he led them to the center of the room where there was a circular rug covering the hardwood floor. "Would you kneel here together, facing me please?"

Lydia's eyes were like great windows of joy and light. With a soft cry, she sank to her knees. Nathan went down beside her, reached out and found her hand and held it tightly against his chest.

Joseph moved around to stand in front of them. "You should know, Sister Lydia McBride Steed and Brother Nathan Steed, that God has manifested unto me that he has accepted of your willingness to live his law. He is pleased with what is in your hearts. Therefore, as the holder of the keys of the sealing power brought back to earth by Elijah of old, I shall now unite the two of you in the holy order of celestial marriage, sealing you together by the power and authority given to me to bind on earth so that it can be bound in heaven."

Joseph's eyes were filled with joy now too. "I should like to first explain to you what this means. The Lord has said that if a man marry a wife by his word, which is his law, and by the new and everlasting covenant, and it is sealed unto them by the Holy Spirit of Promise, then it shall be done unto them in all things whatsoever his servant hath put upon them, in time and through all eternity.

"And this shall be of full force when they are out of the world; and they shall pass by the angels and the gods, which are set there, to their exaltation and glory in all things. And this glory shall be a fulness and a continuation of the seeds forever and ever."

Lydia was weeping as she looked into Nathan's eyes and listened to the powerful words, but she was tingling now as well. His eyes were glistening too as he listened to what Joseph was promising them.

"Then shall you be gods," he went on, still quoting but now addressing it directly to them, "because you have no end. You shall be from everlasting to everlasting, because you continue. Then shall you be above all, because all things are subject unto you. Then shall you be gods, because you have all power, and the angels are subject unto you."

He stopped and let the silence fill the room. Then with great joy he nodded down at the two of them. "If you will face one another and take each other by the hand, we shall proceed."

———————◆———————

When it was over, Joseph watched happily as they kissed and then stood together, their arms around each other's waist. Then he stepped forward to congratulate them. He gave a soft laugh as he kissed Lydia on the cheek. "Now do you see why I had to go and change my clothes? It wouldn't be proper to do something this important in my work clothes."

She laughed. "I'm glad you did."

Joseph turned to Nathan now, sobering. "There's something else you ought to know, Nathan. Today the high council voted to remove John C. Bennett from his fellowship in the Church."

Chapter Notes

Joseph does not speak a great deal in his own history about his personal feelings concerning plural marriage. But he did share his inner feelings with some of his most trusted associates. The words he uses here—the repugnance he felt toward the idea at first, his keen awareness of the troubles this would bring upon them, how the world would react to it—come from those other sources. The report of the angelic visits which resulted in his deciding to move forward, no matter what the cost, also comes from the men who knew him best. These include such men as Hyrum Smith, Brigham Young, Lorenzo Snow, and Joseph B. Noble. (See *Encyclopedia of Mormonism*, s.v., "plural marriage"; Danel W. Bachman, "A Study of the Mormon Practice of Plural Marriage Before the Death of Joseph Smith" [master's thesis, Purdue University, 1975], pp. 74–75.)

Joseph's words prior to sealing Lydia and Nathan come from the revelation which is now D&C 132. He quotes from verses 19 and 20.

It should be noted that at this stage of the Church's development, when the endowment was just being introduced, some people were sealed together for time and eternity before they had received their endowments.

Joshua Steed arrived back in Nauvoo on the *Orleans Queen*, which docked at the north riverboat landing shortly after one o'clock in the afternoon on Saturday, May twenty-first. When he had realized back in St. Louis that he would be gone about twice as long as he originally thought, he had written a letter to Caroline in which he informed her of the approximate date he planned to be home. Now as he moved toward the gangplank, his eyes searched the crowd, and he felt a twinge of disappointment. Caroline and the children weren't there to meet him. It was not a great surprise, but still a bit of a letdown. Nauvoo was now a major city along the upper Mississippi. With the river clear of winter ice, sometimes there could be as many as five or six boats stop there in a day. Though schedules were pretty loose, the boats would always blow their great steam whistles—one long, two shorts, one long, two shorts—to alert the populace that they were coming in. That would give all interested persons a chance to make their way to the landing in time to greet disembarking passengers.

But there was no familiar face, no little redheaded imp waiting to dash up to him as he came down the gangplank. *No Will,* he thought, though that was even less surprising to him. Well, he would be home soon enough. He picked up his valise and a small suitcase and followed the crowd off the boat and onto the wooden pier. He pushed his way past various groups who still lingered in greeting, then stopped short. Nathan and Carl stepped out from behind the small shelter at the end of the dock. "Hello, Joshua," Nathan said.

———•—•———

They found a shady spot under a large cottonwood tree just a block from the landing and sat down on the grass. Carl spoke first. "Caroline was going to come, but as we talked about it, we felt that you should know what's been going on before you see her. That's why we met your boat today."

"All right," Joshua said, still a little puzzled.

"There's been a lot going on here since you left almost three weeks ago. I suppose the first thing you ought to know is that your father is now a member of the city council."

Joshua's eyes snapped open. "What?"

"Yes," Carl said. "How's that for a surprise? We also have a new mayor."

He whipped around. "Bennett's gone?"

"Yes," said Nathan. "He offered his resignation on Tuesday. The city council met Thursday and appointed Joseph as the mayor. Hyrum is the vice-mayor. That created some openings on the council. Pa's name was put forward and he was selected."

"Well, well," Joshua said, completely astonished. "What brought all that on?"

Nathan explained. "As Carl said, there has been a lot happening since you left. The council met about ten days ago, and Joseph told them that there were houses of infamy in the city and that action had to be taken against them in order to protect the innocent and stop the corruption of the morals of the citizenry. Bennett didn't dare oppose that of course, and so the council passed an ordinance that any or all brothels immediately be closed down. That put Bennett on notice that he was in big trouble. He started scrambling to undo the damage. He made a public statement denying that Joseph ever gave him license to have immoral relations with the women of the city. He said that anyone who was saying that he had said those things was an infernal liar."

"He said that?" Joshua said, tight-lipped.

"Yeah," Carl said with equal grimness. "Since that is exactly what he told you and me, I guess that makes both of us infernal liars."

Nathan went on. "He even swore out an affidavit attesting to the same kind of things—Joseph never taught anything contrary to the strictest principles of the gospel or of virtue, Joseph had never countenanced any of Bennett's immoral conduct and had never taught him in public or private that illicit relations between the sexes was justifiable."

"That's a pretty important confession," said Joshua.

"Yes, it is. Then he offered his resignation as mayor and also to have his name withdrawn from the Church. Pa thinks he was hoping that the council would not accept it and give him another chance. Instead, they accepted it, thanked him for his service, and had a new mayor elected before Bennett had a chance to blink. Pa says Bennett was stunned."

"It couldn't happen to a more deserving man," Joshua drawled sarcastically. Then, sensing that Nathan was suddenly hesitant, he asked, "Can I assume from the fact that you and Carl are both here that you've found some answers on that question you were going to investigate?"

"We have. But there's something else you need to know too. The women know everything."

"What!"

"Just hear me out first, then you can ask all the questions you want."

Joshua was fuming, but he finally nodded. "This had better be good."

There was a quick, darting glance at Carl; then Nathan

knew there was no delaying it. He plunged in. He only omitted two things—first, he was careful not to say anything that would give away the identity of Brigham Young or Heber and Vilate Kimball as he told Joshua about the meeting they had gone to that night. Second, Nathan said nothing of his own personal struggle and search. All the rest came out dispassionately and calmly. Carl said little, only adding a detail here and there as Nathan talked.

Nathan saw Joshua's eyes narrow and his heavy black brows knit closer and closer together as he told him what they had learned. But when Nathan got to the part about their deciding to let the wives know everything, Joshua blew up. "So much for your word."

"Father told them," Nathan said. "Once we learned about the assassination attempt, we decided they had a right to know."

"You can do whatever you please with your wife, mister," Joshua snapped angrily. "But you made me a promise. Caroline was not to know until I got back."

Carl leaned forward. "Joshua, it was a joint decision. I concurred. I thought it was best."

"Oh, really?" he said with deep irony. "You waited until I was gone and then you made a *joint* decision."

Nathan had spent a good part of the night and most of the morning steeling himself for this confrontation. He vowed he was not going to let Joshua goad him into a fight. "You think what you want, Joshua. I promised I would investigate this issue for you. I've done that. You now have a full report. We thought it best to tell you all of this before you talk to Caroline and Will. You—"

"Will too?" Joshua cried, the betrayal heavy in his voice. "You two have really been busy, haven't you?"

Carl slapped his open hand with a fisted one. "I'll not be having your insults, Joshua. We did what we thought was right. It was Caroline who decided Will had a right to know too. If that somehow messes up your little scheme to stop them from being baptized, then that's your affair."

His sharpness caught Joshua by surprise, and Joshua backed down slightly. "I'm sorry, Carl. It's just that—" His mouth tightened. "You shouldn't have told her. That was my place."

"It wouldn't have made any difference," Carl said flatly. "None of this has changed Caroline's mind one bit. Will's either."

"Of course not," Joshua nearly shouted. "The whole family has had three weeks to convince her there's nothing wrong here."

Carl shot to his feet, his mouth working. But finally he just turned to Nathan. "I've got work to do at the brickyard."

Nathan held up one hand, still looking at Joshua. "The whole family doesn't know," he said quietly. "Only the seven of us and Caroline and Will."

Carl sighed, looking at Nathan in resignation. "I told you this was going to tear the family apart. I know Joseph is sincere, but you go tell him that. It is going to tear this family apart." He glared at Joshua. "And it's your bullheaded blindness that is going to do it." He gave Joshua a curt nod and moved out of the shade and into the sunshine, not looking back.

Stunned by such a vehement reaction from normally reticent Carl, Joshua just stared after him. After a moment, Nathan turned back to Joshua. "Look, Joshua. I'm not trying to convert you to this principle. You have your feelings and I have mine. Carl has his feelings—and in case you haven't guessed it by now, they are much closer to your feelings than to mine. But he's not lost his balance over it. He's not ready for war with the family."

Joshua stiffened a little. "Anything else?" he finally asked in a tight voice.

Nathan got to his feet slowly now. "No. We just thought you ought to know what has been going on before you went home. The rest is between you and Caroline."

———— ◆ ————

They waited until Savannah and Charles were both asleep. Joshua's welcome home had been warm and sincere, even though they all sensed the underlying strain. He spent most of the afternoon playing with the children and catching up on the news since he had left. Then he left for a couple of hours to go to the freight office and check in there.

There was no family supper at his parents' house as was traditional after someone returned home from an extended trip, and he was glad for that. Though many of the family had no idea what all lay behind it, they knew that the question of baptism for Caroline and Will was coming to a head. By unspoken agreement, they left them alone to work it out. So after a quiet supper of their own, Joshua took the two smaller children upstairs, read them stories, kidded and played and teased, getting them more worked up than sleepy. But they loved it, and it postponed the inevitable for Joshua. Finally about nine o'clock he came back down the stairs again to find Caroline, Will, and Olivia waiting for him in the sitting room.

Wearily he came in and sat down in a chair across the room from Caroline. "Livvy, your mother and Will and I need to talk. Would you excuse us please?"

There was a moment's surprise; then she looked to her mother. Caroline was torn. She had hoped to lay some groundwork before it came to this, but she saw little chance of that now. So she turned to Joshua. "Olivia is in on this too, Joshua. She would also like to be baptized."

There was a sharp intake of breath, and then his mouth hardened. "Sounds like a lot of things have gotten decided in my absence."

"Pa!" Will cut in sharply.

But Caroline gave Will a look that silenced him. She spoke again to her husband. "Are you going to ask her about it, or should we just pretend she isn't here in the room with us?"

Joshua's eyes pinched in, but he finally turned to Olivia. "All right."

Nervously, almost stammering, she started in. She looked very much like Caroline at that moment—beautiful, nervous, but very determined. "Papa, I know you think this is all Mama's doing. Well, it's not. I've been reading the Book of Mormon. I've asked Heavenly Father if it is true. And I've had a very strong feeling that it is true."

"And your mother and brother have nothing to do with your decision?"

"Of course we do," Caroline shot back at him. "Don't try to trap her with a question like that. How could we not have been an influence? But the real question is, Are we the *only* reason Livvy feels this way? Or has she come to know for herself that this is what she wants?"

"I have, Papa," Olivia said, her voice forlorn. "I know it's true. I want to be a member of the Church."

Joshua hardly flickered. He turned to Will. "And I suppose your mind is all made up now too?"

"Yes, Pa, it is."

"So why are you talking to me? You're going to do what you want anyway."

"I don't want to fight you on this."

"Really?" Joshua said, the sarcasm like a grindstone against a knife blade.

Will just blew out his breath and looked away. Then he stood abruptly. "Come on, Livvy. Pa knows how we feel now. He and Mama need to talk."

Olivia stood and moved to Will's side, but she was giving her father a beseeching look. "Please, Papa?" she whispered.

"We'll talk about it, Livvy," Caroline said softly. "Let Papa and me have some time."

Olivia nodded, looking stricken, and followed Will out. When the door shut, Caroline turned to him. "I really am sorry, Joshua. I didn't mean for it to be like this your first night back. If you'd rather wait until tomorrow, that's fine."

"No, let's settle it once and for all."

She met the coldness of his gaze with equanimity. "All right, let's do."

"Nathan said you know everything."

"Yes."

"And that doesn't bother you at all? It doesn't bother you that we have men in this town now who are living with more than one woman and supposedly doing so in the name of the Lord?"

"Why is it you always ask questions that leave only one answer? Of course it bothers me. This comes as much a shock to me as it does to Melissa or Lydia. So why don't you ask me the real question? 'Caroline, knowing it all now, do you still want to be baptized?' "

He met her gaze but he wouldn't ask it. "I already know the answer to that."

"Not from me, you don't!" she cried. "Why won't you ask me?"

"Because I already know the answer."

"Thank you, Joshua," she said in soft mockery. "Thank you for caring enough to ask me."

"Then that's it," he said shortly. "I made a bargain with you. Clearly I have lost. Go ahead and be baptized. Take your children with you. You keep reminding me that they are *your* children, after all."

She shook her head. "So it was all empty words, after all."

"What?" he asked suspiciously.

"Your so-called bargain."

He flared angrily at that. "I just told you. Go ahead and be baptized. If you still are fool enough to want to join that church after what you've heard, then I'm not going to stop you."

"No, Joshua!" she flung back at him. "That's not what you said. You said I wouldn't just have your permission, I would have your blessing."

She dropped her head and he thought she was going to cry. But when she looked up again it was flint-hard coldness he saw in her eyes. "You were so sure it would change my mind, weren't you? That's the only reason you made the bargain in the first place. You were sure you would win."

"That's not true," he said lamely, knowing even as he said it that it was exactly true.

She stood, thoroughly weary now. "I'm sorry it didn't work out as neatly as you planned, Joshua." She moved toward the door.

He watched her, feeling a curious pull of conflicting emotions—anger, guilt, sorrow, they all stumbled over one another inside him.

At the door she stopped and looked back. "Is there anything else you want to say?"

He just looked at her, not knowing what words could possibly bridge the gulf that had opened up between them now.

She watched him for a moment, her eyes unreadable; then she turned and started out.

"So?" he blurted.

She paused. "So what?"

"Are you going to be baptized?"

She turned back slowly. "I don't know, Joshua."

"You don't know?" he echoed in surprise.

Her head moved up and down slowly. "Everyone in Hancock County keeps telling me that Joshua Steed is a man of principle, a man of his word. 'If he says it,' they say, 'then it's as good as a contract.' I guess I was making my plans based on that assumption. Now that I've learned that this is not the case—at least where his family is concerned—I'm going to have to rethink things. I don't know what I'm going to do."

———•———

For the next five days, an uneasy truce prevailed in the Steed family. On the surface there was a cheerful amiability and life went on as usual. Below the surface there was a dark pall. At Joshua's home, the subject of baptism did not come up again, at least not while he was there. Unbeknownst to him, two days after his return, Will announced that he was going ahead, whether or not his mother could join him. When Will asked her if she was going to be baptized, Caroline just shook her head sadly and said, "Not yet, Will."

Adding to the overall strain in the family was the turn that Melissa had taken. She flatly refused to discuss the Church, her feelings, or anything to do with Joseph Smith. Carl was almost embarrassed by the depth of her alienation and tried valiantly to keep their family conversations steered away from any dangerous shoals. This was particularly puzzling for those family members who did not know any of the story behind Melissa's sudden turn.

Fortunately, on the Monday following Joshua's return, Jennifer Jo called everyone to her home just before sundown and took them into Kathryn's room. To lusty cheers and jubilant yells, Kathryn proceeded to demonstrate that she could lift one hand an inch or two off the bed without help and could now grasp a book in the other hand without aid. There was no question about it. It had been a little over five weeks since the accident and she was getting back some use of her limbs.

Almost as if in celebration of that piece of good news, that same night Jennifer Jo McIntire Steed went into labor, two weeks sooner than expected. At 9:37 the next morning, May twenty-fourth, 1842, she gave birth to a small but robustly healthy girl. The parents immediately announced that they would name her Betsy Jo Steed.

Those two events, one on top of the other, did much to restore some joy to the family circle and also to provide much-welcomed safe topics of conversation. But in a certain respect these happenings were only a diversion, for they did nothing to solve what was simmering in the family of Joshua and Caroline Steed.

———◆———

To Joshua's surprise, on Friday morning Benjamin was waiting for him on the narrow porch of the freight office, even though it was not yet six-thirty. Joshua's eyes narrowed suspiciously as he grunted a greeting.

"Good morning, son," said Benjamin.

Joshua stopped short of the porch step, leaving Benjamin looking down on him. "You're up early," he commented.

"Got some things that need saying," Benjamin said shortly, not willing to ease into this.

Joshua showed no surprise. He had guessed that such was the case the moment he saw his father there. "I've heard it all, Pa," he said, not really in a mood to go through this again, particularly with his father, who was primed to call him to task for what was happening.

"Are you telling me to leave?" Benjamin asked evenly.

There was a long sigh. "No, of course not." He stepped up on the porch. "Come in."

"If it's all right, I'd like to stay out here. It's a beautiful morning." There was a wry smile. "Maybe the fresh air will keep things cooler between us."

Joshua laughed shortly. "I doubt it." He moved up to stand beside his father on the porch. He waited a moment, then sent up a warning flag. "Pa, if you're going to try and convince me that what Joseph's doing is right, we may as well end this conversation right now."

"I'm not. Wasn't even going to bring it up."

"Good."

"Don't imagine Caroline has tried to do that either, not if I know her."

"No, she hasn't," Joshua admitted, somewhat grudgingly. He waited; then when his father said nothing, he went on. "So, what is it? Are you gonna remind me of the promise I made to Caroline and talk to me about being a man of my word?"

Benjamin chuckled softly. "You've sure got a lot on your mind about what you think I've got on my mind."

There was an answering laugh in spite of himself. "All right, Pa. What *do* you want to say?"

Benjamin's smile slowly faded. "Just one thing, Joshua."

"I'm listening."

"I've been thinking about that night in Palmyra."

Joshua nodded slowly. He didn't have to ask what night. Fifteen years before. Raining. Black. Joshua and the Murdock boys had tried to jump Joseph in the forest and steal the gold plates. Then his father had come to the saloon. Harsh words. A slap across the face. A drawn pistol.

"That man back then, that Benjamin Steed or whatever his name was, was absolutely dead sure he was right. There was no way that he was going to back down and let his son get away with something as foolish and just plain stupid as what he'd done. And so—" His voice caught and he suddenly looked away.

Joshua was staring at him, frightened all of a sudden. He wasn't sure he wanted to hear this. Not now. Not with everything else.

Finally Benjamin turned back. His eyes were like two great pools of pain. "Eleven years," he whispered. "That's what being right cost me, Joshua. Eleven years when you and I could have been having what we have now. Eleven years of your mother crying herself to sleep and wearing holes in the rug from kneeling there and pleading with God to bring you home again."

One hand came out and started to reach for Joshua's arm, but Joshua was not looking at him now. He was staring at his hands, his head low, his eyes half-closed. The hand drew back again.

"I almost hit him, Pa."

Benjamin started a little. "Who?"

"Will. Up in Wisconsin. I almost hit him. He dared me too. Taunted me by reminding me how I had struck Jessica and let Nathan be whipped." Now at last his head came up. There was a haunted look around his eyes and mouth. "He still thinks that's what stopped me. But it wasn't."

"What did?"

"I had my fist pulled back, blind with anger and hurt. Then suddenly I remembered that night too."

Benjamin nodded, strangely satisfied by that. "I understand."

They sat quietly for over a minute, each deep in the recesses of his own mind, counting costs, longing for a chance to relive those few moments over again in order to change them and make things turn out differently. Finally Joshua looked at his father. "You think I ought to let them be baptized, don't you?"

Benjamin shook his head without hesitation. "I know what you're feeling inside—misunderstood, angry, like you're the outcast."

"Frustrated, betrayed," Joshua added with a touch of bitterness.

"I don't know what is best to do, Joshua. Somehow you've got to find a way through this. I only know this. If you refuse to bend, it won't stop Will from being baptized. It may Caroline, but it won't Will. And then it will be Palmyra all over again. He'll leave you. He'll go back to sea."

"That's just talk," Joshua started, but then he shook his head. Down deep he had this gnawing fear that it was more than just talk. Will wasn't a boy anymore. He could leave and make his own way now. Hadn't Joshua at about that same age?

"That's exactly what I told myself about you," Benjamin said forlornly. " 'It's just talk,' I said. But I was wrong, Joshua. I was eleven years wrong."

"So I just push aside my feelings and let them all be baptized?" Joshua cried softly. "What about what matters to me?"

"You do what you have to do," came the answer. "All I'm saying is, maybe there's some value in sitting down by yourself for a while and counting the cost of doing what you think you have to do. Maybe after that, you'll decide that living with a house full of Mormons is not the worst possible thing that could happen to your family."

Joshua had gone to the freight office early that morning because he had a wagonload of cotton goods come in from St. Louis that needed transport to Plymouth, a small settlement about thirty-five miles southeast of Nauvoo. To the astonishment of his foreman, about ten o'clock that morning Joshua appeared in the stable and abruptly announced that he would be driving the wagon. He borrowed a coat and a bedroll from the previously designated driver, sent the man for some bread, cheese, and dried fruit, sent a hastily scrawled note to Caroline, and was off half an hour later.

He did not return until the following Tuesday, just at dark. Weary, stubbled, dirty, he left the team with the stable hand to unhitch and feed, and headed up the street for home.

He stood facing them. Will sat beside Olivia, holding her hand lightly. Caroline sat on the sofa. Their eyes were wide with curiosity. Above them, he could hear Savannah and Charles thumping around playing "bear" or some such thing that Savannah had engineered.

"There's no sense making this harder than it is," he started, then stopped, realizing that his voice sounded forced and clipped. He took a breath and started again. "I'm sorry I ran off like that to Plymouth, without warning. But I needed some time to myself, to think things through."

They nodded, not daring to ask what things he was talking about.

There was a fleeting smile. His father was right. No matter who was right here, it was costing them dearly. He could see it in their eyes and on their faces.

"My feelings about the Church and Joseph Smith haven't changed," he continued, "and I suppose they never will. But—" As he stopped, he saw the first flicker of hope flash across Caroline's eyes. "But no one's asking me to be baptized. If they were, I guess I'd have cause to balk a little."

Now Will had caught it. His eyes were round and filled with wonder. "What are you saying, Pa?" he asked softly.

"I think you know what I'm saying."

"Thank you," Will breathed softly.

Olivia leaned forward eagerly now. "What about me, Papa?"

He turned to her, wanting to reach out and touch her so she would know how much he loved her. "Are you sure that's what you want?" It was all he could do to keep his voice even.

Great tears welled up and spilled over. "I'm sure," she whispered.

He nodded, feeling as if a knife had just sliced through him when he saw the joy infuse her face.

Now he turned to his wife. Caroline's eyes were like two green emeralds, glowing in soft sunlight. She was staring at him in great wonder. "I gave my word," he said simply. "And Joshua Steed is a man of his word."

She started to speak, then couldn't. Her head dropped and her hands began to twist in her lap. Will went to her quickly and put an arm around her shoulder. With that, her head came up again.

"I already have your permission," she said softly.

"I know. Now you have my blessing."

There was a soft, choking sob, and then the tears began to flow.

"Why, Pa?" Will cried, still not quite believing.

"You don't need to know why," he answered. "That's just how it is. Isn't that enough?"

With the Mississippi surrounding Nauvoo on three sides, there were many places where a baptismal service could be held, but they decided to hold it near the ferry landing at the west end of Parley Street. Not only was there a large open area there, free of trees and undergrowth, but the water itself was mostly clear of the reeds and lilies that clogged so much of the riverbanks around Nauvoo.

By six o'clock, the time scheduled for the service, there was a crowd of nearly a hundred people. By unspoken agreement, especially among the family, Will and Olivia were at the center of most of the attention. Caroline stood back, content to know that her day had finally come. She didn't need anything more than the quiet joy that burned within her. Joshua was nearby, but thankfully, Carl and Melissa moved over to stand by him so that Joshua had someone he felt comfortable with.

All the Steeds were there, of course. They had sent a rider to Ramus, and Jessica and Solomon and the children had come immediately. Jessica now stood beside Kathryn, her hands resting on the handle of the wheelchair. There were thirty-three of them—thirty-four with Solomon, and thirty-five if you counted Rebecca's baby, due almost any day now.

But the crowd consisted of far more than just the family. Emma and Joseph Smith were there with their children. Mother Smith came with them. Hyrum and Mary Fielding Smith had come with their four oldest children. Brigham and Heber were there, though their wives had not come. George A. and Bathsheba Smith and John and Leonora Taylor were two more representatives from the Twelve. Friends, neighbors, customers at the store, people who were purchasing lots from Benjamin and Nathan, English Saints who had come across on the ship with Will, people whose friendship with the Steeds went all the way back to Palmyra—all had come to celebrate with the family on this happy occasion.

Abigail Pottsworth had come too, bringing Jenny and Andrew Stokes. Jenny was with child now and starting to show. There was a brief, awkward moment between her and Will, but warm and sincere congratulations from Andrew. Then they moved back to stand with the others.

Brigham came up to Will, who stuck out his hand. Brigham brushed it aside and swept him up in a crushing hug. "See, young Will?" he growled in a low voice. "I told you that day on the ship that you just had to be patient and you'd come to know."

"You were right," Will laughed back at him. "I wish I had just trusted you."

Heber followed, nearly crushing Will's hand as he congratulated him on his decision. Joseph said nothing, just gripped Will's hand and smiled broadly at him. Then he moved to Olivia and gave her a hug. He whispered something in her ear that made her smile.

Finally, Joseph came to Caroline. Brigham and Heber were over with Joshua and Carl, reminiscing about the time Carl and Melissa had put the two Apostles up in their home in Kirtland. It gave Joseph the opportunity he was looking for. He reached out and touched her hand briefly. She smiled radiantly at him.

"You are right, you know," he said softly. "I know that you are filled with doubts about the wisdom of your course of action, but it *is* right that you should accept this gift that Joshua's offered you."

"I know. I worry that he still resents it down deep inside, but it is his gift. And I've waited so long."

Joseph leaned forward a little. "He's a good man, Caroline. Don't give up on him."

"I won't." She had to blink quickly to fight the sudden burning in her eyes.

"This is not an easy thing he's done here. Just remember, *you* don't have to make him a Mormon." He smiled gently. "That's the Lord's work. You just love him."

She nodded, unable to speak.

By quarter past six, all the greetings and the congratulations were done. Gradually everyone stepped back, the anticipation rising as Joseph stepped forward. Joseph spoke briefly from the third chapter of John, where Nicodemus was told by Jesus that except a man be born of water and the Spirit, he cannot enter into the kingdom of God. Then he just simply reaffirmed that what these three good people were doing was pleasing to God. Though several shot sidelong glances at Joshua at that point, Joseph did not, nor did any of the family. Joshua took note of that and was grateful. He sensed that while Joseph was not skirting around what he wanted to say because of Joshua, neither was he using his talk as a way to preach to Joshua.

In less than five minutes Joseph was through. He signaled for Matthew. "I think you are going to baptize this young lady and young man, are you not?"

Matthew grinned happily. "I am."

"Then let's proceed."

Matthew came forward, took Olivia by the hand, and led her into the water. The water was brown and sluggish and still quite cold from the spring runoff. Olivia walked out until she was waist deep. Then she turned, smiling brightly at her mother.

Matthew gave her a quick smile, then took her arm. His right arm came up, the elbow bent, the arm pointing straight at the sky. He bowed his head and closed his eyes, and Olivia did the same.

"Olivia Mendenhall Steed," Matthew intoned, firmly

enough that those on shore could hear, "having been commissioned of Jesus Christ, I baptize you in the name of the Father, and of the Son, and of the Holy Ghost. Amen."

His eyes opened, his hand came down. Matthew tightened his grip on her right arm now, holding her back with his other arm. Down she went. The water engulfed her, and Matthew looked quickly to make sure her long hair had gone completely under. Then he pulled her up. She flung her head from side to side, whipping water away from her eyes and spraying Matthew. He just grinned and held out his arms. She came into them, laughing and crying. "Congratulations, Livvy," he whispered.

"Thank you, Uncle Matthew."

Will was next. He strode out boldly, almost as though he would push the river aside now that he had his answer. *Do my will and you will know.* Well, that was what he was here for. It was time for doing. He gave Matthew a broad smile. Up came the hand. Both closed their eyes. The brief but significant prayer was repeated. Again a body was immersed in the river's water so that a soul could be cleansed.

A smattering of applause rippled through the crowd. Caroline could barely see Will and Matthew hugging, so swiftly her tears were flowing. Then she felt a hand on her arm. She turned. Benjamin was standing beside her. "Are you ready, Caroline?" Then with a soft hoot of derision he added, "What a question!"

Caroline was barely aware of the water's touch as she followed Father Steed into the water. She turned, feeling as if the warmth of the Spirit was already racing through her every vein. She started to look at the encircling faces but then changed her mind. She turned to Benjamin, wanting to watch his face, wanting to let him see hers. This was the man who, perhaps more than any other person, was responsible for her being here on this day. She loved and respected him so deeply. Only if Joshua had been a Church member would she have wanted someone else standing by her side at this moment.

Benjamin smiled, then gently took her arm in his left hand

as he raised his other hand to the square. "Caroline Mendenhall Steed," he began. She closed her eyes. "Having been commissioned of Jesus Christ, I baptize you in the name of the Father, and of the Son, and of the Holy Ghost. Amen."

Down she went, the water enfolding her; and then almost before she could comprehend its embrace she was up again. Benjamin released her and she reached up and wiped the water from her eyes; then her hands continued upward, pulling her hair back away from her face. "Thank you, Father Steed," she whispered.

He put his arms around her and pulled her to him softly, even as she started to cry. "No, thank *you*," he said, weeping unashamedly with her.

She came out of the water and back up on the bank. Will started toward her. Olivia stepped forward. But she only smiled at them. She walked straight forward, past the outstretched towel that Mary Ann was holding, past Nathan and Lydia and Joseph and all the others. She walked straight to Joshua and into his arms, soaking the front of his shirt and vest. "Thank you, Joshua," she cried in a hoarse whisper. "Thank you for allowing this day."

It was late in the afternoon of June fourth when the midwife and Mary Ann Steed came out of Derek and Rebecca's house. Most of the family were standing in the front yard talking quietly to each other. Derek swung around and went swiftly to the two women. All the others went instantly quiet and turned eagerly to listen.

"You have a new baby, Derek," Mary Ann said in weary happiness.

"I do?"

"Yes, and Rebecca is fine."

"What is it?"

Mary Ann smiled at him. "What did you want?"

He hesitated a moment. "Rebecca thought it was a girl. All along I've felt it was going to be a brother for Christopher."

She nodded thoughtfully. "And do you have names picked out?"

He grinned and looked at Father Steed. "If it's a boy, we

thought it was time we had a little Benjamin around here. We'll call him Benjamin Derek Ingalls. If it's a girl, we'd like to call her Mary Ann Ingalls."

The midwife was beaming now, enjoying Mary Ann's little delaying game. Mary Ann nodded again at Derek, then looked to her husband. "I think you win this one, Benjamin."

There was a soft gasp from those around him, and then they clapped their hands. Derek let out a whoop as Mary Ann said, "Come in and see your new son, Papa."

———•◦•———

The record does not clearly state what happened between the end of May and the third week of June. Bennett had made his public confession and things seemed to be settling down again. Perhaps further evidence of Bennett's misdeeds came forth. Perhaps Joseph felt his repentance was not sincere. Whatever the reason, on June eighteenth Joseph spoke to a huge group of Saints assembled near the temple. In the words of Wilford Woodruff, he "spoke his mind in great plainness concerning the iniquity, hypocrisy, wickedness, and corruption of General John Cook Bennett."

Furious, Bennett went to Joseph and threatened to expose him to the world unless he publicly retracted what he had said. He would write letters to newspaper editors. He would write a book telling all of Joseph's secrets. Joseph, no stranger to calumny and false witness, was unmoved and unmoveable. Even though he had already voluntarily taken his name off the rolls of the Church, on June nineteenth John C. Bennett was formally excommunicated from The Church of Jesus Christ of Latter-day Saints. Three days later, Bennett abruptly left Nauvoo.

In what came to be known as the Wentworth Letter, Joseph Smith had boldly declared: "No unhallowed hand can stop the work from progressing. . . . The truth of God will go forth boldly, nobly, and independent, . . . till the purposes of God shall be accomplished, and the Great Jehovah shall say the work is done."

Being a man of enormous and preening ego, when Bennett fell from grace he struck back in fury. The prophetic promise was that no unhallowed hand could stop the work. There was no promise that the unhallowed hand would not try.

Learned, articulate, suave, charming, and with considerable talents, John C. Bennett came into the Church like a summer storm, quickly moving into its highest circles—mayor, major general in the Nauvoo Legion, chancellor of the newly formed University of the City of Nauvoo, Assistant President of the Church. Then secretly, insidiously, treacherously he began to work the works of darkness. By the time the Church realized just how unholy his hands truly were, he had wreaked enormous damage.

On May sixth, 1842, Lilburn W. Boggs, ex-governor of the state of Missouri, was nearly assassinated by an unknown assailant. At first, no one even thought of the Mormons. Boggs had been a vastly unpopular governor and, at the time, was in the midst of a hotly contested state senate race. In Jackson County a suspect was found—the "many corroborating circumstances leave no doubt of this man's guilt," the papers stated.

Enter John C. Bennett.

In a series of letters to the editor of the *Sangamo Journal*, a Springfield paper, Bennett rehashed all of his previous charges against Joseph—spiritual wifery, Nancy Rigdon, Melissa Schindle, and so on. Swearing that he had left the Church voluntarily after he saw the corruption in the leadership and that his former confessions of guilt had been given under severe duress, he now took a new tack. In one of the letters, he said that Joseph had paid Orrin Porter Rockwell fifty dollars to assassinate Lilburn Boggs. The timing was perfect. Rockwell had been in Jackson County with his wife, who had returned to her family there to have a baby. And Rockwell's name was perfect. Known to be fiercely loyal to Joseph, Porter was fearless in battle, was a crack shot with pistol or rifle, and had become legendary during the Mormon War. He was hated by the Missourians and was still wanted on charges stemming from the war.

Bennett, seeing a rich opportunity, traveled to Independence and introduced himself to Boggs. Almost overnight the story now changed. The suspect already in hand was suddenly acquitted of all charges, and Boggs went before a justice of the peace and swore out a deposition accusing Porter Rockwell and Joseph Smith of attempted murder.

———————◆·——————

It was a blistering hot afternoon in late July. The humidity was high and the sun shone down from a cloudless sky. Trees, flowers, bushes, cornfields, and humans all wilted under its merciless rays. Joshua had his shirt unbuttoned and fanned himself continuously as he sat in the office of his freight business working over the books. The windows were opened, but no breeze stirred and the air was heavy and ripe with the smell of his own sweat.

Though the office for the freight yard was still where it had always been, near the west end of Sidney Street, the corrals and stables were now empty and in the process of being dismantled. With the population of Nauvoo still soaring—it had been announced a week earlier that it topped nine thousand—Joshua's freight business was booming. He now ran almost thirty wagons all over the state of Illinois and back and forth between Nauvoo and St. Louis. He was up to almost a hundred horses and mules and oxen. Land within the city had grown too precious to consume with stables and corrals. So, using the handsome profit he had made on his raft of lumber, he purchased a large parcel of land east of town and built new corrals, stables, barns, and storage sheds. Next week, when the ones here were gone, Joshua would deed the land over to his father and Nathan, and they would begin to develop it into prime building lots, sharing half the profits with him.

In truth, he reflected, all of the Steeds were prospering. The Steed family store was doing a brisk business. Nathan was working on putting another row of storerooms across the back and opening up some of the front ones for more store space. Lydia and Caroline still supervised the running of the store, but with its success, they now had hired a full-time woman and three part-time clerks to attend to the daily working of it. Matthew and Carl were both richly benefitting from the booming growth in the city. The woodworking shop run jointly by Matthew and Brigham Young had such a high demand for cabinets, furniture, railings, fireplace mantels, and a hundred other products, that they too had become employers as well as owners. Brigham was still heavily involved in his work as President of the Quorum of the Twelve, so they hired two men—one full-time, one part-time—to help Matthew at the shop.

Carl's two brickyards were working double shifts six days a week. He opened another kiln in early June but still could not keep up with the demand. Carl was now one of Nauvoo's more well-to-do citizens. Even Derek, who was content with his ten acres of farmland down near the river, was doing well. His assignment of acreage in what had once been a swamp proved to be a blessing. The rich soil was producing some of Nauvoo's finest corn, beans, squash, and tomatoes. His produce sold readily as soon as it was harvested.

It was a good time, even for him, Joshua had to concede to himself. His father had been right. His decision to withdraw his opposition to the baptism of his family had paid off in rich dividends. Caroline was radiantly happy. Will had not said another word about going to sea, even though Joshua knew there was a growing restlessness in him. Olivia was like a child again, and the love between her and her father blossomed into something very special to Joshua. That didn't mean that his feelings about the Church and plural marriage had changed at all. He made no attempt to hide those feelings, but neither did he feel that he had to keep waving the flag in front of his family to remind them of where he stood. And they in turn did not try to persuade him that he was wrong. In a way, the whole issue had become like a room in their marriage that had been shuttered up and closed off. It was always there. They passed back and forth by it a dozen times a day, but they never opened the door to step inside or to try and air it out.

He set his pen down and leaned back, fanning himself more swiftly with a book. It was an interesting contrast between himself and Carl. Melissa had never rebounded from the shock of what she had heard that night in Heber Kimball's home. Though she claimed she was still saying her prayers and reading the Bible and the Book of Mormon, she and the children had not been to a worship service since that night. She still steadfastly refused to talk about it. This was far more than a closed room for them. It was a sealed tomb. It was as though she had erased any memory of it from her mind. On those few occasions when Caroline or Lydia or Mary Ann did try to talk about her feelings, she would simply turn away, as if they hadn't spoken.

Carl had come to some kind of inner resolution with what the Mormons were doing—not acceptance, but a wary tolerance. He too spoke little of it. But things had changed. He still loved living in Nauvoo and being part of the Steeds, but it had been several years since he had been with his family. His sons and daughter had a wonderful relationship with all their cousins here, but they also had cousins in Kirtland. They loved Father and Mother Steed, but they had another set of grandparents they barely knew. More and more, he and Melissa started talking about maybe making a visit back to Kirtland. An extended visit.

With a sigh, Joshua set the book down and went back to work. The sooner he was finished here, the sooner he could leave the unbearable heat of the office.

Ten minutes later, Joshua was startled when the door to the office opened and Joseph Smith stepped inside. "Hello, Joshua."

"Well," he said, standing up, "this is a surprise."

Joseph nodded and came across and shook his hand. Since the whole thing with plural marriage, Joshua had not seen much of Joseph. This was partly because of the press of matters on Joseph's mind now, partly because Joshua had avoided Joseph whenever possible. Their relationship was still amiable, but there was also a definite coolness in Joshua now. Joseph had not seemed to notice or, if he did, had not let it affect his feelings at all.

"I was out east of town yesterday," Joseph said. "That's quite an operation you've made for yourself out there."

"Yes. We really didn't have a lot of choice. We had to expand and there just isn't room here."

"That's wonderful," Joseph said heartily.

Joshua pointed to a chair. "Come in and sit down."

Joseph did so, and Joshua went around behind his desk again and took his chair. "I heard about Bennett going to Missouri and meeting with Boggs. Believe it or not, I'm sorry about that, Joseph."

"Thank you."

"What do you think will come of that?"

There was an enigmatic shrug. "The Missourians aren't after legal redress, Joshua. If they get me back to Jackson County, I'm a dead man. So we'll fight it in the courts."

Joshua accepted that. He knew Jackson County well, and Joseph was not being overly dramatic. "So," he finally asked, "what can I do for you?"

Joseph's demeanor smoothed a little now, but there was still concern in his eyes. Only now it was for another reason. "Joshua, I know how you feel about everything that has gone on. I want you to know that I respect your right to believe as you choose. I really do. I am a firm believer in the doctrine that every man should be free to choose his own way in matters of religion. It disturbs me a little that some of our number tend to shun those who don't believe as we do."

That much Joshua had to admit was true. Joseph was a tolerant man. "I know that, Joseph, and I appreciate it."

"So," Joseph went on, "I know that what I am about to say may not be well received. I could tell you that I come only in response to the whisperings of the Spirit, but I know that doesn't cut much leather with you either. But I still wanted to come to you first."

"First?" Joshua asked warily.

Joseph straightened, his face determined now. "Yes. I'd like to call Will on a mission to England, Joshua."

Joshua shot to his feet. "*What?*" He stared at Joseph angrily. One of the reasons why Joshua had given in on the baptism was to stop Will from leaving. Joseph knew that. And now . . . He couldn't believe what he had just heard.

There was a sad, slightly sardonic smile now on Joseph's face. "Doesn't seem fair, does it?"

"Fair?" Joshua cried. "How could you even think of doing such a thing, Joseph? After all that's happened, how could you even think it?"

"Well," Joseph pointed out with equanimity, "I know this isn't very helpful, but it's not me who is asking this, Joshua. It's the Lord."

"Don't give me that business," Joshua snapped. "I don't care if it's the president of the United States who's asking. You're not taking my son."

"I'm sorry, Joshua, but I have to ask him. The Lord has called him to England. It will be for at least one year, maybe two. Whether he'll accept the call or not, I don't know. But I have to ask." He stood. "I'm sorry. This is something I've been dreading having to do for three days now. I'm sorry."

———◆———

In the end, it was not as hard a decision as Joshua thought it would be. He went home that night, grabbed Caroline, and took her for a walk. He told her everything, his anger rising all over again with the retelling of it.

"What more does this man want of me?" he fumed, throwing his hands out in frustration. "Haven't I given enough?"

He turned to look at his wife when she didn't answer. Her eyes were filled with tears and she was biting her lower lip.

"Now, Caroline, don't start that on me," he began. "I've bent over backwards—"

But she shook her head firmly. "I don't blame you, Joshua. You've been wonderful, and now this."

That took him aback. If she wasn't crying because of his reaction, then why? He reached out and took her hand. "Then what's the matter?"

"You're the one who said it," she reminded him, "just the other night."

"What?"

"About how restless Will is getting."

He frowned. He *had* said that, and it had been worrying him. Will was pretty well running the freight yard now and was making an occasional trip to St. Louis for Joshua. But the itch was on him as if he had rolled in a patch of poison oak. "Yeah," was all Joshua said.

"He won't say anything to you, Joshua," she went on, "not after what you did for him in letting him be baptized. He's very grateful to you for that. But it's still there, this whatever it is. It's not from anger anymore. It's just that . . ."

He nodded glumly. Joshua knew exactly what it was. After the blowup between him and Benjamin, Joshua had headed west. For the next two years he had been totally on his own—working the river rafts up and down the Ohio, starting a freight business in Independence. Though he missed his family, the freedom was exhilarating. Will had experienced that too, only at an even younger age than Joshua had. He had been all through the Caribbean—Mexico, Cuba, the Bahamas. He had been to Europe and then on around the world to China. Nauvoo had to seem pretty confining after that. "Yeah," he said again.

"You know what it means to me to have him here, don't you?"

He looked at her and finally nodded. She had gone through months of agony when Will had been shanghaied and sent to sea. She had missed him terribly for the months he was with Joshua in Wisconsin. Now he would be gone again. "Yes, I do."

"If he goes to sea, that will be it. You know that, don't you?"

He thought about that and finally grunted. "Yes. I know he loves it."

"Is having him gone to England for one or two years any worse than losing him forever to being a sea captain?" she asked softly. "At least this way he'll come back home to us."

So in the end, Joshua had to admit that she was very probably right, and he stepped aside and let Will go. Accepting it, however, did not mean that Joshua liked it. His resentment against Joseph and the Church now had one more thing added to it. He could live with it, but it still galled him deeply that Mormonism kept intruding itself into his life.

Will caught a stagecoach headed east on the second of August. The whole family had come to the stage station to see him off, and it was a tearful farewell. But when he had finished with Charles and Savannah, Olivia and Caroline, Will finally turned to his father. Nothing was said. Neither of them could have spoken at that moment had they wished to. Will just threw his arms around his father and they held each other tightly for almost a full minute. Finally, he pulled back, wiping at his eyes. "I love you, Papa," he whispered. "I'll miss you."

Joshua nodded and stepped back. "I love you too, Will. Come back to us."

"I will, Papa. I will."

There was no question but what John C. Bennett was proving to be a formidable enemy. His decision to go public spread the poison of his lies like thistle pods blowing in a windstorm. The anti-Mormon factions were jubilant. They had long known there was a great wickedness in this accursed church; now at last they had the "proof" for which they were seeking.

In Nauvoo, Joseph and other Church leaders worked vigorously to undo the damage. Depositions were taken which directly contradicted Bennett's claims that he had been forced to make his confessions. Letters were written to Governor Carlin of Illinois and Governor Reynolds of Missouri outlining Bennett's slanderous nature and immoral conduct. Affidavits from those who had been seduced by Bennett and his associates were brought forward to support those claims. The Relief Society sent a petition to Governor Carlin with signatures from almost a thousand women testifying that Joseph was not immoral in any way. Another petition, signed by many non-Mormons as well as members, also testified to Joseph's integrity and morality.

But it was like throwing shovels of sand at a raging torrent. Sometime during that summer, Orson Pratt finally learned about what had been going on with his wife while he had been in England. The problem was, he was only told the Bennett version of events. Feeling wounded and betrayed, Orson withdrew into a shell, refusing to discuss the matter with Joseph. When the Twelve drafted the paper announcing Bennett's excommunication, Orson refused to sign it. When the general petition to Governor Carlin was passed around, Orson refused to sign that as well. Joseph confronted him directly. "Have you personally a knowledge of any immoral act I have committed toward the female sex or in any other way?" he demanded to know. Orson admitted that he did not, but he would not budge. Joseph asked Brigham and the Twelve to labor with their brother. He was unreachable. Before August ended, Orson Pratt, one of the senior members of the Quorum of the Twelve, was excommunicated. The casualty list had now reached into the highest circles of the Church.

On the sixth of August, Nathan and Benjamin crossed the Mississippi and accompanied Joseph and Hyrum Smith and several other brethren to Montrose, Iowa. Joseph had come with the deputy grand master of the second Grand Lodge of Illinois, from Springfield, to create a Masonic lodge in Montrose. Benjamin was a member of the Masonic lodge in Nauvoo, but Nathan was not. Nevertheless, Benjamin had convinced him to come over with him so they could look at some land while they were there.

They met at a small block schoolhouse, where the ceremony was to take place. While the grand master and Hyrum went in to train the new officers—only Hyrum was high enough in the order to participate—the rest of the men moved around to the east side of the school where they were shaded from the afternoon heat. The day was stifling, and the hosting brethren had thoughtfully filled a large barrel with water, then brought several chunks of ice from one of their icehouses to put into it. The shade was a welcome respite from the sun. The ice water was like a gift from heaven.

The men stood around the barrel, dipping their tin cups and drinking deeply. In the easy company that he kept with his brethren, Joseph stood among them, talking quietly. The talk turned to the whole thing with Boggs. Would Governor Carlin respond to the request of Missouri's governor and issue a warrant for the arrest of Porter Rockwell and Joseph Smith? That generated a rumble of angry mutterings and shaking of heads. Would the Missourians never give up? This had been going on now for almost ten years, ever since the Saints had been driven from Jackson County. Would they never leave them in peace?

Joseph slowly shook his head. "Brethren, it isn't over yet."

That brought an immediate quieting among the men.

"It has been a constant annoyance which has followed us since we were driven from that state, but I tell you, we have not seen the last of our persecutions. We shall yet suffer much affliction. We shall yet be driven from our homes."

"No!" someone said in a shocked whisper.

Anson Call had at that moment been reaching into the barrel and refilling his tin tumbler with water. Joseph turned to him and laid a hand on his shoulder. "Anson, don't be too free with this wonderful water."

That brought Anson up and caused even more surprise among the group. They had barely lowered the level of the water in the barrel; there was plenty for everyone. Then suddenly,

Nathan started. Joseph was not looking at Anson Call any longer. He was gazing beyond him, as though looking at something very far away. His own cup was still in hand but forgotten now. "Brethren," he said solemnly, "this ice water that has so kindly been provided for us today is a wonderful thing. The water tastes much like the water from the crystal streams which tumble down from the Rocky Mountains. I see those mountains now, with their snowcapped peaks and the broad and beautiful valleys."

Nathan glanced at Benjamin with a look of wonder. There was a light on Joseph's face and in his eyes now that was remarkable. Nathan had seen this before, this transformation when Joseph was wrapped in the spirit of inspiration and vision. "We shall go to the Rocky Mountains and there we shall become a mighty people."

He swung around suddenly, now looking at them. "There are some of you here who shall do a great work in that land." His hand was still on Call's shoulder. "Here is Anson," he said. "He shall go and shall assist in building up cities from one end of that country to the other." His gaze swept over them, the blue eyes almost fiery now in their power as he looked from face to face. "You shall perform as great a work as has been done by man. The nations of the earth shall be astonished, and many of them will be gathered in that land and assist in building cities and temples, and Israel shall be made to rejoice."

"When, Joseph?" Benjamin breathed.

It was as if Joseph hadn't heard him. "Oh, the beauty of those snowcapped mountains! The cool, refreshing streams that are running down through those mountain gorges!" He turned, as if looking in another direction, and a shadow crossed his face. "Oh, the scenes that this people will pass through! The dead that will lie between here and there."

Nathan was transfixed. Everyone else was too. Horror and shock filled their faces, and yet it was as though Joseph had set them on fire as well.

Again the Prophet turned his head, seeming to gaze on yet

another scene. "Oh, the apostasy that will take place before my brethren reach that land!" Then suddenly there was a confident smile. "But," he went on, "the priesthood shall prevail over its enemies. We shall triumph over the devil and be established upon the earth, never more to be thrown down!"

The light in his eyes faded and gradually his body relaxed again. He drank deeply from his cup, then set it on the bench that stood beside the barrel. No one moved. Every eye was on him. "Brethren," he said finally, "I charge you with all the force and power I have within me. Be faithful to those things that have been and shall be committed to your charge, and you will have the promise of all the blessings that the priesthood can bestow. Remember these things and treasure them up, and all will be well." He paused, and there was a gentle smile. "Amen," he said softly.

"Amen!" came the amazed and yet answering affirmation from those around him. "Amen!"

On August eighth, a deputy sheriff and two other men arrived in Nauvoo. With them they brought a warrant signed by the governor of Illinois for the arrest of Joseph Smith and Porter Rockwell. The intent of the law officers was to carry their two prisoners to Missouri and turn them over to the authorities there.

When the Nauvoo Charter had been passed by the state legislature, Joseph worked hard to ensure that the city courts would have the power to issue a writ of habeas corpus. This legal document was a powerful weapon in protecting a person from illegal arrests or being dragged off to another venue where the person's rights would not be protected. Joseph immediately obtained a writ for both him and Rockwell, preventing the law officers from carrying out the arrest. Not sure what that meant, the law officers returned to Springfield for further instruction. Fearing that their legal rights might be compromised, Joseph went into hiding near Nauvoo, and Porter Rockwell took an assumed name and fled the city, heading east.

The failure to arrest Joseph and his "Destroying Angel," as Bennett had labeled Rockwell, raised a howl of protest from the enemies of the Church. They had long claimed that the Mormons had carved out for themselves an independent kingdom with their Nauvoo Charter. Here, they said, was proof that the Mormon prophet was above the law.

———•———

By late summer John C. Bennett had made an interesting discovery. Sensationalism paid handsomely. After his successful trip to see Lilburn Boggs, Bennett headed east. Writing letters to the editor, composing articles for newpapers, and offering lectures in the evening became his pattern. Louisville, Cincinnati, Cleveland, Buffalo, New York, Boston—he moved from city to city, embellishing his story as he went. The claims got more and more fantastic. Members of the Church were required to consecrate all their property—including their wives—to Joseph Smith for his personal gratification. Joseph had often been seen roaring drunk and falling into the sewers of Nauvoo, he said. Joseph claimed to be Jesus Christ and Sidney Rigdon was the Holy Ghost. When Sidney got sick, Bennett told his shocked audiences, he (Bennett) had become Holy Ghost pro tem. There was a secret lodge of women in Nauvoo, ran another of his claims. This was Joseph's seraglio, his private harem, and the women were totally given over to satisfying Joseph's every desire.

Though Bennett was drawing huge crowds, not all who read or came to listen were totally taken in by Bennett's lectures. The editor of the New York *Sun*, though glad to see the delusion of Mormonism exposed, suggested that Bennett was "just about as big a rogue as Joe." Others asked why Bennett had not come forth sooner to expose the wickedness of the Mormons. Why had he stayed in a leadership position for over a year? Bennett neatly sidestepped that question. The fact that he was making healthy profits from these lectures also was noted with suspicion. One editor said of him, "I know of no man who invents testimony so fast as he who makes his living from his testimony."

By late August, word of Bennett's writings and lectures were filtering back to Nauvoo. These kinds of scurrilous lies could not simply be ignored, lest the honest in heart believe that the Church had no answer, no defense for the charges being leveled against it. On August twenty-sixth, Joseph met with the Twelve and decided that it was time to send missionaries out to "deluge the earth with a flood of truth." Three days later Joseph made his first public appearance since the attempt to arrest him and spoke at a conference of the Saints. There he issued the call for elders to go forth and refute the lies of John C. Bennett. When the meeting was finished, about three hundred and eighty brethren stepped forward to answer the call.

Unquestionably, Bennett turned many against the Church, even some members who lived in the cities where he lectured. But as time wore on something else became evident. Sometimes the suspicious were led to investigate further and found the Church to be something far different from what Bennett was representing it to be. In Chicago, after a debate between Bennett and one of the elders, large numbers started coming to the meetings where the elder was teaching and eventually twelve people were baptized.

Nathan, Derek, and Matthew all stepped forward on August twenty-ninth and volunteered to go out as missionaries. Peter Ingalls also answered the call, but John Taylor persuaded him that his work with the *Times and Seasons* was a mission of its own. The newspaper was publishing a great deal of information about Bennett, and while it wasn't reaching much of the world, it was an effective voice to the Saints. Reluctantly, Peter agreed and withdrew his name.

Most of the elders left almost immediately, knowing the urgency of the mission. With Joseph's encouragement, the three men of the Steed family delayed their departure until September fourth. The reason for the delay was that they wanted to be present for the wedding.

On the third day of September, 1842, on a cool, late summer afternoon, Solomon Garrett and Jessica Roundy Steed Griffith were married by Hyrum Smith. Rachel, now a maturing ten years old, and Kathryn in her wheelchair flanked Jessica on both sides as maids of honor. Several families had come from Ramus to share in the celebration, and with the large number of guests from Nauvoo, they decided it would be best to hold the ceremony in the grove west of the temple. Hyrum jokingly told Benjamin that at the rate he and Mary Ann were going, the Church would have to deed the grove over to them just to handle their family gatherings.

The original plan had been to have Joseph perform the marriage. He had long admired Jessica's unwavering faithfulness in the face of great trials and wanted to be the one to participate in this happy time for her. But on that very day, as Joseph was eating with Emma and the children, three law officers suddenly burst into the main room of the Homestead. While the intruders were delayed by one of the brethren standing watch, Joseph slipped out the back door and went into hiding again.

The news that their prophet was being hounded cast a pall over the wedding celebration, but Hyrum would not let it linger. Nor would Emma, who, once she was sure Joseph was safe, came to the grove shortly after the marriage had been performed. The Lord had once again delivered Joseph from the hands of his enemies, she said, and this was cause for rejoicing. Legal action was under way to overturn the warrant and prove its illegality. Until then, the Prophet would simply stay out of the grasp of his enemies. Soon the mood brightened again. The festivities celebrating Jessica's newfound happiness went on until late into the evening.

The following morning, Nathan, Derek, and Matthew kissed their families good-bye and accompanied Solomon and Jessica and the children on their return to Ramus. At Ramus, they split up—Nathan moving south to intersect the Ohio River, Derek and Matthew traveling together on a more northerly route.

The week following the departure of Nathan, Derek, and

Matthew, Carl and Melissa received a letter from Kirtland, Ohio. Hezekiah Rogers had taken ill. Carl's mother was gravely concerned. She and the brothers begged Carl to come home for a visit. This was all the nudge they needed to help them make up their minds. Leaving the brickyards in the hand of his partner, Carl left with his family five days later.

Mary Ann felt a great sense of sadness as she watched the wagon disappear down the road. For many years her family had been apart—Joshua lost to them, Carl and Melissa in Kirtland. But for the last two years the family had been reunited. It had been a season of great joy for her and Benjamin. Now suddenly once again the family was scattering to the four winds. Will was gone to England for at least a year, maybe two. Nathan, Matthew, and Derek were on their missions in the East and wouldn't return until just before Christmas. Carl and Melissa were now headed to Kirtland for an extended stay. They would not even commit as to whether they would be back for Christmas.

———◦———

During the Christmas season of 1840, with the help of the Pottsworths and their English Christmas traditions, the Steed family started some traditions of their own. On Christmas Eve they gathered all together at Joshua and Caroline's house for dinner. Then after dinner, the children made their Christmas stockings and hung them on the fireplace mantel in preparation for a visit from Santa Claus, or Father Christmas. Names had been exchanged among the cousins, and simple gifts had been made in secret over the past two weeks. These were now exchanged to the accompaniment of oohs and aahs, much applause, and happy hugs. Then Benjamin read the Christmas story from the Gospels of Matthew and Luke as the small children acted it out with shining eyes. An occasional unique innovation by this child or that—one of the Wise Men telling King Herod, for example, that if he tried to kill the infants, he'd knock him off his throne—brought smiles to the faces of the adults.

The circle of the family had dwindled now. Nathan had returned just after Thanksgiving, Derek and Matthew two weeks following that, so they were back again, but that was all. The Pottsworths, who had been with them during the two previous Christmases, were not there. With Jenny's marriage to Andrew Stokes and her new baby, Sister Pottsworth had moved across the river to Zarahemla and rarely came over anymore. Carl and Melissa decided to stay on in Kirtland until the weather broke, even though Carl's father was better again. Will, of course, was only represented by a letter propped up on the mantel.

Though the absence of Carl and Melissa and their children was a source of sadness to all of them, there was compensating news. Gladly, Jessica and Solomon had come over from Ramus, and in addition to adding their numbers to the circle, they announced that the following July they would have a child of their own. Jessica was thirty-eight now and her child-bearing years were limited, so this was received with particular joy. Lydia and Nathan added their own announcement to that, revealing that they were expecting to add a fifth child to their family in June.

The most joyous surprise came early in the evening's celebration. All the family had arrived except for Matthew and Jennifer Jo and Kathryn. Dinner was ready and they were all seated waiting for the late arrivals. Benjamin was about to send someone over to Matthew's house looking for them when there was a sound on the porch. They all turned as the front door opened. A moment later Matthew wheeled Kathryn down the hall to where it opened up into the large sitting room where they were preparing to eat. Matthew and Jennifer Jo—Jenny now again to everyone but Matthew—waved their greetings and offered their apologies as they shed their coats and tossed them onto the bench in the hall. But then to everyone's surprise, Matthew and Jenny left Kathryn sitting there in the hallway as they came over to the table and sat down. Jenny handed the baby to Mary Ann as an embarrassed hush swept over the group. Peter leaped to his feet to go bring Kathryn in as well, but

Matthew grabbed his hand and pulled him back down. "We have an announcement," he said solemnly.

Seeing their looks, Matthew grinned broadly. "No, I'm not talking about another baby. Actually, it's not our announcement. It's Kathryn's."

All eyes turned to her. Kathryn's face was glowing and she had a teasing smile in her eyes. "As you know," she said, "when Matthew left for the East, Jenny got pretty lonely. She and I decided we needed to do something to keep us both occupied." Casually, almost as if she weren't even thinking about it, she raised her arms above her head, stretching lazily.

There was a collective gasp. In the past few months, Kathryn had regained a limited ability to use her hands, but her arms were still barely able to lift an inch or two off the bed. Everyone was stunned.

She smiled all the more broadly. "Jenny has been helping me do some exercises. I think it's paid off." Then, milking the moment for every drop of emotion she could get out of it, she slowly lowered her hands to the wheels of her chair. Gripping the rims tightly, she proceeded to propel herself into the room. Now there wasn't a sound. Even the children gaped in astonishment. Laughing and half crying, she pulled up alongside Benjamin, who sat at one end of the table. She reached out and punched him gently on the shoulder. "How's that, Father Steed?" she asked.

There were tears in his eyes as he looked at her. Without a word, he pushed his chair back and stood on his feet. He bowed slightly toward her and began to clap his hands. In an instant the whole family was up and applauding thunderously.

That had set the mood for the rest of the evening, and now as they gathered around the piano, three and four deep, to end the night by singing carols, they still basked in a warm glow of happiness and contentment. Nathan was at the back of the group, holding Josiah in his arms. Benjamin stood by his side. As Olivia began playing the last verse of "Silent Night," Nathan looked around, then in a whisper said to his father, "Where do you think next Christmas will find us, Pa?"

Benjamin too looked around at the crowded room, then half turned so that the others would not hear his reply. "Are you thinking about Joseph's prophecy?"

Nathan nodded soberly. "Yes."

"He didn't say it was coming right away."

"I know, but—"

"I predict that come next Christmas, we'll be standing right here again, singing carols around the piano."

Nathan smiled, cheered by that thought. "I hope so." He let his eyes turn to where Kathryn sat beside Olivia, singing in full voice with the rest of the family. "And maybe Kathryn will be standing here by our side."

They had started their last song now, the carol that always closed their evening's celebration. Suddenly the words registered in Nathan's mind.

> Joy to the world! the Lord will come!
> And earth receive her King;
> Let ev'ry heart prepare him room,
> And saints and angels sing.

He felt his heart lift and the melancholy push back. There might be difficult times ahead, but there was also that other great day to look forward to as well.

> Rejoice! rejoice! when Jesus reigns,
> And saints their songs employ:
> While fields and floods, rocks, hills and plains,
> Repeat the sounding joy.

It was true that Carl and Melissa were gone and might not return, but there stood Joshua, one arm around Caroline, one hand resting on Livvy's shoulder. At least that crisis had been averted. And Jessica was married to a good and decent man. Kathryn was pushing herself around the house on her own. Wasn't that joy worth repeating?

No more will sin and sorrow grow,
   Nor thorns infest the ground;
He'll come and make the blessings flow
   Far as the curse was found.

He moved away from his father now, over to stand beside Lydia. Slipping his free arm around her waist, he pulled her closer to him. She looked up in surprise, but he just smiled down at her and now sang without restraint.

Rejoice! rejoice! in the Most High,
   While Israel spread abroad,
Like stars that glitter in the sky,
   And ever worship God.
   And ever and ever worship God.

Chapter Notes

The large number of historical references in this chapter cannot all be singly documented. The story of these turbulent months—including the details of John C. Bennett's apostasy and his bitter campaign against the Church, the attempted assassination of Lilburn Boggs and its aftermath, the Orson Pratt incident, and the response of the Church to the threats against it—is accurately portrayed here (see such sources as Andrew F. Smith, "The Saintly Scoundrel: The Life and Times of John Cook Bennett" [unpublished ms., Brooklyn, N.Y., 1994], pp. 125–71; Danel W. Bachman, "A Study of the Mormon Practice of Plural Marriage Before the Death of Joseph Smith" [master's thesis, Purdue University, 1975], pp. 223–60; Richard Lloyd Dewey, *Porter Rockwell: A Biography* [New York: Paramount Books, 1986], pp. 49–59; CHFT, pp. 263–71; HC 5:18–146).

Joseph's remarkable prophecy about the Saints going to the Rocky Mountains was given on 6 August 1842 to a group of brethren (see HC 5:85–86).

Joseph remained in semi-hiding through December 1842, working with the courts and the governor to resolve the legal problems stemming from

Boggs's deposition against him. In December, the case went to the Illinois Supreme Court, which threw out Boggs's deposition as groundless and illegal. On their way back to Nauvoo after that wonderful news, Joseph's carriage slipped on icy, frozen roads and went over an embankment, breaking the fore axle-tree. In high spirits, the company agreed that the bill for the repairs ought to be sent to Lilburn W. Boggs. Joseph arrived back in Nauvoo on 10 January 1843, and his people joyously proclaimed a day of jubilee to celebrate the triumph of their prophet.

In one of those interesting twists of fate, John C. Bennett wrote a letter to Sidney Rigdon and Orson Pratt in January of 1843. He said he was planning to go to Missouri to help a grand jury find enough evidence to indict Joseph again. Sidney, who for months now had vacillated back and forth between loyalty to Joseph and sympathy for Bennett, did not say anything to Joseph but passed the letter on to Pratt. It had been six months since Orson was excommunicated. In that time, his wife had repented and so had Orson. They wanted to come back to the Church. Thus when Orson got the letter from Bennett, he went straight to Joseph with it. Seeing his action as proof of his sincerity, Joseph and the Twelve accepted Orson and his wife back into the Church and Orson was reinstated to the Quorum. Ironically, this changed his order of seniority in the Quorum, a fact that much later would bring John Taylor to the presidency of the Church instead of Orson Pratt.

Porter Rockwell was not as fortunate as Joseph. Because of his reputation, a reward was posted and by spring of 1843 it had climbed to three thousand dollars. As he was returning to Nauvoo in March, he stepped off a riverboat in St. Louis and walked right into the hands of a bounty hunter. Thus instead of rejoining the Saints in Illinois, Orrin Porter Rockwell was clamped in leg irons and taken to Independence for trial. When he brought forth witnesses who testified that he had been several miles away from Independence on the night of the attempted assassination of Lilburn Boggs, the charges that he had shot Boggs were dropped. But Porter Rockwell was wanted on other charges stemming from his part in the Mormon War. Tried on those charges, he was found guilty and was thrown into a filthy, unheated jail cell. He would not see freedom again for another ten months.

"Joy to the World" was included in the first LDS hymnbook. Today its lyrics have been slightly modified so that it is a carol of the first coming of the Savior. Originally it was a hymn of the Second Coming: "Joy to the world! the Lord *will* come!"

They were out behind Nathan's house, chopping wood for the winter. Nathan and young Joshua had started; then about half an hour later Matthew came to help, followed ten minutes after that by Benjamin, who had heard the noise of their axes. Together they now had almost a full cord cut and stacked up behind the big house that Nathan and Lydia had finally moved into during the summer. It was the fourth Saturday in November 1843, but the weather had turned quite warm again. The sun was full, and they worked in their shirt-sleeves. They were all sweating, and shortly after noon Nathan called for a break and they went to the well for a drink.

As they finished, Matthew stretched lazily and looked around. "I love these Indian summer days. Isn't this glorious?"

"It sure is," Nathan agreed. He took one last swig from the dipper and stepped back. "I could live with this right up through March."

"Uncle Matthew?" young Joshua said. "Why do they call it Indian summer?"

Nathan looked at Matthew and smiled. This was so like his son, always wanting to know things, always asking why.

"I don't know, Joshua," Matthew answered. "They just do."

"Well, actually," Benjamin cut in, "there is a reason."

"What?" young Joshua asked.

"There is?" Matthew said.

"Of course, and it's quite an interesting story, actually."

Nathan gave his father a suspicious look. "Are you making this up, Grandpa?" he asked.

Benjamin looked offended. "Of course not."

"What is it, Grandpa?" Joshua pressed.

"Well, when I was a boy, when you said Indian summer, it was a dreaded phrase."

Nathan cocked his head and gave his father a warning look. "Pa, don't you be pulling his leg, now." Which was one of Grandpa's favorite things to do.

Benjamin grinned mischievously. "You just listen, Brother Steed, and maybe you'll learn something too." He turned back to young Joshua. "You see, when the colonists first came to America and began to tame the frontier, it was a very dangerous time. The Indian wars were going on. Many settlers would be out on their own, miles from any town or village. Indians would attack these isolated homesteads and kill or capture the people."

He paused, but Joshua was hanging on his every word now. Nathan and Matthew were also listening with interest.

"Well, when winter came—and I'm talking about New England winters here, fierce, cold—it drove the Indians to their wickiups and their lodges. All the settlers were grateful. They loved winter for that reason alone. But if the weather suddenly turned warm again—not for just a day or two, but long enough for the snow and ice to melt—the Indians would come out again. Thus it came to be called . . ." He was looking at his grandson now.

"Indian summer!" young Joshua cried.

"Yes. And as I say, it was not something you looked forward to."

Seeing Nathan's dubious look, Benjamin quickly raised one hand up. "I swear. I can still remember as a little boy how the very mention of it struck fear into the hearts of some of those old settlers."

"That's really interesting, Grandpa," Joshua said without any trace of doubt. "I'm going to ask my teacher if I can tell that in school. Do you know any other interesting things like that?"

Benjamin tried not to look too pleased as he gave that question some thought. Then he smiled. "Well, I could tell you about a lake in the south part of Massachusetts with a name almost as long as the lake itself."

"Really?" Joshua said with wide eyes.

Matthew was laughing. "Now I've got to ask, Pa. Is this true too?"

Benjamin put his hands on his hips. "You scoffers. Of course it's true."

"What was it called, Grandpa?"

With a grin, Benjamin looked at his grandson. "Now, listen carefully, for this is how you have to say it. *Chargoggagoggman-chaugagoggchaubunagunganaugg.*"

"What?" young Joshua cried, his eyes like saucers. Matthew and Nathan started to laugh.

"Char-gogga-gogg, man-chau-gagogg, chau-buna-gunga-naugg," Benjamin intoned solemnly. "It's an Indian word, meaning, 'You fish on that side, I'll fish on this side, and no one fishes in the middle.'"

Matthew was laughing openly now. "How long did it take you to learn how to say that?"

There was a twinkle in Benjamin's eye. "Nigh on to a year, I reckon."

"Spell it, Grandpa."

"Oh, dear," he said, "I haven't done that for years. Let's see—"

Suddenly he stopped, his eyes going very wide. He was staring past young Joshua, eyes narrowing now to see better.

They all swung around to see what it was that had caught his attention. From where they were standing, they could see past the first house and into Granger Street. A tall figure was walking toward them, evidently coming from the direction of the south river landing. He was tall, dressed in a black coat and hat, and carried a suitcase in one hand. Nathan leaned forward, staring in astonishment. Then he gasped. "Will?"

At that moment Will Steed saw them as well. He was headed for his own home, which was across from Nathan's, but he immediately changed directions, raising one hand to wave.

"It's Will!" young Joshua cried, darting away.

"Oh, my word!" Benjamin breathed in astonishment. "It is Will. Will's home."

———— • ————

Benjamin had been right. Exactly one year before, as he and Nathan had stood with the family around the piano singing Christmas carols, he had said that he fully expected that the next Christmas Eve would find them in that same place doing exactly the same thing. And so it had been. The previous night they had had their traditional Christmas gathering for the children. Now, on Christmas Day, the adults were getting their turn. Joseph and Emma invited about fifty couples to the Mansion House on Christmas Day for a sit-down dinner. As the evening wore on, the party continued. In the largest room, the furniture had been moved out and members of the Nauvoo Legion band played music while sets of couples danced the quadrille. It was a merry and noisy crowd that spilled over into almost every room on the main floor.

When the Saints first came to Commerce in the early summer of 1839, Joseph and Emma had purchased an existing cabin on the south part of the great bend, right next to the river. They called it the Homestead and had lived there ever since. During that time, it had served as Church headquarters, family gathering place, hotel, and infirmary, as well as their residence. But the rapid growth of the Church was bringing Joseph Smith and the Mormons to the attention of the world, and more and more visitors were stopping off at Nauvoo. And the Homestead just wasn't adequate to house them.

With the temple taking the full efforts of the Saints, work on the Nauvoo House—the large hotel across the street from and a bit to the south of the Homestead—was stalled. In light of that, Joseph decided to build another residence, one that would better serve his family's needs and his requirements as frequent host until the Nauvoo House could be completed. Kitty-corner to the northeast from the Homestead, the "Mansion House," as it quickly came to be called, was a beautiful two-story frame building and had twenty-one rooms, including a spacious area for entertaining guests. Joseph and his family had moved in about the first of September. Emma Smith finally had a home worthy of the demands placed upon her as wife of the Prophet.

Nathan looked around. Through the hall and into the next room he could see his own family dancing now. He saw Matthew and Jenny march by, with Rebecca and Derek opposite them. In the far corner Kathryn watched from her wheelchair, with shining eyes, clapping in time to the music. Jenny had her head tipped slightly back, and her long hair bounced lightly as she moved. Matthew looked down at her, handsome and smiling too. Rebecca was trying to look appropriately sober, but Derek was exaggerating his steps so that he looked very much like an English dandy and finally she couldn't hold back—Nathan heard the burst of her laughter above the noise.

"Who would have guessed that of Derek?" Lydia said, smiling beside him.

"I guess the music brings out the boy in him," Nathan said. And then as he looked around at the crowded room filled with laughing, smiling, chattering people, he frowned slightly. "It would have been so good for Melissa and Carl to be here."

Lydia instantly sobered too. "I know. Melissa really wanted to come and see the Mansion House."

The music stopped and applause filled the two rooms. As the next group of dancers moved out and took their places, Nathan saw Will with a young woman on his arm preparing to join the next set. Nathan smiled. Will had been gone for almost sixteen months, and yet in many ways it seemed as if he had aged five years. He was fully a man now, mature, wise, slow to speak unless he had something to say. As the music started, Will remained quite serious, obviously concentrating on the step. The girl, a daughter of a recently arrived family from the East, was gazing up at him with rapturous eyes. There was little doubt about what she was feeling, but Will seemed not to notice.

Lydia was watching all of this too and laughed softly. "Will could about have his pick of any young lady in the city."

"Yes," Nathan agreed.

"Well, I could name you half a dozen that would like him to pick them," a deep voice said behind them.

They turned and Joseph and Emma were there. Joseph laid a hand on Nathan's shoulder and peered into the next room. "What a fine young man. The reports from the brethren in England about him were very complimentary."

"And he's so handsome," Emma said. "He looks so much like Joshua."

"I know," Nathan said. "It's hard to remember that they aren't actually father and son."

"By the way," Joseph said, "I was told that Joshua and Caroline are expecting another baby this summer."

"Yes," Lydia said, "about mid-July. They are so pleased. Little Charles will be four in February. Caroline was starting to worry that they might not be able to have another one."

"And how's my little namesake doing now?" Joseph said to Lydia.

"Doing fine." She grimaced. "Except he's the biggest little pig you've ever seen. I may have to run home here in a bit to feed him again, even though I fed him just before we left."

"And he's how old now?"

"He was born on the eighteenth of June," Nathan answered, "so just six months." The little boy they had lost to the ague in the summer of 1839 had been named Nathan Joseph Steed and they had called him little Nathan. That tragedy was now far enough in the past that Lydia had decided she wanted to use the name again when their baby turned out to be a boy. It was Nathan Joseph, only in this case they called him little Joseph instead.

"And how is Jessica doing with her new little one?" Emma asked. "I heard there were problems."

"There were for a time. The poor little thing wouldn't eat, kept throwing up whatever she did. But Solomon and Father Steed gave her a blessing and that seemed to do it. She's fine now. Cute as can be. She's just a month younger than little Joseph."

"That's wonderful," Joseph said. "I'm so glad they're happy."

"They are," Nathan agreed. "I've never seen Jessica happier. They wanted to come over here for Christmas so badly, but with the baby they thought maybe it was better if they didn't."

Emma turned, going up on her toes. "Oh, it looks like we need to get some more cake out."

"I'll help you," Lydia said.

As they moved away, Joseph looked around the room, his demeanor sobering. "I noticed that Carl and Melissa didn't come tonight. And of course no Joshua."

Nathan shrugged. "Carl told Melissa he didn't mind if she came, but she wouldn't come without him. If Caroline waited for Joshua to come with her, she'd never come to anything."

"I've noticed Melissa at worship services again from time to time."

"Yes, I think she really missed not coming. She's still troubled by everything, but she's trying. In fact, Rebecca thought it might be a good idea if they had Mary Fielding come over and talk with Melissa. To my surprise, Melissa's agreed to that."

"Really? That's good. There aren't many finer women than Mary Fielding Smith."

"I know. Melissa told Carl and he didn't seem to mind. I think he's hoping it won't change her mind, but you know Carl.

He's always been very open about her following her own conscience."

"Carl's a fine man," Joseph said earnestly. "A fine man. Benjamin told me that the rest of the family were finally told all that was going on."

Nathan nodded. "The adults, anyway. We decided they needed to know so they'd understand what had changed Melissa and Carl all of sudden, but we haven't told any of the children, not even Olivia or Kathryn."

There was a sadness now in Joseph's eyes. "Did you know that if Joshua sees me coming up the street, he'll turn and go the other way, or cross to the other side?"

That surprised Nathan and his face showed it.

"Oh, if he knows that I've seen him, he'll say hello, but even then I can feel the coolness in him. I don't think he's forgiven me for sending Will to England."

"Probably not, and yet he admits it was probably the best thing for Will. After being in England, Will has decided he doesn't want the life of a sailor."

"Yes, that's what he told me as well."

Just then a man and a woman came up to shake hands with Joseph. Nathan touched Joseph's arm. "I'd better find Mother and Father and see how they're doing." And with that, he moved off.

Hyrum and his wife, Mary Fielding Smith, were standing with Derek and Rebecca and Mary's sister, Mercy Fielding Thompson, in the parlor. Hyrum was only half listening. His eye was on the band leader in the next room. As the song finished and the dancers applauded, the leader turned his head, looking around for someone. Hyrum raised his hand and waved. When the man saw him he mouthed one word. "Now?"

Hyrum nodded, and the leader whispered something to the others and they started to set aside their instruments. Hyrum nodded in satisfaction, then turned to Mercy. "He's going to stop now for a minute or two. Are you ready?"

She brushed her hands against her dress, looking slightly flustered. "Yes, I suppose so."

Hyrum and Mercy moved out into the center of the room and Hyrum raised his arms. "Could I have your attention please?" he said loudly. He waited and the noise began to drop off. People shushed one another and started to move into the room where Hyrum and Mercy were. Some crowded into the hallway between the two rooms so they could hear better.

"Hyrum's got an announcement to make," Mary said to Rebecca. "I think you'll be surprised. And pleased."

"Brothers and sisters," Hyrum said in a loud voice, "if I could have your attention, we have a special announcement."

All eyes were on Hyrum now. He looked around, smiled, and then began. "Brothers and sisters, as you know, not long ago I was asked to serve on the building committee for the temple. Work there is progressing well, but there is still much to do."

That started heads nodding up and down.

"We've reached the point where we soon will need to purchase glass for the windows. And once we start on the roof, we are going to need many nails. Neither of those items comes cheaply, nor are they things which we can do ourselves, simply because we don't have sufficient funds."

Now there were murmurs of assent. Cutting stone and timber, hauling rock to the temple site, putting the great walls up—all of these were difficult, but the Saints could do them on their own. Making nails by hand in the blacksmith shops would be tedious and very expensive. Kegs of ready-made nails were also expensive. And glass—that was almost as precious as gold.

"I have worried much about this," Hyrum was saying, "and I suppose it became evident to my family that I was greatly weighed down by my anxiety. My sister-in-law, Mercy Thompson, has come up with a wonderful idea. She has discussed it with me and with Brother Joseph, and we give our hearty approval to the idea. I should like her to tell you what she has in mind." He turned to Mercy and nodded for her to begin.

"Thank you, Hyrum," she said, smiling at him.

The Fielding sisters were handsome women, dark, tall, with striking eyes and open features. Mercy was the younger of the two by six years, but the loss of her husband, Robert Thompson, two and a half years before had aged Mercy noticeably and so the sisters looked closer in age than they were. Both still spoke with their distinct British accents in clear, precise tones.

"Brothers and sisters," Mercy began, "Brother Hyrum is right. I think we have a wonderful idea, but it is not mine. I want to make that clear. Recently my sister and I were discussing what we might do to help out with the temple. We are as anxious as you are to see it completed so that we can have the blessings of the temple for all of us. I was so concerned about the matter that I began to earnestly seek to know from the Lord if there was anything I could do. One day, as I was praying, a most pleasant sensation came over me. And then the following words came into my mind: 'Try to get the sisters to subscribe one cent per week for the purpose of buying glass and nails for the temple.' "

That brought a low murmur from the group as the idea struck them. They began to nod their approval and whisper one to another. She waited until it was quiet again. "I went immediately to Brother Joseph and told him I had felt what I thought were the whisperings of the still small voice. He agreed and told me to proceed and the Lord would bless me. So next I came to Hyrum and we decided that we should make a public announcement."

She stepped back, blushing slightly as the applause broke out again.

Hyrum raised his hands until it quieted. "With this announcement, let the subscription begin. Here is a way for the sisters to have a direct part in building the house of the Lord. I know that many of you are in poverty. But this is only one cent per week, fifty cents per year. It is not much, but if we can get two thousand subscribers, in a year we shall have a thousand dollars. Mary and Mercy shall keep a careful record of all who subscribe and the amounts given. And I tell you, all of you who subscribe shall have your names recorded in the book of the Law of the Lord and you shall be blessed."

When Emma, Lydia, and Caroline finally came back out after replenishing the refreshment tables once again, they found Joseph and Nathan standing with Brigham Young, John Taylor, and Benjamin. Lydia saw Mary Ann in the next room in a circle with Matthew and Jenny, Derek and Rebecca, Hyrum, Mary, and Mercy, and excused herself to go and join them. Caroline did the same and went with her. Emma moved off to visit with their guests, giving Joseph a look that suggested that he shouldn't spend too long in one place either.

Benjamin watched her go, then turned to Brigham. "Have you had any response to your letters to the presidential candidates?"

Brigham nodded in disgust. "Henry Clay suggests we go to Oregon Territory. John C. Calhoun was not any better. The rest have said nothing."

"What is this?" Nathan asked.

Brother Taylor explained. "Back in November, in a meeting with the Twelve, Joseph asked us to consider writing to each of the five leading candidates for president of the United States to see where they stand on protecting our rights and getting us redress for what happened in Missouri."

"Really?" Nathan said, surprised at that.

"Yes," Joseph answered. "With the brethren's help, I wrote to each of them." He started ticking the names off on his fingers. "John C. Calhoun, Henry Clay, Martin Van Buren, Richard M. Johnson, and Lewis Cass."

"And Calhoun answered?" Benjamin said. "I hadn't heard that."

"If you can call it an answer," Brigham snorted. "He said that redress of the wrongs against the Saints does not come under the jurisdiction of the federal government."

"And he's right," John Taylor said dryly, "unless of course you believe that upholding the rights guaranteed by the Constitution of the United States of America comes under the jurisdiction of the federal government."

"Are you going to answer him back?" Nathan asked.

Joseph gave an emphatic nod of his head. "I am. I shall answer him in the strongest terms."

"Like what, Joseph?" Brigham asked.

"I shall remind him that his oath as a United States senator binds him to support the Constitution, which protects all creeds and religions alike. I should like to ask him that if his statement about our government having limited jurisdiction is true, then does he also agree that a state can at any time expel any portion of her citizens with impunity and the government can do nothing for them, because it has no power? Why not? For the renowned senator from South Carolina, Mr. J. C. Calhoun, says the powers of the federal government are so specific and limited that it has no jurisdiction over the case."

He stopped and grinned a little sheepishly. "As you can tell, Mr. Calhoun's brief note has got me considerably exercised."

"Rightly so," Brigham said. "Rightly so."

Joseph sobered again. "Well, I will tell you this much. We have petitioned the executive branch, we have petitioned the Congress, we have sought redress in the courts of this land, and we have received no satisfaction. In most cases, we have not even had so much as a sympathetic hearing. But I tell you, if the Latter-day Saints are not restored to all their rights and paid for all their losses, according to the known rules of justice, judgment, reciprocation, and common honesty, I say that God will come out of his hiding place and vex this nation with a sore vexation. Yea, the consuming wrath of an offended God shall smoke through the nation with much distress and woe."

A hush had now fallen over the room and every eye was on Joseph, whose eyes were blazing. "I will go further. I will go so far as to prophesy, by virtue of the holy priesthood vested in me and in the name of the Lord Jesus Christ, that if Congress will not hear our petitions, they shall someday be broken up as a government."

"My goodness, Joseph," Emma said a moment later as she pushed through the hushed crowd to stand by his side. "What have you done to get all these people so serious?"

He smiled and slipped an arm through hers. "Brigham and John got me talking politics," he said apologetically. "They should know better than that. But I shall desist now and—"

At that moment, there was a noise behind them, in the hallway that led to the front door of the Mansion House. "I beg your pardon, sir," a man's voice said loudly, "but this is a private party."

There was a scuffling noise, and a gruff voice shouted, "Let me pass!"

Jonathan Dunham, a colonel in the Nauvoo Legion and also one of Joseph's personal guards, hastily set his glass down and started pushing through the crowd toward the door. Joseph followed, the crowd falling back now to let them through.

"Sir!" The first voice sounded a little frightened now. "You can't go in there."

"Get outta my way!"

Suddenly into view in the hallway a man appeared. The city marshal, who had been standing watch at the door, was right behind him, grabbing at his coat, but the man shook him off easily. There was a gasp of horror from the assembled guests. The man looked like an apparition from some foul, dark place. He wore filthy buckskin breeches and shirt. There was a tattered hat, equally filthy, pulled down low over his eyes. His face was covered with a full beard, greasy and matted, leaving only dark, glittering eyes peering out from beneath the brim of the hat. What hair showed from beneath the hat was long, worn past the shoulders, and looked as though it hadn't been washed for months. He was weaving back and forth, his mouth partly opened, a small hole in a thicket of hair.

"It's a Missourian!" someone said, loud enough for all to hear.

"He's drunk!" cried another.

"Put that man from my house, Mr. Dunham," Joseph called over the heads of the people, who were shrinking back away from the intruder now as quickly as possible.

Dunham reached the hallway and blocked the man's path.

Joseph was right behind him. As Dunham reached for him, the man sidestepped him, thrust him aside, and stepped forward to stand directly in front of Joseph.

"Watch out, Joseph!" Nathan exclaimed. Beside him, Emma gave a low cry.

But Joseph needed no counsel. His hands shot out and he grabbed the man's arms, pinning them to his side in a powerful grip. Dunham and the marshal had both recovered and were coming in behind them. But Joseph had gone rigid. He was staring at the man. It was a startling contrast. There was Joseph, face smooth and clean shaven, well dressed in a long tailored coat and neatly creased trousers, with boots that were highly polished. And facing him was this filthy apparition of a man with wild eyes, long, matted hair, and thickly tangled beard. For a long moment, they just stared at each other, and then suddenly, the intruder began to laugh. It was soft and low, but in the shocked silence, it was such a startling sound, so totally unexpected, that everyone froze.

Joseph reared back, staring even more intently at the man. Then his hands dropped away, his eyes widening in stunned surprise. "Porter?" he gasped. "Porter Rockwell?"

Chapter Notes

Joseph and Emma Smith began moving into the Mansion House on 31 August 1843. The first reception was held a few weeks later. They did hold a dinner and Christmas party there for a large number of guests on Christmas Day (see *HC* 6:134–35).

The plan for the penny subscription fund was first proposed by Mercy Fielding Thompson, who said that it did come as a direct answer to her prayers. It was immediately endorsed by Joseph Smith and by Hyrum, who was by then a member of the temple building committee. Word spread quickly and the response from the sisters was immediate and consistent. Whether it was first announced at the Prophet's Christmas party is not clear, but the letter that the two sisters Mercy and Mary wrote to encourage their sister Saints in England to participate, along with Hyrum's accompanying endorsement, is dated 25 December 1843. (See Don Cecil Corbett, *Mary Fielding Smith: Daughter of Britain* [Salt Lake City: Deseret Book Co., 1966], pp. 155–57.)

By December 1844, one year later, they had received about five hundred dollars, or fifty thousand pennies. About that same time, when a note came due on some Church lands, the money was used to make a payment and protect the credit of the Church at a critical time. That money was replaced from other sources, and eventually the pennies donated by the women of the Church helped fund the purchase of both glass and nails for the house of the Lord. (See Corbett, *Mary Fielding Smith*, pp. 177–78.)

On 2 November 1843, in council with several members of the Twelve, Joseph discussed the idea of writing to potential candidates for the 1844 national elections. It was favorably received and two days later the letters were written. In a brief letter dated 2 December 1843, John C. Calhoun responded as here indicated. Joseph was so incensed at his answer that on 2 January 1844 he wrote a long and blistering reply. The things he says here in conversation are taken directly from that letter. (See HC 6:155–60.)

Joseph's prophecy about the calamities that would come upon the United States if they did not redress the Saints for the crimes committed against them in Missouri was actually given about nine months earlier than shown here (see HC 5:394).

Orrin Porter Rockwell was released from jail in Independence, Missouri, on 13 December 1843 after Joseph raised and sent two hundred dollars with Porter's mother to help pay for legal counsel. Warned that he might still be in danger, Porter traveled by foot and horseback night and day until he arrived in Nauvoo on Christmas Day, showing up at the party as described in this chapter. It was most likely on that same occasion that Joseph promised Rockwell that if he never cut his hair his life could not be taken. (See Richard Lloyd Dewey, *Porter Rockwell: A Biography* [New York: Paramount Books, 1986], pp. 73–77.)

Chapter Thirty-Four

Four days following the Christmas party at the Mansion House, a large group of men gathered together at the behest of Mayor Joseph Smith. With the population of Nauvoo now approaching about eleven thousand souls, the city council decided that the time had come to form a city police force. Joseph had asked his trusted friend and servant Jonathan Dunham to serve as the captain of this new force and requested that he submit a list of names of those who could possibly serve.

At four o'clock on the afternoon of Friday the twenty-ninth of December, the forty men who had been selected to be on the force, along with members of the city council, assembled in the lodge room of Joseph's store to be formally sworn into office and to receive their charge from the mayor of Nauvoo.

With mixed emotions, Benjamin Steed watched them come in. He was thrilled in a way, for here was a constabulary force that would raise their right hands and solemnly swear to uphold the Constitution of the United States, sustain the laws of the state of

Illinois, and enforce the ordinances of the city of Nauvoo. Since the first days of the restored Church, the Saints in general and Joseph Smith in particular had too often been at the mercy of merciless officers of the law. With this police force, that would not happen again.

But Benjamin was saddened in a way as well. For some months now, the various wards, or districts, in the city had been asking for a police force. The population was getting too large. There were too many questionable characters coming in off the riverboats. It wasn't safe to leave doors open any longer. Stock had been stolen. Personal property had a way of simply disappearing. Some of the rowdier youth were starting to pilfer things from stores and homes. Such things were discouraging enough; indeed, the council had been considering the move to create a police force for some time. But the thing which had finally motivated them to action was something of far graver consequence.

Porter Rockwell had brought back a very disturbing report from Missouri. He told Joseph that he had been told by a person friendly to the Church—Benjamin guessed it was Alexander Doniphan, Rockwell's lawyer—that someone from Nauvoo was conspiring with the Missourians to betray Joseph into their hands. For years now, the Missourians had been trying to arrest Joseph and extradite him back to Jackson County for trial. This past summer they had nearly succeeded, and it had taken a group of men from the Legion to intervene or Joseph would have been gone. And everyone—Mormon and Missourian—knew that if they ever got Joseph back to Missouri, he was a dead man.

What was most alarming about Rockwell's report was that this person (or persons) was someone in the highest councils of the Church. Joseph had shared that news with the city council two days before, and that is when they decided it was time to create the police force. Not only would they be charged with the responsibility to make the city a safer place to live, they would specifically be given the responsibility to protect the person of the mayor and prophet. It would be a great relief to Benjamin to see them sworn into office and out on the streets. Things were starting to get tense again, and he couldn't get memories of the days prior to the fall of Far West out of his mind now.

The ceremony was simple and short. The officers were sworn in with great solemnity; then Hyrum, who was conducting, invited Joseph to address them. Joseph arose with great dignity and walked to the front of the council room. Every eye was on him, and when he reached the small desk there, he met the gaze of every man, each in turn. Then he finally nodded.

"Brethren, this is a historic day, and my heart rejoices at what I see before me. As of this afternoon, we now have forty brethren who are sworn to uphold the law and protect our city. We have called forty of you so that there will be enough to always have some on duty while the others rest. I note that we have not done as some city councils have done. You have heard the expression, 'Set a rogue to catch a rogue.' That is what some cities have done. They have taken thieves out of the prisons and set them up as their policemen, thinking there is some truth in that adage. This is wrong and decidedly a foolish policy."

Benjamin watched him with open admiration. Joseph was not only a prophet of remarkable vision and spiritual power but also a wise and prudent civic leader, a man whom most of the men in the room had an unswerving loyalty toward because they loved him and knew that he loved them in return.

The men were rapt in their attention as he charged them with their duties, a charge that Benjamin suspected had not been heard in many cities across the country. He spoke of purity and integrity. He reminded them that they were to be at peace with all men, even the Missourians, so long as those men would mind their own business and leave the Saints alone. He warned them that they were not to cross over into Missouri under any circumstances, for they would be in grave danger. As proof of that, he briefly rehearsed the sufferings of Porter Rockwell and the injustices he had been forced to endure.

"And if the Missourians will not leave us alone," he concluded, "and you are compelled to strike, you must do it with decency and order." He counseled them to keep a strict account of the time they served as policemen, to have the ordinances of the city always in their possession so they could study and learn them. He warned them against bribery. He specifically charged them to ferret out the grogshops, the gambling houses, any brothels and to stamp them out. They were to watch for disorderly conduct, and he added, with a smile, that if anyone tried to resist them, they were to cuff that person's ears. That brought a smile to several faces, for Joseph had been known to do that a time or two with young boys who ran afoul of the laws of the city.

Then, just as Benjamin thought he was ready to conclude, Joseph paused. Now his eyes showed grave concern. "Now, brethren, there is one more thing that I would say to you."

The very gravity of Joseph's voice brought everyone forward slightly in their chairs.

"You need to know that part of your responsibility will be to keep your mayor safe. And when I say that, I am sure you will think first of the Missourians or some of our enemies down in Warsaw or over in Carthage. But I tell you with all soberness, my life is more in danger from some dough head of a fool in this city than from all my numerous and inveterate enemies abroad."

There was no sound, but suddenly the men were exchanging startled glances with one another.

"Yes," Joseph said wearily, "I am exposed to far greater danger from traitors among ourselves than from enemies without. Even though my life has been sought for many years by the civil and military authorities, the priests, and the people of the state of Missouri, make no mistake. If I can escape from the ungrateful treachery of assassins, I can live as Caesar might have lived. But Caesar had his Brutus, and I have pretended friends ready to betray me."

Now a murmur was rippling across the assembled men. Brutus, supposedly the closest and most trusted of Julius Caesar's associates, had led those who thrust their daggers through Caesar.

Joseph straightened, his voice ringing with challenge. "Know this, brethren. All the enemies upon the face of the earth may roar and exert all their power to bring about my death, but they can accomplish nothing, unless . . ." He stopped and his voice rose sharply, sending a little chill racing up and down Benjamin's back. "Unless they are helped by some who are among us. All the hue and cry of the chief priests and elders against the Savior could not bring down the wrath of the Jewish nation upon his head and cause his crucifixion, until Judas said unto them, 'Whomsoever I shall kiss, he is the man.' You remember that, and be on watch. Judas was one of the Twelve and dipped his hand with the Master in the dish. Yet it was through his treachery that the Savior was killed."

He stopped again, looking slowly around the room. His words hung there, as though he had emblazoned them with fire on the wall. *Traitors in our midst. Brutus and Caesar. Judas. Treachery.* There was not a sound now, not even a breath taken. Slowly the fire in Joseph died and his shoulders slumped.

"Brethren, how it pains me that I must tell you of this, but it is something you must know. I shall say it as plainly as I know how. *Brethren, we have a Judas in our midst.* Part of your duty will be to see that this man, these men, are not able to work their will. That is your charge."

"Easy," Joshua called as he pulled on the rope looped around the large ice block. "Not too fast."

Will stood up now, letting Savannah and little Charles give the block—easily four feet by four feet, and three to four inches thick—the last heave up onto the sleigh.

Joshua walked around, tying the rope down to the nubbing posts on each corner. He turned to Will. "You want to take this or do you want me to?"

"I'll do it."

"Can Charles and I ride on the ice, Papa?" Savannah said, her blue eyes peering out from beneath her woolen cap.

"Yes, Papa, please?" Charles piped in.

"It's slippery, Savannah. Will you hold on tight to the ropes?"

"Yes, Papa."

"I'll go slow, Pa," Will said.

"All right." Joshua reached down and lifted his little son, a three-foot wad of padding in his winter clothing. He set him right on the center of the top block and made sure his hands had a good hold on the rope. Then up went Savannah beside him. "Now, hold on, Savannah. And watch Charles close." Caroline would likely be very unhappy if she looked out the window and saw her two youngest riding atop the sleigh in this manner, but there really was very little danger. Even if they fell off, it was only about a three-foot drop to the snow.

Will climbed up and took the reins. He looked back once to make sure all was secure, then snapped the reins lightly. The horses leaned into their tugs and the sleigh moved away.

Joshua watched it for a moment, then went back down to the river. He picked up the long saw and walked out a few feet to where the water beneath the ice would be clear of reeds. He paused and looked up and down the river. For as far as he could see in either direction, men and boys were out cutting ice blocks. He raised his head and looked west. Across the river, the people from Montrose and Zarahemla were doing the same thing. Though later than usual, this was the first really hard freeze they had had, and people were anxious to replenish their supplies in the icehouses of the city.

As he lined up the saw blade with the previous cut and began a few preliminary strokes to start a clean track, he heard a sound behind him. He stopped and turned. A man had stepped out of the thicket of willows just down the bank from where Joshua's team had been standing a few minutes before. It was barely nine o'clock and the morning sun was directly behind them, and so Joshua couldn't see clearly who it was.

"Hey, Steed," a voice called. "Can we have a word with you?"

He squinted a little, recognizing now Doctor Robert Foster. He grunted to himself, half frowning. Foster had been there that day when John C. Bennett had tried to convince Joshua to throw in with him. Later, as Bennett spiraled out of control, Foster had backed away, claiming that he had been duped. He had been disciplined by the Church but was now back in good favor, or so Joshua had heard.

"Yes, what is it?"

"We'd like to talk with you if we can."

We? That was twice he had used that word. Joshua peered more closely and now he saw other men partially hidden in the thicket. Foster was motioning for him to come over now, looking over his shoulder to see if anyone close by was paying them any attention.

Joshua hesitated for a moment, then laid the saw back down again. As he approached the man, Foster melted into the brush and Joshua had to go in after him. Once there, he understood why. There were five other men with him, standing around, skulking in the thick growth, staying out of sight. Four he knew well enough to call them by name. The fifth he recognized but knew only slightly. The first two were the Higbee brothers, Francis and Chauncey, who had also been there that day with Joshua and Bennett. According to what Carl had found out, these two had been right up to their necks in Bennett's little scheme for sweet talking women into submitting to them. Their father, Judge Elias Higbee—who had died just the summer before—had been an honorable man and a close friend of Joseph Smith's, but these two . . . Joshua looked away. The other two were brothers as well, but this was a surprise for Joshua to see them associating with Foster and the Higbees. William Law was Second Counselor in the First Presidency. He had replaced Hyrum when Joseph had called Hyrum to be Patriarch to the Church, whatever that happened to be. His brother, Wilson Law, had replaced John C. Bennett as major general in the Nauvoo Legion and was second in command only to Joseph.

The fifth man, William Marks, was also a Church leader. Caroline talked about him sometimes. He was president of the Nauvoo Stake, a geographical division within the Church. That didn't put him in the general Church leadership, but just beneath it.

Foster seemed to read Joshua's thoughts. "I brought these men with me so you'd know what kind of support we have, Steed. There's also about two hundred more of us. Other members of the stake presidency, high council members, officers in the legion, a member of the city council."

"Support for what?" Joshua asked bluntly. He knew what had been going on in the city the last few days. The previous evening, during their traditional Sunday night supper at his father's house, Benjamin had given the family a full report.

"Look, Steed," Foster said, "I'll come straight to the point. I understand you and your son are leaving tomorrow to go back up to Wisconsin and check on your lumber operation. We wanted to talk to you before you left."

"Then talk."

"As you know, for a long time a group of us have suspected that Joseph Smith has fallen from grace, that he no longer speaks for God, that he is a fallen prophet."

"Foster," Joshua cut in, "by my definition you can only be a fallen prophet if you've been a true one. I don't believe Joseph Smith is a prophet. I never have. I really don't give one tinker's damn for the Church and all their foolishness, so if you're here to enlist my help in that, you're wasting your time."

Chauncey Higbee's face darkened and he muttered something to his brother, but Foster went on blandly, undisturbed by Joshua's sharpness.

"I am well aware of your feelings, Steed, but I would submit that you do have an interest in seeing Joseph discredited. I think it might go some way in influencing your wife and children in their feelings toward the Church."

"You leave my wife and children out of this," Joshua growled, but his eyes belied his words. This could be of interest to him after all.

Foster saw it and went on smoothly, and more confidently

now. "We are making plans to expose Joseph. When the time comes, we could use the support of influential nonmembers. A man of your reputation and position could be very . . . umm, how shall I say it? . . . helpful."

"I'm not sure of that," Joshua said, "but I'm listening. Tell me what you are thinking."

Now William Marks stepped forward. He was a smaller man, with a pinched face and hard, narrow eyes. "We need you to tell people that our lives are in danger, that Joseph Smith is trying to have us assassinated."

Foster swung on Marks, cursing, but the damage had been done. Joshua laughed right out loud. "You think you're in danger because a few policemen built a fire outside your house trying to keep warm?"

"It was a warning," Marks half snarled. "I know the police are denying any such intent, but I'm telling you, it was a warning to me."

"Shut up, Marks," Foster hissed. "We're not here for that." Marks flushed angrily, but Foster swung back to Joshua. "You know about all of this?" Then he snapped his fingers. "Of course, your father is on the city council."

"Yes, that's right. He told me all about it last night." Joseph's call to the police to watch for a traitor in their midst had immediately triggered a surprising reaction among Joseph's enemies. Evidently one of the policemen had guessed who the traitor might be and began telling people about it. In a matter of hours, surmise had become truth, and sympathizers were warning the Fosters, the Laws, and Marks that not only was Joseph on to them, but he had also ordered their assassination.

"You don't believe there's anything to it, do you?" Wilson Law sneered.

Joshua snorted in disgust. "A couple of policemen build a small fire outside one of your houses and you go all weak in the knees and are sure your life is forfeit? No, I don't believe that."

Marks was sputtering now. "That's not true! They were going

to kill me." Chauncey Higbee stepped in front of him, his face a mask of anger now. He grabbed Foster's arm. "I told you he wouldn't listen. Let's get out of here."

Foster shook him off. "Just shut up, all of you." He whirled back around. "You think what you like, Steed, but I'm telling you, Joseph Smith is trying to silence us. He won't succeed. There are too many of us now. We have close to two hundred in the Church who are with us in this. We know too much. We are too great a threat to him. And if we can't stop this abuse of power, then your life is in danger too. How long do you think they'll tolerate non-Mormons among them? They're after ultimate power, Steed. *Ultimate power.* And that includes power over life and death."

"I'm terrified," Joshua said dryly.

"Maybe that's why you gave your wife and kids permission to be baptized," William Law sneered. "That way you'll be sure to be safe."

William Law was a large and powerful man, but that never entered Joshua's mind. His hand shot out and grabbed the man's shirtfront. He yanked him in close, and shoved his face up next to his. "What did you say?" he asked in a menacing whisper.

Foster leaped forward, shoving himself between Joshua and Law. "He didn't mean that, Steed. He's just upset." He jerked around. "Did you, William?"

Law was furious, but he finally shook his head. "I'm sorry, Steed. It was a foolish thing to say."

Joshua let him go and stepped back, still breathing hard. "Let me tell you something, Foster. You know how I feel about the Church. But you're making a big mistake if you underestimate Joseph Smith. I think he's a fool and a charlatan when it comes to religion, but he's also a strong leader. He's a good man, smart as any man I know. He's kind and caring. He knows his people."

Chauncey Higbee was gaping at him. "You sound like one of his followers."

"I'll tell you this," Joshua shot right back. "If it weren't for this whole thing on religion and plural marriage, I could be

Joseph Smith's best friend. I admire the man. Not the prophet, but the man. Only a fool can't see Joseph Smith for what he is— a powerful leader, a brilliant strategist. Come on!" he said in dis- gust. "Do you think he's come to all of this"—he waved an arm in the direction of Nauvoo—"by being a fool? If you don't take the measure of your enemy, you're going to have your tail whipped."

"We know what we're up against," Foster muttered sullenly.

"Do you? Shall I tell you something, Foster? Something you don't know?"

"What?"

"You know what Joseph called you people when he gave the policemen their charge from the mayor? He called you 'dough heads.' Do you want to know why? Because at that point he didn't know who the traitors were. He had no names."

At the flash of astonishment in Foster's eyes, Joshua laughed contemptuously. "That's right. Rockwell was told that someone here was trying to betray Joseph, but . . ." He paused for effect. "He didn't get any names."

"Or so he says," Foster muttered.

"You want to know what Joseph is saying now, after your friends here started bawling to the city council that they had been unjustly accused and that their lives were in danger?" Joshua said, boring in.

"What?" It came out with complete insolence.

"Joseph's asking questions like this. 'Why is it when I say we have a traitor in our midst, but name no one, William Law and William Marks start squealing like pigs in a panic?' In fact, here's a direct quote from Joseph, according to my father. 'Is it that the wicked flee when no man pursueth? Could it be that it is the hit bird that always flutters?'"

Joshua hooted derisively. "Talk about dough heads! At first no one wanted to believe Rockwell's report that someone in the highest councils was betraying Joseph. It was too wild. Too improbable. And now? You have managed to convince the whole city that it's true. Well done, I say! Well done!"

"Listen, you—"

Joshua's face was a cold mask now. "No, you listen. I'm not sure I'd want to be part of this even if I thought you could succeed, but I always make it a rule of thumb to stay away from fools." With that, he spun on his heel and walked out of the trees.

Francis Higbee started to swear loudly, hoping Joshua would hear him. Chauncey gave one expletive and spun around. He moved away in the opposite direction, thoroughly disgusted with the whole farcical situation. But Foster ignored them both. He was still staring at Joshua's disappearing figure. The two Law brothers came forward to stand beside him.

"There's no way you're going to get him to throw in with us," Wilson said. "Chauncey's right about that part at least."

"It'll never happen," William Marks said in disgust. "His whole family are Mormons. He claims he's no lover of the Church or Joseph Smith, but he isn't going to turn against his own kin either."

Foster swung on them, angry at their stupidity. "You still don't see it, do you?"

"See what?" Wilson Law said.

"Joshua Steed is known up and down this river. He's got friends from St. Louis to La Crosse. A lot of people respect him. We need that kind of influence."

"Well, let's offer him a dollar or two and see if he'll come in with us," Francis said with sneering sarcasm.

Now it was Foster who was disgusted. "He's right. You are dough heads! Don't you see? We don't have to turn Steed against the Church. He's already there. All we've got to do is give him a good reason to join up with us."

"And just how do we do that?" William Law asked.

"I don't know," Foster admitted, turning to where they could see through the willows that Joshua was back out on the ice, cutting the next block. "But I'm going to give it a lot of thought. You can count on that."

Mary Ann stopped as they reached the door of Caroline's house. "Are you sure about this, Melissa?" she asked, watching her daughter with concern. "You know that none of us want to press something on you that you are not comfortable with. They all wanted me to make sure you understood that, especially Mary."

Melissa hesitated for a moment, then nodded. "I'm sure, Mama. I would like to hear what Mary has to say, but . . ." Her head dropped slightly. "I don't think it will make any difference."

Mary Ann watched her daughter, thinking back across the years. Mary Ann had given birth to ten children—six girls and four boys. But Melissa and Rebecca were the only girls who had survived, so in a way, Melissa was Mary Ann's first daughter. Melissa would celebrate her thirty-third birthday in about four weeks, and she was now the mother of four children and in the first stages of expecting her fifth. Maturity and motherhood had been very good to her, Mary Ann thought as she studied her. She was still a very lovely woman.

"Melissa, all that Lydia and Caroline and Rebecca want for you is to help you see how it's possible to accept the doctrine of plural marriage. That's all. If you can't accept that, they won't love you one bit less. And neither will I."

"I know, Mama, and I appreciate that. They've all been so good not to try and push me faster than I wanted to go." She sighed. "I want to understand. I want to feel like I used to feel before we went to Brother Kimball's house. Why can't I?"

"Maybe this tonight will help," Mary Ann said. She raised her hand and knocked on the door.

There were sudden tears in Melissa's eyes. "I've always been the weak one in the family when it comes to believing, Mama."

"That's not true!" Mary Ann cried.

Melissa smiled sadly. "I love you, Mama. Don't ever give up on me."

Mary Ann squeezed her hand. "You know I won't."

They heard footsteps, then Caroline opened the door. Seeing the tears, she just nodded and held the door open more widely so that they could come in.

———•———

Olivia had the children gathered around her in the main room of Lydia's house. Emily, at eleven, was "far too old" to need a baby-sitter for herself, so she was helping out by rocking little Joseph, who was nearly asleep. Young Joshua sat on the floor beside Olivia, also ready to provide what help she needed. Savannah and Elizabeth Mary sat together holding hands. There was only fourteen months' difference in their ages and these cousins had long been the best of friends. Josiah, now three, and Charles, almost four, likewise sat together.

"What stories would you like to hear tonight?" Olivia asked. She had promised them that once they had washed the dishes, read their scriptures, and said their prayers, she would read them whatever stories they wanted.

Four hands shot up.

"Elizabeth Mary?"

" 'The Emperor's New Clothes.' "

Olivia's face fell. "I'm sorry, Lizzie, but I didn't bring the fairy tale book. How about something from the Bible? Noah's ark, perhaps?"

"No!" Savannah cried, ready to stand firmly by her cousin. " 'The Emperor's New Clothes.' That's our favorite story."

"I thought David and Goliath was your favorite story," young Joshua laughed.

"It is," she replied, the impish eyes beneath the red hair shining with determination. "But the Emperor is my very, *very* favorite."

"Yes," Charles chimed in. "Tell us that one, Livvy."

"Yes, yes, yes!" the others were chanting now.

"Well, I don't have the book. I'll just have to tell it as best I can."

"No," Savannah said, her voice pleading now. "You've got to read it, Livvy. I'll go get it."

"No, Mama is having a meeting and we can't disturb her."

"Then you go get it," Savannah implored. "Please."

Olivia looked at young Joshua, who grinned. "I'll tell them the story of David and Goliath while you go get it."

"All right," she said, which won her an enthusiastic round of cheers.

She stood and went to the hallway for her coat. "I'll be right back."

———•———

There were four women waiting for Melissa and Mary Ann when they walked into Caroline's parlor. Caroline and Lydia sat in two armchairs. Rebecca and Mary Fielding Smith were on the sofa. Caroline had set two more chairs so they faced the sofa, and Mary Ann and Melissa sat down in them.

Melissa was in no mood for small talk or delaying this further. She immediately turned to Mary Smith. "Well, shall we start? My family tells me that you have things to say that might help me better understand all that is going on."

"I should just like to say one thing first," Mary Ann spoke up.

They all nodded and waited.

"Melissa, we just want you to know that accepting this has not been an easy thing for any of us. It is probably the most severe test of our faith any of us have known. But the thing which has made the greatest difference to us is knowing the feelings of some of the women who have been asked to live the law. Especially Vilate Kimball. You were there that night. You know what it was that finally convinced her that this was truly a principle from God and not just Joseph's doing."

"Yes," Melissa said quietly.

"We"—she waved at Rebecca and Caroline and Lydia—"we feel that Mary has a unique perspective as well. If it can—"

Melissa had turned to Mary Smith. "Has Hyrum taken another wife?" she asked quietly.

Mary flinched a little but did not look away. "Yes." There was a long silence; then she spoke again. "I would like to tell you about that in a few minutes, Melissa, but I would like to say some other things first."

———•———

Remembering her mother's admonition that she didn't want to be disturbed, Olivia went in the back door, opening it with the greatest of care. She tiptoed past the hallway, where she could clearly hear them talking, then went up the stairs to her bedroom, avoiding the places where she knew the floor would creak. In a moment she had Hans Christian Andersen's book of fairy tales under her arm. With the same care, she came back down the stairs. She was just passing the hallway when she heard Melissa's question: "Has Hyrum taken another wife?"

Olivia stopped, staring, not sure she had heard it right. Then came the answer. Olivia was thunderstruck. Any thoughts of fairy tales or reading to the children were forgotten. She stood riveted to the spot, too dumbfounded to even feel guilty about the fact that she was eavesdropping.

———•———

"I would like to say two things to begin with," Mary Fielding was saying. "The first is that just because you are having difficulty accepting it, Melissa, doesn't mean you are a person with no faith."

"Well, that's how I feel," Melissa answered. "I look at Caroline and Lydia, Rebecca, even Jenny. I know it wasn't easy for them, but it hasn't knocked them clear off balance as it has me."

"Do you know who it has knocked off balance?" Mary asked quietly.

"Who?"

"William Marks and Austin Cowles, two members of the Nauvoo stake presidency. Leonard Soby of the high council. William Law of the First Presidency." She let that sink in, then added one more name. "And Emma."

"And yet, Mercy had an unshakeable testimony of Joseph's calling. She knew he was a servant of the Lord and that if she rejected his counsel she risked fighting against God. And then there was the matter of her husband. Joseph told her that when Robert appeared to him, he came with such power that it made Joseph tremble."

She was staring past Melissa now, and her eyes were shining. "Joseph married them in August. As Robert had requested, Mercy was married to Hyrum for time, but not for eternity. Hyrum had to make a covenant as part of the marriage ceremony that in the morning of the first resurrection he would deliver Mercy up to Robert Blashel Thompson, along with whatever offspring had come of their union."

Mary had finished all she wanted to say. After a long pause, she looked at Melissa. "That's it. I don't know that saying anything more will make any difference. I don't know if you believe all of it. All I can say to you is that I know it is true. Otherwise, I would never have accepted what has happened."

Just then there was a noise out in the hallway and Caroline raised one hand.

"What?" Melissa asked, turning.

"I thought I heard the back door close," Caroline said. She got to her feet, walked out into the hallway, and stood there for a moment. Everything was quiet now. Finally she turned back with a shrug. "I guess it was just my imagination," she said.

When Olivia stepped back inside Lydia's house, she was greeted with a chorus of disapproval. "What took you so long, Livvy?" Savannah said petulantly.

"Yeah," Emily said. She no longer had the baby in her arms. He had fallen asleep and she had put him down some minutes before. "Joshua has told us five Bible stories already."

She looked at them, her eyes vacant; then finally she raised the book in her hand. "I . . . I couldn't find it," she mumbled.

"Read us 'The Emperor's New Clothes,'" Charles exclaimed. "We've been waiting."

Olivia turned and looked at her cousin. "Could you read it to them, Joshua?" she asked. "I . . . I've got a bad headache."

"Sure." He got up and took the book; then he peered more closely at her. "You don't look very good, Olivia. Maybe you'd better go lie down."

She nodded numbly. "Yes, that's a good idea." And without another word she walked upstairs and threw herself on Lydia and Nathan's bed.

Chapter Notes

In his speech to the new police force given on 29 December, Joseph did not give any names when he told them there was a Judas in their midst. But his speech sent the dissidents, who up to that time thought they were operating without Joseph's knowledge, into a panic, which in turn brought some of their activities to light. After the city council heard testimony on both sides about the accusations that Joseph had charged the police to kill William Law and William Marks, the conclusion was that it was speculation and surmise, along with a healthy dose of gossip, that led to the false accusations. The whole affair did serve to confirm Joseph's fears that he did have enemies in the highest councils of the Church. (See HC 6:166–70.)

It should be noted that as a result of his disaffection, William Law was dropped from the First Presidency during the early part of January 1844.

In the summer of 1843, while Joseph was telling some of the brethren of the difficult time Emma was having with plural marriage, Hyrum asked Joseph to write the revelation down for him. Though much of it had been received some years before, Joseph had not put it into writing for fear that it might fall into the wrong hands. Hyrum said to him, "Joseph, if you will write the revelation on celestial marriage, I will take it and read it to Emma. With the revelation, I think I can convince her that it is true." Joseph demurred. "Hyrum, you don't know Emma like I do." But Hyrum was certain he could do it. "The doctrine is so plain," he said, "I can convince any reasonable man or woman of its truth, purity, and heavenly origin." Joseph then had William Clayton, his scribe, come in and he dictated the revelation to him word for word. When Joseph was done, he had it read back to him and pronounced it correct. With that, Hyrum went to Emma and tried to reason with her.

Hyrum returned saying that he had never had such a tongue-lashing in his life. Later, Emma coaxed the copy of the revelation from Joseph and then tore it up. By then, Newel Whitney had made another copy, but Joseph said that the revelation had been so emblazoned in his mind that he knew it by heart and could repeat it at any time. (See Danel W. Bachman, "A Study of the Mormon Practice of Plural Marriage Before the Death of Joseph Smith" [master's thesis, Purdue University, 1975], pp. 161, 205–6; *Restoration*, pp. 525–26.)

The description given here of Hyrum's marriage to Mercy Fielding Thompson, his sister-in-law, after Joseph had been visited by her deceased husband, is based on testimony given by both sisters (see Don Cecil Corbett, *Mary Fielding Smith: Daughter of Britain* [Salt Lake City: Deseret Book Co., 1966], pp. 152–54; Bachman, "A Study of Plural Marriage," pp. 123, 187).

Olivia Mendenhall Steed was mature beyond her sixteen years in many ways. She was a woman now, and a beautiful one at that. She turned heads wherever she went, and there was more than one young man in Nauvoo who lay awake at nights with visions of her face before him. But in other ways she was still a young girl. She was the daughter of one of the most prosperous men in western Illinois. Even back in Georgia, when her natural father died and left her mother a widow with two children, Olivia had lived above the normal standard of living for most girls of her age. To say that she was spoiled would be far too strong, for Caroline went to great lengths to see that she kept a balanced view on life. But there was no denying that she was pampered. She had never gone to bed hungry. She had never lived in circumstances where everyone—men, women, and children—rose at first light and worked the fields until dark just so that the family could survive.

Had she been raised in such circumstances—an experience which can give children a natural maturity by the time they reach puberty—she might have made some different decisions, chosen a more rational way of coping with the shock she had received that night standing furtively in her mother's hallway. But she had not been raised that way, so in her turmoil her emotions took over. She knew that she had done something terribly wrong in listening to a forbidden conversation, but instead of coming forth and confessing her transgression to her mother, which would have given Caroline a chance to clear up any misconceptions, she withdrew into herself. And as she lay awake night after night, or stared at nothing in the day, the questions multiplied like puddles after a heavy rain.

Why hadn't she been told about plural marriage? Everyone else in the family seemed to know about it except for her. She was certain that most members of the Church didn't know either, so why did her family know? Were they part of it? What were they trying to hide? Was that why her father had been so bitterly opposed to their joining the Church? Was her mother being asked to be someone else's wife? Who else in the family was living this law? Nathan? Derek? *Matthew?* That one really caused her to blanch. Kathryn was right there in the home. Had Matthew now married both Jenny and Kathryn? Now Olivia better understood why Melissa had become so distant and strange during this last year and a half. Had she been asked to be someone else's wife and refused? If so, that would explain why Carl didn't come to Church anymore.

On and on the questions went, and she became more and more depressed as the specters danced in her mind. And so finally, as young girls often do, Olivia, after extracting a vow of absolute secrecy, confided in Amy Appleby, her best friend. Amy was seventeen now, and though she was a good girl and a wonderful friend, she was also at that stage where young men and love and courtship filled her mind with fleecy clouds of romantic fantasies. Amy's horror at Olivia's revelations about plural wives knew no bounds. That night, still reeling, Amy told her mother everything, swearing her to absolute secrecy as well.

Unfortunately, Liza Appleby was married to John David Appleby. And John Appleby was good friends with Leonard Soby, a member of the Nauvoo Stake high council. Soby didn't even let Appleby finish his story. He took him straight to Wilson Law, who immediately called his brother William and Robert Foster.

When Appleby was done retelling the story, a general rage broke out among the group. Hyrum Smith, long thought to be a moderating influence for Joseph, was clearly right in the middle of it all too. Now what did they do? What more evidence did they need? But Foster, with his usual cunning, let them rage on around him while he half closed his eyes and withdrew into his thoughts. Finally, William Law noticed that Foster wasn't in on the conversation.

"Foster, what do you think about all this?"

Foster straightened, smiling triumphantly as his mind worked it over. He turned to Appleby. "John, here's what I want you to do. You go back to that daughter of yours. Don't let her know you've told anyone else about this. She told your wife, your wife told you, and that's as far as it went. But you tell her that she needs to get that Steed girl to go to Joseph Smith."

"Are you crazy?" Wilson Law exploded. "That will just warn Joseph."

Foster ignored him. "Tell her to tell the Steed girl that only Joseph can give her the counsel she needs. That's important."

William Law was suddenly giving Foster an admiring look. "Yes, he's crazy," he said to his brother. "Crazy like a fox."

Foster bowed slightly, accepting the praise as his due.

"I don't get it," Wilson said. Soby and Appleby were also perplexed.

"Tell Amy," Foster went right on, "to be sure and find out when—and I mean *precisely* when—this Olivia plans to go see Joseph. And have Amy tell you immediately. That's very important. Very important."

"All right," said Appleby.

Now Wilson Law had it too. "I see."

"Look," Soby suggested, thinking he understood, "if you want to get at Joshua Steed, why not just tell him that his wife has been preaching plural marriage right in his own home? That'll do it for sure."

Foster rubbed his hands gleefully. "Oh, brethren, we can do better than that. Much, much better." He turned again to Appleby. "Remember, as soon as you learn when it is that the Steed girl plans to go to Joseph, you come straight to me, so we can be ready."

———◆———

"Sister Emma?"

Emma Smith was behind the counter in the store sorting through a box of buttons. There were two women across the room looking at bolts of material, but other than that, the store was empty. She looked up, then immediately smiled. "Hello, Olivia."

"Good afternoon. Uh . . . I was supposed to meet Brother Joseph here today." She looked around. "Is he here?"

Emma laughed lightly. "Well, not here. He's upstairs in his office." She pointed to the back of the store. "Just go up those stairs."

"Thank you."

"You're welcome." Emma turned back to the box and continued her sorting. But she had just begun when the front door to the store opened and three men came in. She frowned. It was Leonard Soby, John Appleby, and Francis Higbee. Emma did not know everything that was going on, but she was aware enough to know that these three men were trying to cause trouble for her husband and the Church.

"Good afternoon," Soby boomed.

"Hello," she said with a cool nod.

They came around the barrels and boxes that filled the inside of the room. "I'm looking for a good wood plane," Appleby said, pushing forward to stand directly in front of her. The other two came up behind him. Higbee leaned on the counter and looked at her with open admiration. He had always found Emma to be a handsome woman. He also knew that she intensely disliked him and that his boldness unnerved her.

"The tools are over there," she said, pointing down the counter to one wall.

"Could you show me?" Appleby asked innocently.

With a shrug, she nodded and started forward. Behind her, Higbee raised an arm and motioned frantically. At the back of the store, the door opened a crack, and then Robert Foster slipped inside. Bent over in half a crouch, he made his way up the stairs and was soon out of sight.

Appleby, who had been following Emma, suddenly stopped and looked at Higbee, who nodded. "On second thought," Appleby said, "I'd like to look at some material for my wife, please."

Joseph listened to Olivia for almost a quarter of an hour and said virtually nothing. Occasionally he would ask a clarifying question, or murmur an assent to something Olivia said, but for the most part he just listened. He was pleased to note that as she got it all out that her voice gradually calmed and her demeanor became less troubled.

When she was finally finished, he sat back, pursing his lips and making a steeple of his fingers. "Thank you, Livvy," he said kindly. "I'll bet it wasn't easy for you to come and see 'Brother Joseph,' was it?"

She smiled back at him, looking so much like Caroline that it was eerie. "No, it wasn't."

"Well, I'm glad you did. The first thing I want you to do when you get home is sit down and tell your mother everything."

Her face twisted with brief pain but also relief. "All right."

"She'll understand. Your mother is a wonderful woman, Livvy."

"I know."

"Now, let me say a word or two about what you heard. But before I do, I must ask something of you, Livvy."

"All right."

"I wish I could reveal all I know to the Saints, but they are not ready to receive it yet. Sometime in the future this will be spoken from the housetops, but for now, we must be wise. Therefore, in a very real way I am about to put my life in your hands by telling you some of these things. So I must have your word that you will not speak to anyone else besides your mother about what we discuss here today. Do you understand?"

"Yes, Brother Joseph. You have my word on it."

"You can't speak of it to anyone—not your dearest friends, not even Will or your father. Not unless I release you from this vow. If you feel that you cannot keep this promise, then we shall finish now and you will be free to go. I will not respect you any less for not wishing to take the burden of such a vow, for a burden it will be. Agreed?"

Olivia was greatly impressed that Joseph would even consider sharing such important things with her. And she found his trust strangely exhilarating. "I swear," she finally said.

"Good." Now he sat back, obviously relaxing. "I'm not going to go into all of how this came to be. Your mother can tell you that if she chooses. But since you know about the general principle now, I must say I'm glad you heard it from whom you did. Mary Fielding Smith is an admirable woman, strong in her devotion to the Lord."

Olivia nodded.

"And to have your grandmother and your mother and your aunts there too. You are blessed to be part of a wonderful family, Livvy."

"I know."

He leaned forward slightly, suddenly quite earnest. "Do you believe what Mary said about Robert Thompson coming to me?"

She bit her lip, then nodded. "I guess so."

"Olivia, I want you to hear it from my own lips. Robert

Thompson did come to me from the spirit world and told me to have my brother marry Mercy Thompson. I testify to you that this is true. It is not something I would lie about." He was watching her closely now. "Do you believe me?"

Now there was no hesitation. "Yes, I do, Brother Joseph."

He visibly relaxed. "Bless you for your faith, Livvy. There are many who think I am lying about all this, that for selfish reasons I say God has commanded me to do this thing. That, or they think I am being deceived by Satan."

"I don't think that," Olivia said, surprised to realize she really meant it. It had done much for her to talk it all through with Joseph, and now his kindly face and positive manner were greatly reassuring.

"I don't know all of the reasons why God has asked this of us, but I am certain of one thing. It is a great test of our faith and obedience. And it is proving to be a great sieve, separating out the wheat from the chaff."

"I—" Her head dropped. "I have to admit that I doubted, Brother Joseph. When I first heard them talking about it, I really wondered if you were still a prophet."

"I understand. If it is of any consolation, you should know that I greatly questioned my own standing with God. God had to be very direct with me before I would obey him."

"Will I ever be asked to let my husband—when I have a husband—take another woman?" she asked, sounding very much now like a little girl.

"I don't know, Livvy," he answered frankly. "I have been surprised at times by those whom the Lord commands me to bring into this order. So far, only a very small number have been asked to live this law. Perhaps a greater test for you would be to be asked to be the second or third wife to someone else."

She rocked back, clearly shocked by that thought. Over the past few days, she had mused painfully over what it would mean to share her future husband with someone else, but she had never considered the possibility that someone else might have to share her husband with Olivia. "But—"

Joseph's eyes were infinitely gentle now. "Only God knows what will test your faith to the greatest, Livvy. What if I were to come to you right now and say, 'Olivia Steed, you are to be wife to Heber C. Kimball, or Brigham Young, or John Taylor'?"

She paled. "I . . . I don't know," she stammered.

Joseph's face immediately softened. "Please," he said quickly, "I'm just using this as an example. Right now the Spirit whispers that you are not expected to live this law. Nor," he said as an afterthought, "are any of your family going to be asked to live it right now."

Her relief was so real she could almost taste it. "That's good," she breathed.

"But do you see what I'm saying, Olivia? That is what I mean by a test. Ask your mother about the test that Heber and Vilate Kimball had to face. Tell her I said that she is free to share that with you. Then you'll begin to sense what I mean. And though you are still young, you must prepare yourself to respond to whatever God may ask of you, whether that's plural marriage or some other thing."

"I understand," she said, a little shakily. "I don't know if I'm strong enough."

"Olivia," he said in great earnestness now, "from this very day I want you to start praying for two things every night and morning."

"What?"

"First, I want you to ask God to give you faith. I don't know what all the future holds for us, but I know it is going to take great faith. Ask your Heavenly Father to strengthen you so you can face whatever comes. Second, I want you to ask your Heavenly Father if I am truly his servant. Not just *was* I his prophet, but *am* I now? Do I still speak for him?"

"I . . . I think I understand, Brother Joseph."

"Good." He stood, and she stood too. He walked to the door and opened it. As she went to leave, he smiled down at her.

"All that matters is that we do God's will, Livvy. And when we do, he blesses us. Even when it seems like he is making our lives so painful we can hardly bear it, he only designs to bring us greater happiness and joy. That is his whole purpose, to make his children happy."

She sighed, feeling as though the weight of a thousand days had been lifted from her. "Thank you, Brother Joseph. I'm glad I came to see you."

On impulse, he held out his arms and she stepped forward. He gave her a quick hug, then kissed her on the top of her head. "I hope my Julia turns out to be just like you, young lady."

"Thank you, Joseph," she said, stepping back. "And I hope someday that I can learn to have even half as much faith as you do."

He laughed. "Let me tell you something, Olivia. If my enemies think I claim to be perfect, they are fools. I am but a rough stone. The sound of the hammer and chisel was never heard on me until the Lord took me in hand. And it has been a painful process at times."

"Really? Even for you?"

"Even for me. Not long ago I told the Saints that I am like a huge, rough stone rolling down from a high mountain. The only polishing I get is when some corner gets rubbed off by coming in contact with something else. The faster I roll, the more I strike with accelerated force against such things as religious bigotry, priestcraft, and all manner of evil." His voice softened noticeably. "So it has always been with me, and so, I suppose, it shall always be—all hell knocking off a corner here and a corner there until I shall become a smooth and polished shaft in the quiver of the Almighty. I ask for nothing more, and hope for nothing less."

<hr />

Amy Appleby was waiting for Olivia as soon as she came out the front door of the store. "What did he say, Livvy! I've been dying. You were in there a long time."

Olivia looked at her friend. "It was wonderful, Amy. He was so kind and so patient. He wasn't angry with me at all for having questions."

"But what did he say?"

Olivia stopped and faced her friend. "I had to promise not to tell."

"But . . ." There was open dismay on Amy's face. "You can tell me, Livvy. We're best friends. I promise I won't tell anyone."

"I know, Amy, but I swore I wouldn't." Olivia had a sudden thought and reached out and grabbed her friend's hand. "You haven't told anyone else, have you, Amy? About what I told you the other day?"

There was a momentary shadow that darkened her eyes, but then Amy shook her head firmly. "Of course not." She pulled her hand free. "Are you really not going to tell me anything?" she said, half pouting now.

"All I can tell you is that I feel so much better now. But I can't say anything more. I swore, Amy. And I must keep that promise, no matter what."

When Robert Foster slipped outside through the back door of the store, he stopped at the corner of the building, checked to make sure no one was coming, then moved quickly down Water Street. He had gone only a block when Appleby, Soby, and Higbee stepped out from behind some bushes.

"Well?" Francis Higbee demanded.

Foster was expansive. Smiling, he laid his hand on Higbee's shoulder. "Well, Frank, let's just say this. When Steed gets back from Wisconsin, I think he'll be very glad to talk to us."

"Did you hear it, then?" Soby demanded.

"Every word," Foster said exultantly. "I was in the room right across from his office, and those doors are as thin as rice paper. Every single word!"

"And?" the high councilor prodded.

"And," Foster said with quiet triumph, "it was everything I hoped for. Everything!"

On Monday, January twenty-ninth, shortly before ten a.m., Nathan Steed walked into the mayor's office. To his surprise, the only other one there besides Joseph and Hyrum and the Twelve was John P. Greene, Brigham's brother-in-law and the city marshal. He stopped for a moment, not sure if he had gotten Joseph's invitation right. But Joseph was up and had him by the hand, pulling him into the room even as he shook it.

"Come in, Nathan, don't let this august and rather solemn group frighten you. I want you here because . . ." He laughed. "Well, actually, I've got several reasons, but I think it best if you don't know them all, lest you bolt and run."

He showed Nathan to a chair, then looked around. "Everyone here, Brother Brigham?"

"All are present, Brother Joseph."

And that was a thrill for Nathan as he realized how unusual it was for Brigham to be able to say that everyone was present. The Twelve were together again. Orson Hyde had returned late in 1842 from his momentous trip to the Holy Land, and Parley P. Pratt finally returned a few months after that, having spent almost three years of service in England.

Joseph nodded and called on Wilford Woodruff to open with prayer. They sang a hymn and then the discussion turned to the subject of a presidential candidate. Joseph frankly declared that he could not in good conscience vote for any of the candidates currently put forth. There was total agreement on that part. The moment Joseph ceased speaking, Willard Richards's hand shot up.

"Brother Willard," Joseph said, inclining his head toward him.

"I hereby move that we nominate another candidate for president of the United States. I move that we, as a body, form an independent electoral ticket and that we have Joseph Smith, mayor of Nauvoo and lieutenant general of the Nauvoo Legion, be a candidate for president of the United States of America. I further move that we use all honorable means in our power to secure his election."

"Hear! Hear!" a couple of them said, stomping their feet on the floor to express their approval.

Nathan was startled, but no one else seemed too surprised. They had obviously discussed this previously.

"Second the motion," Brigham called.

Joseph was very solemn. "We have a motion and it has been seconded. All in favor?"

Every hand in the room shot up.

He smiled, a trifle wanly, Nathan thought. "Thank you, brethren, for your confidence. This is truly an honor. Who would ever have thought that a young boy from a small village in Vermont would come to this position in his lifetime? But I must say that if we attempt to accomplish this, we must send every man in the city who is able to speak in public throughout the land to electioneer and make stump speeches. I propose that after the April conference we have general conferences all over the nation, and I will attend as many as convenient. Let us tell the people we have had Whig and Democratic presidents long enough. We want a president of the United States and not the president of this party or that. If I ever get into the presidential chair, I will protect the people in their rights and liberties."

Again there was the rumble of feet. "Hear! Hear!" called one. "Bravo!" cried another.

"Thank you, brethren. It is important that we draft a platform stating our position and that we mail it out immediately. As I have considered that problem, I have decided that I shall dictate my ideas to Brother W. W. Phelps. He and Brother John M. Bernhisel, both men of considerable literary skills, can then make us a draft that will be acceptable to the people. The election is only a few months away and there is much to do."

He turned now to Nathan. "My old friend, you have a good head for boiling things down to their essence. Would you be so kind as to assist me in reviewing the statement once it is finished? Then I would like a brief summary of the document that outlines its major points."

Nathan dropped his head slightly, surprised but pleased. "I would be honored to help in any way possible, Joseph."

"Good. We shall reconvene in a few days to consider the draft and make revisions thereto."

———•———

Nathan was in the mayor's office, working laboriously from the long draft that Phelps and Bernhisel had titled "General Smith's Views of the Powers and Policy of the Government of the United States." He made a mistake in spelling and muttered something under his breath as he crossed it out.

"Now, careful, Brother Nathan," a voice said from the door. "You wouldn't want a menial task to drive you to profaning, would you?" Nathan grunted as Joseph came into the room to stand beside him. "How is it coming?"

Nathan pushed his chair back, frowning deeply. "You have other scribes, Joseph. They are so much better than me in these kinds of things."

Joseph peered over his shoulder at the sheets of paper. "Nathan, you're not to be worrying about correct spelling or if a sentence sounds just right. What I need from you is a simple summary of what our position is. You and I have been friends for many years. You know what is important to me, how I think, what I feel. That's what I need you to do. Then we'll let the literati fix it, all right?"

Nathan sighed. "I suppose." He reached over and retrieved his previous sheet. "It's right here."

He started to hand it to him, but Joseph waved him off and dropped into a chair. "Read it to me, Nathan. I want to hear how it sounds."

"All right. I have summarized it into seven points."

"Good. Let me hear them."

"Well, first of all, the noble sentiments on the purpose of the United States government are reviewed. This part draws heavily on the words of Benjamin Franklin, as well as statements from several of the inaugural addresses of some of our previous presidents—Washington, Jefferson, Madison, and so on."

"Good, good. Go on."

"Second, the proposal is made that the size of Congress be reduced by two-thirds, with two senators per state and only two representatives per million population. Also that congressional pay and power be reduced so that our officers serve the people more faithfully."

Joseph chuckled. "That should raise some hackles in those hallowed halls. But pay them two dollars a day, I say. That is more than a farmer gets, and he lives honestly enough."

Nathan nodded. "Third, let there be significant prison reform, and in this vein it is proposed that many people now in prison be pardoned, that public service sentences be established for lesser crimes, and that our prisons be turned into seminaries of learning rather than places of rigor and seclusion, which change no man for the better."

"Yes, that's good."

"Fourth, that the United States government abolish slavery by 1850, not by mere fiat but by raising money through the sale of public lands and through the reduction of the salaries for congressmen. Then with that money the government will purchase the slaves from their masters so that the slave owners will not be economically ruined."

"That will be very popular in the North but totally rejected in the South," said Joseph. "But be that as it may, I say break off the shackles from the black man and let him earn his bread for wages as is the privilege of other men and he shall be blessed."

Nathan continued. "Fifth, let military court-martial for desertion be abolished. Make honor the standard of the soldier and desertion will cease to be a problem. Sixth, practice greater economy in state and national government so that the people are not so heavily taxed. And finally, number seven, let Congress grant the creation of a national bank, with branches in each state and territory. One of the purposes of this bank would be to circulate a standard medium of exchange."

Nathan laid the paper down. "That's it."

"Good, good," Joseph said again. "I am meeting with the Twelve again on Wednesday. We will read the entire document, but I would like you there to first give your summary. It will help clarify their minds on the matter."

"I'd be happy to, Joseph." He started to straighten the papers. "Is there anything else you need?"

Before he could answer, there was a knock at the door. Joseph got up and opened it. William Weeks, the temple architect, was there. He had a thick roll of plans under his arm. "Oh, Brother Joseph," he said, obviously not in a jovial mood. "Do you have a minute that I may talk with you?"

"I was just leaving," Nathan said, standing up.

"No you weren't," Joseph said. "Sit down. Brother Weeks doesn't have any great secrets he's trying to hide, do you?"

That won him a brief smile. "No, Brother Joseph." Weeks looked at Nathan. "And how are you, Brother Steed?"

"I'm fine. It's good to see you again. The temple seems to grow higher with every passing day."

"Thank you."

"What can I help you with, Brother Weeks?" Joseph asked.

Weeks withdrew the plans from beneath his arm and waved them at Joseph, instantly agitated again. "It's about those circular windows, Brother Joseph. We simply must discuss this matter further."

He started to unroll the plans but Joseph shook his head. "I don't need to see them, William. I am very familiar with them. And as I have said on more than one occasion, the circular windows are designed to light the offices in the dead work of the arch between the two stories."

"Brother Joseph, begging your pardon, sir, but I have been an architect and builder for many years. I had a reputation of some renown back in New England. And I tell you, round windows in the broad side of a building are a violation of all the known rules of architecture. The building is too low for round windows. They must be semicircular or the whole will look completely out of balance."

There was a patient smile, and then Joseph laid his arm across Weeks's shoulder. "Brother William, I tell you again, I will have the circles, even if we have to make the temple ten feet higher than we originally calculated. Close your eyes for a moment. See if you can't picture this in your mind. Inside the temple there will be one light at the center of each circular window sufficient to light the whole room. From the outside, when the whole building is thus illuminated, the effect will be remarkably grand."

"But Brother Joseph—"

"No buts, Brother William," he said, cutting him off. "I wish you to carry out *my* designs. This is not just a whim of Brother Joseph's, you see. If you remember, in the revelation which commanded us to build another temple here, the Lord said, 'And I will show unto my servant Joseph all things pertaining to this house.' "

"I know, but—"

Joseph shook his head at the man, chiding him gently. "William, William, the Lord has kept his promise. I have not wanted to say this before, lest you think I was trying to force your hand, but you need to know that I have seen this house in vision, and what I saw there were circular windows. I saw the splendid appearance of that building when it was all illuminated." There was a long pause. Weeks had bowed his head in submission now. "And," Joseph concluded firmly, "I will have it built according to the pattern shown me."

"Yes, Joseph, I understand."

Joseph smiled easily. "Maybe in future architectural books they will amend that silly rule about circular windows and say that it was William Weeks, the Mormon architect, who overturned it."

———◆———

When Nathan arrived back at Steed Row, Lydia was baking bread. He walked into the kitchen, gave her a quick kiss, won himself a frown by pinching a healthy wad of dough from the kneading board, then sat down.

"How was the summary?" she asked.

"Joseph seemed pleased."

"Good."

"It's interesting, isn't it?" he said quietly.

"What's that?"

"Living next door to a prophet of God."

She gave him a strange look.

"Well, I don't mean literally next door to him. But close by."

"Yes. So?"

"We see him every day. We go to his store and buy things from him. He wears an apron and dusts the shelves. We go to his home and sit around the table with him and eat bread and cheese." He smiled, remembering snow fights and ice sliding. "He plays with our children."

She wasn't yet sure exactly where all this was leading, but she nodded anyway.

"And yet he is still the Prophet. He gets revelation. He teaches us the doctrines of God. He tells us how to extend the gospel to those who have died." He looked up at her now, his eyes contemplative and filled with wonder. "He sees circular windows on a building that hasn't even been built as yet."

"What? What do you mean, circular windows?"

He chuckled softly. "I'll tell you about that tonight, but for now I'd better go find Father. He probably thinks he's running this business all by himself anymore." He stopped again. "But it's easy to forget he's the Prophet when he's also your next-door neighbor, isn't it?"

Chapter Notes

Joseph's words about being a rough stone and becoming a polished shaft come from his own description of himself (see HC 5:401, 423). The statements were actually made in May and June of 1843, about six months before the time depicted here.

The position paper outlining Joseph Smith's platform as a presidential candidate was dictated to W. W. Phelps by Joseph and then evidently polished by Phelps, John M. Bernhisel, and others under his jurisdiction. There is no known summary paper such as Nathan was writing, but what is done here by Nathan encapsulates the major points of Joseph's candidacy. (See *Restoration*, pp. 269–70.) On 7 February 1844, the full draft was read to the Twelve, and the following day W. W. Phelps read it publicly at a political meeting in the assembly room of the Red Brick Store (see HC 6:197–211).

The story about the circular windows is recorded in Joseph's history (see HC 6:196–97; see also Richard O. Cowan, "The Pivotal Nauvoo Temple," in *Regional Studies in Latter-day Saint Church History: Illinois* [Provo, Utah: Department of Church History and Doctrine, Brigham Young University, 1995], pp. 116–20). The revelation referred to by Joseph is now D&C 124:42.

With the exception of John David Appleby, who is fictional, the names of all the conspirators are real, although the situation involving Olivia is of course the author's creation. It should also be noted here that William Marks (mentioned in earlier chapters), who was president of the Nauvoo Stake, was upset by Joseph's teachings but did not join the conspiracy. After the Martyrdom, he did take the side of Sidney Rigdon in the succession question and eventually was dropped from the stake presidency and the Church. (See Andrew Jenson, comp., *Latter-day Saint Biographical Encyclopedia*, 4 vols. [1901–36; reprint, Salt Lake City: Western Epics, 1971], 1:283–84.)

Joshua and Will Steed returned to Nauvoo from Wisconsin late in the evening of the twentieth of February. They came overland by stage and rented carriage. The weather had turned quite warm for this early in the year, and even the ice along the riverbanks was about gone now. Farther north, the ice on the river was breaking up and there were great chunks of it in the main current. It would be a few more weeks before the riverboat traffic would open up and start plying the great inland highway again, and so overland routes had been their only choice.

Caroline sent word to the family the next morning that her men were back home and that there would be a family dinner that evening to celebrate their return. As usual, immediately the women put their heads together to decide who would bring what, and then spent the better part of the day preparing the food to feed such a group.

They met at six and ate heartily. Then, protesting that it was too warm for coats but losing the battle with their parents, the children went outside to play. Over warm blackberry pie and raspberry ice cream whipped up by Derek and Peter earlier in the afternoon, the adults settled in to visit.

The news from Wisconsin was good. Jean Claude Dubuque, now in full partnership with Joshua, was proving to be an able businessman. There had been a good harvest of trees through the winter, and the sawmill now had great stacks of sawn lumber ready to be made into rafts once spring broke. Joshua announced that the Frenchman felt confident enough in his crews that he could bring the rafts down without Joshua's going back up again. At that, Caroline stood and applauded enthusiastically.

Will won a clear frown from his father when he announced that Jean Claude had been traveling to the Mormon lumber camps each Sunday for worship services and that he would be baptized when he came down with the rafts in May. After that, the conversation turned to what had been happening in Nauvoo during their absence. Inevitably, the question of Joseph's candidacy was raised. Joshua, who had seen the newspaper articles about it in Peoria, was openly scornful. "Talk about naivete."

"Joshua!" Caroline cried.

He jerked around. "What? Because I'm in the minority here I can't say what I'm feeling?"

She shook her head, dismayed at the emotion she saw in his face. "You can say what you please, but you don't have to be unpleasant about it."

"It's unpleasant only because it is the truth," he retorted. Then turning back to Nathan, he went on. "I know that here in Nauvoo there was probably a great celebration. Joseph Smith for president! Hip hip hooray! At last a candidate we can believe in. But out there"—he threw out his hand to include all of the world to their east—"don't you realize how people feel about the Mormons? Especially after Bennett spent a year going around the country telling all? Most people are not sure whether you are a joke or a menace. And then to hear that your prophet is running for president?" His laugh was harsh, mocking. "Let's just say that the reception out there wasn't quite as warm as here in Nauvoo."

Caroline was looking at the floor now, her face flaming. Will was watching his father, his mouth tight. "Pa's been grumping about this ever since Peoria," he said.

His father's nostrils flared and he swung on Will. "That's right. Will thinks it's grumping only because he can't face reality either. Tell you what. You take a snowball and toss it into one of Carl's brick kilns. That's how much chance your Joseph Smith has of winning this election."

Melissa spoke up now. "Do you think it's wrong of Joseph to try and win?" she asked.

"I think Joseph has his head in the clouds," Joshua snapped. "That's all I'm saying."

To everyone's surprise, Carl jumped in to support his wife. "Maybe they would rather have a man they can vote for in good conscience, even if there's no chance he will win."

"That's it, exactly," Nathan said, pleased that Carl had seen it. "Who else would you have us vote for? John C. Calhoun? Martin Van Buren, whose only answer to our cry for help was, 'Your cause is just, but I can do nothing for you'?"

Grudgingly, Joshua backed down a little. "All right, I'll grant you that. I'm just saying that you are being very naive if you think Joseph has one chance in ten thousand of winning."

Benjamin decided to change the subject. "Did you know that in Warsaw, Thomas Sharp has called for a day of fasting and prayer to remove Joseph Smith from power?"

That brought everyone's head around.

"That's right," he said. "March ninth. And I understand that in Carthage on that same day they're calling for a 'wolf hunt.' "

"A wolf hunt?" Joshua asked. "What's that supposed to mean?"

"Well," Benjamin said, "on the surface, it's just that, though no one has seen a wolf in these parts for many years. But talk to anyone in Carthage and they know exactly what it means. It's nothing but a thin excuse to go out and terrorize the Mormons."

Joshua looked dubious.

"They already burned some haystacks a month or so ago," Benjamin said. "A home of one of the members in the outlying settlements was burned to the ground under very suspicious circumstances. That's why we feel that we have to have a candidate we can vote for with our hearts."

"Either that or leave the country," Matthew said.

Nathan gave him a quick look, then glanced at Derek. Before dinner they had wondered how to break into this. Now Matthew had just given them the perfect opening. Nathan took a breath. "Joseph has asked the Twelve to organize a party to go to California and Oregon."

He might as well have dropped a buffalo through the roof. There were exclamations of shock and astonishment. Even Joshua was staring at him.

"California!" Lydia exclaimed. "But why?"

"To find us a place where we can be safe." Nathan shot a look at Joshua. "Where we're not dependent on the United States to protect us. Where we can build a temple and worship in peace." He took a breath, looking at Lydia now. "Just yesterday, Joseph charged the Twelve to start putting together a delegation. I may be asked to go."

"No!" she cried. "Oh, Nathan, when?"

Derek looked at Rebecca. "Brigham has talked to Matthew and me as well."

"When would you go?" Jenny cried in dismay.

"We don't know," Nathan answered. "It will take a while to organize something. Maybe later in the summer after the elections are over."

"Is he serious?" Joshua said, sobered now out of his irritation.

"Serious enough to tell the Twelve to start working on it." Nathan took a breath, staring at Joshua now with unwavering eyes. "I understand your disdain for our feeble efforts to find a solution to our problems, Joshua. And you're probably right. Joseph will very likely never be the president of the United States. But at least he's looking for solutions. And that means enough to me that I'll vote for him whether I think he can win or not. And if that doesn't work . . ." He took a breath. "Then I'll follow him to California or Oregon if he asks me to."

Doctor Robert Foster was waiting on the front step of the Steed and Sons Freight and Portage Company when Joshua rounded the corner and started up the street. At the sight of him, Joshua's mouth tightened. Did these fools never give up?

"Good morning, Steed," Foster said with little attempt at cordiality.

"If this is more of what we talked about before I left, I'm a very busy man today, Foster."

Foster's mouth curled slightly at the corners, and there was a serpentine look in his eye. "Give me five minutes and I think you'll agree that you're not that busy."

When the front door slammed, Caroline jumped, nearly dropping the frying pan. She turned toward the door as Joshua came clomping down the hall and entered the kitchen. "Joshua?" she said in surprise. "Did you forget something . . . ?" Her voice trailed off when she saw his face. "Joshua, what's wrong?"

"Where's Olivia?"

"She's upstairs helping Charles get dressed. Why, what's the matter?"

He just glared at her. "And Will?"

"You told him to go out to the Peterson place and check on that load of corn coming in from Keokuk."

"So he left?"

"Yes, about a quarter of an hour ago."

There was one curt nod. "You get Olivia and both of you come out to the barn."

"The barn? But—"

"Savannah can watch Charles for that long. I don't want the young ones hearing what I've got to say. Now, just do it!" And with that, he spun around and stomped out again.

———•———

As they left the house and started across the yard, Olivia looked at her mother, fear openly written on her face. "Do you think he knows about my going to see Joseph?" she asked.

"I don't know how he could," Caroline answered. She was pale. Her stomach was one huge, twisted knot. The fury in Joshua's eyes was not for some slight infraction by one of the children. And why did he want Olivia too? "Have you told anyone about that, Olivia?"

"No, Mama. Not anyone. I promised Joseph."

"Not even Amy?"

"No, Mama. I mean, I didn't tell Amy about what Joseph and I discussed, but she knows I went to see him, because she's the one who first gave me the idea."

This was news to Caroline. "Amy told you to go to Joseph? Why would she tell you—"

Olivia had suddenly stopped. She looked stricken. "Because I told her about that night I heard you and Grandma and Mary Smith talking about plural marriage." Olivia had confessed to Caroline about having eavesdropped that night. But—whether it was out of forgetfulness, negligence, or guilt, she wasn't sure—she had not told her mother that she talked to Amy about it.

Caroline's mouth opened and she almost wanted to gag. "You told Amy about that?" she half whispered. Just yesterday, Benjamin had taken Caroline aside and whispered a word of warning to her about Olivia's friendship with Amy Appleby. John Appleby was known to be friendly with Foster and Soby and the Laws, he said. Olivia needed to be careful about what she said to her. Caroline had been planning on talking with her about it this very morning.

"I'm sorry, Mama," Olivia said in a low voice that was now trembling. "She promised me that she hasn't told anyone." Her eyes said that she no longer believed Amy Appleby's promises.

Caroline thought about that, trying to assess the damage. At least Amy didn't know what had transpired in Joseph's office. Caroline looked up as a movement caught her eye. Joshua had come to the door of the barn and was watching them with a baleful stare. She took her daughter's hand and raised her head high. "I'm here, Livvy. It will be all right."

Joshua stepped back inside as they reached him. He waited until they were in, then shut the door behind them. When he turned to face them, his lips were pressed into a thin, hard line, and his eyes were like glittering pieces of coal. "All right," he said in a low, menacing voice. "I'm going to ask some questions and I want no more lies."

Caroline's chin lifted slightly and she met his gaze with calmness. "No more lies? Does that mean you think I have been lying to you, Joshua?"

"Don't be cute with me, Caroline!" he snapped.

"The last thing in the world I have tried to do is be cute, Joshua."

He thrust his jaw out, addressing Caroline now. "Is it true that while I was gone you used our home as a meeting place to try and convert Melissa to the idea of plural marriage?"

She had expected no less. "One night Mary Smith visited with me, Lydia, your mother, Rebecca, and Melissa. And yes, we did meet here. You and Will were gone, it was quiet, so—"

He threw up his hands and whirled away. "And knowing how I feel about this whole damnable doctrine, it never occurred to you that I would object to that?"

"I . . . no, Joshua, I guess it didn't. I'm sorry."

"Sorry?" he raged, swinging on her again. "*Sorry?* I caved in about your being baptized, Caroline. I didn't stand in Will's way. I agreed to let Olivia join the Church with you, even though I felt that she had been duped into believing all this nonsense. And this is how you repay me? You bring Mary Smith right into my home to do this?"

"Somewhere I had it in my mind," Caroline said evenly, "that this was my home too. But I am sorry, Joshua." Then there was a steeliness in her own voice. "Would it have made any difference to you if it had taken place at your mother's house? or Lydia's?"

He exploded at that. "If it had taken place at my mother's house," he yelled, "at least my daughter wouldn't have come back and overheard the whole thing."

Now Caroline's head dropped. On that he had her. It had been a foolish thing to do and Olivia had been badly shaken because of it. "You're right, Joshua. I was wrong. I'm sorry."

He just snorted in disgust. Then he swung on Olivia. She shrank back a little, her eyes wide with dread. "Now, you answer me, Livvy, and you answer me honestly. Is it true that you heard everything Mary Smith was saying about plural marriage?"

"Yes, Papa, all but the very first part."

"And is it true that you went to see Joseph Smith to ask him about it?"

That stunned her.

"Did you?" he said, his voice snapping like the crack of a whip.

"Yes, Papa."

"And did you ask"—the sarcasm was heavy now—"*Brother* Joseph about plural marriage?"

She could no longer bear the heat of his eyes. She stared down at the floor. There was a numb nod.

"And what did Joseph tell you, Olivia?"

There was a quick, frightened look at her mother. "I promised I wouldn't tell," she said.

He jerked forward, mouth twisting. "What did you say?" he asked.

"I swore I would not speak to anyone about it."

"Not even to your mother?" he shot right back.

"No, I— Joseph said I could tell Mama."

"But not me, right?"

She didn't answer.

"Look at me!" he commanded. "You look at me when I'm talking to you."

Olivia's head came up. Her eyes were shining, her lower lip visibly trembling.

"Did Joseph tell you not to tell me?"

For a long moment there was silence, then a bare whisper, "I cannot say."

He whirled, took three steps to the half wall of the nearest stall, and slammed it with his fist, causing both Caroline and Olivia to jump. "She can't say," he cried.

"There's no need to terrorize her, Joshua," Caroline said softly.

Now he spun on her, so angry he could hardly speak. "Is that what it is? Because I want to know the truth, I'm terrorizing her?"

"You're frightening her, Joshua, can't you see that?"

He turned, ready to snarl out an answer, and then he saw the fear on his daughter's face and felt ashamed. He moved closer, his face softening now. "Livvy," he pleaded. "Don't you understand? I'm trying to protect you. I don't want anything awful happening to you."

Her eyes flooded with relief. "I know, Papa, but it wasn't what you think. It wasn't anything bad."

"Did Joseph speak to you about the possibility of marrying Brigham Young or Heber Kimball?" he asked.

It was like being slapped in the face again and again. Caroline couldn't believe it. This was more than just knowing about Olivia's trip to see Joseph. He knew every word that had transpired.

"I can't say, Papa," Livvy whispered.

Now his face went cold. Very quietly, he said, "I see. And did Joseph suggest that you pray about this so you would have faith enough to live it when you're asked to?"

She looked away. Caroline jumped in. "Joshua, I don't know who told you all of this, but they've twisted it all around. It's not what—"

He whirled like a bull, his head weaving, his chin down. "No, Caroline. You stay out of this! This is my daughter and I'll not have her duped into thinking this is from God." He swung right back to Livvy. "Did he ask you to pray, Livvy?"

"It is not what you think, Papa," Olivia said with a sob. "You make it sound ugly and awful, but it wasn't like that."

"Then tell me!" he pleaded. "I'm listening, Olivia. I'm trying to understand. If it was so beautiful and wonderful, why won't you tell me what happened?"

Her head was down now. Tears were streaming down her face. She didn't answer.

"I see," he finally said, totally wearied now. "Just one last question, then. Did Joseph Smith take you in his arms and kiss you?"

Olivia's head came up with a violent jerk. "No!" Then remembrance came rushing back and horror filled her eyes. "He hugged me, Papa. That was all. He kissed the top of—"

"You don't have to lie, Olivia," he said, wanting to cry now. "Someone was there. Someone saw you!"

There was one tortured glance at her mother, and then Olivia's body twisted in a racking sob. She whirled and plunged out the barn door, hugging herself as though she were in unbearable pain.

Joshua watched the door shut behind her. He didn't turn around to meet Caroline's eyes.

"I don't know who told you all of this, but they're lying," she said quietly.

"Caroline, we're leaving tomorrow."

She stiffened as if thrust through with a sword. "*What?*"

His voice was dull, lifeless, as though he were exhausted from a long journey. "We'll have to go to Warsaw for now, until I can find a buyer for the freight yard here."

One hand flew to her mouth and she bit down hard on her fingers. She felt her stomach lurch, the growing weight of the baby twisting inside her.

He went on as if he were dictating a letter to a secretary. "I know Warsaw is not ideal, but I've got to be close to Nauvoo until I can make the arrangements to sell the business. We'll just give the house to my family. Then we'll move to St. Louis. We could even go back to Georgia if you'd prefer."

He turned. She was standing there, hand still to her mouth, staring at him from eyes sunken with shock.

"Don't try to fight me on this, Caroline. You may get Will and Olivia to stay with you, but no court in the land will give you Charles and Savannah and the baby. Not with plural marriage on the table."

There was no response.

"You'd better start packing some things. I'll be at the office most of the day getting things ready there." He turned and went out the side door, leaving Caroline to stand there alone, staring out at nothing. She held her arms across her body and began to rock very slowly back and forth as the tears started to flow.

Joseph and Hyrum heard the footsteps on the stairs, then the heavy thud of boots coming down the hallway toward the office. They were reviewing a copy of the political statement, talking about what needed to happen now. They both looked up and Hyrum started to rise to go to the door, but the latch turned and suddenly it was thrust open. Joshua Steed filled the frame.

Totally surprised, Joseph stood quickly. "Joshua, I heard that you had returned. I was—"

"Joseph, I know about your little talk with Olivia."

His eyes widened.

"Oh," Joshua flung at him, "she didn't break her word to you. You're really quite amazing, actually. It didn't matter that her father wanted the truth behind all this. It didn't make any difference when I asked her straight out what was true and what was not. She was a faithful little Mormon right to the last. She wouldn't tell me anything."

Joseph started around the desk. Hyrum was rooted to where he stood. "Joshua, I can explain. I—"

"No!" Joshua cut in sharply. "I've heard quite enough of your smooth talk and your silky ways. I'm here to warn you. You even so much as talk to my daughter again, and you'll wish to heaven that the Missourians had gotten you instead of me. Do you understand me, Joseph?"

"I don't know what you think went on between your daughter and me, but if you'll sit down, I'll tell you anything you want to know."

Joshua raised a hand, his forefinger jabbing at the air. "You heard me, Joseph. You stay away from my daughter. You leave my wife alone. Or you will rue the day you were ever born into this world."

———————

When Caroline opened the back door to her home and saw Nathan, her eyes widened with concern. He smiled reassuringly. "Caroline, I'd like to talk to you and Will and Olivia. Can you leave Charles with Savannah for a time?"

She looked frightened all of a sudden. "Joshua could come home anytime now and . . ." She didn't have to finish that. It would be like setting a keg of black powder on an open fire if Joshua thought the family was trying to intervene at this stage.

"I know," he said quickly. "I've got Matthew and Derek watching the road. They'll give us plenty of warning if he decides to come."

Will had come to the door to stand by his mother. "If he sees you talking to us," he said, "it will be Jackson County all over again, Nathan."

Nathan nodded and managed a smile. Without thinking, one hand stole up and he rubbed the scars beneath his shirt. "Most of the wounds are healed now. Besides, for all the outer fireworks, it isn't the same Joshua now that it was then. I'm not trying to sneak around behind Joshua's back, but I'd really like to talk to you before you have to leave."

She hesitated, and then her head bobbed quickly. "All right. Knowing Joshua, I don't expect him until late, after I'm asleep. Where do you want to meet?"

"In our barn." He moved away, not waiting for her answer.

———————

They sat almost in semidarkness, the only light coming from a small candle Nathan had brought from the house. Olivia's eyes were still red and puffy. Will sat like death itself, staring at the ground, his mouth in a hard line. Caroline was still half-dazed. Nathan had brought a chair out for her and made her sit in it. She was only four months with child, but this time she was having a more difficult time of things, probably because she was now almost thirty-eight years old.

Nathan took a long, slow breath. His shoulders lifted and fell. Then he cleared his throat. He carried the family Bible in one hand. "I have no right to say what I'm about to say. You're already facing enough challenges."

If he wanted to get through to them, he had just said the right thing. Their heads were up and they were watching him curiously now.

"You know," he said thoughtfully, "each week we go to worship services and there we partake of the sacrament of the Lord. We partake of the emblems and promise that we will always remember the Savior. And we do this so we can always have his Spirit to be with us."

They were still watching him, but no one spoke.

"Always remember him," he said, almost to himself. "I've often wondered what that means. If I remember the Savior always, what difference would it make in how I react to an angry neighbor, a selfish friend—" He stopped, and then very softly added, "Or a bitter, angry father." He met their startled gaze now, feeling a touch of shame that he was reminding them of the cost of discipleship when they were already paying such a terrible price for it. But he had no choice. He had thought long about this all afternoon.

"What difference would it make if I were to *always* remember the one who said that we should love our enemies and pray for them which despitefully use us? What difference would it make if I were to always remember the one who, even as the soldiers were driving great spikes through his hands, said, 'Father, forgive them, for they know not what they do'?"

The silence in the barn was total. No one moved as their eyes were held by Nathan's. He sighed, feeling their pain. "I know that you have every right to feel betrayed, to feel that you have been wronged. I suppose when you three were baptized no one talked about this part of living the gospel, did they? No one told you that right at the toughest time of your whole lives, you'd still be expected to keep the covenants you've made with the Savior. Covenants like taking his name upon us. Always living his commandments. Forgiving others."

Will's lip was suddenly trembling and he looked away. "I don't know if I can, Nathan. I don't know if I can forgive him for this. For taking Mother and Olivia away from the family."

Nathan wanted to go to him and take him in his arms and tell him it was all right to feel that way, that they had just cause. But he couldn't. "You must, Will," he said. "Because if you don't, if you can't live the gospel now, even when things are terrible, then your father's right. The Church really isn't that important to you."

"But he's wrong!" Olivia cried. "He thinks I'm lying to him. He thinks those awful things about me and Joseph. He won't listen!"

"Do you love him, Livvy?"

Her head came up with a jerk.

"Right now? After all he's done? Do you still love your father?"

"Of course, but—"

"Do you, Will?"

There was a long moment, then a slow nod. "Yes."

"Then you must show him that you won't let his anger and his bitterness turn your love away. Show him what a true disciple is like."

Nathan opened the Bible and withdrew a folded sheet of paper from it. He handed it to Caroline, and as she took it she gave him a quizzical look. He motioned for her to open it. She did, scanning the lines in the dim light. Suddenly her eyes were brimming with tears. "Yes," she said. "I understand."

"What is it, Mama?" Olivia asked.

She turned to her children now. "This seems like a very dark time for us right now," she began. "It seems like everything has just collapsed in around us."

"Yes," Will said, curious now too.

"Well, these are the words which God spoke to Joseph when he was going through a very difficult time too." She turned the paper to the light and began to read, slowly and with much feeling. " 'If thou art called to pass through tribulation; if thou art in perils among false brethren; if thou art in perils among robbers; if thou art in perils by land or by sea—' " She looked at Olivia. " *'If thou art accused with all manner of false accusations;* if thine enemies fall upon thee; if—' " Suddenly her voice faltered and the paper dropped to her lap. She looked away.

Nathan reached down and took the paper from her. " 'If they tear thee from the society of thy father and mother—' " He too had to stop for a moment, his hands trembling slightly. But then he went on with deeper resolution. " 'If they tear thee from the society of thy father and mother and brethren and sisters, know thou, my son, that all these things shall give thee experience, and shall be for thy good.' " He lowered the paper slowly, speaking mostly to himself now. " 'The Son of Man hath descended below them all. Art thou greater than he?' "

"Thank you, Nathan," Caroline said. "Thank you for reminding us of who we are and what is expected of us. We will be fine now."

"There's something else," Nathan said. "We had a family council this afternoon. You need to know that each week all of us, including the young children, will be having a special fast for your family. And we'll not just be fasting and praying for you three. We'll also be fasting for your father."

Chapter Notes

Mention is made here of the family's eating ice cream. Dating back to George Washington and colonial times, ice cream was a favorite dessert in America. It would be 1846, two years from the time of the action in this chapter, before a woman named Nancy Johnson would invent the simple hand-cranked freezer which allowed ice cream to be made at home with relative ease. Until then, ice cream was made by filling one large bowl with ice, then nesting another bowl inside that and whipping the mixture—eggs, cream, sugar, and some kind of fruit or syrup for flavoring—vigorously until it froze. (See *Discovering America's Past: Customs, Legends, History, and Lore of Our Great Nation* [Pleasantville, N.Y.: Reader's Digest Association, 1993], p. 56.)

It was on 20 February 1844 that Joseph told the Twelve to organize an expedition to go west in search of a possible location for a new home for the Saints (see *HC* 6:222, 232). This decision likely stemmed from his Rocky Mountain prophecy mentioned earlier in this book. Some men volunteered and some preliminary efforts were undertaken for this expedition, but with the press of the election and the growing problems with the dissenters, nothing more came of it.

Ⅰt said a great deal about the depths of Joshua Steed's feelings that within twenty-four hours of his visit from Robert Foster he had his family out of Nauvoo. Shortly after eight o'clock on the morning of February twenty-third, he loaded Caroline, Will, Olivia, Savannah, and Charles into a wagon filled with enough essentials to last them until they could find a home in Warsaw, fifteen miles south of Nauvoo. He stood back, quiet but resolute, while the family bid their farewells to his family. When that was done, he gave his mother a brief kiss on the cheek. "I'm sorry, Mama," was all he said. He shook hands with his father.

"I'm sorry it had to end this way, Joshua," Benjamin said.

He shrugged, his face impassive. To everyone else he simply lifted a hand, said good-bye, then climbed up on the wagon seat and drove away. Will sat beside him on the wagon seat, Caroline and the other children rode in the back.

Upon their arrival in Warsaw, Joshua checked his family into the hotel, the same one he and Will stayed in each time they came through Warsaw, and saw to getting them supper. First thing the next morning, he went in search of Thomas Sharp, editor of the *Warsaw Signal*. Three nights later, Joshua Steed was the featured speaker to a capacity crowd at a rally of the anti-Mormon political party in Warsaw. By then, word had spread as far east as Carthage and across the river into Missouri, and Joshua had a wildly enthusiastic crowd. Joshua Steed, the famous and wealthy businessman from Nauvoo, had come out in open opposition to the Mormons.

After the rally was over, the masses surged up and down the streets of Warsaw, chanting, shouting, shaking their fists in the air. With each hour the barrels of beer and the kegs of whiskey emptied and the mood of the crowd grew more jubilant. Or, one might say, the mood grew uglier if one viewed it from the Mormon perspective, as Will, Olivia, and Caroline did from their hotel room. Savannah and Charles were asleep in the next room, but the three of them stood at the window of the second floor. The curtains were pulled open and they had no lamp or candles lit, so they could watch from the darkness what was going on in the streets. Olivia stood close to her mother, her shoulder touching hers for reassurance, her eyes wide and showing fear.

After several minutes, Olivia looked up at her mother. "They really hate us, don't they?"

"Yes," Caroline murmured. She felt cold and sick and dead inside. One hand strayed down to run across the swelling of her stomach. Was this what her child would be born into? How would she even find a sympathetic doctor or midwife in this town?

Will stared numbly out into the night. He had faced hostile ministers in England. He had spoken to more than one taunting street crowd. He had been splattered with eggs and tomatoes, and once had even had a vicious dog set loose on him. But he had never felt anything like this. "Now I know how Grandma and Grandpa and Nathan and all the rest must have felt in Missouri," he said quietly. His voice trailed off and they stood there together, staring out into the darkness.

———•———

"May I speak with you, Pa?"

Joshua looked up from reading the paper. Will stood in the door of the small room at the back of the *Signal* building. Thomas Sharp was providing Joshua with a temporary office until he could find something to rent. He laid the paper down. "All right."

Will moved inside and shut the door. Joshua watched him warily, noting that Will looked tired and drawn. Will sat down and leaned forward, peering at his hands.

What his father didn't know was that Will had been awake for a good part of the night. He had carefully considered every facet of what he was about to do. He wished fervently that he could have counseled with Nathan on this. Or Joseph. Nathan's counsel to Caroline, Will, and Olivia before they left weighed heavily upon them. On the other hand, Will was also deeply concerned for the welfare of his family, and he had finally decided there was a matter of principle too.

"I'm listening," Joshua finally said.

Will sat up straight, then nodded. "All right. I have something I would like to say."

"Oh, really?"

Will's jaw tightened a little. "Look," he said, "we can do this like adults, or we can toss out our sarcastic little jabs and make the whole thing very unpleasant. You choose."

Joshua leaned back, then nodded. "All right, I'm sorry."

Will blew out his breath. "Thank you."

"So?"

"I want to explain something to you, something that may not make much sense to you."

"I'm listening." Then he had a thought. "Does your mother know about this?"

"No. This is just between you and me."

Joshua grunted and motioned for him to go on.

"All right. I'll try and say this clearly. First, let me say that I understand how you feel about what happened and why you insisted on our leaving Nauvoo."

"Do you?" Joshua asked sardonically.

"I do. I don't agree with it, but I think I understand. I tried to imagine last night what I would feel if it were my daughter and I thought she was being taken advantage of by unscrupulous men."

"Not *think*," Joshua snapped. "*Know!*"

Will sighed. "Maybe you ought to sit down and listen to Olivia—really listen—then maybe you'd change your mind." He held up his hand quickly as Joshua started to reply to that. "But that's not what I'm here to talk about. I'm just saying that I think I can understand some of your feelings. That's one of the reasons why we are here with you now."

"You're here because you had no choice," Joshua said flatly.

Will just looked at him steadily, calmly, and after a moment, Joshua backed down. "Well, not you," Joshua said. "You didn't have to come. But your mother and Olivia, they knew what would happen if they didn't come. They had no choice."

Will sighed wearily and stood up. "Look, Pa, why don't you just call me when you're ready to talk to me like I'm a man, and not like I'm some little boy anymore."

Joshua watched him through furrowed brows, taking his measure, recognizing something he hadn't seen before. "All right, sit down. I'll just listen."

Will, not surprised, did so. "Mother came because she loves you a great deal," he said. "She will miss the rest of the family, but she loves you, Pa."

He finally nodded. "All right, yes. There's been a lot of strain between us lately, but yes."

"And I do too," Will said, his eyes open and wide and vulnerable.

For a long moment, their eyes held; then Joshua nodded slowly. "I'm glad, Will. I love you too. Very much. Believe it or not."

"I know, Pa. That's why I've got to say this."

"Then say it."

There was a curt nod. "Did you know that Savannah came home from school this morning crying?"

Joshua's head came up. "No, why?"

"You tell me why!" Will shot right back at him.

There was a momentary start, then a flash of anger. "Then I'll take her tomorrow. I'll talk to her—"

Will shook his head. "Mama and Olivia are going to teach her at home."

"They'll not be treating my family like this. Sharp will help me in this. I've already talked to him about it."

"And will Sharp stop the angry looks on the street every time Mama steps outside? Will you and the good editor of our newspaper follow along behind Olivia and stop the whisperings and the catcalls from the young men? Oh, I know, you never see it happen, Pa. Joshua Steed is the most popular man in Warsaw right now. It's just too bad that all of his family are Mormons. No one dares do anything outright, of course, but that doesn't stop them from hating us."

Joshua opened his mouth, then shut it again, thinking he knew what was coming next. He was wrong.

"We're not asking you to go back to Nauvoo, Pa. And we understand that you've got to get the freight business sold up there before we can leave here."

"Then what? What are you asking?"

"Stop working with them."

Joshua looked puzzled. "What? Working with whom?"

"You're going to tear us apart, Pa. It's bad enough to stand by and cheer when you see a ship sinking, although we can even live with that. But when you go on board and kick holes in the planking to help it sink just a little faster, especially when your own family is on the ship . . ." There was a grimness to him now that was sobering. "Well, that's something else again."

"You fight for what you believe in. I'm fighting against what . . ." Joshua caught himself, seeing where he almost stepped.

"You're fighting against what you *don't* believe in," Will finished for him with bitter irony. "That's just it, Pa. You're not fighting *for* anything. You just want to destroy the Church."

Joshua flushed. "I'm fighting to keep my daughter out of the clutches of some very evil men."

"I know that's what you think, and even though I think you're wrong, I understand that. That's why we're here with you. We'll live with Warsaw and its anger for a while. And we'll move with you to St. Louis or whatever. But when you start working with those who are trying to destroy everything we believe in, it's not just saving Olivia anymore. Or me or Mama. It's destroying the Church. It's destroying part of us."

Now at last Joshua understood. "You want me to simply back away from all of this?" He gestured around, including the city and all that it implied in the movement. "Be a dispassionate observer?"

"That would be nice, but I can even live with a passionate observer. But not a participant, Pa. That's what I'm saying." He leaned forward, wanting so badly to help him see. "Let me ask you a question, Pa. Do you still feel guilty about what happened to Nathan that night in Jackson County?"

Joshua looked away. "You know the answer to that," he said shortly.

"But why?" Will came right back. "You never lifted a finger against him. You never touched the whip. All you did was walk away. Why are you feeling guilty?"

Now Joshua was watching him intently, and Will finally nodded. "It's because you were responsible. You don't have to hold the whip to be responsible for the whipping, Pa."

They both sat there, staring at nothing, their chests rising and falling softly as the emotions surged through them.

Will stood now. "I wasn't there in northern Missouri, Pa, so I don't know. But the rest of the family were. And they're scared, Pa. Grandpa says right now it's just like it was then. This is how it all started."

He leaned forward now, hands on the table. "You think about that the next time you've got that crowd howling for the blood of the Mormons. You think about young Joshua and Emily and Betsy and little Joseph and Rachel and young John. You think about them facing another Haun's Mill." He straightened and passed a hand before his eyes. "You told me about the horrible things that happened to women there. Well, not all of those kind of men live in western Missouri, Pa. I saw some of them on the street, right here, last night."

"I . . ." Joshua shook his head.

Will straightened, turned, and walked to the door. He stopped there, his hand resting on the knob. "It's Far West all over again, Pa, and right now, you're part of it. It makes me sick enough, to think that you want to stand by and cheer when you see that happening, but I can live with that, I guess. What I'm not sure I can live with is knowing that you're not just standing on the side anymore, that you've gone and got yourself right in the middle of it and that you're whipping up the mobs all over again."

Ten days following the departure of Joshua and his family, Mary Ann and Benjamin had a second devastating blow. Just after supper, Melissa came to their house. At the look on her face, Mary Ann jumped up, but Melissa handed her a letter. It was very short.

Carl—

I know Mother has written you about Pa's health. I know also that she worries too much, but this time she is right. If you do not come immediately, you will likely not have the privilege of seeing Father alive again. Hurry!

David

It was dated about ten days before.

"Oh, Melissa," Mary Ann said, sinking back into her chair.

Melissa started to cry. "We'll be leaving day after tomorrow."

Benjamin stood up and took her in his arms. "We're so sorry, Melissa."

Now her body began to shudder and she threw her arms around his neck. "I don't know if we'll ever come back, Papa. I don't know."

———•———

On the ninth of March, the citizens of Warsaw joined in a day of fasting and prayer. They made no excuses about the object of their petition. They wanted Joseph Smith brought down and the Mormon church destroyed, and they were appealing to God to help it happen. That night there was another massive rally planned. By late afternoon, the streets were thronged with people. Joshua now had his family in a small rental house near the northern edge of town, but Caroline still locked the doors and pulled the drapes.

To her surprise, after dinner Joshua got down a large book of stories and offered to read to Savannah and Charles. "Aren't you going to the rally?" she asked.

He looked up, ignoring the sudden piercing look Will was giving him.

"No, I don't think so," he said, then patted the sofa and motioned for Charles to climb up beside him.

———•———

As spring gradually spread across the Great Plains, and the efforts of the dissenters increased, Joseph spent more and more time in council with the Quorum of the Twelve. His journal became peppered with entries like, "Spent the day in council," or "In the afternoon, met with the Twelve in prayer."

In keeping with that pattern, on Tuesday, March twenty-sixth, he and nine members of the Quorum of the Twelve met for most of the afternoon in the upper room of his store. It was a long meeting devoted to instruction and counsel and correction.

As the afternoon wore on, Brigham watched Joseph with growing concern. He could see that Joseph was getting tired. Of equal worry was the fact that he seemed to be more and more pensive of late, often withdrawing into his thoughts or sometimes even sorrowful. Since that day some twelve years before when he had finally decided it was time to be baptized a member of the Church, Brigham had never wavered. There had never been a day when he had doubted Joseph and never a day when he had doubted that God was at the helm. But in these past few weeks, he had felt Joseph's power and calling as never before. It was as if Brigham were filled to overflowing each time the Prophet taught, then renewed all over again the next time they met. "When I think that I am sitting at the feet of Joseph and being tutored by him," he told his Mary Ann one night, "I feel to shout, Hallelujah! all the day long."

He felt that way now, and as he looked around at the faces of his brethren in the Quorum, he saw that they felt that way too. Joseph was finally done. He stepped back and laid his scriptures on the table, then reached up and pinched the bridge of his nose, closing his eyes wearily. "Thank you, brethren," he said, his eyes still closed. "It has been another wonderful time together. I appreciate your attentiveness."

They watched him, the weariness etched into their faces now too. Then Joseph's hand dropped and he opened his eyes. For what seemed like an eternity, he let his eyes move from face to face, searching, probing, commending—and all without a word. Finally, he nodded. "Brethren, I feel to say something to you and I would like you to pay special heed."

That banished any thoughts of tiredness in an instant. Every eye was on him now.

"Brethren, the Lord bids me hasten the work in which we are engaged. Some important scene is near to take place. I do not know what it is. It may be that my enemies will kill me."

There was a soft collective gasp.

"You know as well as I that even before the Church was organized, the Lord intimated to me that I might have to die for the work. In March of 1829, while I was still translating the Book of Mormon, the Lord said to me, 'Be firm in keeping the commandments, and if you do this, behold I grant unto you eternal life, *even if you be slain.*' Less than a month later, the Lord called attention to his own death, telling me, 'They can do no more to you than they did to me.' "

Seeing their faces, he smiled briefly. "Oh, there have been the reassuring promises as well. You remember that during those dark days in Liberty Jail, he told me that my days were known and that my years would not be numbered less."

Hyrum was nodding. "And there was Father's blessing too."

"Yes, that's right." He turned back to the Twelve. "On the day my father died, he gave each of us his blessing. To me he said, 'Joseph, you shall even live to finish your work,' at which I cried out, 'Oh! my father, shall I?' 'Yes,' came the answer. 'You shall live to lay out the plan of all the work which God has given you to do.' "

"And that you shall," Wilford Woodruff spoke up. "There is still much to do, Brother Joseph."

"Aye, that there is," he agreed. "But if you suppose that Brother Joseph cannot die, this is a mistake. It is true there have been times when I have had the promise of my life to accomplish such and such things, but, having now accomplished those things, I have not at present any lease of my life; I am as liable to die as other men."

"No, Joseph," said John Taylor, "please don't talk that way."

He shrugged. "I understand my mission and business. God Almighty is my shield, and what can man do if God is my friend? But fear not; I shall not be sacrificed until my time comes. Then I shall be offered freely."

Brigham stiffened. Joseph had made intimations like this before, but never so direct and never so extensive. He shook his head, stunned by the implications of what Joseph was saying.

Joseph saw that look and turned now to speak directly to Brigham. "If that should happen, and if the keys and powers which rest on me were *not* imparted to you, they would be lost from the earth." He stopped, his face as grave as Brigham could ever remember seeing it. Then he seemed to straighten a little, as if resolved to the task before him. "But if I can only succeed in placing them upon your heads, then let me fall a victim to murderous hands if God will suffer it. Then I can go with all pleasure and satisfaction, knowing that my work is done and the foundation laid on which the kingdom of God is to be reared in this, the dispensation of the fulness of times."

No one moved. No one spoke. Every eye was searching the face of their beloved Joseph. Now his head turned and once again he was speaking to them all. "Upon the shoulders of the Twelve must the responsibility of leading this church henceforth rest until you shall appoint others to succeed you."

After a long silence, Orson Hyde spoke up. "Joseph, you make me want to weep when I hear you speak like that. Never fear, we shall not let your enemies have you." Others immediately nodded and murmured assenting comments.

Now Joseph smiled, and it was almost dazzling in contrast to what had preceded it. "Weep?" he asked incredulously. "Brethren, I feel to rejoice. Now if they kill me, you have got all the keys and all the ordinances and you can confer them upon others. Now the hosts of Satan will not be able to tear down the kingdom as fast as you will be able to build it up. Is not that indeed cause for rejoicing?"

He clapped Brigham on the shoulders. "Come," he said with sudden exuberance. "A good stick wrestle out in the air would get us all out of this gloomy mood. What say ye? Can any of the Twelve—or all of you together, for that matter—outpull Brother Joseph?"

It was on the evening of April fourth, shortly after sundown, that a knock sounded on the door of Joshua Steed's rented home in Warsaw. He was in the washroom giving Charles a bath. "Caroline, can you get that? I've got Charles in the tub."

He heard her footsteps come down the hall, and then she was at the door to the washroom. "I'll watch him," she said.

He grunted, irritated. She refused to go to the front door anymore. It was always someone for him, and she did not like the looks she got from the people who came to see him. He got up and pushed past her without a word. He knew it was time to move, to wrap up the business in Nauvoo and leave. The atmosphere in Warsaw was oppressive to his family. Even Savannah, he thought—his little toughy who stood up to just about anything life could toss at her—had grown silent and morose.

Well, it would be over soon, he thought. He had a group of five men who were very interested in buying his freight business in Nauvoo. They would take it lock, stock, and barrel, and were even now trying to raise the funds. Caroline had gotten a letter from Lydia saying the family was not going to do anything with the house yet. They had covered the furniture and locked the doors, nothing else. But as far as Joshua was concerned, that was their affair. He had deeded it over to his father and was free of it now. When the sale of the business was final, then Joshua and his family would leave! In St. Louis he'd buy Caroline a house like she had never had before. Or maybe build one. In a neighborhood where being a Mormon wouldn't matter. But then, too, he was still toying with the idea of striking out for somewhere new. Philadelphia maybe. Or Boston—the opportunities there were rich enough for about any businessman. Maybe he could open up a shipping company and rekindle Will's interest in the sea.

He crossed the small living room and went to the door and opened it. To his utter surprise, Robert Foster and Wilson Law were standing there. Behind them was Chauncey Higbee and another man Joshua didn't know.

"Hello, Steed."

"Yes?"

"May we come in?"

They had so caught him by surprise that he was still just standing there. "Uh, of course." He opened the door wider.

As they filed in, Joshua heard a soft noise behind him. He turned. Caroline was standing at the point where the hallway started. Her mouth was tight and she was staring at the four men.

"Evening, Mrs. Steed," Foster called out jovially.

She didn't even flicker in response. "Joshua, may I speak with you for a moment?" She immediately disappeared again.

Startled, Joshua turned to Foster. "Sit down, I'll be right with you." He left the room and went down the hall. He found her in the kitchen. Savannah was in the washroom now, sitting with Charles. Will and Olivia were with Caroline.

"What?" Joshua asked.

"I won't have those men in my home," Caroline said quietly.

He was momentarily shocked, then quickly recovered. "Well, I didn't invite them, they just showed up."

"Well, I won't have them here while we are in the house."

The irritation he had felt earlier flared again. It had not been easy to extricate himself from Thomas Sharp's plans for Joshua Steed, and it had cost Joshua considerable prestige when he refused to be an active participant in the rallies any longer. "Why not?" he snapped. "You don't even know what they want."

"Why not?" Will cried. "Do you even have to ask that? They're opposed to everything we believe in."

"Oh, I see," he said haughtily. He swung on Caroline. "If I remember right, there was a time when you let Mary Fielding Smith into our home and she was opposed to everything I believe in."

Caroline bowed her head briefly. "Yes, of course. You're right." She turned to Olivia. "Go help Savannah get Charles dressed. Will, you find their coats."

A momentary look of dismay crossed Joshua's face. "Where are you going?"

"I don't know. We'll return when your guests have gone."

"Caroline, there's another political meeting tonight. There'll be lots of people out on the streets. I don't like you out there on a night like tonight."

She turned to Olivia, who was still standing there, watching her parents lock wills. "Olivia," Caroline said, "I asked you to do something."

"Yes, Mama." She moved swiftly away.

"Caroline, come on. It's not like I knew they were coming. Don't be—"

"Will, get our coats please."

"Yes, Mama."

"Well, suit yourself!" Joshua snapped. "I have a right to have guests in my home, same as you."

"Yes, you do," she agreed. And he knew she meant it. She walked past him and went to help Olivia.

———◆———

When Joshua came back into the living room, Foster looked concerned. "I hope our showing up like this unexpectedly isn't a problem," he said, glancing toward the hallway.

"It's not," Joshua said shortly. "What brings you here?"

"We've something we thought you needed to hear. By the way," he went on, "this is Leonard Soby."

Soby stood and came over and shook Joshua's hand. Joshua nodded briefly at him, then took a seat. "What is it?" he asked.

"Well, first of all, let us congratulate you on what you've been doing down here. We keep hearing reports of your good work. I—"

"I'm not in that anymore. I've got too much business to take care of."

"Yes," Foster said smoothly, "I got a long letter from Thomas Sharp telling all that."

Joshua's eyes narrowed. "You're in touch with Thomas Sharp? Does Joseph know that?"

"Joseph is going to know everything soon enough," Higbee sneered. "Tell him, Foster."

Foster nodded and smiled. It was a triumphant smile. "That's why we're here. Day after tomorrow is general conference."

For a moment Joshua looked blank, then remembered the large meetings the Church held twice a year. "So?"

Foster leaned forward, eager now. "Joshua, we're going to depose Joseph."

One eyebrow came up and he leaned forward. "Depose him?"

"Yes," Higbee jumped in. "At the conference. We're going to have him declared a fallen prophet. We'll vote him out and put in William Law instead."

"Wait a minute. As I recall, you claimed you have about two hundred people who are sympathetic to your views. And Joseph has thousands. How do you think you'll be able to depose Joseph with that kind of a vote?"

"You don't understand the principle of common consent in the Church," Foster said with a condescending smile. "It doesn't take a majority, just a few votes from people with the courage to defend their position. We've got him, I tell you."

Joshua sat back. He had heard the family talk about their strange way of sustaining and upholding the officers of the Church. "And you really think that will work?" he said dubiously.

"Yes!" Foster cried. "Why don't you come up to Nauvoo? You don't want to miss this." There was a sudden cunning look. "Bring your family. Maybe that will finally convince your wife that this church will no longer tolerate the doings of a wicked man at its head."

"Caroline?"

She was at the small dresser, brushing out her hair. She stopped, watching him in the mirror.

"They want me to come to Nauvoo."

There was a slight lift to her eyebrows.

"I won't lie to you. They want me to come to the general conference. They say they're going to declare Joseph a fallen prophet and have him voted out."

There was a soft, derisive laugh. "Don't get your hopes up, Joshua."

"I'm not," he said snappishly. "But Joseph is in more trouble than he knows."

She turned around now, totally incredulous. "What are you saying, Joshua? That you want to go to the conference?"

"Yes. I don't have any part in this, I want you to know that. But if it's going to happen, I'd like to be there."

"It won't happen, Joshua. I'd love to go back and see your family, but I'm telling you, it won't happen."

"Do you want to go or not?" he asked pointedly.

Now her eyes narrowed. "With the children?"

"Of course. I worry about you traveling that far in the wagon in your condition, but . . ."

"I'll be fine." Then, still thinking quickly, she added, "The conference will last for four days."

"I know that. We'll stay at the house. That will please Pa."

"And what if your precious Mr. Foster is wrong? I won't simply turn around and come back to Warsaw again after the first five minutes prove how utterly foolish these friends of yours really are. If we go, Joshua, we stay for the whole four days."

He considered that. He needed time in Nauvoo anyway to conclude things with the freight business. And if things went as Foster planned, if they really did throw Joseph out, staying in Nauvoo for a while longer wasn't an unattractive prospect. It would certainly make Caroline happy again. He nodded. "Fair enough."

It was late, after ten, when Benjamin and Nathan knocked softly on the door of Joshua's home.

Tired from the journey up from Warsaw, Caroline and the children had gone to bed. Joshua was working on a summary of the business for his potential buyers. At the knock, he looked up, then stood and went to the door. If this was Foster again, he thought . . .

"Evening, Joshua. Can we have a word with you?" Benjamin asked when Joshua opened the door.

Joshua gave his father a long look, then finally shrugged.

"Surely you're not going to try and change my mind about this whole thing," he said with a touch of irony.

"About going to see Joseph's 'downfall'?" Nathan asked with a smile. "No, that's not why we're here, though I think you're in for a surprise tomorrow."

"Maybe, maybe not," Joshua grunted. But he stepped out on the porch and shut the door behind him.

Nathan stepped back. "First of all, I think in all the excitement today we forgot to tell you. Yesterday we got a letter from Melissa. Carl's father died a couple of weeks after they got to Kirtland."

"Oh," Joshua said. "Sorry to hear that."

"She says Carl wants to stay through the summer at least."

Joshua caught the significance of the last two words. "So, that makes two of us Joseph has driven away."

Benjamin decided not to comment on that. Instead his shoulders lifted and fell. "Joshua, there's something we think you need to know about Foster and that bunch."

"Why? You think I'm somehow associated with that group? No thank you."

Benjamin didn't try to hide his surprise. "That's not what they're saying."

Joshua's eyes narrowed. "What are they saying?"

"Foster is bragging about how they went to Warsaw and convinced you to come up here. He hasn't said it right out, but he's hinting strongly that you are in this with them and—"

"Well, I'm not," Joshua cut in sharply. "They came and told me that Joseph's going to be voted out this conference. If that happens, I'd like to be here. That's the only reason I came."

There was a long appraising look from Nathan, and then he nodded. "I'm glad, Joshua. Will told me that you're not actively participating in the anti-Mormon party either. That means a lot to us."

"Will talks too much," Joshua muttered. But down deep he was secretly pleased that his family knew he had made that choice at least. In that, Will had been right. He couldn't lead a fight that might hurt his family. "So, knowing that I'm not a part of it, what else did you have to say?"

"Did you know that they are conspiring to murder Joseph?" Benjamin asked.

Joshua jerked a little in spite of himself, then shook his head. "They're going to try to get Joseph declared a false prophet, but murder? I think you're seeing ghosts in the graveyard."

"No, it's far more than that," Nathan said, glad to see Joshua's genuine shock. "We have testimony that Foster and the Laws and the Higbees have sworn on a Bible that they will not rest until Joseph is destroyed."

Joshua didn't want to believe any of this, but he had to admit that it rang true. It was just the kind of melodramatic nonsense that Foster and his cronies would dream up. He finally nodded. "That wouldn't come as a great shock. But I am not a part of it, Nathan. Not in any way. I want no part of them or their dough-headed schemes."

Benjamin gave him a sharp look, then smiled. "Dough heads. You know who called them that, don't you?"

Now Joshua smiled. "Yes," he said ruefully, "it's the only thing I've ever heard that makes me think Joseph is a prophet."

The three of them laughed at that and the tension was gone.

"It's good to see you and the family again, Joshua," his father said.

"Thank you. It feels good to be back." Then before they could draw any conclusions from that, he went on. "But make no mistake, Pa. If Joseph is not turned out of office in the next couple of days, I'll not be coming back to Nauvoo. Not ever."

Benjamin nodded, the sorrow clearly written on his face. "I understand, Joshua."

Chapter Notes

Just as the Savior knew of his coming crucifixion and spent increasing time with his Apostles preparing them for when he would no longer be with them, in a similar manner, during the spring of 1844 Joseph Smith felt an increasing intimation of his coming death; and like the Master whom he served, Joseph worked feverishly to make sure the Twelve were ready for the responsibility that would soon rest upon them. Once that was done, it was as though a great burden had been lifted from his shoulders, and, in the words of Orson Hyde, "he rejoiced very much." Some of the comments Joseph makes in this chapter are drawn from things he said at an earlier date about the fact that his mission might be coming to a close. He did speak at this March 1844 meeting about his coming death, however, and then went on to speak about the Twelve now having the keys of the kingdom so they could carry on the work if Joseph was taken. (See HC 4:587; CHFT, pp. 273–74; Draft Declaration of the Twelve Apostles, reporting March 1844 meeting of Twelve, as cited by Boyd K. Packer, " 'The Shield of Faith,' " Ensign, 25 [May 1995]: 7.)

Late in March of 1844, Joseph Smith told an assembly of the Saints that there was a conspiracy against his life. Hyrum counseled him not to publicly inflame the situation, but Joseph said that these men couldn't "scare off an old setting hen." (See HC 6:271–72.) Joseph's source of information on this conspiracy seems to have been two young men, Dennison Harris and Robert Scott. When they were invited to the meeting of the conspirators, they went to Joseph and asked him what to do. Joseph advised them to go but sternly warned them against making any covenants with the conspirators. At the meeting, all in attendance were required to put a hand on a Bible and swear "before God and all holy angels" that they would not rest until Joseph Smith was destroyed. The boys refused to make the oath and were threatened with their lives. When they finally escaped, Joseph was waiting nearby. After hearing their report, he swore them to secrecy and made them promise they would not tell their story to anyone for at least twenty years, so as not to put their lives in jeopardy. (See Restoration, pp. 590–91.)

The temperature during the morning of Saturday, April sixth, was pleasantly warm for this early in the month. With the mild winter and recent warm spells, spring had definitely come to Nauvoo. The fields and roadsides were a dozen different shades of green. Many of the trees were now in full leaf. Gardens were filled with the last of the tulips, and the crocus and hyacinth were gone now. Here and there, the brilliant splash of purple and white lilac bushes caught the eye.

They had assembled in a grove about a quarter mile east of the temple site, and the crowd was huge. As they waited for the meeting to begin, Joshua tried to get a rough estimate of how many were there, but finally gave it up. Thousands for sure. Most were seated on wooden benches, but some were in wagons and carriages and even on rocks. The Steeds weren't right at the back, but about two-thirds of the people were in front of them. He knew that the family would have liked to sit closer to the front, but he did not want to and they stayed with him.

Through the crowds, Joshua caught a glimpse of the Higbee brothers but immediately turned his head so they wouldn't see him. He didn't see Foster at all and didn't really look for him. He had come to see if they were right, if this would be the day that Joseph fell from leadership. That was all. He wanted nothing more.

At quarter past ten, Joseph and Hyrum Smith appeared and moved toward the raised platform that most of the Saints referred to simply as "the stand." As soon as they were seated, Brigham Young stood up and in a loud voice called the congregation to order. He announced that their prophet would say a few words after the choir sang a hymn. When they were done, Joseph stood and moved slowly to the front part of the stand.

"He's been sick, you know," Benjamin whispered to Joshua.

"Oh?"

"Yes, quite ill. It takes a strong pair of lungs to speak to a group this size."

He nodded without comment, then turned back to watch Joseph. Joshua was not familiar with how a conference worked, and so he wasn't sure when Foster's group would make their move.

"Brothers and sisters," Joseph said, "how good it is to see you this morning. Before we have prayer, I would just like to say a word or two. Perhaps you have heard that it has been expected by some that the little petty difficulties which have existed in our city of late would be brought up and investigated before this conference. But this will not be the case," he said firmly. "These things are of too trivial a nature to occupy the attention of so large a body. I intend to give you some instruction on the principles of eternal truth, but in consequence of the weakness of my lungs due to my recent illness I shall wait until later in the conference. The elders will give you instruction, and then, if necessary, I will offer such corrections as may be proper."

Now his eyes swept across the congregation and his voice rose in volume, but he still spoke calmly. "Those who feel desirous of sowing the seeds of discord will be disappointed on this occasion. It is our purpose to build up and establish the principles of righteousness and not to break down and destroy."

Joshua was watching intently now. *He knows! Joseph knows what they're up to and he's uncocking their pistol before they can even take it out of the holster.* Say what you would about Joseph, he wasn't stupid. This was a wiser strategy than going for an open confrontation. Simply get up and state that this was not a crisis, it was a petty thing. Trivial. Those were good words. Who could get up a revolution over something trivial?

"The great Jehovah has ever been with me, and the wisdom of God will direct me in the seventh hour. I feel in closer communion and better standing with God than ever I felt before in my life, and I am glad of this opportunity to appear in your midst. I thank God for the glorious day that he has given us. We shall now have Brother William W. Phelps give us an invocation, after which the choir will sing another hymn for us, and then we shall hear from President Sidney Rigdon."

He sat down and there was a collective, inaudible sigh of relief. The crowd had felt it too. They had come expecting trouble. Joseph had neatly sidestepped it by simply assuming there would be none.

When it became obvious that Sidney Rigdon was going to go on for as long as his lungs were capable, which seemed to be forever, and that nothing other than that was going to happen, Joshua whispered something to Caroline, then stood and slipped away. Nathan, sitting directly behind them, leaned forward. "He doesn't like Sidney's sermon?" he asked with a straight face.

There was a quick smile from Caroline as she shook her head. "I guess not."

———◆———

During the midday intermission, Joshua heard voices coming up the street and hurriedly went to the window. Now that the freight yard was east of town, he wasn't too far from the temple site and he wondered if his family were coming to get him. He stood and walked to the window, then frowned deeply. Robert Foster and a man Joshua didn't know were coming down the street. He looked around, considering locking the door and simply ignoring their knock, but then decided it was time to make a few things clear. He stepped out on the porch just as the two men arrived.

"Afternoon, Steed," Foster said in surprise as Joshua came out on the step.

Joshua nodded.

"Joshua, this is Joseph H. Jackson. Jackson, meet Joshua Steed."

They exchanged curt nods. Joshua gave him a quick appraisal. He was the kind of man Joshua had met on many a trail or in the saloons of America, or slinking around the back alleys of America's big cities. A big man, he wore a brace of pistols, had a bowie knife on one hip, and swaggered as if he were daring someone to invite him to use them. If this group had murder on their minds, this looked like the kind of man who would do it for them.

Joshua looked at Foster. "Sure glad I came up from Warsaw for conference."

"The conference isn't over yet. We'll get him." He took a breath. "Look, we wanted to talk with you about something."

"Foster," Joshua cut in flatly, "I never was much for working with men who are all talk and no action."

Foster flushed and Jackson's face instantly darkened. The big man took a step forward, one hand moving toward his pistol. "Hey, mister, you better watch your mouth."

"Foster, call your dog off or be prepared for the consequences."

There was a moment's hesitation while Foster considered what those consequences might be; then he grabbed at Jackson's arm. "It's all right, Joe," he said. "Evidently Steed has lost his nerve and doesn't want in on the game."

"I never did want in on your game, Foster, and if I hear that you're telling people I am in it with you, I'll be coming to work it out between us. You understand me?"

Jackson's eyes were like pig eyes now—tiny, hard, glittering with hatred. One hand was hovering just above his pistol butt. "Get outta the way, Foster. This dandy needs a lesson or two in manners."

Joshua didn't even glance at him but kept his eyes fixed hard on Foster. He lifted his right hand slowly up to his waist and hooked his thumb in his belt, pushing the coat back just a little. He wore no weapon, but he knew they couldn't be sure about that, because his coat was long enough to conceal a pistol.

Foster blanched a little. "You're making a big mistake, Steed," he yelped.

"Maybe so," he agreed, "but it's my mistake, isn't it? Now, I'd suggest you get, Foster. And I don't want to be seeing you at my door again, understood?"

"Come on, Jackson," Foster blurted, yanking around. "He's no good to us anymore."

Jackson's hand fell away from his pistol, but his mouth was twisted and hard. "This ain't between you and Foster anymore, Steed," he warned. "You and me have a score to settle."

When the conference reconvened Saturday afternoon, Joseph again did not speak, and the time was turned over to President Rigdon to continue what he had started earlier that day. Joshua, who had returned to the grove, rolled his eyes and left immediately. Then about five o'clock, Brigham dismissed the assembly because rain was threatening. The Steeds barely reached home before the heavens opened and it began to pour. Had it not been for his promise to Caroline, Joshua would have packed them all in the wagon and headed back to Warsaw that very night. But he said nothing, and quietly determined he would push the sale of his business as quickly as he could so that he could leave Illinois once and for all.

It was about an hour after their return home that afternoon that Emily burst into the kitchen. "Mama! Papa! Come see."

She didn't wait to tell them what they were supposed to come see. She darted out again. Lydia smiled at Nathan and set aside the pan of potatoes she was peeling. Nathan was setting the table for her. He stopped and they both went out after her.

When they stepped out on their front porch they saw

instantly what it was that had got her so excited. The rain over Nauvoo had mostly stopped now, but to the east the sky was still black and dark. Out over the west the sky had cleared and rays of sunshine slanted in at a shallow angle, catching the last of the rain squall. The result was that there was a brilliant double rainbow directly over the temple, as though it had been placed there by some divine artistic hand.

"See, Mama?" Emily cried. "Isn't it beautiful?"

"Oh, yes," Lydia breathed.

Up and down Steed Row others were coming out now as the word spread. Those on the west side of the street stood on their porches. Those on the east came out in the street so as to see it better. Mary Ann and Benjamin came over to join Lydia and Nathan.

"That's breathtaking," Mary Ann said.

"I don't think I've ever seen one that bright before," Nathan said.

"Me neither," said Benjamin. Then he nodded in satisfaction. "Well, there's another year we don't have to worry."

Nathan turned, puzzled. Both Lydia and Mary Ann gave him a quizzical look as well. "What's that supposed to mean?" Mary Ann asked him.

"That's right," he said, "I forgot to tell you."

"Tell us what?" Nathan asked.

"It was just about a month ago now. Joseph was talking about the second coming of the Savior. And then he made a most unusual prophecy. He told us that one day he had been inquiring of the Lord concerning His second coming. Joseph said it was made known to him by the Spirit that the rainbow was a sign given to Noah as a promise that in any year in which the bow is seen, there will be prosperity, seedtime and harvest."

Mary Ann peered at him to see if he was teasing them, a habit not unknown to Benjamin. But he was not. He was quite serious.

"Really?" Lydia said, totally fascinated by that concept.

"Yes. He said that in any year the rainbow would be seen the Savior would not come. But in the year when the bow is withdrawn, or not seen, then will commence desolation, calamity, and distress among the nations, and there shall be no seedtime or harvest, but we can look for famine."

Nathan was listening as intently as his wife and mother now. "That's amazing," he said. "A simple thing like a rainbow can signify all of that?"

"Yes," Benjamin said. Then a slow grin stole across his face. "Since hearing that, as a matter of fact, I have become an avid rainbow watcher."

Sunday morning dawned bright and beautiful. The rain had cleared the sky and deepened the colors of spring. Joshua almost didn't go to conference, volunteering to stay home and watch the children. But by unspoken agreement the family wouldn't let him use that as an excuse. Still wondering if Foster was going to pull something off, he finally went up to the morning session.

The crowds were huge, at least half again what there had been on Saturday. Joshua was amazed. Was it the weather? Was it the fact that it was the Sabbath and everyone had the day free? Was word about this silent contest going on between Joseph and his enemies bringing in the flock to see what was going to happen?

But Joseph didn't give a sermon at this session either. The only thing of interest at all was a brief announcement Joseph made right at the beginning. "Brethren and sisters"—he was almost shouting to make his voice carry across the vast throng— "I would remind you that we have a very large group here this morning. As mayor of the city, I ask you all to keep good order. You have probably noticed that we have policemen all around the outskirts of the congregation to help keep order and to assist you if you need help."

Joshua's head came up. *To keep order?*

Joseph's voice rang out across the congregation with authority now. "And you brethren who are our policemen, I want you to exercise your authority. I know this is a Church meeting but it is also a meeting of our citizens. Don't say that you can't do anything for us, for the constitutional power calls on you to maintain good order. God Almighty calls upon you to maintain good order. And we command you to do it!"

Joshua was shaking his head slowly, feeling a grudging admiration for the man. If Foster and his bunch were planning anything today, Joseph had just put them on notice that it would not go uncontested. There were forty policemen. That was sufficient to discourage about anyone.

He didn't even wait for the announcement that Sidney Rigdon would continue his speech outlining the history of the Church for yet a third conference session. He murmured something to Caroline and left again.

As he slipped through the crowd, Nathan leaned over to Lydia. "How come he always gets to leave just when Sidney starts talking?"

"Nathan Steed!" she whispered sternly, but he could see the twinkle in her eye.

———◆———

Joshua surprised them all by returning for the afternoon session. They all knew why he had come. Though the likelihood was getting ever more remote, there was still a chance there would be some action. But despite his motives, they were still glad to have him there. Joseph had promised to speak, and maybe he would do so this session.

Joshua settled in beside Caroline as he looked around. He noticed with some disappointment that Joseph was not up in the row of chairs on the stand. After the hymn and prayer, Hyrum stood and talked to the congregation about the women's "penny fund," encouraging them to continue to contribute so that they could purchase the glass and nails they would need for the house of the Lord.

Just after three, a stir went through the crowd as Joseph and Emma finally arrived and Joseph took his seat up front. Hyrum ended immediately and had the choir sing another hymn. Then he turned the time over to Joseph.

The Prophet stood and moved forward with a firm step and his chin up. He looked stronger and quite composed. If he was worried about someone challenging his position as prophet and leader of the Church, you could not tell it by looking at him.

"My glorious brethren and sisters, what a wonderful sight it is to see so many of you here this afternoon. I feel to call the attention of this congregation while I address you on the subject of the dead. As you know, some weeks ago, a dear brother, a faithful elder in the Church, Brother King Follett, was crushed in a well by the falling of a tub of rock as he sought to repair it. I had planned to preach the funeral sermon of Brother Follett last Friday, but ill health would not allow it. I should like to do so now, if I may."

Six or seven rows forward of where the Steeds were and off to the left, Joshua saw movement. It was Robert Foster. He had turned his head and was looking right at Joshua. There was a quick, triumphant nod. "This is it," Foster seemed to be saying. "He shall preach and then we shall have him."

His interest piqued again with that, Joshua leaned forward to listen more closely.

"I have been requested to speak by Brother Follett's friends and relatives, but inasmuch as there are a great many in this congregation who live in this city as well as elsewhere who have lost friends, I feel disposed to speak on the subject in general and to offer you my ideas, so far as I have ability, and so far as I shall be inspired by the Holy Spirit to dwell on this subject.

"I ask for your prayers and faith that I may have the instruction of Almighty God and the gift of the Holy Ghost. I wish to set forth things that are true and which can be easily comprehended by you, and I pray that the testimony of the Spirit may carry conviction to your hearts and minds of the truth of what I shall say. Oh, my beloved Saints, pray that the Lord may strengthen my lungs and stay the winds and the weather. Let the prayers of the Saints to heaven appear, that they may enter into the ears of the Lord of Sabaoth, for the effectual prayers of the righteous avail much. There is strength here, and I verily believe that your prayers will be heard."

Joshua was watching Joseph's face. He was about fifty or sixty feet away, but Joshua could see that he was very determined. His body was erect, his shoulders back, his voice strong. This certainly wasn't a man looking over his shoulder to see what enemy was lurking there.

"I do not intend to please your ears with superfluity of words or oratory, or with much learning; but I intend to edify you with the simple truths from heaven. In the first place, I wish to go back to the beginning—to the morn of creation. There is the starting point for us to look to, in order to understand and be fully acquainted with the mind, purposes, and decrees of the Great Elohim, who sits in yonder heavens as he did at the creation of this world. It is necessary for us to have an understanding of God himself in the beginning. If we start right, it is easy to go right all the time; but if we start wrong, we may go wrong, and it will be a hard matter to get right.

"There are but a very few beings in the world who understand rightly the character of God. The great majority of mankind do not comprehend anything, either that which is past, or that which is to come, as it respects their relationship to God. If men do not comprehend the character of God, they do not comprehend themselves. I want to go back to the beginning, and so lift your minds into a more lofty sphere and a more exalted understanding than what the human mind generally aspires to."

Joshua had to admit it. The contrast between Joseph Smith and Sidney Rigdon was dramatic. There was power in Joseph, and you could feel it energizing the hearts of his people. They were fixed on him now, every eye turned to him. The children had quieted, and only the fussing of a baby here and there could be heard.

"I want to ask this congregation—every man, woman, and child—to answer this question in their own hearts: What kind of a being is God? Does any man or woman know? Have any of you seen him, heard him, or communed with him? Here is the question that will, peradventure, from this time henceforth occupy your attention. The scriptures inform us that 'this is life eternal, that they might know thee the only true God, and Jesus Christ, whom thou hast sent.' There can be eternal life on no other principle.

"It is my privilege to be the man who comprehends God and to explain those principles to your hearts, so that the Spirit seals them upon you." His head came up now, his voice hardened in sudden challenge. "And if that be the case, then let every man and woman who does not know God henceforth sit in silence. Let them put their hands to their mouths, and never lift their hands or voices, or say anything against the man of God or the servants of God again. But if I fail to do as I plan, to teach you about the character of God, then it becomes my duty to renounce all further pretensions to revelations and inspirations. It means I am no longer a prophet and should be like the rest of the world—a false teacher."

As the faces all across the group registered shock at that, Joseph paused to take a drink from a glass of water that Hyrum handed to him. He finished and continued. "There are those who would say that my life should be forfeit because I am a false teacher—"

Benjamin swung around and shot Joshua a quick glance, and to his own surprise, Joshua nodded. Joseph was taking them on. The gloves were off now. This was a bare-knuckled, head-on refuting of the men who were furtively trying to bring him down. Joshua couldn't tell for sure, but it seemed that Joseph was looking directly at Foster now. The doctor seemed to sink down in his seat, aware that many people were staring at him as well.

"There are men who have pretensions to godliness, but when their ignorance of the knowledge of God is made manifest, they will all be as badly off as I am. If any man is authorized to take away my life because he thinks and says I am a false teacher, then, upon that same principle, we should be justified in taking away the life of every false teacher. But if that were the case, where would be the end of blood? And who would not be the sufferer?

"I will prove that the world is wrong, by showing what God is. I am going to inquire after God, for I want you all to know him and to be familiar with him. And if I bring you to a true knowledge of him, all persecutions against me ought to cease. If I teach you truly of God, you will then know that I am his servant, for I speak as one having authority."

Another pause, another quick drink. "I will go back to the beginning before the world was, to show what kind of being God is. What sort of a being was God in the beginning? Open your ears and hear, all ye ends of the earth, for I am going to prove it to you by the Bible and to tell you the designs of God in relation to the human race and why he interferes with the affairs of man. God himself was once as we are now, and is an exalted man, and sits enthroned in yonder heavens! That is the great secret. If the veil were rent today, and the great God who holds this world in its orbit, and who upholds all worlds and all things by his power, was to make himself visible—I say, if you were to see him today, you would see him like a man in form—like yourselves in all the person, image, and very form as a man.

"I am going to tell you how God came to be God. We have imagined and supposed that God was God from all eternity. I will refute that idea, and take away the veil, so that you may see. These are incomprehensible ideas to some, but they are simple. It is the first principle of the gospel to know for a certainty the character of God, and to know that we may converse with him as one man converses with another, and that he was once a man like us—yea, that God himself, the Father of us all, dwelt on an earth, the same as Jesus Christ himself did."

He stopped, once again letting his eyes move from face to face. "Do you wonder if I am right? Well, I shall show it to you from the Bible. I wish I were in a suitable place to tell it and that I had the trump of an archangel, so that I could tell the story in such a manner that persecution would cease forever. What did Jesus say? Mark it, Elder Rigdon! The scriptures inform us that Jesus said, 'As the Father hath power in himself, even so hath the Son power.' To do what? Why, to do what the Father did. The answer is obvious—in a manner to lay down his body and take it up again. Jesus, what are you going to do? To lay down my life as my Father did, and take it up again. Do we believe it? If you do not believe it, you do not believe the Bible. The scriptures say it, and I defy all the learning and wisdom and all the combined powers of earth and hell together to refute it.

"Here, then, is eternal life—to know the only wise and true God; and you have got to learn how to be gods yourselves, how to be kings and priests to God, the same as all gods have done before you. And how do we do that? Namely, by going from one small degree to another, and from a small capacity to a great one, from grace to grace, from exaltation to exaltation, until you attain to the resurrection of the dead and are able to dwell in everlasting burnings. Then you shall sit in glory, as do those who sit enthroned in everlasting power."

Joshua turned to his family. Caroline was leaning forward, her lips slightly parted, her eyes totally focused on Joseph. He suspected that even if he spoke to her she would not hear him. And in that moment, Joshua Steed understood with perfect clarity that he had come to Nauvoo for naught. He looked around. Nathan and Lydia had the same expression. Matthew and Jenny, and Kathryn in her wheelchair, were almost mesmerized. Derek, Rebecca, Will, Olivia. Men, women, teenaged boys and girls, even the older children—they were all fixed on their prophet, and he was indisputably teaching them with great power. It didn't matter that what he was saying didn't make much sense to Joshua. Now he understood why there were the huge numbers of people here. Now he understood that a group like Foster's fools chirping in the background would hardly be a distraction. Nothing they were doing would bring Joseph down. Nothing!

"The Bible tells us," Joseph went on, his voice sounding a little hoarse now, "that we shall be heirs of God and 'joint-heirs' with Jesus Christ. What does that mean? It means that we inherit the same power, the same glory, and the same exaltation as the Savior did, that we can ascend the throne of eternal power, the same as those who have gone before. What did Jesus do? 'Why, I do the things I saw my Father do when worlds came rolling into existence. My Father worked out his kingdom with fear and trembling, and I must do the same. And when I get my kingdom, I shall present it to my Father, so that he may obtain kingdom upon kingdom, and it will exalt him in glory. He will then take a higher exaltation, and I will take his place, and thereby become exalted myself.'

"Can you not see it, my brothers and sisters? It is plain beyond disputation. When you climb up a ladder, you must begin at the bottom and ascend step by step, until you arrive at the top. So it is with the principles of the gospel. You must begin with the first and go on until you learn all the principles of exaltation. But it will be a great while after you have passed through the veil before you will have learned them. It is not all to be comprehended in this world. It will be a great work to learn our salvation and exaltation even beyond the grave."

Joshua stood once again, winning himself irritated glances from those around him and a surprised look from Caroline. He ignored both, making his way slowly through the people, careful not to step on anyone. Once clear, he walked quietly back toward his house.

He had come to watch Joseph dethroned, he thought with some sense of irony. Instead he had just witnessed him entrench his position as leader of the Church more powerfully than ever before. Now Joshua knew there was only one thing to do. It would take him a month or two to finish up the sale of his business here in Nauvoo. Then he and his family would leave Warsaw. And now he wasn't so sure that St. Louis was the answer anymore. They would leave and go somewhere far away. Maybe eventually that would make the difference. And yet, even as he formulated those thoughts, he knew it was foolish thinking. He had seen Caroline's face. He had watched Will and Olivia. They would follow Joshua wherever he said, he knew that now. But what of it? Their hearts were here. Their confidence was fixed on the man speaking of how to achieve celestial glory. Joshua understood now that he was never going to turn their hearts away from that. Never! And it left him filled with a great emptiness and sense of loss.

Though nothing was declared openly or brought before the full congregation of the Saints, the April 1844 general conference proved to be a pivotal moment in the ever-widening split between Joseph and his enemies. The opposition group was openly recruiting members of the Church to join them, but Joseph had hard evidence of their secret conspiracies now and moved quickly against them. The break was swift, inevitable, and final.

On the eighteenth of April, just a little over a week following the conference, Robert D. Foster, William and Wilson Law, and William's wife, Jane, were excommunicated from the Church for unchristian-like conduct. Though not unexpected, it nevertheless came as a tremendous shock to the Church. William Law had been Second Counselor in the First Presidency. Wilson Law was a major general in the Nauvoo Legion.

Two days later, Emma Smith, who was now about three months pregnant with another child, took a riverboat south to St. Louis to purchase goods for the store and for the Mansion House. Immediately upon hearing that, some of Joseph's enemies spread the rumor that Emma was extremely bitter over the whole issue of plural marriage and was leaving Joseph for good. This was the real reason for her departure, they said. Unfortunately for the rumormongers, five days later she was back in Nauvoo and went right back to the Mansion House.

On April twenty-sixth, Foster and his brother came to the mayor's office and threatened Joseph with a pistol. They were arrested, disarmed, and fined one hundred dollars each. Now the spirit of rebellion was out in the open and growing uglier almost daily. That next Sunday evening, while the Saints gathered for a prayer meeting for the sick, the apostates gathered at the home of Wilson Law. After several affidavits attesting to Joseph's "fallen" state were read, it was proposed that a new, reformed church be created. The proposal was greeted with enthusiasm, and immediately steps were undertaken to formalize it. William Law would be the new president; Austin Cowles and Wilson Law would be his counselors. Robert Foster and Francis Higbee and others were nominated to be apostles in a new "quorum of the twelve."

During all this trouble, Joseph did not abandon his candidacy for president of the United States. His platform statement had been mailed to about two hundred leaders throughout the country in an attempt to build a base of support for his candidacy. It was decided that elders would be sent on missions throughout the United States to promote his run for the presidency. By mid-May, Brigham Young and Heber C. Kimball and all the rest of the Twelve, except for John Taylor and Willard Richards, had left Nauvoo to go east.

As summer came, the Saints were alienated from virtually everyone else in Illinois. Many communities were jealous of Nauvoo's explosive success; others resented the city's liberal charter and the fact that the state legislature would not grant them similar license. With the Nauvoo Legion numbering five thousand strong, there was growing fear of the Mormons' power. Criticism continued to grow that the municipal court system was more protective of Joseph than it was of the law. And the distaste for the unique Mormon doctrines—particularly the growing knowledge of plural marriage—only deepened the alienation and isolation.

But in spite of all that, the danger lay elsewhere. When he had addressed the newly formed police department back in December of 1843, Joseph Smith said: "All the enemies upon the face of the earth may roar and exert all their power to bring about my death, but they can accomplish nothing, unless some who are among us and enjoy our society join with our enemies." As June 1844 began, the stage was set to prove how prophetic Joseph's statement would be.

When Foster and the Laws formed their new church, two actions were decided on. The first would prove to be a minor annoyance. The second would have far greater consequences. First, a committee was appointed to visit different families in the city to see who would join the new church. They had some limited success, but nothing more. Second, the group also resolved to begin publishing their own newspaper to provide a countervoice to the papers published by the Church. Immediately they sent off for a press. There had to be a suitable name, they reasoned. This newspaper would be the means of bringing all of

Joseph's nefarious acts to the attention of the world. A name was proposed and eagerly accepted.

They would call it the *Nauvoo Expositor*.

Chapter Notes

Joseph's comments about the rainbow being a sign related to the second coming of Christ were given on 10 March 1844 and were recorded by several different men (see Joseph Smith, *The Words of Joseph Smith*, comp. and ed. Andrew F. Ehat and Lyndon W. Cook [Provo, Utah: Religious Studies Center, Brigham Young University, 1980], pp. 332, 334, 335, 336; also found in *Teachings of the Prophet Joseph Smith*, sel. Joseph Fielding Smith [Salt Lake City: Deseret Book Co., 1938], pp. 305, 340–41). On 6 April, shortly after the afternoon session of conference was dismissed because of imminent rain, a brilliant double rainbow appeared in the heavens (see *HC* 6:297).

What has come to be known as the King Follett Discourse—which some have thought to be one of the most important doctrinal discourses ever given, and which was in the eyes of the Saints the consummate proof that Joseph was not a fallen prophet—was delivered on the afternoon of 7 April 1844, the second day of the conference (see *HC* 6:302–17; also in *Teachings of the Prophet Joseph Smith*, pp. 342–62). Less than half of the total sermon is cited here.

The doctrine that God is an exalted man and that man may someday become a god himself was first taught by Joseph Smith in the King Follett Discourse. Though the doctrine has been widely criticized by some other churches, it is based solidly on biblical concepts as well as on latter-day revelation. Paul taught that God is the Father of our spirits (see Hebrews 12:9). This is why we refer to him as our Heavenly Father (see Matthew 6:8–9).

It is part of Latter-day Saint theology that this is a literal fatherhood and not just symbolic terminology. Elder Boyd K. Packer, a member of the Quorum of the Twelve, suggested why this concept of fatherhood is pivotal to the idea that we may someday become gods. "Since *every living thing* follows the pattern of its parentage, are we to suppose that God had some other strange pattern in mind for *His* offspring? Surely we, His children, are not, in the language of science, a different species than He is? What is in error, then, when we use the term *Godhood* to describe the ultimate destiny of mankind? We may now be young in our progression—juvenile, even infantile, compared with Him. Nevertheless, in the eternities to come, if we are worthy, we may be like unto Him, enter His presence, . . . and receive a 'fulness.'" (In Conference Report, October 1984, p. 83.)

Other biblical references support this concept. For example, we are commanded to be perfect, just as our Father in Heaven is perfect (see Matthew 5:48). Paul taught that the faithful can become "joint-heirs with Christ" (see Romans 8:14–18). A joint-heir is one who inherits the same rewards as another heir. Since Christ was given all that his Father has (see John 16:15), to be joint-heirs with Christ means that we may inherit all that the Father has also. Paul confirmed this when he said that through Christ, God would "freely give us all things" (Romans 8:32). And John the Revelator taught that those that "overcometh shall inherit all things" (Revelation 21:7). In another place, John wrote: "Beloved, now are we the sons of God, and it doth not yet appear what we shall be: but we know that, when he shall appear, *we shall be like him;* for we shall see him as he is" (1 John 3:2; emphasis added).

This doctrine is taught clearly enough in the New Testament that C. S. Lewis, that wonderful Christian theologian and writer (and not a Latter-day Saint!), wrote: "It is a serious thing to *live in a society of possible gods and goddesses,* to remember that the dullest and most uninteresting person you can talk to may one day be a creature which, if you saw it now, you would be strongly tempted to worship. . . . There are no ordinary people." (*The Weight of Glory and Other Addresses,* rev. ed. [New York: Macmillan, Collier Books, 1980], pp. 18, 19; emphasis added.)

This does not mean that Latter-day Saints believe they will someday supplant God the Father or ever take his place as the Supreme God of the Universe. The Father, the Son, and the Holy Ghost will ever, eternities without end, be held in the utmost reverence and worshipped as God. But Latter-day Saints do solemnly affirm, as they believe God himself stated in a revelation given to Joseph Smith, that if certain conditions are met, through the glorious grace of Christ, "then shall they be gods, because they have no end; therefore shall they be from everlasting to everlasting, because they continue. . . . Then shall they be gods, because they have all power, and the angels are subject unto them." (D&C 132:20.)

President Spencer W. Kimball, twelfth President of the Church, taught: "Man can transform himself and he must. Man has in himself the seeds of godhood, which can germinate and grow and develop. As the acorn becomes the oak, the mortal man becomes a god. It is within his power to lift himself by his very bootstraps from the plane on which he finds himself to the plane on which he should be. It may be a long, hard lift with many obstacles, but it is a real possibility." (*The Teachings of Spencer W. Kimball,* ed. Edward L. Kimball [Salt Lake City: Bookcraft, 1982], p. 28.)

For an excellent summary of the time period between April and June 1844, see *CHFT,* pp. 269–71. The quote from Joseph Smith about enemies within the Church is found in *HC* 6:152.

N athan burst into his father's house without knocking. He stopped just inside, looking around. "Anybody here?"

"I'm in the kitchen."

He strode down the hall and found Mary Ann at the kitchen
table writing a letter to Melissa and Carl. "Where's Father?" he
blurted.

"He just left to go find Joseph." Her eyes dropped to the
paper in his hand. "The *Expositor?*" she asked grimly.

"Yes. Has Father seen it?"

"That's why he was going to find Joseph. He thinks there'll
be a call for the city council to meet."

"At the very least," Nathan cried, shaking the paper at her.
"This is outrageous! Did he read any of it to you?"

"No, Brother Harris of the city council came by. He had a
copy. Said they needed to talk to Joseph immediately."

Nathan came over and sat down in a chair, positively fuming. He spread the paper out on the table. "Listen to this. They

say—" He turned the paper to the last page and scanned quickly. " 'A part of its columns will be devoted to a few primary objects, which the Publishers deem of vital importance to the public welfare. Their particular locality gives them a knowledge of the many gross abuses exercised under the pretended authorities of the Nauvoo City Charter—' " He slammed his fist down against the table. "They're calling for the unconditional repeal of the Nauvoo Charter."

Mary Ann nodded. "They put all that in their original prospectus published about a month ago. The city council has been waiting to see if they would really carry through with it."

He snatched the paper up again and turned it back to the front page. "Well, listen to this. Talk about slander! 'We are earnestly seeking to explode the vicious principles of Joseph Smith, and those who practice the same abominations and whoredoms.' " He turned the page. "Here's more. 'It is a notorious fact, that many females in foreign climes, and in countries to us unknown, even in the most distant regions of the Eastern hemisphere, have been induced, by the sound of the gospel, to forsake friends, and embark upon a voyage across waters that lie stretched over the greater portion of the globe.' It then goes on to say that once they arrive, these women are taken to some secret place down by the river or to some room with a No Admittance sign. There, expecting to be given a blessing by Joseph, they are instead forced to submit to him and become his spiritual wives. If they don't, then Joseph pronounces them damned for all eternity."

Mary Ann's eyes were wide. "How can they say things like that? Those are outright lies."

"The whole paper is full of lies!" He was so angry he couldn't sit still. He stood and began pacing. Then he remembered something else and grabbed the paper again. "Look! Read this right here. See if this describes how you or Lydia or Rebecca would describe your life here in Nauvoo." He stabbed his finger down to show her the place.

Mary Ann bent over and began to read. " 'It is difficult—perhaps impossible—to describe the wretchedness of females in this place, without wounding the feelings of the benevolent, or shocking the delicacy of the refined; but the truth shall come to the world.'" She looked up. It wasn't very often that Mary Ann Steed exhibited anger, but now she had a deep anger in her eyes. "That is horrible!"

"Yes, it is. But how many of our enemies out there will believe it is a lie? None. This is what they want to hear. And these men are giving it to them."

He picked up the paper and jammed it under his arm. "I'm sorry, Mother. I didn't mean to come in and upset you. But this has got me so angry. This has got to be stopped, Mother. It has to be stopped."

———•———

For two full days—Saturday the eighth, and again on Monday the tenth—the city council met in long sessions to discuss what should be done about the *Expositor*. The newspaper had thrown the whole city into an uproar and now the council had to determine what to do. The list of publishers came right out of the group of conspirators—William and Wilson Law, Robert and Charles Foster, Francis and Chauncey Higbee, and Charles Ivins.

For two solid days, Benjamin sat as a member of the council and listened to sworn testimony about the character of the men behind the newspaper. He studied the ordinances of the city and was convinced that legally they had a right to take action against something which so flagrantly threatened the peace of their city. He listened as they read from Blackstone, the esteemed English jurist, and found a basis in the law for moving forward. He listened to all of that, and at the same time knew in his heart that this was going to have grave consequences. The enemies of the Church would howl over this one, and so they had to be very wise in how they proceeded.

He knew all of that, but the thing which finally helped Benjamin make up his mind was the testimony of Phineas Richards, another member of the city council. "Brethren," he said, "some of you know that my son was killed at Haun's Mill. I have not forgotten what transpired there. I have not forgotten that my son's body was dumped into a well without a winding-sheet, shroud, or coffin. Now the same spirit is raging in this place. I, for one, cannot sit still while that happens. I am ready to stand by our mayor to the last in whatever he chooses to do. Whatever we do, brethren, the quicker this thing is stopped, the better."

Thus it was that on the afternoon of June tenth, Joseph Smith, as mayor of Nauvoo, following the directive of the city council, issued the following order:

STATE OF ILLINOIS,
CITY OF NAUVOO
To the Marshal of said City, greeting.

You are here commanded to destroy the printing press from whence issues the *Nauvoo Expositor*, and pi or scatter the type of said printing establishment in the street, and burn all the *Expositors* and libelous handbills found in said establishment; and if resistance be offered to your execution of this order by the owners or others, demolish the house; and if anyone threatens you or the Mayor or the officers of the city, arrest those who threaten you, and fail not to execute this order without delay, and make due return hereon.

By order of the City Council,
JOSEPH SMITH, Mayor.

A few hours later, city marshal John P. Greene handed the order back to the mayor and the city council with the following written at the bottom:

Marshal's return—The within-named press and type is destroyed and pied according to order, on this 10th day of June, 1844, at about 8 o'clock p.m.

J. P. Greene, C. M.

"Pa?"

Joshua looked up in surprise. "Will? What are you doing back already?"

Caroline was equally surprised. "I thought you went to Carthage."

Will nodded. "I did. Something's come up. Can I talk with you, Pa?"

Caroline knew her son too well. He was supposed to be gone with the other teamsters for a full three days. She laid the book down that she had been reading. "Is everything all right, Will?"

He fumbled at that. "It's . . . well, it's just something I need to talk with Pa about, Mama. Can you come out to the wagon, Pa? I need to show you something."

Caroline started to rise, pushing up with both hands, the awkwardness of her body clearly discernible. But Joshua was up and laid a hand on her shoulder. "I'll go see what it is, Caroline. Don't you be getting up."

She frowned at him, and yet beneath it she was pleased at his concern. "I've got another full month, Joshua. I'm not going to break in pieces."

"We'll be right back. You just sit there."

But Joshua's calm demeanor disappeared the moment they stepped outside. Will's wagon and team were tied up close by, but Will made no move toward them. "What's wrong?" Joshua asked in a low voice.

"You've heard about the *Expositor* affair?"

"Who hasn't? The whole county is in an uproar."

"Did you know that one of the men who helped publish it went to Carthage and swore out a warrant against the Nauvoo City Council for destroying private property? They sent a constable from Carthage to serve the warrant."

"No, I didn't know that. I've been at home all day. With all the furor, your mother is very nervous. Warsaw is like a war camp."

"We should have moved, Pa. We should have moved weeks ago."

Joshua's first reaction was to flare back at him, but the worry was too heavy on his mind. "When the sale of the freight yard fell through, I had no choice but to stay. But maybe it's time to leave. I'll just have to come back and handle the other."

Will wanted to lash out at him. In Carthage, Will had actually been frightened. Four different times he had been accosted by men on the streets, demanding to know where he was from. When he told them he was from Warsaw, that had ended it. But he was grateful they had not asked the more pertinent question. Are you a Mormon? But things were heating up rapidly. Word in Carthage was that Joseph would probably slip out of the warrant by once again going to the municipal courts of Nauvoo. If that happened, it would be like pouring kerosene on a fire.

"Pa, we've got to go now. Tonight!"

"Tonight! Are you crazy? Your mother has to be moved very carefully. We'll have to put a bed in the wagon. Find a place to stay and—"

Will turned on his heel and walked to the wagon, where he retrieved a large sheet of paper. In the darkness, Joshua couldn't see clearly what it was. When he returned, Will was obviously afraid. "If you've been in the house all day, then I assume you haven't seen the latest issue of the *Signal*."

Joshua felt his stomach drop a little. "No."

"Well, let me just read you one small paragraph from your friend Mr. Thomas Sharp, and then you tell me if you think we ought to wait for things to calm down a little." He moved closer to the house again where there was sufficient light from the lamps coming through the window. He looked at his father. "In the first part of the article, Sharp talks about what happened in Nauvoo. He's incensed, of course. He rails on and on about how the Mormons have destroyed freedom of the press and all that. But then, this is how he concludes it."

He lifted the paper and began to read: " 'We have only to state that this'—this meaning the destruction of the *Expositor*—

'is sufficient! War and extermination is inevitable! Citizens arise, one and all! Can you stand by, and suffer such infernal devils to rob men of their property and rights, without avenging them?' "

He stopped, his voice a hoarse whisper now. "There's his question, Pa. Want to hear his answer?" He dropped the paper. He knew the last part almost by heart. " 'We have no time to comment,' he says. 'Every man will make his own answer. *Let it be made with powder and ball!*' "

For what seemed like a very long time, Joshua stared past Will into the darkness.

"Pa, it's come. Just like Missouri. We can't wait. We've got to get out of here. Now! Tonight!"

There was a heavy sigh, filled with pain. "We can't just leave, Will. Not like this. Your mother is going to have a baby in a few weeks. We have to get a better wagon. Fix a bed for her."

"Then in the morning. No longer!"

"Yes," Joshua finally said. "In the morning."

"To Nauvoo?"

Joshua shook his head emphatically. "No, absolutely not. We'll go to Quincy. It will be better there."

"Pa, she's going to need family."

He just shook his head.

"*Pa!*"

"No, Will!" he said flatly. "Aside from my feelings, Nauvoo is not the place to go for safety right now."

"It is for us," Will said softly. But he knew there was no changing his father's mind, and he turned away.

They went to the small livery stable—one they had not used before—early the next morning. They came almost ten minutes apart, pretending not to recognize each other, and Will gave his name as Will Mendenhall. Joshua rented a black surrey with a single bay mare to pull it and drove away. Will asked for a wagon to haul some furniture and said he needed it for a full day. With it came a team of two big mules large enough to handle any load.

Once they reached Quincy, Joshua would send everything back, along with a fat bonus for the liveryman for the inconvenience of losing his equipment and stock for a couple of days.

As Will handed the man the money, the liveryman jerked his head toward the wagon. "The tarp's in the back."

"Yes, I see that. Thank you."

"Don't look like rain," he observed.

Will nodded. "Hope not. But I can't take any chances."

"Suppose not."

Will thanked him, walked to the wagon, climbed up into the seat, and drove away.

Five minutes later and two blocks away, Joshua snapped the reins and pulled the carriage out into the street behind Will's wagon. Will reined up and jumped down quickly. Joshua climbed out too and they spread the tarp over the wagon bed and started to tie it down. Now Joshua was all business. His words were clipped and came out in staccato bursts. "All right," he said. "You go first. The mattresses are all ready. Be sure your mother is comfortable. It's going to be hot under this canvas, but once we get out of town we'll take it off."

"Yes, Pa."

"I'll be right behind you to get Savannah and Charles." His brow was deeply creased. "I don't like this, Will," he suddenly said. "Maybe we should just risk it and all go together."

Will shook his head. "If they think you're trying to get us out, Pa, there's no telling what they'll do. I know they don't like you much since you refused to help them, but you're still respected. And you're not a Mormon. No one is going to bother you."

"It's not me I'm worried about," he said, scowling deeply as he stared down the empty street.

———◆———

Everything went smoothly at the house. Olivia stood in the alley, watching for anyone who might be coming, while Will fixed the bed beneath the tarp. Then he nodded to his mother. She had already said her good-byes to Savannah and Charles inside. She didn't want to leave them alone but Joshua was waiting just around the corner; the minute he saw the wagon leave, he would come for them.

Will held the tarp up while his mother climbed onto the tailgate. She rolled over awkwardly, then crawled in under the tarp onto the mattresses. Will lifted the tailgate, pulled the tarp over the edge of it so that no part of the wagon bed was open, and tied it down. "I'll hurry, Mama."

"I'm all right," came the muffled reply.

Will climbed up on the wagon seat. Olivia took one last look up the alley, then climbed up beside Will. "Let's go."

Will snapped the reins and the mules started forward. As they came out into the street, Joshua was approaching from their left. Will raised his hand. "See you tonight, Pa."

"Bye, Papa," Olivia called.

As they approached Main Street, Will gave his sister a sidelong glance. "Don't look at anyone, Livvy. Not even if they're staring at you. Just look straight ahead."

"I know, Will. I'm not afraid."

"That's good."

It was not even eight o'clock yet, and the streets were still mostly empty. Will felt himself relax a little. But as they started through the downtown part of Warsaw, he suddenly tensed. There was a small knot of people standing halfway down the block. Instantly he knew what they were doing. They were clustered around the big display window of the *Warsaw Signal* office reading the latest issue of Thomas Sharp's newspaper. Will felt his skin start to crawl. They were reading words like "war" and "extermination," and "let it be made with powder and ball." He moved his team as far out into the center of the street as he dared and looked straight ahead. There was no choice but to drive right past them. "Don't look, Livvy," he hissed again. "Don't look."

For a moment he thought they had made it. Several people turned at the sound of the wagon and glanced at them, but then immediately turned back. He saw a flash of recognition on a woman's face and an instant frown, but then she too looked away.

But just as he was pulling past the group, there was a shout. "Hey!"

Will didn't turn and he grabbed Olivia's hand to stop her from doing so.

"Hey you! On the wagon!"

There was no ignoring that. He didn't stop, just turned his head. What he saw sent a shudder running through his body. It was a big man, bald, with heavy features and tiny eyes looking out from paunchy cheeks. He knew the man instantly. It was the typesetter from the *Signal*. This was the man whom Will had insulted almost three years before right here in the street, and had ended up feeling the blunt end of one of those huge, ham-like fists. He looked away, debating whether to whip the mules into a run.

But the man broke into a run and darted around to the head of Will's team, grabbing at the near mule's bridle and bringing them to a halt. He looked up, grinning wickedly. "I thought it was you."

"Let go of my team," Will said evenly.

"I understand you're a Mormon now. Where you going, Mormon!" he cried. The crowd at the window had turned to watch, and the big man's last words brought a low, angry rumble. The people started to move in his direction.

"My sister and I are on our way to get some furniture. Please let go of my animals."

"Hey, you know who this is?" the man chortled loudly. "This is a Mormon boy. From Nauvoo." That won him instant cries of anger and a low, menacing muttering.

"That's Joshua Steed's children," a woman called out. "You'd best leave them alone."

The porcine eyes narrowed into even tinier slits. "Steed? That old bag of wind who makes all the promises, then never delivers?"

In one quick flash of clarity, Will knew what he had to do. People were moving in now. In a moment, the wagon would be surrounded and someone just might ask what he had in the back.

He leaned over, handing the reins to Olivia. "When I say, Olivia, you whip those mules and get out of here."

She gaped at him. "No, Will," she cried.

"Yes!" he hissed. "You go! I'll catch up." And then he stood up and jumped lightly down into the dust of the street.

There was an instant look of pure joy on the typesetter's face. "Well, well. Come to finish what you couldn't do before, Mormon?"

"Somebody get the sheriff," a voice cried anxiously.

"Look," Will said reasonably, moving up toward the man. "I don't want trouble. All I want to do is go get some furniture."

"This here is a Mormon," the man yelled, looking around him. "One of them that burns down newspaper offices."

There were several angry cries, and that's when Will acted. With a single shout of, "*Now, Livvy!*" he lowered his head and charged. It caught the man by surprise and Will's shoulder slammed into his chest at full force, knocking the man back several steps. "Go, Livvy!"

The man's surprise was short-lived. With a cry of betrayal, he charged. As a great fist came clubbing down against the side of his head, Will heard Olivia's piercing yell and saw the reins snap. The mules leaped forward, scattering the people in front of them.

Will, half-dazed from the blow, rolled clear of the slashing hooves. The bigger man was not so lucky. The hind leg of the nearest mule, kicking back for traction in the soft dirt, caught the man on the back of his leg. He screamed and went down, writhing in pain. Tasting dust and blood, Will staggered to his feet. The wagon was racing away and he hobbled after it, knowing that once the big man got up, it was finished. But he only made it about ten feet when three young men leaped in front of him. "Going somewhere, Mormon?" The one was licking his lips. Will went into a crouch, but he was much too slow. The nearest man darted in behind him and pinned Will's arms. The other two waded in, fists doubled, arms already pumping.

Joshua had taught Olivia how to drive a team, and occasionally she still drove one of his wagons for him. But it had never been any kind of serious driving. Usually it was just here and there about town, or occasionally for short stretches out on the open road. Now she had two startled mules running at full speed down a city street. The wagon careened back and forth, the tail end whipping dangerously. Fortunately, the street was straight and almost empty.

A block away, two men coming out of the blacksmith shop looked up. They had no idea what had just happened at the newspaper office. All they saw was a runaway team headed straight for them. It barely even registered in their minds that it was a woman at the reins. It said something about their courage that they didn't hesitate. They darted into the street, waving their arms and shouting, trying to slow the team. But all Olivia could think of was that people were trying to stop her family from leaving Warsaw. The sight of two men out in front of her, waving for the team to stop, only terrorized her. She whipped the mules harder. Then her eye caught sight of a side street coming up fast on the left.

"Hang on, Mama!" she screamed as she yanked on the reins.

The mules alone might have made the turn, but the weight and forward speed of the wagon was too much. As the team jerked left in response to Olivia's command, the wagon tongue turned sharply, following their lead. The right front wheel bit sideways into the soft dust of the street, starting into a broad slide. With that kind of force, the spokes on the wagon wheel might as well have been made of straw. Three of them snapped clean and the wheel crumpled like paper. The sheer force of the weight and the momentum ripped the whole front axle and tongue assembly out from under the wagon bed. The wooden tongue whipped around like a giant scythe, cutting the legs out from under the mules. With a horrifying shriek, they went down, kicking and thrashing.

When the front wheels snapped free of the wagon bed, Olivia hurtled skyward, tumbling end over end. Even before she hit the ground, the front corner of the wagon dropped, ploughing into the earth. For a moment it skidded along, but then the corner dug into the soft earth. The tail end of the wagon box flipped up and over, bouncing like a tumbleweed in a windstorm.

For a second or two the silence was total. Dust boiled up in great clouds. But there was not a sound. The two would-be rescuers stood frozen in horror, staring at the carnage and destruction before them. Two blocks away, near the offices of the *Warsaw Signal*, a small knot of people also stood rigid, staring toward the shattered wagon. And then out of the silence came one long, drawn-out scream. "Mama! Livvy!"

Nathan got up as quietly as he could, so as not to wake Lydia. Normally, the sound of a horse outside his window on a summer night would not have brought him up with a jerk, but these were not normal times in Nauvoo. He tiptoed to the open window and peeked out. Their bedroom faced Ripley Street, and as he looked down, he could see a dark figure just sliding off his horse. There was a grunt of pain as the man got off the horse and hit the ground. He hobbled forward and started tying the reins to Nathan's fence.

Behind him, Lydia sat up. "What is it, Nathan?"

He waved her to silence. "Who goes there?" he called down loudly.

The man jumped, then straightened, looking up at him. "Nathan? It's me, Will."

"Will?" And then in the soft moonlight he could see that Will was hunched over, holding one arm across his chest, and he moved slowly. "Will, what's wrong?"

"Can you get Derek and Matthew? Bring them to Grandpa Steed's."

Nathan didn't ask any more questions. He whirled around and went to the chair for his clothes.

"It's Will?" Lydia said, up now and moving quickly as well.

"Yes. And it looks like he's hurt."

When they came into the main room of Benjamin and Mary Ann's house, Lydia stopped and one hand flew to her mouth. Will sat at the table beside his grandmother, who had a wet cloth in her hand and was dabbing gingerly at his face. And what a face it was. His cheeks and jaw were a mottled mass of ugly bruises. One eye was nearly closed. Over it, a smear of blood pointed to a cut in his eyebrow. His lips were puffy and split in one place. "Oh, Will!" Lydia gasped. "What happened?"

"Did you get Derek and Matthew?" he asked Nathan.

"Yes, they're coming. What happened, Will?"

He just shook his head and Benjamin looked up. "Let's wait until everyone gets here; then he'll only have to say it once."

Nathan nodded and strode to the door. Derek and Rebecca were just coming into the yard. Up the street he could see two more forms running toward them. "They're coming," he said over his shoulder.

There was a similar horrified reaction from the others when they saw Will's face, but Benjamin waved them to silence and got them all seated. "Now," he said, very gently. "Tell us what happened, Will."

He did. He didn't look at them, but just stared at the floor. His voice was low, and sometimes they had to lean forward to hear him. He started with a report of his trip to Carthage and what he had found there and of his quick return to Warsaw. They nodded grimly at that. Rumors were flying like bullets in Nauvoo too. The whole city was in a state of panic.

Still not meeting their eyes, Will went on. He explained the decision to leave Warsaw as quickly as possible. Now, in a wooden, lifeless voice, he described in great detail the arrangements he and his father had made. He told about the livery stable and the tarp. He described the wagon and explained how careful they had been, how he had filled the whole bed of the wagon with mattresses for his mother, how he made sure she had a pillow for her head.

With a growing sense of horror, Benjamin finally reached out and laid a hand on Will's arm. Will stopped, almost startled as his eyes came back into focus. "What happened, Will?" Benjamin asked gently. "Tell us what happened."

For several seconds he stared at his grandfather, and then suddenly his eyes were filled with tears, his swollen lip began to tremble.

Rebecca was shaking her head, not wanting to hear the answer. "Oh, please," she whispered, sensing what was coming.

Will's face crumpled now and a great sob was torn from deep within his body. He buried his face against Mary Ann's shoulder. "Livvy's dead, Grandma. Livvy's dead!"

"No!" Lydia cried, leaping to her feet. Rebecca and Jenny gasped, then burst into tears. Nathan rocked back, stunned into silence. Derek turned away, his eyes burning.

"What about your mother, Will?" Benjamin asked, in that same soft voice.

Will pulled away from Mary Ann, brushing at the tears with the back of his hand. He spoke swiftly now, telling them about driving past the newspaper office, about the typesetter blocking the way, about the runaway wagon. As he started to describe how Olivia had tried to turn the wagon, Mary Ann dropped her head now, her body shaking. "Oh, dear Lord, no!"

"What about your mother, Will?" Benjamin said again. "Is she all right?"

He shook his head. "Mama's real bad, Grandpa. That's why I came. Papa didn't want me to. Said it's too dangerous for you to come to Warsaw right now. But you've got to come. You've got to help her."

Lydia's face was drained of color. "What about the baby, Will?"

He looked up, remembering that part, and there was a momentary brightening. "The baby came this afternoon. We thought it would be dead. A little girl. She's very tiny, but I think she's all right."

Then the enormity of it settled in again and he started to shake his head, the shock making his voice hollow. "If we hadn't put the mattresses in and tied the tarp down real tight, Mama would have been killed too. It was like she was in a cocoon. But the wagon flipped completely over. She's got a broken arm, and one ankle is also broken."

Lydia had to look away, biting down on her lip to stifle the cry within her.

"Your father? Charles? Savannah?" Derek asked now.

"They're all right. They went another way." He shook his head. "We were going to meet once we got out of town." He swallowed hard, fighting for control of his voice again. "Papa's in shock. I've never seen him like this. I can't get him to talk to me. He just sits by Mama, holding her hand, and rocking back and forth."

Nathan was up in an instant. "Derek, you get your wagon. Rebecca, Jennifer, Lydia, get blankets, pillows, mattresses. We'll need medicine, stuff for the baby. Matthew, see if you can borrow a wagon from someone. We'll need another wagon for the rest of the family."

"I'm going with you to Warsaw," Lydia said to him.

Nathan jerked around and gave a quick, hard shake of his head.

"No, Aunt Lydia," Will cried. "Pa's right. Warsaw is no place for Mormons. We've had a doctor come. But there are a lot of men in town. They're drinking hard. You don't want to be a Mormon out on those streets tonight."

Lydia folded her arms and planted her feet. "There's a baby down there," she said evenly, "and Caroline can't be nursing it. I'm still nursing little Joseph. I'm going."

"But—"

"For two days little Joseph can survive with a bottle."

Benjamin stood, looking at Nathan. "She's right," he said.

Nathan's face was twisted with fear. "I know." He looked at Lydia. "All right. We'll get things ready. Will, you stay here and rest for as long as you can."

But Will didn't rest. He sat between his grandfather and his grandmother, holding each other tight, and they all wept together.

———•———

"Joshua?"

There was no response. He was standing by the window, staring out into the darkness.

"You've got to decide, Joshua. We can't wait much longer."

He turned, and Benjamin was shocked once again with what the last two days had done to him. His eyes were sunken and old. Two days of black stubble covered his chin, making him look all the more like a tormented man. His mouth was drawn, his skin pallid.

"I can't, Father. She'll die if we move her."

Nathan stepped forward. "She'll die if we don't take her back, Joshua. We've got to risk it."

Joshua's head jerked up, weaving drunkenly now. "I've already killed my daughter," he cried hoarsely. "I won't kill my wife too."

Nathan moved forward and took him by the shoulders. "Joshua, you were trying to get them out. You can't blame yourself."

"I should have moved them. I knew it was bad. People were even starting to yell at me on the streets. Now my Olivia is gone." He looked away. "She's gone, Nathan, and I never got to tell her I was sorry for not believing her."

Nathan shook him gently. "Joshua, nothing can bring Livvy back now. We've got to think of Caroline and the other children."

That finally got through. "Yes. Savannah is terrified. I could hardly get Charles to sleep."

The others stood by, content not to intervene. Matthew was by the door. Derek stood near the other window. Will sat beside his mother's bed, looking very tired now. Lydia had just finished nursing the baby and was rocking her slowly in one corner.

Joshua turned and looked toward the bed. His hand came up, as if in supplication. "The doctor says she is bleeding internally. If we try to move her . . ." He passed a hand before his eyes, not able to say it. "You'd better just go. It's too dangerous."

Nathan turned and looked at Lydia and shook his head. It was clear that Joshua was still in shock. He was almost babbling, jerking from one subject to another.

"I tried to tell Will not to go get you, but . . ."

"Did you think we really wouldn't come?" Lydia asked gently.

He turned. Now his eyes were haunted. "You had every right not to. I—" He dropped his head. "If only I hadn't made *them* come here," he cried. "If only I hadn't been such a fool."

Will stood and limped over to stand beside his father. "Pa, I was the one who sent Livvy on the wagon alone."

Joshua swept him up and clung to him. "No, Will, it wasn't your fault. It wasn't your fault."

Benjamin watched them, feeling a growing sense of urgency. "Joshua, dawn is in a few hours. We have to decide. We can give her a priesthood blessing to help her make the trip."

"No," he said shortly.

"Yes!" Nathan said fiercely. "That's how we got you out of Far West and up to the McIntires. You were hovering between life and death and we took you twenty-five miles on a travois."

"No, Nathan."

"How can you say no?" he said, angered by this kind of blindness. "You were with Joseph that day across the river. You watched him raise Elijah Fordham from his deathbed. How can you say that power isn't real?"

"Because," Lydia answered for him, "Joshua doesn't think God will let that power be used in his behalf. He's afraid that Caroline will die because God wants to punish him for bringing them here."

Nathan and Benjamin both turned around to stare, first at her and then at him. Joshua fell back a step, then moved to the window, turning his back on them. Nathan looked at his father, then made up his mind. "Joshua, we're blessing your wife and taking her back to Nauvoo. If you don't like that, you're going to have to fight me to stop me."

"Joshua?" The faint murmur brought them all around.

Caroline's eyes were open and she was trying to raise her one hand. In an instant Joshua was across to her and clasping her hand. She fell back, her breathing shallow and rapid. "Joshua?"

He leaned over her, trying not to look at the battered face. "Yes?"

"Take me home."

He reared back. "But—"

"Please, Joshua."

He looked over at Lydia, torn with indecision. She was crying now, but she smiled at him through the tears and nodded. "Just say yes, Joshua. That's all she wants to hear."

He turned back to Caroline. "Yes."

She closed her eyes, her face smoothing; then suddenly she rose up sharply. "Olivia. Can't leave her."

A cry of anguish was torn from Joshua's throat.

"We won't, Caroline," Nathan said, his own voice strained now. "We'll take her back and give her a proper burial."

Joshua stood up, suddenly decisive. "All right, let's take her home."

"Good," Nathan said. He turned to Derek. "Make sure the teams are ready. Matthew, you'll have to get Savannah and Charles when we're ready. Will—"

But just then a soft knock sounded on the door. For a second everyone froze, then there was a scramble. Nathan whipped out a pistol from his belt. Will hobbled over to the corner and grabbed his rifle. Derek leaped back to stand behind the door. Matthew instinctively moved over to shield Lydia. Joshua also drew a pistol, then held up a hand for quiet. "Who is it?" he called.

"Joseph Smith."

If the knock had stunned them, this absolutely dumbfounded them. They gaped at one another, not believing their ears. Only Lydia responded aloud. "Brother Joseph?" she cried.

"Yes, Lydia, is that you?"

"It *is* Joseph!" Derek cried, stepping out and undoing the

catch that locked the door from the inside. He threw the door open and Joseph strode in. Behind him was Orrin Porter Rockwell.

Nathan's eyes registered total shock. "Joseph?"

"Hello, Nathan. Benjamin." Then he strode over to Joshua. There was not a moment's hesitation, even though Joshua shrunk back at his approach. Joseph threw his arms around him. "Joshua, I'm so sorry. I can't tell you how the news of your tragedy has torn at my heart."

Rockwell came inside and shut the door behind him. Joseph released Joshua and immediately went to Caroline's bedside, leaving Joshua dazed. He dropped to one knee and took Caroline's hand. Her eyes fluttered open again, then widened perceptibly. "Joseph?"

"Yes, Caroline." He bent down and laid his cheek against hers. "It's all right, Caroline. Everything is all right now." There was the barest nod.

Nathan moved over to Rockwell. "What are you doing here?" he hissed. "There are a hundred men out there howling for Joseph's blood right now."

Rockwell gave an enigmatic shrug. "You know Joseph. Your mother came and told him what happened. There's no other explanation needed."

"I can't believe it. This is crazy. He could be killed."

Rockwell let one hand come to rest on his pistol butt. "That's why I came." He looked at Joseph with a mixture of admiration and exasperation. "He wanted to come alone." He reached up and removed his hat, running his hand through his long hair. "But we've got to hurry, Nathan. If we're not out of here by first light . . ."

"We're just getting ready to leave."

Joseph heard that and straightened. "Have you given Caroline a blessing yet?" he asked Benjamin.

"We were just getting ready to. Would you do it, Joseph?"

He turned to Joshua. "Are you in agreement with that?"

"Joshua," Joseph said, his voice rising in warning.

"My daughter is dead because of him," he said in a tight voice. "I'll not be forgetting that very soon."

"You listen to me, Joshua. If you do go out alone some night to talk to Livvy, don't you tell her about that, because it will make her want to weep. You think about that, before you go after Doctor Foster."

Joshua stood, feeling the tiredness seeping into his soul. Joseph didn't move. He was lost deep in his own thoughts now. "Joseph?"

He looked up.

"I guess you know that Mormonism will always test my patience and strain my credulity."

That won him a deep chuckle. "I thought as much."

"And I guess I'm going to have to wait until I get on the other side and have God tell me directly that he allows a man to have more than one wife before I will accept it."

"That doesn't surprise me either, Joshua."

He pulled his shoulders back, looking up at the stars that filled the sky above them. "But know this, Joseph Smith. While those things are true, they shall no longer stand between our friendship. I am in your debt for what you did this day, and I shall never forget it."

"I didn't do anything, Joshua. I just felt like I needed to be with your family."

"You came, Joseph," he said with quiet finality. "That was enough."

Chapter Notes

The first and only issue of the *Nauvoo Expositor* was published on Friday, 7 June 1844. The prospectus promised that a new issue would be published each week thereafter. Sylvester Emmons, not a Church member but nevertheless a member of the Nauvoo City Council, was hired by Foster and the others to serve as editor and because of that was expelled from the council. Ironically, beneath the title of the paper, the motto on the masthead reads: "The truth, the whole truth, and nothing but the truth." (See *CHFT*, pp. 275–76.)

The proceedings of the city council meeting, including the testimony mentioned here and the order to destroy the press, are given in great detail in Joseph's history (see *HC* 6:432–48).

With the Steed family not being historical figures, obviously Joseph's trip to Warsaw is not based on actual historical events. The idea was suggested by several journal entries about this time which indicate that Joseph would go out riding with Porter Rockwell (see *HC* 6:227, 399, 424, 451, 472).

Chapter Forty

Joshua tiptoed quietly to the bedroom, then stopped when he opened the door. So much for thinking Caroline might be asleep. It might as well have been a meeting of the Relief Society. They had turned the downstairs sitting room into a bedroom so that Caroline would not have to worry about negotiating stairs when she began her recuperation. Now it was packed with people. Lydia and Mary Ann sat on chairs beside Caroline's bed. Mary Ann had the baby. Jenny and Rebecca sat on the floor directly beside Caroline. Kathryn was in her wheelchair behind the others. Jessica and Rachel stood at the foot of the bed.

When the men had gone to Warsaw to get Caroline and bring her home, Mary Ann had paid a young man to ride to Ramus and tell Jessica of the tragedy. Solomon Garrett had immediately packed his family into a wagon and come to Nauvoo. Aside from their being there with the family in an hour of need, their presence had proven to be a blessing in another way. Jessica's little Miriam had been born just a month after

Lydia's baby, and so Jessica and Lydia were now alternating nursing Caroline's baby.

Caroline's head was turned as she listened to the conversation and she saw Joshua before the others. "Hello," she said weakly.

As they all turned, he went right to her. "How are you feeling?"

"Better," she said. "I slept all the time you were gone."

"That's good." He laid a hand on her cheek.

"The fever's down," Mary Ann said, "don't you think?"

"Yes, I think it is." He was encouraged. Caroline's voice wasn't so tremulous now. Her eyes were bright again; her cheeks had good color.

"They tell me that the funeral was very nice," Caroline said to Joshua.

He nodded. "It was. And there were hundreds of people there. That's why I've been so long getting back. Everyone came up afterwards to express their condolences and to tell me they are praying for you." There was a touch of awe in his voice. "I couldn't break loose."

She looked away, her eyes tearing up. "I wanted so much to be there."

He squeezed her hand. "I know."

Mary Ann stood and walked to the bassinet. She carefully laid the baby down and smoothed the blanket over it. Then she turned to Joshua. "We'll go now. We don't want to tire her."

"Thank you, Mother. Thank you all."

As they started to file out, Jessica touched his arm. "I've just fed the baby, so she'll be all right for a time."

Lydia nodded. "I'll come in a couple of hours and feed her again."

"Thank you."

Kathryn maneuvered her wheelchair so that she faced both Joshua and Caroline. "Have you decided what you're going to name her?"

He shook his head. "Not yet, but I know what I *want* to call her."

Caroline's eyes rose a little. "What?"

He spoke very quietly. "Caroline Steed."

There was a soft murmur of approval from the other women, but Caroline moved her head back and forth on the pillow.

"No?" he asked.

"Livvy," she said. "I want to call her Livvy."

Joshua's eyes were instantly burning. He looked away. "I don't know if I could bear to call her Olivia, Caroline," he said in a low voice.

"Not Olivia," she answered, a tear trickling down one cheek. "Just Livvy. I want to have another Livvy."

Joshua knelt down beside her and began to stroke her hair. Then he looked at Kathryn again. "I think we'll name her Livvy Caroline Steed," he said huskily.

He walked them to the door and bid them good-bye, then came back to sit beside Caroline. He took her hand.

"Tell me all about it, Joshua."

"Are you sure you're not too tired?"

"No, I want to hear it from you. I want to hear everything."

He talked softly and with an occasional tear or two. She too wept as he spoke. He spent the most time telling her about what Joseph had said—how he had talked about the spirit world, and that Livvy was there now, still with all of her personality, her laughter, her love of music. Finally, Joshua had to stop.

She looked up, and when she saw his eyes, she started to cry again. "You're not sure it's true, are you?" she asked.

He stared at her for several seconds, then looked away.

"Oh, Joshua," she cried. "How can you bear it if you don't know?"

He had held it back for so long—speaking at the services, accepting the kind wishes of all the people, keeping his emotions in check. Now his hands began to tremble and his lip quivered. "I don't know if I *can* bear it, Caroline," he said in a hoarse whisper. "I . . . If only I could see her once more. Take her in my arms and tell her how terribly sorry I am for being such a fool."

"She knows, Joshua," Caroline said, taking his hand in both of hers. "She knows."

Finally, he pulled free, sniffing back the tears and wiping at his eyes with his fingertips. "I can see why the gospel is so appealing to you, Caroline, but . . ." He took a deep breath and shook his head, the stubbornness in him not allowing him to let it lie. "But just wanting something, even desperately wanting something, doesn't make it so. I wish it did." His voice cracked again and he dropped his head. "I wish it did. It would be so simple then."

Caroline reached up and pulled his head down against her chest and began to stroke his hair. "Oh, my poor dear Joshua," she whispered. "My poor dear Joshua."

By the evening of June seventeenth—the day of the funeral for Olivia and a week following the destruction of the *Nauvoo Expositor* press—the rumors were flying as thick as a swarm of hornets. A group of men in Carthage were supposedly preparing to attack Nauvoo. Fifteen hundred Missourians had ferried across the river to join the Warsaw anti-Mormon party; Thomas Sharp was whipping them into a frenzy and they too were going to march on Nauvoo and get Joe Smith. The Laws, the Fosters, and the Higbees were bringing a mob to smash the printing offices of the *Nauvoo Neighbor* in retaliation. With all of that, Nauvoo was like a tinderbox. Joseph had companies of the Nauvoo Legion watching the roads. He detailed some of the police to stand guard over the printing office. Other companies of the Legion started to dig fortifications around the perimeter of the city.

It was in that air of tension that Joshua appeared at the Red Brick Store late that afternoon. Joseph was in council with city officials and Church leaders, but when he was told Joshua was outside, he came out immediately. Joshua didn't waste any time with small talk. "Joseph, I understand Nathan is going to Springfield."

Joseph wasn't surprised that he knew. "Yes. I'm sending a letter to Governor Ford along with affidavits describing recent threats against the Saints."

"I want to go with him."

Joseph looked at him for several seconds, then shook his head.

"Why? Caroline is much better. She's got all the women here to care for her and—"

Joseph just kept shaking his head.

"Why? Lydia's very worried about Nathan going alone."

"He'll not be alone. There are others going." Joseph motioned to a couple of chairs that were out in the hallway and they sat down. "Joshua, Caroline is better only because we blessed her by the power of the priesthood. Do you believe that?"

Joshua hesitated. This was the other thing that kept him going around and around. The rational part of him knew that there was no way that Caroline could have made the fifteen-mile journey in a wagon and survived. The doctor in Warsaw had feared for her life even without moving her. And yet she was not only still alive, she was healing. But on the other hand . . . He shook his head angrily. There was no "on the other hand." "Yes," he said. "I don't understand it, but I believe that what you did made the difference."

"It was not me, Joshua," Joseph reminded him softly. "It was the Lord. But the point is, your wife has been through a terrible ordeal. She *is* healing, but she needs you, Joshua. She can't be worrying about you being in danger. To be out anywhere in Hancock County is a threat right now, and I can't make her have to face that too. I can't."

Joshua sat there, staring at his hands, and finally he nodded. "I understand." He looked up. "I hear you've called out the Legion."

"I have. They'll assemble first thing in the morning. The threats grow more ominous with every passing hour."

"I would like to help."

Joseph leaned back, appraising Joshua with that long, steady look that Joshua had come to know. "Joshua, you don't have to prove to me that you're sorry for what happened. You don't have to prove to God that it's not your fault that Olivia was killed."

Joshua was stung. "The city is in danger. And if that's true, my family is in danger. I want to help. I want to join the Nauvoo Legion. I'm not asking to be an officer or anything. Just let me help."

Joseph was silent for a long moment after Joshua finished; then he spoke quietly. "Your father is a wise and wonderful man, Joshua, but he's getting older now. As a member of the city council he is under indictment too. Your mother is worried sick about this. Remember, once before he was marched off to jail and very nearly didn't come back. With Nathan going, your family needs someone strong, Joshua, someone to steady things. That is your place right now. It is enough."

"I'm not strong!" he cried bitterly.

There was a kind smile, a gentle touch on the arm. "You have to be strong, Joshua. We all have to be strong now." He stood and Joshua stood too. "You watch over your family, Joshua. If more is required of you than that, I will come to you. Fair enough?"

Joshua finally nodded. "Fair enough." He started toward the stairs and Joseph turned to go back into his meeting, but Joshua stopped. "Joseph?"

"Yes?"

"Just tell them you were wrong."

"About destroying the press?" he asked in surprise.

"No." Joshua hesitated. "About plural marriage." Seeing Joseph's reaction, he rushed on. "I'm not being critical, Joseph. I'm just telling you, that's what has got everyone so stirred up. The way out of this is to just admit that you were wrong."

A slow, sad smile stole across Joseph's face. "Oh, Joshua, Joshua. Would that it were that simple." And with that, he turned and went back into his office, leaving Joshua alone in the hallway.

At eight a.m. the next morning, the men of the Nauvoo Legion began to gather on the assembly ground up near the temple. Matthew, Derek, and Will came together as members of the First Cohort. Benjamin, too old to be in the militia itself, served as an aide-de-camp to Joseph and was not there when the troops began to assemble. Nathan, now a lieutenant, should have been there as well, but he had left for the state capital the previous evening.

By nine o'clock, after much shouting and yelling, they were formed up into their respective cohorts. And then, as has been true of military organizations from time immemorial, they settled down to wait. By noon, any semblance of their former organization had dissipated again and they were scattered here and there, sitting or lying in the shade. Then at about one-thirty, all of that changed. The order came that their commander-in-chief wanted the Nauvoo Legion to form up in the streets by Joseph's home. Once again they formed into their companies, and their companies into the cohorts. At two o'clock, Joseph appeared.

Across the street from the Mansion House another building was under construction. It was still only framed, but the flooring for the second story was laid down and it provided a perfect platform from which the commander-in-chief could address his troops. The streets in all four directions around the Mansion House were filled with soldiers, and every head turned in Joseph's direction as he stepped out on the building above them.

At Joseph's request, W. W. Phelps, one of Joseph's clerks, began. He had a newpaper in his hands and held it up high. "Men of the Legion," he cried in a loud voice, "I have here a copy of an extra edition of the *Warsaw Signal*, which has just been put in our hands. The editor, our longtime enemy Mr. Thomas Sharp, has called upon all the 'old citizens' of western Illinois to rise up against us. In specific and direct terms, he exhorts the citizens to exterminate Joseph Smith and the other leaders of the Church and to drive the rest of the Mormons from the state."

That brought an angry rumble from the assembled men.

Phelps went on quickly. "We also have received word that various militia groups are even now undergoing drills in preparation for an attack upon our city. Therefore, at one forty-five p.m., on this eighteenth day of June 1844, Mayor Joseph Smith proclaimed that Nauvoo is now under martial law. We shall now be pleased to hear from our mayor and our commanding general." He stepped back, lowering the paper.

Joseph moved forward right to the edge of the unfinished building so that he could look down into the faces of the men. Matthew could hardly bear to look up at him. He felt physically ill. Like most of the men here, he had been there when word came of Governor Boggs's extermination order. He had seen the results of that when Jessica came stumbling into Far West after the massacre at Haun's Mill. He had lived through the seige and fall of Far West. But then he hadn't had a wife and two-year-old girl to worry about. He hadn't had a sister-in-law who was paralyzed from the waist down and who couldn't even get out of bed without someone to help her.

He glanced at Derek and saw that his jaw was clamped tightly shut and that his fingers were clutching the handle of the sword Benjamin had given him—clutching it so tightly that his knuckles were white.

"Brethren, it is with considerable concern that I stand before you this afternoon. Would that the circumstances which bring us here together were more pleasant. But they are not. As you know, enemies now threaten our city. They say it is me that they want. If that were true, I would give myself up to save all of you. But such is not the case. It is thought by some that our enemies would be satisfied with my destruction; but I tell you that as soon as they have shed my blood, they will thirst for the blood of every man in whose heart dwells a single spark of the spirit of the fulness of the gospel. Make no mistake. The opposition of these men is moved by the spirit of the adversary of all righteousness. They wish to destroy not only me, but every man and woman who dares believe the doctrines that God hath inspired me to teach to this generation."

His voice was sharp with anger now.

"You and I both know that we have never violated the laws of our country. We have every right to live under their protection and are entitled to all the privileges guaranteed by our state and national constitutions. We have turned the barren, bleak prairies and swamps of this state into beautiful towns, farms, and cities by our industry. I call on God, angels, and all men to witness that we are innocent of the charges which are brought forth against us by our enemies."

There was a great stamping of feet, their way of applauding their commander.

"We have forwarded a particular account of all our doings to the governor. We are ready to obey his commands if we get the protection which we know to be our just due. We have been tried before a civil magistrate on the charge of riot—not that the law required it, but because the judge advised it as a precautionary measure—and we were legally acquitted by Esquire Daniel Wells, who is a good judge of law and who"—he added pointedly—"is not a member of our church. We are American citizens. We live upon a soil for the liberties of which our fathers periled their lives and spilt their blood upon the battlefield. Those rights, so dearly purchased, shall not be disgracefully trodden underfoot by lawless marauders without at least a noble effort on our part to sustain our liberties."

Now the men, besides stamping their feet, pounded heavily on their rifle butts or slapped their hands against their legs. The ground trembled and clouds of dust rose around them.

Joseph was visibly touched. He let his eyes sweep in each direction where the men stood. "Brethren of the Nauvoo Legion, will you all stand by me to the death and, even though your lives may be in peril, sustain the laws of our country, and the liberties and privileges which our fathers have transmitted unto us, sealed with their sacred blood?"

"Aye!" It was a mighty shout torn from thousands of throats.

Now his shoulders pulled back and one hand dropped to rest upon the handle of his sword. "I call upon all men, from Maine to the Rocky Mountains, and from Mexico to British America, to come to the deliverance of this people from the hand of oppression, cruelty, anarchy, and misrule to which they have long been made subject." His voice rose in a great shout. "Come, all ye lovers of liberty, break the oppressor's rod! Loose the iron grasp of mobocracy, and bring to punishment all those who trample underfoot the glorious Constitution and the people's rights."

With one swift motion, Joseph drew his sword and thrust it upward, as if he wanted to pierce heaven itself. "I call upon God and angels to witness that I have unsheathed my sword with a firm and unalterable determination that this people shall have their legal rights and be protected from mob violence, or my blood shall be spilt upon the ground like water, and my body consigned to the silent tomb."

Matthew felt a little thrill run up and down his body, and without realizing it, he squared his own shoulder and laid a hand upon his pistol.

"Bear witness, one and all," Joseph cried, the sword still thrust upward, catching the afternoon sun on its steel. "While I live, I will never tamely submit to the dominion of cursed mobocracy. I do not regard my own life. I am ready to be offered a sacrifice for this people. What can our enemies do? Only kill the body, and their power is then at an end."

The sword lowered slowly, and Joseph looked around, his face suddenly sad. "God has tried you. You are a good people. Therefore, I love you with all my heart. Greater love hath no man than that he should lay down his life for his friends. You have stood by me in the hour of trouble, and I am willing to sacrifice my life for your preservation. May the Lord God of Israel bless you forever and ever. I say it in the name of Jesus of Nazareth, and in the authority of the holy priesthood, which he hath conferred upon me. Amen."

With a mighty roar the nearly five thousand men of the Nauvoo Legion answered their prophet. "Amen!" they cried as if with one voice. "Amen."

On the seventeenth of June, Hyrum Smith had written a letter to Brigham Young suggesting that, due to the deteriorating
situation in Nauvoo, the Twelve ought to come home as quickly as possible. When Hyrum showed the letter to Joseph, his
brother advised him not to mail it. Three days later, conditions
had reached the point that Joseph changed his mind. He sat
down and dictated ten letters to those members of the Twelve
who were out on missions promoting Joseph's candidacy for the
presidency. Only John Taylor and Willard Richards were in
Nauvoo. The message was the same in each letter. Conditions
are very serious here. Return home immediately. With the mails
in disarray because of the martial law, Joseph sent a special rider
to take the letters beyond the confines of the county and see
that they got posted.

As the rider left with the letters, Joseph turned to Hyrum.
"Hyrum?"

"Yes, Joseph?"

"I want you to leave."

Hyrum was stunned. "What?" he cried.

"I want you to take Mary and your family and go to Cincinnati. Hyrum, I want you to live through all of this."

"Joseph, I cannot leave you." There was complete finality in
his voice.

Joseph sighed and turned to the others in the room with
them. "I wish I could get Hyrum out of the way so that he could
live to avenge my blood." He turned back to the brother who
had stood by his side for so long. "But I will stay with you and
see it out."

———◆———

With the news from Hancock County growing more grim
with every day, Governor Thomas Ford finally decided to try to
get control of the situation. He left Springfield, unknowingly
passing somewhere along the trail the delegation Joseph Smith
had sent to meet him. When Nathan's group learned that the

governor was no longer in Springfield, they decided they would rest for a day before starting back. But Nathan himself felt too much anxiety for his family to do that. He slept for a couple of hours, bought some extra grain for his horse, and started back.

Springfield was normally a four-day ride from Nauvoo, being about a hundred and fifty miles. But they hadn't gone the full way and Nathan pushed hard on the way back, sleeping in quick snatches along the road, then moving on. When he reached Carthage, however, which was still about twenty miles from Nauvoo, he knew that both he and his horse had reached their limit. Just before midnight on June twenty-first, he pulled up in front of the Hamilton House, a hotel, and stiffly slid off his horse. Inside, as he signed the register book, his eye was caught by the two signatures just above his. John Taylor and John Bernhisel, both of Nauvoo, had checked in just an hour before. He determined that he would seek them out before going on the next morning, to see what was happening.

The hotel clerk had been right. As Nathan approached the courthouse, he saw Elder Taylor and Brother Bernhisel just coming out of the building. With a shout and a wave, he caught their attention and moved quickly over to join them.

"I thought you were in Springfield," Elder Taylor said.

Nathan explained briefly what had happened. The Apostle nodded. "When Joseph received a message from Governor Ford, stating that he was here and requesting to hear the Mormons' version of matters, we realized that you had probably not reached Springfield in time. So Joseph asked Brother Bernhisel and me to bring another letter and some additional documents down to the governor. We've got an audience with him at ten. Why don't you stay for that, then we'll ride home with you."

Nathan nodded immediately. He would feel much better about riding in this part of the county with someone else.

"Do you know who else is here?" Bernhisel asked.

"No, who?"

There was a short explosion of disgust from Brother Taylor. "Robert Foster, Wilson Law, the Higbees. Joseph Jackson."

"Here?" Nathan said in surprise. "What are they doing here?"

"Just what you'd expect. Stirring up as much trouble as possible."

Bernhisel was angry now. "They saw us when we came in last night. Chauncey Higbee came to our room and tried to get me to come over to the courthouse and post bail for one of our brethren."

"In the middle of the night?" Nathan asked in surprise.

"Exactly," Elder Taylor muttered. "I told John it was a ruse to get us separated from each other. I think they wanted to get the papers we're carrying. We've just come from the justice of the peace right now to see about the bail. He won't accept bail from either of us. Never planned to. It was all a lie."

Joseph Jackson was a proven murderer and a man of violent temper. Knowing that gave Nathan a quick chill. "You were wise not to fall for it."

John Taylor nodded. "We lay awake all night with our pistols in hand, just in case."

"I'll be glad to be out of here," Bernhisel said. "This is not the place for Latter-day Saints right now."

It was ten minutes after ten when they were finally invited into the dining room of the Hamilton House, where the governor was holding audience. As his aide ushered them into the room, all three men stopped dead at the sight of what was before them. Governor Ford was there, all right, with his secretary and a few others of his staff, but there were almost twenty other men in the room as well. And it took only a moment to know which group these men represented. On the front row of chairs, leering delightedly in their direction, were Robert Foster, Wilson Law, Francis and Chauncey Higbee. Joseph Jackson sat directly behind them.

"That's Frank Worrell," Bernhisel whispered. "He's one of the officers for the Carthage Greys." Nathan felt a sudden bleakness. The Carthage Greys were the local militiamen, and among their number were some of the most bitter of Joseph's enemies. That alone said mountains about where Governor Ford was going to stand.

The governor's secretary stood and came to meet them. "Come in, gentlemen. Governor Ford is ready to receive you."

"And so are we!" Jackson yelled. Then he cackled fiendishly.

"Bring on the Mormons," someone else shouted. "We're ready for them."

Governor Thomas Ford seemed not to even notice the outcries. He motioned them forward. "Come sit down, gentlemen."

Ford was a handsome man, in his mid-forties, with full dark hair, neatly barbered. He was clean shaven, and well dressed in a black suit and white shirt with a black cravat fastened at the collar. Nathan, feeling shabby in his trail clothes, saw that Thomas Ford had the kind of face that politicians longed for—pleasant, honest, trustworthy. He had come to the governor's chair through years of distinguished judicial service, first as an Illinois state attorney, then as a circuit judge, and finally as a justice of the Illinois Supreme Court. There was no question but what he had won the election with the help of the Mormons. There was also no question, as Nathan looked around the room, that he wanted to distance himself from that "tainted" influence as much as possible now.

As the three men took seats in front of the governor, the catcalls continued. "Hey, why didn'cha bring ol' Joe Smith? We'd have given him a warm welcome." "Get ready for some heavy lying, Governor, sir." "Where's your prophet now, brethren? Out marrying him another wife?" That brought a chorus of guffaws. "No wonder he's too busy to come down and answer to the courts."

Finally, Ford raised a hand. "Gentlemen, please. They've come to be heard. Let's not let this get out of control."

Nathan shook his head. The wave of the governor's hand was like that of a tired mother chiding a particularly malicious young boy, and both boy and mother knew that it would never amount to any more than just a tired wave of the hand. Ignoring the stream of gibes, John Taylor went forward and handed the governor Joseph's letter and the packet of documents. "In response to your call for further information, the mayor has sent me and Mr. Bernhisel to report to you on the happenings of recent days. Mr. Steed here was part of a delegation on their way to Springfield to give you a similar briefing, but you had passed them on the road coming here. There are also copies of several documents which will substantiate the truth in this circumstance."

"Joe Smith ain't never told the truth in his life," someone shouted.

"Infernal liar," Francis Higbee snorted. "Always has been."

Again it was as if Ford weren't even aware of their presence. "Proceed," he said to Elder Taylor.

John Taylor began to outline in brief the events surrounding the destruction of the *Nauvoo Expositor* press. It was a cruel joke. Governor Ford was leafing through some of the documents, only half listening. Meanwhile, the crowd jeered, swore, pounded their chairs, and interrupted constantly. "That's a damnable lie!" Wilson Law shouted after a sentence or two. "Lies! Lies!" shouted Robert Foster when the Apostle started to talk about the slanderous nature of their paper. Jackson stood up and shook his fist at Taylor, swearing loudly. "An infernal falsehood," he screamed into Taylor's face. And through it all Governor Ford went on reading and half listening, as if they were alone in a forest glade with nothing but the soft hum of an occasional bee to break the silence.

Finally, when a highly frustrated Elder Taylor stopped, Governor Ford looked up. Now the men in the room leaned forward, tensing. This would tell where their governor stood. "Gentlemen," he said, looking at the three of them, "I understand your position, but I think under the circumstances, the only way we can satisfy all parties in the matter is to bring Joseph Smith and the others here to Carthage where they can answer to the charges laid against them."

"But, Governor—"

He raised one hand quickly, the most energetic response he had yet shown. "I know how repugnant this may seem to your feelings, but you must realize that the public excitement has reached a dangerous pitch here. We must do something to allay the fears of the people and show them that you people are willing to be governed by law."

"Sir, this matter has twice gone before the courts in Nauvoo and—"

"The courts in Nauvoo are lackeys of Joe Smith," Foster yelled.

The governor, for the first time looking irritated, waved him to silence; then to Elder Taylor, he continued speaking, his voice unctuous and smooth. "I know all that about Mr. Smith going before your courts. But the people view it differently. Therefore, notwithstanding your opinions, I think we must satisfy the people. Joseph Smith must come here to face his accusers. He is accused of riot in destroying the press of a public newspaper. He must face those charges here."

John Taylor straightened to his full height. Joseph had once called him the "Champion of Right," and now he looked and sounded every bit the part, with his white hair and dignified majesty and his rich British accent. "Sir, should Joseph Smith comply with this request, it would be extremely unsafe. Considering the present excited state of the people that you yourself have alluded to, unless he comes with a sufficient force of armed men he could never be safe."

"Never!" Wilson Law shouted, shaking his fist. "He's already a dictator, a demagogue. If he brings his legions down here, there shall be all-out war."

"And if he doesn't," Taylor thundered back, "he shall be in the gravest danger."

Ford stood now, signaling that the audience was at an end. "Mr. Taylor, you go back to Nauvoo and tell Mr. Smith that he and the others accused in this matter must come here to answer the charges, but that I strongly advise you not to come with any armed men. I pledge to you my word as governor and I pledge the faith of this state—Mr. Smith and those who come with him shall be protected. I guarantee your perfect safety."

Foster sat down, smiling triumphantly at Nathan.

"Gentlemen, I shall draft a letter for Mr. Smith. Please wait outside and then you may return to Nauvoo. Tell your mayor that I shall send Captain Gates and a squad of men to Nauvoo to ensure that he may come to Carthage in safety. That will be all."

———— • ————

In the end, the governor kept the three of them waiting until almost five o'clock. It was a clear slap in the face, letting them know where they stood with their chief executive. They finally set out, pushing their mounts hard, and arrived in Nauvoo about dusk. They went straight to the Mansion House to report to Joseph. Joseph immediately sent for others to come and hear John Taylor's report and moved them to the upper room of the store. Willard Richards came. Stephen Markham, a commander in the Legion, was there. John Greene, city marshal, and several officers of the police force were also there. It was a grim group that watched as John Taylor handed Joseph Governor Ford's letter.

The room was completely silent as Joseph's eyes scanned the neatly written lines. Then the corners of his mouth turned down and his eyes narrowed. Finally, Joseph lowered the letter, slowly shaking his head. Hyrum, watching him closely, leaned forward. "What, Joseph? What does he say?"

"There is no mercy," Joseph said, his voice heavy with discouragement. "No mercy here."

John Taylor quickly told them of how they had been received by the governor and then how they had been humiliated by the long delay.

"Well, the same spirit fills his letter," Joseph murmured, his face downcast.

Hyrum took it particularly hard. He looked at his brother. "No, Joseph," he agreed. "You are right. There is no mercy here. Just as surely as we fall into their hands we are dead men."

"Then what shall we do, Brother Hyrum? He is insistent that we come."

There was a long silence; then, "I don't know."

The gloom settled in heavily on all of them. Nathan watched Joseph's face, lined now with weariness and anxiety. Then suddenly, Joseph sat up. His eyes widened and his countenance brightened. "The way is open. It is clear to any mind what to do."

They all came to attention with that.

"Yes," he said, his voice rising now with excitement. "All they want is Hyrum and myself. Tell everybody to go about their business, not to collect in groups, but to scatter about. There is no doubt they will come here and search for us, but let them search. They will not bother you in person or property. Not even a hair of your head shall be harmed."

"But," Nathan blurted, "where will you go?"

Joseph stood now, too excited to remain seated any longer. "We will cross the river tonight, and go away to the West."

Nathan's mouth opened as he stared at the Prophet. Hyrum and the others were equally stunned. Joseph had talked about going to investigate the areas of California and Oregon back in February, but with the press of his candidacy and then the growing crisis, little more had been said of it.

Stephen Markham looked up. "But Joseph, are you sure that's wise?"

Joseph swung on him. "Brother Markham, I tell you, if Hyrum and I are ever taken again, we shall be massacred, or I am not a prophet of God. I would go to Carthage alone, but I want Hyrum to live to avenge my blood and he is determined not to leave me."

Now he turned to two of the policemen. "Abraham, John, you go and get the *Maid of Iowa*. Get it to the upper landing. Take Hyrum's family and my family and put them on it. Then go down the Mississippi and up the Ohio River to Portsmouth. There we will send word on where we are and how to get our families to us."

Joseph turned, ignoring their shocked looks. "Will you come with us, Brother Nathan?"

Nathan wasn't terribly surprised. Joseph had specifically requested that he be part of the Oregon expedition. "Of course, Joseph. Do you want any others of my family?"

Joseph almost immediately shook his head. "With all of Joshua's trail experience, he would be of great value, but no. He must stay here with Caroline now. Will too. She could not bear to lose either of them just now. No, just you, Nathan. Tell Lydia I'm sorry."

"She'll understand."

"You mustn't tell her where we're going, Nathan," he added quickly. "For her own safety."

"Where shall I meet you?"

"Across the river in Montrose. Try Brother Killien's home, or William Jordan's."

Nathan stood. "I shall be there before morning."

Chapter Notes

Not only would Joseph's address to the Nauvoo Legion on 18 June 1844 turn out to be his last address to them, but it would prove to be his final public discourse to the Saints as well. The words he uses here come directly from the record of his address on that date (see HC 6:497–500).

The attempt by Higbee and Jackson to separate John Taylor and John Bernhisel on the night of 21 June 1844 and the shabby treatment of the two brethren by Governor Ford the next day are recorded in John Taylor's biography (see B. H. Roberts, Life of John Taylor, Collector's Edition [Salt Lake City: Bookcraft, 1989], pp. 122–25; see also HC 6:542–45).

Lydia stood watching her husband thrust things into the small valise. The tears had stopped now, but her cheeks were still wet. "Can't you even say farewell to the children?" she asked.

He stopped for a moment, his throat constricting. "I dare not," he finally managed. "The officers may question them. Kiss them for me, especially our little Joseph."

"I will."

He finished, then straightened, looking around the room. Then with a low cry of pain, he took Lydia in his arms and pulled her to him. "I shall miss you, my darling."

"And I you," she said fiercely, gripping him tightly.

He kissed her. "Joseph has said that if he can get away clear, there will be no danger here. Not one hair shall be harmed."

"We'll be fine," she managed, pushing down the anxiety that was like a great knot in her stomach.

He kissed her again. "We shall find us another home, where we can be safe once and for all."

She nodded, reaching up to wipe her cheeks. "You must go, Nathan." She kissed him one last time, hard and with longing. "Be careful."

"I will. And may God watch over all of you while I am gone."

⸻

To Nathan's surprise, Joshua was waiting for him at the front gate. Nathan instantly started shaking his head. "Joshua, you can't. Caroline needs you."

"I know that," he said. "I'm not trying to go with you. But knowing how easily my little brother gets lost, I thought I would just row you across the river."

Nathan felt a quick lump in his throat and clasped Joshua's hand. "Thank you. Will you give Caroline and Will my love? And Mama and Papa and all the rest? I wish I could tell them all good-bye."

"I will," Joshua said gruffly. "Now, let's get going before you get me bawling like a baby here."

⸻

Dawn was just coming when Nathan raised his hand and pointed about two hundred yards upriver from where they were. "There!" he said. "There's the landing." He held his oar out of the water for a few moments while Joshua leaned into his, turning the nose of the rowboat into the current. Then together they started rowing hard, moving the craft toward the landing.

When they were still about fifty yards out, they saw figures moving around on the bank. Nathan peered more closely. "I think it's Joseph," he said in surprise.

Just then Porter Rockwell's voice came floating across the water. "Nathan, is that you?"

"Yes!" He waved an arm, then went back to rowing. In another couple of minutes they nosed the rowboat in beside the one already pulled up on the bank. Joshua stood, then hopped nimbly out. He pulled the boat in further and Nathan followed him. Nathan noticed the other boat had about two or three inches of water in it. "Looks like you had a wet ride last night."

Rockwell shook hands with them. "Just about didn't make it. Joseph and Hyrum had to use their boots to bail water all the way across." He pulled a face. "Some favor, lending a man a leaky rowboat."

"We thought you'd be long gone by now," Joshua said.

Joseph came down. He was in stocking feet and walked gingerly. "We got a late start," he said, in answer to Joshua's comment. "By the time we said our farewells to our family, it was about two o'clock this morning. Then with the boat nearly sinking on us, we've only been here a few minutes."

Joshua looked at Nathan. "I'd better leave again. I promised Caroline I'd come right back."

"How is she?" Joseph asked.

"Remarkably good," Joshua answered.

Hyrum and Willard Richards had come over to join them now too. "Your wife is a very lucky woman," Elder Richards said.

"Yes." Joshua turned to Nathan and stuck out his hand. "Good luck, little brother. Be careful." Then to the others, "Keep your powder dry." He chuckled, looking down at their stocking feet. "Don't put it in your boots."

"Say," Joseph said, "can Porter go back across with you? He's going to get us some horses and come back after dark tonight. Then we'll be off in the morning."

"Sure."

Rockwell grinned. "You mean I don't get to have another adventure going back across?"

Joseph stepped forward and laid a hand on Joshua's shoulder. "Thank you, Joshua. Tell Caroline she is in my prayers daily."

"I shall, Joseph. And when you find yourself a new home, will you let us know?"

There was a momentary start among the small group of men.

"Does that mean that you'd come with us?" Nathan blurted.

There was a sheepish grin. "Well, I think I've sold my freight business for the second time. I know it's not final yet, but I can't simply back out on them. Maybe it's time for a change."

"I would like that, Joshua," Joseph said. "I would like that very much."

The original plan had been to stay at the home of John Killien, a man whom Joseph trusted deeply. But Killien wasn't home, and so they went on to the Jordan home, where Sister Jordan prepared a full breakfast for her unexpected but welcome guests. About nine o'clock, John Bernhisel and Reynolds Cahoon came to the house. Cahoon was highly exercised and reported that early that morning the posse promised by Governor Ford had arrived in Nauvoo to provide escort for Joseph and the other prisoners. When they learned that Joseph and Hyrum were gone, the captain was furious. Sending the others back to Carthage for reinforcements, he vowed that they would guard the city until Joseph surrendered, even if it took three years.

Joseph was neither surprised nor upset by that news and told them to go back and stay calm. Clearly unhappy, Cahoon finally relented, grumbling all the way back to the boat. Then Joseph and his companions set to work. There would be the five of them—Joseph and Hyrum, Rockwell (once he got back), Willard Richards, and Nathan. That took considerable supplies. Joseph had brought some over in their boat; Joshua and Nathan had done the same. The Jordans and Willard Richards went from house to house among the Saints in Montrose to get more. By noon they had flour, salt, sugar, some ammunition, blankets, dried fruit, and a dozen other items to divide between them.

They were in the midst of debating how best to do that when Brother Jordan appeared at the doorway. "Brother Cahoon is back. And Porter Rockwell."

Joseph stood. "Porter? He wasn't supposed to come until after dark."

Actually there were four men waiting for them outside. In addition to Cahoon and Rockwell, Lorenzo Wasson, Emma's nephew, had come. The fourth man was Hiram Kimball. Though Sarah Granger Kimball was a wonderful, faithful sister, her husband had joined the Church only about a year ago. A wealthy businessman, Hiram owned one of Nauvoo's most prosperous stores and several pieces of property. He had been known to be sharply critical at times. Like many wealthy men, he assumed that his wealth gave him privileges with others.

Before Joseph could say anything to Rockwell, Porter withdrew a letter from his shirt. "Emma asked me to give this to you," he said.

Joseph opened it and read it quickly. His eyes darkened as he did so, but he folded it again and put it inside his shirt without comment. Cahoon, watching him closely, spoke first. "Joseph, Emma asked us to come and persuade you to come back. She's terribly frightened."

"Come back!" Nathan cried. "Are you joking?"

Cahoon glared at Nathan for a moment, but then spoke to Joseph again. "It will be all right," he said earnestly. "The governor has given his pledge and the pledge of the state that you shall be protected and that you will get a fair trial."

"In Carthage?" Willard Richards sniffed. "You must be mad."

"Look, Uncle Joseph," Lorenzo Wasson jumped in, "Aunt Emma is badly frightened. She had to do this once before, remember? You were in Liberty Jail. She had to leave Missouri completely on her own."

That was somewhat of an exaggeration, since Stephen Markham and others had helped her leave Missouri, but there was no question but what Emma had seen this kind of terrible experience before. And she was almost five months with child again. If Joseph went west, he would likely not be back when the baby was born. After her last stillborn experience, that would surely be terrifying to her as well.

And yet, even with all that, Nathan had to say what he felt. "Lorenzo, I understand your concern, but you haven't been to Carthage and seen what's going on down there. The governor is listening to the mob. He's not going to give Joseph any protection."

Hiram Kimball waved that off. "That's just the kind of talk meant to frighten people. The governor sent a posse to give you escort. He's given his word." Now he leaned forward, his jaw set, his chin thrust out. "This is no time for cowardice, Joseph. If you don't come back, they'll destroy Nauvoo. We'll lose our homes, our—"

"Cowardice?" Hyrum exclaimed. "You think we are leaving because we are afraid?"

"All I know is that Emma is begging you to come back," Wasson said.

There was a momentary pause, and then Cahoon spoke. "There's an old fable. When the wolves come, the shepherd flees and leaves the flock to be devoured."

Joseph looked as though he had been slapped. He just stared at them, his eyes suddenly haunted. "Is that what you think?" he whispered.

No one answered, but it was clear what they thought.

Joseph's shoulders slumped. His voice was hollow and drawn. "If my life is of no value to my friends," he said to no one in particular, "then it is of none to myself."

"No, Joseph!" Nathan exclaimed.

But Joseph didn't even turn to him. In the silence Cahoon, Wasson, and Kimball looked at the others with stubborn defiance. Joseph looked like a beaten man now. Hyrum was pale and staring at the three men in great dismay. Joseph finally turned to Rockwell. "What shall I do, Porter?"

Rockwell shook his head. "Joseph, you are the oldest and know best. But I'll say this—as you make your bed, I will lie with you."

Joseph then turned to Hyrum. "Brother Hyrum, *you* are the oldest. What shall we do?"

For a long moment the two brothers gazed at each other; then Hyrum sagged, the heart gone out of him. Cowards? It was a bitter lance indeed. "Let us go back and give ourselves up and see the thing out," he said woodenly.

"No," Elder Richards cried.

But Joseph waved him to silence. His eyes never left Hyrum's face. "If you go back I will go with you, but we shall be butchered."

"No, no!" Hyrum said, more resolute now. "Let us go back and put our trust in God and we shall not be harmed. The Lord is in it. If we live or have to die, we will be reconciled to our fate."

Joseph turned away, looking out toward the west. His face was drawn, his eyes shadowed with pain. Finally he turned back around and spoke to Cahoon. "Tell Captain Davis to have a boat here at half past five. We shall cross back over and surrender ourselves then."

Before crossing back to the eastern side of the river, Joseph and Hyrum drafted a letter of response to Governor Ford. Immediately upon reaching Nauvoo, Joseph dispatched Theodore Turley and Jedediah M. Grant to Carthage to deliver it. They arrived in the county seat about nine p.m. and immediately took the letter to the governor.

Pleased to hear that Joseph was willing to surrender, Ford promised to send the posse back again as an escort. But the enemies of the Church had gotten wind of the new developments. Wilson Law and Joseph Jackson strode in and launched into a diatribe against the Prophet and the Mormons. Everything was lies, they shouted. Other prisoners didn't get a private escort. Why should Joe Smith be given privileges that no other prisoner would receive?

Ford caved in. Rescinding his previous decision, he told Turley and Grant to return to Nauvoo immediately and tell Joseph Smith that he was expected to present himself in Carthage by ten a.m. the following day—without escort—or the city of Nauvoo would be destroyed with every man, woman, and child in it.

The disheartened men finally arrived back home at four a.m. the next day and went straight to Joseph with their report. Not really expecting much better than that, Joseph sent runners throughout the city. At half past six, Joseph and Hyrum and all other members of the city council would depart Nauvoo. They would ride to Carthage and there surrender to the authorities as requested.

"Papa!"

"Shhh!" Nathan said, putting a finger to his lips. "Don't wake the others."

Young Joshua dropped his voice. "Why do you have to go, Papa? You aren't named in the warrant."

Lydia shushed him now. "Your father is going to help Grandpa Steed and to be with Brother Joseph." She was making a valiant effort to keep her voice even and the fear from her eyes. But when she turned to Nathan he could see it clearly.

He walked to young Joshua and took him by the shoulders. "You help Mama. You watch the children when she has to be over with Aunt Caroline and baby Livvy."

"Yes, Papa."

Then he went to Lydia and took her gently in his arms. She buried her head against his chest and he kissed the top of her head. "It's going to be all right," he said softly. "At least I'm not going west. We should only be a few days."

She looked up, her eyes glistening. "I know," she said. "Just be careful, Nathan."

"I could go, Pa. One of us needs to be with Joseph. We owe him that."

Joshua looked away, the pain tearing through him. "Will, we are needed here. Both of us. Joseph will understand."

"But Grandpa Steed, Pa . . ."

"Nathan is going to be with Grandpa. Our place is here."

Will's head dropped in resignation. "Yes, Pa."

Joshua walked to him and laid a hand on his shoulder. "You know that I'd be proud to ride with you, don't you?"

"Yes, Pa."

He squeezed his son's shoulder. "We need to make sure everything here is ready in case of trouble. That will be our ride today, Will."

"At least it's summertime," Benjamin said, trying to keep his voice light.

Mary Ann was surprised by that unexpected comment.

"Last time I marched off to jail it was November. I think I prefer June."

"Please, Ben," she whispered. "Don't talk about it."

"This isn't like last time," he said, trying to sound hopeful. "We've got the law on our side now. We've got the Nauvoo Legion standing by. Don't worry."

She laughed through the sudden tears. "Do you know how much I hate it when I'm worrying and you tell me not to worry?"

He tried to smile, but his face betrayed him. He stepped to her, took her in his arms, and then just held her tightly for a long time.

The farewells at the Mansion House and at Hyrum's home were no less painful. Nathan watched with heavy heart as Emma and her two oldest children clung to Joseph's coat. Emma was nearly hysterical, and Nathan wondered if she was having regrets about what had happened yesterday. Joshua had been incensed when he learned that Emma was part of stopping Joseph from escaping to the West, but Nathan, understanding the terrible cost that Emma had paid in the past, was willing to leave judgment to the Lord in the matter.

There were nearly thirty in the party of horsemen that finally rode away from the Mansion House. Eighteen were under indictment—Joseph and Hyrum and sixteen members of the city council—and the rest were friends and associates who would provide the escort that Governor Ford refused to send. Nathan and Benjamin rode side by side. A deep gloom was upon them all, and few words were spoken.

They moved slowly out of town, turning north on Durphy Street, then east again on Mulholland, which would take them past the temple before they turned onto the Nauvoo-Carthage

"Are the other militia groups giving up the arms furnished to them by the state?" someone called out.

Captain Dunn just looked away, obviously a bit ashamed. The answer to that was clear. Only the Mormons were being asked to give up their arms. Joseph spoke up now. "Captain Dunn here has given me his word as a military man that we shall be protected as we return for these arms, even if it costs him his life."

"That's right," Dunn said, looking at the angry faces before him. Then he turned to face his own men. "Men," he called, "we have given our pledge that we shall protect them. And General Smith has assured me that the Nauvoo Legion will not oppose us."

That must have been weighing heavily on the minds of these men. Sixty armed soldiers seemed like a lot of men until you considered marching into Nauvoo where five thousand members of the Nauvoo Legion awaited you. It was not surprising, then, that when Captain Dunn made the announcement a ragged cheer went up and down the line.

Joseph made a quick designation, indicating that about half of his group should wait here until they returned. Nathan and Benjamin were among those assigned to stay. Nathan was just as glad. His father looked tired, and making a trip to Nauvoo and back would be an additional six or more hours of riding. And besides that, facing more farewells was not something Nathan would look forward to.

Joseph walked to his horse and mounted. Captain Dunn did the same. As the others mounted and turned to Joseph for the signal, he looked around at those that were with him. The wide blue eyes were clear and composed. The deep sorrow of the morning was gone. He seemed relaxed and completely at ease. That made what he said next all the more startling.

"Brethren," he said in a voice soft enough that it wouldn't carry to the soldiers, "I am going like a lamb to the slaughter." He ignored the collective gasp. "But I want you to know that I am as calm as a summer's morning. I have a conscience void of offense toward God and toward all men." He glanced toward the militia now. "If they take my life, I shall die an innocent man, and my blood shall cry from the ground for vengeance. It shall yet be said of me, 'He was murdered in cold blood!' "

With that, not waiting either for comment or for the militia to follow, he wheeled his horse around and started back toward Nauvoo.

Governor Ford had originally demanded that Joseph be in Carthage by ten a.m. With the order to return to Nauvoo for the arms, that deadline was extended. It was nine o'clock that evening before Joseph and his company returned to where Nathan and the rest were waiting. They decided to rest and eat for a time, and as they did so, Captain Dunn and his troops caught up to them. After half an hour's respite, the whole party—almost a hundred in number now—set off again.

It was five minutes before midnight when the long column finally rode into Carthage. Nathan took some comfort in the lateness of the hour, thinking that at least they wouldn't have to face the clamoring mob that they all knew awaited them. He couldn't have been more wrong. All that the long delay had done was make the waiting crowds all the more impatient. Gathered in Carthage, in addition to the locals, were townsmen and farmers from the surrounding communities, as well as several hundred militia from various parts of the state. The delay had also given those crowds the afternoon and evening to consume prodigious amounts of beer and whiskey. The shout went up while Joseph's party, accompanied by Dunn's men, were still four or five blocks from the public square. They could hear it jump from house to house, voice to voice. In seconds, torches and lamps came pouring out of the houses and saloons of Carthage. The rising roar of hundreds of angry voices swelled like a hurricane.

"All right, men!" Captain Dunn shouted. "Form in around the prisoners. Stay steady. We've made a promise to bring them in safely and that's what we'll do." He brought his rifle out of its saddle holster and held it at the ready. His men did the same.

The Mormons left theirs where they were, lest they inflame the emotions of the mob even more.

Benjamin looked at Nathan, and without a word having to pass between them, they spurred their horses forward a little, coming in closer together. Benjamin stared forward, his face pale, his hands gripping the saddle horn until his fingers showed white. A stream of shouting, cursing, fist-shaking humanity surged forward and enveloped them like a flood. Benjamin felt as if he were going to faint. He wanted to clap his hands over his ears. It was a reenactment of Far West. It was a scene from hell itself, with all the fiends of a thousand years unleashed at one foul moment. "There's Joe Smith!" "There's that damnable prophet of theirs!" "Step aside, Dunn! Give us a clear shot at him." "Kill them all!" "Hey, Joe, hope you said good-bye to Nauvoo. You'll never see it again!" "Let's see the false prophet now!"

Profanity was like thick smoke in the air around them. Some of the mob tried to push through the surrounding militia riders and grab at the boots or legs of Joseph's group, but Captain Dunn was true to his word and his men drove them back. The Carthage Greys were the most frightening of all in the stream of abuse and invective that they hurled at the Mormons.

Benjamin leaned over toward Nathan until their heads almost touched, but even then he had to yell to make himself heard. "I never thought I'd have to see this again," he cried. "It makes my blood run cold."

Nathan nodded, one hand on his pistol butt, his eyes scanning the crowd in nervous flicks back and forth. They were just coming up on the Hamilton House, and suddenly a window in the upper story opened and a man's head came out.

"It's the governor!" someone shouted, and in moments the cacophony died away. "Hey, Governor," one of the Carthage Greys shouted, "we want to see Joe Smith. Why are you taking him away?"

Ford glanced down at Joseph momentarily, then looked away. "Gentlemen," he said in soothing tones, "I know your great anxiety to see Mr. Smith, which is natural enough, but it is quite too late tonight."

Someone booed, but Ford raised his hands, smiling generously down at them. "But I assure you, gentlemen, you shall have that privilege in the morning, for I shall cause him to pass by you upon the public square."

A ragged cheer and scattered applause swept across the crowd.

"Now, with that assurance, I ask you all to return quietly and peaceably to your quarters until then." He drew in his head again and shut the window.

"Hurrah for Tom Ford!" someone called.

"Yeah," Nathan muttered, "hurrah for Tom Ford."

———•———

Carthage, Illinois, June 25th, 6:30 p.m.

My dearest Lydia,

I am writing this quick note to send home with Father. He and most of the others who were under warrant have been freed on bail and are returning to Nauvoo. Joseph and Hyrum are being bound over for reasons I shall explain in a moment. Joseph has asked that some of his friends and associates remain with him. I am honored that he has requested that I be one of those.

Our arrival last night was not a pleasant one, but I shall let Father tell you about that. This morning, at 8:00 a.m., we went to the courthouse and surrendered all those named in the warrant to Constable Bettisworth. As you know, he is the one that first came to Nauvoo with the warrant after the press was destroyed. To our surprise, Bettisworth arrested Joseph and Hyrum again, this time not on the original charges of riot for destroying the *Expositor* press, but on charges of treason against the state for putting Nauvoo under martial law. This later proved to be important. This afternoon, when all of the prisoners appeared before the justice of the peace, he set bond at five hundred dollars each.

Incidentally, he set this outrageously high, thinking we could not meet it. But some of the brethren pledged all their property, and the total of seventy-five hundred dollars was met almost immediately. Pa and I put up our building lots as surety and bonded for Pa and two other men.

But anyway, while all the others were being freed on bond, Joseph and Hyrum could not be. Treason is a capital crime and only a circuit court judge can set bail on capital crimes. The nearest circuit judge is at least a day's ride from here. So Joseph and Hyrum have been bound over for trial in a few days.

True to his promise to the mob, Governor Ford marched Joseph and Hyrum and a few others before the various militia formed up in the public square after we finished at the court-house this morning. Instead of satisfying them, it almost caused a riot. The Carthage Greys went wild when Joseph and Hyrum were introduced as generals. They started to scream and yell and toss their hats in protest. One man grabbed his sword and pulled it out, waving it toward the two prisoners. "Bring them here," he shouted. "I'll show you the proper way to introduce these Mormons to real officers." We feared for their lives, but finally they were taken back to the hotel again. The most chilling thing? Ford, in trying to satisfy the crowd, said, "You have my word on it, you shall have full satisfaction in this matter." For the Carthage Greys, full satifaction will be nothing less than the blood of our beloved brethren.

Well, I must close. All of those that were freed are ready to go. I send with this letter my deepest love. Please do not worry. Joseph continually assures me that all shall be well. I love you eternally.

Nathan

———•———

They were in the larger of the two hotel rooms in the Hamilton House given over for the billeting of the Mormon group. Those who had been released were bidding farewell to the others. Those staying behind, like Nathan, were sending letters and notes and personal messages back with them.

Joseph moved from man to man, shaking hands and thanking them. When he came to Benjamin, he went to speak, wanting to say something light and filled with humor. They had joked together so often, the two of them, even in the grimmest of circumstances. But Joseph's voice caught and suddenly he couldn't speak. Finally, he just opened his arms and the two of them embraced, clapping each other on the shoulders. "Good-bye, old friend," Joseph finally managed in a hoarse whisper.

"Good-bye, Joseph," Benjamin answered in a voice equally choked with emotion.

Chapter Notes

When John Taylor and John Bernhisel returned from Carthage with the governor's letter and the gloomy report of how they were treated, Joseph immediately felt impressed that fleeing Nauvoo was the solution to the dilemma. He and Hyrum, along with Willard Richards and Porter Rockwell, crossed the river during the early morning hours of 23 June in a leaky rowboat. While they waited for horses (which Porter went back across the river to obtain) and prepared for their departure, they received a delegation from Nauvoo. The three men mentioned here came across the river with Porter Rockwell to ask Joseph to return. They carried with them a letter from Emma. That letter no longer exists and it is not known exactly what Emma said. She did ask Joseph to return. While it is not recorded exactly who said what at that point, the record does state that "Reynolds Cahoon, Lorenzo D. Wasson and Hiram Kimball accused Joseph of cowardice for wishing to leave the people" (HC 6:549).

Carthage Jail, Hancock County, Illinois
June 27th, 10:00 a.m.

My dearest Lydia,

This may be brief, as Joseph is sending Cyrus Wheelock back to Nauvoo to gather witnesses in his behalf and Cyrus will carry this with him. When he is ready to leave, I will have to close. Much has happened in the day and a half since Father left us. I shall try to catch you up on the most important things.

Yes, as you see, I am in the Carthage jail, but do not be alarmed. I am not a prisoner, only a companion to Joseph and Hyrum, who are now in jail. When I last wrote, we were being billeted in the hotel, but much has changed since then. Shortly after Father and the others left on Tuesday evening, a constable came with a mittimus in hand. A mittimus is a legal order committing a person to jail or prison. This came as a great shock to us all. Mr. Wood and Mr. Reid, the lawyers who are representing

Joseph, said this was completely illegal, since prisoners are entitled to be brought before a justice of the peace for examination before they can be sent to jail.

Mr. Wood and Elder Taylor immediately went to Governor Ford to appeal. But to their amazement, the governor said it was purely a judicial matter and that the executive branch could not interfere. Remember, Ford is a former state supreme court justice. He knows that this is totally wrong, but will do nothing against it. So illegal or not, we are now in jail. Fortunately they allowed the others of us—John Taylor, Willard Richards, Stephen Markham, Dan Jones, John Fullmer, and myself—to stay with them and give them some protection.

And it is a good thing. As the guards marched us to the jail, the mobs lined the streets, screaming and shouting, trying to get at Joseph and Hyrum. Stephen Markham has a stout hickory cane which he calls the "rascal beater." Dan Jones also carries a walking stick. We used both to fend off the crowds as we walked to the jail. I know this report will worry you, but in a way, we are glad now for the mittimus. We are actually safer here than in the hotel. We have at least some protection and there is a guard posted outside.

Yesterday, the legal farce continued. Joseph spent over an hour with Governor Ford trying to explain our case. He also told the governor that we are in great danger here. Ford brushes that aside and says there is no danger here with his troops to protect us. I find it hard to believe that he takes the threat so lightly. He has been here for several days. He has seen the troops in near riot. The governor is no fool, and therefore that leaves me only one conclusion—he has no intention of interfering.

Last night was both a wonderful and a terrible experience. The jailer, a kind man, has allowed us to sleep in an upstairs bedroom rather than forcing us into a cell, so we are somewhat comfortable. There is only one double bed, but we have some straw mattresses to sleep on. The bedroom is not secure, and that worries us somewhat, but it is far more comfortable than being in a cell.

We read scriptures together, particularly scriptures from the Book of Mormon that talk about prophets being in prison, such as Alma and Abinadi. In this setting, that was most touching. Then sometime after we had retired—Joseph and Hyrum in the bed, the rest of us on the mattresses on the floor—we heard a gunshot fired outside. That caused us some consternation but things quieted again. Joseph came and lay down on the floor with us, I'm sure to quiet our fears. As we were lying there, he turned to Dan Jones. I don't know if you know him. He is from Wales. A fine man. Anyway, Joseph asked Brother Dan if he was afraid to die. That brought us all up short, but Dan answered without hesitation. "Engaged in such a cause," he said, "I do not think death would have many terrors." Joseph seemed pleased with that, then surprised us all by saying, "Brother Dan, you will yet see Wales again and fulfill the mission appointed you before you die."

Do you remember what I said some time ago about having a prophet as your next-door neighbor? I have thought of that often these last few days. Here we are in the most terrible of circumstances, and even now, prophecy comes as natural to him as hammering steel does to a blacksmith. Though I find myself anxious at times, I consider it a great privilege to be at his side.

When we rose this morning, Joseph sent Brother Jones to inquire about the gunshot. He encountered Frank Worrell of the Carthage Greys outside. Worrell openly bragged that he was a better prophet than old Joe Smith, for he (Worrell) prophesied that before the day is over, Joseph and everyone with him will be dead. He warned Jones that he'd better flee. Jones went directly to the governor and reported this conversation. Ford told him that he was unnecessarily alarmed, that the people "are not that cruel." Then he refused to give Jones a pass to come back inside the jail. We talked to him briefly but they wouldn't let him stay.

Most alarming to us, however, is that we received word just a few minutes ago that the governor has left for Nauvoo this morning. He took Captain Dunn's troops with him. This is not good. Captain Dunn and his men are the one militia group that has remained impartial in all of this. The governor also dismissed all the other militia groups except the Carthage Greys, who are left to guard us. This is very much like leaving the fox to guard the henhouse.

Twice yesterday the governor talked about going to Nauvoo today, but both times he pledged his word that if he went, he would take Joseph with him. Once again we learn that the solemn word of the highest executive of our state means nothing.

Just a few minutes ago, we learned that— Never mind. Brother Wheelock is here. I must close. I know not what this day shall bring, my beloved Lydia. I am determined to stay by Joseph's side and see it through. I love you and rejoice in the knowledge that not even death can separate us, for we are bound together by eternal ties. Kiss the children for me. Pray that all will be well. I love you.

Nathan

———•———

There were just six of them now. In addition to Joseph and Hyrum and the two Apostles, only Nathan Steed and Stephen Markham remained. John Fullmer had left with Cyrus Wheelock to help secure some witnesses for the upcoming trial. The morning had been a little rainy, but it had cleared now and the early afternoon air was heavy and humid. The jail was sweltering and the mood was one of dark depression. When lunch was brought up, they ate mostly in silence.

Earlier that morning, wearing a long coat because of the rain, Cyrus Wheelock had managed to smuggle in a pistol to Joseph. It was called a "pepperbox" because it had six barrels which fired in succession. As they finished lunch, Joseph went and got the pistol and brought it back to where they were sitting. He also got the single-shot pistol which John Fullmer had left with them. He laid both weapons on the table and looked at his brother. "We may have to use these, Hyrum."

Hyrum looked distressed. "Joseph, you know how I hate to use such things, or to see them used."

"I know, so do I. But we may have to defend ourselves."

With reluctance, Hyrum reached out and took one of the pistols. Joseph took the other pistol for himself and looked at it with distaste. "You know, we are much like the Savior in this regard. We have the revelations of Jesus and the knowledge within us to organize a righteous government on the earth and to give universal peace to all mankind. But we lack the physical strength to do so, just as Jesus did when he was a child. We have of necessity, therefore, to be afflicted and persecuted and smitten. And we must bear it patiently until Jacob, or Israel, comes of age. Then we shall be able to take care of ourselves."

It was just a short time later. They were stretched out on the floor or the bed, each man either sleeping or withdrawn into his own thoughts. From the bed there came a soft moan. Nathan and Joseph, lying side by side on one of the mattresses, went up on one elbow. Willard Richards groaned again, rolling over on his side.

"Willard?" Joseph said. "Are you all right?"

"I don't know, Joseph. My stomach is greatly upset. It must have been something I ate." With some effort, he turned onto his other side, holding one arm across his stomach. Joseph sat up now, and for several minutes watched the Apostle with growing concern. It was obvious that Elder Richards was greatly distressed. Finally, he turned to Markham. "Brother Stephen, would you be willing to go out and try and find some medicine for Willard?"

"Of course." Markham sat up and began to pull on his boots.

Nathan sat up now too, glad for a chance to do something. "Perhaps I should go with him, Joseph. It may be safer if two of us go rather than just one."

"Yes," Joseph said immediately. "Both of you must go. But go with care."

They went downstairs and explained their mission to the jailer, and he unlocked the door and let them out. After being inside the jail all day, they found the light outside to be blinding, and they stopped there for a minute, blinking and shading their eyes.

There were some thirty or forty of the Carthage Greys deployed around the jail, languishing in the hot sunshine. A sergeant, on hearing the door open and seeing Nathan and Markham come out, sprang to his feet. "Hey! What are you doing?" He reached for his rifle. Others were coming to their feet now and doing the same.

"One of our number is sick," Nathan said evenly. "We are going out to obtain some medicine."

Markham showed him the pass which allowed them to go in and out of the jail.

"Let him die," one of the guards snarled. "Serve him right."

The sergeant muttered something under his breath but, after examining the pass closely, nodded and stepped back. With hearts pounding, Nathan and Markham pushed through the Greys, ignoring the catcalls and the jeers all around them. Once free, they walked swiftly away. "This is not good, Nathan," Markham muttered under his breath. "Not good at all."

"We shall see it through, Brother Markham." But even as he spoke, Nathan had to lick his lips, feeling a sudden dryness in his mouth.

It took them nearly an hour to find what they needed. As they rounded the corner and started back toward the jail, they were met by a line of guards blocking the street. Nathan and Markham were cut off, with the jail still a block away. It was obvious that the guards had made a decision since the two men had passed through the ranks before. Without any verbal command, the guards tightened ranks, completely cutting off any passage farther up the street. The sergeant watched Nathan and Markham for a moment through hooded eyes; then he turned and shot a stream of tobacco into the dust. Nathan took a deep breath, feeling the prickle up and down his spine in spite of the fact that he was sweating heavily. He looked at Markham. "Are you ready?" he said in a low voice.

"I am," Markham answered. "Let us be resolute."

They moved forward. The sergeant spat again, then stepped forward, looking at Markham. "Hey, old man," he shouted at Markham, "you're not going back there. You've got five minutes to leave town."

Just then, two men came around the corner behind them leading two horses. To his surprise, Nathan saw that one of them was the mount he had stabled at the Hamilton House. From Markham's sudden intake of breath, Nathan guessed that the other horse was his. "What is this?" Nathan whispered.

Markham just shook his head, still moving forward. Nathan stayed with him, feeling his heart thumping heavily in his chest. The Greys had unshouldered their rifles now, and the tips of their bayonets glinted in the sunlight. "I have medicine for the prisoners," Markham said firmly. "I have a pass from the governor that allows us to go in and out of the jail. Please step aside."

"Please step aside," another man mimicked.

"Wait, wait!" another man cried in a mocking voice. "They have a pass from the governor."

"Ain't that too bad?" jeered a third. "The governor ain't here no more."

The sergeant lowered his rifle so that the bayonet pointed straight at Markham's stomach. "You two have only got one pass that's good today," he snarled, waving to the men with the horses to come forward, "and that's your pass out of town." He made a menacing gesture with his bayonet. "Mount up and git!"

Markham didn't move, and Nathan stood shoulder to shoulder with him. "We have every legal right to go in," Nathan said, fighting to keep his voice steady. The men were circling in, and their mood was growing uglier with every passing second. More were coming from the jail now. This was more than just the usual taunting. They were determined not to let them pass.

"Show them their legal rights, men," the sergeant shouted.

A man lunged forward, bayonet flashing. Nathan jumped

but not quickly enough. The tip of the blade caught him in the calf just above his boot. There was a searing pain and he jumped back, backing into the side of his horse. "You heard the sergeant," the man screamed into Nathan's face. "Now, git!" From behind him, unseen this time, a second man jabbed in. Nathan yelped as the fiery pain slashed through his other leg. He saw Markham fall back, men rushing in on him like boys jabbing sticks into a dying rabbit.

"All right," Markham yelled, grabbing the saddle horn and trying to pull himself up.

Three, four, five more times, Nathan felt the lancing pain. Twice they missed and hit the boot, but with such force that the leather was pierced and the flesh cut open. There was no alternative. His legs were on fire now and he could feel the blood trickling down into his boots. As he mounted his horse, out of the corner of his eye he saw Markham's face, twisted in agony.

"Get out of here!" the sergeant yelled. Someone slapped the rump of Nathan's horse and the animal leaped forward, almost throwing Nathan off. Grabbing the saddle horn, he managed to hang on as his horse pounded away. He looked back and saw that Markham was right behind him, also trying to hang on as his horse charged forward at a hard run.

They let the horses have their head until they reached the outskirts of the city. Then Nathan pulled up, breathing hard. Markham reined in beside him. "Are you all right?" Nathan gasped. He could see that all around the top of Markham's boot was dark red. He looked down at his own legs and saw the dark stains.

"I'm all right," Markham said, wincing even as he did so.

"What do we do now?" Nathan said, looking back toward the town.

"If we go back, they will kill us," came the reply.

There was no disputing that. Getting back to Joseph and Hyrum was out of the question. Nathan thought quickly. "I say we ride for Nauvoo to get the governor. Either he sends help or we bring the Legion back with us."

Markham hesitated for only a moment. "Yes," he said. "We've got to get help."

The Carthage Jail was started in 1839 and completed two years later at a cost of $4,105. Made of thick rock walls, the solidly built structure served as jail, debtor's prison, and residence. Most of the main floor served as living quarters for the jailer and his family. There was a living room, a smaller dining room, and a kitchen. In the northwest corner of the main floor was the debtor's cell, a cell used for those who were charged with lesser violations of the law, such as nonpayment of debts. Also on the main floor, attached to the outside of the building on the northeast corner, there was a frame addition that served as porch and "summer kitchen" for the jailer's family. Just to the front of that was the well that furnished the jail with its water.

Upstairs, the entire back of the building was occupied by a long room with thick steel bars. This was called the dungeon, or the criminal's cell. Here those charged with more serious crimes were kept. The rest of the second floor, except for the stairwell, was taken by the spacious bedroom that the jailer had offered to the prisoners. It had one window facing east and two on the south. These provided some movement of air if there was a breeze blowing.

By quarter to four on the afternoon of June twenty-seventh, there was no breeze and the upper room was a sweatbox. All three windows were open but it made little difference. Joseph and Hyrum Smith and Willard Richards and John Taylor had all removed their coats and were in shirtsleeves. They said little now. Their mood was one of growing melancholy. Governor Ford was gone. Nathan and Markham had left almost two hours before and had not returned, which was an ominous sign. Outside, the Carthage Greys were becoming increasingly raucous and irritable. Through the open windows came a constant stream of profanity, filthy stories, and endless bragging about what they planned to do with old Joe Smith now that the governor was

702

gone. Tempers were short. Someone made an insulting comment and in an instant they were at each other's throats.

Suddenly John Taylor could bear no more. He sat up and began to sing in a low, sorrowful voice.

> A poor wayfaring man of grief
> Had often crossed me on my way,
> Who sued so humbly for relief
> That I could never answer, Nay.

The others turned in surprise, then sat up to listen. John Taylor had a rich tenor voice, and his British accent made it seem all the more full and resonant.

> I had not power to ask his name;
> Whither he went or whence he came;
> Yet there was something in his eye
> That won my love, I knew not why.

The melody was somber and thoughtful, a perfect choice for the mood that filled the room. The words told the story of a stranger who appeared again and again, and always in desperate need of help—he was without food, he was near death with thirst, he was caught in a howling storm, he was found beaten and wounded by the wayside. And again and again, the words told of reaching out, usually with great sacrifice, to help meet the stranger's needs.

Joseph was transfixed, watching Elder Taylor with wide, impassive eyes. Hyrum sat with his head down on his arms. Willard Richards's head was tipped back, his eyes closed. It was as though Brother Taylor's voice had pushed back the obscene sounds of the outside and now filled the room with a quiet reverence.

> In pris'n I saw him next—condemned
> To meet a traitor's doom at morn;
> The tide of lying tongues I stemmed,

And honored him 'mid shame and scorn.
My friendship's utmost zeal to try,
He asked, if I for him would die;
The flesh was weak, my blood ran chill,
But the free spirit cried, "I will!"

At the mention of prison, Brother Taylor's voice faltered momentarily, but he pushed on. Now Hyrum's head was up. Willard Richards opened his eyes. Each one watched John Taylor. Coming to the seventh and final verse, he sang now with sudden joy.

Then in a moment to my view,
The stranger started from disguise:
The tokens in his hands I knew,
The Savior stood before mine eyes.
He spake—and my poor name he named—
"Of me thou hast not been asham'd;
These deeds shall thy memorial be;
Fear not, thou didst them unto me."

The last note ended and hung in the air. If there were sounds coming from the mob outside, they did not hear them. The song had transformed them. Finally, Hyrum stirred. "Thank you, Brother John. I love that song. Will you sing it again for us?"

Elder Taylor seemed almost surprised that there were others in the room with him again. He looked at each of them, then shook his head. "Oh, Brother Hyrum, I do not feel like singing."

Hyrum leaned forward. "Never mind, John. Commence singing again and you will get the spirit of it."

For a long moment, the Apostle stared at the others; then finally he nodded and began again.

It was about two miles west of Carthage. There were four or five dozen men milling around. Horses were tethered to a thick

In Carthage Jail

patch of brush off to one side. Again and again single riders, or groups of two or three together, would come cantering up to join the others. They were welcomed with loud calls and bursts of laughter. Several jugs of whiskey, most nearly empty now, were passing here and there among them.

As four o'clock approached, suddenly someone shouted. They all turned. The man was pointing to the west, down the Carthage-Warsaw Road. A cheer went up and down the line. Coming toward them in a ragged line was a body of horsemen. The Warsaw boys were coming, and Thomas Sharp, editor of the *Warsaw Signal*, was riding at their head.

As they rode up—there were about as many newcomers as there were those waiting for them—they were welcomed enthusiastically, with backslapping and handshaking and passing of the jug. Finally, the leader of the waiting group raised his hands and shouted for silence. "Men," he cried, "the hour has arrived."

A shout went up and he let it roll for a moment, then raised his hands again. The men instantly quieted. "As you know, Joe Smith and his brother are seeking a solution to this problem in the courts." An angry muttering rose from the group.

Thomas Sharp swore, then lifted his rifle high above his head and shook it at the sky. "The only courtroom that matters today is powder and ball."

There was a triumphant roar.

The first man smiled thinly, waiting for it to quiet again. Then he turned to Sharp, pointing to where several buckets were lined up in a row. "Some of our men are a little nervous about being identified. We've mixed up some buckets of mud and gunpowder." He turned to face the crowd around him. "If any of you are of a mind to, here is something to blacken your faces. If you want to ride in as you are, so be it. We leave in half an hour."

Hyrum was seated at the table reading quietly from *Antiquities of the Jews* by Flavius Josephus. Joseph was sitting in the chair opposite him, listening without comment. John Taylor was stretched out on the bed. Willard Richards stood at the window that looked out to the east. Suddenly, he cocked his head, listening. "Do you notice anything?" he asked. They all turned to look at him.

"Like what?" Hyrum asked.

Elder Richards moved away from that window and started toward the two windows that were on the south wall. "Like how much quieter it is now."

Hyrum set the book down. Joseph turned in his chair. "Yes," Joseph said. "It *is* quieter all of a sudden."

The Apostle moved to the window that looked almost straight down on the entrance to the jail. He pulled the curtain back a little so he could see out. There was a soft grunt of surprise.

"What?" Elder Taylor asked, sitting up now.

"They're gone."

Joseph stood and moved toward him. "Who's gone?"

"The guards. All but"—he counted quickly—"eight."

Joseph came to stand beside him, looking down at the men who stood or sat near the front entrance to the jail. He too counted, then shrugged. Before, there had been enough to completely encircle the jail. Now there couldn't be enough to even adequately cover the front entrance.

Brother Taylor lay back down again. "They changed the guard yesterday about this time too." He checked his watch. "Yes, it's four o'clock."

Elder Richards nodded, accepting that, but he stood there, looking down on the greatly diminished numbers. Finally, he too moved away, feeling vaguely uneasy.

———◆———

There were several thousand people gathered in the streets around the Mansion House. Governor Ford, immediately upon arriving in Nauvoo, had asked the city leaders to call the Saints together. In a city already gripped by fear, the word spread rapidly. Like most of the population, the Steeds had dropped whatever it was they were doing and flocked to learn what was happening. Now Ford stood atop the partially completed building that Joseph had used to address the Legion a week before.

They stood in gloomy silence as Ford imperiously harangued them. There was no conciliatory gesture toward the Saints here, not even an attempt to find some middle ground for a solution. He spoke as though every man, woman, and child in Nauvoo had shared in the act of riot. It was condescending, insulting, demeaning. They should be praying Saints, he said, not military Saints. If they sought to retaliate in any way against those who were bringing their leaders to justice, every man, woman, and child in Nauvoo would be exterminated, he promised. The Saints didn't like it, and a low undertone of angry muttering could be heard throughout the large audience.

Joshua stepped closer to Benjamin. "This is not good, Pa. Why is he here and not in Carthage where his presence is needed?"

Benjamin shook his head. "The city council was told that the people of Carthage are afraid we're going to call out the Legion and send them to free Joseph. He's supposedly here to see that doesn't happen."

"My fear," Derek growled, "is that they're *not* going to call them out."

Joshua started to respond to that when a movement caught his eye. Porter Rockwell was near the edge of the crowd motioning frantically for him to come. Joshua pointed at himself, with a questioning look, and Rockwell vigorously nodded. Joshua slipped through the crowds to where he stood.

"What's the matter?" Joshua asked.

"Something's afoot here," Porter said in a low voice, "and I don't like it."

"What do you mean by that?"

Rockwell lowered his voice, looking around. "Well, right now, for example. Are you catching the gist of his message? He's warning us against any retaliating. For what? Nothing's happened yet. Joseph and Hyrum are still awaiting trial, and yet he speaks as if something has already taken place."

Joshua turned to stare suspiciously up at the man who was the governor of their state. There was an element of that in his words.

"There's more. As you know, the governor and his staff went to the Mansion House when they first arrived here to rest and refresh themselves."

"Yes."

"Well, as I was about to come over here, I realized I had left my hat in the room where they were staying. I was just going to slip in and get it and then slip right out again. But when I walked in, a man was standing by the governor. This man was the only person speaking. He had one hand raised high. Just as I opened the door, he dropped his arm, like he was chopping something off. And as he dropped his hand he said, 'By now, the deed should be done.'"

"The deed?" Joshua asked. "What deed?"

"I don't know," Rockwell admitted. "The moment they saw me they cut off any further talk. But they all looked as guilty as a bunch of boys caught smoking a pipe out behind the barn. Now the governor is warning us not to strike back. I don't like it, Joshua. Not one bit."

Joshua's mind was racing. Then he came to a decision. He reached out and gripped Rockwell's arm. "I'm going to Carthage, Porter. I'm not leaving Nathan and Joseph down there without help. Will you come with me?"

There was instant relief on the younger man's face. "Yes. Gladly."

Joshua reached into his vest pocket and pulled out his watch. "It is half past four now. I'll meet you at my place at five o'clock. If we ride hard, we can be to Carthage by dark."

"I'll be there." He turned and strode away.

———◆———

The one hundred and fifty men with blackened faces were about a quarter of a mile west of the outskirts of the city now. They were all on foot, having left their horses in a grove of trees a few hundred yards back. Their leader raised his hand and the group came to a halt, not in any rank-and-file order, but milling about him like a flock of goats. They looked like caricatures of children in Halloween masks. The mud-and-gunpowder mixture left only round circles of white showing around the eyes, the nostrils, and the mouth. Here and there, white streaks had been cleared by beads of sweat running down from beneath their hat brims. Some had painted their faces to make themselves look like Indians. It only added to the macabre, surreal appearance of the whole assembly.

"All right," the leader bawled. "It's five o'clock. Form up on me."

The leader faced forward as the men fell in behind him. Then as he moved them out with a wave of his arm, he looked over his shoulder and cried out in a singsong voice:

> Where now is the Prophet Joseph?
> Where now is the Prophet Joseph?
> Where now is the Prophet Joseph?
> Safe in Carthage Jail!

The men took it up instantly, and in moments, it was a throaty, chilling chant.

> Where now is the Prophet Joseph?
> Where now is the Prophet Joseph?
> Where now is the Prophet Joseph?
> Safe in Carthage Jail!

———————

At five p.m., the four men in the bedroom heard footsteps coming up the stairs, and then there was a knock at the door. John Taylor was standing next to the door, and on a signal from Joseph, he opened it. Mr. Stigall, the jailer, was standing there, hat in hand. "Mr. Smith?"

Joseph, who sat on the edge of the bed, stood and came over. "Yes?"

"I thought you should know. The two men that you sent out for medicine earlier this afternoon, well, they were driven out of town by the guard. I'm sorry."

Joseph's head dropped. "I see," he finally said. "Thank you for telling us. We've been greatly concerned."

"I'm feeling much better now," Willard Richards said, as if it might help. "I'll be all right."

The jailer turned to go back down the stairs, then stopped again. "Begging your pardon, Mr. Smith, but it's my opinion that you'd be safer in the cell tonight."

Joseph was surprised and then touched. "Thank you, Mr. Stigall. That is most considerate of you. And I think you are right. We shall go in right after supper."

"All right." He turned and went back down the steps.

As Elder Taylor shut the door again, Joseph turned to Richards. "Willard, when it is time to go into the cell, will you go in with us?"

Willard Richards looked surprised and a little offended. "Brother Joseph, you did not ask me to cross the river with you. You did not ask me to come to Carthage. Do you think I would forsake you now?"

Joseph didn't speak, just watched his friend steadily.

Suddenly, Elder Richards had a thought. "But I'll tell you what I will do. If you are condemned to be hung for treason, I will be hung in your stead and you shall go free."

Joseph's eyes widened, then were instantly glistening with tears. "You cannot, Brother Willard," he said in a husky whisper.

"I will!" the Apostle said emphatically.

Joshua was giving the girth on his saddle one last jerk, when the door to the barn crashed open and Will came running in.

Joshua looked up in surprise. "Is Porter here already?"

"Pa, it's Nathan!"

Joshua whipped around. "What?"

"Nathan just came home, Pa. He and Brother Markham were driven out of Carthage."

"No!" He sagged back. "What about Joseph?"

"He's still there."

"But—"

"You'd better come, Pa. Nathan's legs are all bloody."

Chapter Notes

The events described in this chapter are told in great detail in various sources (see HC 6:575–616; CHFT, pp. 276–81). Dan Jones served a mission in his native Wales from 1845 to 1849, during which he helped to bring into the Church about two thousand people in only a couple years' time. He served a second successful mission in Wales from 1852 to 1856. Thus was fulfilled Joseph's remarkable prophecy. (See CHFT, p. 280; Andrew Jenson, comp., *Latter-day Saint Biographical Encyclopedia*, 4 vols. [1901–36; reprint, Salt Lake City: Western Epics, 1971], 3:659–60.)

The evidence that Governor Ford had a good idea of what was about to happen in Carthage is pretty strong, and, in fact, there is testimony that would imply that he (1) deliberately went to Nauvoo and left Joseph in Carthage; (2) discharged all of the militia except for the Carthage Greys, the most violent of all the groups opposed to Joseph; and (3) took Captain Dunn's company, the only truly impartial troops on the scene, with him so as to clear the field for Joseph's enemies to operate without restraint (see HC 6:587–90).

Having Thomas Sharp with the group from Warsaw is supposition. However, he was later indicted by a grand jury for participating in the murder of Joseph and Hyrum, so it is very likely he was there. As with the others indicted for the work of that day, Sharp was never found guilty or punished in any way. (See Dallin H. Oaks and Marvin S. Hill, *Carthage Conspiracy: The Trial of the Accused Assassins of Joseph Smith* [Urbana: University of Illinois Press, 1975], pp. 36–38.)

The jailer had been gone only a few minutes when once again the four men in the upper bedroom of the Carthage Jail heard footsteps on the stairs. Willard Richards, who was closest now, opened the door. It was one of the guards from outside. He carried a bottle of wine.

"Yes?" Elder Richards asked.

"You need to taste this wine before I'll drink it," the man said gruffly.

There was no way that the prisoners could have bought poisoned wine while in a jail cell, but Joseph smiled and came over to the door. Half an hour before, the jailer's son had brought them a pitcher of water and told them that the men outside were demanding that the four prisoners buy a bottle of wine for their guards. There was just reason for protesting such gross inequity, but Joseph did not. He simply told Willard to give the guard a couple of dollars to buy some wine. Now the man was back, evidently suspicious of Joseph's abilities to influence others.

Joseph brought one of the water glasses over and Willard Richards uncorked the bottle. He poured in about a finger full, which Joseph tasted. He handed the glass to John Taylor and he sipped it too. Then Elder Richards did the same. The man grunted, took back the bottle, and corked it, satisfied that it was safe. As he backed out the door onto the upper landing of the stairs, a voice from below began calling. "Frank! Frank! Get down here! Quick!"

Willard—half-amused, half-disgusted—stood at the head of the stairs and watched the man go out again. But then as the main door to the jail shut behind the man, there was a rustling sound outside, and muffled voices could be heard urgently crying out to one another. Startled, Willard leaned over the railing to hear better, then quickly stepped back inside the bedroom and shut the door. He turned to Joseph with a puzzled look.

But before he could say anything, from outside, they heard the sound of running feet, then a loud cry. "Surrender! Surrender!" As they swung around to stare toward the open window, a rifle fired, making them all jump. It was just outside their window. Then another exploded and another. Now men were shouting and yelling loudly. "Lay down your arms! Get out of the way!" Someone swore and there was the crash of metal on metal.

In two leaps, Willard Richards reached the window that looked down on the entrance. What he saw shocked him deeply. A hundred or more men were running toward the jail from every direction. Their faces were blackened and horrible to behold. All had rifles and were brandishing them wildly. Even as Willard watched, eyes widening in horror with the realization of what was happening, the guard directly below him raised his gun and fired it harmlessly into the air. Another did the same. The eight guards were laughing and shouting, falling back to make way for their oncoming brethren.

"We're under attack!" Joseph yelled. He darted to the bed where he had laid his coat and grabbed for the pepperbox he had hidden in the pocket. Hyrum leaped to his feet, pawing for the single-shot revolver in his coat.

Now the crash of gunfire outside was coming so fast they could barely distinguish one shot from another. Out of the corner of his eye, John Taylor saw one of the curtains jump violently and a round hole suddenly appeared in it. Above his head another hole appeared in the ceiling and plaster rained down in a little puff of white. "They're shooting through the windows," he yelled.

Below, the front door to the jail crashed open and men pounded up the stairs. "The door!" Hyrum shouted. He leaped across the room to the closed door and threw his weight against it. Joseph went running toward it too. Elder Taylor dived for the corner where Stephen Markham and Dan Jones had left their walking sticks. His hand fell on Markham's "rascal beater" and he tossed the smaller one to Willard Richards.

There was a solid thud as a body slammed against the door. Through the thin panel they could hear men swearing and shouting. "Get the door! Get the door! Get out of the way! Gimme a clear shot!" Both Apostles dashed across the room and threw themselves against the door too. Now the lack of a secure latch would prove telling. The gunfire outside the jail was one continuous roar now, and bullets were whizzing in through the windows like angry hornets.

Hyrum grabbed the door latch and held it fast. The latch rattled momentarily, then he jerked his hand back as someone on the other side put the muzzle of a musket right up against the latch and fired. It shattered and the door jerked open a couple of inches. The four men didn't have a chance to slam it shut again before several rifle barrels were shoved into the narrow opening. Seeing the danger, Joseph leaped to the left side of the door, trying to pull it shut. John Taylor did the same and began striking at the muzzles with the rascal beater, knocking the rifles down to keep them from firing directly into the room. Elder Richards, pushing against the door from behind, flailed at them as well.

Outside the door they could hear the men who were farther back screaming profanities and yelling for the ones up front to go on through. Above their heads, holes were blossoming as if by magic in the ceiling, raining down a fine powdery dust into the room. The glass of one window shattered. The curtains were riddled with holes now. With more men crowding onto the landing, the attackers began hurling themselves against the door. Willard Richards was a big man, but he couldn't hold it against that kind of force. The door opened another couple of inches and instantly more rifles were shoved through the gap. Now the men on the other side of the door began to fire. Inches from Hyrum's nose, one rifle came up and fired, narrowly missing his face. He gasped and fell back a few steps, blinded and deafened by the near miss.

Backing toward the center of the room, Hyrum raised his pistol, preparing to fire. At that instant, someone, frustrated by his inability to get to the bedroom door because of the crowd, fired directly at the door. The ball tore through the thin panel, showering Elder Richards with splinters. It also caught Hyrum full in the face, just to the left of his nose. He staggered back. "I am a dead man!" he cried. At that precise moment, a ball was fired from outside by someone far enough away to give it a fairly flat trajectory. The projectile barely cleared the window sill and caught Hyrum in the left side of his back. It hit with such force that the bullet passed clear through his body and slammed into the back of the watch he carried in his vest pocket, totally smashing it. So many bullets were now being fired into the room that, even as he fell, another shot from the doorway caught him, entering his head through the throat.

With a great tortured cry, Joseph sprang across the room and knelt beside the fallen form. Bullets were flying all around them but he gave them no heed. He reached out and took his brother by the shoulders. "Oh dear brother Hyrum!" he sobbed. But there was nothing more he could do for him. With a cry of outrage, Joseph sprang to the door, right into the face of the muzzles. He shoved the pepperbox around the frame and pulled the trigger as fast as he could. Three of the six barrels failed to discharge, but the other three had the desired effect. There was a howl of surprise, a scream of pain, and then a heavy crash as someone fell.

Elder Taylor and Elder Richards were still frantically trying to parry the gun barrels, but there were too many outside trying to force the door. It was almost half-open now, and the rifles were extending farther and farther into the room, giving the men who were holding them more control over their aim. Now John Taylor backed away from the door. There was no way to hold them. Maybe there were friends outside. If only he could get clear of the withering fire. He turned and raced to the east window. He climbed onto the sill, crouching so as to get through the opening. The well was right below him on the ground. He would have to jump clear of that. He saw that it was a leap of fifteen or twenty feet and wondered momentarily if he might break his ankle.

Whether it was deliberately aimed or was another unfortunate shot from someone firing blind didn't matter much. Just as he poised himself to leap outward, a ball from the doorway struck John Taylor in the left thigh, smashing into the bone and almost going out the other side. With a scream of agony, he collapsed onto the window sill. Even then he would have fallen outward, but a man standing near the well heard the scream. He looked up, saw the figure there, snapped up his rifle, and fired. The ball caught Elder Taylor just below the right breast, exactly in the location of his watch pocket. John Taylor always carried a fine pocket watch that kept excellent time. The watch took the hit squarely, and the force knocked Elder Taylor backwards again. With a crash he toppled off the sill and onto the floor.

With only Elder Richards now trying to fend them off, the rifles were firing directly into the room now with one continuous roar. Unfortunately John Taylor fell to the floor directly in the line of their fire. He screamed again as one ball hit him in the left wrist and flattened itself against the bone. In agony not comprehensible to most men, but still conscious enough to realize his danger, he pulled himself under the bed. Now the bed took several balls, but there was still one more meant for John Taylor. A rifle was brought down low as its owner shoved it between the legs of the man in front of him and blasted away. The ball skimmed the floor and struck John Taylor in the hip, tearing away a fist-size chunk of flesh.

Seeing that there was no safety in the room and thinking that only by fleeing could he save the lives of the two Apostles, Joseph suddenly straightened. Calmly he moved back, dropping the pistol on the floor. He turned and sprang to the same window where John Taylor had tried to gain freedom. It was like trying to walk through a hailstorm without being struck. As he leaped onto the sill, someone from below fired up at him, striking him in the right breast. As it had happened to John Taylor, so it was here. The force of the shot might have knocked Joseph back into the room, but at that same instant, from the widening gap in the doorway, two muskets belched fire and two balls flashed across the room. Both caught Joseph squarely in the back, smashing into him with the force of two mighty blows.

"O Lord, my God!" he cried, and pitched head first out the window.

"He's jumped the window!" someone at the door yelled. There was a shout and instantly those at the door were gone, tearing down the stairs lest they lose their quarry. Willard Richards heard the yell too. He crossed the room to the window, staring down at the horrible scene before him. Joseph's body was lying near the well. "We got 'im! We got Joe Smith!" someone was yelling. Heedless of the danger he was putting himself in, Elder Richards thrust his head out the window, wanting to see more clearly. Joseph's shirt was a mass of blood. There was no movement in his body. Men were coming around the corner of the jail on the dead run, screaming in triumph. One man was dancing up and down, howling fiendishly.

With a sob, Elder Richards drew his head back into the room. Looking around wildly, he sought escape. In moments they would be back for him. Sure that his life was forfeit at any moment, he rushed across the room to see if the door to the criminal's cell might be open so he could find refuge there.

"Take me!"

He whirled in astonishment. "John?"

"Yes!"

"Hold on!" Racing now, he went out of the bedroom, pushed open the door to the cell, then went back for his companion. Taking Elder Taylor by the arms, trying to inure himself to the wounded man's groans of agony, Willard dragged him across the floor of the bedroom, out onto the landing, and then into the criminal's cell, leaving a long smear of blood across the floor. The cell was empty except for a filthy straw mattress on the floor. Puffing heavily, Willard pulled John into the far corner of the cell. Then he yanked the mattress up and over him, taking care to make sure his body was completely covered. "This is a hard case to lay you on the floor," Willard gasped, "but if your wounds are not fatal, I want you to live to tell the story."

He took one last look around, then moved swiftly back to the outside door to the cell room to await the next onslaught. He didn't have long to wait. Joseph Smith was dead, but the mob knew there were three more men still up there. The entrance to the jail crashed open and heavy footsteps came running up the stairs again. They reached the landing, not five feet from where Elder Richards stood, holding his breath. He heard the door to the bedroom being flung open, then heard a cry of joy. There was a scuffling sound, then, "This is the brother! This is Hyrum. We got his brother!"

"Where's them other two?" someone shouted.

"Check the cell!"

Holding the cane high, knowing how futile it would be, Willard Richards stepped back.

Then another cry went up. This time it came from outside. It was filled with sheer terror. "The Mormons are coming! The Mormons are coming!"

Someone right outside the door swore. "The Mormons! We've gotta get outta here!"

Once again there was the thunder of boots on the wooden stairs, then the sound of panicked flight outside. In less than a minute, all was silent.

———•———

"Are you awake?"

Nathan turned his head and nodded.

Lydia reached out and took his hand. "Will you hold me?"

"Of course." He half turned, wincing a little, and opened his arms to her.

"I don't want to hurt your legs."

"My legs are fine. They're just superficial wounds."

She nodded and slid into his grasp, laying her head against his chest. He pulled her close, holding her to him, wanting the comfort that her presence gave him. They lay there for a long time, neither one speaking, both wide awake.

"What is it?" she finally said.

He turned and looked at her.

"You feel it too, don't you?"

He nodded, not having to ask what "it" was.

"Why, Nathan? What is it? It's like a great chill has fallen on the city."

"I don't know. Worry, maybe. Knowing Joseph and Hyrum and the others are down there alone now." He turned his head away from her.

"Nathan, you had no choice. You were driven out. They would have killed you if you went back. Joseph would have wanted you to go, you know that."

"Yes," he said, not comforted at all with knowing she was right. "And yet . . ."

She snuggled in against him even more tightly. "I know," she said.

He closed his eyes, picturing the jail's bedroom, wondering if the night had brought a breeze to cool it down at all, wondering if the governor was back in Carthage yet to bring at least some rein over the Carthage Greys.

"What do you make of what happened with the animals tonight, Nathan?" Lydia asked after a few minutes.

He reached down and began to rub her shoulder softly. "That was very strange," he admitted.

That evening, just before sundown, the animals around the city began a most peculiar thing. Somewhere a dog started to howl—a low, mournful sound that carried for blocks. Another took it up, and then another. And if that were not odd enough, very quickly the cattle joined in, lowing and bellowing from stables and pastures, barns and milking sheds. Soon the whole city was filled with the eerie sound of animals crying out in seeming pain. It had sent chills running up and down Nathan's back and only added to the great heaviness that seemed to lay upon him.

"Have you ever seen that happen before?" she asked.

"No. I saw a dog mourn for his master like that once, after the man died, but nothing like this. Tonight it seemed like animals all over the city were howling."

She gave a little shudder and squeezed in more closely to him. "It frightened me, Nathan."

He wanted to soothe her, tell her it was just an odd coincidence, but he couldn't. He just gently rubbed her shoulder over and over and held her close.

Nathan woke up with a start, sitting straight up in bed. Light flooded through the windows and he realized that the sun was up already. After lying awake for so long last night, he had overslept by an hour or more.

Lydia stirred and then the loud knocking started again and she too jerked up. "What is it, Nathan?"

"Someone's downstairs." He tossed back the sheet and got out of bed, moving to the chair where he had hung his pants. Lydia rose now too, putting a robe on around her nightdress. Then, even as they moved toward the bedroom door, they heard the door downstairs open. "Nathan? Lydia?"

"It's Joshua," he exclaimed. He turned. "Coming!"

As they came quickly down the stairs, Nathan saw that Joshua was fully dressed. He had his back to them, staring out the window. He turned and Nathan stopped. Joshua's face looked exactly as it did that night when they had arrived in Warsaw to help with Caroline. He looked haunted, half in shock.

Lydia recognized that look too. "Joshua! What is it? What's wrong?" One hand flew to her mouth. "Not Caroline!"

He shook his head. "I was going to the freight yard, when . . ." He held out a paper, staring at them mutely. Nathan took it and moved closer to Lydia. It was in Joshua's scribbled handwriting on the back of another letter, obviously a hastily made copy. The first line read: "Carthage Jail, 8:05 o'clock, p.m., June 27th, 1844."

Then Lydia gasped. Her knees buckled and she started to crumble. Nathan grabbed her around the waist, too dazed to do more than that, reading on in a numbing shock of his own.

> Joseph and Hyrum are dead. Taylor wounded, not very badly. I am well. Our guard was forced, as we believe, by a band of Missourians from 100 to 200. The job was done in an instant, and the party fled. This is as I believe it. The cit-izens here are afraid of the Mormons attacking them. I promise them no!
>
> W. Richards
> John Taylor

"No!" Lydia wailed, tears streaming down her face. "No!"

Half stumbling himself, Nathan led Lydia to a chair and sat her down. She dropped her head into her hands and began to shake violently as the sobs tore at her body. Dimly, barely seeing him through his own swimming eyes, Nathan turned to Joshua. "I should have stayed with them, Joshua. I should have stayed."

Eight blocks away, in one of the sitting rooms of the Mansion House, a terrible cry of pain was torn from the lips of Emma Smith. "No! Oh, dear God, please! No!" She dropped her head in her hands, rocking back and forth in violent jerking motions. "No! No! No!"

John P. Greene, Nauvoo city marshal and long a trusted friend and associate of the Prophet Joseph Smith, dropped to one knee beside the huddled figure. He reached out and clasped her hands, his own face stricken with grief. "Oh, dear Sister Emma, God bless you." Then laying his hands upon her head he bowed his head and poured out a fervent blessing upon her. Gradually she calmed under his hands, but he could still feel the trembling in her body. When he had finished blessing her with comfort and peace and the ability to accept what had happened, he stepped back.

She looked up at him, her face wet with tears. But when she spoke, she didn't speak to him. "Why, O God, am I thus afflicted?" she burst out. "Why am I a widow? Thou knowest I have trusted in thy law."

Feeling as if his very heart was breaking, John Greene kneeled beside her again. "Oh, Sister Emma, I know this is difficult for you, but this affliction shall be a crown in your life."

Her head came up, her eyes wide and dark with pain. "Joseph was the crown of my life!" she whispered. "For him and for my children I have suffered the loss of all things. Why, O God, am I thus deserted and my heart torn with this tenfold anguish?"

She turned away, hunching over, hugging herself tightly as she wept for her lost Joseph.

———◆———

For Mary Fielding Smith the shock was as severe, but not totally unexpected. Her little Martha, who was three, was recovering from the measles. Mary nursed her long into the evening of the twenty-seventh of June, rocking her and telling her stories, trying to appear cheerful. But something was wrong. Mary could feel it. Long after Martha was asleep, Mary walked back and forth across the floor of the living room, or moved to the front window and stared out at the darkness, unable to shake the sense of foreboding that hung over her like a great pall.

When the knock came shortly after first light and she saw the two men standing there, she nodded numbly. Calling the children around her, she sat down slowly in her rocking chair, then nodded for the men to give her the news that they carried. As the children burst into tears, Mary sat in a stupor of grief, rocking slowly back and forth, remembering the terrible feelings of the night before.

———•———

At eight a.m. on the morning of June twenty-eighth, two wagons left Carthage. Branches cut from trees shaded two bodies from the summer sun. No one was there to bid them good-bye. By morning, Carthage was a ghost town. Fearing that the Nauvoo Legion was coming to sack the city, the populace fled. And thus the dead left their place of dying without fanfare or farewell.

At three p.m., the wagons approached Mulholland Street, about a mile east of the rising Nauvoo Temple. Here the dead were welcomed home. Thousands lined the streets in mute grief or wailing sorrow. An entire city was in shock.

The bodies were taken to the Mansion House and the doors closed behind them. The Saints were instructed to return the next morning when the bodies of the leaders would lie in state.

That afternoon, Elder Willard Richards, his left ear still showing smears of blood from where a ball had grazed it, spoke to the grieving Saints. With John Taylor grievously injured and the rest of the Twelve in the East, he was the senior acting Apostle. He spoke earnestly and with authority. He reminded them that they were Saints. He spoke of the importance of keeping the peace. He told them that he had pledged his honor and his life on the promise that the Saints would not retaliate in kind. And then he asked for their sustaining vote.

Red-eyed with grief, numb with shock, the eight thousand people present raised their hands in resolution. They would trust the law to provide a remedy for the assassinations, and that failing, they would call upon God to avenge their slain leaders of the wrongs committed against them.

Then they quietly returned to their homes to try to comprehend the terrible loss that had been wreaked upon them.

That evening, four brethren labored in silent grief to prepare the bodies of the fallen martyrs. They had been carefully washed. Cotton soaked in camphor was put into each of the several wounds both men had sustained. The brothers, not separated now in death any more than they had been in life, were dressed alike in their finest trousers and white shirts. White neckerchiefs were placed at their throats, white cotton stockings put on their feet, and white shrouds draped across their chests.

Tomorrow, the Saints would gather to say their last good-byes. Tonight, the family and some close friends would spend a few moments with their beloved Joseph and Hyrum.

Lucy Mack Smith stood quietly in front of the door that separated her from her two sons. She steeled herself with all the power of that mighty will that had sustained her through so many trials and so much hardship. Since the first word of the tragedy had reached her she had braced herself for this moment, roused every energy of her soul, and called on God to give her strength. She was not sure that she could bear to look upon the bodies of these two sons struck down so cruelly in the prime of life.

Beside her stood Mary Fielding Smith, tall and straight, her eyes red and puffy but her face composed. Clinging to her hands or her dress were her children, who, like their mother, were trying to be brave.

There was a noise behind them and Mother Smith turned. Emma and her four children were coming down the stairs. Dimick Huntington, a longtime friend of the family, walked beside her, holding her arm. The roundness of Emma's stomach was evident, a painful reminder that the unborn child would never know its father. At the sight of her mother-in-law and sister-in-law, Emma stopped. She swayed and nearly swooned, and Huntington had to grab on to her to hold her. Lucy Mack started toward her, but Emma straightened again and waved her back. This was not the first time she had started down to join them, and Mother Smith wasn't sure but what once again she would have to turn back and return to her room. Emma was shattered, totally devastated by this latest and most terrible calamity in her life. And who could blame her? Mother Smith thought. This woman had seen enough trials and challenges for any five other women. As Emma came up to stand beside her mother-in-law, Lucy Mack reached out and took her hand. "We'll make it, Emma," she whispered, not sure if it would be true for either of them.

"I'm ready, Mother Smith."

Lucy straightened to her full four-foot-eleven-inch height, then turned to Brother Goldsmith, who stood guard at the doors, and nodded. Gravely he stepped aside and they went in.

The bodies were lying together side by side on a long table. As the families moved into the room, Emma cried out and threw her hands over her eyes. Her son Joseph the Third broke from her gasp and ran to his father's body, crying out, "Oh, my father! My father!" That was too much for the rest of the children—Emma's and Mary's—and they burst into tears and started to wail and cry.

Emma, barely able to walk, let Brother Huntington take her forward to stand beside the table. She fell to her knees and threw her arms around Joseph. "Joseph! Dear Joseph! Speak to me! Just once speak to me. Oh, Joseph! Have the assassins killed you?" She dropped her head and began to weep with mighty, shuddering sobs.

Mary Smith moved forward slowly, trembling at every step. When she reached her husband, she too could no longer hold the anguish in. She reached out and touched Hyrum's face, not wanting to look at where the ball had struck him, yet not able not to. "Oh, Hyrum," she gasped. She ran her fingers through his hair. "Oh, speak to me, Hyrum. I cannot believe that you are dead."

Lucy Mack Smith stood back, listening to the sobs and cries of her daughters-in-law and her grandchildren. Tears streaked her cheeks too and finally she had to look away. After a few moments, Emma was taken out, on the verge of hysteria, barely able to walk. A great wrenching cry welled up inside Mother Smith. She could not give voice to it, but neither could she stop the question from bursting forth in her mind. She did not know it, but it was very much like the cry of Emma earlier that day. "My God, my God, why hast thou forsaken this family?" She dropped her head, covering her eyes with her hands.

And then it came, as clearly as if someone stood at her elbow. It was not an audible voice, but one inside her mind. It spoke softly but with perfect clarity. "I have taken them to myself, that they might have rest."

Her head came up with a start and she looked around. In an instant, peace flooded through her soul like a summer's rain. She stood there, almost too overcome to move, letting the wonderful realization of the words sink into her soul. In her crushing grief she had momentarily forgotten that it was only the flesh that lay before her now. Joseph and Hyrum still lived. And at a future time they would take these bodies up again and live forever. Their Savior would bring them forth again someday, and in the meantime, they would have rest.

Slowly now, still mindful of the great grief around her, she moved forward to stand before the table. She looked down at her sons. She saw the evidence of the violence that had snuffed out their lives. She saw the paleness of their faces and felt the coldness of the flesh. But now she saw something more. Though tears were still streaming down her face, as she looked down upon them she saw the calm repose on their faces. Their eyes were closed in death but they were also closed in peace.

She marveled. And as she marveled she cried out in her mind, this time not with grief but with longing, "Oh, my sons, how I shall miss you."

And once again it came. Quiet, peaceful, clear. Only now it was the voice of her sons that came into her mind. "Mother, weep not for us. We have overcome the world by love. We carried to them the gospel, that their souls might be saved. They have slain us for our testimony and thus placed us beyond their power. Their ascendency is for a moment. Ours is an eternal triumph."

For a long time, Lucy Mack Smith stood there, saying goodbye to her sons, no longer grieving as she had when she came in. And then she turned and moved over to stand beside her daughter-in-law. Mary looked around in surprise. Mother Smith slipped an arm around her waist. Together they stood and looked at the two men who lay before them.

———————

The six of them walked slowly along in the darkness. No one spoke. Seeing the bodies lying there on the table was so stark, so shattering, so totally, irrevocably real, that they could not put words to their grief.

They had gone together to the Mansion House at the specific invitation of Mother Smith, Emma, and Mary. The rest of the Church would come tomorrow, when the doors would be thrown open and ten thousand Saints would move past the coffins in long, silent lines, paying one last sorrowful tribute to their leaders. But tonight only the extended family and a small group of intimate friends were invited to come in after the immediate families had their chance to say farewell to their husbands and fathers.

That the Steeds had been included was silent testimony to the bonds that had been forged between these two families. Emma and Mother Smith had asked for Benjamin, Mary Ann, Lydia, and Nathan. In addition, Mary had requested that Rebecca and Derek be included because of her longtime friendship with Rebecca.

As they approached the first houses on Steed Row—Nathan and Lydia's on the left, Derek and Rebecca's on the right—they stopped. It was almost ten o'clock. The streets were deserted. Most of the homes were dark now. A great reverential hush seemed to lie over the city. They were reluctant to speak and break the silence, and yet they could not simply part without giving word to their sorrow.

"It was seventeen years ago this spring," Mary Ann said softly. "Remember? Martin Harris suggested that we hire those two Smith boys to help us clear the land. He said what good workers they were."

Nathan's voice was husky as he nodded and spoke. "I walked partway home with them one afternoon. That was when Joseph first told me about his going to the grove to pray."

"And I fired them," Benjamin said with shame in his voice, "because everyone in town was saying that Joseph was a charlatan. I didn't want people to think I was believing anything Joseph said."

Rebecca was still crying softly, but she smiled through it. "Do you know what I remember? Joseph pulling sticks with me and with Matthew and letting Matthew win."

"He didn't let you win too?" Lydia asked.

"No. I was giggling so hard before we even started, Joseph just pulled me over and started to tickle me. I loved him from that moment on."

"I feel as if part of me has died," Lydia said in a hoarse whisper.

"It has," Benjamin said, his voice also trembling. "A part of all of us has died. But in another way, it is a part that will always live too."

Mary Ann moved closer to Benjamin and slipped under his arm, as though she were cold, but her chin was up and her eyes were radiant through the tears. "Do you realize how fortunate we are to have had Joseph and Hyrum be that much a part of us for all these years? Future generations will call us blessed. We walked and talked with the Prophet. We ate with him. We sat at his feet."

"We were his next-door neighbors," Nathan murmured.

Only Lydia understood all that he meant by that comment, and that brought the tears flowing again for her. Nathan slipped an arm around her and held her tightly. Rebecca turned to her too. "How is Emma, Lydia?"

Lydia had gone upstairs with Dimick Huntington to see Emma while the others were viewing the bodies. She shook her head. "She is totally, completely devastated. I've never seen her like this. It seems all of her reserves are gone. She has nothing more to draw on."

"Those reserves have been tapped too many times," Mary Ann said sadly.

"But she's a strong woman," Lydia went on. "I predict that tomorrow she'll be there with her head high to greet the people. But tonight, she is just completely lost."

"Oh, I hope this doesn't make her lose the baby," Rebecca said.

"I asked her about that and she says she's all right. The baby seems strong and healthy."

"Mother Smith was the one who surprised me," Derek put in. "She was obviously grieving, but there was such a peace and serenity about her tonight. I felt like she was comforting us instead of the other way around."

"She was, wasn't she?" Nathan said. He had been struck by the same thing quite powerfully.

"Mother Smith is an incredible woman," Benjamin said.

Suddenly, Rebecca moved away from Derek and into her mother's arms. "Oh, Mama!" she cried. "Why did this happen? We needed Joseph so much."

"I don't know," Mary Ann said. "I don't know."

"What is going to happen now?" Lydia cried, giving voice to her own fears. "How can we go on without Joseph?"

"Oh, we'll go on," Nathan said, "but it will never be the same again."

"But who will even lead us?" Rebecca asked in anguish. "Who could ever take Joseph's place?"

Benjamin suddenly straightened. "May I speak for Joseph and answer that?"

They all turned to him in surprise.

"If Joseph were here at this moment, I think I know what he would say." And then he began to quote something. It was something that had so impressed Benjamin that day when Peter had burst into the house to read it to them, that he had committed it to memory. Earlier in the day, as he walked out on the prairie by himself, trying to cope with the shock of knowing that Joseph was dead and wondering what that would mean now, it had come back to him with great power.

" 'The standard of truth has been erected,' " he began; " 'no unhallowed hand can stop the work from progressing.' "

He stopped, letting that sink in for a moment. "Yesterday, many unhallowed hands tried to stop the work, and I suppose today they are celebrating their supposed triumph. But Joseph said that no unhallowed hand could stop this work. Not one!"

As they nodded now, he went on. " 'Persecutions may rage, mobs may combine, armies may assemble, calumny may defame, but the truth of God will go forth boldly, nobly, and independent till it has penetrated every continent, visited every clime, swept every country, and sounded in every ear, till the purposes of God shall be accomplished and the great Jehovah shall say the work is done.' "

Benjamin looked at each one in turn. "I think that's what Joseph would say to us if he were here."

Mary Ann's head came up now in wonder. "He would, wouldn't he? He would chide us, remind us that what we are engaged in wasn't *his* work and *his* glory, or it would die with him. It is God's work and God's glory. And it is not done!"

Nathan now understood Mother Smith's serenity and peace. "Do you remember Joseph's prayer? The one given him by revelation back in Ohio?"

They all looked blank.

"I can't quote it verbatim, but it goes something like this. 'The keys of the kingdom are given unto man on the earth, and from there the gospel will roll forth to the ends of the earth.' "

He hesitated, trying to remember the exact wording, and then Derek came in softly " 'As the stone that was cut out of the mountain without hands shall roll forth, so shall the gospel roll forth until it fills the whole earth.' "

For a long time they stood there in the darkness and in the quiet. Each was lost in their memories, each was immersed in their thoughts. Then Rebecca pulled away from her mother and stepped to her father. She went up on tiptoes and kissed him on the cheek. "Thank you, Papa," she said softly.

Chapter Notes

The guard's coming to the bedroom door and the prisoners' sampling of the wine were the last things to happen prior to the attack on the jail. The story is accurate; the motive the guard had in having Joseph and the others test it as given here is a surmise. (See HC 6:616.)

The details of the Martyrdom are retold in many sources, but all are based on the eyewitness accounts of John Taylor and Willard Richards (see HC 6:616–21; B. H. Roberts, *Life of John Taylor*, Collector's Edition [Salt Lake City: Bookcraft, 1989], pp. 137–40). Even though he was terribly wounded, John Taylor remained conscious throughout the attack. It is likely that when Elder Richards put the mattress on top of Elder Taylor, the straw and ticking helped stop the bleeding and saved his life.

Willard Richards, who was a very large man, miraculously had only the lower tip of his left ear grazed by a bullet, even though he stood in a room into which hundreds of shots were being fired. This fulfilled a remarkable prophecy made by Joseph over a year before. "Willard," Joseph said, "the time will come when the balls shall fly around you like hail, and you shall see your friends fall on the right and on the left, but there shall not even be a hole in your garments." (See HC 6:619.)

Hyrum Smith's watch was smashed completely by the ball that hit it from behind. But the bullet that hit John Taylor's watch hit the face, his life thus being saved in two ways: the watch stopped the bullet from entering his body, and the impact of the ball threw him back into the room. The hands of the watch were stopped at sixteen minutes and twenty-six seconds after five p.m., marking forever the exact time that the tragedy struck. (See Roberts, *Life of John Taylor*, pp. 149–50.)

Joseph did hit some of the mob when he fired the pistol (see Don Cecil Corbett, *Mary Fielding Smith: Daughter of Britain* [Salt Lake City: Deseret Book Co., 1966], pp. 166–67).

The first message written by Willard Richards concerning the tragedy was not delivered to Nauvoo until sunup the next morning. By then, other riders had come in during the night with the news. But the first official confirmation was Willard's letter. Elder Taylor had asked Elder Richards that in writing the message he downplay Elder Taylor's wounds so that his family would not worry. (See HC 6:621–22.)

On the night of the Martyrdom, long before the first word of the tragedy came to Nauvoo, a spirit of death pervaded the city. Bathsheba Smith—wife of George A. Smith, a member of the Twelve—said, "Such a barking and howling of dogs and bellowing of cattle all over the city of Nauvoo I never heard before nor since." (See *Restoration*, p. 621.)

The reactions of both Emma and Mary Fielding Smith are drawn from historical records (see Gracia N. Jones, *Emma's Glory and Sacrifice: A Testimony* [Hurricane, Utah: Homestead Publishers and Distributors, 1987], pp. 158–60; Corbett, *Mary Fielding Smith*, pp. 171–72). Mother Smith's experience when first seeing her two martyred sons and the answers she received come directly from her own record of the events of that day (see Lucy Mack Smith, *History of Joseph Smith by His Mother*, ed. Preston Nibley [Salt Lake City: Bookcraft, 1954], pp. 324–25). Having the Steeds visit the Mansion House on that first evening that the bodies were brought back to Nauvoo—the evening of 28 June—is based on the statement in the historical record which says, "Relatives and particular friends were also permitted to view the remains during the evening" (*HC* 6:627).

The prayer quoted by Nathan and Derek is now found in D&C 65.

Joseph Smith, the Prophet and Seer of the Lord, has done more, save Jesus only, for the salvation of men in this world, than any other man that ever lived in it. In the short space of twenty years, he has brought forth the Book of Mormon, which he translated by the gift and power of God, and has been the means of publishing it on two continents; has sent the fulness of the everlasting gospel, which it contained, to the four quarters of the earth; has brought forth the revelations and commandments which compose this book of Doctrine and Covenants, and many other wise documents and instructions for the benefit of the children of men; gathered many thousands of the Latter-day Saints, founded a great city, and left a fame and name that cannot be slain. He lived great, and he died great in the eyes of God and his people; and like most of the Lord's anointed in ancient times, has sealed his mission and his works with his own blood; and so has his brother Hyrum. In life they were not divided, and in death they were not separated! . . .

. . . The testators are now dead, and their testament is in force.

. . . They lived for glory; they died for glory; and glory is their eternal reward. From age to age shall their names go down to posterity as gems for the sanctified.

. . . Their innocent blood, with the innocent blood of all the martyrs under the altar that John saw, will cry unto the Lord of Hosts till he avenges that blood on the earth. Amen.

—John Taylor, Doctrine and Covenants 135:3, 5, 6, 7

1844

N

W ⊕ E

S

Missouri River

Sugar Creek

Des Moines River

IOWA TERRITORY

MISSOURI

UNORGANIZED TERRITORY

● Far West

● Liberty

● Independence

Missouri River